Watch Me Grow: I'm One-Two-Three

provides reassurance and information for parents and childcare providers about the development of toddlers by:

- Exploring all the amazing accomplishments and challenges a child is likely to experience between ages one and three, year by year.

- Incorporating cutting-edge research on the unparalleled brain development that occurs between the ages of 12 and 48 months.

- Translating scientific knowledge into recognizable day-to-day moments.

- Assuring and informing parents about typical developmental milestones and the individual needs of their child.

- Acknowledging how each new change in behavior can affect the entire family.

- Explaining what the world is like from the toddler's point of view to help inform parental choices.

- Helping parents adjust their parenting styles to the ever-evolving needs of their child.

- Sharing the incomparable wisdom and experience of actual parents in touching and often humorous anecdotes.

- Involving readers with "Reader's Notes" sections where parents can chronicle their child's unique strengths and challenges.

Praise for
Maureen O'Brien

"This is a lovely book. It contains fascinating stories about children. It gives parents a chance to understand what is going on in their development. A rare combination!"
　　—T. Berry Brazelton, M.D., Professor Emeritus, Harvard University and
　　　　Codirector, Brazelton Touchpoints Center, Children's Hospital, Boston

"O'Brien combines a rich child development background with her own joys and challenges as a parent to produce this infinitely helpful text. . . . [It's] like living next door to a child developmentalist with a sense of humor."
　　—Claudia Quigg, M.Ed., Founder and Executive Director, Baby TALK

"Dr. O'Brien brilliantly weaves the latest information on brain research into each chapter of this wisdom-filled book. There are many child development books on the shelves these days—*this* one's a keeper."
　　—Patricia Lawrence, M.S., P.N.P., Boston Medical Center

"What a delight to find this book on 'wonderful ones.' Dr. O'Brien's observations are easily conveyed through her skills as a clinician, but even more by her upbeat personality and experiences as a mom."
　　—Agnes W. Williams, Executive Director, Greenville's Child, Inc.

"An amazingly insightful book. . . . With a reassuring and informative tone, this feels like sharing parenting stories with a best friend who is also an expert on child development."
　　—Dr. Melanie S. Percy, R.N., C.P.N.P., University of Texas, Austin

". . . Captures the essence of the child from age one to two. A refreshing and essential book for parents and anyone who cares for young children. A must-read!"
　　—Dr. Fran Sterling, pediatrician

"This book blends a mother's insight and compassion with the knowledge and wisdom of a professional. . . . A phenomenal resource for parents, teachers, and others."
　　—Amy Tishelman, Ph.D., licensed clinical psychologist, Children's Hospital,
　　　Boston

"I love this book! It is a gem. . . . A mixture of the most current research, information on development and age-appropriate behavior, the sound advice of an expert, and the empathy of a friend. I will be using this book as a resource in all the classes that I teach and recommend it to others."

—Marlies Zammuto, Deputy Executive Director of Education and Program Development, Child Care Circuit

"This book is by far the best of its kind on the market and a must-have for any parent of a two-year-old. Dr. O'Brien takes the most up-to-date concepts in the field of child development and renders them completely accessible with her fun-to-read style. She totally demystifies the terrible twos."

—Rose DiBiase, Ph.D., developmental psychologist and Associate Professor, Suffolk University

"An exceptional resource for all parents. You feel comforted and nurtured by her understanding of the challenges and frustrations in parenting a two-year-old. I will recommend this book to my students preparing to work with children and families."

—Claire M. White, M.S., C.C.L.S., Assistant Professor of Child Life, Wheelock College

"As the father of five children long past age two, I remember enough about those years to know how much this book would have helped us and any parent. This book is wisdom well told."

—David Lawrence Jr., President, the Early Childhood Initiative Foundation

"Dr. O'Brien and Ms. Tippins have written a warm and comprehensive view of the wonder of development in the two-year-old. Every parent can relate to these scenarios that bring a sometimes humorous but always enlightening view of life with a terrific two-year-old."

—Dr. Kristie Brandt, Director, Napa County Health and Human Services

". . . Enlightening and compelling. O'Brien's conversational style is effective in communicating complex developmental theory in a manner easily understood . . . and parents will recognize the many developmental milestones addressed through the use of touching anecdotes."

—Gregory Hall, Chair, Department of Behavioral Sciences, Bentley College

Elise S. Donoghue

About the Author

Maureen O'Brien, Ph.D., is a recognized expert in child development and former research associate in pediatrics at Harvard Medical School; a consultant to, and the former head of, the Brazelton Touchpoints Center at Children's Hospital in Boston; and an adjunct assistant professor at Bentley College. She is the mother of twins, and she lives with her family in Canton, Massachusetts.

Sherill Tippins is the author of a number of books for parents and children, including *Two of Us Make a World: The Single Mother's Guide to Pregnancy, Childbirth, and the First Year*. She lives with her family in Brooklyn, New York.

WATCH ME GROW

I'm One—Two—Three

WATCH ME GROW

I'm One–Two–Three

A Parent's Essential Guide
to the Extraordinary
Toddler to Preschool Years

MAUREEN O'BRIEN, PH.D.,
WITH **SHERILL TIPPINS**

Quill
An Imprint of HarperCollins*Publishers*

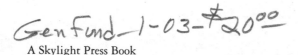

A Skylight Press Book

A hardcover edition of *Watch Me Grow: I'm One* was published in 2000 by William Morrow, an imprint of HarperCollins Publishers.

A hardcover edition of *Watch Me Grow: I'm Two* was published in 2001 by William Morrow, an imprint of HarperCollins Publishers.

First Quill edition published 2002.

Photographs by Elise Sinagra Donoghue

Designed by Gretchen Achilles

Library of Congress Cataloging-in-Publication Data is available.

ISBN 0-06-050787-X

02 03 04 05 06 ❖/RRD 10 9 8 7 6 5 4 3 2 1

TO OUR CHILDREN

ALEXANDER AND MATTHEW (M. O'B.)

AND

VINCENT AND DASH (S. T.)

Contents

WATCH ME GROW: I'M TWO
**Every Parent's Guide to the Lively and
Challenging 24- to 36-Month-Old**

WATCH ME GROW: I'M THREE
Every Parent's Guide to the Charming and Demanding 36- to 48-Month-Old

Preface

A WORD TO THE READER

One-year-olds differ tremendously from two-year-olds, who in turn are vastly different creatures from three-year-olds. We initially wrote the Watch Me Grow series one volume at a time to reflect this fact. We envisioned parents of one-year-olds buying the first volume and then returning for the second volume when their child turned two. But as a parent myself, it made greater sense to put the books together as a set. Why? Well, one reason is because all infants are not created equal. One-year-olds may be right-on-track physically, but have more toddler-like verbal skills. Some two-year-olds are slower to seek out their peers, while others are more eager to socialize like preschoolers. Because children develop at slightly different rates, and parents often like to peek ahead at what to expect next, we decided a single, comprehensive set of resources would be ideal. Thus, *Watch Me Grow: I'm One-Two-Three* was born.

Now parents who have fast-maturing children can get a "heads up" on their child's upcoming developments. Families with more than one child under age three can compare their sons' and daughters' advances, or remind themselves of the amazing progress their child is making from year to year. As a "one-stop-shopper" myself, my goal is for the Watch Me Grow series to meet busy parents' legitimate need for quality, value, and convenience by having as much child development knowledge available as possible in one place. I genuinely hope this series serves as just such a resource for your growing family!

—*Maureen O'Brien, Ph.D.*

WATCH ME GROW

I'm One

Every Parent's Guide to the
Enchanting 12- to 24-Month-Old

The two women sat talking on a park bench in the playground, so near that I couldn't help but overhear. They were discussing a parent support group that they had been trying to organize but were frustrated because they'd had difficulty getting experts to come speak to them.

"It's not fair," one of them said, only half joking as she gently pushed her baby's stroller back and forth. "My sister's receptionist has a really bad home situation, and she has all kinds of help with the kids. She gets counseling, parenting classes, lists of baby-care services. It makes me feel guilty to say it, but I need help sometimes, too, and there's nobody there for me!"

As the mother of twin five-year-old boys, I could sympathize with her frustration. She was doing her best to adjust to her new situation as a mother, trying to raise her child in a responsible way and enjoy doing it at the same time. But sometimes one feels so isolated as a new parent—trying to get by on instinct, contradictory advice from friends, and generic advice from child-care books that often seem dated—that it seems impossible to do a good enough job. As a developmental psychologist and former director of the Touchpoints Project, a nationally known child-development program at Boston Children's Hospital, I'm well aware of the constantly growing bank of research on how babies and young children learn and grow. I appreciate how this information can help parents help their children reach their full potential while enjoying a richer, smoother family life. The trouble is, I also know how often this priceless information fails to find its way to the parents who need it most.

Years of experience working with a wide variety of parent support groups have taught me much about universal parent concerns. The crucial advantage any parent, regardless of background, can have is the knowledge that he or she has a supportive, informed person to turn to—whether that person is a child-development expert, a pediatrician, a relative, or a competent friend. When we feel overwhelmed by a situation, failing to understand why our child is behaving a certain way, a well-informed support person can help us step back from the conflict.

Ideally, he or she can help us to understand how the child feels and what he is trying to communicate, and to consider which of a number of solutions might both alleviate the problem and reinforce the relationship between parent and child. Again and again, I have observed how just knowing that that friend was there for them, ready to lend a hand when necessary, has helped parents recover their equilibrium and improve their family life.

When I became a parent, I came across the challenges we all experience—conflicts with my little ones that I hadn't anticipated when pregnant, even situations I'd never run into in my work. Like most parents, I turned to books at times when I needed backup, for either information or reassurance. The classics were helpful—particularly Dr. Spock's *Baby and Child Care* with its reminder that parents know more than they think they do. My day-to-day interactions at work with Dr. T. Berry Brazelton brought to life the importance of considering the unique aspects of each parent-child combination. What I felt was missing from many of the sources I'd found, though, was a voice to which I could personally relate— the voice of another mother who had the background of a career in child development and who had recently been through these early years of parenting and could apply her knowledge to real-life, practical situations.

My parenting experience deepened my formal training in a way that only hands-on trial and error can. My twins taught me how important it is to respect the individual nature of each child and why a one-size-fits-all approach to parenting is doomed to fall short in a world in which every child develops at his own rate. I also saw, over and over, how knowledge unearthed through recent research on brain development could be used in everyday situations to help babies and young children build healthier, happier lives. Most importanr, I understood from personal experience that both children and parents are growing, changing beings who learn from *each other,* and that both child development and parenting are processes that evolve over time.

Now, with this book, and all the books in the *Watch Me Grow* series, I hope to offer you the fruits of my training and experience—to act as *your* supportive, well-informed resource, helping you to understand exactly "what's going in that little head" on those days when you feel at odds with your child. Ir is my firm conviction that you don't need a Ph.D. to be the best parent you can be. All you need to do is observe your little one, get to know her individual style, and take advantage of the wonderful array of scientific and practical information provided here. Together we will explore all the amazing accomplishments and challenges your baby is likely to experience between twelve and twenty-four months—acknowledging how each new change in behavior can affect the entire family while also looking at the transformation from the *child's* point of view. By alternating sensible approaches to common concerns such as sleep disruption and speech delays with clear, useful explanations of how your child's body is learning to work in conjunction with her brain, I can share with you all the knowledge and confidence that my formal training has given me. Anecdotes collected from other parents may provide you with new insights and remind you that you're not the only person to have traveled this road. "Q&A" sections address some of the more challenging dilemmas that arise when parenting a one-year-old. Descriptions of toddlers at work at the toy box will show you how young children learn and grow. Finally, a "First-Person Singular" section at the end of each chapter allows you to write down your observations of your own child's behavior—comparing it to the descriptions you've found here, contrasting it with earlier behavior, and noting any questions it brings to mind. Here you can record what kinds of activities your child likes best, how her energy level tends to fluctuate throughout the day, how she responds to your various parenting "experiments," and what the warning signs are that she's used up her energy and needs a break. This accumulated knowledge will help you adjust your parenting style to her ever-evolving needs.

Every child is a unique being, with his or her own personality and way of growing. The best use of this and other books is as a departure point for your own research into why your child acts as he or she does and which parenting techniques work best. The new knowledge and fresh insight offered here will give you much of the information you need to parent your one-year-old successfully. Direct observation will do the rest. It is my hope that by showing you new ways to look at, listen to, and, respond to your little one, this book will lift some of the weight of parenthood from your shoulders, empowering you to do what you naturally want to do—share the joy of living with your delightful one-year-old and introduce your child to all the wonders of the world.

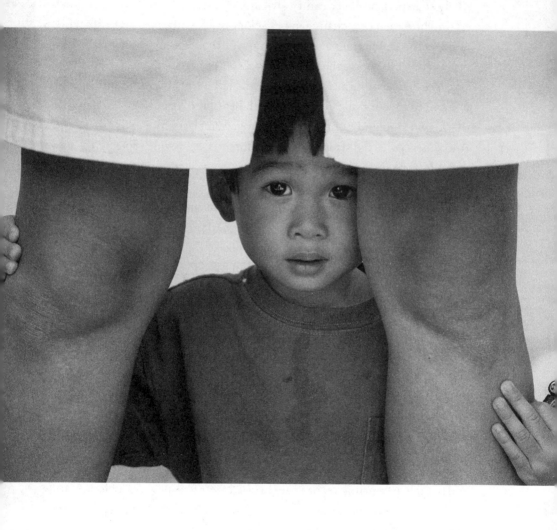

CHAPTER 1

What I'm Like

A t birth your baby's brain is one-fourth its adult size. By his second birthday, it will be three-quarters its adult size.

What a pleasure it is to see a child move from the nearly total dependence of his first twelve months toward a life filled with exploration, verbal communication, and active learning. Mom and Dad watch proudly as fifteen-month-old Philip sits on the floor of their living room, babbling happily as he plays with the plastic rings and spindle they gave him for his birthday. Over the past three months, he has learned to bang the rings against the spindle, pull himself to his feet so he can throw a ring to the floor, and then, when Dad picks up one of the rings, stagger over to try to take it from him. Now, as he puts the first ring on the spindle, then the next, Philip's smile grows in amazement—and so do his parents'. He dares to reach for a third. Uh-oh. This one doesn't fit. Philip furrows his brow. He pushes, hard. It won't budge. Suddenly, to his parents' dismay, Philip lets out a yell and sends the toy flying across the room. *It won't let me put the ring on!* he's thinking. *Bad toy! I hate it!*

Such is the dilemma of the one-year-old—determined enough to know what he wants, but increasingly aware that he's not quite able to get it. No wonder the generally eager, sunny disposition of the twelve-to fifteen-month-old begins to succumb to bouts of angry tears, yelling, and "acting out" more and more as he approaches midyear. Who wouldn't want to cry if his feet slipped out from under him every time he tried to run? Who wouldn't protest loudly if Mom disappeared for work with no clear indication of when she'd return? And who wouldn't kick and squirm if his caregiver pinned him down for a diaper change just when he wanted to chase the cat?

Being the parent of a one-year-old is all about reveling in those exciting periods when your child's physical and mental capabilities suddenly take a giant leap forward. It's also all about supporting him through the difficult periods—the times when he knows what skill he wants to master (walking, asking for his blanket, putting on his shoes) but hasn't quite done yet. Certainly, there are plenty of rewards in store for you this year. During the next twelve months, your baby will begin to appreciate what's out there in the world for him: the colors of a flower, the pleasure of sipping apple juice on a hot day, and the joy of watching a bird fly. He'll discover the satisfactions of banging on the kitchen pans while you cook dinner, clutching a favorite blankie as he learns to lull himself to sleep, and eagerly climbing stairs, furniture, and even people. As he approaches age two, he will grow increasingly interested in others. He'll begin to learn how to converse with his caregiver, his grandfather, and the lady next door, and he'll learn to play happily alongside other children, even if he's not always directly interacting with them. His increasing social awareness will help him begin to sense other people's emotional states, learn to take turns (sometimes), and begin to control his negative impulses in ways that will encourage friendship.

Nevertheless, there will be times—probably around the middle of this year—when his whining, banging, or loud, repeated "No!" will baffle and discourage you. These negative behaviors are not a sign of naughtiness or rebellion; rather, they are natural expressions of frustration as your child learns to cope with a tidal wave of new feelings and developing (but not fully developed) capabilities. In fact, those times when your one-year-old seems to fall apart without any visible provocation are some of the surest indicators that he is developing at a healthy, normal pace. (It might also help keep things in perspective to know that, according to a 1986 study by T. Power and M. Chapieski, toddlers are *told* no every nine minutes on average.) By focusing on how to arrange and manage his environment so that he encounters as few no-win situations as possible—by erecting a supportive scaffolding of predictable rules, practices, and routines—you can help him realize his new goals in ways that won't overwhelm him, and that will help you maintain your own equilibrium as well. Fortunately, this is far from a thankless task. By supporting him in his growth, you'll have the pleasure of participating in his transformation from alert but profoundly dependent babyhood to the active, eager, increasingly independent state of early childhood. Best of all, by the time he turns two, your little one will be able to communicate his appreciation by telling you he loves you in his very own words.

A BABY'S-EYE VIEW

Where's Grandma?

"Beh!" Twelve-month-old Jeffrey points to the teddy bear in his toy basket and looks expectantly at Grandma, who's baby-sitting tonight.

"Bear!" she responds with gratifying enthusiasm, picking up the bear and handing it to him. "Is this your favorite bear, Jeffrey? What's his name?"

Jeffrey doesn't understand the word "favorite" but is about to respond anyway, when abruptly the noise of a telephone cuts through the air. *Loud!*

Jeffrey claps his hands over his ears. The muffling effect intrigues him. Focusing on his hearing, he shifts his attention away from Grandma. Then the telephone stops ringing. Jeffrey looks up.

No Grandma. Jeffrey looks around, stunned. The room suddenly looks enormous. He feels chilled and frightened. *Alone!* Instinctively, he starts to crawl toward the doorway. At the door, he stands up and peeks into the hall. *Grandma's voice!* He can hear it! Too eager to try walking, he drops down again and crawls down the hall at top speed.

There she is, in the dining room, talking on the phone. *Grandma!* At the sight of her Jeffrey pauses, overcome with relief. He crawls over, grabs her skirt, and pulls himself to his feet. "Aaah!" he says, holding on to her knees.

"Hello, Jeffrey," she says, smiling, and puts a hand on his head as she turns back to the phone. Jeffrey basks in the pleasure of her touch. *Wanted Grandma,* he thinks with great satisfaction. *Got her!* He looks down at his feet and stamps the floor with satisfaction.

STAGGERING TOWARD INDEPENDENCE: YOUR CHILD'S PROGRESS IN THE SECOND YEAR

There is something about a one-year-old's taking his first unaided step that invites parents to sit back, take a deep breath, and congratulate themselves on how far their little one has come. This feeling of pride is well deserved. Your wide-eyed neophyte of a year ago has learned an amazing amount in his short lifetime. He has developed from a contented little bundle to a rolling, then reaching, then sitting, creeping, crawling, and perhaps even staggering dynamo. He has moved from responding instinctively to random stimuli toward anticipating certain actions, recognizing familiar objects and surroundings, and developing a rudimentary memory. He has learned to tell the difference between speech and other sounds, to play with "ba-ba-ba" and "da-da-da" sound combinations, to babble constantly in his own jargon, and even to say a word or two in real language. Most enjoyably, he has moved from communicating mostly through crying to seeking eye contact, smiling at loved ones, fussing to demonstrate his displeasure when they leave, and engaging in simple games and play with others. By his first birthday, real signs of his unique character have emerged, giving you some tantalizing hints of just what kind of child—and adult—he may turn out to be.

In fact, your twelve-month-old probably appears as supremely pleased with himself as you are with him. His pride in his new ability to communicate his desire for a cookie, to reach and control the television set, and to crawl after a ball if it rolls away gives him a typically cheerful disposition. The reality, though, is that beneath this placid self-sufficiency rumbles the drumbeat of major change. As we will see in Chapter 2, the body of that twelve-month-old playing happily on the floor has already begun gearing up for the enormous transformation into an upright, habitually walking state. The urge to practice walking will become practically irresistible between twelve and eighteen months—though his actual progress may be sporadic, involving "plateaus" in skill development that last several weeks or even longer. Whether or not he can yet get around on his own two feet, a child this age experiences great frustration at being confined and frequently expresses his feelings with tears and anger. As my colleague Dr. T. Berry Brazelton has pointed out in his book *Touchpoints,* the need to keep moving can even disrupt a one-year-old's sleep. Fortunately, these motor drives and their attendant side effects fade somewhat after about eighteen months in the face of a new focus on language and cognitive growth. After that, your little one may be better able to relax into a car seat, for example, if you talk with him or give him something interesting to play with.

Your one-year-old's increased ability to move around, explore, and experiment with objects will expose him to an enormous variety of fascinating new information. In Chapter 3, we will see how this interaction will teach him the concepts of empty and full, here and not-here, cause and effect. Predictable routines that you and others provide will help his brain develop the idea that events often take place in sequence—a discovery that will eventually help him understand the passage of time. As his memory improves, he will be able to learn more efficiently from daily experience. A better memory will also allow him to frame thoughts in his mind and hold on to them long enough to plan actions and carry them out deliberately.

Though he may already be able to say one, two, or even several recognizable words at the age of twelve months, your child's verbal abilities will really take off by around the middle of the second year, as his ability to frame thoughts improves. Though his verbal progress may be as sporadic as his motor development—and will only really progress when his ability to walk has been achieved—you can rest assured that even if he says nothing, he always understands much more than he can say. As we will learn in Chapter 4, your child could probably already respond to simple, two-word commands ("Come here") by his first birthday. By fifteen months, he will probably know, but not yet be able to say, the names of "his" people and pets. When children reach eighteen months, their spoken vocabulary often starts to increase at a rapid pace. "No" frequently becomes a favorite word. By the end of the second year, most will probably be able to speak in two-, three-, or four-word sentences (though the variance among children is very wide at this age) and understand perhaps two hundred words.

Much of your child's emotional development during this year wouldn't be possible without the physical, mental, and verbal progress that accompanies it. As we will see in Chapter 5, the twelve-month-old is just becoming aware that his thoughts are separate from those of others and are hidden from them unless he expresses them. This ability sharpens his interest in others' emotional states. Your child will begin to respond more to your emotional expressions. As the year progresses, his emotional energy will become increasingly focused on his desire to control his environment. Beginning at around fifteen to eighteen months, he will become easily frustrated when he cannot make things go the way he wants them to go. There may be howls of frustration as he decides *he* wants to be the one to leave when he feels like it; *he* wants to choose whether he wears shoes; *he* wants to decide whether he feels like eating. Since he is not yet able to reason or to consider long-term benefits, this can be a difficult time for you and your child. By the end of the year, though, his physical, mental, and verbal abilities will have caught up somewhat to his desire for independence, and he may become easier to get along with.

Your one-year-old's determination to walk, talk, think, and feel like a "big kid" will leave little room for socializing with other children during the first half of the year, but as his verbal, emotional, and mental growth continues, he will become increasingly able to turn outward and begin interacting with others. I will point out in Chapter 6 that the second half of the second year is an excellent time to begin arranging play dates, so your child can explore the idea of having a friend and so you can help him through the inevitable lessons in sharing, taking turns, and settling differences in acceptable ways.

All of this growth—physical, cognitive, verbal, emotional, and social—proceeds more comfortably for your child and your entire family if you are able to provide reliable routines for his daily life and enforce consistent limits that take his developmental stage into account. Chapters 7 and 8 are devoted to exploring ways in which to create predictable, but not rigid, routines for sleeping, eating, and other everyday activities and to begin teaching your child which behaviors are unacceptable to help him learn to govern himself.

Of course, there is no way to predict exactly when your child will achieve a particular milestone and no way to significantly hasten its arrival. "My friend Kathy and I had our first babies almost a month apart," a mother in a Washington, D.C., suburb recalled recently. "She and I grew up together, and the whole time we were pregnant, we talked about how much fun it would be to have kids who were best friends. The problem is that her son, Gabriel, always seems to accomplish things before mine does, even though he's three weeks younger than my Kevin. Gabe just had his first birthday, and when we're over at his house for a visit, he walks around like he owns the place, while Kevin sits in one spot and babbles. I just wonder sometimes what Kathy is doing that I'm not doing."

The answer, quite probably, is "Nothing." Despite our tendency to compare our kids to others, until a child is ready, there is not really much you can do to help him move forward except be patient and encourage the efforts he does make. Rest assured that he is not just sitting idle; he's working on other skills that you aren't focused on. Observe him carefully, looking for clues to what his current interests are so you can encourage them. Understand that his entire being is concentrated on learning to do precisely what you want him to do, but that the challenges of these very difficult and complex growth spurts will sometimes require him to rest, review old skills, and vent his frustration. And next time your best friend's one-year-old talks circles around your babbling little one, pick up your baby, give him a hug, and tell him he's the best conversationalist you've ever known.

Toddlers love to experiment with new textures, and self-feeding is a wonderful advance this year.

Planning Ahead

As your baby faces the enormous challenges of learning to walk, talk, and understand others' points of view, he is bound to run into frustrations practically every waking hour of his day. At times it is tempting just to impose circumstances on your toddler and let him wail (putting him in a playpen while you're on the telephone, for example, instead of letting him practice toddling around the living room), telling yourself that he needs to learn to deal with frustration in any case. Though it's true that learning to postpone gratification is a necessary skill, it's better learned at a later age. During this year, forcing your child frequently to endure a frustrating situation that makes him cry just wastes valuable time he could have spent developing his walking, communicating, or thinking abilities. Experienced parents and other caregivers will tell you that a more productive approach is to *think ahead,* arranging your child's environment as much as possible to prevent unnecessary conflicts before they happen.

Placing your child's toys at his eye level (in boxes or baskets while he is crawling, on low shelves when he starts to walk) will save him from having to cry when he wants to play with something new. If he constantly pulls the books off your lower bookshelves, start storing his own picture books there. If he loves to play with your dishwasher, plan to use dishwashing time as an exercise in learning cooperation, letting him help you load and unload the silverware and open and close the dishwasher door. You can plan ahead for a finicky eater by keeping a variety of his favorite easily prepared foods on hand and letting him decide what he'd like to eat for lunch that day. Taking him outside will be easier for everyone if you pack extra food in case he gets hungry and give him his nap before you go (or plan to bring him home before he begins to get sleepy). Of course, in some cases frustration can be a good thing (out-of-reach toys motivate babies to stand up!), but most of the time a little forethought will prevent many a nonproductive, exhausting battle.

LEARNING EVERY SECOND: HOW YOUR CHILD'S COMPREHENSION GROWS

Imagine what it must be like to be a twelve-month-old. Just as his body is bursting to move forward, his mind is making quantum leaps in its own development—taking in information like a sponge and literally re-forming itself around the kinds of stimulation it receives. Where once he perceived only a chaotic jumble of color, light, and sound, certain reliable patterns have emerged. He has figured out such basic concepts as up and down, here and there, and the differences between people and objects but is only beginning to understand that a parent who leaves the room continues to exist, that a plate pushed to the edge of a table will fall off, that the baby he sees in the mirror is himself.

Each of these vital neurological advances, and many more, will occur in your child's second year, propelled by the phenomenal brain development that began before birth and continues at the same rapid pace until about age two. During this period, the brain expands more rapidly than at any other time of life. Its 100 billion neurons, only loosely wired for the processes of vision, speech, movement, and touch at birth, have been building synaptic connections ever since, creating a network of interactive parts that has transformed your watchful newborn. He is now an observant individual capable of understanding the world around him and acting on what he knows. His brain has grown physically as well, from one-fourth its adult size at birth to three-fourths of its full size by age two.

Between the ages of six and eighteen months, your baby's neurological net grows increasingly dense, until it contains approximately one and a half times more branches (used to transmit messages within the brain) than he could ever use as an adult. At this point, most of the branches are still unused. Recent research by a large number of experts, including Drs. Craig Ramey of the University of Alabama at Birmingham and Harry Chugani of Wayne State University in Detroit, has revealed that which branches become permanent and which ones die away in early childhood depends *almost entirely* on the quality of physical, emotional, and cognitive stimulation a child receives before the end of the third year. Once a neuronal passage is stimulated by experience, its connections are reinforced and it becomes stronger. The stronger it becomes, the more likely it is that it will spring into action the next time a similar experience occurs—and the more easily it will integrate the new information. This cycle of experience and neuronal integration is how learning takes place.

In other words, your one-year-old is a bubbling cauldron of pure human potential, perhaps never more open to learning than right now. It is both exciting and daunting to consider how great a difference you can make from now on in the quality of his inner world. By playing peekaboo, reading stories, and sharing nursery rhymes with your baby, you are not only having fun with him and deepening your emotional connection, but you're also literally improving the quality of his mind. This is especially important now, because, as we will see throughout this book, certain "critical windows" of neurological development open between ages one and two (in, for example, the areas of language and some aspects of emotional growth) that will never open quite as wide again.

A PARENT'S STORY

Mastering the Software

"I have to tell you about the major breakthrough I had last week about my daughter, Kendra, and what she's going through," Giselle, the mother of a thirteen-month-old in my parenting group, told me recently. "I had just bought a new computer with all this really great new software that I had to learn from scratch. So I set it up on the dining-room table and started practicing. Meanwhile, Kendra was playing on the floor nearby, or staggering around the house, or watching her brother Jared play with his toys, and it seemed like every fifteen seconds she started wailing. Either she was mad because Jared had left the room, or she was mad because he had a toy and she wanted it, or she was mad about something none of us could figure out. And there I was, trying to work with this software that I couldn't make go, and the harder I tried, the less it seemed to work.

"Then, in the middle of all this frustration, Kendra crawled over to me, pointed at the fruit bowl, and said, 'Orange!' I turned to her and yelled back, 'No!'

Toddlers' newfound skills allow them to explore their expanding world in exciting ways.

"Of course, she burst into tears, and I hated myself for yelling at her. *I sound just like a one-year-old,* I thought. And then it hit me like a bolt of lightning: *Of course I do. Kendra and I are going through exactly the same thing!* Her trying to figure out how to make me give her that orange was exactly like me trying to make a command work right on my computer.

"I was overwhelmed with sympathy for both of us. Believe me, next time she gets upset because she can't run after the dog or reach something she wants, I'll be more sympathetic. And I'll understand how happy she is when she finally accomplishes those things, too."

LEARNING THROUGH THE SENSES: THE IMPORTANCE OF PLAY

For a one-year-old, the world is a jumble of kaleidoscopic sensations, and all of his energy is directed toward piecing the fragments of sound, image, movement, texture, taste, and emotional expression into a satisfying picture of how the world works. Tell a one-year-old that you'll be back in a minute and he'll quite likely begin crying the moment you leave the room. Play peekaboo with him—letting his eyes register your appearance, disappearance, and reappearance—and he will eventually come to understand that when you go away, you *will* come back. Other concepts that a child this age must master can best be learned through sensory experience as well. Causality—the notion that a specific action leads to a predictable result—can be experienced by stacking two blocks and knocking them down, kicking a ball and watching it roll away, or (unfortunately) snatching a toy from a sibling and watching her cry. The one-year-old's obsession with imitation may have something to do with this need to learn through physical sensation. Mimicking a parent's vocalizations or a sibling's behavior tells a toddler more about that experience—how it feels, on many levels—than passively witnessing it ever would. Repeating the words or behavior over and over gives him the same sense of "learning by doing" that helps us adults learn most effectively, while providing a sense of comfort and predictability.

A love of sensory experience also feeds the one-year-old's explosion in language development. Just watch your little one babbling to himself in the morning before you pick him up out of his crib, and you will see that the physical pleasure of creating different sound combinations is a big part of his motivation for learning. Language gives him the satisfying feeling of control he so craves at this age. His first words are likely to be labeling words (nouns such as "doggie" and "ba-ba"), and in a very real sense, his ability to name an object is equivalent to "owning" or controlling it. By eighteen months, he may begin to incorporate labeling words with actions ("Truck go") and to relate an object to a place ("Truck here"). This mastery of language gives him a way to reach beyond his body for the first time, moving toward a more symbolic relationship with his world—a relationship that will also reveal itself in his new ability to pretend that a box is a house, a doll a baby, or Daddy's shoulders a horse to ride.

Meanwhile, though, it is important to understand how close the links are among your toddler's physical, cognitive, and emotional worlds. His block-stacking and ball-kicking pursuits help him not only to understand the concept of cause and effect but also to develop his gross-motor skills. The games of peekaboo that lead to a cognitive understanding of object (and person) permanence also provide the emotional reinforcement of warm, pleasurable parent-child interaction. Your awareness of these activities' invaluable bonuses can help you guide and support your child's emotional and social development throughout this period as effectively as you nurture his body and brain.

When rolling a ball back and forth to each other, you can talk about and demonstrate "taking turns." When you are coloring together and he wants your red crayon, you can give it to him while introducing the concept of sharing. Not all of these attempts to ground your child emotionally will "take" the first, second, or even third time, of course, but this is the age to begin experimenting with ways to help him understand and manage his emotions. In any case, as recent research causes scientists to push the age of comprehension back further and further toward infancy, it makes sense to introduce any concept just a little earlier than you think your child can understand it. At the very least, you'll be ready when he is.

THE TOY BOX

At Twelve Months

It is morning, breakfast is finished and Sam is crawling happily across the living-room floor. At the far end is his toy basket, and he can see his favorite toy—a plastic disk with brightly colored buttons that play animal sounds when you press them—sticking out over the edge. He reaches the basket, rises to his knees, and tugs on the toy until it comes free. It slips out of his hands and lands on the wooden floor with a loud, satisfying bang. Intrigued, Sam moves closer to the toy. He picks it up, then lets it drop again. *Bang!* Sam can feel the vibration from the noise in his legs and feet. He giggles and picks the toy up again. *Bang!* Sam continues picking up the toy and dropping it, fascinated by the relationship between the object's falling and the noise it makes. Every sense is busily taking in this information and feeding it to his curious brain.

Letting the toy drop to the ground one last time, Sam falls on top of it, exhausted. His arm accidentally pushes one of the buttons, and the toy emits a rooster's crow. "Sam!" says his mother's voice somewhere above him. "You made the rooster crow! That's wonderful!" Astonished, Sam looks from the toy to his mother's smiling face, to the toy again. He swings his arm down and hits another button. The toy meows like a cat. "Look," says his mother. "You made the cat meow." Amazed, Sam stares at the toy. A great number of connections—in the cognitive, emotional, and physical areas—are being stimulated in his brain. Soon Sam crawls away to look for other amusement. But the seemingly random, undirected play experience has not been wasted. Sam's brain will build on this experience of dropping something and watching it fall, of performing an action and receiving praise, of pushing a button and hearing a sound, and of hearing such words as "Look," "cat," and "meow"—moving him along in his development in a natural, pleasurable way.

MANAGING HIS WORLD: YOUR TWENTY-FOUR-MONTH-OLD

When you stop to consider how much your child is learning every single moment he's alive, a toddler starts to seem like a truly wondrous being. Draining as his enormous energy can be at times, frustrating as his determined "No!" or even his tantrums can be, it is impossible (in our calmer moments) not to admire him for his sheer determination and drive. It's been a very eventful year for Philip and for his parents, too, as they learned to deal with his frustration at his limited ability to control events, to communicate his feelings to others, or to make himself feel better. As his skills developed, his level of frustration decreased. As his parents got to know him better, they found ways to prepare for and deal with many of the difficult moments that did arise. Now, as his second birthday approaches, they are more relaxed as they watch him play, knowing that he is less likely to throw away a challenging toy in anger than to gesture at them to make it work, that he will use his past experiences to help him solve its mysteries, and that he knows that whether or not he can master the toy, he is a smart little boy.

As you read more about your child in the chapters that follow, keep in mind how exciting this period is for him. Support him in his admirable attempts to learn, develop, and grow. And be patient. Remember that your child is different from all others. He is not likely to follow exactly any developmental checklist put forth in parenting books and magazines (including the timetable that follows, which is intended not as a "test" but as a general guide). In the end, the vast inconsistencies in the ways children grow are what keep them fascinating. So appreciate him as he is, and be glad that he can still—and always will—manage to surprise you now and then.

ADVANCES

Major Achievements in the Second Year

Here are a scattering of behaviors that parents often see at these ages. If your child doesn't demonstrate them at the time indicated, don't be alarmed. Think of these as new territory he will probably visit soon.

12 MONTHS	Stands alone
	Responds to very simple commands
	Indicates what he wants mostly with gestures
	Plays alone when with other children
15 MONTHS	Tries hard to communicate
	May walk with more confidence
	May enjoy saying no

18 MONTHS	Likes to look at books
	Displays increased vocabulary
	Gets frustrated easily
21 MONTHS	Can climb stairs
	Likes to help with household chores
	Can carry out a simple plan
24 MONTHS	Can probably form two-, three-, or four-word sentences
	Engages in basic pretend play
	Is much more confident on his feet

FIRST-PERSON SINGULAR

In the next twelve months, your child's progress will amaze you, as he advances in walking, talking, feeding himself, and interacting with new friends. Take a moment now to fantasize about what sort of person is about to blossom from the seeds of personality you've already been observing. What will he be like—risk-taking and adventurous, sociable and chatty, curious and intense, shy and sensitive—more like his mother or his dad? What will he like to do most? How do you expect to structure his days? By writing down your ideas now, you can compare them to how you feel about your child twelve months from now, when you reflect on what an exciting time the two of you have just gone through.

CHAPTER 2

Starting the Motor—
My Physical Abilities

B y the time she's two, she will be walking, feeding herself, punching buttons, hammering pegs, and opening every cabinet door in the house.

For weeks, twelve-month-old Tara has been cruising around the house on her own two feet, keeping one hand on a piece of furniture, the wall, or a friendly adult's pants leg as she experimented with walking upright. Rob and Liza, her parents, have pulled out the cameras half a dozen times already, convinced she was about to take her first unaided step, but each time Tara thought better of letting go of her support and turned back toward the coffee table or dropped onto her hands and knees. Last night would have been the perfect time for her to cross the walking threshold: Grandma, Granddad, and Rob's brother's family were all over for dinner and put a lot of energy into encouraging her to take a few steps across the room. Tara reveled in their attention—sitting on the floor, waving her hands, and chortling—without providing the expected "entertainment" in exchange. Tonight Rob and Liza sit slumped together on the couch, watching television, a little discouraged over Tara's progress, though nether one will admit it.

Meanwhile, Tara sits in front of her toy box in the corner of the living room, playing contentedly with a wooden hammer and pegs. If she senses her parents' suppressed frustration, she has no idea what's causing it. Searching for another toy, she grasps the edge of the toy box and pulls herself to her feet. While she's digging around, she hears a pleasant tinkling sound and turns to see her mother lifting a glass of iced tea to her lips. The ice in the glass is what's making the soft, pleasant sound. It glistens as it moves around inside the glass. Tara is filled with an overwhelming desire to touch it.

She grunts to express her desire for the glass. Then, without thinking, she starts moving toward it. The ice continues to glisten tantalizingly inside the glass. By now Tara has walked as far as she can toward the couch without letting go of the toy box. She hesitates, looking from the box to the glass in her mother's hand. Then, just like that, she lets go.

"Liza!" Rob has glanced away from the television in time to see Tara take a first, tentative step. "Liza, look!" Liza watches, too, as Tara staggers forward again. The momentum of this second step sends her plopping back down to the floor. Her surprise is magnified by her parents' sudden, inexplicable explosion of applause, and she starts to howl. "You did it, Tara!" Rob shouts, rushing over to scoop her up. "Liza, where's the camera! I can't believe we left it in the dining room!" He gives her daughter a big hug, while she continues wailing—little realizing that she's just made a literal "first step" into the world of adult human beings.

Over the next year Tara will continue to develop and refine her walking ability—not all at once, and not in a smooth, regular sequence, but in uneven spurts of activity that will alternate and overlap with other advances. Soon, motivated by her parents' praise, her desire to examine objects that are otherwise out of reach, and her inner drive toward motor development, her first unsteady steps will progress to a wide-legged, swaybacked, staggering toddler's gait. By her second birthday her posture will have begun to straighten somewhat, her movements become smoother, and her feet taken her to practically every nook and cranny in the house in a constant search for new stimuli for her hungry mind. She will have learned to feed herself with a spoon, empty and fill containers, punch buttons, pull levers, hammer pegs, and open cabinets and drawers. So much of her parents' energy will be spent looking out for their child's safety as she plows ahead from room to room, sidewalk to playground, and parking lot to department store, grasping and manipulating any object within reach, that they'll no doubt marvel over that first-birthday lament, "I can't wait until she walks!" But even the weariest parent has to admire the tenacity with which the one-year-old moves forward through her environment, utterly determined to learn about every aspect of the world—and of her brand-new walking, learning, exploring self.

THE TOY BOX

At Twelve Months

Sonya has found her favorite new toy in her toy box—the plastic shape box Mommy gave her yesterday. She smiles and sits down on the floor with it, babbling to herself. She likes the rattling noise the shapes make inside. Mommy appears, says something in a pleasant voice, and opens the lid of the box. Delighted, Sonya holds up the box, then tips it over. The different-shaped plastic blocks fall out! *Wow—that was interesting.*

Before Sonya can investigate further, Mommy puts the lid back on and hands her one of the blocks. "Circle," Mommy says. She points to a round hole in the box. Frowning in concentration, Sonya tries to maneuver her hand toward the hole. After some trial and error, she manages to get the circle into the round hole. The nice noise it makes when it drops in and the happy sounds Mommy makes echo Sonya's feeling of satisfaction at having made her hand do what she wanted it to do.

Mommy hands Sonya another shape. "Square," Mommy says. Sonya confidently moves the square toward the round hole. But it won't go in. Sonya tries several times to solve this problem, but her fine-motor and cognitive skills aren't quite up to it yet. She smacks the box with the plastic square. Suddenly the muscles in her legs call to her. It's time to move on! Sonya pulls herself to her feet and toddles off. She'll learn more about shapes another day.

EXPLORING THE BODY: MOTOR ACHIEVEMENTS IN THE FIRST YEAR

It's tempting to date your one-year-old's walking life from the moment she took that first wobbly step, but in fact she's been developing the muscle control required for walking and other advanced motor skills since she first learned to sit up, if not before. At six to seven months, she managed to operate her stomach, leg, and upper-body muscles sufficiently to sit while propping herself with her hands. Sometime between seven and ten months, she was able to sit without props, freeing her hands to reach out for and grasp the things she wanted. Meanwhile, her spine began to straighten from the six-month-old's slump to the greatly improved posture of the older baby. Soon afterward she contrived to get both knees under her abdomen, push up off the floor, and start creeping or crawling—perhaps backward at first.

By her first birthday, her body and brain have developed to the point at which walking becomes her top priority, whether or not she's actually taken a step. Eating, sleeping, and even cuddling will take a backseat to her urge to move until she satisfies her now overwhelming desire. A skilled creeper-crawler, she will amaze you with the speed at which she can cross a room on hands and knees. But her skill on all fours doesn't impress her any longer. She is now obsessed with the drive to pull herself upright.

You will not be able to predict exactly when those first steps will occur, and they will not necessarily follow her ability to stand and to cruise the furniture in a regular, smooth progression. She may cruise for a couple of weeks before venturing forth without help, or she may move straight from crawling to walking. This uneven, almost jerky progress is typical of the way all of us humans develop new physical skills. An adult learning to ice-skate, for example, might actually start by crawling on hands and knees until he feels comfortable standing on the ice. Just staying upright is a challenge for a while. Then, at some unpredictable moment, he will begin walking awkwardly. Several practice sessions later, the skater will begin to learn to balance "naturally" and start to pick up speed.

Learning to walk presents exactly the same challenges for a one-year-old—and proceeds in the same bumpy, uneven manner. There is probably no need for concern if your child continues cruising for weeks or even months after her first birthday without ever accomplishing that first step. Late walkers are just developing according to their own inner schedule; sooner or later that step will come. Keep in mind that heavier babies, and those with older siblings, tend to walk later than others. Your child's need to focus on one skill may cause her to appear "stuck" for a while. This is perfectly normal. She may even fall back temporarily, crawling again when she'd already learned to stand. This probably just means she needs a rest—like a skater who stops and holds on to the railing for a moment before moving on.

Whenever she does start to walk, your baby will be extremely proud of her accomplishment. Her face will be wreathed in smiles as she looks to you for the approval she rightfully expects. In the weeks that follow, she will devote nearly all her energy to refining her primitive walking skills, even "practicing" walking in her dreams to the point where her muscle movements wake her up.

A PARENT'S STORY

Car-Seat Blues

"Running errands used to be a breeze with Marisol," Connie, mother of two, told me. "She'd fall asleep three minutes after I started the engine. The vibration would just put her right out." Now, though, Marisol was twelve months old, and Connie said that her daughter screamed every time she even heard the word "car."

It's easy to imagine how infuriating it must be for a one-year-old, whose deepest desire is to remain constantly on the move, to be buckled into a confining baby seat and forced to sit in a car for half an hour or longer at a time. "She kicks and screams the whole time I'm trying to close that buckle," Connie said, "even when I promise she'll just be there for a little while."

Connie wondered if her daughter was "acting spoiled" by screaming every time she rode in the car. She wasn't, of course—

she was just acting normal. As I pointed out to Connie, trying to force a one-year-old to sit quietly in confinement is like trying to teach a cat not to purr. The best way to handle this unpleasant situation is to minimize the number of times you'll have to go through it. Consider how many stops you plan to make while doing your errands—and how many times you plan to take your toddler out of her seat and then (horrors!) put her back in. Is there any way to minimize the number of stops—by, say, walking instead of driving between two nearby stores, using the drive-through windows at banks, restaurants, photo developers, etc.—or perhaps skipping one or two errands until you can go alone?

When you do have to buckle her in, distract her from her horrible "I'm out of control" feelings by showing her a snack and telling her she can have it "as soon as you're in your seat." Keep a tape of her favorite songs in the car to play as you drive along, or sing to her and encourage her to join in. Some activities designed especially for car-seat use may be appropriate, as long as she can manipulate them on her own: busy books that fasten onto the seat, a plastic steering wheel that will make her feel as though *she* is driving the car, or a noise-making toy that she can hold. Remember, if you can turn car time into a fun experience *before* she starts to resent sitting in her seat, she may continue to look forward to riding around with you and not initiate the pattern of resistance that can make running errands so difficult.

Remember, though, never leave your child in the car unattended. Always take her with you, even if you are just dropping off a package at the post office. Don't take a chance with your baby's health or safety.

YOU CAN'T STOP ME NOW: LEARNING TO WALK IN THE SECOND YEAR

By fifteen months, your child may well be able to walk with relative ease even while holding something in her hands, though she continues to use a wide-legged gait and falls easily and frequently. Knowing how shaky her new skill still is, she's likely to drop down to her hands and knees and crawl when she's in a hurry. (I remember watching my own toddler, eager to pick up a ball and run, drop to his knees, put the ball in his mouth, and then crawl across the room at top speed.) This new ability to motor around means that the child is much better able to explore her world in multifaceted ways—reaching for and grasping new objects, climbing up and over things, and opening cupboard doors. Clearly, it also means she has many more opportunities to seriously hurt herself by falling or handling dangerous objects. It's time to fence off stairways, since she can probably crawl up them. Install baby locks on cabinets that contain dangerous substances, or move the substances to a cabinet that's out of reach. It's fine to use a playpen when you need to wash your hair, concentrate on a phone call, or otherwise be unavailable to keep her safe—as long as you "set her loose" afterward to continue satisfying her healthy urge to explore.

Rhythm and patterns of all kinds become increasingly interesting to one-year-olds as they continue to practice walking, climbing, and moving in other ways. Your child will find interruptions in rhythmic clapping very funny—as when you sing "Pop Goes the Weasel" or chant "This Little Piggy" and end with a tickle. As soon as she can walk easily, she's likely to climb onto your leg for a game of "This is the way the ladies ride" or onto your lap for a bounce on your knee. She'll also begin to move spontaneously to rhythmic music, expressing her pleasure in the beat by bouncing, swaying, and trying to sing a word now and then. This rhythmic involvement is important for enhancing such cognitive growth as the comprehension of sequence and time, as well as motor skills. You can encourage your little one's participation by joining in, moving joyfully to the music yourself.

By around eighteen months, your toddler will begin to exude a new confidence in moving her body. She will look more at ease as she stands and examines objects or walks toward a loved one. She will still stagger a bit and continue to fall frequently, but her movements will have become noticeably smoother and more deliberate than they were even three months earlier. At this point, her greatest joys will center on running (still stiffly, and just a little bit at a time), climbing and descending stairs (placing two feet on each step), and climbing into, up, and over any object in her path. Her movements are still mostly big ones (lugging, pulling, pushing). When she throws a ball while sitting, her legs will kick out at the same time. Her entire body is still involved in nearly every movement. Refinement will come later.

Don't expect her to direct her own activities consciously at this age. Ceaselessly wandering around, she tends to bump into objects at random, then start to investigate them. In fact, the eighteen-month-old's motto must be "Do before you think." She will run into the next room and then decide to explore it, instead of the other way around. She will put an object into her mouth and then decide whether or not she wants to taste it. Because of this do-first-think-later mentality, and because she's in almost constant motion, it's still vital to monitor her activity with great care. It takes only an instant for her to pull on an electrical cord in an effort to learn about it or to make a big leap forward on the "down" escalator just because she feels like moving.

During this period—during her entire development, for that matter—your child will progress through each stage of growth largely through a process of trial-and-error experience. In other words, chances are excellent that she did not grab that electrical cord to aggravate you, but because she needed to find out what would happen if she did. Repetition—and experiencing minute variations with each repetition—is another one of a child's most powerful tools for integrating physical and other kinds of knowledge. Your toddler may run back and forth the length of the house fifty times in a given hour or bang on pots and pans for five minutes at a stretch—not to drive you crazy, as it sometimes seems, but because she needs to practice until she gets it right.

Vital as they are, these approaches to learning can truly test parents', caregivers', and other family members' patience during this year. It may help to look forward to the day—at around twenty-one months—when you first see how this sometimes maddening behavior has begun to pay off. By that time, your child will start to exhibit new smoothness and self-confidence in walking and running. The pleasure she has learned to take in her body will be apparent in her desire to run, dance, twirl, jump, and climb whenever she gets the chance. Her new skills will instill a healthy sense of independence that will expand as she enters her third year.

If the first steps she took toward you around her first birthday filled you with well-deserved satisfaction, her first steps *away* around her second birthday should make you feel equally proud. You have given her the room she needs to measure herself against the world and see what she (and it) is made of. She now has the confidence to move ahead on a more sophisticated level, comfortable with her body and with what she can make it do.

Walking Delays

It's difficult to remain calm when your one-year-old is still crawling long after her friends have begun walking erect. But, as I will emphasize throughout this book, the *rate* of development among one-year-olds varies widely, even if the *sequence* of steps is nearly always the same. There is probably no need for concern when your child has not begun walking by thirteen or fourteen months, if her other developmental skills seem to be on track and there is no family history of physical developmental problems. You may be able to spur her progress somewhat by regularly holding her hands and "walking" her to rhythmic music or nursery-rhyme chants in a fun, nonpressured manner. One thing to avoid: using a walker to encourage her to take her first steps. The American Academy of Pediatrics (AAP) strongly discourages the use of walkers because they are responsible for a huge number of accidents among five- to fifteen-month-olds (25,000 accidents in 1993). Walkers roll down stairs; tip over, causing children to hit their heads; and allow babies access to dangerous objects that parents had thought were out of their reach. In any case, the AAP reports, walkers have no effect on babies' walking development and may even delay it, since they prevent children from practicing the movements necessary to get to their feet and start moving on their own.

Certainly, if your child appears slow in several other areas of physical development and you have a "gut feeling" that something is wrong, monitor her progress (but don't panic), and call your pediatrician's office or mention your concerns at her next checkup. Your pediatrician has probably been tracking her development all along, and chances are that the two of you can figure out together whether anything's wrong. Remember, you know your child better than anyone else does, and as with all other aspects of raising your child, your instincts regarding her physical development are a valuable tool, not to be discounted.

I CAN DO IT MYSELF:
FINE-MOTOR DEVELOPMENT

Though walking is a primary aspect of physical development this year, it's not the only way your child is growing. Fine-motor development—her ability to grasp and manipulate objects and control other aspects of movement—is phenomenal right now, helping her become almost as independent as she'd like to be. From the beginning, this development has been aided by advances in her movement skills. At age four months, when she was limited to lying on her back or sitting in her bouncy seat, she concentrated on learning to wave her hands, kick her legs, and hang on to objects that were handed to her. At seven to ten months, she could grasp and manipulate only objects that were within her reach while sitting up. At ten to twelve months, her crawling ability gave her better access to new objects, and her hands became increasingly active and helpful.

By her first birthday, her fast-speed crawling and hesitant first steps have given her more opportunities to refine her grasping and reaching ability, thus exploring her world in new ways. Now that she can grasp tiny objects between her thumb and forefinger, now that her hands have learned to grasp and release, she delights in comparing the textures of various objects and trying hard to figure out "how things work" in general.

The confidence that increased movement affords her extends to all other aspects of your one-year-old's life. At twelve months, she's likely to start being very demanding about wanting to do things herself. Often, she thinks she can do more than she can, and her unexpected failure proves very frustrating. Providing her with experiences at which

Safety is still a critical issue, as toddlers continue to explore objects with their fingers and their mouths.

she can succeed—allowing her to finger-feed herself, letting her "pretend" to feed herself with a spoon, cooperating with the seemingly endless games of drop-the-toy-and-make-Daddy-give-it-back, and showing her how to use fat toddlers' crayons—not only will further bolster her confidence but may lessen the number of outraged cries.

By age twelve months, your baby can form her hand around the shape of an object, such as a spoon or a marker, and she can tell if an object is out of reach. If you give her a ball, she can fling it awkwardly or roll it along the floor. She can wave bye-bye, and her continued involvement in old games such as peekaboo and patty-cake help her improve her hand-eye coordination, her ability to clap, and other skills.

At around fifteen months, your child will probably become fascinated by the process of emptying and filling containers—though she'll still be much better at the emptying part. Handing her a big bowl full of tennis balls (or any other objects big enough not to choke her) will keep her occupied for a surprisingly long time. This process of putting in and taking out will help her begin to understand the concept behind a shape box, if she has one; at this age she should be able to fit a round block into a round hole. Hammering pegs into holes (as with toolbench toys) provides the same kind of satisfaction on a more whole-body level. Stacking blocks has also become great fun. Your child can probably stack at least one small block on top of another. It's a good idea to keep the toys out in the open, at eye level, so she can get to them easily when she's in the mood. Your child's enchantment with putting objects inside other objects will motivate her to help you put things away—though she may want to dump them right out again!

At eighteen months, your baby's ability to walk, grab, push, and pull has improved greatly, but her hand and arm movements are still a bit awkward. She still uses whole-arm movements in throwing a ball or playing with her toys. She often drops things. When she tries to turn the page of a book, she usually turns three or four instead. Still, her muscles are beginning to work together better. She can now build a tower of three or four small blocks, though she fusses when they fall over. She can pull a pull toy, but it's frustrating when it keeps tipping over. She can even use a spoon or fork, though she may still prefer her fingers.

During the last few months of this second year, your child's hand-

Toys that both encourage physical interaction and show concepts are best for toddler learning

eye coordination will continue to improve. She will experiment and learn to fit plastic or wooden rings onto a spindle in order of size. She will be able to bring a full spoon to her mouth (sometimes right side up). She'll get better at helping you put the silverware, pots and pans, and books in their proper places. She'll also learn to be more efficient in her movements: When holding two objects, for example, she'll figure out how to store one under each arm in order to take a third. This gradual (though not necessarily regular) improvement in coordination and fine hand movements will increase through the third year, as she learns to throw a ball; string beads; cut with scissors; hold a cup of milk without spilling; pull on pants, shirt, and laceless shoes; and build an even taller tower of blocks. But the grace with which she moves and the skill with which she manipulates her small body are grounded largely in the experiences she has had this past year. Practice makes perfect for children as well as adults. The more opportunities she has to experiment with physical movement, with handling objects, and with self-care skills such as feeding and dressing herself, the more at ease she will become with her body and its place in the world.

Physics at Lunchtime

Mmm. Smells good. Naomi, fourteen months old, sits in her high chair, gazing at her plate of rice and chicken. *If I can just get my hand on it . . . There.* Naomi has a nice handful of chicken, but how can she get it to her mouth? *Hard to do—like holding my spoon without dropping it.* Concentrating hard, she moves her fist toward her face, using her arm like a crane. Uh-oh! She's knocked her sippy cup of milk to the floor.

Dad picks up the cup, puts it back on the tray, and says something to his daughter. Naomi smiles at him, though she doesn't understand his words. *Hmm,* she thinks. *Naomi make cup fall again . . .*

Her eyes wander to her hand. *Uh-oh! No chicken!* In her fascination with the fallen cup, she has let go of her food. *Get milk,* she decides, and slowly maneuvers her hands toward the cup, wholly engrossed in her task as her dad looks impatiently on.

I CAN GO ANYWHERE: SAFETY CONCERNS

To the one-year-old, the world is a fabulous playground that begs to be explored, yet her concepts of what is and is not physically safe haven't yet developed sufficiently. For this reason, the second and third years are two of the most difficult in which to keep your little one safe. Speeding cars, steep stairways, candy-colored pills, and intriguing bottles in the cabinet under the kitchen sink all beckon, inviting her to touch, climb, taste, probe, and otherwise investigate. Since you can't watch your child every moment of every day for the rest of her life, the sooner you begin to teach her the "habits of mind" with which she can ensure her own safety, the better off she and you will be. Fortunately, young children are largely creatures of habit, so if you focus on just a few rules that can never be broken, your child will most likely accept them.

To this end, make sure that *every* time you go out walking, she holds an adult's hand before she crosses the street. Teach her *never* to touch the stovetop, because it may be hot. *Never* allow her to play with cleaning-fluid containers, even if they've been washed out and refilled with sand or water (use soda bottles instead). Don't assume that she will follow these rules on her own just because you've repeated them to her. You probably baby-proofed your home to a certain extent once she learned to crawl, covering electrical sockets, removing heavy and/or dangerous objects from coffee tables, etc. Now that she is walking, you will need to "raise the height" of baby-proofing to her eye, reach, and exploration level, installing baby gates, placing rugs or other padding under stairs, putting cushions under the crib when she starts trying to climb out, and installing lockable latches on kitchen and bathroom cabinets. Lots of parents suggest literally getting down to her level and looking around to discover all the tempting but dangerous or breakable items within her reach. (Did you remember the computer? Is there spare change lying around?) Remember, now she can get her hands on many more small objects that could choke her if she puts them in her mouth, and she is likely to do so. Keep a constant eye out for these objects and place them up high. The one-to-two-year-old doesn't worry about the consequences of climbing a ladder, popping a marble into her mouth, or toddling out into the street, so as the adult, you have to.

Q & A

Don't Touch or Can't Reach?

Q: My sister and I have a difference of opinion about how much parents should baby-proof their houses when their kids learn to get around on their own. My sister, who has a nine-month-old, has put every single breakable or dangerous thing out of reach in her house. I feel that my one-year-old needs to learn how to deal with these things and get to know what's fragile and what's dangerous, so I put only serious poisons like household cleaners out of reach and leave the rest. Which of us is right?

A: To a great extent, you both are. Baby-proofing works not only to protect your toddler from obvious dangers such as electrical sockets and bleach but also to allow your home life to proceed smoothly without repeated, avoidable minor crises. If your one-year-old has become so fascinated by the telephone that she can't resist constantly taking it off the hook, for example, moving the phone will prevent her getting into trouble constantly and your losing your temper. Later, you can demonstrate the phone's purpose by helping her call Grandma. In general, it's best to create as varied and rich an environment as possible for your child (including opportunities to learn how to handle some breakable objects), while protecting her safety and the family's peace of mind. So put away your favorite breakable objects, but leave out a few less precious and less dangerous things for her to practice with. In this way, she can learn while you can spend much less time saying no.

I TRY IT NOW: LIVING WITH EXPERIMENTATION

As your child approaches her second birthday, she will become increasingly aware of the progress she has made in becoming an independent person, just like her older siblings, parents, and caregivers. This feels very good, and she will naturally want to augment that good feeling by acting as independently as possible. As parents, our job is to encourage this healthy drive toward independence without pushing too hard. It's a good idea to applaud your baby's efforts to feed herself with a spoon, for instance. It's not a good idea to *make* her use a spoon at every mealtime or to tell her she's acting like a baby because she decides she needs a break from practicing that skill and reverts to feeding herself with her hands. Keep in mind also that young children cannot develop fully without a great deal of trial and error, repetition, and just plain mess. It's unpleasant to have her throw her food on the floor on days when you're already feeling stressed, but it's an inevitable part of a one-year-old's growth.

The happiest parents, it seems, are those who accept the fact that a mess will occur and prepare for it by placing newspaper under the high chair, using plastic dishes with suction cups to keep them on the high-chair tray, and keeping cleaning supplies nearby. By doing this, you free yourself to observe your child's progress and share in her delight over the new discoveries she's making amid the chaos. One mother of three whose home I visited had clearly devoted some thought to avoiding chaos in the playroom. She had arranged play areas and toy shelves at three different heights, so that the seven-year-old's toys were usually out of the three-year-old's reach, and the one-year-old could get to her own toys and no one else's. Imagine how many potential conflicts she eliminated with that single design effort! You will find that your child's life is increasingly full of such opportunities to maximize pleasure and minimize stress. Take advantage of them.

Just as there's no point in resenting the inevitable messes and repetitions of babyhood, it doesn't make much sense to confront head-on a little person so determined to control her environment. Maddening as it can be to watch the clock tick while your determined eighteen-month-old struggles to put on her own shoes, such attempts at self-sufficiency are a healthy, admirable, and utterly necessary part of growing up. The solution to these "I can do it myself!" dilemmas lies in what I call "the power of Velcro": making it as easy as possible for your child to manage her environment, so that she feels in control while you still manage to get to work on time. Keeping her snack food and dishes in a lower cabinet at her height, providing clothes with few buttons or snaps, placing a step-stool in the bathroom so she can stand at the sink while you help wash her hands—these are all ways to help your child feel independent while allowing you to get through the day efficiently. No, you are not spoiling her by waiting for her to manage on her own. You are giving this new human being the room she needs to grow.

EASING THE WAY

A Work Space of Her Own

If she hasn't already, your fifteen-month-old will soon enter her first age of perceived self-sufficiency, in which she believes she can do practically everything herself and will certainly insist on doing so. Since healthy self-confidence and a can-do attitude are positive qualities to encourage in any child, this might be a good time to provide your little one with a table and chair just her size. Sitting at a table enables her to play "office," to draw, to play with clay, and to manipulate stuffed animals more comfortably. By pulling up your own chair (or better yet, sitting on one that's her size), you can keep her company, observe her daily development in a thousand fascinating ways, and reinforce her sense of herself as a "big girl" who "works hard," just like the grown-ups in her world. As she practices with the fat crayons she probably prefers (you can tape down the edges of the paper to make it easier for her), you may notice that she can now imitate a stroke you make. Reading a picture book together, you may be surprised to see her try, and sometimes succeed, in turning a page. Her table can also be used for solitary snacks, where she can have her meal on a tray, practice holding her cup in both hands, and otherwise rehearse for the big-girl years ahead.

LOOK—I DID IT!: STEPPING INTO A WIDER WORLD

It's been a year since Tara took her first steps, surprising herself at least as much as her parents. Now, on her second birthday, she runs from room to room with all the energy and excitement of a growing girl. Over the past twelve months, her body has developed from that of a baby to that of a young child. Thanks to her parents' efforts to let her "do it herself" as much as possible, her coordination has improved; her gait is smoother and more efficient than it was just three months ago; she is able to feed herself, drink from a cup, and scribble with a crayon; and her precious sense of independence and self-sufficiency has been bolstered by her new (sometimes still flawed) ability to tend to herself, obtain what she needs, and explore her world. Her emotional and cognitive gains have been well served by her developing body—as her mom and dad know from having watched for signs of progress. She is a unique individual now, poised to take her first giant steps into the exciting world just outside her front door.

Fine- and Gross-Motor Achievements in the Second Year

12 MONTHS

Stands alone

May take a few steps

Stacks two blocks

Grasps and releases objects more easily

15 MONTHS

Walks with staggering gait

May like to climb

Holds a crayon

Turns pages of book

18 MONTHS

Walks; perhaps runs and jumps

Climbs more easily

Needs a hand going up stairs

Pulls toy while walking

Likes fitting shapes into matching holes

May try to draw with crayon

21 MONTHS

Runs faster

Squats frequently

Needs a hand going down stairs

Throws more accurately

Enjoys scribbling and finger painting

24 MONTHS

May climb and descend stairs alone

Is much sturdier on feet

Likes to dance

Can stack five or more blocks

May show preference for one hand

Now, while the issues of physical development are fresh in your mind, take some notes about your child's latest advances in areas relating to movement and other activity. How is her mobility changing? Is she attempting to feed herself? If you have a photograph or videotape of her six months ago, look at it and write down some of the ways in which her skills have advanced since then. How is her behavior different from that described in this chapter? How is it the same? What do her physical strengths and weaknesses seem to be at this time? What is her most exciting accomplishment so far? What do you really look forward to seeing her do next? If possible, videotape her now, crawling, walking, eating, and playing, so you can monitor her changes next year.

Remember, it isn't necessary to actively play with your child every moment you're in her company. Often, it's just as important to step back and observe quietly. These moments of observation can greatly increase your understanding and help you work with her more effectively in the future.

READER'S NOTES

_____

_____

_____

_____

_____

_____

_____

_____

CHAPTER 3

Thinking for Myself—My Cognitive Development

Duering the first three years, a child's environment literally helps build his brain.

When Leah was pregnant, she had dreamed that her son Craig's first birthday would be just like this: a sunny July afternoon with family and friends gathered in the backyard to celebrate. While the guests help arrange the gifts and peek in at the birthday cake in the kitchen, Leah sits on the back porch with Craig, blowing bubbles so he can watch them waft away on the breeze. Craig's round eyes track each floating orb with utmost seriousness. Each time a bubble bursts, his mouth makes a little O shape, his brow furrows, and he ducks his head to search for it. Leah laughs. "Look at this," she says to her husband, Jerry, who is video-taping the two of them. "Craig can't seem to get the idea that the bubbles are gone."

A friend calls Leah inside to help her set up the refreshments table. Leah leaps up, hands the bubble paraphernalia to Jerry, and runs inside. Behind her, Craig, who has been balancing unsteadily on his two chubby feet, falls back onto his bottom in surprise. *Where has Mommy gone?* his stunned gaze seems to say. *Has she disappeared forever, like the bubbles?* Craig stares at the empty space where his mommy just was. His eyes fill with tears and he starts to cry but stops the moment Mommy comes back to check on him.

It is sometimes very difficult for us adults to comprehend how a one-year-old views the world—especially since that view evolves constantly as he moves through this dynamic year. In this chapter we will examine your child's growing understanding of object permanence—the knowledge that people and objects continue to exist when they're out of his sight, his sense of where he is in space, and his concept of the passage of time. All of these concepts will be tested and refined as he becomes able to move about with greater ease, communicate more freely with others, and otherwise explore his world. The quality and variety of his encounters will largely define how complex and rich his thinking becomes. Gazing at bubbles is one of thousands of ways he might ponder the concepts of "here" and "not here." Your own natural coming and going is another. One of the greatest satisfactions—and responsibilities—of this year of parenting lies in providing your child with as wide an array of stimulating situations as possible and watching his understanding increase at a truly astounding rate.

NEW KNOWLEDGE ABOUT THE DEVELOPING BRAIN

Until recently most scientists believed that a baby's brain structure is for the most part determined by his genes, that it is virtually complete by the time he is born, and that this "inherited" aptitude determines in very large part how the child will interact with the world. Most of these assumptions were derived indirectly from animal research and observation and from interpretation of human behavior. As we know now, earlier scientists quite often underestimated how the brain works. Over the past few decades, new uses of noninvasive brain-imaging technologies, such as the positron emission tomography (PET) scan and magnetic resonance imaging (MRI), have allowed researchers to actually watch the brains of infants and children in the process of learning. These amazing windows into the working brain have created an explosion of new knowledge about human brain development—and have proven unequivocally that environment plays a much greater role in determining a child's intelligence quotient (IQ), emotional state, and destiny than scientists had ever imagined. In other words, during his first three years, your child's environment literally helps build his brain.

When your infant was born, his brain consisted of a jumble of neurons, most of them still waiting to be woven together into a fully operational mind. Some of this wiring had been accomplished through the genes, a little more was created via messages from the mother's hormones, and still more was the result of the sounds, rhythmic movements, and other "environmental" influences in the womb. After birth, the environmental input to the brain increased astronomically. Each new sight, sound, personal encounter, touch, and smell created a new connection in your child's developing neural web. The more often an experience was repeated—the more times your baby reached out for his rattle and grasped it, for instance—the more likely it was that the related "brain connections" would be reinforced and made permanent.

Even now, at twelve months, the building of your child's brain is far from complete. During this year, he will learn most of the fundamental concepts that allow us to move through the world easily—that objects can be hollow or solid, that containers can be full or empty, that one event can lead to another in a predictable sequence, and so on. To a large extent, these facts must be learned through interaction with the environment; they do not just appear in the brain through genetic programming. This is why it is so important that your child be exposed to as wide a variety of stimulation as possible (without overdoing, of course) during this year. Each of the physical, emotional, and intellectual experiences he has during these twelve months will affect to some degree the way his brain will be wired for the rest of his life.

This does not mean that the absence of any single experience or learning opportunity (say, playing with a shape box) will make a crucial difference for your child, but a general absence of stimulation in a particular area (practically no talk about shapes or no opportunity to categorize objects by shape) can certainly hold him back. The *timing* of these experiences is important also. Certain types of stimulation are much more effective at certain times than at others. Dr. Janellen Huttenlocher of the University of Chicago has repeatedly demonstrated that a child who is spoken to a great deal and allowed to practice responding during his first two years is more likely to develop good language skills. On the other hand (as twenty years of research by Drs. Alan Sroufe, Byron Egeland, and others at the University of Minnesota has shown), a child who is abused or emotionally neglected very early in life may never fully develop a sense of empathy or secure attachment, and this can translate into problem-solving difficulties, relationship and school problems, and other cognitive deficits as the child grows.

Neurologists call these prime-time opportunities *critical periods.* They are the developmental reason your child suddenly becomes so focused on mastering a particular skill such as walking, communicating through language, or strengthening emotional attachments. Though of course it is never too late to help a child improve his ability, children learn best when caregivers take note of where their attention is focused and support their learning in that area *at that time.* Therefore, general checklists of a one-year-old's developmental interests and achievements (such as the one at the end of this chapter) are much less important in helping your child learn than are your own observations of his current interests.

A PARENT'S STORY

Setting the Stage

"Okay, I admit it. I'm an ambitious mom, and I know it's gotten in the way of helping my kids sometimes," a colleague said over coffee the other day. "With my older son, Andrew, I truly bordered on the ridiculous—reading to him while he sat on the potty during toilet training, introducing him to toys that were designed for children years older than he was. In one sense I don't think it was energy wasted. At least Andrew knew that I loved him and that I cared a lot about what he thought and did. But the fact was, his brain wasn't ready to try to recognize the letters of the alphabet on a page, for instance, when he was eighteen months old. He was interested in stacking blocks at that time. Now I realize that back then he needed to learn about balancing objects, not about how to read.

"With Cass, my daughter, I've tried to do things another way—letting *her* decide when it was time to learn something. I knew I couldn't predict exactly when she'd be interested in what activity, and I was busier now with two kids, so I couldn't follow her around every minute to find out. Sometime around her first birthday I decided to set up the house so that she could play with what she wanted when she needed it. I put a sandbox in the backyard, a hammer and pegs in her little play space, and some books with pictures of characters she knew and liked on her bookshelf. My house looks like a little Montessori classroom now, but I really think it's better letting her choose her 'lessons' instead of my forcing them on her. She learns when she's ready—and that's the best way to learn."

YOU'VE COME A LONG WAY, BABY: NEUROLOGICAL ACHIEVEMENTS

"It's endlessly fascinating to me, trying to figure out how Emily's brain works," a mother in my parenting group mentioned the other day. "You can see how it develops from the way her behavior changes month to month, or sometimes even from day to day." It's true. You can gauge pretty accurately where your child is in his developmental sequence simply by watching how he behaves. Nearly everything a one-year-old does literally expresses his "state of mind" at that particular moment. If he focuses intently on eye contact as you play peekaboo with him, and looks concerned when your hand covers your eyes, he's at a very basic level of attention. If he giggles with delight when you disappear behind your hands, wait a few seconds, and then reappear, he's at a distinctly more sophisticated stage. As he gets up on two feet, opens a drawer, and dumps out the contents on the floor, he's moved toward knowing that objects exist even when they're out of sight.

Of course, this process of actively studying his environment did not begin on his first birthday; its pace has simply quickened now that he has greater physical opportunities to access new information. From the first day of life (and even before), he has been busily processing the data he receives through his senses and through interaction with the people and objects within his reach. As an infant, when his reach was obviously very limited, his learning focused for the most part on repeating actions that first occurred accidentally (or that you instigated for him). He first noticed his hand because it happened to pass in front of his face, for example; only after he noticed it did he begin trying to put it into his mouth. Between eight and twelve months, as he became able to grasp things while sitting and to crawl, his interest turned to repeating actions that created intriguing sights or sounds—shaking a noisy toy, for instance, or making "ba-ba-ba" sounds that tickled his lips and felt good in his mouth.

By his first birthday, your child's increased range has allowed him to begin behaving in more actively experimental ways, varying his actions and noting their effect on his environment. This is the age when he enjoys punching a variety of buttons on a plastic toy and watching different objects pop up. As the year unfolds, he will also enjoy experimenting on you—spinning the knobs on the stereo, for example, and looking to see how you react.

As your baby's understanding of the world increases and his brain continues making new connections, an important change takes place in his thinking sometime between eighteen months and two years. He becomes capable of thinking about something without its actually having to be there. This new ability to "think symbolically"—to picture playing with his ball without having just seen the ball right there in front of him—means that he will be able to cook up more predicaments to get himself into, because he can imagine scenarios and plan ahead a little. But it also means that he might avoid pinching his hand in the cupboard door because he can remember how much it hurt last time he did that, or can even generalize from the time he caught his finger in the toy box. Your toddler's developing language ability is a great help in enabling him to frame these concepts and scenarios in his mind. In the second half of the second year, his symbolic thinking and language abilities combine with great strides in imaginative play, empathy, and a host of other vital skills to bring him to an entirely new level of comprehension.

Hearts and Minds

Q: I have been taking my fifteen-month-old child to the same child-care center since he was eight months old. It's a small center, and fortunately the turnover is very low. My son has made some good friends among the child-care workers, and I think he feels very loved and secure there. However, I wonder whether he's getting enough intellectual stimulation. The staff are very good about holding the kids on their laps, cuddling them, and so on, but I don't really see much "teaching" going on. My question is, Should I look for a more stimulating environment or leave him where I feel he's loved?

A: You are the only one who can decide whether your child would do better in another situation. And naturally, all parents who work outside the home dream of finding a caregiver who is both nurturing and stimulating for their children. When making your decision, though, there are some developmental facts about children this age that you might want to keep in mind. First, studies have shown that children this age learn best—that is, their brains develop most efficiently—when the learning takes place in the context of secure, close relationships. Your one-year-old may be more open to learning where he is than with a new, unfamiliar, and possibly less nurturing caregiver. Second, much of what a child needs most to learn between twelve and twenty-four months— rock-bottom concepts including the dependability of loved ones, the predictability of daily routines, the near-certainty that when he communicates to another person the person will respond—can best be instilled through relationships that stay as stable as possible. This is not to say that a change in child-care arrangements would necessarily be a poor choice. But talk to the caregivers about their methods first to be sure your assumptions about them are correct. Visit the center at various times of day, so you don't just see the kids during rest time or lunch. And don't discount the neurological benefits of loving friendship. You can always make a point of "stimulating his brain" during your own time with him at home.

OUT OF SIGHT, OUT OF MIND: OBJECT PERMANENCE

For the very young infant, the world is less like a movie than like a photo album—a series of snapshots that seem only vaguely related. Infants focus on and comprehend what they can see right now, paying little or no notice to what has passed or what is coming. If an object moved out of your three-month-old's range of vision, he immediately forgot about it. If your five-month-old dropped a toy, he was perfectly happy to accept a replacement. Likewise, babies up to about six months of age are often quite complacent about being left with a caregiver. Once Mommy or Daddy has left the room, the infants' minds are fully occupied with the person who has taken the parent's place. As with other aspects of babies' cognitive development, the age at which researchers consider children able to begin to understand that an object continues to exist even when they can't see it has been pushed back a number of times (due mainly to more sophisticated tests devised by child-development researchers) and is now believed to be at around six months.

In any case, by age eight to twelve months, a typically developing baby will search for a toy if you take it from him and hide it within reach. If you move the toy to another hiding place while he is watching, he is likely to look for it in the first hiding place rather than the second, unless the time between hiding and searching is very short. By twelve to sixteen months of age, he will look for the toy in the new hiding place—but only if he saw you move it. Only after his eighteenth month or so will he be able to recall his previous experiences with this game and look for the hidden toy even if he didn't see you hide it. Psychologists call these actions "displacements," but such appearances and disappearances are an important part of your child's everyday experience.

Trying experiments like the one above with your child can be fun and interesting for you both. It is amazing how clearly you will see the progress your little one makes as you experience the same situation together from one week or month to the next. While on an airplane recently, I watched an eighteen-month-old passenger demonstrate his own progress splendidly. The little boy sat by the window, the mother was in the middle seat, and a stranger sat by the aisle. At one point during the flight, the stranger left his seat. Naturally, the toddler's eyes lit up—he saw this as an opportunity to escape into the aisle, giving his stifled, motor-driven body a chance to explore. Unfortunately for him, his mom (who naturally wanted him to stay where he was) blocked his way to the aisle with her legs. She held up a toy to try to distract him, but her little one was clearly not satisfied with that.

How would he solve this problem? I wondered. At twelve months, he could have done nothing about it but push harder on her leg. He wouldn't have been able to plan an escape strategy in advance and then carry it out. Nor would he have been able to remember similar situations well enough to draw on those experiences for help. Pretending to read a magazine, I watched, fascinated, as the toddler took the toy from his mother, then tossed it gleefully into the aisle. Quickly, he checked his mother's face for her reaction.

How clever! Now his mother either would have to let him go into the aisle to get the toy or get up and get it herself, thus moving her legs and enabling him to escape. Clearly, his mother was exasperated by his behavior, but it was all I could do not to rush over and tell her what a bright and creative son she had. In just a few months, no doubt, he would try to talk his mother into letting him go (an even better solution than this one, which was foiled when another passenger simply handed the toy back to Mom), but in the meantime he had used every neural connection he had to solve the problem at hand. Parenting can feel like a thankless chore on many, many occasions, but at least we can sit back and marvel sometimes at how cleverly our children work to control their worlds and how impressively their brains develop to help them.

LEARNING BY DOING: FROM IMITATING TO CREATING

If the young child's journey of discovery leads from observation to imitation, experimentation, and finally symbolic thought and creativity, your one-year-old is already surprisingly far down the road. With months of more or less silent observation and study behind him, he has already begun imitating your sounds and actions with increasing skill.

As you reward his attempts to behave "like a big boy" with smiles, hugs, and praise, his longing to be just like you increases exponentially. By the time he is around twelve to fifteen months, his desire to follow you out of the room is almost irresistible, he insists on feeding himself the way his big sister does, and he struggles daily to converse successfully with his sitter, no matter how long it takes.

This determination to do the things his caregivers and family members do is the fuel behind much of his neurological development and is the reason babies and toddlers learn better from those who love them than from strangers. At twelve months, he will watch you pour sugar into the sugar bowl and want to do that himself. Later, in the sandbox, you will show him how to pour. His delighted repetition of this motion that is "just like Dad's" will lead to all kinds of learning—about the characteristics of various material substances, about gravity and weight, about "empty" and "full," and so on. As the months pass, he will experiment with various ways of pouring sand, filling the sand bucket over and over and over, each time emptying it and stomping on the pile he's made. Still later, he'll concoct schemes to build a sand pile somewhere else in the yard and actually carry out his plans. By age two, he might direct you to do it and clearly communicate his disapproval if you don't comply. Without the initial drive to imitate that you can spot in the last half of the first year and the insistence of trying things out for himself, none of this learning would take place.

Q & A

Who Teaches Best?

Q: My son, Jonathan, is eighteen months old and an incredible mimic. Whatever he sees my husband or me doing, he has to try to do it, too. We've been able to use "copycat" tendencies to teach him all kinds of behavior patterns and new ideas.

Lately I've been thinking about arranging for a child-care situation for him so I can start working again. The problem is, I can't decide between hiring an in-home caregiver just for him or placing him in the group child-care center in our neighborhood. Is it better for him to spend most of his time five days a week observing and imitating an adult caregiver or other children his age (who might introduce him to negative behaviors and might not teach him much that's new)?

A: Imitation is a powerful, ever-present way in which children learn. The fact is, no matter where you place your child for care, he will imitate and learn much from others. The critical issue then, is not *whom* he will be imitating but the *quality of nurturing* and the *variety of activities* to which he will be exposed. A caregiver who takes him to the grocery store or to play with other children in the playground, or one who simply creates exciting play opportunities in your yard (bubbles, Play-Doh, music) can be a wonderful provider of stimulation and fun. In a center, as you point out, your son is guaranteed to have lots of peer interaction—with positive and negative behaviors galore to imitate—but odds are he won't form as exclusive a relationship to the caregiver, who needs to divide her time among several busy toddlers.

When deciding on the best child-care arrangement for Jonathan, consider the following: Does he have other opportunities to spend time with other children—for example, on weekend visits with family? Is he sensitive to overstimulation, which groups of children invariably provide? How well does he handle transitions, such as a change in caregiver or location? Has he already formed strong attachments to other adults in his life (so that he doesn't particularly need more such attachments now)? Which child-care arrangement will be less stressful (emotionally and financially) for your family?

Since research shows that quality of child care is the key ingredient, focus your decision on what matters most to your child at this point in his life, and most to you as a parent, and you will no doubt find a situation in which your child will thrive.

LANDMARKS IN THE WILDERNESS:
THE SENSE OF SPACE AND TIME

Have you ever gotten lost while driving through a part of town you didn't know? If so, you know that bewildering sense of moving aimlessly through unknown territory, searching for landmarks that will point the way. As soon as you find one building you know, you feel considerably more at ease. After that, a second landmark seems to appear more quickly. Then a third—until you know right where you are, and your confidence returns.

This is one way of imagining what the world might feel like to a very young child as he ventures forth on his hands and knees—and, eventually, his two feet—into the vast and mysterious external world. Just one "landmark"—his mother's presence, for instance—can provide him with enough confidence to venture a little further out into the unknown. As he explores, seeking new knowledge, another person or object becomes familiar to him, and then another and another. The more known objects and people fill his space, the more his world becomes defined—and the more confident he becomes that he can continue exploring further without undue risk, though he will still check his landmarks occasionally.

Your child must identify not only physical landmarks but cognitive ones as well. He must familiarize himself with a number of "obvious" laws of physics that affect the world he is exploring but that don't appear obvious to him at all. Having already begun to sense the fact that space exists in three dimensions, the nine- to twelve-month-old crawls to the kitchen cupboard to discover for the first time that objects often have an inside and an outside, that they can be hollow or solid. By twelve months, he has become fascinated by the idea of putting something inside something else. At around fifteen months, he will understand how to stack one block on top of another. By eighteen months, he will clearly comprehend "up" and "down," "open" and "closed," and such sentences as "Where's Duncan? There he is!" By the end of his second year he will understand "big" and "little" as well as "all gone." Each of these new concepts is a welcome landmark helping to make your child's world more predictable and comprehensible. The more landmarks he can rely on, the more confident he will feel about seeking out new information.

A baby's sense of time is "bumpy" in ways very similar to his awareness of the space around him. To a six-month-old, time passes not like a flowing river but in an endless series of milliseconds, each separate and distinct from the moments before and after. There is not really a concept of time other than the present. That is one reason it is often easier to leave a baby in the care of a sitter at that age. He isn't quite able to get his mind around the idea that once you were here and now you're gone—much less understand that you'll be back in four hours. By twelve to eighteen months, your baby has begun to develop at least a minimal sense of both cause and effect and immediate sequences of events. That is, he is aware that if he drops a toy, someone is likely to give it back to him, or that if he holds his arms up to Daddy, he will be picked up himself. These "bumps" in his temporal landscape are like landmarks he can return to again and again. If the expected sequence doesn't happen, his confidence is shaken, and he may start to cry or withdraw. His sense of time's progression has been violated.

As he gains experience during the first half of his second year, your child's collection of landmarks increases; he is able to remember and predict sequences of events that occur over a longer period of time. By eighteen months, he understands that the arrival of bath time means that bedtime is approaching. Mommy's arriving home means it will soon be time to eat. As with spatial landmarks, these met expectations increase his confidence tremendously and give him a greater sense of control. In general, though, when outside the framework of daily routine, a toddler this age still lives in the moment. Saying he can go to the park "tomorrow" or that you'll be off the phone "in a minute" doesn't mean the same thing to him as it does to you.

The concept of "later" does begin to seep in as your child approaches his second birthday, however. By now, he has heard you say you'll give him another cup of milk "in just a second"—and then received it—often enough to at least begin to understand that the milk will eventually arrive. But even by age two, it is still hard for him to conceive of time in the abstract. It is still more effective to ground your comments in terms of concrete actions. Saying, "First we'll put on your coat. Then I'll take you to the playground" is clearer than "We'll leave in ten minutes, okay?" The two-year-old's concept of time is still somewhat uneven, in other words—defined more by sequences of events than by a smoothly progressing clock.

By the end of the second year, you will be astounded at how far your child has come in his understanding of what his environment consists of, how it works, who is in it, and what his place in it is. His transition from determined explorer, to frustrated beholder of all he doesn't yet understand and can't yet do, to a stronger, smarter, and infinitely more capable twenty-four-month-old is truly astonishing. Providing him with reliable landmarks on his journey toward self-sufficiency is one of the greatest gifts you can give him.

A BABY'S-EYE VIEW

"Go Home!"

It is almost lunchtime, and fourteen-month-old Eugene is shopping with Lisa, his mom, at the mall. He feels his tummy rumble. *Hungry. High chair.* He looks around. The high chair is not here. He feels panicky—his tummy hurts! He starts to cry.

"I know, it's lunchtime," Lisa murmurs, glancing at her watch. She's irritated with herself for forgetting the snack bag, and her annoyance can be heard in her voice. "Just ten more minutes, okay, Eugene? We have to get some sheets at Sears, and then we'll go to a restaurant."

Mommy mad. Tummy hurts. Crackers! Eugene cries even harder.

His loud cries force his mother to stop and look at him. She realizes that this violation of the expected sequence—hunger to food—has really upset him. She doesn't have any crackers, but . . .

"Okay, Eugene," Lisa says, trying to keep her impatience out of her voice. "Here's your teddy." She winds it up, and its familiar melody starts to play.

Eugene hugs the stuffed bear. It smells good, feels good. The music and Mommy's calmer tone of voice comfort him. For now he forgets about the crackers.

A little later, Eugene and his mom enter the restaurant. Mommy says something to the lady. He smells the food. Hungry! He heads for a chair just as the lady brings menus and a pack of crackers for him. His physical need for food—and his cognitive need for predictable sequence—are both about to be satisfied, and thanks to Mom's ability to think on the fly, his need for comfort was met in the meantime.

PEEKABOO!: THE IMPORTANCE OF PLAY

"I wonder sometimes if I'm doing everything I can for Hanna," I overheard a mom say at the clinic one day. "I mean, she's nearly two already, and all she ever seems to do is hang around the house and play. I like hanging out with her, but I wonder if all the other parents in the neighborhood have started taking their kids to art classes or working with flash cards or something."

It can seem a little endless sometimes, as your child's second year progresses, to see him puttering about the house, happy as a clam but not obviously *doing* anything constructive. One minute you might find him scribbling on a pad of paper with the fat crayons you've provided; the next he might be tasting the crayon or squashing it beneath a block or sticking it into a ball of clay to see what happens. *Is this serious?* you ask yourself. *Can he possibly be learning anything?* The answer is yes, absolutely. For a toddler, play is work, and it is quite a serious matter. Your child may look as if he's just fooling around with a crayon, but he's actually gaining invaluable experience about the relative strength and plasticity of various objects while refining his motor skills! Every activity he's doing voluntarily must be teaching him something, or he wouldn't do it.

On the other hand, there are specific ways you can use your little one's love of play to extend his knowledge and reinforce those neural connections that will enrich his thinking. As you know, by the time he is one, your child will have become capable of moving beyond simple repetition in his play. He will be able and eager to expand his horizons through experimentation, constantly seeking new variations on experiences he has had before. This act of expanding on previous experience is the key to both pleasurable play and efficient learning. Encourage it whenever possible. Instead of stacking rings on the spindle with him the same way every time, encourage him to try stacking the rings without the spindle to see what happens. When they topple over, ask,

Note the joy on this toddler's face when he is in charge of this tried-and-true game of peekaboo.

"What else can we do with the rings?" Maybe you can string them on a shoelace or toss them into the toy box one by one. Narrate what you're doing: Name the color of each ring as you stack them, count how many you've stacked, or talk about which one is biggest and which smallest. Or have your child rub the rings with his fingers, note their texture, then rub the carpet he's sitting on—and invite him to compare the two.

All of this new information taken in through the senses will start those thousands of neurons firing away. He will add the new input he's just received to what he already knows, and make connections that will prepare him for even greater understanding the next time. The idea is always to start where the child is in his play and then "push the envelope" just a little, leading him ahead one step after another in the learning game.

What kinds of games does a one-year-old like to play? As always, you can best find out by observing your own child and following his lead. Keep in mind that it isn't necessary to have a large number of toys to keep your toddler occupied. Not only can he find a nearly infinite variety of ways to play with a limited number of toys, but most objects in his environment look like "toys" to him. He's as happy (or even happier) banging pots and pans on the kitchen floor as he is hitting a toy drum.

This is a good thing, because children this age tend to spend only brief periods with one object before moving on to another. In general, the one-year-old will use objects in play much as you use them in real life: He'll pretend to brush his hair with your brush (probably holding the brush upside down), whack on things with a toy hammer, and so on. As the year progresses, he'll increasingly partake in "symbolic" play—rocking a doll or pretending to drink from an empty cup. As his brain grows more complex, so will his pretend play. By his third year, he may insist that a wooden block is really a race car or that he is a horse and you are the horse's mommy or daddy.

The one-year-old particularly enjoys any game that involves being face to face or having physical contact with those he loves—such as peekaboo, "This Little Piggy," and acting out favorite stories together. Even when he can't perform all the parts of the game, you can see how focused he is on taking in information by the way he studies your face. Watch how delighted he is when you smile and tickle him at the end of "This Little Piggy," just as he'd predicted you would. Now try playing the game without the expected smile and tickle, and see how surprised he looks. He will probably try to get you to perform the game correctly—maybe by vocalizing—demonstrating his earliest problem-solving skills. Reward him with a new game of "This Little Piggy" and a bigger tickle for his trouble!

As mentioned earlier, studies have shown that toddlers' play is especially productive when a baby's parents, other caregivers, or siblings participate. The pleasure of interacting with loved ones motivates them to pay more attention to what's going on. Children's play tends to last longer when parents join in than when they're alone, especially when Mom or Dad adjusts the play to the child's level.

Brothers and sisters make even better playmates, since they usually enjoy the play more than adults do. Toddlers love to imitate other children and can learn a lot from them, especially in the realm of practical skills. (You may have heard of a neighbor's one-year-old who toilet-trained himself early by imitating his older siblings.) This ability to learn from other children is one of a number of reasons it is a good idea to begin arranging play dates for your child in the second year. An early-childhood music or dance program, which combines stimulating rhythmic games and melodies with child-to-child and parent-child interaction, might be a fun activity for you both. But don't forget to let your one-year-old play on his own as well. He needs to learn to entertain himself to some degree, to enjoy his own company and have the satisfaction of discovering things for himself.

THE TOY BOX

At Fourteen Months

It's Saturday, and Josh is enjoying a deliciously unstructured morning hanging around the house with Mom and Dad. Dad has been helping him stack some blocks. Josh can make a stack of two, but Dad can add even more blocks on top of that. He picks up a cylinder. "Look, Josh. Those blocks are square, but I can put a round one on top," Dad says, and he demonstrates.

Suddenly Josh feels tired of blocks. He toddles off, heading by habit toward the toy basket. Ah! There's his duck—the plastic one that squeaks when he squeezes or punches it. He grabs it and smacks it on the edge of the basket, listening for the squeak.

"Oh, you found your yellow duck," Dad says, going over to him. He knows better than to insist on continuing with the blocks. "Look." He points to one of the duck's eyes and traces it with his finger. "The duck's eye is round, like the round block. It makes a circle shape."

Josh looks from the toy to his dad and back again. "Wownd." He's heard the word before but didn't know what it meant. He still doesn't—but he knows it has something to do with both the block and the eye.

"And look," Dad continues. "That button on your overalls is round, too. Daddy's buttons are round. There are lots of round things in this house."

Josh listens intently. He likes Dad's happy tone of voice. He also likes the connections Dad is making among different objects in his world. He drops the plastic duck. "Wownd!" he says, and giggles as it squeaks.

HOW HARD SHOULD YOU PUSH?: PACING YOUR CHILD'S PLAY

Sometimes at the playground I've heard parents suggest that the kind of directed play I've described might place an unnecessary burden on their children. They watch other parents asking their very young toddlers questions, nudging them on toward more experimentation, providing new words for their vocabulary, and they wonder whether this kind of "pushing" is just a reflection of the parents' ambition and not in the best interest of the child. They prefer to let their children move along at their own pace, they say. Childhood is short enough without parents pushing babies to do better from the very beginning.

Of course, pressuring a one-year-old to achieve for his parents can get out of hand. No one advocates "drilling" an eighteen-month-old, insisting that he perform a new skill in order to receive a reward, and so on. But the fact is that while parental coaching doesn't have much effect on how quickly a baby acquires motor skills such as crawling or walking, stimulating play inspired by the child's existing interests does literally encourage brain development. It is not necessary to pressure a child to "make him smarter"—young children love to learn! It is his caregivers' job to offer him the *opportunity* to learn more about what interests him whenever possible, in the context of a loving, supportive environment. Just as Andrew and Cass's mom pointed out in "A Parent's Story" earlier in this chapter, letting your child know you're available and following his lead is the best way to expand his understanding of his world.

Whether your child picks up new skills more or less quickly than your co-worker's child, both one-year-olds will learn them in roughly the same sequence. Children with Down's syndrome and other developmental conditions follow the same blueprint toward maturity, though not with the same speed or richness as children who are spared those challenges. In most cases there is no need to worry if your child is not yet putting things into containers at fifteen months. He's probably just not interested in filling things up right now. Keep in mind also that, as we saw in the previous chapter, the second year is filled to the brim with physical challenges; during periods when your little one is obsessed with learning to walk or develop certain fine-motor skills, he will probably spend less time playing with non-movement-related toys and games.

It is a fact, too, as Dr. Howard Gardner pointed out in his groundbreaking book *Frames of Mind,* that we humans display a wide variety of types of intelligence. Your child may be a genius at discerning emotions but not particularly advanced in his ability to categorize shapes. He may "specialize" in musical ability but possess a less than dazzling visual sense. Many of these abilities will develop only with time, and your child's performance in any one area will probably rise and fall as the years progress. It makes sense, then, to enjoy and encourage whatever skills manifest themselves and not to worry too much about his "slower" areas.

In the end, the most important lesson for your child to learn at this age is that he is well loved and that his world is a reasonably predictable place, nevertheless full of delightful surprises. The wisest parents are those who think for a bit about the ways in which they can enrich their child's experience and then, after implementing those ideas, devote themselves to having fun. Remember, whatever your toddler's intellectual level turns out to be, it can only be enhanced through time spent interacting with you.

Playing with Your Child

Playing with a young child doesn't always come naturally. In most cases, doing it well takes a little focus and practice, and maybe even letting go of some grown-up expectations. In general, your one-year-old will play most happily when his entire body is involved. His brain is literally not capable of taking in much information "symbolically," through abstract concepts or talk (though, in my estimation, educational computer games are moving even one-year-olds toward such concepts sooner). This is why nursery songs and children's chants are such a delight for a child—they provide new information through his senses in the form of pleasing rhythms and sounds, movement (such as hand-clapping), and direct interaction with other people.

When playing, make sure to get down on the floor with him as often as possible, playing "at his level" rather than talking down to him. Listen to what he says about what he's doing, and respond by taking the play one step further in an interesting direction. Make eye contact. Avoid distracting stimuli, like a television going in the background. Give him plenty of positive reinforcement, and he will come to view play—and learning—as one of life's greatest pleasures.

BOOKS:
TOYS THAT TALK

Parents sometimes become so conditioned to playing actively with their infants that they forget to initiate book-reading until late in the second year, or they read books only at bedtime. This is a shame, not only because

This pair enjoys the experience of reading together, even though they're not on the "same page."

storytime can be used very effectively in establishing daily routines and encouraging language development (as we will see in later chapters), but because books are literally "toys that talk," and they provide the perfect opportunity for the two of you to engage in some stimulating play. Pulling your one-year-old onto your lap for a story sets up just the kind of loving, focused interaction your child loves best. The feel of the book, the challenge of turning its pages, the brightly colored story illustrations, the coziness of sitting close to you, and the sound of your narration all pleasantly engage the senses. Meanwhile, each new page brings a host of concepts and images for a curious one-year-old to ponder. Your involvement—naming objects in the pictures for him, asking him questions now and then, and comparing bits of the story to people, animals, or situations he already knows—keeps his neurons firing and his brain working hard.

As with other aspects of parent-child play, even when your little one doesn't seem to be paying attention—even when his gaze wanders or he flips through the pages, skipping half the story in the process—he is learning something. So be patient. Don't worry about the storyline so much right now, and don't insist on reading to the end. Just focus on introducing the pleasures of storytime to your child, not only at bedtime but often throughout the day, and use it to demonstrate once again how loved he truly is.

IF YOU'RE CONCERNED

Developmental Delays

As I have pointed out before, performance checklists for toddlers are often inaccurate when applied to a specific child, but they do give a very general idea of the steps your child must take to achieve cognitive maturity. If he is less than two months behind the chart in achieving a certain skill, there is probably nothing to worry about. However, again, your own instincts are the most reliable diagnostic tool. If your one-year-old does seem to be falling behind cognitively—if he is not mastering skills at all as opposed to accomplishing them slowly—or if he appears listless, unfocused, or uninterested in exploring his world, he might have a hearing, vision, or other problem. Increasingly, children's hearing is tested at birth—a good thing, since a lot can be done to correct such problems if they are diagnosed early. But if your child's hearing and vision haven't yet been tested, it's certainly not too late to discuss your concerns with your pediatrician and perhaps set up an evaluation. The sooner your child receives the help he needs, the sooner he can resume his place on the road to greater understanding.

SEE YOU LATER, MOMMY!

Nearly a year has passed, and it's almost time for Craig's second birthday party, an event that Leah hopes will be as much fun and as memorable as the first one. Feeling a little nostalgic, she pops the videotape of his first birthday into the VCR while twenty-three-month-old Craig busies himself with his toy box nearby. Suddenly there on the screen is Craig at twelve months, staring in wide-eyed wonder as a bubble drifts past his face. Leah giggles, watching his expression as, on the TV screen, she gets up and goes inside the house.

How different he is now, Leah thinks as she looks from the teary one-year-old on the screen to the busy two-year-old at the toy box and back again. *His understanding of how the world works has progressed by light-years. Now when I blow bubbles, he watches them pop, then orders me to make some more— that is, when he doesn't insist on blowing the bubbles himself. His understanding of what happens to me when I'm gone has changed completely, too. Now when I leave him at the child-care center, most days he waves good-bye and tells me, "Mommy go work!" He still cries once in a while when I drop him off or even pick him up, but I think he knows now that I'll always be back at the end of the day. All that talk and repetition has paid off, I guess.*

Leah nestles deeper into the sofa cushions, watching her televised self rush back to reassure her crying one-year-old that she's still there— she just stepped out of sight for a while. She glances over at her two-year-old son. "Where my car?" he says without looking at her, poking around in his toy box. "Help, Mommy." And a moment later, "Oh. I got!"

He holds up the car and gives her a big smile. He did it! Leah grins as she watches him cross the room with his prize. He knew that his toy was somewhere around here, and he found it. He solved the problem himself. What an independent little boy.

Common Cognitive Achievements in the Second Year

12 MONTHS	Turns pages of a book
	Puts objects in a container
	Can sometimes stack two cubes
	Uses toy telephone like a real telephone
15 MONTHS	Likes to scribble
	Builds tower of two or three blocks
	Closes container
	Names one picture
	Points to two pictures
	Becomes interested in cause and effect
	Practices new tasks over and over
18 MONTHS	Can tell the difference between circles and squares
	Can point to doll's body parts
	Names three objects
	Identifies objects in a photograph
	Follows simple directions
	Memory improves

21 MONTHS	Can tell difference between circles, squares, and triangles
	Shows greater accuracy with shape box
	Attends to story longer
	Matches shoes with correct family member
	Is beginning to understand concept of "now"
24 MONTHS	Builds tower of blocks, train of blocks
	Engages in fantasy play
	Begins to plan behaviors
	Engages in creative problem-solving
	Begins to understand concept of "soon" or "after lunch" (but not "next week" or "at four o'clock")

FIRST-PERSON SINGULAR

Now record your observations of your own child's neurological development. What are his all-consuming obsessions as the months pass? How has his play evolved? When did you first see that he had planned an action ahead of time? Has he started to play imaginary games with his dolls or action figures? Keeping in mind the variety of kinds of intelligence, make a note of any evidence you see of the emergence of musical, visual, interpersonal, or other non-mainstream skills or interests. As his neurological and verbal abilities develop side by side, you will see a merging of intelligences that leads your child to a new level of thinking. He will let you know through his words what steps he's made. Write down those funny little sentences before you forget. You'll enjoy recalling them in the years to come!

_____

_____

_____

_____

_____

_____

_____

_____

_____

_____

_____

_____

_____

_____

_____

_____

_____

_____

CHAPTER 4

"Listen to Me!"—My Verbal Abilities

Between twelve and twenty-four months, your child is likely to progress from understanding (but not yet saying) a dozen words to knowing two hundred or more.

Sharon's firstborn, Dana, was just over a year old when Sharon discovered that she was pregnant again. Initially, Sharon was delighted at the idea of having two children so close in age. But as the pregnancy continued and became increasingly difficult (Sharon was confined to bed for the last couple of months), she felt guilty about how often Dana's needs had to take a backseat to the developing baby's. Sharon became particularly concerned when she realized, after baby Jacob's birth, that twenty-one-month-old Dana was hardly speaking yet. Checking the standard parenting books, Sharon was horrified to see that according to the lists of developmental milestones Dana should know more than a hundred words by now and be able to say a few dozen. It seemed to Sharon that Dana hardly ever said more than "Mommy," "dog," and a few other nouns! Worried that she had not spent enough time with her daughter (who had gone to stay with her grandparents several times during the pregnancy), Sharon began reading to her several times each day. When she pointed to a picture and asked Dana what it was, both mother and daughter became increasingly frustrated by Dana's inability to say the word. Soon the reading sessions became so unpleasant that Sharon feared they might be working against Dana's speaking ability rather than encouraging it.

Sharon's situation is not unusual. In my clinical experience, I've seen how difficult it is not to worry when a child's verbal development seems to lag behind that of others the same age. Concerns about how a non-speaking child's relative silence relates to her intelligence, anxiety over whether a recent life change or other difficulty might have slowed her progress, and guilty thoughts about how we might have stimulated more verbal development if only we'd known—all of these get in the way of observing the child objectively to see whether there really is a problem. In fact, though, children's verbal development varies widely and can stop and start for a number of reasons. What we had assumed would be a steady progression of nonsense sounds to single words to two-word sentences to fluent speech is instead a journey full of leaps and regressions, often influenced by the child's passing emotional or physical state. More important than the *number* of words your child can say is whether she frequently gets frustrated because she can't think of the word she wants, whether she can say more words now than she could a month ago, whether she understands a good deal of what you say to her, and whether her hearing is satisfactory. Certainly, such events as a difficult pregnancy, a change in caregivers, or a move to a new house are likely to slow or even temporarily stop a child's progress in speaking. If her development does not pick up again after a couple of weeks and you truly feel there's cause for concern, it wouldn't hurt to check with her pediatrician. But in most cases, children catch up verbally within a year or so. Meanwhile, if you actually count the words she says (in her own way) over the course of a few days, you may be surprised at how many she already knows.

In this chapter, we will examine the ways in which your child's verbal abilities have been developing since before she was born. We will see how quickly she learned to distinguish her parents' language from foreign tongues and how she picked up the rhythms and characteristic sounds of your language before she learned to speak actual words. We'll follow her development as she learns first to understand words, then to say some of them. We'll see how gestures and facial expressions often precede language, and the funny ways in which she may confuse words and their meanings at first. The basis of all her learning in the area of communication is, first, listening to your speech and then imitating you. We will explore the importance of talking a great deal to your child in order to stimulate her own speech development. Finally, we will discuss adults' regrettable tendency to confuse a one-year-old's verbal ability with overall intelligence. Many other issues and concerns—such as a new baby in the house or an individual child's simple tendency to think things through privately—can get in the way of a toddler's desire to talk out loud. Between the ages of twelve and twenty-four months, your child's ability to communicate should be measured not by how many words she can say at any given time but by how content she seems to be with her own progress.

"BA-BA!":
VERBAL ACHIEVEMENTS BEFORE
AGE ONE

If you've ever tried to learn a foreign language, you have to be impressed by your one-year-old's comparative ease in picking up yours—particularly since she learns most of what she knows from the natural context of conversation, not from specific lessons aimed at systematically increasing her knowledge. Many parents have decided that their child must simply be a genius because of her ability to internalize and use a language at such a phenomenal rate. In fact, though, language acquisition is an instinct, like learning to walk, and all normal babies' brains are superwired for the task. Your one-year-old finds it easier to learn English than you ever found it to learn French because, from birth to age three, she is experiencing one of those neurological "critical periods" for language. Her ability to acquire her mother tongue (or any other language) will never be as primed as it is right now.

Recent studies by Dr. Patricia Kuhl of the University of Washington and others have shown that very young infants can already recognize the sounds of their mother tongue, responding differently when they hear a foreign language spoken. By approximately seven months of age, they have grown sufficiently familiar with their language's typical rhythms and sounds to begin separating distinct words from the stream of ordinary conversation. This ability to hear distinct words leads very quickly to the nine-month-old's first wordlike vocalizations. At this age, she begins limiting her babbling to sounds that "make sense" in terms of phonemes, or sound combinations, in her native language (though they don't actually mean anything). The daughter of an English speaker, for example, will say "Ga-ga," but probably not "Gda-gda." A Polish baby, on the other hand, is very likely to practice the latter sound. At around this age, your baby probably also began to understand and respond to some words and expressions, such as "Do you want your teddy bear?" and "Wave bye-bye!"

Toward the end of the first year, babies begin *jargoning*—that is, babbling in a way that sounds like your language (it has the same rhythms and sounds) but still isn't actual words. Sometimes jargoning seems to be an actual language itself, since a child this age may regularly use a certain word ("da," for example) to denote a specific object (such as a teddy bear). Later, her approximation of the real word will grow more accurate ("beh" for bear), and the original term transferred to an object whose name sounds more like it ("da" will come to mean "Daddy"). All of these developments set the stage for the language burst that takes place in the second year.

EASING THE WAY

Word Games

Moving into her second year, your child continues to benefit from focused attention as you converse. As she watches and listens to you speak, she is taking in not only your words but your inflection, pitch, and speech rhythms as well. Playing with your words—varying each of the qualities listed above—will make learning language into a pleasant experience while it "tunes up her ears" for better expression. Here are some specific "talking games" for parents and toddlers from "Read*Write*Now*," a wonderful guide for parents available on-line at www.ed.gov.

All parents enjoy trying to teach their one-year-olds to sing the

ABCs. Next time, try singing the song to your little one in a variety of funny variations—pausing dramatically between phrases; singing it in a high, peeping voice like a bird; and then singing the song in a deep, dark voice like a bear. Let your child try to mimic you if she likes. By playing this game, you will not only familiarize her with letters but expand your own range of expression.

You can help your child increase her vocabulary by reading to her often. When reading one of her favorite stories, use your voice to draw attention to a special, new word. Say the word in a funny way, sing it, say it loud or soft, and make funny faces when you say it. For the rest of the day, show your child different ways the word can be used. The next time you read together, choose a new word.

If your child hasn't yet started saying her own name, play this game: Ask her, "What's your name?" If she answers correctly, say, "Yes, that's your name. Your name is [Dana]." If she doesn't say her name, you say, "Your name is [Dana]. What's your name?" and repeat again until she says her name correctly. Once she knows her name, you can have fun with it. Look at your child. "What did you say your name was? [Dana]? I thought your name was Snicklefritz." Of course, you can also play with your own and other loved ones' names, as in "My name is Mother Goose. Is that my name?"

Ways to encourage speech at any time include using short sentences, speaking slowly, talking in a higher register than usual, and demonstrating your love of communicating by varying your inflection and saying new words or phrases with careful attention and enthusiasm. (Speak and read aloud to your child a bit more dramatically than you might to an adult.) Just as important in encouraging speech is learning to listen to your child and responding appropriately to what she's trying to tell you. By echoing her inner experience with your own verbal response (watching her eat her favorite food and remarking, "Dana *loves* broccoli!"), you will demonstrate to her the power of words to create a bond of understanding between human beings.

"MORE COOKIE!":
VERBAL ACHIEVEMENTS FROM
ONE TO TWO

Between the ages of twelve and twenty-four months, your child is likely to progress from understanding (but not yet saying) perhaps a dozen words to knowing two hundred or more. How many of these words she actually says is not the critical issue at this age—although the fact that words, unlike other developmental progressions, are easy to count often results in comparisons with other children. Some one-year-olds are quite happy comprehending speech without feeling a need to talk back. In any case, there will be some kind of progression from her more sophisticated comprehension ability toward better speaking skills. However many words she can say by her second birthday, the number will certainly be more than she could say on her first.

Receptive speech is the term for the kind of communication your child has probably already begun to learn by the time she turns one. This means that if you ask her to get her "blankie" out of the laundry basket, she'll show you that she understands by either getting the blanket or by shaking her head no. She has begun to understand, if not always to name, a number of people and objects as well—usually those most meaningful to her such as "Mama," "Dada," "blankie," and "dog."

Twelve months can be a funny period for language, because your child is likely to spend quite a bit of time "pretending" to hold conversations, declaiming away like a seasoned orator, her inflections and rhythms stunningly accurate but her words for the most part nonsensical. This is one instance when you will be bowled over by what brilliant mimics children are—she will sound *exactly* like your mother or her brother without actually saying one English word! Still, only her family and caregivers are likely to know what she means.

The word "no" may become an object of endless fascination at around this time. As she says "No!" to this and "No!" to that, you may wonder whether your generally cheerful twelve-month-old is hitting the "terrible two's" alarmingly early. In fact, though, she's just reveling in the power of this easy-to-say word and watching, fascinated, for listeners' reactions. Chances are that "No!" will take up quite a long residence in your household from now on. Its inherent power can be irresistible to very small children, who must sometimes feel it's all the power they've got.

In most cases, the first half of the second year is a bit slow in terms of verbal ability. This is partly because your child is so focused on learning to walk and develop other motor skills that there's little energy left to focus on language. You may wonder at times whether she's making any progress, as she seems content to use her handful of nouns and just point and grunt for anything else she wants. Never fear, at around eighteen months, having mastered her ability to walk, she will likely begin spewing forth an absolute explosion of words. According to many scientifically documented child-development scales, children acquire on average half a dozen or more words per day between age eighteen months and six years. This is truly amazing when you think about it. Her word use will also become more reliable—you won't have to figure out what a sound means quite as often. She will begin at eighteen months with a vocabulary of anywhere from three to fifty words and an ability to say short sentences of two or three words ("More milk," "Dana go home," etc.), and end up at age two telling you quite clearly what she wants or needs with words.

THE TOY BOX

At Fifteen Months

Anne is mopping the living-room floor, so she has parked fifteen-month-old Petra on the other side of the baby gate dividing the living and dining rooms. Petra stands at the gate frowning, as Mommy moves back and forth, back and forth, with the mop. "Tull!" she says, raising an imperious arm and pointing at the toy box at the opposite end of the living room. Anne looks up at her. "Turtle?" she asks. She walks over to the toy box and pulls out a stuffed turtle. "Is this what you want?"

"No!" Petra says with great relish, a grin playing around her mouth. She points again. "Petra, tull!"

Perplexed, Anne holds up a teddy bear. "Tull?" she asks, trying not to feel silly.

"No!" Petra says with even greater relish.

Anne suspects that this entire exercise is taking place just so Petra has the excuse to say "No!" Still, she pulls out the well-worn toy phone. "Telephone?" she asks tentatively.

"No! Tull!"

Suddenly Anne experiences a moment of blazing insight. "Tull" means *"pull"*! Petra wants the caterpillar pull-toy her grandfather bought her last week. She's been obsessed with it ever since, pulling it everywhere as she works on her walking skills.

"I know," Anne says, smiling at Petra. She gets out the pull-toy and holds it up. "Pull the caterpillar, right?"

"Tull!" Petra is probably thinking, *Finally, Mom.* She stretches her arm over the baby gate. She *must* get that pull-toy now. Better word skills can wait their turn. Right now she needs to walk and pull.

"THAT'S WHAT I SAID": HOW LANGUAGE DEVELOPS

We tend to think of our children's language development as something they accomplish pretty much on their own. But, of course, when you think about it, learning to communicate verbally is impossible without people to communicate *with*. Your one-year-old's speech skills are the result of a joint effort between herself and those around her. When she first tries to "speak" to you by repeating sounds you don't recognize as words, you nevertheless naturally make an effort to imagine what the sound might mean. When you speak to her, she goes through the same process. It is this focus on each other's efforts to communicate—the guessing at meaning, the questioning repetition, and the mirroring back of comprehension or puzzlement at the sound of a word—that lays the groundwork for speech.

If you have ever visited a foreign country where you had a very limited command of the language, you probably remember what a bewildering cacophony of sound seemed to envelop you everywhere you went. Think back to how you managed to get the things you needed while you were there. Probably you just pointed at objects, such as items at a market, nodded a lot, and tried to say their names. If you

More and more, your toddler's pointing gestures will be accompanied by actual words.

heard a word (such as *"grazie"* or *"playa"*) often enough, you would probably start to use it yourself once in a while and feel pretty good about your ability to participate in all the "noise" surrounding you.

Your child deals with her world in much the same way. Just like you in a foreign land, she points at things and tries to name them. At around twelve months, her initial vocabulary consists of words that mean a lot to her: the names of people around her, her favorite objects, and things that fascinate because they move or make interesting noises (such as "cat" or "car"). Soon she will announce the names of foods she eats, articles of her clothing, and the names of people outside her immediate circle. At first, her parents (or even a sibling) may be the only ones who understand what she's trying to say. To these loved ones, "ba" means "bottle," *obviously.* Parents' tendency to repeat the word their baby says, their faces lighting up with pride, helps refine the child's pronunciation while reinforcing her desire to keep talking. Through this "name, echo, name" process, the one-year-old's utterance will gradually come to sound more and more like the actual word—though often a child is three years old before just about everyone can understand her.

Clearly, even learning the names of objects is not an easy task, and it's something of a miracle how easily babies manage to get it done. Just think about how perplexed you might be in that hypothetical foreign country if the person standing next to you pointed at a bird in the sky and said, "Yah!" What does "yah" mean? you'd wonder. Does it refer to the bird, to an aspect of the bird (its long wings or its blue color), to the act of flying, or to how high it is in the sky? As research by Dr. Ellen Markman, author of *Categorization and Naming in Children,* and others has shown, babies solve this initial problem by assuming that a naming word (such as "juice") refers to a whole entity (the juice) rather than to just one aspect of it (the color). Once they know the word "juice," they can go on to learn the subsidiary words, such as "sweet," "orange," and so on. This system doesn't always work. A one-year-old might *over*generalize, calling cups of water, milk, and soda "juice," too. (They all come in a cup, don't they?) They can also *under*generalize, calling only the drink in their own cup "juice."

Of course, these sources of confusion straighten themselves out over the months as children's brains develop, thanks to feedback from you and with more observation on their part. By eighteen months, language skills have often progressed to the point at which your child can start ordering you around with a technique called *telegraphic speech,* so called because it's as simple and urgent as a telegram. If your child is this age already, you are no doubt well accustomed to hearing "Mommy come" and "Daddy go" and "Get ball" around the house. Even telegraphic speech can be confusing to parents, though. What does "truck me" mean, for example? Does the child want the truck? Is she saying that it's her truck? Does she mean the truck is small like her? Trying to guess the message in those two little words can get pretty funny at times. It helps, parents historically have found, to pay attention to the child's gestures and other nonverbal communication as well. But even then, expect quite a few misunderstandings at both ends of the conversation during this year.

Dr. Steven Pinker, author of *The Language Instinct: How the Mind Creates Language,* and other experts point out that no matter what culture your child belongs to, the steps she takes in language development remain more or less the same. Babies name objects before moving on to verbs, no matter what language they use to say those first words. They generalize in the same way, assuming that a word refers to an entire object rather than a part of it. And they make the same mistakes as they begin learning how to construct their sentences.

A BABY'S-EYE VIEW

Look Over There!

Sun, fifteen-month-old Irene thinks as she and her mom go out for a walk in the neighborhood. She sees something move on the sidewalk ahead. A word pops out: "Dog!" "Yes, dog!" her mother repeats, giving her hand a squeeze. "Big dog, right, Irene?"

But Irene's attention has already wandered. As the two of them stop at an intersection, Irene watches the traffic light change and a truck drive off. She pulls on her mother's hand and points at it. "Tuck!"

"What's that, sweetie?" her mother responds. "Oh, yes. The truck goes! The light turns green and it goes."

Irene feels a physical tingle at the sound of Mommy's

words. She has seen cars go but hasn't had the word to describe what she sees. Mommy has used that word before. But now the sound of it has connected with a meaning for the first time. "Go," she says experimentally, looking off toward the disappearing truck. "Tuck go!"

Her mother looks down at her. She gives her a big smile and squeezes her hand again. "Yes, Irene. The truck goes!" she says.

Irene smiles, too, as mother and daughter start to cross the street. "Tuck go." She feels the sound of the words in her mouth. She sees another dog. *Maybe dogs go, too . . .*

LISTEN TO ME: FROM IMITATING TO EXPRESSING THROUGH WORDS

By eighteen months of age, your child will have become quite an accomplished mimic, in both her behavior and her words. If you have a tendency to say "Awesome" or some other somewhat unusual word or phrase when in her presence, expect to hear it back from her very soon. She may not use it appropriately, but she will almost certainly get the inflection and facial expressions exactly right. As she practices her speech, she will not only talk to other people, but will often talk to herself. Just as she babbled happily to herself in her crib in the morning when she was younger, so she will chatter away to no one as she plays with her toys, walks around, etc. Often she narrates her activities as they happen. Some theorists believe that children do this not just to play with words but to make sense out of their day, re-creating their experience through language. This is a truly sophisticated accomplishment, involving the use of mental symbols and abstract thought, and it is fascinating to watch.

By around twenty-one months, many children move from the apparent self-involvement of narrating their actions to themselves to the more spontaneous conversation of the two-year-old. At this point, your child may initiate much more of the conversation than before. She will be more likely to notice if you aren't really interested in what she's saying or if you are distracted. She'll increasingly respond to the tone of your voice more than just the words (stopping what she's doing when she hears a sharp-toned "Sweetie," for example).

By this time, "Mine!" has probably long been a popular staple of her verbal repertoire. But she may now become interested in who owns the other objects in her world. "Mommy comb!" she may tell her father, outraged, when he starts to borrow his wife's comb one morning. And she will happily wander the house calling, "Where Daddy keys?"

Q & A

Simon Says

Q: My eighteen-month-old has suddenly begun spouting a number of "inappropriate" words at the worst possible times. She shouts "s—t" whenever she falls down or stubs her toe. The other day my mother-in-law was visiting when my daughter cruised through the room yelling, "Where damn phone?" What's a parent to do?

A: It's a fact of life that one-year-olds are incurable mimics. In general, if a word gets said in your house, you can bet your child will be saying it herself soon—particularly when the word is invoked with the level of emotion with which most people use curse words. Your angry or embarrassed "Don't say that!" will only make the word more fascinating, an irresistible temptation at this age.

If you are uncomfortable with the idea of your sweet-faced child's cursing like the proverbial sailor, either at home or in public, your only recourse is to avoid using those words your-self. You will have to do this long before she is able to repeat them. Children often understand and "learn" words far earlier than they begin to speak them. If, as in your case, your child has already begun using such words, your best bet is to gently and nonchalantly give her alternatives. Next time you stub your toe, say "sugar" instead, loud enough for her to hear.

LET'S TALK:
THE RHYTHMS OF CONVERSATION

Watching your child learn the meaning of word after word is a joyful experience, but verbal communication consists of more than just the formation of words and letters, more than just putting sounds together. Your child naturally understands that she must not only expand her vocabulary and learn the basic rules of grammar and semantics but also pick up the art of when to pause in conversation, when to talk, comprehend why it's useless for both people to talk at the same time, and so on. You have heard her practice with the rhythms of speech since she began to babble. Now she must work on how and when to modulate the volume of her voice (reminding her to use her soft "inside voice" or louder "outside voice" can be helpful) and on the meaning and value of eye contact.

This is not an easy set of rules to learn, so be patient if your child stutters at times in her eagerness to get her idea across to you or looks away sometimes while you're talking. Don't rush her. Let her work out what she needs to say in her own good time. Then respond naturally, clearly, and with enthusiasm. Keep in mind that stammering is quite common at this age— it's just a sign of temporary overload, a momentary inability to keep pace with what is happening in her brain. Refusing to run roughshod over her during these awkward moments will give her the chance to practice her verbal skills and increase her confidence in her ability to communicate.

By the time she reaches her second birthday, your child will probably have mastered many of the social, speaking, and listening skills it takes to carry on a successful conversation. She will have had experience in taking turns, recognizing her own turn to talk, and knowing when the person to whom she's speaking doesn't understand what she's said. She will know the signs of attention and willingness to continue talking—eye contact, body posture, and so on. (I've seen two-year-olds in the hospital waiting room, for example, notice that their parents have stopped listening to them while they're filling out paperwork. The children literally turn their parents' heads toward them with their hands to get their attention, then blithely continue talking.) Your two-year-old will still be more likely to converse with adults than with other children, but that will change remarkably soon. In just a few months more, you will see her carrying on earnest tête-à-têtes with her equally verbal peers.

Pillow Talk

"From the time Bobby was about eight months old, he loved to babble to himself at bedtime," his mother, Elise, told me. "He was quite a talker. I used to laugh, hearing him in his crib chatting to the walls. After he started talking, I'd hear him in bed at night muttering about his day. He'd talk about what he'd had for lunch and what he'd done with his sitter and how he'd made birthday cakes out of sand at the playground that afternoon. Starting when he was about eighteen months old, I got into the habit of passing by his door every once in a while to hear what new words he was using or find out what events of the day he was reviewing. I was often surprised by what he'd focused on or seemed to be processing. It helped me figure out where his interests were at that particular time, so I could expand on them the next day. Listening to him at bedtime is also how I found out that he was picking up some Spanish words from my husband, who's from Puerto Rico. My husband usually speaks English to Bobby. I didn't even know he'd heard Spanish!"

SMART TALK: HOW LANGUAGE REFLECTS COGNITIVE ADVANCES

Because language takes its big leap forward at the same time as several other cognitive skills—that is, at about eighteen months—its appearance is generally considered a sign of the progress infants and toddlers make on their way to early childhood. Your child's increased verbal ability does not *cause* the other cognitive leaps of this period (the idea that she can make things happen, the concept of the "self" versus "other," etc.), but it is a *sig-*

nal that a number of separate skills have begun coming together to make a greater whole, a consequence of the brain development described in the previous chapter. Basically, increased verbal sophistication signals the one-year-old's ability to think symbolically—to begin to play out past, present, or future events on the stage of the mind.

What language does do is radically restructure your child's world, mainly by dividing it into nonverbal and verbal experience and introducing a new and more refined sense of categories. It introduces a sense of the passage of time—of past, present, and future events. And it frames experiences in words that can be retained as conscious memories—separate from the preverbal, but extremely important—daily accumulation of unconscious impressions such as "Mom loves me" or "Mom doesn't love me." This new ability to "log" thoughts and experiences and re-create them in her mind allows your child to ponder and respond to a much wider variety of data and leads to even greater and more varied cognitive growth.

IF YOU'RE CONCERNED

Verbal Delays

As with all aspects of development at this age, a very broad spectrum exists regarding the language development of perfectly "normal" children. If your twenty-month-old seems to prefer looking at picture books rather than engaging in conversation all the time, she's probably perfectly fine. Keep in mind that she may be currently focusing on another area of development or that she simply isn't particularly extroverted by nature.

It's also vital to remember that all children this age understand much more language than they can speak. If your child has older siblings, she may not feel the need to say much, since others are speaking for her. (The same is true if you provide her with all her needs before she has to ask for them.) Children in bilingual homes also tend to spend some time sorting out the different sounds before beginning to speak either language. (This is not a cause for alarm; such a child is usually back on track by the time she enters school.) Generally, if your child listens to you, responds to your questions or directions ("Where is your juice?"), and otherwise demonstrates that she understands your words (pointing to an object you name), you can be sure that her "window of opportunity" for language is being put to good use.

If you have explored all these possibilities, however, and continue to feel that your child may be speech-delayed, consider whether she might have a hearing problem. (She should have had her hearing tested by her pediatrician, but if she hasn't, make sure it is tested now.) If her hearing is normal, she could conceivably have a speech or learning disorder that should be diagnosed by a professional. By age two, most significant problems can be either accurately identified or ruled out by a speech pathologist or other specialist.

HOW SMART IS SHE?: VERBAL SKILLS AND GENERAL INTELLIGENCE

Because we place so much importance on the ability to communicate through words, it's not surprising that any hesitation in the process of learning to talk often has parents panicking over their child's intelligence level. As I've said, it is crucial to keep in mind that there is truly an enormous range in the rate of language acquisition during this year.

I know from personal experience how hard it is to separate the concepts of verbal performance and intelligence, as well as the ideas of verbal *ability* and verbal *performance.* My own son, Alex, appeared to be speech-delayed when he was two years old, and I was the only one who wasn't worried. Alex didn't seem frustrated by his limited range of speech, and he and his twin brother, Matthew, were communicating just fine. However, my friends and relatives continued to point out to me that Matthew was comparatively advanced in his verbal skills, so surely Alex's relative silence was a source of concern. Finally—partly through peer pressure and partly through guilt (what kind of a mother was I not to worry?)—I did start to doubt my own gut feeling that Alex was okay, and I made an appointment for him at the hospital where I work.

The hospital staff tested Alex's hearing first. They played a tape of a cow mooing. Alex easily tracked where the sound was coming from and handled the other tasks well, so his hearing was fine. Next, Alex's expressive speech was tested through a speech and language evaluation. In the end, the verdict was "He obviously understands us. He has several words and lots of the right signs are there. He's just not ready to talk much yet."

In fact, Alex's verbal development started to kick in less than six months later. Now he talks much more than his twin brother. But he continues to be the very thoughtful boy he always was, pondering a new situation first, then talking his way through the activity.

The moral of the story is that I could have trusted my intuition in this situation, since it was based on what I knew about him, but having a trained professional check his hearing turned out to be a big relief. Language skills are such a loaded issue for us, connected as they are to how we think the child will do in the world, that it's probably better just to quell all the fears we can.

One fact to consider is that, in general, girls talk sooner and more fluently than boys. Even at twenty-one months, many boys may still speak chiefly in one- or, at most, two-word sentences. Many may still be using jargon. Others will communicate chiefly through pointing, gesturing, and grunting. A twenty-one-month-old girl, by contrast, might already be speaking in short sentences, though still with a "babyish" pronunciation that's often difficult to understand.

Language, like other areas of development, proceeds at its own pace. It does not make sense to jump to the conclusion that a one-year-old who is slow to begin talking has a cognitive delay. If the cause isn't her current focus on motor skills or the fact that she has a new baby brother at home, she may simply be in an environment in which the adults don't talk to her a great deal. (Though there is no evidence that specifically trying to teach a child to talk speeds up the *rate* at which she learns, it is known that the wider the variety of language experiences she has, the more enriched her vocabulary will become.) Or she may simply have a quiet nature.

As I pointed out earlier, even most two-year-olds stammer and stutter at times. Their speech is coming in so rapidly at that age that it's just very difficult to keep up with it. Talking at this age must feel to a child sometimes like falling over her feet while learning to walk. Again, it's important to help her along during this phase without always saying the words for her. Try to stay attuned to when your child wants your help expressing her thoughts (maybe when she's tired) or when she'd prefer to struggle along on her own. In general, it's best not to voice her thoughts before she's tried to do so herself, but if it's clear she's about to lose it, try asking a leading question that provides her with some of the words she needs. (If it's obvious that she's hungry, for example, ask, "Do you want cereal or a banana?" instead of "What do you want?") Trying to express oneself at this age, when there's so very much to say, can be quite frustrating. Your efforts to help her ease the frustration will probably be met with gratitude, if you don't crowd in too close.

Without question, the leaps your child will make in language acquisition between twelve and twenty-four months will amaze and delight you. Just keep in mind the broad range that exists in the rate of this development, and resist the urge to compare your child's progress to another's. Remember also that learning to talk is not a steady process. As Dr. T. Berry Brazelton points out, there will probably be periods of regression when your chatty two-year-old reverts to the speech patterns of her younger self. (This frequently occurs after the appearance of a new baby or a new caregiver, for example.) There are also bound to be breakdowns in communication once in a while, leading to frustration on both sides. Clearly, the frustration is worth the reward, however. By the time she's two, your child's world has grown dramatically, embracing both her sensory experience and whatever information she takes in through language. It's a fact—as you might make a point of telling your little one—that her exciting steps forward in learning to talk mean she's truly "a big girl" now.

Q & A

What Did You Say?

Q: Our fifteen-month-old daughter, Melissa, has been talking up a storm since before her first birthday. She talks to her stuffed animals when she wakes up in the morning, to us all day, to the mailman, to her older brothers and all their friends, to the trees, to herself, and to anyone else who happens by. The problem is, no one can understand more than a word or two of what she says! Even those of us in her family who have listened to her talk for months now have to ask her to repeat herself over and over again, and most of the time we end up just guessing what she said or nodding sagely and saying, "Yes." We can tell that she's using actual words rather than jargon, but her pronunciation is so vague that she has to gesture and act things out to get her point across. Obviously, this hasn't affected her confidence so far, but we worry about how things will go when she starts spending more time in groups with other kids. Will they make fun of her? Should we take her to see a speech therapist before then?

A: Your daughter sounds like quite a conversationalist, in her own way! It appears from your description that she is using language skills quite appropriately for her age in several ways. She uses her speech to engage people in social situations, she narrates her everyday activities, she even talks to things that don't talk back. When all else fails, she uses gestures to supplement her requests. The fact that she can't articulate words clearly so that adults always understand her is also quite common at this age. Given how early she started babbling, though, I would be surprised if her articulation doesn't improve quite soon. In the meantime, when she vocalizes, listen carefully to her speech. Pay less attention to the exact pronunciation of the word than to the variety of sounds she makes, her intonation (Does her voice go up when she asks a question, mimicking adult speech?), and whether she makes eye contact during conversations. Read to her and reward her efforts to refine her speech whenever they naturally occur. If you're confident that she hears well and is able to communicate what she wants well enough, don't worry so much about how precise her language is at the moment. Do track her progress, though, and if you're still concerned, make it a priority for your next pediatric visit to discuss whether further steps need to be taken.

TEA AND SYMPATHY: LEARNING TO CONVERSE

Several months have passed, and baby Jacob is struggling to roll over. His older sister, Dana, loves to watch him work at trying to control his brand-new muscles. As she watches him, Jacob looks up at his sister, and his face brightens into a smile. "Mommy! Look!" Dana cries. "Jacob smiling!"

Sharon joins her daughter and laughs at Jacob, trying so hard to charm his sister into picking him up. *It's certainly easier when you can ask with words,* she thinks. She glances at Dana, who has gone back to playing quietly with her dolls and her miniature tea set. It was amazing, once the uproar of a new baby had faded away, how quickly Dana had begun to spout new words. After the first month or so, her feelings about Jacob had seemed to stimulate her desire to speak rather than stifle it. Her sudden interest in imaginary play also seemed to open a new avenue for speech. (Sharon can hear her talking to her dolls even now.) True, she still doesn't chatter away like some of the two-year-olds she plays with, but she talks much more than she did even six weeks ago. Sharon is glad, though, that she discussed her concerns with Dana's doctor. He was able to put her mind at ease, and that took the pressure off both of them.

Sharon's thoughts are interrupted by Jacob's sharp cry. "Oh, Jake!" Dana says before Sharon can respond. "Don't cry." Dana picks up a toy cup and holds it out to her brother. "Want tea?"

ADVANCES

Verbal Achievements in the Second Year

12 MONTHS	May babble in sentences that sound like your language but aren't
	May say two or more words— usually "label" words ("dog"), greetings ("hi," "bye-bye"), or over-generalized terms ("wa" for water and juice)
	Responds to your simple commands
15 MONTHS	Knows (but probably doesn't yet say) names of people, pets, body parts, favorite objects

	Points to certain objects when you ask her to
	Comprehends many more words than she says
18 MONTHS	Frequently says, "no"
	Vocabulary starts steadily rising
	May refer to herself by name
	May know the names of two colors
	Loves to repeat a word she is learning
21 MONTHS	Uses two-word sentences
	Says "me" and "mine"
	Can name own body parts
	Continues learning new words every day
24 MONTHS	Uses two-, three-, and four-word sentences
	Uses "and"
	Uses "I," "me," and "you"
	Says many more words
	Mimics adult inflections, gestures, etc.

FIRST-PERSON SINGULAR

Don't let this year go by without making audiotapes and, if possible, videotapes of your one-year-old's endearing efforts to speak as you do. Not only will you benefit from watching the many ways she works to get her thoughts across to you, but your child will enjoy listening to or watching herself on tape as well, studying her own inflections, her successes and failures at communicating, and your verbal responses. In contrast to her response a year ago, she'll realize that the girl on the screen is her. Two-year-olds enjoy the sounds of their own voice on audiotape at bedtime. Such a tape might ease the going-to-sleep struggle, but she may stay awake a little longer.

Don't forget to record your child's verbal "firsts" here as well. These are some of the most common milestones parents and children want to look back on later. You will probably also want to compare her rate of verbal acquisition to her other cognitive advances later on. Write them down now, before she comes over and starts a conversation.

READER'S NOTES

CHAPTER 5

Tears and Laughter—My Emotional Growth

His frequent outbursts are a result of his disorientation as he struggles with an environment he is only beginning to understand.

It's a beautiful, brisk autumn morning, and Carla has taken Victor, her one-year-old, to the playground. It's crowded there today. Babies sit wide-eyed on grown-ups' laps, toddlers try to climb up the little kids' slides, and older children run shouting to and fro. Carla parks her stroller near an empty bench, unbuckles Victor and sets him on his feet. "Go play," she says cheerfully, and sits down on the bench to keep an eye on him. Though he has only been walking for about a month, Victor is happy with the "long leash" his mother gives him. He has an adventurous temperament and loves to go exploring on his own.

Tentatively, Victor takes a few steps toward the center of the play area. A large red autumn leaf has fallen onto the pavement. Victor is fascinated by its gradations of color and wants to pick it up. He takes one step and then another, concentrating fiercely despite the noise of children playing nearby. Finally he is only a step or two from the leaf. Its colors are so vivid! It's still wet from last night's rain, and the rainwater makes it glisten in the sun. Victor wants to show it to his mom. He looks back toward the bench. But another woman has moved a baby carriage between Victor and his mother. He can't see her!

In an instant, all Victor's confidence, courage, and curiosity vanish. *Where is Mommy?!* He starts toward the spot where she was, staggers, and falls on his bottom. Strangers rush from all directions, all around him. No one is familiar. He starts to wail.

Just then, the woman with the stroller moves on. There's Carla, sitting on the bench. Still crying, Victor reaches for her. "Sweetheart, what's wrong?" she cries, going over to him. She picks him up and gives him a hug. "See, I'm here," she says. "You're okay."

Victor settles down a bit, comforted by his mother's touch and the sound of her voice. He remains in her arms a moment longer, letting the feelings she gives him of confidence and safety build up inside him. Then, emotionally fortified, he struggles to get free. Now that the bond between his mother and himself has been tested and found still strong, he feels comfortable venturing forth again, ready to explore his world. He sees the leaf and starts toward it—but this time he keeps part of his attention on Mommy's presence.

As your twelve- to twenty-four-month-old learns to maneuver— both literally and figuratively—through the wider world of the toddler, he is bound to experience all the tension, excitement, and discomfort of any "new kid on the block." In an environment that he is only beginning to understand, he will necessarily feel disoriented and out of his depth at times. (His panic may feel much like yours when you lose sight of him momentarily in the supermarket or the playground, though perhaps even more unsettling, since he doesn't have the experience to know that the situation will probably be resolved.) His frequent confusion and constant new discoveries this year will cause him to display an entire range of emotions—delight, sadness, fury, frustration, joy, and more—often heightened and sometimes unpredictable. You won't always know the reasons for his outbursts, since it's difficult to fully assess the emotional state of a child with limited language skills. But whatever the cause, his emotions will probably not be well modulated. When unhappy about something, most eighteen-month-olds cannot yet limit themselves to a frown or a pout. Instead, they'll start to cry or even erupt in a tantrum over what may actually be a minor frustration.

This behavior doesn't mean they're "spoiled" or "difficult." Putting the brakes on their emotions is just a new experience for them, and they will need plenty of practice before they improve.

The good news is that, as the year progresses, your child's emotional world will grow more sophisticated and, to some degree, manageable. Dr. Daniel Stern, author of *Diary of a Baby: What Your Child Sees, Feels, and Experiences,* and others have written eloquently about how one-year-olds increasingly respond not just reflexively to direct experience (such as having a toy snatched away) but to their own and others' emotions as well (Mommy's disapproval when they snatch the toy back). By the end of the year, your little one's tears and laughter may even be inspired by his private thoughts, memories, and dreams. As his emotional life begins to deepen and change in this way, you'll witness the emergence of his unique personality. You'll learn that he is a sensitive, thoughtful child, or an adventurous, even reckless one. You'll realize that he is somewhat fearful or remarkably placid. This "blossoming" of his character is the great reward for the emotional challenges and frustrations that your little one— and his entire family—may have to endure this year. In the months to follow, you will have the pleasure of really getting to know your child, and enjoying all the intricate ways in which your personalities interact.

A PARENT'S STORY

Warm and Cuddly

"When Vicki was about fifteen months old, she started having trouble going to sleep all over again, even though she'd been on a pretty good schedule for months before that," her mother, Jeannine, told me. "She kept trying to get me to stay in the room with her while she fell asleep, but I wanted her to learn how to go to sleep on her own. I had avoided trying to get her to use a security blanket or stuffed animal before, because I'd heard so many stories about kids who'd lost their blankets or worn them to shreds and then were inconsolable. Vicki finally ground me down with her constant whining at bedtime. I reached under her changing table and got out one of the cloth diapers I used to use as a spit-up cloth. I gave that to her to cuddle up with while she listened to a tape of children's songs, and it actually worked pretty well. She got really attached to that diaper over the next few weeks. I didn't care, because I had plenty more to replace it when it got dirty. It helped her settle back down to her routine, and when she started having the occasional tantrum later, her 'blankie' helped calm her and worked great for me, too. I just wish I'd thought about using something replaceable like that long ago."

A LOVE OF SAFETY: EMOTIONAL PATTERNS IN THE FIRST YEAR

Since the day he was born, and even before, much of what your child has learned about emotions he learned directly from you. Over and over during the first eventful months of your child's life, you demonstrated that you were there for him by responding promptly to his cry, feeding him when he was hungry, smiling back and talking to him when he smiled at you, and so on. Each successful encounter between the two of you deepened the attachment, bolstering his confidence that you would support him when he needed you and that even if he turned his back on you for a bit, you would be there waiting when he returned. You no doubt watched him experiment with this concept as he began to crawl. He probably enjoyed creeping out of your sight, then crawling back and "finding" you. He enjoyed checking your expression to see if his absence had worried or frightened you. Above all, though, then as now, he wanted to be in control of the leaving; he didn't like your disappearing on him at all! Through these games, the two opposing desires of your baby's emotional life—the urge to explore versus the need for a sense of safety—were first examined.

Sometime between seven and nine months of age, your baby became aware of the presence of strangers—that is, the fact that some people were "his" people, to be trusted, while others definitely were not. This realization signaled a major shift in his concept of his world, threatening his newfound sense of safety and awakening anxieties about whether you were in this sea of unfamiliar people and whether you would come when he needed you. Often during this period, he would carefully gauge your reactions to brief separations (such as when you left him with a caregiver) and other potentially emotional situations. If you appeared anxious, he would most likely become anxious, too. If you seemed calm, he might feel somewhat reassured that even if you left, he would be okay. However, he would probably cry for a little while as you left in any case, simply because he was watching his "secure base" walk out of the room. This crying behavior might have been disappointing on some levels, because he was no longer the "cute bundle" who could be passed from person to person, but it has deep roots as a survival tactic.

As your child approached his first birthday, his experiments in leaving you and finding you, his frequent observations of your own emotional responses, and his experiences weathering your own disappearances and returns instilled in him the belief that though you cannot be at his side every second, you will probably be there when he needs you. His level of confidence in this arena determines to a great degree how free he will feel to venture forth and explore his world in his second year. Ideally, he will be able to deal with a bit more distance from you as he progresses through the months to come. As in all dimensions of development, young children vary tremendously in their abilities to tolerate separation, to self-comfort, and to settle down after feeling upset. One handy idea is to leave behind a "token" of your presence (your purse, for example, or some other object that reminds him of cozy times he's spent with you), to help him move toward greater self-reliance.

This gradual shift from dependence toward independence is not just a physical process. As Dr. Judy Dunn has pointed out in her book *The Beginnings of Social Understanding,* your baby is exploring his own emotions as he explores his physical world. At seven to nine months, he studied your face to gauge your emotional response, then responded in a similar way himself. At twelve months, he may begin experimenting with his own feelings about people and events. He responds differently to people and situations depending on whether or not they are familiar. He demonstrates attachments to others as well as to you—a great advantage as he approaches the superenergetic toddler phase. He also starts to show that he feels differently from you about some things, and as his tastes become clearer, both of you get to know him even better.

Throughout this second year, your baby will continue to move back and forth between his attachment to you and other significant caregivers and his desire for independence. While the two urges coexist within him, one emotion often activates the other. When your baby feels confident and secure, for example, he sets out exploring. But when he goes too far and loses sight of you, his attachment mechanism is activated, and he must make contact again. Once he has "found you," he settles himself until his confidence returns, and he sets out exploring again. As the months pass, the reassurance he needs shifts from physical touch to eye contact and a smile to a casual acknowledgment as he shows you a toy from across the room. But the road to independence is fraught with pitfalls. There are bound to be times when your little one panics because he feels too far away from you (physically or emotionally), and times when he rebels because he feels you are holding him too close.

Though it is hard sometimes to be aware of where on the spectrum your child happens to be emotionally at the moment—and to make allowances for it amid the clamor of daily life—the more understanding and supportive you can be throughout this challenging period, the better for your child in the long run. His ability to rely on you to be there has been shown again and again in scientific studies to have a real long-term impact on his sense of well-being. One such study with which I was associated, called the Minnesota Parent-Child Project, followed 180 children from birth through age twenty. With comprehensive information on each child's social, cognitive, and emotional development, including his or her temperament, IQ level, and other distinct traits, the researchers found that no matter what their individual differences, the kinds of attachments the children formed with their primary caregivers *at one year of age* predicted: (1) their teacher ratings, behavior problems, and quality of relationships with peers in preschool, (2) their social competency as ten- and eleven-year-olds in summer camp, (3) their ability to empathize with others as they grew older, (4) their resilience in the face of personal difficulties, and (5) their school achievement level as teenagers.

A Friend Indeed

Strangers, twelve-month-old Tony thinks as the people enter his house. The smells, sounds, and shapes of these newcomers alert him that they do not belong here. Mommy looks happy as she ushers them inside. *Why is she looking at them and not at me?* Tony holds his arms up for his mom. "Uh!" he grunts. He knows the word "up," but at times when he feels uneasy it doesn't always come out right. He wants Mommy to pick him up and cuddle him. "Uh!"

Finally Mommy notices Tony. She smiles and picks him up. "There you are, big boy," she says. Tony feels better. But then she turns her face away again! "Look how big he's gotten," she says proudly to the strange ones. Tony looks warily at their big, unfamiliar faces all leaning forward, staring at him. *Go away!* he thinks. He starts to cry.

"May I hold him?" one of the strangers says. She reaches out for Tony. At the touch of her hands, he starts to scream. *Mommy!* he wants to say, *Make her stop!*

Now Mommy is frowning. "I don't know what's wrong with him. He's usually friendlier." She hands him to the stranger briefly.

Help! Tony feels as though his ties to Mommy have just been snapped. He struggles in the stranger's arms. The unfamiliar texture of her clothes rubs irritatingly against him. *Must have Mommy!* He feels himself losing control. His fear washes over him, and he starts to scream and kick.

"Okay, Tony, here I am." Mommy's arms are suddenly around him. He feels safe again. He snuggles against her and relishes the sense of warmth and security. A moment later, as Mommy carries him into the living room, he peeks over her shoulder. *Who are these new people anyway? They're all smiling and laughing. Oh. One is carrying a stuffed bear. Hmm. Nice bear,* he thinks as his eyes follow it across the room.

THE AGE OF DISCOVERY: EMOTIONAL GROWTH IN THE SECOND YEAR

Your one-year-old's first steps out into the world are a poignant reminder that sometime around the beginning of his second year, he has begun to realize that the two of you are not one indivisible unit. Increasingly, as he begins walking on his own two feet and thinking about the world around him in terms of words and ideas (rather than just responding instinctively to each sensation), he plays with the notion that his own mood, emotions, and thoughts can be separate, and even different, from yours. An interesting experiment by Dr. Joseph Campos and his colleagues demonstrated this change in perspective for the developing child. Babies of different ages were encouraged to crawl across a flat Plexiglas surface (called a "visual cliff") with what looked like a sharp, step-like drop underneath. As far as the babies could tell, they would tumble over the edge of the step if they continued crawling forward. When the babies were around nine months old, they would crawl toward the apparent drop-off, see the "step," and start to turn around to descend the step backward—but if they saw their mothers smiling encouragingly at them, they would change their minds and crawl blithely ahead, over the drop, instead. (If their mothers instead looked suddenly anxious or frightened, the babies would stop in their tracks.) After twelve months, on the other hand, some babies would note their mothers' reactions, hesitate while they weighed their mothers' assessments of the danger against their own, and then, even if their mothers were smiling, would turn around to descend the step backward. In other words, though the older babies still looked to their mothers to gauge their emotional responses, they no longer automatically shared them.

In the 1980s, Dr. Megan Gunnar of the University of Minnesota devised an experiment in which twelve- to thirteen-month-olds were shown three toys, one frightening, one pleasant, and one "ambiguous"—that is, it could be frightening or pleasant, depending on one's attitude. Gunnar found that the one-year-olds checked their mothers' responses to the toys before playing with them. If their mothers smiled encouragingly, the babies would play with the ambiguous toys, but they would not play with the frightening toys even if their mothers looked unafraid and encouraging. Again, these children were interested in their mothers' emotional responses but did not always mimic them.

When he is between twelve and fifteen months of age, your own child's emotional state will revolve around this amazing, dawning realization—that he has his thoughts and you have your thoughts, and they might not always be the same. The idea of emotional separateness is truly mind-boggling for a child who until recently assumed that you and he were in some sense a single whole. During this time, you will see him start to test your emotional responses to his own and others' actions, not only to determine how he himself should feel but to see whether you feel the same way he does.

Still, during this period, when motor development is so dramatic, there is not as much energy available for examining feelings as there will be later in the year. Your child is beginning to very roughly "feel out the emotional territory" in his newly discovered separate self—but only when he isn't distracted by his efforts to get the bleach bottle off the shelf in the laundry room or to stagger at top speed down the sidewalk just out of your reach. Until about eighteen months, much of his emotional life still centers on his own physical activity. He sees something (a bird or a cat) and is filled with a determination to catch it. He laughs with pleasure when he falls down on purpose, rocks on a rocking horse, pounds on things, or throws toys around.

Between eighteen and twenty-one months, however, as his focus on motor activity begins to relax, he starts to notice more what your own responses are to his activity. It may dawn on him at this point that though he finds it quite amusing to drop the entire contents of your jewelry box into the dog's water bowl, you don't seem to think it's so funny. Over the next few months, he becomes increasingly fascinated by this disparity between your responses and his own. He begins to get a keener sense of what's expected and unexpected. Over time, he figures out that if he changes his behavior, your (and others') responses will change. This is a wonderful discovery for toddlers, who so desperately yearn to control their limited environment. You may chuckle as you watch him reach his hand toward the hot-water faucet in the bathtub, then pull away, then reach for it, then pull away—while staring fascinated (as in the crawling-off-the-step experiment) at your mouth turning down and up, down and up. But you are experiencing a wonderful early opportunity to show your toddler how to behave. Make it clear to him now, in gentle, informative, consistent, nonpunitive ways, what you expect from him in specific situations (such as brushing his teeth twice a day, putting on his pajamas at night, going to sleep once the lights are out, and holding your hand when he crosses the street), and you may avoid a lot of conflict later on.

During this period, your toddler's cognitive (thinking) and affective (feeling) skills are deeply intertwined. The more he is aware of his separateness from others, the more sensitive he can become to the feelings of others. Gradually, his understanding will grow sufficiently to target and predict others' feelings with some accuracy. This is why, after snatching a toy from another child's hand, your eighteen-month-old will stare in fascination at the crying child without looking particularly sorry or even sympathetic, while at twenty-four months he may try to remedy the situation or even burst into tears himself. Within that six-month

Emotional outbursts can be avoided by letting your toddler experiment, under close supervision.

span he has begun to empathize—that is, to understand, not just recognize, others' emotions. His empathy may also prompt him to hug you when you're feeling blue or even tell you fondly that he "wuvs" you when you sing a happy song or do something funny to amuse him. This development comes as quite a relief to those parents (and there are many) who've had to fend off fears that they were raising a rather chilly person during those earlier months, but evolution from emotional experimenter to empathizer is quite natural.

As your child approaches his second birthday, you will see him interact emotionally with others on an increasingly sophisticated level. His social and emotional development has now reached a more complex stage. "I can't believe the difference," one mother told me. "A year ago, he pretty much depended on *us* to control his emotions. If he was frightened, we needed to fix it. Now he's so much better at calming himself down when he's upset or even soothing his baby brother." It's true—your two-year-old has assumed his place as a unique member of your family. He may pretend to take a bite out of the table to amuse you, offer to share a toy with his brother, and laugh with delight at the cartoon characters playing happily on TV. He has entered a generally sunny time for children altogether, in fact—a rewarding plateau after the steady climb from an undifferentiated "oneness" toward proud individuality.

THE TOY BOX

If I Had a Hammer . . .

At eighteen months, Max can go over to his toy box and pull out his favorite toy all by himself, thank you. He rummages around until he finds the plastic animal noisemaker. Confidently, he punches one of the big plastic buttons, and the toy barks like a dog. He punches another. The toy moos. This is old stuff for Max now.

Dad walks into the room in his bathrobe, settling down on the couch to read the paper. Max waits for him to play, but Dad hasn't had his first cup of coffee yet. Max thinks for a moment. Then he pounds his plastic toy on the floor, making a big, satisfying bang.

The newspaper slams down, and there's Daddy, looking at him!

"Max!" says Daddy loudly. Max laughs impishly. He slams the toy on the floor again. Daddy frowns even more. "I said stop that, Max!"

This is fascinating. Every time Max pounds the toy on the floor, Daddy looks at him and says something. *He sounds angry!* As soon as Daddy has started reading the paper again, Max crosses the room toward him. He stops a couple of feet away, hesitates, then pounds the plastic toy—just a little less hard— on the coffee table.

The newspaper slams down again! Max watches in wide-eyed anticipation. Daddy starts to yell, then manages to restrain himself. "Don't hit the table," he says instead, still annoyed. "You'll hurt the table and break your toy. If you want to pound something, I'll get your hammer and pegs. Come on." Seeing that his son looks apprehensive, he gently removes the toy from his hand and adds, as he sets up the new game, "Tell you what. After I've had my coffee, we can go work on that bench I'm building for the backyard. You can help Daddy, okay?"

Max takes the toy hammer from his father. He didn't understand everything Daddy said, but he liked his tone better. He glances toward the coffee table. It would be fun to hit it, but he knows Daddy would really get mad if he did. *Daddy said "yard,"* he thinks. Max heads for the back door, toy hammer in hand— not willing to wait for coffee.

"IS THIS CHILD *MINE*?": YOUR CHILD'S TEMPERAMENT

"I don't know what to do about him," I overheard a mother confess to a friend in the children's play area of a pediatrician's waiting room recently. She had her two-year-old son in an iron grip as he was struggling to get free. A few feet away, the mother of a younger child was trying to comfort her while inspecting the bite the boy had just given her. To her credit, the boy's mother looked just as distressed as everyone else who had witnessed the incident. "He's always been this way," she said to her friend. "I don't know why he always acts so angry. It's not like we ever spank him. We hardly ever even raise our voices at home!"

Often parents express bewilderment over how their children "got that way"—both in a negative sense and in other ways, as with a child who is sociable and friendly though his parents are painfully shy. Developmental psychologists, including Dr. Jerome Kagan of Harvard University, point out that this basic emotional makeup—called temperament—is essentially part of a child's genetic inheritance and is separate from his life experience. Precisely because it is out of their control, temperament is a source of some of parents' greatest fears and greatest pleasures—in a sense, it really is the great parental lottery. Your child's natural rhythms, his level of activity, his sociability or lack thereof, his general optimism or pessimism are all largely determined (and even, in some cases, expressed) before he is born. Equally important, however, is how well his temperament fits with yours, how well you are "attuned" to his general emotional state, and how successfully you are managing to work with his basic temperament in ways that are good for him. In other words, nature is a vital key in determining what sort of personality your child has, but "nurture" plays at least as great (if not greater) a role in your child's behavior.

Certainly every parent-child combination is unique. Some mothers are fortunate enough to have given birth to a child they understand perfectly and who "understands" them. Parent and child are able to communicate and get along together without really having to think about it. Other mother-child couples seem somehow out of sync. You may not feel quite comfortable and secure with your child, or he may not feel that way with you. As did the mother in the waiting room, you may even feel embarrassed or shocked by your child's apparent temperament and expressed behavior, finding that you don't even like him at times. This is a sad situation and a difficult one. But it is not your child's fault, nor your own. If you find yourself in this position, it's important to assess the situation as objectively as possible, examine the ways you can change your child's environment to gradually shape the ways in which his temperament is expressed, and try as much as possible to make clear that it's his behavior (and not him) that you dislike.

If your eighteen-month-old has started biting children on the playground, it doesn't mean he's bad or that you are a bad parent. Difficult as it is to keep in mind when other parents are throwing disapproving looks your way, the fact is that the second year is a time when children naturally experiment with all kinds of behavior just to find out what kinds of responses they will create. In fact, no matter how much you "like" your child or how good the relationship is, this is an age that tends to be difficult for everyone. Your child is active enough to create all kinds of emotional drama, yet he has not yet reached that empathic stage when he completely understands how his actions make others feel. So when your one-year-old behaves badly, don't be too quick to decide that that's "just the way he is." Your child is still in an extreme state of flux. Many of his apparent personality traits, such as stubbornness, selfishness, and negativity, may really be just phases that every child goes through and that will fade away if you don't pay too much attention to them. Even the more permanent aspects of his character are open to parental guidance and "retuning." So don't judge his character or assign him particular characteristics too early (as in, "Reed's such a *loud* boy").

It also makes sense to keep in mind that just because this child is very different from his brother, his sister, or the child next door, that doesn't mean he's better than or inferior to the other child. Each child is different, with a fascinating mix of good and bad traits that are continuously reshaped by his life experience (much like us adults). In addition, many children create a first impression that is very different from how they really are. Your child may put people off at first with his apparent hyperactivity, but those who know him better understand that he is just a very exuberant, happy child.

Whatever your child's temperament—whether he talks a mile a minute, spends much of his time contentedly puttering about on his own, gets unnervingly "physical" with kids he's just met, or leaves the room the instant a new person enters—try to drop your own assumptions for a moment and see the world from his point of view. He may not be the typical kind of person you'd pick to be your friend (he may chatter all day when you'd rather read a book), but he is a one-of-a-kind individual with his own strengths and his own worth. Sharing his childhood with him means you'll get to know a person "like him"—a type of person you'd ordinarily never mix with—in a very intimate way. Giving him a chance to express himself in your presence allows you to show your appreciation and respect for him and will give you ideas for ways to channel his negative energy into more positive outlets. As he grows, he will deeply appreciate this effort at attunement and will repay you a thousandfold with his own respect and desire to do well. If he is truly a challenging child by nature, he will need your understanding and patience more than ever. Look at it as your best shot at unconditional love.

Try as they might, it has been difficult for developmental psychologists to tease out precisely where inherited temperament ends in an infant and where environmentally influenced traits begin. Certainly, as any mother of twins or more than one child can tell you, there are obvious behavioral differences among babies even in utero. From the moment of birth, some cry a lot, some are quiet, some sleep regularly, others wake at all hours. Though it is also possible to "create" irritable or active babies by interacting with them in particular ways, babies are undeniably biased toward certain moods and emotions. However, the fact is that practically from the first encounter, parents react to what they perceive as the infant's temperament and change their own behavior accordingly. If a baby smiles and makes plenty of eye contact with his parents, they tend to smile and make eye contact back. If he sleeps most of the time or looks away frequently, the parents may not interact with him as much. This shaping mechanism continues as the child grows older. A study designed by pioneering researchers Drs. Alexander Thomas and Stella Chess demonstrated that mothers of twelve-month-olds responded similarly to their babies whether they were categorized as "difficult" or "easy" but exerted far less effort in trying to control the difficult children as little as six months later. It pays to be aware of this tendency to adjust to a baby's apparent character and change your responses when they aren't productive.

One way to work at managing the "mutual shaping" process so that it works in your and your child's best interests is to be aware of behaviors that are typical of a particular age and are therefore probably not specifically due to your child's basic temperament. If you can avoid reacting too much to these temporary behavior patterns, they will eventually settle down. In the second year, your child's most challenging time is likely to fall somewhere between age fifteen and twenty-one months. During this period, he is old enough to formulate very strong desires but isn't always able to satisfy them. This clearly creates frustration and leads to all kinds of difficult behavior, including shouts of "No!," refusals to cooperate with your wishes, and outright tantrums. Frankly, much of this behavior is part of the territory for this phase of his life. Your best response is to do what you can to gently curb his excesses (by refusing to give in to overly rude demands, by modeling and discussing appropriate ways to express his anger, and especially by avoiding frustrating scenarios whenever possible) and to remind yourself that this behavior isn't going to last forever. Remember that a child needs to try out *all* his new feelings, negative as well as positive. In fact, he will probably save his most intense feelings (good and bad) for you. This is why, even after a placid day with his caregiver, he will completely disintegrate when you arrive, behaving as though he's not happy to see you. Depressing as that can feel when it's happening, keep in mind that he's actually demonstrating the strength of his love for you, using his sense of safety with you to have the meltdown he was holding back all day. "My mother used to give me such a look when I picked Carl up from her house after work, when he was around one and a half," one mother told me. "A lot of the time he'd see me and just start screaming. My mom would say something like 'We did nothing but laugh and play all day.' After I realized that he was just letting go of all his pent-up feelings at once, I felt a lot better about it, and he stopped doing it soon enough."

Your "Challenging" Child

The second year is a particularly difficult time to tell if your child is just "going through a phase" or if he is dealing with a more lasting emotional (or behavioral) challenge. If you have been worrying that he seems overly aggressive, angry, frustrated, listless, or reclusive, even for his age, confront your feelings now and begin researching their validity. One way to do this would be to ask others who know your child for an honest reading. Do they believe that he has a problem or that he's just acting like a typical toddler? Next, monitor your own responses to his questionable behavior. Do you aggravate the situation—making too big a deal out of his refusal to cooperate, for example—and thus reinforce his actions through your increased attention? In many cases, his behavior may simply be a case of being exposed too often to the triggers that happen to set him off. Pay attention to what time of day he usually falls into the behavior pattern that worries you. Does he begin "acting that way" when he hasn't eaten for several hours, when he's missed his nap, when he's in a room with a lot of other children? Correcting his behavior may be just a matter of avoiding those "trigger" situations whenever possible.

In the meantime, keep in mind that a "challenging" child, as Dr. Stanley Greenspan, co-author of *The Challenging Child: Understanding, Raising, and Enjoying the Five "Difficult" Types of Children,* terms such children, is not directing his behavior at you but is responding to stress at some level within himself. Sensitive or very active children can have particular trouble during this year, when they must deal with so much internal change. Failed interaction with others his age will only lead to more frustration in the future, so it's best to try to deal with the causes of his misbehavior now, before his world widens even more.

"NO!":
DEALING WITH TANTRUMS

Alisha had been taking her daughter, Maia, to a child-care center near her workplace since Maia was six months old. From the beginning, Maia seemed to enjoy the center, and Alisha was confident in the quality of care that her daughter received there. Whenever Alisha dropped in for a visit at lunchtime or came to pick Maia up, Maia was busily engaged in an activity by herself, with other children, or with one of the caregivers. Alisha especially enjoyed reading the daily summary of Maia's activities and accomplishments. One day, though, when Maia was about twenty months old, something went wrong. Alisha took her to the child-care center in her stroller, as usual, but when they reached the front door, Maia refused to get out of the stroller and go inside. "No!" she wailed as Alisha tried to pull her out of her seat. Her cries were so loud they made Alisha's ears ring, and the other parents stared as they passed by with their own (well-behaved) children. Mortified, Alisha asked Maia to lower her voice. But Maia was oblivious to the effect she was having on everyone else; she was completely caught up in the feeling of panic she was experiencing. Alisha tried asking Maia what was wrong, to no avail. She mentally reviewed the summary of Maia's activities from yesterday, but nothing seemed out of the ordinary. In the end, Alisha had no choice but to pick Maia up and carry her into the child-care center. After checking in with the teacher, she left Maia with a promise to call later. "I feel like the worst parent on the planet," she told me over the phone from work. "I feel like I'll never be able to set foot in that center again."

Of course, as Alisha learned when she returned to pick Maia up that day, the child-care workers had seen far worse tantrums than that one in their careers. Maia was her old cheerful self by then, throwing herself affectionately on her mother as soon as she saw her. Alisha was relieved as she hugged her little girl to know that she had kept her own temper in check sufficiently during the tantrum not to have said anything damaging that she would now regret. Reviewing the situation on the ride home, Alisha decided that the tantrum must have resulted from the rush they had been in that morning. Everyone had overslept, and Maia had been snatched out of bed and jammed into her clothes without her usual wake-up routine. Then they realized that they were out of the raisin bread that Maia liked for breakfast. Finally, it was raining, and Maia had had to sit inside the plastic stroller cover, which she hated. As a result, she'd passed her frustration threshold and just disintegrated.

Alisha knew she could expect rough drop-offs and pickups from the child-care center occasionally, but she never wanted to go through another tantrum like that one first thing in the morning. She made plans to avoid future tantrums before they happened. "I tried waking Maia a little earlier for the rest of the week, to give her time to awaken gradually," she told me. "It's amazing what a difference that little change made. She's never had another tantrum like that one. I just didn't realize how out-of-control any little change in her routine made her feel at that age. Now I make sure we have extra raisin bread, just in case!"

Experts generally agree that a tantrum is your child's way of telling you when he's reached his limit of frustration and needs you to help him make things right. Usually resulting from the gap between his desire to do something (grab a handful of candy at the grocery-store checkout, for example) and his ability to do it, this frustration builds until he is unable to express it in any other way. Tantrums at this age are in no way signs that your child is "spoiled" or that you are a bad parent. They are simply symptoms of your child's development as he learns to cope with a complex new set of feelings.

One of the worst aspects of a tantrum is its potential to embarrass the parent, but there's no need to suffer unduly if and when your child has a tantrum in a public place. You can be sure that the large majority of people passing by (or even glaring disapprovingly at you) have been or will be in exactly the same situation one of these days. Hard as it is, one of your primary challenges is not to let your embarrassment lead you to "punish" your child. Spanking him, telling him he's acting like a baby, yelling, or otherwise getting highly emotional yourself will only make matters worse. Right now, he needs to know you're the "rock" he can cling to as he tries to find his bearings. He can only climb out of his chaotic state if you remind him (through your own behavior) what it feels like to be calm.

Children respond differently to various comfort techniques, so you may have to try several before you figure out how you can best calm your out-of-control child. If you're at home, you have the option of letting him work out his emotions himself. Either pick him up and hold him quietly or gather him up and carry him to a safe spot where he can cry and kick to his heart's content. Then go about your business while checking in verbally once in a while ("Are you feeling better, Patrick? Would you like me to read you a story?"). Basically, he needs to figure out how to get control of himself again, and there's not much more you can do to help him. Moving away from him may also help you resist the very real temptation to go over the edge yourself. You are in more danger of behaving in ways you'll later regret at home where no one is watching. If necessary, leave him for a few moments until you're sure you've regained control.

In public places, it's important to stop the noise as soon as possible. Of course, the best solution to these tantrums is to try to avoid them in the first place. But if your child loses it, perhaps it's best just to concentrate on getting him out of there as quickly as possible. (Try to avoid well-meaning strangers who try to help and may foil your escape.) As you hustle your child out of there, remind yourself that this, too, shall pass. Later, when everyone's calmed down, try to figure out what might have caused the tantrum. Often it's a minor occurrence that you never would have suspected meant so much to your child. One father who loved to take his one-year-old grocery-shopping after work had a wonderful time picking out vegetables and treats with her, but each time they reached the checkout area, she fell into a tantrum for no reason he could understand. Finally he realized that the moment when he was unloading the grocery cart onto the conveyer belt was the only time he turned his back on her. Apparently this made his daughter feel suddenly alone and lost. As soon as her father learned to face her as he unloaded groceries, her behavior cleared up. When such behavior inevitably happens, ask yourself what's different in the way you or your child approached the situation. You might come up with a clue that could prevent future episodes.

EASING THE WAY

Avoiding Tantrums

Tantrums are extremely unpleasant for parent, child, and anyone else within earshot. The best way to avoid them is, as always, to think ahead a little. The first rule in preventing an uncontrollable level of frustration from building up in your child is to stick to his daily routine as much as possible. If he is used to having lunch at noon and then taking a short nap, delaying lunch or the nap will raise his stress level. When you do need to change the order or occurrence of his usual activities, inform him ahead of time and be ready to fall back to a simpler schedule (such as skipping the trip to the library or having a quieter than usual afternoon). Transitions are another common situation that is hard on toddlers. Try to move from one activity to another gradually, rather than just placing your child abruptly in another environment, among a new group of people, or even in a new outfit without warning. Sometimes toddlers lose control because they feel they are over-restricted. (That's why strollers, grocery carts, and car seats are often the places where things erupt.) Try giving your little one as much freedom as possible to explore his world without placing him in physical danger. Finally, when he absolutely refuses to go along with your wishes, ask yourself what the long-term goal is and aim for that. For instance, if you want to give him a bath but he refuses to take off his underwear, ask yourself what's more important—taking off his underwear or the bath? There's nothing fundamentally wrong with letting him wear his underwear in the bath once or twice so he can find out what it's like. That way he will have figured out that it's not really much fun, and you won't have had to fight about it.

Many tantrums can be avoided or alleviated just by maintaining awareness of your child's level of maturity and specific skills— in other words, how much change, challenge, and "strangeness" he can take. If you learn to recognize the signs that he is about to lose control, you may be able to distract or comfort him before the yelling starts. Positive reinforcement during the good times works very well, too. When he's been particularly well behaved say, "I'm proud you're being so patient waiting your turn." (Not, "You're a good boy for being so patient.") He may remember your praise and strive to hear it again on a more challenging day.

A WIN-WIN SITUATION: LETTING THE OTHER PARENT PARENT, TOO

Mothers are of vital importance in one-year-olds' busy lives, but don't forget that fathers and other male caregivers can also contribute a great deal. Landmark research by Dr. Ross Parke of the University of California at Riverside and Dr. Michael Lamb, author of *The Father's Role: Cross-Cultural Perspectives,* has focused particularly on what fathers bring to families. The results indicate that fathers' involvement in their babies' caretaking leads to gains in the babies' cognitive and emotional development. School-age children whose fathers spent a higher than average amount of time with them as infants have been shown to have significantly higher IQ scores, longer attention spans, more eagerness for learning, and even more of a sense of humor than those whose fathers did not participate. In his recent book, *Fatherneed: Why Father Care Is as Essential as Mother Care for Your Child,* Dr. Kyle Pruett of Yale University points out that fathers help enrich their children's self-image and contribute to a more stable family-support structure for the child. Looking ahead, father involvement in the teenage years gives the adolescent a stronger sense of his inner "locus of control"—the ability to resist peer pressure because he is sure of his own values.

Certainly, having a helpful partner around can greatly lower the stress level in your household. Involved partners can also temper the intensity of the mother-infant relationship once your child is ready to become a little more independent. Finally, any two caregivers are bound to have different approaches to raising a baby. It helps a developing child to witness a variety of behavior patterns and interact with adults in different ways—as long as the adults don't argue incessantly about whose approach is better.

Some dads are completely natural, involved caregivers, but especially with a first child, dads are subject to the same insecurities and misconceptions as moms are. As you watch him toss your eighteen-month-old up in the air (practically giving you a heart attack as the child's head almost touches the ceiling) and order him to clean up his toy closet (when he's obviously much too young), keep in mind that your partner may not have had all those years of baby-sitting experiences, conversations with his mother about child care, talks with pediatricians, and other experiences that have traditionally prepared many women for parenthood. He may well feel self-conscious as he tries to establish his separate relationship with his child—especially if you're watching him every second. Surely you can empathize with his feelings when your child screams for you and (at least for the moment) rejects him. Support him in his continued efforts, resisting the temptation to criticize but making yourself available for advice if he asks for it. The

Nothing can ease your toddler's anxiety like the security provided by loving, involved parents.

rewards—a more cohesive family, a more secure child, and someone to talk to about that fascinating child—are worth the effort.

She Doesn't Want Me . . .

Q: When my wife became pregnant, we agreed that I would take on half of the parenting duties whenever possible. I have tried to do that, but from the beginning, my one-year-old daughter has preferred her mom to me. When I try to take her for the afternoon, she whines that she wants to be with Mommy. When I go in to tell her bedtime stories, she refuses to let me. What am I doing wrong?

A: Regardless of dads' good intentions, infants' attachment to their primary caregivers, who in this society tend to be the mothers, is so strong that sharing the child-care duties can sometimes be difficult. Some babies and toddlers resist being "passed off" to Daddy at first, and they aren't usually very tactful about expressing their preferences. Too often this resistance causes dads to throw up their hands and retreat in frustration to the office or the TV set. This is a real shame, because a relationship with your child is vitally important for you, for her, and for the family's health. If you can, try to overlook your little one's stubborn resistance to changing hands. Make a point of doing some of your child's favorite activities together (not just the chores), so that she will learn that time with Dad is often fun time. Taking on some of the more serious responsibilities of parenting, such as bringing your child to the pediatrician for her checkups, may also add more dimension to your relationship with your child. If you are unsure about some aspect of parenting, you can talk with the doctor or with other actively involved parents, as well as your wife, about effective methods that have worked for them.

It might help to know that as they grow, young children throw their allegiance back and forth from one parent to another, each time with great passion and loyalty. Your little one may be Mommy's baby now, but—as I overheard one father of a four-year-old assuring a toddler girl's dad at a child's birthday party the other day—"Don't worry, pal, your time will come."

AND THE CAREGIVER MAKES FOUR: EXPANDING YOUR CHILD'S FAMILY

As the months pass, your child's world will continue to widen to include more caregivers, friends, and other family members. It is good to know that no matter how many people he learns to love, there's always enough love to go around. A great deal of recent research, including a seminal long-term study published in 1997 by the National Institute for Child Health and Development, has shown that *quality* child care does not affect the security of a baby's attachment to his parents. In other words, babies don't confuse the caregivers in their lives or choose only one person to whom to attach themselves. Your child will always know and appreciate the fact that you are his mom or dad. Of course, it is sometimes easier to *tell* yourself that your baby will always love you most than it is to believe it when he starts screaming the moment you challenge his desire to stay and play with his caregiver. Remember that, as any parent can tell you, children this age routinely save up their emotional demonstrations until the moment they can unload them on their parents—and that his "show" is one way of telling you how much you mean to him. Count yourself lucky that your child is so attached to his caregiver. Think about how sad his life would be if he were not! For your own mental health and your child's sake, try not to compete with your caregiver—or allow her to compete with you— over who is the best "parent" to your little one. Focus instead on your shared love for him and on what you can learn from each other about how to deal with the behavioral challenges that arise.

Oddly, parents sometimes forget how important a particular caregiver can become to a one-year-old, no matter how temporary they assumed that caregiver to be. Transitions from one caregiving situation to another can be very upsetting to your child, as difficult for him as you might find moving to a new house in your own life. When possible, it's best to phase out one caregiver gradually and phase in the next, so that there's a time when your child spends time with each of the participants and doesn't experience an abrupt transition. Be sure to talk about the change with him ahead of time, while it's happening, and afterward—keeping in mind the fact that he can understand many more words than he can say. Even the transition from the babies' room to the completely different and initially strange toddlers' room at the child-care center can throw him out of balance. As his second year progresses, make sure that any such transitions are handled with tact and an awareness of your child's very real emotional attachments.

Q & A

Where Did She Go?

Q: My twenty-month-old son, Luke, was very close to his full-time sitter, Andrea, who began taking care of him when he was four months old. He cried when she left at the end of each day, so much that I had to work hard to keep from feeling jealous. Two months ago, Andrea's family suddenly had to move back to their native country. We told Luke she was leaving, of course, but I'm not sure he really understood. Now that she's gone, he keeps asking where she is, and I don't know what to tell him. How can I help him deal with Andrea's not being in his life anymore?

A: Changes in relationships are hard for everyone, but this is especially true for toddlers. Your son's asking for his caregiver is only natural, given the strong relationship they shared for most of his life to date. Frankly, at this age, preparing him for her sudden departure was probably all you could do at the time. Now, though, there are several ways to help make this physical loss of a special person a bit easier for him (and you!). Continue to talk about Andrea routinely or when your son asks for her, keep photos of her nearby and refer to them visually, even after you have a new caregiver in place. When he colors a picture, tell him you're going to send it to her, and let him help you mail it. He won't understand the logistics of distance or how long it will be before he sees her again, but he will make the connection between talking about her, seeing her face, and his happy associations with her. If at all possible, an occasional phone call would be a wonderful opportunity to hear her voice again and strengthen that connection. As hard as it is, think of this separation as an important lesson in life—that special people come and go in ways we cannot control but physical distance does not mean that important relationships have to end.

"SEE YOU LATER!": EXPANDING THE EMOTIONAL BOUNDARIES

Frank, the little boy down the street, is just two weeks younger than Victor, and today is his second birthday party. Carla and Victor have been invited, and they are pleased to visit Frank's house for the first time. When they arrive, Carla ushers Victor into the playroom with the other children. She sees that several parents she knows have already taken charge of monitoring the room, so after lingering for a while until she sees that Victor is comfortable, she gives him a quick, reassuring wave and she slips out of the room to grab a soda.

A brief time later, Carla peeks back into the playroom. She finds the kids all gathered around Frank's dad, who is blowing up balloons. Carla watches Victor stand with the other children, entranced by the sight of so many balloons. A balloon pops. Victor looks startled, and a child next to him starts to cry. Carla watches Victor give the crying child a concerned look. Then he sticks his thumb in his mouth, soothing himself as Frank's dad comforts the crying child and starts blowing up another balloon.

What a difference, Carla thinks. A year ago Victor could hardly let her out of his sight. Now he has learned all kinds of ways to manage his emotions. *He's becoming so independent,* Carla thinks as she smiles across the room at an adult acquaintance. Sometimes it's nice for grown-ups to enjoy some independence, too.

Emotional Achievements in the Second Year

12 MONTHS	Emotional states tend to vary easily
	Is easily distracted from source of discomfort
	Enjoys looking at himself in the mirror
	Begins to understand that his feelings are separate from his parents'
	May mirror others' emotions
15 MONTHS	May experiment with sharing, but then want object back
	May cry often but is easily comforted by a loved one
	May notice when familiar people are missing
	Starts to prefer certain clothes and routines
18 MONTHS	Becomes easily frustrated
	Finds it difficult to manage his emotions
	Acts impulsively
	Uses blanket, stuffed animal, or favorite toy to comfort himself
21 MONTHS	Begins to recognize others' emotions

Expresses love for parents through hugging, etc.

Starts to understand concept of "good" and "bad" behavior

Makes some attempts to control crying

24 MONTHS Is generally less impulsive

Thrives on a reliable routine

Can be bossy at times

Self-confidence has increased

Takes pride in doing things himself

FIRST-PERSON SINGULAR

As you watch your one-year-old grow more independent and learn to recognize and manage his own emotions, take some time to write down your observations here. What was his confidence level on his first play date? His fifth? How did he and you weather that change in caregivers? What is his favorite comfort object? How has he learned to show you he loves you? Who are his favorite people? What activities does he particularly enjoy doing with Dad?

It is fun to look back at these notes later and see which traits turned out to be a part of your child's ongoing personality and which were just a sign of a temporary phase. Though difficult to see at the time, these differences eventually become very clear.

_____

_____

_____

_____

_____

_____

_____

_____

_____

_____

_____

_____

_____

_____

_____

_____

_____

_____

_____

CHAPTER 6

Where I Stand—My Social Development

She's learning to share experiences and compare her reactions with others'.

A new family has moved in next door, and Marian and Bill have invited them over for dinner. Marian is glad they're bringing their two-year-old son, Pete, as well. Her own daughter, Clara, hasn't had much experience with other children, since she's an only child and only twelve months old. Marian looks forward to watching her daughter play with a brand-new friend.

Pete turns out to be a very nice boy, and Marian and Bill like his parents, too. As the adults drink coffee after dinner, Marian turns Clara loose to practice her walking skills in the dining room. Bill has already brought the toy box into the dining room, so Pete will have plenty of things to play with.

Constantly admonished by his parents to "be nice to Clara," and "show Clara the toy," Pete does try to interest the one-year-old in playing with him. But Clara brushes right past him, focused on her movement and determined to walk all the way across the room. Most of the time, the two children don't even seem to notice each other; each is absorbed in his or her own activity. "Mommy, look!" Pete says, going to his mother, holding up one of Clara's toys to show her. "Turtle!"

Distracted from her walking by the sound of Pete's voice, Clara turns to see Pete holding aloft one of her toys. He's heading toward *her* parents (it seems) with *her* toy! Clara lets out a yell of protest. She heads straight for Pete, clearly intending to get back the toy. Sighing, Marian and Bill both get up to deal with her. Obviously, Clara is no good at winning friends and influencing people. *Will she ever learn?* Marian wonders.

The fact is, social skills with peers are not a top-priority aspect of development for this young a child, compared to the obvious need to form attachments to Mom and Dad. Though children in this country seem to develop certain social skills earlier now than in previous generations, your one-year-old is not likely to start appreciating the joys of friendship until the end of her second year or even later. In general, your child will move from a preoccupation with *physical* skills toward *psychological* issues. She needs to proceed in her development from the inside (her own body and feelings) out (her relationships with others). She demonstrates this not only in her behavior but through her body language; most infants' first "bye-bye" wave is directed inward, as though waving to themselves, but over the year they turn their pudgy hands around and start greeting the outside world.

Your child cannot progress far in her social skills until she begins to come to grips with the distinction between herself and others. This important step generally occurs in the first half of the second year. As she gradually comes to understand that she is a separate individual, that other people have feelings, and that their feelings "feel" much like hers, she can start to learn the different ways of interacting with parents, siblings, grandparents, friends, and strangers. This is a complex series of behavior patterns to master, yet your child will be well on her way toward successful interaction with practically anyone by the end of her second year.

Q & A

That Bad Girl . . .

Q: Recently my twenty-month-old, Richard, has been coming home from his child-care center rambling on about "bad girls" and "blocks." I finally figured out by going there and watching that Richard's upset because a small group of older girls occasionally monopolize the block corner. The staff doesn't seem to think it's an issue that they should get involved in. They say Richard doesn't have any trouble with the other kids, that the blocks are available to him sometimes (thought not always when he'd like), and that this situation will work itself out.

I understand that the girls should be allowed to play by themselves with the blocks if they want, but on the other hand I don't like to see my child repeatedly rejected by a group at such a young age. What really worries me is the fact that I can't seem to get my son interested in finding other friends. He seems completely caught up in his desire to get those girls to let him play with them. What should I do about this?

A: It's hard not to want to rescue your toddler from an unpleasant situation with other kids, but the caregivers at your child's center may have taken the correct approach in this case. In general, your child can best explore the complex ins and outs of playing with others and making friends if the adults who care for him are watchful but not intrusive (unless, obviously, someone is about to get hurt). Interfering in such interactions as you've described harms a child's ability to learn to help himself. At your child's age, observing and interacting with older kids can be a plus, even if they aren't particularly friendly. Anyway, he's probably more focused on the blocks right now than the fact that the girls are trying to exclude him.

For all these reasons, it might be best to wait and see how the situation works out. Ask his caregivers to monitor your child's interactions with others, though, and make sure this exclusion scenario doesn't get too prolonged. Meanwhile, try to drop in occasionally at lunch or a little early at the end of the day and read a story to your child—so that he will know that he has your support—and point out and discuss interesting friends his age once in a while. Quite soon, the attraction of playing in the block corner when the older girls are there will probably fade. They may even tire of the block corner eventually and leave it all to him!

"LOOK—IT'S ME!": SOCIAL ACHIEVEMENTS IN THE FIRST TWO YEARS

The age at which scientists believe that infants are aware of their separate selves has been pushed back repeatedly, as methods of determining developmental advances are regularly improved. The ability to move at about six to nine months certainly provides babies with more experience of their separateness and opens up new opportunities to encounter objects and other people. Gradually, your baby transfers her focus from her own physical sensations toward these objects outside herself. (At about this time, she uses her first words to name them, further demonstrating that her attention is moving outward.)

As she proudly masters the names of one object after another, your child becomes increasingly aware of, and interested in, your responses to her actions. By now she is cognizant of the fact that her thoughts are separate from yours and that they may be very different. She will begin the process of *social referencing*—that is, looking to you after she performs an action or, if the two of you witness an event, checking your reaction to it. This is one of the first clear signs of her growing awareness of her social world.

At around eighteen months, a number of cognitive advances come together to move your child forward in her social development. Whereas she was previously instinctively attracted to videotapes of babies' faces (and to babies' faces in picture books), she now becomes aware that the faces belong to "others" who are not herself. Likewise, while she loved to look at herself in the mirror at six, nine, and twelve months of age, she now understands that she is actually looking at a reflection of herself! At twelve months, she would point at an object (and perhaps name it) even if no one else was in the room. At eighteen months, she will point out the object only if someone is there. Her developing language skills have helped her realize that she can share experiences and compare reactions with others through gestures and words.

The period between eighteen and twenty-four months is a time of deepening social relationships. With the great jump in verbal ability, your child is able to attempt more sophisticated social interactions. She becomes fascinated by others' emotions and gradually begins to realize that other people can experience the same kinds of preferences and feelings that she does. By her second birthday, she will have begun enjoying play dates, will learn a great deal by imitating other children, and may even refer to her friends by name when they're not there. Still, unless her parents encourage her to engage actively with other children, her play will remain largely parallel with theirs until well into her third year. She may sit literally back to back with her best friend as they play, even when they're doing the same thing.

THE TOY BOX

At Twenty Months

Tally's friend Theo has come for his third play date, and the two are happily pulling one toy after another out of the toy basket, as though they're competing to see who can get them out the fastest. Suddenly Theo stops, entranced by the red ball he has found at the bottom of the basket. "Ball!" he announces with satisfaction. Theo and Tally's moms, who are chatting nearby, glance at him and smile.

"That's a funny ball, Theo," Tally's mom, Ruby, says, going over to demonstrate. "Look, it makes a jingly sound when you roll it." She rolls the ball. Theo laughs when he hears the sound and runs after it. Ruby turns to smile at her daughter, but Tally has a frown on her face.

"Mine!" Tally says, getting up and racing toward the ball. She grabs it and holds it aloft just before Theo reaches it. "My ball!" she tells him sternly.

Theo reaches for the ball, starting to wail with frustration. "Theo, it's Tally's ball," his mother, Holly, says. She moves toward the toddlers as Theo's wails get louder.

Ruby can see that this situation will only get worse. The

parents will have to physically separate the children, and Tally and Theo will lose their chance to practice playing together. But she has an idea. "Tally, look!" she says, reaching into the toy box for another ball. "Here's your blue ball with the sparkles! You love these sparkles, don't you?"

Gently, she manages to exchange the pretty blue ball for the red one in Tally's hands. As soon as Tally's attention is diverted to the blue ball, she drops the red one to the floor.

"Ball!" Theo says. He sits down on the floor, placing the red ball between his legs with great satisfaction. Tally sits down, too, her back to Theo, making her blue ball roll away.

Ruby and Holly exchange relieved glances. A potential problem has been avoided without the adults trying to force their children to "share" when they're not yet able. Tally and Theo are not playing together, but at least they are successfully playing side by side. Perhaps there will be a good opportunity to experience taking turns or sharing later in the play date. If not, at least the playtime will end without any practice in hitting.

"PLAY WITH ME": LEARNING TO BE WITH OTHERS

The road toward successful interaction with other human beings is a long and challenging one for any child. Your one-year-old will be grateful for all the support and social interpretation you can provide. One way you can help is to be aware of where your child is developmentally, in order to avoid demanding too much or expecting too little in her social interaction. Between twelve and fifteen months, for example, it probably isn't possible to curb your child's behavior by pointing out its effect on someone else. The fact that her hitting Sarah on the head "hurts Sarah's feelings" will certainly fascinate your child (and is important for her to hear, so that she can eventually begin to understand it), but it probably won't convince her to stop hitting Sarah. In fact, if you make too big an issue of the incident—snatching your child away, getting emotional, and otherwise giving her more and richer attention than usual—you will actually encourage the behavior by focusing her attention on it. A better response would be to model good behavior by apologizing to the other child on your child's behalf, make sure she is cared for, then separate the two of them and explaining calmly but firmly to your child why her action was wrong. (She isn't likely to understand the abstract concepts as you tell her that her behavior was "bad" or "mean," but she will learn from your tone of voice that you do not approve.) You can then put the children back together (if both are willing), remaining there yourself to make sure that they don't fight again. If you see that they're headed for another confrontation, gently guide their interaction in positive directions. In general, it's best to work on preventing such situations rather than trying to deal with them after they've occurred.

By eighteen to twenty-one months, your child has begun to perceive the fact that another person's feelings are much like her own. This can certainly help with biting and hitting issues, if you continue to monitor them calmly and consistently. However, other issues come to the fore during this period that can also cause difficulty on the play-ground or during play dates. These spring from your toddler's low frustration threshold and her increasing need to try to control situations. At this age, for example, your toddler is more likely to bite a child because she took away her toy, or because she hit her, or because she's tired and is losing it emotionally than just because she wants to see what happens when she bites. By repeatedly showing your child specific ways to interact with others—what to say, when to share, how to get the other person to cooperate—you ease the way toward friendship and social ability.

By the end of her second year, your child will have become more interested in the concept of "good" versus "bad" behavior. Unfortunately, she will probably be quicker to judge the behavior of others before her own; this is an age when your child is likely to protest loudly when another child behaves "badly" toward her but blithely do the same thing herself a few minutes later. This is to be expected and can be gradually remedied by continuing to consistently (but not relentlessly) discuss the good and bad behavior the two of you witness in other children and in herself. Your own example—behaving calmly and fairly as often as possible in stressful situations—will instruct her even more effectively than words. Meanwhile, her deepening perception of the emotional world of

A back-to-back position enables each child to stay focused on his or her own play, although others' play will invoke curiosity.

others will lead her to express her affection for her friends more frequently, making for more pleasant and rewarding interactions.

As we have seen, forming emotional connections with other children is a long process, and social interaction is not a particularly interesting idea to your child until her second birthday or even later. Just as when in an unfamiliar city you would probably want to familiarize yourself with the layout of the area before venturing forth, your child needs to get to know herself a bit before she's ready to connect with others. At twelve months, she doesn't especially enjoy meeting strangers (though she will probably show more interest in other children than in adults). Between eighteen and twenty-one months, she is still likely to enjoy solitary or parallel play and spend a lot of time "talking" to herself in jargon or early words. By this time, though, her stranger anxiety has probably abated, and she may begin to enjoy playing with familiar adults for longer periods of time. This greater ease with adults other than parents is why, as you may notice at the child-care center, children this age tend to cluster around the caregivers rather than play with each other. In general, your child knows that the other children are there, and they are becoming more important to her, but her drive to experiment with objects and master her environment is still stronger than her desire to make friends. In other words, if your eighteen-month-old is more interested in her cousin's toys than in her cousin when he comes to visit, at least you know she's developing right on schedule.

The social situation changes dramatically, though, at the end of the second year. Finally your child is ready to begin exploring the social realm. Toddlers at this age are often quite eager to meet other children, and they begin imitating and learning from their behavior at a tremendous rate. If you have been considering putting your child in a group child-care situation, this might be a good time. A high-quality setting with a caregiver for every three or four toddlers can provide structured play that incorporates lessons in such social skills as turn-taking, sharing, and controlling negative behavior.

EASING THE WAY

Play Dates

Getting together with another parent and child is nearly always a good idea, but at first the benefits may well be more yours than your child's. As the year begins, you can watch other parents with their children, learn some new techniques, and offer some of your own insights to them. At this point, your children won't play together much at all, but they are interested in the fact that other children like themselves exist. If your child has no siblings, it's especially helpful to introduce her to children in her neighborhood. As she progresses past the middle of the year, they still won't be "friends," but they will benefit from their familiarity with one another. You and the other parent will be able to monitor their social experiments (transfer of objects, hitting, etc.) in a safe, well-controlled environment. Meanwhile, you'll be plugged in to the neighborhood grapevine, picking up information on which child-care centers, children's programs, and nursery schools various parents prefer. By the time she reaches age two and actually begins to show an interest in the idea of having a friend, she'll already have one contact. Since both of you will be familiar with the other parent's and child's temperaments and behavior habits, guiding both children through their first real lessons in social give-and-take will be easier for everyone. Later, when your child begins preschool or kindergarten, she may find she has this life-long friend in her class.

It's important to note, though, that not every random play-date arrangement works out for the best. You may find that your child and your neighbor's child experience a fundamental incompatibility (yours may be quiet and solitary, for example, while the other child is very physical and assertive). It's also possible that your parenting style and that of the other parent clash (perhaps you believe in intervening only when necessary, while the other parent constantly "hovers"). If you really feel that these play dates won't work out, there's no harm in just admitting this to the other parent and looking for another play-date partner. Some parents prefer to develop play-date relationships with two or three different children over the course of the year, so that undue pressure is not put on one relationship and so that their children can be exposed to different behavior patterns as they learn their own style of relating to others. If one child or parent causes frequent problems during play dates but you're reluctant to give up the chance to socialize, try limiting your social interactions with that family to more public places like the park or playground.

In short, no play date is mandatory at this age, and few turn out to be perfect, but most can be informative and even fun. These days, when children are rarely just "sent outside to play," play dates may be the best early tool for beginning the socialization process.

LEARNING ABOUT GOOD AND BAD: THE SEEDS OF MORALITY

The morality of children is a hot-button topic for many parents these days, especially around those times when the media provide us with new evidence that some children seem never to have learned the difference between right and wrong. The months on either side of a child's second birthday are rife with opportunities to fear for your child's moral future, if you allow yourself to run with those emotions. There are bound to be hitting, pushing, and screaming incidents; she may step on a bug just to see what happens; she may seize a candy bar from the grocery checkout stand and refuse, red-faced and tight-lipped, to give it back. It is vital, then, to keep these incidents in developmental perspective; they are *perfectly normal* incidents for children her age. Instead of seeing them as the first "warning signs" of a sociopathic disorder (a syndrome that clearly springs from much more serious beginnings than this), treat your child's social transgressions for what they are: *opportunities* to begin showing her better, more productive ways of interacting with others.

Your child will show you that she is ready for these lessons by the increase in her ability to empathize as the year progresses. More and more over the months, your toddler will try to comfort others in distress rather than mimicking their behavior or becoming upset herself. As she nears her second birthday, she may even begin to act on her empathic feelings by bringing a toy (even one of her own) to a crying child or feeding a doll that she believes is hungry. This is your chance to encourage these positive, or *prosocial,* behaviors—praising her for her kindness and generosity, describing how much better the child (or doll) she's helped feels, and treating her in similar ways so she can experience the pleasure she's learning to provide for others. If you believe that the basis of a moral life is the Golden Rule, now is the time your child can begin to learn the value of "doing unto others as she would have them do unto her."

Though your child's capacity for empathy can be greatly encouraged now, its origins lie to a large extent in how securely her attachment to her key caregivers was established in her first year of life. From you she learned the pleasure of being loved and attended to and the behavior patterns surrounding caring for another person. As she approached her first birthday, she increasingly checked your own responses to incidents you both witnessed and noted when you reacted in empathic or nonempathic ways. In the second year, your calm, consistent parenting has given her the support she needed to lock on to others' emotions as well as her own. Now, as she experiments in a wide variety of ways with interacting with other children (positively as well as negatively), you can make the greatest impact of all by clearly explaining the consequences of her actions, stating your rules of behavior, and giving her an emotional response. (For example, "Look what you did. Can you see that that hurt Amy? That's a 'no.' " Or, just as important, "What a nice idea. Grandma loves kisses. Look how happy she is.")

When she's reached age two, your child's ability to empathize is still limited, but with your encouragement it will increase dramatically through her elementary-school years. Her ability to share, help others, and sympathize will blossom with your good example and her own increasingly confident social experiments.

A BABY'S-EYE VIEW

Poor Daddy

Ice cream, twenty-two-month-old Esther says to herself with great satisfaction, running down the sidewalk holding Daddy's hand. *Esther like banilla.* Daddy's stride is enormous, and it is difficult but fun to try to keep up. She enjoys the differences in his movement compared to Mommy's. "Stop!" she shouts proudly when they reach the corner. "Good, Esther. We stop and look both ways for cars, right?" Daddy responds. They wait for the "walk" sign, then proceed across the street. But as they step up onto the sidewalk, Daddy trips and falls!

"Ouch!" Daddy says (altering what he would have said if he were alone). He sits on the ground and inspects his knee. His pants are torn, and he has a cut. "Daddy needs a Band-Aid," he says a bit harshly, trying to clean up the small amount of blood.

Esther stares at the cut on his knee. She feels a familiar feeling well up inside her—it's a mixture of fear and sadness. Her lower lip quivers. She is going to cry!

"I hurt myself, didn't I, Esther?" Daddy says, more in his normal tone of voice. Esther looks at him. Her panicky feeling is replaced by a new feeling, a kind of sympathy. "Poor Daddy," she says. "Ouch." She puts her head two inches away from his and stares at his knee. She gives him a long hug, just like

Mommy does when she gets hurt. She feels better now, so Daddy must. She pulls on his arm. "Up, Daddy," she says briskly. "Ice cream."

The two-year-old's increasing focus on how things are "supposed to be" also informs and supplements her first attempts at moral behavior. At around twenty-four months, your child may begin to insist adamantly that toys should not be broken, shirts should have all their buttons, and her hands should be clean. In one well-known study by Dr. Jerome Kagan of Harvard University, fourteen- and nineteen-month-old children were put in a playroom with a large number of toys, some of which were purposely flawed. None of the fourteen-month-olds paid any special attention to the damaged toys. The nineteen-month-olds, on the other hand, were very interested. They took those toys to their mothers, pointed out the damaged parts, stuck their fingers in the place where the animal's head had been removed, for example, and in many cases asked that the toys be fixed. This new concern for the "correctness" of things increases as children approach their second birthday. It may cause your two-year-old to object passionately to the clothes you've chosen for her that day, but it can also bring lessons in correct behavior zinging home.

At about the same time that correctness becomes an issue, the one-year-old begins to comprehend the concept of *agency*—that is, that something (some kind of "agent") caused a thing to happen. Your child will demonstrate this ability not only through her interest in toys that do something when she punches or manipulates them, but in her triumphant cries of "I did it!" and her murmured "Uh-oh," when she flips the sugar bowl upside down. It is a wonderful experience to watch your child internalize the positive aspects of this concept—to see her private smile as she completes a simple puzzle, indicating that she knows she's succeeded at something even though you haven't said a word. This understanding of the fact that she can cause things to happen, coupled with her desire to keep things "correct," makes for very powerful motivation toward learning positive behavior in the final months of the second year. It is yet another fundamental basis for your child's developing moral sense, a skill that, while still primitive, will soon grow by leaps and bounds.

Social Challenges

It is really too soon to worry about such issues as whether your child fits in with children her own age or even whether she'll ever learn to share. But if you consistently feel that your child is not taking a normal interest in interacting with other people—if she is unusually withdrawn, timid, aggressive, or off-putting in ways that don't seem to be changing over time—talk to her other caregivers about how she is when you're not present. Remember, no one, not even adults, is always the same in every social situation. Often (to our chagrin), our children behave differently when we're not around. If your child's caregiver or any other adult who knows your child well shares your concerns, however, it can't hurt to discuss them with your pediatrician. In almost every case, time will tell if your child is experiencing social challenges—and in most cases, time will alleviate the problem. But it is never a good idea to ignore deep-seated concerns that arise from interaction with your own child.

"WE DON'T BEHAVE THAT WAY": EXPLORING PROPER LIMITS

Every parent knows that teaching a child new skills is an uneven process, with just as many regressions as breathtaking leaps forward. The second half of this year, when your child proves just as eager to experiment with the limits of acceptable behavior as she is to test everything else in her world, can prove especially difficult. Add to that the especially painful embarrassment many parents feel when their children misbehave in social ways, and you have a potent brew for discord in your life with your toddler. If you can put aside your own emotional investment in wanting always to appear "correct," though, this time can be used to help your child experiment with limiting her behavior, and learning how to interact with others in positive ways.

The first step in this process is to help your child distinguish between

Learning to express angry feelings without using aggressive behavior is a major hurdle for toddlers and parents.

angry *feelings* and aggressive *behavior.* All children feel angry now and then; at this age, your child probably feels angry several times a day. Anger can arise as a result of the natural frustrations of this point in her development, or it might be the result of such major events as a new caregiver or a new baby in the house. As with most such situations in life, acknowledging that the emotions exist rather than trying to deny or stifle them is the first step in addressing them. You can then sympathize with your child's anger, and help her express it in words, while simultaneously trying to guide and shape the ways in which that anger is expressed. It may be acceptable in your family to punch a pillow or yell in one's own room, for example, but not to punch or yell at the baby. Helping your child distinguish between her emotions and her expression of those emotions—and between good and bad forms of expression—helps her learn to channel her anger without feeling that she's a bad person for feeling that way.

Some children seem to attract more attention to their "difficult" behavior because they are larger than other children their age or because they tend to act out when others are present rather than when they're alone. If you have a larger than average child who frequently seems to be at the center of social disruption, start talking to her about how her large size affects her behavior. You may need to gently dissuade her from enthusiastically hugging other children, roughhousing with siblings, or leaping into Grandpa's lap. Tell her, for example, "Allegra's smaller than you. You need to be gentle." Then model the desired behavior yourself by showing her how to, say, roll a ball to Allegra instead of throwing it. She may continue to be too rambunctious a lot of the time, but she'll get the point eventually.

Just as you can parent more efficiently once you discover which situations are likely to cause your child to lose control, so she can begin to monitor her own stress level by learning what her limits are. If you see your child beginning to lose it on a day when she's missed her nap, point out nonjudgmentally that she must feel overwhelmed because she's tired. If she's close to two, she'll say, "Not tired!" Rather than argue, say, "Well, I'm tired," and offer to read her a story or start some other restful activity. If you know that she tends to become fearful in large crowds, talk to her about any upcoming group occasions and stay with her while they're in progress until you're sure she's comfortable. Debriefing her afterward— as in, "Did you like the clown? He had a big red nose that honked loud"—

will help her process the experience and prepare her for the next one. If you know that your child has difficulty sharing her toys with her friends, prepare ahead for a play date by helping her choose ten toys to place in a basket and carry into the living room (away from her other toys) for the play period. (Encourage any fledgling impulses toward sharing by saying, "Sally might like this toy," as you drop it in the basket—and try to include pairs of similar toys to keep both toddlers happy.) Keep in mind that losing control is frightening to the child; she would like to avoid it, too. Labeling the causes of her behavior and showing her how to deal with it will help her monitor her own behavior later on.

This is a good time to show your child how to *rechannel* socially maladaptive behaviors as well. If your child constantly pounds on other kids, provide her with some pounding toys during play dates or group child care. If she is a sensitive child who cries a lot, show her that words work better than tears in gaining the attention and care of others. If she refuses to mind you or acknowledge that she hears you, give her something to do by herself until she's ready to come back and be part of the group.

As your child learns to limit her negative behavior, be sure to give her plenty of examples of positive behavior to take its place. Whenever you happen to catch her doing something right, take a moment to offer her some praise. When working out better ways to deal with specific social situations (such as taking turns or dealing with teasing), acting out the situations for her with puppets or toys can supplement the example you yourself are setting ("Look. Elmo's sad that you're not sharing."). Repetition has great value at this age as well. We sometimes forget that our children don't automatically know the rules of social interaction in our culture. They need to hear, over and over until they learn it, that hurting others is not acceptable, that crying to get one's way is not appropriate, that it is not necessary to put up with someone else's hurting us, and that helping others is a highly valued trait.

A PARENT'S STORY

Don't Push!

"I always used to have a problem with my sister-in-law, Michelle," Annette, the mother of twenty-four-month-old

Liana, told me. "Michelle is the kind of mom who can never leave well enough alone with kids. She always has to intrude on their play, showing them how to play a game better or telling them 'interesting facts' when they're just trying to have fun. I've watched her do that with her own kids for years, and after I had Liana, she started right in with her. I know she means well—she probably thinks she's enhancing their experience and making them smarter. But I'm the kind of parent who likes to let kids learn on their own as much as possible, and it really bothered me whenever Michelle interfered.

"Still, I never worked up the courage to say anything about it to her. I remember when Liana was about nine months old, Michelle gave her a jack-in-the-box. Liana was happy just watching someone else turn the crank until the clown jumped up, but Michelle kept forcing her little hand to turn the crank and saying, 'See, Liana? This is how it works. You turn the crank, and that makes the latch open on the lid.' It was driving me crazy, but I was still more concerned about offending Michelle, I guess, than rescuing Liana, because I didn't say anything and just let Michelle ruin the game.

"Then, the other night, when Michelle was over with her family, the kids had gotten out a set of blocks and marbles to play with. Liana doesn't really get the concept of stacking the blocks yet so that the holes in the middle line up and a marble can run from top to bottom. She just likes stacking a few blocks by herself, without the marbles. Needless to say, Michelle had to get right down on the floor with her, saying, 'No, Liana, look, you can line the blocks up so that the marble goes through this way—see?' I kept talking to her husband like nothing was happening, but I was really seething inside. Then, all of a sudden, I heard Liana shout, 'No, my game! Stop!'

"There was dead silence in the room for a second. But Michelle got the message. She came back and joined us grown-ups, and Liana went back to playing with her cousins her own way, looking very pleased with herself. I know that Liana was rude to her aunt, but it was so satisfying to me to hear her *express* what she felt. If she were older, she could have said, 'I'm fine, thanks,' but at her age she did the best she could to express her need for her own space. In some ways the incident really made me understand how much she's learning about how people interact and how much she can teach me—not just the other way around. It gave me a good feeling as a mom to know she can handle herself so strongly with others. We'll just have to work on finessing her manners a little better, I guess."

"LET'S BE FRIENDS": A WIDENING WORLD OF RELATIONSHIPS

A year has passed, and two-year-old Clara has grown and developed in ways Marian and Bill could hardly have imagined twelve months ago. Once again, they are having a dinner party, this time with a couple down the street whose daughter, Kenya, has visited several times before on play dates. Because Clara continues to have problems sharing her toys, Marian has discussed with her beforehand which possessions she's willing to share with Kenya tonight. They've laid out half a dozen "acceptable" playthings and put the rest of the toy box away. As they were doing so, Marian was touched by Clara's picking up a Raggedy Ann doll, saying, "Kenya's doll," and putting it in the stack of things to be played with. *Maybe Clara is starting to think of her friends' wishes after all,* Marian thought.

The dinner goes well, and the girls play happily together, falling into the rhythm established on their play dates. They jump together on Clara's little trampoline. Marian keeps one eye on them as she chats with the grown-ups, knowing that Kenya can get aggressive and that Clara will start screaming if she's pushed. By the time coffee is served, Clara and Kenya have just about worn each other out. They continue to keep busy with the toys, but their voices have become somewhat shrill and their behavior a little testy. A few minutes later, Clara suddenly appears at Marian's side. "Blankie," she says and lays her head on Marian's lap. Marian looks down at her in surprise. Did Clara just realize she'd reached her limit and figure out what to do about it? Whether or not that was Clara's intention, her ploy worked. Kenya's parents are getting to their feet, saying it's about time they got home. A few minutes later, Marian, Bill, and Clara stand at the door, waving their guests good-bye. As the door closes, Marian gives Clara a hug. The evening went so well! And part of the credit had to go to her two-year-old, who amazingly enough was able to enjoy social time with a peer, regulate her own level of stimulation, and know on some level when to call it quits.

ADVANCES

Social Achievements in the Second Year

12 MONTHS	Social "style" begins to emerge. May be friendly, reclusive, a tease, weepy
	Likes to be read to
	Sometimes enjoys turn-taking activities
	Enjoys a wider circle of people
15 MONTHS	May try to direct others' behavior
	Teases family members
	Usually plays independently but makes sure a familiar person remains nearby
18 MONTHS	Communicates emotions physically more than through words
	May have difficulty with transitions
	Begins to obey some family rules
21 MONTHS	Starts to become interested in playing with other children
	Doesn't like to share favorite toys
	May give back toy that belongs to another child

24 MONTHS

Imitates other children's behavior

Enjoys playing with older children

May begin to share

Sometimes empathizes with another's emotions

Manages transitions better but sometimes has trouble with separation

FIRST-PERSON SINGULAR

Later, your child will enjoy looking back on the notes you keep about her social life in her second year. Be sure to write down the names of her first friends here, and note what activities they liked to do together the most. If you and another family go out on an excursion, describe it briefly and include photographs. Note when you first witness your child sharing her own toy, when she first offers a toy or a kiss to a crying friend, and when she first seems aware of your own, separate feelings. Watching the ways in which her empathy and kindness grow can comfort you on days when she's feeling a little less sociable.

READER'S NOTES

CHAPTER 7

Predictability Helps—
My Need for Routine

Your child needs to know what the rules are and that he can depend on them.

Angela's favorite grandmother lives 150 miles away in another state and has never had a chance to see Spencer, Angela's little boy. Angela hesitated to take the trip earlier in the year, but now that Spencer is twelve months old, she feels he's ready to interact well with a new relative. Angela is so excited about the meeting that she forgets to plan important details for the trip itself. To her dismay, Spencer begins crying the moment he is put into the car seat and hardly stops until they reach her grandmother's house. He starts crying again when he is introduced to his great-grandmother, he wails when he's offered the creamed corn she cooked for him, and when it's time to put him in the portable crib Angela has placed near her bed, he screams for so long that Angela fears he will have convulsions. "He's a real handful, isn't he?" Angela's grandmother remarks grumpily the following morning, as Spencer hiccups miserably in his mother's arms. "He must take after your mother's side of the family." Angela may not be happy with Spencer's behavior during her vacation, but at least she can console herself with the knowledge that it's quite normal for his age. One-year-olds take comfort from familiar surroundings and daily activities. To understand what they're going through when their world is suddenly altered, imagine how shaken you would feel if you'd just started a new job and discovered that your boss had been fired, your office moved, or your lunchtime changed to 5:00 P.M.

By establishing routines, sticking to them whenever possible, and providing acceptable substitutes when the usual routines are not possible, you help your one-year-old feel confident in his world; he learns to view his life as predictable and secure. Knowing that naptime will always follow lunch (even if that nap occasionally takes place in a stroller), that he cannot have a cookie if he didn't eat breakfast, and that you will sing him a song or read him a story before he drifts off to sleep will literally take a load off his mind and free up his energy for more constructive thoughts. This doesn't mean you have to be absolutely rigid about feeding times, behavioral rules, and so on. Everyone needs to learn to deal with a certain amount of unpredictability in life. But general *consistency* is a great boon to children this age. Singing familiar songs when your child must ride in the car during naptime, providing familiar toys and books when he must sleep away from home, and bringing along a snack when he will be out of the house at lunchtime are all ways to keep his routines consistent without having to be a complete slave to them yourself.

Routines would be very easy to follow if everybody stayed in the house all day and our children's needs and desires never changed. Obviously, that is not the way the world works, however. Such routines as sleeptime, mealtimes, and even toilet training are frequently disrupted by daily demands and must evolve as the child's development progresses. Trying to come up with a proper philosophy for, say, getting your child to sleep through the night on his own is made even more difficult by the mountains of conflicting advice thrown at you by friends, relatives, parenting magazines, books, on-line services, and so on—many of them not appropriate for your child at his particular stage of life. It does not make sense, for example, to impose the "just put him to bed and let him cry himself to sleep" routine on a three-month-old infant, who is not yet physiologically able to sleep through the night without a feeding. It may not even make sense at twelve months, when, as we saw in Chapter 2, a child's overwhelming urge to practice walking may cause him to wake up in the night and need to be soothed a bit on his way back to sleep. Well-timed routines can set the stage for happy, secure children who can sleep, eat, and use the bathroom on their own, but routines that ignore a child's temperament and developmental stage or a family's lifestyle are likely to fail.

In the end, only you know which routines will work with your child at any particular stage. Which routines you choose (assuming that they work reasonably well) is not as important as the fact that you have them. Your one-year-old may not always be eager to take a bath before bedtime, but in the long run it will help him learn that bath-and-then-bedtime is a normal, inevitable part of life. Meanwhile, he will look to this predictable sequence of events as a welcome landmark in what is often a confusing array of daily events. Bit by bit, routine by routine, you can thus build a secure platform from which he can "take off" toward eventual independence.

"IS IT MORNING YET?": SLEEP PATTERNS IN THE SECOND YEAR

Because of the developmental factors that control and often disrupt a young child's sleep patterns—and because of the wealth of contradictory theories about how best to handle sleeptime routines—figuring out how to get a one-year-old to sleep is one of the most challenging aspects of this stage of parenting. Certainly, a sleep routine is necessary if your child is eventually going to learn to go to bed and stay there. He will need to figure out how to let go of wakefulness without his parents present, to get himself back to sleep if he wakes in the night, and (eventually) to get up and go to the bathroom and then return to bed if he has to. The best way to reach that goal from where you are at the beginning of the first year is to (1) observe your child's developmental state; (2) decide where, when, and how he will go to sleep depending on your family's lifestyle, needs, and personal preferences; and (3) stick to your routine until you see that it is no longer getting your child to his goal, and then gradually change it.

Developmentally, your child has some good news and some bad news for you this year. The good news is that by around twelve months, he is probably physically able to sleep through the night. His sleep cycles have lengthened since infancy, and his tendency to sleep at night more than in the day has been established, to the point at which he is able to actually get a good night's sleep. The bad news is that a number of external factors can intrude to disrupt this physical ability to sleep all night. At around twelve months, when he is learning to walk, the increased physical exertion and mental stimulation that result may prevent him from falling asleep easily and may wake him up in the night. (Think of how hard it is for you to sleep when you're in the midst of an exciting or stressful period at work or at home.) At fifteen months, his body has calmed down a bit, but more than one daytime nap (or a single nap that's too long) may keep him from sleeping well at night. At eighteen months, the frustrations and emotional challenges of the toddler begin to impinge on his ability to sleep—he starts to feel a need to resist and control his routines, and he may need a comfort object to hold on to. At around twenty-four months, nightmares—and even, for a minority of toddlers, night terrors—can happen.

A PARENT'S STORY

Bumps in the Night

"I'll never forget the first time Eliza woke up screaming," Mary, her mother, told me. "She was nearly two, and we were visiting our parents' summer house. She slept in a little toddler bed in our room, and her screams jolted Bob and me bolt upright at three in the morning. She was sitting up in bed with her eyes open, crying so loudly it was as if someone was hurting her. I rushed over to her and took her in my arms, but she didn't pay any attention to me. I realized she was still asleep, even though her eyes were open, and I tried to wake her up, but I couldn't. (I found out later that it's best not to wake children from night terrors anyway, because they get disoriented if they're snapped out of sleep, and that may scare them even more.) It was so creepy, seeing her sort of 'there but not there,' in the dark room. But after a few minutes, her screams turned into whimpers, and then all of a sudden she sighed and snuggled back under the covers. It was as though nothing had ever happened.

"The next morning, she seemed perfectly fine. When I mentioned her 'bad dream,' she didn't know what I was talking about. I decided that was just as well and didn't mention it again. We had a few more nights like that over the following few months, and then they went away just as suddenly as they'd come. I talked to her pediatrician about them. She says they're not really dreams, but something called 'night terrors'—that they're not the result of anything particularly traumatic that's going on in her life. They're just something that happens to some kids at around their second birthdays, maybe because they were overstimulated during the day. They come and then they go, usually when there's some big disruption in their lives.

"The whole episode made us more aware of how abrupt changes affect her and to plan for them a little more. Now, when we travel, we always bring her night-light along. These episodes have happened only twice more since then, and they weren't quite as scary because we all understood them and could handle them better."

When deciding on (or changing) your child's sleep routine, take these developmental stages into consideration. He may not experience all of these challenges, but by observing him you can learn what obstacles to nighttime sleep do exist and work around them. If he is currently sleeping in bed with you, for example, and your long-term goal is to get him into his own room by age two, it might be best to wait until he's fifteen months old and then move him into a crib. At that point, his motor drives will have receded somewhat (reducing the need for you to be there to pat him back to sleep), and his toddler's resistance to change may not yet have kicked in. If you want his bedtime to be a reliable 8:30 P.M. by his second birthday, start reducing his naptime as soon as he's ready (between ages fifteen and eighteen months), and be sure to wake him up early in the mornings. If you want him to learn to put himself back to sleep when he wakes up at night (so you don't have to get out of bed and comfort him yourself), check to make sure he still has his security blanket, teddy bear, or other comfort object at around eighteen months, and encourage him to use it to help soothe himself.

Developmental stages have their advantages, too. During much of this year, your child will probably remain in a crib, for example, where his ability to disrupt the household at 2:00 A.M. will be somewhat limited. Take advantage of this natural tool to enforce his sleeptime routine, and don't get rid of the crib until you feel that his routine is firmly established—probably sometime after his second birthday. After eighteen months, your child's increasing ability to comfort himself means you need to comfort him yourself less and less at night. In fact, at this age it's best to let him whimper by himself for a while, since he is probably only partly awake and will fall asleep naturally if you don't intrude. At twenty-four months, he will probably begin to resist bedtime in earnest, but by then his bedtime routine should be so firmly entrenched that he will begin to realize there's no avoiding it. Verbal and cognitive abilities help at this age, too, since he can discuss with you (to some extent) his concerns about sleep, can engage in imaginary play relating to bedtime, can flip the pages of a book by night-light, and can talk himself back to sleep when he needs to. (You can also help him understand that it's sleeptime by saying as you leave the room, "I'll be back when the tape is over," or "You can come wake me up when it's light in here.")

Q & A

Making a Break for It

Q: I am a big supporter of the idea of letting a child learn to get himself back to sleep. My twenty-month-old son, Jason, has slept in a crib in his own room from birth. Increasingly over the past months, I've noticed that if I don't go in right away when he starts whimpering at night, he usually falls back asleep. However, recently he's begun climbing out of his crib in the middle of the night. He's had a couple of falls. Now I'm up half the night worrying that he's going to hurt himself—and besides, his acrobatics keep him from falling back asleep. What should I do?

A: There's not much you can do about convincing him to stay in bed. Once he has learned that he can get out of his crib, he will continue to try to escape. The only solution is to change his environment so that he can't get out or get hurt. Once your child starts consistently climbing out of the crib (not the first time he accidentally finds his way out), lower the mattress as far as it will go. Make sure there aren't any large toys or other objects he can use to boost himself over the edge. Place the crib so that one side is against the wall, and then put some kind of cushion or pad on the floor where he might land if he does find a way to climb out. Some parents lower the side of the crib so that if the child does climb out, he's less likely to hurt himself—but the trade-off, of course, is that it's easier for the toddler to make his escape. In general, for safety reasons, it's a good idea to try to keep your child in a crib until at least age two or two and a half. (Of course, having another child might mean reevaluating this timetable.) When he's in his crib, you know he's safe, and you can complete the process of teaching him his sleep routine while he has no choice but to stay in one place.

"MORE STORY!": CREATING AN EFFECTIVE SLEEP ROUTINE

Your child's evolving sleep needs are not the only factor to consider in establishing an effective routine that will both satisfy his need for predictability and move him toward the sleep pattern you want him to have. When deciding *where, when,* and *how* your one-year-old should go to sleep, it's also necessary to take into account his temperament, your needs and your family's, the realities of your lifestyle, and even the size of your home.

Where is an issue for many parents who, for a variety of reasons, prefer to keep their babies in bed with them but are afraid people outside their family will disapprove or are finding that their child's presence is preventing them from getting enough privacy or sleep. Though the "family bed" is less common in the United States than in many other countries, there are plenty of justifications and advocates for it. Keeping the baby in bed with you allows you to tend to him at night without completely disrupting your sleep, it allows for a physical closeness that many parents (especially those who must work away from home all day) greatly enjoy, and it offers perhaps the only initial solution for parents who don't have an extra bedroom for their child. As the need for night-time feedings recedes, however, and your growing child starts to toss, turn, and perhaps even talk in his sleep, you may start to think about the long-term goal of having him sleep in his own bed, if not in his own room. Again, fifteen months of age is a good developmental "window of opportunity" for moving your child out of your bed and into his own crib (or out of your room and into his own). However, his own temperament—how much he likes to cuddle versus how much he likes to be on his own—may become an overriding factor at any age, as may your own and your partner's desires, the size of your bedroom, etc. The point is that there is no right or wrong place for your one-year-old to sleep. What's important is to take into account his needs and yours, decide on a place for him to sleep, and then be consistent about it so that he can know where "his place" is.

When a child goes to sleep can be another emotional button for parents, especially if their child tends to fall asleep at midnight and their neighbors' children are all in bed by eight. Increasingly, it seems, parents do allow their toddlers to stay up until quite late at night, probably because so many work all day and want to spend some time with their kids once they're home. On the other hand, many parents dream of the time when they'll have their evenings to themselves again, when the children have a regular bedtime and Mommy and Daddy can relax alone once they're sleeping. (They may also worry about how they'll ever get their kids used to going to bed early so they can get up in time for school.) It's up to you whether or when you decide it's time to work toward that long-term goal of an early bedtime, but whenever you do, you'll need to take your child's particular situation into consideration. Developmentally speaking, by the time your child reaches fifteen months, you can probably cut out his morning nap and begin shortening his afternoon nap, but you will still need to consider whether he is naturally a morning person or a night person, whether you still want him to stay up late at night so you can see him, and whether it's possible for him to get to sleep early, given the size of your home, if the grown-ups are still making noise and moving about. Of course, even if he's a night person, your child can still learn to go to bed at eight-thirty—he can stay quietly in bed without falling asleep right away. You can spend more time with him early in the mornings and weekends if you don't see him enough in the afternoons, and you can be quieter in a small house if he needs to get to sleep—but these elements do need to be considered when deciding on a reasonable bedtime for your child.

How your child goes to bed is yet another aspect of the bedtime routine that changes as he gets older, yet its general consistency may be the most important. Reading your child a story before bedtime, for example, can soothe him through the motor excitement of the twelfth-month period, his emotional eruptions at eighteen months, and the general resistance at twenty-four months. Whether he is still sleeping in your bed, has been moved to his own crib, or is sleeping in a room of his own, that story will signal to him that it is bedtime and that all is right with the world. It matters less, then, whether you snuggle under the covers with him after the story, put him in his crib, play recorded music, or close the door of his room and walk away. As long as the transition from one sleep routine to the other is gradual (rather than your sleeping with him one night and leaving him alone the next), the consistency of how he goes to sleep will get him through the changes.

Again, it's important to consider all your child's circumstances, not just his developmental stage, in choosing a sleep procedure. A warm bath before bedtime is a good idea at any age—but perhaps not if you get home from work late most nights and have to cook dinner for three kids before you put the baby to bed. Putting your child in his crib at a set time and leaving him to fall asleep by himself is a reasonable practice as he nears his second birthday—but not if he shares a room with siblings who may interrupt him as he's falling asleep. As we've seen, a comfort object often works well during this year—but not if your child happens to be the type who would rather throw the blankets and toys you provide. In deciding how your child should go to sleep each night, then, think about all the sleep-ritual possibilities available to you at each developmental stage—audio-tapes, teddy bears, books, baths, a nighttime walk with Daddy, a stroller ride with Mom, a rock in the hammock and a special song—eliminate the ones you don't feel you or your child could live with for the next couple of years (or more), and introduce the ones that remain, bit by bit, until you've found the routine that works best.

A predictable sleep routine is not impossible, if you keep your long-term goals firmly in mind and are consistent about the rules along the way. Whether his bedtime is seven o'clock or eleven, whether his crib is in the living room or his own bedroom, he will be grateful on some level for your predictable, reliable announcement, "Time to go to bed," at the end of the day. This explicit statement will help him begin to prepare himself for his nightly separation from you, which is understandably difficult at this age. The relaxing rituals you have incorporated in his routine will comfort him as he resigns himself to sleep. He knows (since you've refused to make exceptions) that once he's in bed, you are not going to get him up again. He may protest this policy, but he knows he can rely on it. And, like all of us, a child who knows he can rely on the rules in his world finds it much easier to fall asleep.

A BABY'S-EYE VIEW

In the Wee Hours

Dark. Michael looks around the empty room. Shadows from the moonlight crisscross the wall. Somewhere a board creaks. From down the hall, he hears the refrigerator start to hum. Mommy! Michael looks around wildly. She isn't here. He starts to sit up, but all the dark, empty space around him scares him, and he lies back down. He starts to whimper. "Mommy," he says out loud. There's no answer, and he grows more frightened.

Gathering up his courage, Michael stands up in his crib. The feeling of empty space behind his pajama-clad back gives him the chills. "Mommy!" he cries, grabbing the rail and giving the crib a shake. He's happy to hear some noise, especially noise that he controls. "Mommy! Here!"

Still there's silence. Michael moves his foot. It knocks against something. He looks down and can make out the dark outline of his teddy bear. *Teddy!* He plops down and picks it up, holding it against his chest. Its smell is so familiar. It's so soft. He rubs the bear's ear over and over in a reassuring rhythm. His breathing gets heavier.

Sleep comes over him like a thick, wooly blanket. Michael tries to keep his eyes open, but it's impossible. He turns over on his side, still clutching his bear. *Teddy.* He falls asleep—on his own.

"NO PEAS!":
THE DEVELOPMENT OF
FEEDING ROUTINES

Feeding probably ranks second only to sleep as a major issue of concern for parents of one-year-olds—largely because we fear that we may actually be starving our children if they don't eat the food we give them each day. It's important to know that for a number of reasons (which we'll explore later in this section), toddlers this age cannot be expected to stick to a traditional rounded diet, that their feeding habits and needs will change frequently during this year, that they don't need as much to eat as we often assume, and that as long as you offer your child a variety of healthy foods, his body will get the nutrition it needs. By paying attention to your child's particular eating habits, you can begin to build a predictable routine around his natural feeding schedule. This routine will eventually provide him with the confidence to experiment with new tastes, practice his self-feeding skills, and monitor his own level of hunger.

The first element to consider in creating a mealtime routine is what you give your child to eat. By his second year, he has already had some experience with solid foods, but this is an excellent time to expand his choices. After he's reached age two, a child's tastes in food are likely to remain largely limited to what he ate while he was one. So, easy as it is to stick to the same foods every day, make a point of putting a little tomato sauce on his spaghetti once in a while and letting him try plums and kiwis as well as apples. Expose him to different food textures as well as tastes. Don't be concerned if he doesn't eat most of these offerings. He doesn't have to like them all—he just needs to know them.

Within this variety of foods, provide a little something from each of the standard food groups sometime during the day—some fruit or fruit juice, some meat, egg, iron-fortified oatmeal or other cereal—and at least a pint of milk a day (if he doesn't like milk, cheese and yogurt make good substitutes). Chances are excellent that he will not eat it all, but he will ingest the food he needs to keep going. The American Academy of Pediatrics points out that according to numerous studies, very young children naturally select foods that add up to the number of calories they need each day. If given a high-calorie yogurt to eat before lunch, for example, they will select a lower-calorie lunch, and vice versa. It's best not to interfere with this wonderful self-monitoring process, but make sure that the food your child has to choose from is healthy, nourishing, and safe.

Keep in mind that one-year-olds need much less food than we adults do. A "handful of peas" wouldn't get us far, but he may manage fine on that on any given day. When structuring his eating routine, take the long view; if he is eating pretty well over the course of each week, don't worry about what he ate on Tuesday. Occasional binges are also to be expected. He *will* tire of peanut butter one of these days. Keep his pediatrician apprised of his eating habits, keep an eye on his rate of growth, provide him with choices, and then leave his eating decisions up to him.

As the year progresses, and you have a better idea of which foods your toddler likes best, you can begin to provide his favorite cereal at breakfast and be certain that something he likes is available at dinnertime. If you continue to let him make his own decisions through this second year about what to eat (from the choices you've provided), he may become more adventurous as he approaches his second birthday. Though he will check to make sure that his potatoes are mashed and buttered just the way he likes them at dinner, he may reach for some of the broccoli that everyone else in the family is enjoying. Secure in the knowledge that he can have a grilled-cheese sandwich for lunch at home tomorrow, he may be willing at least to try the stir-fried vegetables his friend's mom has served. You will have provided a "standard menu" he can rely on, in other words—the perfect platform from which he can venture forth toward new gustatory adventures.

Of course, what's on the menu is not the only concern when trying to create a mealtime structure for your child. Issues of *where, when,* and *how* are almost as important in eating routines as in sleeping, and these requirements tend to change over the course of the year. Your child's desire at twelve months to practice walking and moving may make it difficult for him to stay in a high chair. You may find it easier to feed him while he's sitting on your lap at the table or standing and facing you. He may eat better if given frequent (and shorter) small meals rather than three larger ones at this age. Finally, finger foods he can take with him on his explorations are an efficient way for him to supplement his diet. There is nothing wrong with any of these practices—and they are all more effective if you stick with one until he no longer needs it, so he will know what to expect. Try to confine feedings to the room with the high chair or dining table, though, so you can move him back to the chair or table easily when he's again able to sit still.

By fifteen months, he will probably feel comfortable in a high chair again. At this point, his focus is more on feeding himself than on moving around. Obviously, this means more of a mess for you, but these attempts at independence are very important and need to be encouraged. To help him stay as relaxed as possible about the process, continue to offer your child finger foods during meals (they're easier for him to eat and aren't as messy), prepare for the messes that will happen (by putting a plastic sheet under the high chair and perhaps feeding your child away from the dinner table if the mess greatly upsets your spouse), and praise him for his admirable attempts to drink from a cup and master the use of a spoon.

Your child's appetite may appear to take a nosedive between eighteen and twenty-one months, leading to a period of increased anxiety for many parents. It may help to keep in mind that one of the reasons for this decline is that your child is probably working hard to feed himself with cup and spoon now, and these utensils naturally transfer less food into his mouth than a bottle and his fingers used to. His increasing drive to experiment may also inspire him to treat his food as a toy; he may prefer to toss a piece of bread to the dog rather than eat it. His growing familiarity with the foods you offer may also have helped him develop some strong preferences. You can help him ingest the food he needs by reliably providing his healthy favorites, offering finger foods along with food that requires a spoon, and perhaps offering him a daily bottle or sippy cup of milk to make up for what he's not getting from a regular cup.

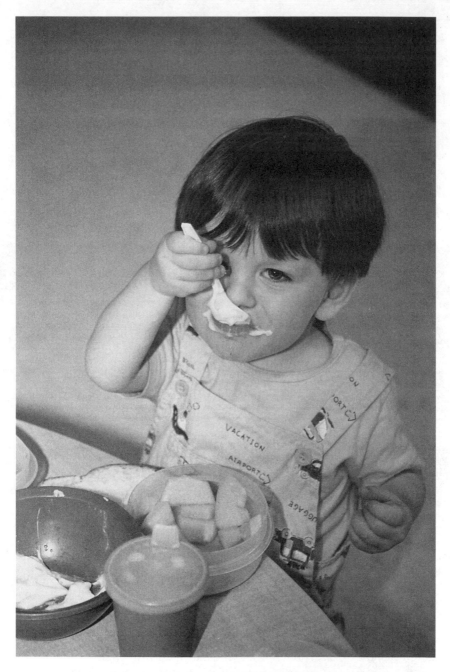

As your toddler's ability to handle a spoon and a cup grows, meals can be a more independent, though still messy, activity.

Because your child is both eager to feed himself and not especially good at it yet, this can be a difficult age at which to take him to a restaurant. True, he does not yet have the capability of controlling his behavior in adult ways and considers all the novel accoutrements of restaurant dining (salt and pepper shakers, menus, coffee creamers) tantalizing toys. He may also resent the violation of a home feeding routine that he has just begun to get to know. The public nature of his "misbehavior" in restaurants may embarrass you more than is called for (though it may help to remember that you were just as disruptive at his age, and so was everyone else in the room!). For this reason, some families choose to avoid restaurants as much as possible during this period. On the other hand, if your toddler has been going out routinely since infancy, he will be used to the restaurant routine and probably easier to take out, especially if you remember to order his meal with your drinks, and not your own entrées, and if a little public disorder doesn't bother you.

By age twenty-four months, your child will probably be very proud of his self-feeding abilities and also very quick to object if you try to help him eat or offer advice. By respecting his attempts to eat as you do and avoiding helping him too much or expecting him to display "good manners" at the table at such a young age, you can prevent the real feeding problems that some children develop as they grow.

Throughout this year, it is possible to create a predictable, supportive feeding routine that also incorporates your child's evolving needs. Whether he eats standing, sitting in his high chair, or sitting at the grown-ups' table, for example, he will know that meals always occur in the breakfast room and not all over the house. Perhaps he will learn that he can decide what he wants for breakfast each morning (since you make a point of stocking his current favorite on the bottom shelf) but that he has to eat what the rest of the family eats at dinner (though, of course, you always make sure that something he likes is included). He may grow used to the fact that breakfast means finger foods (because you're in a hurry in the mornings), but lunchtime, when he's with the sitter, is a perfect time to practice using a spoon. In other words, the nature of the routine matters less than its *consistency*—but this consistent routine must also continue to suit your particular child and family. In this as in all everyday routines, the more your toddler can predict what will happen, the more secure he will feel, and the more open you are to changing the rules when necessary, the better cared for he will be.

"He Just Won't Eat!"

In my work at Boston's Children's Hospital, I have found that an inevitable source of anxiety for parents of one-year-olds (and especially for grandparents) is feeding. Toddlers' ability to get by on what appears to be astonishingly little food sparks families' fears that they aren't caring for their children properly. If you are anxious about how little your child eats, he is likely to have picked up on your emotional state, and this could cause him to resist eating even more. In many households, this combination of a parent's anxiety and a child's resistance creates an intense power struggle that becomes an unintended part of the "mealtime routine."

You can best avoid this kind of vicious cycle by allowing your child to eat what he wants (and no more) during mealtimes, then removing him from his high chair and not giving him more food until the next meal. (Remember, though, that given your toddler's desire to move and limited attention span, four or five mini-meals work better at this age than three large ones.) Once he has realized that when he's done eating, the meal is over and that he gets to eat only during mealtimes, he'll learn to eat then. A toddler can hold out for an astonishingly long time, though, if he senses that his behavior creates a response in you, so be consistent—and stay calm. His hunger will eventually overcome his resistance.

"GO POTTY":
TOILET TRAINING

Unlike sleeping and eating routines, using the potty is a wholly elective activity rather than one that springs from a physiological need. As with other developmental accomplishments, however, there are windows of opportunity for toilet training that make the process easier for everyone at some times than at others. The best way to spot such an opportunity is to know your child. Has he become interested in the fact that you (or his big brother) use the potty? Does he seem intrigued when you read him a book about a child learning to use a potty or when you show him the new underwear you bought for him? If he seems aware that he is about to have a bowel movement—if he stands stock-still and stares at you a moment before his face turns red, runs behind the couch, or simply tells you he's about to "go"—he's certainly showing signs of readiness for toilet training. However, there's no need to push the process. Toilet training usually occurs between eighteen months and four years. Avoid starting when you're far along in a pregnancy, when there's a new sibling, or when your child has some other major change to deal with. Those issues aside, it's best to bring the subject up gently once in a while, see if your child's interested, and wait to start the process until he's clearly ready.

The end of the second year is often the time when a clear window of opportunity for toilet training (also called "toilet teaching") occurs. By that time, your child is no doubt over the excitement of learning to walk and is willing to sit down for short periods of time. He is probably verbally advanced enough to understand you when you explain that the new potty seat is his and that he can use it just as you use yours. "Mine" is often an important concept at this age, and the mere fact of having his own seat may be enough encouragement for him to begin using it. Toddlers nearing their second birthdays also love to imitate behavior, particularly that of older siblings. Many younger siblings train themselves to use the potty just so they can "be like" their brothers or sisters. This is also an age at which your little one may begin to demonstrate a sense of order. If he likes putting things away sometimes and enjoys knowing the proper places for objects, he may be ready to transfer that sense of order to his potty.

The first requirement for proper toilet training is physiological readiness. Research has shown that most children can't voluntarily control their bladder and rectum until at least eighteen months of age. Once your child has passed this milestone, you must also wait for him to show some sign of interest in or awareness of what's happening in his diaper. If

Later in the second year is a good time to introduce concepts such as sitting on the potty, although toilet training success is no doubt far away.

he grunts and pulls at his pants while having a bowel movement, he is aware, and if he tells you what has happened, he is clearly interested in your reaction and in getting cleaned up. Finally, he must have reached the "imitative" stage and not currently be in one of the resistant, negative stages that are so common for toddlers. Trying to toilet-train your child when he is in the midst of a "No!" stage will not only doom you to failure but may cause such reactions as his withholding his stool altogether, which can lead to painful constipation.

Once your child has entered a relatively tidy, compliant, and imitative developmental stage, however, he is ready for a first attempt at learning to use the potty. (If this attempt is not successful, don't worry—there will be plenty of other opportunities later on.) You might begin by getting one of the many children's books dealing with this issue and reading it a number of times to your child. Point out the potty pictured in the book, and talk about how all children learn to use one eventually. If your child knows older children who use the toilet, remind him of this fact. (With his concrete toddler mind, it's much better if he can actually see another child complete the process.) Speak admiringly of that child's underwear (or the underwear of the child in the potty-training book), and then buy some for your child. Place a potty in the bathroom near your toilet, and talk about how soon your child will be "big" and able to use the potty and wear underwear just like the other big kids. In the interests of keeping the process as simple as possible, boys should be taught to urinate sitting down. This way, they will be in place to defecate as well. After your boy has learned to use the toilet consistently, he can move on to urinating while standing.

Don't expect all of these ideas to take hold right away. Keep in mind that using the toilet is not a simple development; it involves a number of new concepts that your child will need time to ponder. Meanwhile, if he signals that he is on the verge of having a bowel movement, offer to help him do it on the potty. He will probably refuse, but the connection will gradually be made for him. Allowing him to wear his new underwear at home sometimes, rather than a diaper (or letting him run around without anything on his bottom), may speed the process, since it will be easier to get him undressed and sitting on the potty in time to use it.

When he first succeeds at using the potty, praise him sincerely but not overwhelmingly. (Then he won't feel too bad when the next, inevitable accident happens.) Proudly tell the rest of the family about it later that day, and let them praise him, too. The more he feels that he is being initiated into the world of "big people," the more effort he is likely to make in completing the training process. Your continued example, the stories about successful potty-using you keep telling him, and his pride in his new, diaperless state will greatly motivate him.

Toilet training is not a smooth process, however, and there are bound to be a number of rough spots. When your child has an accident on the floor, wets his pants, or loses interest in the potty, be careful not to scold him about it. Getting upset will only make the training process unappealing, and he may stop trying. Though it doesn't hurt to remind him exactly what he's supposed to do when he senses he needs to use the potty (he may actually have forgotten) and to reiterate the positive effects of potty-using, criticizing him or losing your temper over a mess can only prove damaging. Be upbeat (as in, "Oh, well, you'll get to the potty next time. Can you get a new pair of underwear from the bureau, please?"). If he continues to have accidents, there is no shame in reverting to a diaper for a time (and he will probably not mind). Now that you have created a *routine* for using the potty, he will be able to make use of it whenever he decides he's ready.

Child-development experts generally agree that the second year is usually not the time to achieve toilet-training success, but it is a time when *preparation* for training can take place. (For ideas on how to prepare, from such experts as Dr. T. Berry Brazelton and toilet-training specialist Ann Stadtler, visit the "Toilet Training 101" site on-line at www.totalbabycare.com.) Ideally, your child will have plenty of time to get used to the idea before he has to put it into practice. As he grows older, preschool requirements may place pressure on him to accomplish this task, but at least the presence of other toilet-trained children will encourage him to follow suit. It is useful to keep in mind the fact that girls often complete toilet training at an earlier age than boys. Even twin siblings may feel ready to go through the process at entirely different times. This just goes to show that of all the routines explored in this chapter, the toilet-training process must remain the most child-driven. Attempts to direct a child's progress when he isn't ready for toilet training simply do not work for you or your child.

ON THE ROAD: MAINTAINING ROUTINES WHILE TRAVELING

Family vacations and out-of-town travel can provide fascinating stimulation for your child, but they can also destroy the well-established routines on which he has just begun to depend. In order to ensure a happier trip for everyone, it pays to think ahead about the ways you can incorporate your child's usual schedule into your temporary life on the road. You can begin by familiarizing your child with your travel destination as much as possible. If you're going to visit a relative or friend, call ahead of time and encourage your child to talk (or listen) to that person on the phone. Show him pictures of the people or places you plan to see. Talk about the plane, car, bus, or train trip, and read him books about other children traveling that same way.

Once you've started on your journey, your goal should be to replicate your child's home and normal routine as much as possible. Take along his favorite food in a separate bag, and try to feed it to him at the usual times. Bringing some of his audiotapes and playing them in the car can comfort him as he starts to fall asleep. Whatever you do, don't forget his "blankie," pacifier, or other comfort object and some of his favorite books and toys! Finally try to allow him something like the amount or kind of movement he's used to as well. If you are traveling by plane, take him for a little walk through the airport and down the airplane aisle if you can, to satisfy his urgent need to explore. If it's naptime, try to arrange for him to sleep a bit, wherever you are (or schedule plane trips at times other than naptime). If you're in a car, take frequent breaks to let him run around. Continue to talk to him about where you're going and when you plan to return home. He won't understand a good deal of what you tell him (and there will inevitably be some settling on both ends of the trip), but your reassuring tone and constant presence will comfort him.

THE TOY BOX

At Twenty-two Months

Charlie is upset. Without much warning, he was put onto an airplane with Mommy and flown to a place called Florida. The flight schedule prevented him from taking his nap on time, he didn't like the food the flight attendant gave him (he'd already eaten the treat that Mommy brought when they were in the airport), and now Mommy's unpacking their suitcase in a strange hotel room. Charlie looks around the room. *Nothing* here looks familiar! All the colors, angles, smells, and sounds are wrong. Feeling completely out of kilter, he starts to wail. But just then Mommy pulls out a bag that he recognizes—it's the bag he uses to carry his things to the child-care center. "Look, Charlie, your toys came to Florida, too," Mommy says. She opens the bag, and out spill Charlie's stuffed giraffe, his dump truck, his toy xylophone, and his favorite blocks. Charlie's body immediately relaxes. He is filled with relief. "Charlie's toys!" he says, plumping down on the floor beside them. He picks up the giraffe and hugs it. Who cares where they are? His toys still make him feel better.

GETTING READY FOR CHANGE: THE ADVANTAGES OF GROUP ACTIVITIES

As your child nears the end of his second year, he will have gained confidence and a sense of security through his reliance on the routine you have created together. Soon he will be ready to turn outward toward those outside his immediate family and meld their attitudes, habits, and routines with his own. Eventually, entry into preschool, kindergarten, or elementary school will require him to move out of the routines of home life and into the established routines of group activity. (For children in group care, of course, this happens even earlier.) To begin to prepare your child for these experiences, you might consider partaking in a group activity this year, such as a weekly story hour at the library, an early-childhood music program, or even a gymnastics or swim class for toddlers.

It is fascinating for a growing one-year-old to realize that other routines exist besides the ones established in his own home and to watch another adult besides his parents take charge of a group of kids. Learning new activities (swimming, singing songs and dancing, jumping on a small trampoline) and incorporating group routines that include greeting a teacher, interacting with other children and their parents, and saying good-bye introduce your child to a wider world of structure and proper behavior. As he participates in these activities, he will gradually begin to realize that other children behave differently or have different "customs" and backgrounds from the ones he knows. Discovering that "Janie hits," "Rose can swing on the rope," or "Eleni likes to dance with her mommy" holds a fascination for the toddler. They also open up ways to talk with your child about how *you* do things, and why. In general, the more your child is able to understand and rely on his own family routines, the greater his ability to tolerate others' is likely to be. As you and your child get to know more and more people together in the coming years, you will be glad you took the time to establish what is "our family way" so that others' ways will prove less threatening and more interesting to compare.

EASING THE WAY

When Routines Differ

These days, it doesn't make sense to assume that a young child lives in only one home with only one "normal routine." If you and your child's other parent live apart or if your child spends a great deal of time with a relative or other caregiver, he may be growing up with two very different sets of daily routines. Problems can arise when these routines conflict or when the adults involved remain unaware of how the other conducts the one-year-old's day. Mom may serve dinner at home every evening, for example, while Dad takes his toddler out to eat on his night with him. A child's parents may not mind if he doesn't eat all his dinner, while the grandparents who care for him when his parents are out of town cannot tolerate his leaving food on his plate.

Frequently a caregiver will have a hard time getting a child to go to bed because she hasn't been told, for example, that he wants his story *before* his bath instead of after. Clearly, the parents' first step in helping their child adjust to a switch between routines is to communicate to the other caregiver what their own routines have been. If your child needs a pacifier to lull himself to sleep at home, by all means tell the other caregiver this before he or she takes charge. Routines and rules involving television, bedtime, meals, and so on should be discussed among all adults concerned—and compromises arrived at in cases where the adults cannot make their routines consistent.

Try to involve your child as much as possible in the process of negotiating the new routines. As young as he is, he will feel better if *he* "agrees" ahead of time that he doesn't have to watch a children's videotape before naptime at Dad's house but can listen to an audiotape instead. (He may still protest, but at least he won't have been taken by surprise.) If he is not allowed to leave food on his plate at his grandparents' house, maybe he'll feel better about it if you ask them to let *him* decide how much he wants put on his plate in the first place. Keep in mind that while it's nice for routines to be consistent from house to house or caregiver to caregiver, young children are very adaptable and learn a lot from encountering new sets of rules and adult attitudes. In the end, the most important issue for your child is his emotional environment. As long as he understands that the adult in charge cares for him and is doing what he or she believes is best, a change in his routine is not likely to do any harm.

"HI, GRANDMA!": LEARNING TO ENJOY NOVELTY

It has been a long year, and Angela's embarrassment over her last visit to Grandmother's house has faded into the past. Spencer's second birthday is now approaching, and Angela is eager to repeat the visit more successfully. This time, though, Angela is more sensitive to the fact that travel is difficult for Spencer, at least at this age. He doesn't like to leave his beloved toys, his room, and the rest of the life he knows so well.

To help ensure that the trip turns out to be enjoyable for everyone, Angela started talking to Spencer about it a couple of weeks before they left home. She told some of his favorite stories about his great-grandmother (stories he'd heard a number of times before) and even called her so the two of them could "talk" on the phone. One day she got out her old photograph albums and showed him pictures of her grandmother and her big old house. To Angela's delight, he seemed particularly excited about the old swing set in the yard.

When it was time to pack, Angela asked Spencer to help her pack a few of his favorite toys. She asked for his input on what snacks to bring in the car. They brought along his favorite tapes to sing along to while she drove. Spencer still threw a fit when she had to actually buckle him into his car seat, but once she'd handed him his Baggie full of Gummi Bears and popped the first tape into the player, he was fine again.

This time the trip took nearly twice as long, because Angela and Spencer stopped so many times along the way. When they finally arrived at Grandma's house, they were both tired and cranky. Once again, when Angela lifted Spencer out of the car and held him up to her grandmother to hug, Spencer burst into tears. But this time, instead of apologizing and feeling embarrassed, Angela comforted Spencer and got out his wind-up musical bear. Then she chatted with Grandma for a few minutes, giving Spencer some time to settle down. Soon Spencer's tears were dry, and Angela's grandmother was actually smiling at the way he cuddled his bear close and stared in wonder at the old swing set. "Come on, Spencer," she said, leading the way. "I'll show you the slide."

How the Need for Routine Evolves
in the Second Year

12 MONTHS	May self-comfort with a security object in strange places
	Appreciates storytime
	May notice when familiar people are missing
18 MONTHS	Needs time to adapt to new situations
	Obeys simple rules
	Develops clothes preferences
	Bedtime routine helps reduce nighttime fears
24 MONTHS	Enjoys family routine
	Major changes (a new sibling, etc.) may trigger regression

FIRST-PERSON SINGULAR

Your child's routines evolve so quickly—while his need for them remains so strong—that you may temporarily forget he will not *always* have to have the blankets pulled over him, then back off, before he can go to sleep at night. Before you forget about them, record his quirky routines on this page. Note when he stops needing a particular comforting routine, and try to figure out why. Record the ways in which routines helped you get through a challenging period, so that you can benefit from your experience with your next child or prepare for later challenges with this one.

READER'S NOTES

CHAPTER 8

Drawing the Line—My Need for Limits

D istraction is a terrific way to avoid unnecessary conflict.

What a morning! The alarm didn't go off, and both Fred and his wife, Linda, are late for work. They rush about the house, pulling on sweaters and searching for shoes. At first, neither of them notices twelve-month-old Emily amid the chaos, toddling into the bathroom with a toy clutched to her chest. She moves closer to the toilet, stops, and slowly lifts the toy over the bowl.

Fred, hurrying past the doorway, sees what she's up to. "Don't throw that in there!" he says, stopping in his tracks. Emily looks up at him, but the hand holding the toy continues its downward curve toward the toilet. "I said don't!" Fred shouts, taking a step toward her. The toy drops into the water.

"Emily, I said no!" Fred yells. Emily looks up at him, then down at the toy, and bursts into tears. Fred hesitates, not knowing what to do. Should he comfort Emily? Spank her? Give her a time-out? Should he blame her for disobeying him, or was this his fault for not having distracted her in time? Finally he picks her up. "That's okay," he mumbles guiltily. But then he thinks, *Why am I apologizing?* She's *the one who dropped the toy.*

Discipline is one of the most difficult aspects of parenting for many adults. Setting limits and enforcing rules makes us feel guilty ("I hate being the bad guy"), particularly if we remember some excessive discipline experiences from our own childhood or if we confuse discipline with punishment. Besides, with both parents often at work all day, we long to come home to a happy, smoothly running family. But, as I've pointed out before, young children tend to save their most provocative behavior until their parents get home in order to try it out in a safe environment. Sometimes we feel as though the "nicer" we are to our kids, the more meltdowns we suffer at home. Facing a relentlessly active toddler, we find ourselves struggling with our tempers and wondering what we're doing wrong.

In fact, children—even one-year-olds—need more than niceness from their parents. Perhaps more than any age group, toddlers require boundaries, rules, and a reliable structure to help them find their way in an often confusing world. Discipline means setting limits—not just taking away a toy when it has been misused but also monitoring with your child how much stimulation she can handle and encouraging and reinforcing positive behaviors. This chapter will explore ways in which you can begin helping your one-year-old learn to control her own behavior, making it possible for the entire family to live under one roof more peacefully. By thinking now about the limits you want to set for your child, in the context of her temperament and its unique challenges, you will begin to give her an idea of what is expected of her and help her continue to grow in a safe, supportive environment.

EASING THE WAY

Trying to Be a Big Girl

Many of your child's behavioral difficulties during this year are likely to stem from the gap between her desire to do things herself and her ability to do them. In trying to put on her pajamas, she may become frustrated, and her inability to verbalize her frustration may increase her anger even more. In such a situation, she's quite likely to throw the pajamas aside, refusing to get ready for bed. Instead of focusing on her "misbehavior," try helping her verbalize her frustration and then talking her gently back through the process of getting dressed. Giving her words to express her feelings ("It's hard to find the sleeve") helps her to calm down, and helping her take care of herself demonstrates to her that she will learn to do so without your help one of these days. Next time you might start to help her (as unobtrusively as possible) before she loses emotional control. In general, staying one step ahead of your child, helping her not get stuck, is one of the best ways to avoid unnecessary conflicts.

"MORE, MORE!": LEARNING ABOUT LIMITS

Discipline—or the setting of limits—begins in infancy, although we don't generally see it that way. From birth onward, a baby's actions are molded by her parents' responses. Gradually she learns to predict the consequences of various behaviors. She may observe, for example, that a smile generates a happy response, while an angry yell inspires a frown or sudden absence of physical contact. Over the ensuing months, social interaction, sleep habits, feeding patterns, and other activities will all be affected by the consequences they tend to generate. In general, though, the more common idea of "discipline"—that is, the conscious teaching of appropriate behavior—does not become much of an issue until around the first birthday. At this point, when your child is becoming much more mobile and is able (and seemingly eager) to get into one dangerous situation after another, it becomes necessary to introduce clear, specific limits to her behavior. She will need to learn to respond to a clearly expressed "No," before she's able to decide for herself whether her behavior is appropriate or not.

Fortunately, at just about the time your child is learning to walk, she becomes very interested in testing your responses to her actions. When she totters over to the radiator or to a forbidden kitchen cabinet and looks around to be sure you're watching her, she's checking to see whether this really is a no-no. Such actions demonstrate that she has figured out that there are acceptable and unacceptable forms of behavior. She is fascinated (if still often mystified) by these boundaries. Her constant repetition of an action that causes you to say "No" is not a sign of naughtiness at this age but a healthy signal that she is focused on learning precisely what her limits are.

If laying out the boundaries for your child were the only hurdle to master, parenting would certainly be simpler. However, a number of developmental issues complicate this cut-and-dried process of setting limits. Some of these are *physiological:* A one-year-old may hear you tell her to stop a physical action (such as throwing a toy into the toilet) but actually be unable to stop the movement of her arm once it's in progress. Some of the issues are *cognitive:* Your child may not yet have developed sufficient experience of cause and effect or sequence to understand that pulling the cat's tail *always* means that the cat will scratch her or that climbing up on the table will *always* make you mad. *Emotional* issues also can come into play: If your child feels that the best way to capture your attention is to misbehave, she will misbehave more and more frequently. It is vital to consider all of these issues when monitoring your child's actions, to ensure that you are not expecting too much in the way of good behavior at any particular stage. Sadly, children this age are physically abused more than virtually any other age group, largely because parents forget to take into account their natural limitations, and confuse verbal ability with true understanding.

As your child begins to move about her world with greater ease, she begins also to develop her own agenda that is separate from and frequently in conflict with yours. Certainly, by fifteen months, she has begun to focus on acquiring as much freedom as possible to explore. When she feels that this goal is being frustrated, she can create a substantial fuss. Parental tactics that work with older children, such as trying to reason with her or making long-term promises ("Sit still until dinner's finished, and then we'll go out for an ice cream cone"), are useless now, when your child cannot yet fully comprehend sequences or think very far ahead. The trick, instead, is to work at combining her agenda with yours as much as possible, arranging her world so that she usually wants what happens to be best for her, thus giving her frequent positive "cooperating" experiences. By allowing her to leave the table when she's finished eating, for example, or letting her eat before the rest of the family, you avoid a conflict that will get the two of you nowhere.

In the end, of course, our goal as parents is to help our children learn to discipline themselves as much as possible. By setting a positive pattern now—allowing your child to experience the pleasure of ensuring her own safety, of eating healthy foods, of "using words" instead of screaming or crying, and of behaving fairly with her peers—you can help her begin to take pride in her ability to set her own behavioral limits. She will move from what psychologists call *situational compliance* (behaving properly in a specific situation because she's been told to) to *committed compliance* (internalizing general rules of behavior because it makes her feel good to behave). As she grows ever more independent in the coming years, you will thank yourself a thousand times for having made the extra effort to help her learn to "monitor" herself from the beginning—by helping her identify what sets her off (feeling hungry, perhaps, or tired), exploring different coping strategies with her (such as getting out a book to look at when she's overstimulated and needs to settle down), showing her how to talk about her feelings so she doesn't simply blow up, and helping her learn to ask for help early when she feels frustrated or angry.

A PARENT'S STORY

Choosing the Rules

"When my son, Raul, and I started getting together with other kids and parents for play dates, I realized that my rules for Raul were a lot stricter than those the other parents had," Maria, a former colleague of mine, told me. "I never let Raul watch any television, and he wasn't allowed to eat junk food. When the other moms found that out, they acted like I was over the top. Their comments made me start to wonder about myself as a parent, and pretty soon I started to make exceptions. I let Raul eat at a hamburger chain a couple of times, and, of course, after that he had a fit when I didn't want to take him there again. After I let him watch children's TV a couple of times, he acted like he was addicted to it. I thought I might have to get rid of the television completely just to make him leave it alone.

"After a while, I decided that being wishy-washy about the rules was worse for Raul than any of my rules would be, as long as I stuck to them. I thought about the reasons I'd come up with those rules in the first place, and I realized that I still believed in them no matter what anyone else said. So I decided to stand by them after all, at least when we were at home or out on our own. After a while, Raul's behavior cleared up a lot. I think he likes knowing what's allowed and not allowed. I learned that being consistent is easier on both of us, and he's learning that hamburgers and french fries aren't the most important thing in the world."

"THANK YOU FOR SHARING": EFFECTIVE WAYS TO SET LIMITS

One reason discipline becomes such a difficult issue is that many parents assume that a one-year-old behaves well in order to please them and misbehaves in order to provoke. In fact, though, your responses to her behavior are not as important to your one-year-old (at least in the first half of this year) as is the overpowering urge to explore. When the opportunity arises to taste the dog's food, her very real need to experiment with what is right in front of her will probably win out over any dimly perceived notion that you might disapprove. Looked at in this way, it's hard to get angry at your child for such an action; she's only following her natural instincts. During this period, when her developmental urges can get her into so much hot water, it's best for everyone to plan ahead for the inevitable by keeping the dog food and any other very troublesome temptations out of her reach. Gradually, you can reintroduce these items as she becomes better able to monitor her own behavior.

Distraction is a terrific way to avoid unnecessary conflict, and one that is often undervalued during this period. Parents may feel that simply changing their one-year-old's activity when she has done something wrong does not teach her anything, overlooking the fact that there are times when a child is simply not cognitively or emotionally prepared to learn about a particular issue at a particular time. It is extremely difficult for a one-year-old to take turns, for example. If your child refuses to give another toddler access to a game or toy, distracting her with a different toy while the other child takes a turn with the first one solves the immediate problem without tears or a scene. Of course, distraction doesn't teach her to take turns, but it allows her to continue interacting at a time when she's not really ready to learn that lesson.

Meanwhile, it's important to show her how she *should* behave, by praising her good behavior as it randomly happens. If your child happens to let another child play with her doll during a play date, thank her for sharing and tell her that "Mommy's proud you shared." If she tells you that a child has hit her (instead of just hitting the child back), tell her how much you admire her ability to "use her words," and then help her solve the conflict. Inevitably, on another occasion, she will refuse to share or will hit another child, but her awareness of what constitutes *good* behavior will increasingly help to curb those impulses as her ability to control her behavior expands.

Because one-year-olds' ability to reason is so limited and their desire to "behave" so sporadic, parents often (understandably) fall back on that tried-and-true behavior modification tool, the bribe. Telling your child she can have a cookie if she eats all her carrots may work very efficiently today. The problem is, you may have to offer her a cookie next time you want her to eat her carrots, too. In the long run, such a reward may even lessen her interest in the related behavior (if she's not in the mood for a cookie, there's no way she will eat those carrots). For this reason, it's best to use such external rewards sparingly and to keep them as minimal as possible. Rewards (such as gold-star stickers displayed on a poster at around age two) can be effective in "hooking" your child on a new means of doing something, but they should not be expected to have a strong or lasting effect without other positive reinforcement.

One of the best ways to guide your child's behavior over the long term is one that is frequently forgotten or ignored by parents—the power of modeling good behavior yourself. Very young children specialize in imitation. They are uncannily observant and learn a great deal from what they see. If you are in any doubt about this, look around at your friends' children. Is their walk similar to their parents'? Do they have a similar sense of humor? The same way of interacting with others? The same serious, fearful, aggressive, or playful approach to life? Quite frequently, children pick up habits from their family members—and social behavior is no exception. The best way to ensure that your child will share with others, then, may be to share with her (and with others) yourself. If you want her to speak to others with respect, make sure you do so as well. In this context, it's a particularly ironic and unproductive parenting tecnique to spank a child because she bit or hit or otherwise acted aggressively.

THE TOY BOX

At Twenty-four Months

It's early morning. Joanna has hopped out of bed and wandered into the living room, eager to play with her new sticker book and stickers, but she hasn't had breakfast yet. "You can play with them after you eat your oatmeal," Mom says. Joanna protests loudly, but she knows from experience that Mommy doesn't relent in these matters, and soon she reluctantly gives up her stickers in favor of the oatmeal. After breakfast is over, Mommy hands over the sticker book. "Good for you," she says. "You ate all your oatmeal! Now you're ready to start your day. Do you want me to play with you?"

Smiling, Joanna opens the book and, with her mother's help, happily places a sticker on the first page. She registers the connection between the pleasure of play, Mommy's positive reaction, and the fact that she finished her breakfast. Cooperating feels good, she realizes—and she's no longer hungry.

"OR ELSE!": CREATING EFFECTIVE CONSEQUENCES FOR BAD BEHAVIOR

Over the years, many parents have told me with great sincerity, "I never spank my child when I'm angry." As I often point out to them, it's hard to separate the emotion of anger from the action of spanking when you really think about it. Look back on the times (if any) when you were spanked as a child. You probably remember one or two spankings very clearly—how scared, angry, or sad you were, how huge and powerful your parent seemed. Now think again. Do you remember what you did to deserve the spanking? Probably not, at least in the early years of your life. The fact is that physical punishment works *against* the parent's interests in that it models the very sorts of aggressive behavior the parent is often trying to prevent and distracts from the original behavior issue. The child stops thinking about what she did wrong and focuses only on the scary and painful experience of being spanked.

For decades, Dr. Murray Straus and his colleagues at the University of New Hampshire have studied physical punishment and its consequences for growing children. They and other leading experts, including Kenneth Dodge at Vanderbilt University, have demonstrated beyond dispute that repeated physical punishment (and even the threat of physical punishment) actually increases children's aggressiveness. Spanking your child may get her to comply with your wishes at that particular moment, but it is likely to discourage her from cooperating with you in the long run. Furthermore, frequent or severe physical punishment such as hard spanking, slapping, and constant verbal abuse affects children's cognitive development. (Just as positive experiences stimulate growth in the brain, so can negative experiences stunt it.) As they grow older, children who have been routinely exposed to negative experiences tend to interpret many situations as hostile toward them when they are not. If such a child is pushed while standing in line for the slide at the playground, for example, she might assume the worst and push back or start yelling, while another child might not like being pushed but wouldn't exaggerate the situation. Clearly, physical punishment is not the answer for your one-year-old. In fact, the more you keep scary, negative emotions and behavior out of the equation, the more productive an enforcement of limits is likely to be.

Of course, it's easier to talk about remaining calm when dealing with a mischievous toddler than it is actually to do so. No matter how serene and "positive" you try to be in encouraging your child to behave well, there will be times when she shocks you with her actions. Biting another child (especially a baby) or poking Daddy in the eye may strike you as alarmingly aggressive, though both are quite normal (if regrettable) exploratory behaviors in this year. Children must try out all sorts of actions, in the same way they need to try out both good and bad feelings. If you overreact to her aggressiveness or other negative behavior during this experimental phase, you may actually end up reinforcing it. Your angry outbursts hold the same scary fascination for your little one as a car wreck on the highway does for adults, and she may be tempted to "test" your anger some more. Refusing to give her extra attention when she behaves badly is the best way to get her to lose interest in the behavior and to stop. Many a father has found that simply clearing his throat warningly can stop a toddler in her tracks—at least long enough for him to explain what the problem is. Against a generally calm emotional background, a slightly sharper tone of voice may correct your child's behavior without tempting her to explore your disapproval further.

Naturally, there are some situations in which you must immediately and forcefully discipline your child, particularly when you are trying to teach her to avoid a specific danger, such as running into the street, playing unsupervised near a swimming pool, or reaching up to touch the stove. Keep in mind, though, that punishment is more effective if it happens rarely. Save it for the really important, safety-threatening times. As with other aspects of parenting, it's best to think ahead of time about how you will enforce limits with your child, so that you're ready with a plan when the situation arises. Do you intend to use time-outs with your child as she grows older? You might as well start with that method now. When she's this age, you may have to sit down *with* your little one—but as long as she understands that she's been taken out of the action until her behavior improves, the time-out will be effective. Withdrawal of a treat is another discipline method that works well at this age and continues to be effective later on. In general, discipline seems to be most effective if it is a more or less natural result of the inappropriate behavior. For example, biting a child (if this is a frequent problem and not a first offense) may mean the abrupt end of a play date; refusal to allow her shoes to be put on may lead to not being able to go outside and play. When deciding on a form of discipline, think about your own needs as well as your child's. A time-out may give you the chance *you* need to calm down, and the physical separation may prevent you from giving in to the truly harmful urge to shake or spank her.

Whatever enforcement method you use, explain calmly to your one-year-old what you are doing and why, and keep the incident brief and low-key. (A five-minute time-out seems like three hours to a one-year-old.) She probably won't understand much of your explanation, but she will appreciate the concern and support she hears in your voice when you explain (preferably before and briefly after the time-out) why it is necessary, and she will understand on some level (despite her cries) that you are acting in her own best interests. Once the act of discipline is over, go on to other things and forget about it. By not dramatizing the incident, you allow your child to ponder the simple cause-and-effect relationship of bad behavior's leading to unpleasant results, rather than focusing on your emotional response to her action. (This cause-and-effect association is strengthened if you respond to her inappropriate action immediately after it happens.) No matter how effective your response to her behavior seems to be at the time it takes place, don't be surprised if you have to repeat the process a number of times. If she's very young, she might have forgotten the previous experience. If she's a little older, she may be "testing you" to see whether you really meant what you said. Again, this is a natural part of being a one-year-old, and it doesn't mean she's deliberately defying or ignoring you.

A BABY'S-EYE VIEW

That's a No-No!

Suzie is playing ball outside with her caregiver, Monique. The ball rolls out into the street. *Get it!* Suzie thinks, and she toddles into the street after it. "Suzie!" Monique calls, running to pull her (and the ball) out of harm's way.

The action causes Suzie to realize what she has done. *Car!* She looks up and sees an SUV speed by the place where she was just standing. Monique's face looks scared! Suzie starts to cry.

Then she feels Monique's comforting arms around her. "You're okay, Suzie. I know you forgot," Monique's voice murmurs in her ear. "But listen," the voice continues in a much firmer tone. "You must *never, never* run out into the street like that again. That is a *no.* You could get hit by a car. Okay? Don't do that again."

Suzie pulls away from Monique and swipes at her tears with her sleeve. She feels less panicky now that Monique has held her. She is able to think about what she did instead of just feeling scared. She has heard the strict tone in Monique's voice. *I shouldn't have gone there,* she realizes. She frowns and shakes her finger at the street. "Bad car!" she says.

"NO MEANS NO": CONSISTENCY COUNTS

Keeping behavioral rules simple for your one-year-old also means keeping them consistent. Smiling and saying, "Oh, how cute," when your little one twists her daddy's nose and then punishing her for doing the same thing to a child her age isn't fair to a toddler who is not yet able to distinguish between the separate circumstances. As with her daily routine, consistent and predictable limits on behavior foster a sense of well-being for a child and free up her energy for more productive pursuits. For this reason, it is a good idea to think ahead about which behaviors you feel violate your bottom line and which you're willing to let slide for now. The clearer you can be with yourself and your child about these boundaries, the easier your discipline decisions will be this year, and the less need you will probably have to enforce them. You may decide, for example, that actions that threaten your child's or others' safety are clear-cut reasons for disciplinary action (hitting a child with a toy will lead to immediate removal from the play area), but childish behaviors in adult environments can be ignored (being a nuisance in a restaurant). Your confidence in your choices is at least as important as the actual choices you make, since your child will sense any indecisiveness in your response and repeat the questionable action frequently just to watch you respond differently each time.

It helps if your decisions spring from clear, simple principles your child can begin to understand. That way, she will be able to generalize your rules more efficiently (not hitting a child with her hand as well as not hitting him with a toy) and adjust her behavior more easily as your rules change (moving from holding your hand every time she crosses the street to stopping, looking both ways, and moving on alone when she's older). By talking to her about these principles and sticking to them consistently, you can help your child begin to internalize your code of behavior, rather than simply respond to arbitrary commands.

Once you feel that you have a clear idea of what constitutes unacceptable behavior for your one-year-old, it's vital to make sure your disciplinary practices are consistent with those of the other adults in her life. Talk with and observe your partner's, caregiver's, and other involved adults' approach to discipline, and if there are disagreements, talk about them when your child is not in the room. Agreeing on general principles of behavior and how they will be enforced is not a one-time action for parents and other caregivers. You will have to have these discussions again and again as your child grows. Just keep in mind that the more you maintain a united front in matters of enforcing limits, the easier it will be for your child to know what's expected of her. In any case, it is usually not a good idea to object to a form of discipline while it is in progress (assuming that it doesn't physically harm your child). By waiting to discuss the incident with the adult in private and agreeing on a proper response for the future, you can avoid confusing your child even more. It is critical to stand up for your beliefs regarding discipline when dealing with both informal caregivers and child-care centers. If you are not in agreement with the adults who care for your child, you may need to find new caregivers who can carry out your wishes. If you are not sure that caregivers are responding as they say they are, try dropping in for a visit right before lunchtime, when toddlers tend to be at their worst, and observe the adults' behavior for yourself. By doing so, you may reassure yourself as well as your child.

Q & A

"My Parents Spanked Me, and I Turned Out Okay."

Q: I was single when I gave birth to my son, David, and married when he was six months old. My husband is a much stricter parent than I am, and he tends to punish David when I feel he doesn't really deserve it. My husband says that's the way he was raised. David is nearly two now, and I've gotten better at arranging things so that he doesn't get into mischief as much as he used to. But my husband occasionally spanks him or hits him on the arm when he thinks he's misbehaving on purpose. I don't like to argue about his parenting behavior in front of David, but I don't like to stand by while he hits my child. What should I do?

A: While it's not a good idea to argue about parenting techniques in front of your child, physical abuse of any kind constitutes an exception. By striking your child, your husband is violating a trust between the two of you and between himself and David. It's best to step in at that point, removing your child from the scene. Once you have separated your husband and child, allow your husband to cool down, and then discuss the incident with him. Ask him if he really believes that hitting is the only answer and if so, why. He may not know that other options work. If possible, provide him with solid evidence (in the form of magazine articles and books) backing up your conviction that physical punishment is a bad idea. Suggest that he talk about this with other parents. If he continues hitting your child, enroll in parenting classes with him or, if the situation warrants, seek counseling as soon as possible. You owe it to your child—and your relationship with your husband—to work out this critical issue as soon as possible, since it will exist throughout your parenting careers.

MOVING FROM DISCIPLINE TOWARD SELF-DISCIPLINE

Of course, we all wish that our children would just behave without having to be disciplined or watched every single minute. Only near the end of this year, though, will your child's cognitive, emotional, verbal, and motor skills come together in a way that enables her to understand and follow rules more consistently. Once she is able to understand, remember, and decide to follow specific rules, she will move gradually toward understanding the principles behind them (that is, she will understand that it's bad to hurt any living thing, not just that it's bad to pull the cat's tail). Her full ability to understand these principles may not develop until she has passed her second birthday, but you can pave the way toward self-discipline this year by creating a structure upon which she can build general concepts of appropriate versus inappropriate behaviors later on.

The kind of reasoning that leads to effective self-discipline is *inductive* reasoning, the kind of thinking spurred by remarks you make such as "When you yell at me, it hurts my feelings," and "Don't push him, or he'll fall and cry." Sharing this insight into the effects of certain behaviors helps children understand the principles behind their parents'— and, eventually, society's—rules. It also allows them to internalize those principles. Though inductive reasoning is a sophisticated form of thinking that does not become possible until around the second birthday at the earliest, you can help your child begin to think this way by stimulating her verbal development (through talking and reading to her), cognitive skills (by playing with her), motor development (through drawing and physical activity), and social/emotional skills (by encouraging interaction with other children, sharing tasks, and taking turns).

Until your child becomes capable of inductive reasoning, prevention is still the best policy. Installing a baby gate at the top of the stairs is more effective with a twelve-month-old than explaining that if she tries to climb down the stairs she may get hurt. As she becomes more aware of the concepts of sequence, and cause and effect, however, you can begin to introduce her to the idea that there are natural consequences to her actions ("If you run away from me one more time, we'll have to go home") and the concept of having to wait before she's allowed to do something ("Don't open your present yet"). As she becomes more verbally adept, she will grow more interested in cooperative and other prosocial behavior ("It's time to clean up now"). These concepts will gradually lead to an ability to consider the other reasons behind most of your behavioral rules.

By age three, your child will be generally capable of understanding why one kind of behavior is good and another is bad. Until then, you will have to work within her limitations, always explaining the reasons behind your rules as simply as possible but understanding that she will not comprehend them fully in this year. In the meantime, your efforts to communicate these reasons to her will let her know that you care about those reasons and that you expect her to adopt them herself someday. This evidence of your concern is worth a thousand unexplained do's

One-year-olds' mobility and natural curiosity are a dangerous combination. Prevention, such as childproofing unsafe areas, is still the best approach.

and don'ts—and will pay off eventually in a self-disciplined, rather than an oft-disciplined, child.

Is My Child Spoiled?

No matter who you are or where you come from, your beliefs and others' regarding proper child-rearing are probably very different. You may deny your toddler's request that you buy her a toy, too, when shopping for her friend's birthday present ("We're shopping for Mary now"), while your mother may casually toss a present for your daughter into the shopping basket. Since your mother is acting according to what she believes is a reasonable belief system, how is it possible to know if she is spoiling your child? Is it even possible to spoil a person at this age?

Yes, it is possible, but definitions vary. It is important to keep in mind that an occasional tantrum doesn't necessarily mean your child is spoiled—it just means she's a toddler. Emotional extremes are a hallmark of the one- and two-year-old's experience, and the occasional meltdown is only to be expected as your child learns to deal with her feelings. Spoiled children, on the other hand, exhibit more deliberate misbehavior, and chances are that when one looks back on these children's lives, one will see that the seeds for their misbehavior were planted early. Inconsistency on the part of the parents is what makes it possible for children to learn to manipulate adults. A child's process of testing the adult over and over to see if the adult will set limits on her behavior can reach the point at which no one (adults included) wants to be around the child. Her behavior can lead to future relationship difficulties, which certainly no one wants.

Experts agree that the spoiled child is expressing a real need for discipline through her behavior, and her caregivers' refusal to provide it leads to increased anxiety and "acting out" behavior. For this reason, deciding on clear limits for your child and sticking to them consistently is a great service to the both of you. The clearer the rules are, the more easily she can follow them. A child who knows your unequivocal position on candy at the checkout stand will probably not bother to tease you about it, but if you vacillate on the issue, sometimes buying candy and sometimes not, you can expect a tantrum if you don't buy it this time. If you find you cannot control your child's behavior on a regular basis, it is time to sit down and work out some ground rules, allowing for a reasonable amount of slack (casually looking the other way when your child sniffs the candy bars at the checkout stand)—and make a point of sticking to them in the future.

"GOOD GIRL!"

It's a year later, and once again the family is in a mad morning rush to get out the door. Emily, now twenty-four months, strides into the bathroom, climbs up on her stool, and plucks her toothbrush from its holder. While looking for her toothpaste, her eyes happen to fall on the open toilet—an especially tempting receptacle since she's started the toilet-training process recently. She leans toward the toilet, lifts her toothbrush to drop it in, and hears her father's voice ring forth: "Emily! What are you doing?"

The sharp tone of her father's voice stops Emily's arm midthrow. In that moment's hesitation, she remembers the last time she tried to throw something into the toilet—and the time before. Straightening up, Emily turns to look at her dad with wide eyes.

Fred knows from experience that this is time to change the subject. "Were you about to brush your own teeth, all by yourself?" he says. "What a big girl!" Emily's face relaxes as she turns back to the mirror. In the reflection, she sees a big girl who can brush her own teeth.

"I do it!" she says proudly. Then, holding her toothbrush high in the air to show her dad, she gets to work on the toothpaste tube.

Fred gives his daughter a pat on the head and starts off to look for his shoes again. But then, on second thought, he returns to the bathroom—and removes the open tube of toothpaste before Emily has a chance to "brush" the entire mirror.

Advances Toward Self-Discipline in the Second Year

12 MONTHS	Begins imitating some adult actions
	Enjoys demonstrating mastery
	Understands that she can cause things to happen
18 MONTHS	May follow simple commands
	May be aware of cause and effect
	Memory starts to improve
	Begins to understand concepts behind simple safety issues (hot stove, etc.)
24 MONTHS	Begins to understand simple time-related concepts ("soon," "after breakfast," etc.)
	Starts to rely more on words to communicate feelings

FIRST-PERSON SINGULAR

No matter how "naughty or nice" your child has been this year, it's sure to have been (literally!) a challenging period. Take a few minutes to record here the triumphs that you most want to remember—the first time your child pulled a chair over to watch while you made dinner or the first time she put away her toys without even being asked. Make a note of the kinds of limit-setting techniques that worked best with her—offering her a choice of acceptable behaviors and letting her pick one or discussing the reasons behind your decision until she felt she understood them. Chances are the techniques that work best now may also work well when she's a teenager. You may be glad later that you took some notes!

READER'S NOTES

CHAPTER 9

Looking Ahead—I'm Two

He can walk, he can talk, and now the real fun is about to begin.

It's been a long year but a very fruitful one for the children we've observed in these chapters. In twelve months, Philip and Tara, Spencer and Clara—and your own one-year-old—have learned to walk, feed themselves, communicate verbally, and deepen their relationships with loved ones as well as with new friends. We have watched clear personalities emerge from their baby selves as they have learned to make their wishes known and their opinions heard. Though your own development as parents might not have seemed quite as mind-boggling on the surface, you know that your skills in effectively raising your child have improved as your knowledge about him has deepened. This knowledge will come in handy as your one-year-old turns two and faces the equally challenging transformations that occur in that year. You may be dreading the two-year-olds' legendary tantrums, refusals to eat, and insistence on doing everything themselves—but don't worry. With the empathy, communication skills, and humor you've developed over these past months, you'll be able to see these new developments as the exciting signs of growth and challenges to your creativity as a parent that they really are.

A LARGER WORLD:
WHAT YOUR CHILD HAS LEARNED

Motor development took center stage in your child's life this year, certainly during the first six months. This is the year in which he began walking with ease, climbing, and even running. His developmental process did not take place smoothly, but in fits and starts and perhaps even with a few regressions (or "touchpoints," as my colleague Dr. Brazelton would say). At its most intense, it might have disrupted your little one's sleep, prevented him from sitting still to eat or to be changed, and led to outbursts of frustration when you buckled him into a car seat or stroller. By his second birthday, though, he has clearly mastered his ability to get around, as well as to perform such fine-motor skills as feeding himself with a spoon and grasping a crayon. Though further refinement of his motor skills will certainly follow in the years to come, they will probably never again dominate his life to such a great extent.

Your one-year-old's great strides in movement skills were strongly linked to his increasingly urgent quest for independence. During this year, he began to test the ground between independence and attachment, as each need triggered its opposite drive. This balancing act between the urge to explore and the need for Mom and Dad will continue into his third year. You are quite likely to continue to hear the proud announcement "I did it myself!" as well as soft bedtime requests for a story and cuddle—and cries of frustration ("I can't do it!") when the balance between not enough parental presence or too much of it feels wrong.

Throughout this year, your child's physical development—and the independent exploration that took place as a result—has stimulated a great deal of cognitive growth. By reaching, grasping, emptying, pushing, banging, filling, and otherwise experimenting with physical objects, your one-year-old learned a great deal about the physical nature of the world around him, including the concepts of space, cause and effect, and sequence. His practice with finding hidden or discarded objects (and his experience with your comings and goings) has led to a new understanding of what happens to things and people when they disappear from his sight. His memory improved tremendously, allowing him to learn more effectively from experience, to make a plan and carry it out, and to begin to learn rules of behavior. His ability to think symbolically led to new skills in imaginary play. At age eighteen months, he might have been able to pretend to drink from an empty cup; by his second birthday, he can imagine that something else (his teddy bear, perhaps) is drinking from that cup, and his imaginary play thus becomes richer and more satisfying.

Of course, all of these cognitive advances have fed into your one-year-old's stunning advances in the ability to use and understand language. He has grown from a babbling baby to a relatively sophisticated individual who expresses his opinions in two- three-, and maybe even four-word sentences. Master of perhaps one or two words at twelve months, he now knows as many as two hundred—and is picking up half a dozen or more each day. Instead of crying to try to convey to you that something is wrong (but *what?*) he can now tell you exactly how he feels. Chances are he can also use his verbal skills to reach out to new friends and frame his thoughts and experiences in conscious memories that will stay with him in the years to come.

All of this development—physical, mental, emotional, and verbal— has set the stage for the magical blossoming of his personality. As his likes and dislikes, needs and wants, and fears and enthusiasms have been made manifest, he has begun to turn noticeably outward to engage with the outside world. His realization at around twelve months that he and others possess a private mental and emotional world led to a growing awareness of (and fascination with) the concepts of the "self" versus "another." His developing verbal abilities increasingly allowed him to express his own inner thoughts and explore those of others. He became aware of his loved ones' separate emotional states and began to respond to their emotions as well as to events that affected him directly. He learned to empathize to some degree with the other children in his life and grew fascinated by their own ways of coping with the world. Gradually, his interest in others' subjective viewpoints led him to sense a pattern of "principles" or beliefs behind your creation of a daily routine and your setting of limits. Increasingly, he moved from mainly wanting to please himself (by satisfying his urge to explore) toward wanting to please you and his other caregivers by being "good" and following your rules.

TRUSTING YOURSELF:
WHAT YOU HAVE LEARNED

The year has been one of great discoveries for you as well as for your child. The months between ages one and two brought with them the miracle of your child's "unveiling." By now, whether you worked at home or away from the house this year, you know your child as no one else does. You know his temperament—whether he is generally calm and easygoing or sensitive and easily upset, active and assertive or shy and secretive, reckless and adventurous or cautious and slow. You also know where his temperament and yours match and where they clash, and you've begun to experiment with ways to accommodate these differences.

Your second year of closely observing your little one's physical and emotional growth has given you a greater understanding of his capabilities and needs. As a result, you can more effectively tailor your expectations and his tasks to suit him. You can avoid pressuring him to master a skill (toilet training, for example) before he's ready and can more easily trust yourself to recognize any developmental or health problems that arise.

After a year of increasingly sophisticated conversation, you have to guess much less about your child's wants, needs, passions, and opinions. By now you usually know what he's saying, even if your friends and relatives don't. The two of you have learned how to communicate effectively; he is better able to understand your speech, and you are continuing to help him develop his. This new level of communication is more than just a skill. Through words, your child can open his mind to you, giving you a much better idea of where he is in his development and emotional growth. This greater knowledge allows you to continue to stay one step ahead of him, leading him toward greater understanding and more complex thought and action.

WHAT'S NEXT?:
DEVELOPMENT IN THE THIRD YEAR

The seeds planted in the second year truly blossom in the third, making age two an especially satisfying time for both parent and child. Your child will experience another great burst of development as his third year begins. The continued refinement of his fine-motor skills will make him more adept at such tasks as dressing himself, drawing, turning the pages of a book, and playing with more complex toys. His increased ability will lower his frustration level (and your own) as he works at these tasks, but his need to "do it himself" means you will have to plan for the extra time (and patience) it takes to get those things done.

After age twenty-four months, toilet training may be begun with greater chance of success. Your child is likely to take quite a bit of pride now in tending to his own bodily functions and become curious about wearing "big kid" underwear or using the bathroom like his older siblings or friends. Though he will be prone to a number of "accidents" this year, your patience and support will help him gradually master this skill. Due to physical limitations, however, he may continue to need pull-ups at night as late as his fourth or fifth year.

Your child's developing social awareness in the third year will help you continue to promote such prosocial behavior as sharing, taking turns, and speaking politely. His desire to live up to your standards (along with his urge to test them) will continue to increase as the one-year-old's irresistible urge to touch everything subsides. Your continued, consistent setting of limits will help him develop self-discipline, and his greater experience with inductive reasoning (pulling Suzie's hair makes her cry; if I run on the wall, I may fall off) will allow him to understand why he can't do certain things. Finally his expanding sense of time will enable you to say "in a minute" or "later" and have a reasonable hope that he will understand and briefly accept the concept.

The third year is a wonderful time for making friends and learning new social skills. As a two-year-old, your child will learn a great deal by imitating others, especially same-age or slightly older children. He will become interested in all the rituals and rules of friendship, from a habitual hug hello to the house rule that cookies be shared. His expanding imagination will allow him to enjoy playing with (rather than alongside) his peers more, and his ability to empathize, laugh at others' jokes, and "be funny" himself will help him cement his bonds with them.

Perhaps the most exciting area of growth in the third year is in language development. Your child's communication skills will advance at

Between ages two and three, peer relationships blossom as children enjoy sharing their discoveries with new friends.

a rocket pace next year. For the first time, he will be able to make use of the basic rules of grammar, and his more sophisticated language skills allow for increasingly complex symbolic thinking. When he becomes a two-year-old, your child's questions will increase in number, and they won't stop coming. Your life will be filled with "Wazzat?" and "Where it goed?" Your child is likely to repeat the same questions over and over, partly to ensure that your answer is always the same and perhaps also to reexperience the pleasure of a successful communication.

If language growth is one of the greatest satisfactions in the third year, emotional swings may turn out to be the greatest challenge. For at least the first half of the third year, your child's negativism may be at its most extreme, caused in large part by his steadily increasing determination to control and manage his world. Spurts of cognitive growth (language and abstract concepts) or physical development (toilet training) may again disrupt his sleep for brief periods, as his mind races so fast or his body can't slow down after a particularly exciting and challenging day. Fortunately, you know your child much better now. Your deeper understanding of his temperament, moods, needs, and desires will go far in helping you weather the inevitable storms of early childhood—and in allowing you, your child, and your family to enjoy the many good days ahead.

FIRST-PERSON SINGULAR

Now is a wonderful time to turn back to the beginning of this book and read the predictions you wrote down twelve months ago about what you thought your child might be like at age two. How accurate were your guesses? In what ways did your child surprise you? This might also be a good time to get out any videotapes and photographs you have and take a look at all the ways he's advanced over the year. Once you've properly appreciated his progress, write down some predictions here about the year to come. What are your goals for your child, for yourself as a parent, and for your family as a whole this year? In what ways would you most like to see your child grow? Have you noticed any particularly strong skills yet, or do you suspect that one or more might develop next year? As we've seen, the better you know your one-of-a-kind child, the better equipped you will be to help him grow. Thinking about him with pen in hand provides you both with tools for a better future as well as memories to look back on in the years to come.

WATCH ME GROW

I'm Two

Every Parent's Guide to the
Lively and Challenging
24- to 36-Month-Old

I don't know if I can take it anymore," the woman in line at the grocery store murmured to her friend. "It took me an hour to get out of the house this morning because Darcy absolutely refused to get dressed. I'd been late for work on Monday for the same reason. I could just imagine the look on my boss's face if he saw me walk in late again. I was so desperate I offered to put Darcy in her best velvet party dress if she'd just let me cover her body with something—but all she did was hide under the covers, wailing, 'No! No! No!'"

The woman's friend lifted her eyebrows in a world-weary way. "She wanted to wear the shirt and pants she wore yesterday, right? The cruddy ones in the laundry hamper?"

The first woman laughed in surprise. "How did you know?"

Her friend shrugged. "Darcy's two."

Hearing this conversation, I couldn't help but sympathize with the mother (what parent doesn't know how frustrated she felt that morning?), but I could see poor Darcy's side, too. It can't always be fun to be labeled part of the "terrible twos" club, whose members are best known for their stubbornness, defiance, and (worst of all) public temper tantrums. No doubt, there were times when Darcy brought great joy to her mother—by shrieking with delight at the sight of a bright balloon, proudly showing off her latest crayon creation, or solemnly telling her parents how much she loves them—but in the rush and pressure of everyday life it is sometimes hard to recall those wonderful moments our children share with us. Two-year-olds can especially try our patience as their improving verbal, physical, and emotional skills make them seem more capable of responding appropriately than they really are. Darcy may have listened attentively as her mother explained that she had to get dressed *now* because Mommy had to get to work on time, but at two she was far from understanding the concept of "getting to work," much less the idea of "on time." Instead, she may have latched on to the memory of how uncomfortably clothes could rub against her skin, decided that she wanted to run and jump freely that morning without being encased in a dress, or resisted cooperating in a certain sequence of events she knew would lead to her mother's departure. Her need to establish her own identity by getting her way may have prevented her from going along with her mother even though she wanted her approval. Unfortunately, at Darcy's age, the only way she could express these intense feelings was to scrunch up her face in defiance and shout, "No!" In other words, the business of being two may be keeping her from getting what she wants nearly as often as it frustrates her mom.

As Darcy's mother and her friend left the store, I thought about all the advice the mother would probably get from well-meaning friends, television, and parenting books and magazines on how to get her toddler to behave. Some of the advice would be good, some bad, but chances are that little if any would be tailored to the needs or circumstances of her particular child. If only someone could help that mother see what caused *her* child's behavior at a given time, I thought—if only she could step back and observe the ways in which her daughter's developmental level, emotional needs, and unique personality meld or collide with those of her caregivers—that mother would be well on her way to creating parenting strategies that actually work.

My goal with this book, as with all the books in the Watch Me Grow series, is to help you step back as a parent and take a look at your child's mind, emotions, and abilities at each phase of development. Only in this way can you begin to understand why your child's behavior appears so remarkably mature at times (comforting a younger child who is crying) but can be so maddening a few hours later (throwing a cup across the room). As a developmental psychologist and researcher, former director of Boston's Brazelton Touchpoints Center, and a university professor, I am well aware of the vast and growing body of research on how young children learn and grow. As the mother of twin eight-year-old boys, I know from personal experience that children are very different from one another, even when they are the same age or in the same family; that they are *growing, changing* beings whose comprehension, skills, needs, and desires evolve over time; and that parenting itself is a constant challenge that can be eased (but not erased) as parents grow to understand more about their particular child.

Not so many years ago, children were seen—by scientists, child development experts, and many parents—as empty vessels waiting to be filled. Recent research into the workings of the developing brain has challenged this assumption, showing that young children are more actively engaged with the world, deliberately interacting with their environment in ways that literally shape their brains. Now that your two-year-old can move about on his own, he is even less dependent on your constant, methodical "teaching" than he was a year ago. Problem-solving and mastery of skills will be his major agenda for the year. Of course, you will want to be there to reinforce what he is learning, but he will lead the way much more often than he used to as he explores the world around him. Parenting a two-year-old is all about this interplay between following and leading—knowing when to let your child make discoveries on his own, and when to elaborate on those discoveries to bring him forward a little bit more.

The key to raising any child successfully lies in observing him accurately, with an educated eye, and then using your knowledge of his temperament, history, and capabilities to help him create what the psychologist Jerome Bruner calls a secure scaffolding that will support his climb toward adulthood. In these pages, I walk with you through the practical situations that you encounter with your child every day. It is my hope that this book will enhance the life of your two-year-old and your entire family, helping you grow together with greater understanding, excitement, and joy.

What I'm Like

Your child is able to take the initiative in learning much more than before. The art of parenting lies in supporting her interests as they develop.

It's hard to believe how much a twenty-four-month-old has already learned about how the world works, what kinds of pleasure, support, and stimulation it can offer her and the many exciting ways she can interact with it. As Maggie and Richard Wolff sit down to dinner with six-year-old Justin and two-year-old Amy in her booster seat, they exchange a glance of relief mixed with pride. Finally, after all the months of milky spit-ups, interrupted sleep, teething dramas, and wordless wails, the Wolffs are starting to look like a functional family again—four individuals with distinct personalities and increasingly effective ways of communicating their needs. Even mealtime seems on the verge of becoming an enriching family activity, rather than a rushed attempt to bolt down food while Amy tries to tip her high chair over or throws her food. As Amy announces, "Butter, pease," stretching out her hand as elegantly as a princess, Maggie dares to look ahead to dinnertimes filled with conversations about each family member's day, perhaps even ending with an offer from the kids to help clean up. She gives her daughter a smile. *Look at her,* Maggie thinks. *She's practically a little girl already. Her hair's all the way down to her shoulders. She sits up straighter in her chair. Her gaze is just as direct and confident as Justin's!*

"Let me help you butter that roll," Richard says to Amy, holding the butter dish in one hand and reaching for Amy's plate with the other.

Instantly, Amy grabs the edge of her plate. "No!" she yells. "My dish!"

Uh-oh. Maggie's heart sinks. That tone of voice is certainly familiar, and Maggie notes that Amy's hunger is what's really getting in the way of her patience. "Amy, let your father butter the roll for you," she says, hoping for the best. "He'll put plenty on, just like you want it."

"*I* do it! Gimme!" Amy's face, scrunched up like a samurai warrior's, has turned bright red. She opens her mouth, and the entire family flinches in the face of her bloodcurdling scream. Her brother rolls his eyes. "Can I be excused?" he asks.

"Amy, let . . . me . . . have . . . the . . . plate." Richard tugs on the dish with each word. But his daughter pulls back. A moment later, the inevitable happens: the dish goes flying off the table, and the family dog pounces on the unexpected treat.

As Maggie and Richard resignedly clean up the mess, order Justin back to his seat, and try to salvage the rest of dinnertime, Maggie has to admit to her husband and herself that, "after all, Amy *is* only two."

However bright their daughter is, and however amazing her progress has been from dependent infant to active, independent toddler, she still has much learning and development ahead of her in all realms—emotion, self-expression, social interaction, advanced thinking, and motor skills. The adults around her, naturally impressed by her advances so far, may assume that she comprehends and is capable of doing more than she really can. But as every parent learns, a two-year-old can *say,* "I do it," but that doesn't mean she can *accomplish* a particular action. She says, "Okay," when you tell her to put her shoes on, but she doesn't necessarily understand that you mean right *now.* She knows what she wants, but she is still often unable to express her desire acceptably in words.

In fact, the central dilemma for both child and parent in the third year springs largely from the normal unevenness of a two-year-old's mental, physical, and emotional development. Although a child this age is certainly making marvelous progress, she still has quite a short attention span, a limited ability to postpone gratification and to plan for the future, and a need for time and patience when learning to dress herself, follow daily routines, share with others, and express her feelings. She still must rely on her caregivers' emotional, educational, and practical support to ease her into early childhood *as she becomes ready,* and not before. Many of the difficulties that so commonly occur during this year—conflicts that can lead to furious impatience on the parents' part and loss of control (and even tantrums) on the child's part—are a result of this mismatch between a parent's or child's expectations and the child's abilities.

Fortunately, the third year of life is a time of profound growth in just those areas that can seem so defeating right around her second birthday. Last year you were able to encourage and applaud your child's very clear triumphs in learning to walk and to say her first words. This year her deepening awareness and refinement of skills may not be as easy to observe, but these advances will improve all of your lives in very important ways. At age one, her one- or two-word utterances frequently left you fishing for their meaning; this year she will learn to express, in increasingly varied sentences, more of what she thinks and feels. At age one, she could sit at the dinner table (in a high chair or booster seat) but did not fully participate in the ritual of the meal. By the end of this year, she will be able to listen to her brother's tales about his school day and perhaps chime in with a simple story of her own ("I went to the zoo. There was giraffes!"). The first, rather awkward play dates of her second year may progress toward budding friendships in her third. And of course, last year's early attempts to establish who she is will lead to this year's full-blown tests of the limits of acceptable behavior and the power of her individual will. Your two-year-old's progress, in other words, will be more a matter of depth than breadth. As the months pass, you'll experience the pleasure of watching her consolidate, integrate, and act on all the knowledge she has acquired, until she is able to master her world and herself with the true dexterity of a growing child.

A CHILD'S-EYE VIEW

"Mommy Home!"

Twenty-four-month-old Isabel is playing with blocks on the living room floor. *Yellow block on top,* she tells herself. She feels happy and busy, sharing her toys with her mom, Diane, who sits stretched out beside her. As she balances a third wooden cube on top of the yellow one, she proudly announces, "Tree bocks!" and enjoys a surge of satisfaction as Mommy applauds.

Just then, she hears the sound of a key in the front door lock. Her hand freezes, hovering over the pile of blocks. *What's that noise?* She searches her memory. *Key in the lock means Mommy's home from work.* She looks at her mother. "Mommy home!" she says with a big smile.

Mommy looks very surprised. "No, silly," she says. "Mommy's right here. That's Daddy!"

Isabel blinks, acknowledging this contradiction between a learned association (key in the lock equals Mommy) and the evidence her mom presents ("Mommy's right here"). The door opens, and she turns toward it to see her father entering the room. Isabel's eyes widen. She looks back at Mommy. "Yay!" she says brightly, demonstrating her deeper understanding of this particular situation. "Daddy home!"

"LOOK AT ME!": YOUR CHILD'S PROGRESS IN THE THIRD YEAR

What great satisfaction we parents take in watching our two-year-olds run, jump, and climb on the little kids' playground, almost as independently as the big kids nearby. The pride they take in their own accomplishments, so obvious each time they rush back to give us a progress report, is hard-won and certainly deserved. Consider the fact that only eighteen months ago your child was just beginning to sit up, babble nonsense sounds, and grasp objects within her reach. She's been walking for only a year or less, and speaking in sentences just recently if at all. As she neared her second birthday, she grew somewhat more aware of the world outside her immediate environment—its attractions, its mysteries, and the other people inhabiting it. Now, early in her third year, she can walk, run, and climb with ease, speak more clearly and be understood, and perceive that others' viewpoints may differ from her own. She stands poised on the brink of true individuality—ready to take her place as a unique member of her world.

Your child will accomplish this feat by continuing to refine a wide variety of skills over the next twelve months, as well as develop some new abilities. As we will see in Chapter 2, her change in physical appearance from potbellied toddler to straight-backed young child during the first half of this year will accompany a similar progression in such gross-motor skills as walking, running, climbing, pushing, and pulling. Delighting in her new sense of physical power, she will soon start to experiment with new variations in movement—trying a somersault after seeing one on TV, spinning in place and falling down dizzy, and squatting and waddling like a duck. Her fine-motor skills—buttoning, cutting, drawing, threading—will progress even more dramatically this year, leading inevitably to demands to "do it myself." One of the most welcome aspects of this new self-sufficiency involves her physiological development. By the middle of the year, if not before, your child will be able to control her bladder sufficiently to allow toilet training to begin, and her drive toward independence may motivate her to go to the bathroom "like the big kids." At the best of times, her burgeoning abilities in all of these areas will lessen her frustration level (and your own). Still, you will want to build in the extra minutes she'll need to try to dress herself, eat meals without help, and help her little brother drink from his bottle.

Just as daily practice improves your two-year-old's motor skills, continued experimentation with objects and people enhances her understanding of her world in new, exciting ways. In Chapter 3, we will trace the two-year-old's journey from simple planning and problem-solving toward a more complex and sophisticated ability to imagine, pretend, and express herself in words and in play. Her world, once an unknown expanse, is now filled with familiar, reassuring landmarks. Her sense of time may have also developed to the point where she understands the concepts of "later," "soon," and "in just a minute," though she still can't wait very long to get what she wants. Her attention span will lengthen considerably this year, as will her ability to notice more than one aspect of an object or situation at a time—two skills that help her follow storylines, make multistep plans, and retain memories for longer periods. Like a child coloring in the outlines in a coloring book, your two-year-old will continue to fill in the details of her immediate environment as the year progresses. She will grow increasingly eager to explore the larger world beyond her front door. Her expanding curiosity may even enable her to benefit from a preschool program or other regular group activity this year.

Your child's cognitive development may reveal itself most clearly in her amazing verbal growth. Not only will her vocabulary grow at a truly astronomical rate, but, as we will see in Chapter 4, she will begin to demonstrate her comprehension of many of the basic rules of grammar as she speaks in sentences of three, four, and even more words. "No nap" will become "I don't want nap," "All wet" will grow to "Look, it's all wet!" and "Baba juice" will develop into "More juice, peeze." From this point onward, her verbal repertoire will expand exponentially, not only in the quantity of her words but in the quality and range of her expression. By the end of the year, you are likely to have a real conversationalist on your hands.

Despite these advances in your child's verbal abilities, she will not always be able to express the frustration she feels at not being able to master her entire world. For this reason, you are likely to hear "No!" and witness angry outbursts even more often after she turns two. In Chapter 5, we will see how, as my colleagues at Touchpoints have shown, temporary surges in cognitive development (speech, concepts) or physical changes (toilet training) may disrupt sleep or lead to emotional scenes. Fortunately, as your child's ability to express herself improves, and as she grows better able to wait for what she wants and accept the fact that others may have a different point of view, her negative behavior will gradually abate. By age three, her emotional life will have grown more complex, encompassing new feelings such as shame, embarrassment, and true pride. She will be better able to show empathy for others and will probably begin to demonstrate a budding sense of humor. Her personality will have established itself, enabling you to better understand her and thus weather the inevitable storms. In fact, her heightened desire to live up to your standards may well lead to a "second honeymoon" of closeness between you and your child.

Your two-year-old's efforts to know and express herself more fully will be enhanced by new relationships with others. During this year, she will begin to pay more attention to the children around her, learning a great deal from them through imitation. In Chapter 6, we will explore ways parents can build on these experiences when reinforcing social rules, including taking turns, sharing, and refraining from aggression. We will see how games and other play activities can also teach these conventions, and we will discuss ways in which your child's new, often highly simplified ideas about boys and girls can be gently guided and shaped. We will also look at the issues of morality and empathy for others and discuss ways to lay the groundwork for this development.

As your two-year-old grows in all of these ways—as she learns to communicate more effectively, wait a bit longer for a treat, and enjoy interacting with her peers—you can bolster her confidence through a support system of daily routines, clear rules, and simple methods for resolving conflicts. Chapters 7 and 8 explore ways to create predictable, but not rigid, structures for such two-year-old challenges as bedtime, dinnertime, and toilet training, as well as ways to cope with behavior that has gotten out of hand.

Of course, life with a two-year-old rarely proceeds according to plan. Discipline issues, disruptions to routine, and uneven development all occur frequently enough to challenge even the most saintly parent's patience. It helps to remind yourself ahead of time that exceptions will surface for every rule—that behavior will sometimes turn erratic, plans will have to be scrapped, and your child will not always "perform" as you would like. Children differ in the areas of development they choose to work on at any particular time. Your friend's twenty-four-month-old may be willing to experiment with taking turns and sharing or otherwise develop her social skills, while yours refuses to do so but is moving along faster in her climbing, hopping, and balancing abilities. Never fear—the two children will switch places more than once in the year to come. During this period when your child moves productively from one type of growth to another and then back again, it's important not to "type" her too soon (announcing, for example, that "Rose is a great athlete but not very social"). As a two-year-old, she is able to lead the way in her own learning much more than before. The art of parenting lies in observing her interests as they occur, and arranging her world so that she can make many of her discoveries on her own.

A PARENT'S STORY

Thinking Like a Toddler

"I'd always heard that girls were better at toilet training than boys," a woman reported at a parenting group meeting I visited recently. "I was really glad to hear it, because I wanted to put my daughter Denise in a preschool program that doesn't accept kids in diapers. About six months before Denise was due to start the program, I began the whole process—giving her a potty to sit on, reading her books about using the potty, asking older kids to let her watch them use the potty, buying her flowery little underpants to wear instead of diapers, and so on. Denise is a smart girl. I figured if I just followed all the steps, so to speak, everything would work out fine.

"But no matter how much I talked about how great that potty was, Denise just would not use it. The weeks passed, and I was at my wits' end. I'd already put down the deposit for the preschool, and I was scared to lose it. Then one day, about two weeks before preschool started, Denise and I were walking through Macy's children's department, and she suddenly stopped dead in her tracks. 'Superman!' she said. I looked where she was pointing, and there was a pair of blue and red Superman underwear lying on a pile of clothes in a sale bin. And it hit me—the little boy next door who'd let her watch him use the bathroom was wearing Superman underwear at the time. He'd done a whole Superman act for Denise that day that had really entranced her. Naturally, I bought half a dozen pairs of that underwear right then and took them home—and from the time I put a pair on her, Denise started really trying to use the potty, just like the boy next door. Apparently, she'd made a strong connection in her mind between Superman underwear and using the bathroom, but I'd never have been able to take advantage of it if I hadn't finally listened to her and followed her lead."

"NOW I UNDERSTAND": HOW YOUR CHILD'S COMPREHENSION GROWS

One of the most gratifying aspects of your child's development this year is her increased ability to make associations—to connect one piece of information with another in her mind and use that link to create new ideas and concepts about her world. Some of these associations lead to truly impressive leaps of insight. A two-year-old might put a handful of snow in her mouth, for example, and when asked what she is eating, answer, "Water." Other links, such as a new ability to see the number 1 on a page and say the word, will pave the way to a higher order of learning. Some connections are so wildly fanciful that they charm us with their originality even as we wonder how they ever occurred—as when a child urged to look at a video camera and say hi to Grandma asks, "Is Grandma in *there?*"

The ability to associate one observation or idea with another is enhanced by your toddler's longer memory and attention span. When she can *remember* the golden retriever your friend Susan brought to visit last week, it's easier for her to link it to the dog she sees in a neighbor's yard this afternoon ("Look! Susan dog!"). When she is able to spend more than a minute or so *focusing* on one object, she is likely to notice more aspects of that object that she can connect with something else ("Doggie has tail—like my kitty!"). Her ability to *classify* objects (this is a dog, not a horse) will also increase significantly this year, helping her to develop general assumptions about all the members of a group ("Dogs like bones") and to predict sequences ("I throw the ball. Daddy catch it"). A two-year-old's verbal development greatly enhances her ability to comprehend and retain the hundreds of associations she makes each day. As she moves through this year, you are likely to see her literally narrating her actions ("Punch the dough!" "Up the steps, up the steps, up the steps . . .") as she learns to link her physical movements with mental activity. All of these connections not only stimulate

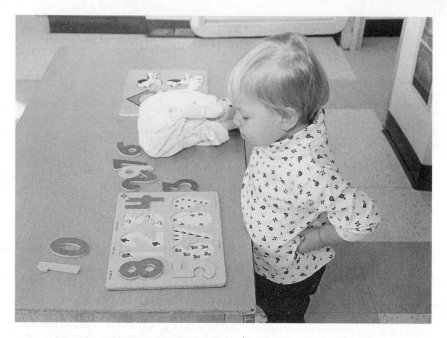

You can almost see "the wheels turn" inside your two-year-old's head as she valiantly tries to solve new dilemmas.

her cognitive development but spur her imagination as she links your behavior toward her with her own behavior toward her dolly, or when she pretends to rake leaves just like Daddy did last weekend.

Amazingly, the countless associations you can see your two-year-old making represent only the tip of the iceberg as far as her mental activity is concerned. Because two-year-olds are still able to communicate only a small portion of what they're thinking, most of their associations take place invisibly. Only recently, as researchers have come up with better-designed experiments and studies, have we begun to realize that toddlers understand, analyze, and retain much more than they have traditionally been given credit for. In short, the two-year-old's "associative machine" virtually never stops working. As a result, this is a year when you as a parent can contribute a great deal to your child's learning. By keeping an eye (and ear) out for the associations that your child expresses, and making the right comments to extend them ("You're right, snow becomes water. The hot sun—or your warm tongue—melts it"), you can stimulate her thinking even more. Certainly, her brain is ripe for such nourishment. A two-year-old's brain is 75 percent as large as an adult's; by age three it will have grown to 90 percent of adult size.

EASING THE WAY

Playing Isn't Everything

Parents are not (usually) preschool teachers, and it isn't necessary or even wise to spend all of your time down on the floor deliberately stimulating your child through games, artwork, play, and other child-centered activities. Children make associations no matter what's going on around them. As long as you and your child spend your time together actively observing and commenting on your surroundings, she can learn an enormous amount by, say, helping you cook dinner, chatting with you in the car as you run errands, or even dropping by your office with you after hours so you can catch up on paperwork. Not only will she learn that beating egg whites makes them foamy, that it's fun to invent a rhyme pairing "car" with "far," or that Mommy goes to a specific place when she "disappears" to work every weekday morning, but she will also begin to accept the fact that hers is not the only important agenda and that a vast array of new adventures await her beyond the playroom.

LEARNING FROM OTHERS: A WORLD OF STIMULATION

If an infant focuses most intently on her own internal experience, and a one-year-old on her evolving relationship with those closest to her, the two-year-old gradually becomes open to expanding her social world beyond her immediate circle. This turning outward, stimulated in part by her growing awareness of her surroundings in general, is a slow, uneven process and requires a great deal of effort. Your toddler may peer curiously at the mailman as he stops by each day but quickly duck

WHAT I'M LIKE | 233

behind you if he so much as looks at her and says hello. This is not necessarily a sign of shyness, but more likely a symptom of your child's attempts to deal with what is still an overwhelming flood of new information. As she grows more familiar with the reassuring rules and common formulas of social interaction (as you show her how to say hello, announce her name when the mailman asks her for it, and so on), such interaction will cease to confuse her and she will begin to make contact with greater confidence.

Your child's fascination with other children will continue to intensify as well, drawing her more and more into social interactions. Just as when she was one, she learns a great deal by imitating her peers. Even when this acquired behavior is "bad" (hitting, snatching toys, yelling), it opens the door for exploration and discussion. By commenting on what has happened ("Look how sad the boy is because he got pushed on the slide"), you help her understand that actions have natural consequences. As the months pass and your child interacts more with adults outside her family and with other children, her focus will move gradually from "me" to "me and sometimes you, too." Her ability to

Imitating peers and pretend play are two activities your two-year-old will engage in more than ever before.

empathize will expand, and as her willingness to wait for what she wants gradually grows stronger, she will begin to share, take turns, and experiment with other social skills.

Your two-year-old's ability to interact with a wider world is largely a result of her greater general awareness of her surroundings. By age twenty-four months, a toddler is all eyes and ears, soaking up everything around her (good and bad) like a sponge. Her longer memory and increased comprehension help her retain and use what she takes in. As a result, she not only learns the social rules and ethical principles you teach her but experiments with the variations she observes in others. Now more than ever it's important to consider your child's presence when you are in conversation with other adults, when you are stressed emotionally or having an argument with your spouse, or when the television is on. Though it is neither possible nor desirable to screen everything that reaches your child, it is only considerate to protect her from information that is emotionally overwhelming or inappropriate.

THE TOY BOX

At Thirty Months

Ever since he was born, Richie has been a confirmed night owl, and his weary parents, Janet and Dave, soon fell into the habit of letting him play with his toys in the living room after dinner while they enjoyed their nightly TV programs with their two older sons. Tonight the family is watching the evening news, and they hardly notice Richie assembling his wooden train set behind an easy chair, talking quietly to himself. Just as Dave leaves to get something to eat in the kitchen, a story about a fatal plane crash in London comes on. "Dave, come here," Janet calls. "Your boss is in London right now, isn't she?"

As Dave returns, Janet feels Richie's hand on her knee for a moment, but she is too engrossed in the news story to pay attention. The two parents and their older sons watch the screen anxiously. Suddenly, Janet notices that Richie's hand is gone from her knee, and his play chatter has changed in some subtle way. Looking over at her son, she sees that he has crammed a small wooden giraffe and a monkey into one of the train cars. He picks up the car, hurls it through the air, and smashes it into the ground. "Boom! 'Splosion!" he announces.

Janet is startled. She had no idea that Richie was paying attention to the news story. Yet he has effortlessly picked up on its emotional content and its effect on his family. Janet stands up quickly. She knows that Richie is too young to comprehend exactly what he's saying, and she doesn't want to increase his interest in the subject by dwelling on it. Instead, she takes his hand and, with a pointed glance at her husband, says, "Come on, Richie, let's go find a book to read."

A PLACE AT THE TABLE: YOUR THIRTY-SIX-MONTH-OLD

It is amazing to consider how much information a two-year-old ingests over the course of a year, and how competent she becomes at mastering her steadily expanding world. As frustrating as it can be at times to deal with her determination to control events around her, and as draining as her constant questions and high activity level can be, you can't help but feel some awe at her sheer determination to perfect her skills and grow. In just twelve months—a year that slipped by for her parents in a mere instant—Amy has evolved from a single-minded toddler, focused on imposing her will, to a more confident, mature young individual with her own clear tastes and opinions, a better sense of verbal give-and-take, and a stronger (if still sporadic) desire to please her parents and to look at things from the point of view of others.

Amy's parents have grown this year as well, Maggie acknowledges to herself as she sits down to dinner with her family. She and Richard have learned to plan ahead to avoid unnecessary conflicts with their daughter. Their growing knowledge of her strong personality has helped them rearrange some of their family habits and customs in ways that ease stress at home. "Would you like a roll, Amy?" Maggie asks her daughter as the family passes around the bread basket. "Yes, please,"

Amy replies—polite as ever. Her father hands the basket to her, and Amy carefully chooses one for herself. This time the rolls have been buttered ahead of time. After Amy tears her roll open and takes a big bite, she passes the basket to her brother. "Here," she says. Maggie and Richard exchange an amused glance. Amy is just as passionate a little girl as she always was, but at least her passion is being directed in a positive way toward her dinner and not wasted in a tearful outburst.

Parenting a two-year-old is all about respecting a toddler's need to control her environment while leading her toward new experiences as she is ready for them. It's not easy to know when your child needs a gentle nudge and when it's time to step back. By observing your unique child—learning the signals she gives when she's beginning to feel overwhelmed, noticing when she's bored or restless, gauging her level of development from her day-to-day behavior—you can support her growth in positive, stimulating, nurturing ways. As you read in the chapters that follow more about how toddlers grow, compare the information I give you with your experience with your own child. How is your toddler different from the portraits I provide? How is she the same? Keep in mind that no child will exactly follow any blueprint put forth in books, including the developmental timetables in the following chapters, which are intended not as a "test" but as a rough guide. It is, after all, the vast inconsistencies in the ways children grow that keep them fascinating. Resist the temptation to push your child to perform every skill described in these pages, but use the information to inspire you to better observe and act on her behavior and to appreciate the fact that your toddler is different from all others. The seeds planted during her earlier years are about to blossom in your child. This is not the time to judge but to open your eyes and see.

KEEP IN MIND . . .

Parenting Concepts for the Third Year

In the rush, chaos, and onslaught of unexpected challenges that fill the lives of families with two-year-olds, it's easy to lose sight of the parenting goals you've created or the new approaches you've been meaning to try. Here you'll find a few general pointers to keep in mind as you guide your child through the months ahead. By considering these general guidelines with your partner and your child's other caregivers, you can start to create a working parenting plan, and improve your family's daily experience as a result.

THINK PREVENTION, MINIMIZE FRUSTRATION. Your two-year-old doesn't profit from repeated experiences of failure. Simplify her environment and avoid overwhelming situations so she will have more chances to succeed.

CHOOSE YOUR BATTLES— YOU CAN'T WIN THEM ALL. Make a list of the behaviors you want your child to change, and focus on only the top one or two at a time. Eventually, you will work your way all the way down the list, but don't expect too much too soon.

LET YOUR CHILD MAKE SOME CHOICES, TOO. Your child will be much less prone to tantrums and other acting-out behavior if she feels she has some control over how her day will go.

THINK SAFETY. Two-year-olds can climb higher, run faster, and get into more dangerous places than you think—yet they are not very aware of the physical dangers that surround them. Overestimate your child's physical abilities and underestimate her level of vigilance when looking out for her well-being.

TALK YOUR WAY THROUGH THE DAY. Two-year-olds soak up new words like sponges. Providing your child with new expressions and ideas stimulates her thinking and helps her manage her emotions better as time goes on.

SEE EVERY DAY AS A CHANCE TO LEARN. You don't have to actively teach your child for her to learn. Children learn from helping around the house, playing in their rooms, and chatting with you while riding in the car. Be aware of the potential for expanding your two-year-old's thinking with each new experience or encounter.

PROVIDE "LANDMARKS." Two-year-olds need to know that the people, places, and things with which they're familiar will be around to support them as they venture forth into the unknown world. By providing your child with predictable routines and offering her a favorite toy or your hand to hold in an unfamiliar situation, you will help her work up the courage to experience something new.

THINK "TODDLER": REMEMBER YOUR CHILD'S AGENDA. Just because you're late for work doesn't mean your child feels rushed. Just because you want to eat a restaurant meal in peace doesn't mean your child understands why she must sit down and stop playing with the silverware. Hard as it can be, consider what your child's needs and motivations are before judging her behavior.

FIRST-PERSON SINGULAR

The most effective tool in successfully parenting your child is your own observation of her particular personality and style. Take a moment now to consider what you know about her already. How is her personality expressed in her day-to-day behavior? Is she generally adventurous, sensitive, placid, or fearful? Is she happiest snuggled up with you, roughhousing with her brothers, attempting a new physical feat, or painting pictures or looking at books alone? Which of her behavior patterns do you find most unproductive, and which would you like to encourage this year? At what times or in what circumstances do the two of you fall into frustrating loops of negativity ("You will!" "I won't!") that you would prefer to avoid? By writing down your thoughts, ideas, and observations now, you can compare them to your feelings about your child twelve months hence—and ponder the ways in which your child's temperament, her environment, and your own expectations have brought the entire family through another year of growth.

READER'S NOTES

_____

_____

_____

_____

_____

_____

_____

_____

_____

CHAPTER 2

Jump, Color, and Dance—
My Physical Abilities

Your child is getting wiser in the ways of the physical universe and more realistic about his own limits.

It's Sunday afternoon, and Peter has taken twenty-four-month-old Jesse to the playground while his wife, Diane, catches up on some housework. The weather is warm, and the playground is packed with children. Peter and Jesse have spent many afternoons here before, and after unbuckling Jesse from his stroller Peter automatically leads his son toward the fenced-off section for toddlers. This time, however, Jesse tugs eagerly on his father's hand. "No!" he says, and points to a tall slide nearby. "Go here."

"But, Jesse," Peter replies over the noise of shouting children, "this space is for the big kids. You could get hurt."

Jesse frowns, then snatches his hand away. "I slide!" he crows, racing through the crowd to the slide's long metal ladder. As Peter hurries to catch up, Jesse climbs the ladder like a pro. Peter is impressed and wonders, *Has Diane been taking Jesse to this part of the playground?* Not wanting to "baby" Jesse, Peter hangs back a little as his two-year-old balances at the top of the slide, then swoops down with a happy shout.

Oblivious to a little bump at the bottom, Jesse leaps up and looks around excitedly. "Swing!" he says, running through an open gate to the older kids' swings area.

"Jesse! Wait!" Peter tries to maneuver between the groups of children to reach his son. As he reaches the gate, one of the swings flies just over Jesse's head, barely missing him. "Jesse!" Peter takes a flying leap and yanks him out of harm's way.

Jesse is not grateful for the help. "I swing!" he shrieks, struggling to break free. "Jesse, stop right now," Peter snaps, hanging on tight while he catches his breath. Then he helps Jesse onto one of the swings and, after making sure his son knows how to hang on, starts pushing. *Was I wrong to let him play here?* Peter asks himself as Jesse swings higher and higher. *He seemed so confident on the slide. But I don't think he had any idea that the swing could have hit him in the head. Am I supposed to make him stay in the babies' area, even if he's sick of it?* Glumly, Peter ponders this dilemma and keeps pushing the swing, hardly hearing his son's shrieks of pleasure.

Peter would be relieved to know that, as the months pass, his two-year-old's cognitive growth and experience will gradually temper his reckless behavior. As he continues to experiment with movement in a variety of ways—leaping, dancing, pounding, painting, brushing, splashing, and undressing with great energy and enthusiasm—he will grow steadily wiser in the ways of the physical universe and more realistic about his own limits. An increasing awareness of his surroundings, from flying swings to speeding cars and angry dogs, will help him build a list of reliable safety rules. The parent's job this year, as his two-year-old focuses more on mastering skills than on apprehending danger, is to act as "spotter"—standing by to rescue him when he needs it, helping him learn to adopt safe habits ("Don't go near the swings without a grown-up"), but allowing him to lead the way whenever possible in his journey of physical discovery.

This journey will involve an improvement in not only his gross-motor skills (running, climbing, squatting, spinning, jumping, and even somersaulting) but in the important finer workings of his hands as well. This is a wonderful year to introduce "busy books" that allow him to practice buttoning, zipping, threading, and other fine-motor skills, especially when he is confined to a car seat, stroller, or crib. Paper, crayons, and kids' scissors will create new opportunities for self-satisfaction as he happily "works" at his table, just like Mom or Dad, or "does homework" like an older sibling. In fact, his desire to be just like you and others he admires will motivate much of his physical activity. Similarly, his inability to satisfy that desire (whether he's prevented from doing so or is simply unable to) will lead to angry outbursts and even tantrums. As trying as his shrieks and tears can be, it isn't hard to understand what he's going through. Just think back to how you felt as a teenager when your parents forbade you to stay out as late as your friends (preventing you from imitating those you admired), or, as an adult, when you were learning to use your first computer program (and were frustrated by the difficulty of mastering a new skill). In the end, despite the two-year-old's frequent inability to control his emotions, it's impossible not to salute his sheer will to perfect his skills in the face of all the obstacles that his safety-minded caregivers place in his path.

THE TOY BOX

At Twenty-four Months

It's a holiday, and Annette is enjoying a morning at home with her six-year-old daughter Andrea and Carlos, who's just turned two. She lays out modeling clay, cookie cutters, and a rolling pin on the dining room table. Andrea immediately starts to work, rolling out the green clay and using a tree-shaped cutter to create a "giant forest." Carlos watches in fascination, then reaches for the cutter. "I do it!" he says.

"Andrea's using that one," Annette points out. "Here's a cat-shaped cutter for you, Carlos. We'll roll out the yellow clay. You can make some wildcats for the forest."

Annette helps her son roll out the clay, and for a while this diversion keeps Carlos happy. He grabs the cat-shaped cutter and smashes it down on the clay. "Careful," his mother warns. "Do it gently, like this." Annette tries to show him how to avoid smearing the clay, but Carlos grabs the cutter back. "I do it!" he says. He smashes the cutter down again, smearing it even worse than before. Frustrated, he looks at his sister's orderly collection of clay trees. "Gimme!" he yells, and this time successfully grabs the tree-shaped cutter out of her hand.

"Hey, quit!" Andrea protests, but before she can stop Carlos, he has smashed the cutter down on her forest, squashing her creation. "Mommy, he's ruining everything."

"Okay, okay, Carlos, that's enough." Annette picks Carlos up and removes him physically from the table. *I should have known better than to expect them to enjoy this activity together, she tells herself. Carlos still gets too frustrated when his hands don't work as well as his sister's.* "We'll make a separate place for you to work, okay?" she adds. "I know—you can make a jungle! I'll show you how to make the snakes, okay?"

Scowling, Carlos grudgingly follows her over to his toddler table. He still wants to do what Andrea can do. But snakes are even better than trees—and anyway, he still has the tree-shaped cutter tightly clutched in his little hand.

"LET ME GO!": EARLY MOTOR ACHIEVEMENTS

What a pleasure it is to observe how happy and comfortable your twenty-four-month-old has become with his active, hardworking body. Now that he moves more efficiently and is sturdier on his feet, he has become less preoccupied with each step he takes and can devote more of his attention to the fascinating world around him. At this age, he may walk up and down stairs by himself (although some children still feel more comfortable crawling or sliding down steps), thus gaining access to cabinets and rooms that he hadn't known were there. He may run to keep up with his siblings rather than remain helplessly behind when they race off down the sidewalk. His greater ease with his body has also allowed him to begin developing more nuanced types of movements— from cutting, drawing with a pencil, and playing with clay to riding a Big Wheel, doing a somersault, and dancing to rhythmic music. As a result, his optimism and ambition have increased enormously. He is determined to master new skills—on his own terms and according to his own schedule.

This is a year when it's especially easy to see how your child's physical skills help him learn more about the world around him. Yet his ability to manage his body has profoundly affected his cognitive growth from his very first months of life. From the moment he learned to roll over on his back, he began to choose some of the stimulating sights and human interactions he would encounter. Once he learned to sit up at around six months, he began to grasp every object within reach in order to explore it with all his senses. When he learned to crawl, his learning opportunities increased a thousandfold, and as he began walking at around twelve months, his explorations expanded vertically as well as horizontally. At the same time, the development of his fine-motor skills allowed him to learn new facts about the physical world. By feeding himself with a spoon he learned that "If I move it too fast, it spills."

At age two, a child can sit still long enough to concentrate on her fine-motor skills, such as cutting with child-safe scissors.

Pounding pegs with a hammer taught him that "If I hit it too hard, it falls all the way through the hole." Drawing with chalk or oversize crayons led to the discovery that "If I move my hand this way, the color goes there, too."

The feelings of power and satisfaction these discoveries provide continue to motivate your child to venture farther into the unknown. As we observe later in this chapter, his abilities are likely to improve sooner than you expect, and his urge to experiment physically will be hard for him to resist no matter what the consequences. Your best strategy, then, is to arrange his environment so that he can experience new movements and sensations without getting into too much trouble. On quiet streets, go ahead and let him run down the sidewalk, but stay close enough to take his hand before he reaches the intersection. Encourage him to climb the stepstool to help you hang a picture, but be ready to help him back down. Let him try to "write" a letter to Grandmom, but help him finish it when his hands get tired and he starts to feel overwhelmed. As you bolster his confidence in these small ways, your two-year-old will learn that the world is a manageable and interesting place—and the link between his physical and cognitive skills will strengthen even more.

A PARENT'S STORY

"Cut the Paper, Not the Curtains!"

"I have to admit, I'm one of those moms who watched my son grow older with a certain amount of regret," a colleague told me while observing my own sons at play nearby. "When he was a baby, it was pretty easy to contain him in a limited space or just pick him up when he got too hyper. Once he became a toddler, his activity level really wore me out—especially after he turned two.

"I remember when he first started using kids' scissors. He was two and a half and just got completely obsessed with them. He had a little desk next to our kitchen table, and every morning he would sit and cut up magazines while I puttered around the kitchen. At first I was grateful that he was sitting still for a while. Then I started noticing little slices in the bottom of the kitchen curtains. A few days later, I found some holes in the knees of his sweatpants. Pretty soon I figured out that practically every time I turned my back, Mike started cutting up everything in sight. Back when he was one, I could have just taken the scissors away and distracted him, knowing he'd forget about them pretty soon. Now he wouldn't forget, and he wouldn't surrender control so easily. He and I had to figure out some compromise.

"The next time I caught him cutting the curtains, I sat him on my lap to talk about it. I realized that he had this urge to practice his cutting skills. On the other hand, I 'needed' for him to stick to cutting paper. We decided to go to the art store at the mall and see if we could find something that would make us both happy. As it turned out, they had some kids' scissors designed to cut only paper—nothing else! Mike loved them, and walked out happy as could be. I was relieved to find a way to limit his behavior without squelching his energy."

"LET ME TRY!": MOVING FORWARD AT AGE TWO

If one word can describe a typical two-year-old, that word is indisputably "active." Your child will be constantly on the move this year and will insist on directing much of his own physical experimentation and activity. As the first months pass, he will begin to pride himself on his ability (or, at least, his attempts) to take off and perhaps even put on some of his clothes, build a tower of blocks, wash and dry his hands, and brush his teeth (with your help). He'll also learn to coordinate the movements of his wrists, fingers, and palms, enabling him to unscrew lids, turn knobs, and unwrap paper as well as draw and cut. Clearly, his increasingly active and experimental nature will keep you very busy and may even become overwhelming at times. As always, the best way to cope with your eager little experimenter is to plan ahead—by putting a mat on the playroom floor for leaping and somersaulting, placing interesting containers full of harmless items in cabinets within his reach (while moving potentially dangerous items higher up), and using a gate to keep him out of non-child-proofed rooms.

As he approaches age two and a half, your child will express his joy in movement through gleeful "catch me" games and, like Jesse, swinging and sliding sessions on the playground. He may enjoy learning to pedal a small tricycle at this time. He will experiment with walking on tiptoe and standing on one foot—though, interestingly, jumping in place will still take great effort and coordination. At around his third birthday, he'll probably grow more interested in drawing with chalk and crayons and can begin learning to hold a marker in the writing position. He may enjoy imitating your vertical and horizontal strokes on a piece of paper, completing simple puzzles with your help, and using plastic kids' scissors with your supervision.

By the end of the year, your child will have graduated from his uncertain toddling to the more assured gait of early childhood—and his physical confidence will increase accordingly. After months of trying out all kinds of movement variations, such as galloping and trotting, and multiple actions, such as throwing a ball while running or eating ice cream while walking, he will come to a new, deeply fulfilling understanding of how his body works. To his great satisfaction, he can now kick a ball where he wants it to go, hit a baseball if it's placed on a tee, imitate a note on the piano, and steer his tricycle around a neighborhood filled with fascinating new people, places, and ideas. Thanks largely to your support and encouragement, he can look forward to a future full of exciting sports, enjoyable games, and one-of-a-kind arts-and-crafts creations.

IF YOU'RE CONCERNED

A Different Drummer

Young children's physical accomplishments are often readily visible to adults. Unfortunately, one often gives in to the temptation to compare one child's progress with another's, so your two-year-old's level of activity may cause you some anxiety this year. Whether your child strikes you as much more active than others his age (so that you wonder if he's hyperactive) or seems disturbingly sedentary and quiet (causing you to worry that he's not developing on schedule), take his natural temperament into account before judging him in this area. As two-year-olds grow, their physical natures assert themselves more and more clearly. For example, your very active child may be overstimulated by crowds and responds to a busy playground by running around shrieking or dumping a pile of sand on another child's head. (If this is the case, it's best to remain near him much of the time, perhaps keeping a soothing hand on his shoulder and moving him to a less stimulating area when he seems overwhelmed or likely to hurt another child.) Or, your generally passive two-year-old may just have a calm, observant nature. If he seems content to sit and watch rather than frustrated by an inability to master a task, he is probably fine. (He could benefit, however, when you bring activities to him and encourage him to join in sometimes. That way, his laissez-faire attitude doesn't keep him from tackling new skills.)

Keep in mind that normal activity levels can often seesaw wildly this year. (Just as we sometimes throw ourselves too enthusiastically into a new exercise routine and suffer aches and pains the next day, a two-year-old may overextend himself one day and feel cranky and exhausted the next.) It is also important to remember that young children pass through many phases, physical and otherwise, before their personalities finally gel. Your very active or rather passive child may behave completely differently three months from now. When observing him, be sure to consider his behavior over the course of many months, or even a year. Don't "type" him too soon, because he will certainly pick up on your judgment. Rather than matching your physical style or expectations, focus on working at a pace closer to his.

If you are truly concerned about his activity level, poll your neighbors, relatives, or other adults who know him for their opinions. Have they also wondered whether something is wrong? If they agree with your sense that your child is not developing normally, talk with his pediatrician before he turns three. A child who is properly assessed before his third birthday can be admitted into an early intervention program and thus has a better chance to profit from corrective therapy.

PRACTICE MAKES PERFECT: REFINING MOVEMENT SKILLS

"Russell, stop taking your shoes off," a weary parent scolded her two-year-old in his stroller as they ate lunch in the food court of a crowded mall. "I said stop," she repeated as he pulled off the other shoe just as she was tying the first one back on. Finally, at her wit's end, she snatched both shoes off the floor where her son had dropped them and stuffed them into the stroller basket. "Fine, then," she muttered, bundling up their food and throwing it in the trash. "If you can't keep your shoes on, we'll just go home. You can stay barefoot all day in your room for all I care."

As his mother marched off with him toward the exit, Russell twisted around in his stroller to give her a puzzled "What did I do?" look. It was obvious to anyone—even to his mother, no doubt, if she had stopped to consider the situation—that Russell hadn't meant to provoke. He had simply felt compelled to practice taking off his shoes, and his fascination with the resulting physical sensations overrode his less urgent need to attend to what she was saying. It is a simple fact of parenting that watching your child *acquire* such skills as crawling or walking is typically very exciting, but standing by as he *perfects* them—fine-tuning the muscles through constant imitation, experimentation, and repetition—can drive even the most patient caregiver up a wall. Your child is not only likely to remove a given item of clothing repeatedly once he learns how but may also learn to love opening and closing the refrigerator door even after you've asked him not to, and jumping off the next-to-last step of the staircase despite the many times you've told him it isn't safe. Despite appearances, however, he isn't flouting your rules out of anger or defiance in any of these cases. He's simply responding to the same kinds of developmental urges that once commanded him to pull himself to his feet and start to walk.

Constantly curtailing your child's experiments with movement prevents him from developing coordination and other motor skills he needs to work on. It is also likely to end in shrieks of protest, futile struggles, and mutual misunderstandings that can establish a negative pattern for years to come. Still, the fact remains that children must keep their clothes on (at least sometimes), refrigerator doors must stay closed, and little ankles must not get sprained. One of your greatest parenting challenges this year is to find a viable compromise between your child's need to practice a variety of movements (even apparently nonproductive ones) and your need to limit his activity level or at least redirect his energy.

One way to meet this challenge is to plan ahead for your two-year-old's need to move. By installing a swing set in the backyard, making sure he has access to age-appropriate play equipment at a public playground or park, and taking him for romps in outdoor areas free of cars, you allow him to try out his muscles in a wide variety of new and exciting ways. It's also a good idea, when possible, to set up one or more areas inside the house where your child can jump, roll, and climb. Certain chairs and sofas might serve as designated climbing areas. Cushions, a carpet, or a mat on the floor can prevent some bumps and bruises when you aren't there to spot him. A large cardboard box makes a fine tunnel or house. Elsewhere, a small table and chair just his size can provide a suitable place for him to practice such fine-motor skills as cutting, painting, and drawing. It isn't necessary to provide expensive equipment; a sheet of paper taped to a tabletop works as well as an easel, and old magazines are perfect for cutting. Maintain the thrill of novelty by rotating these objects now and then, or introducing an occasional new find. Music provides another kind of variety because it helps your child learn to move to the beat, explore his body through leaping, bouncing, jumping, and spinning, and experience the pleasure of singing along.

You can help your child move creatively during everyday activities as well. By assigning him regular chores, such as watering a plant or putting his empty cup in the sink, you introduce him to the satisfying experience of familiar, oft-repeated movements. He can develop new motor skills by helping you in your own work, too—tearing up lettuce leaves for a salad, pushing the "start" button on the dishwasher, using his toy broom to help you sweep, digging in his own flowerpot-sized garden while you transplant some shrubs, and even "organizing" a variety of important-looking objects you've loaned him from your desk. Participating in these grown-up activities will fill your child with pride even as they help him develop his motor skills.

Encouraging your child to use his body in as many ways as possible may not only cut down on less productive activity but also stabilize his sleep rhythms. Particularly when his sleep routine is in flux, physical activity can help him use up excess energy that would otherwise prevent him from falling asleep. (Of course, it's also important to watch out for times when he risks getting overtired and becomes unable to sleep for that reason.) Though it's true that even a well-exercised child may repeatedly pull off all his clothes, open and shut the dresser drawers, and resist bedtime, these activities are likely to become shorter-lived and less frequent as he finds more interesting ways to move.

Meanwhile, the key to weathering this type of activity is, again, to plan ahead for the kinds of situations you know are likely to happen. If your child hates being buckled into a car seat, be sure you bring along a tape of children's songs when it's time to do errands so he can at least exercise his lungs and kick his legs to the beat. If you know he is likely to climb the furniture during a visit to a friend's house or perform chemistry experiments with the condiments at a restaurant, don't forget to pack an activity book or paper, crayons, and stickers to keep him occupied. (Better yet, frequent restaurants that cater to kids—providing crackers to munch on and plastic cups with lids.) Some activities, such as Russell's shoe-removal experiment at the mall, are probably better off simply tolerated or ignored. By tossing the shoes in the stroller basket and letting her son just wear his socks, Russell's mom could have finished her lunch in peace. Likewise, a two-year-old who eases his boredom by repeatedly squatting and jumping up, squatting and jumping up while in line at the bank with Mom, is dealing with confinement as best he can—despite the disapproving looks of the adults around him.

Throughout this year, it's important to remember that your child does not yet know how to regulate his own activity level—he is not necessarily able to slow down when he is exhausted or when he sees that you are losing patience. Just as you "spot" him on the playground to protect him from harm, it's important to guard him from excesses in activity level as well—setting healthy limits and helping him channel his energy in ways that are productive, tolerable, and fun.

EASING THE WAY

Coping with Your Own Physical Limits

Given the fact that your two-year-old will need to keep moving in all kinds of ways, it's wise to consider your own level of energy and tolerance and to think of ways to cope during those times when you feel worn out. The good news this year is that your child is finally fully able to understand your words when you tell him to "stop that right now." The bad news is that he is still frequently *unable* to make himself stop on command, since brain and body don't always work effortlessly together at this age. The confusion caused by this apparent paradox is one of the reasons why two-year-olds tend to suffer abuse at the hands of their caregivers more than infants or older children. For this reason if no other, anticipating your own limitations is just as important as accommodating your child's.

If you know you simply do not have the patience or energy to put up with a two-year-old's energy all day (and few people do), think now about introducing a few pinch hitters—by turning your child over to your partner at appointed times, arranging for play dates or playground sessions where he can expend his energy on his peers, or finding enough quality child care to allow you to recharge. If caregiving relief is not an option for you, consider the ways in which you could structure and pace your day with your two-year-old so that the two of you reach your breaking points less often. Take care not to plan too many errands for a day when you're together. Call up a friend for a grown-up chat and a chance to blow off steam. On those occasions when you're simply exhausted and your child isn't, put him in a bubble bath and take a break nearby with a magazine.

Interestingly, many parents find that the strain of their two-year-old's activity level affects them emotionally more than physically. All that movement leaves little opportunity for the cuddling that felt so good in the past. If you feel this way, make sure you take advantage of the quiet moments to get the hugs and kisses quotient you need while your child is open to the idea, or indulge in gentle tickle games instead. After all, you are only human. If a sign of affection from your child can help you cope with his more typical "running-away" behavior later, it's important for you to have it.

ON THE RUN: KEEPING YOUR CHILD SAFE

"I had to take Jay to the emergency room again," Rebecca, a former client, told me when I asked her how her weekend had gone. "This time he tried to jump to the bottom of an escalator. Four stitches in his forehead." I could hear the dejection in Rebecca's voice, and no wonder. Just two months before, Jay had cut his leg badly while trying to climb a wrought-iron gate, requiring several stitches in his shin. "People must think I'm a terrible parent," Rebecca said in a low voice. "I try to watch him. He's just so active, I feel like I spend all my time running after him, yelling, 'Watch out!'"

Though it was true that Jay was an unusually active, adventurous toddler, nearly all two-year-olds prefer to be constantly on the move. Their eagerness to practice new skills—along with their ability to acquire these skills very quickly—often leaves parents a bit behind the curve, struggling to keep abreast of their child's latest achievements. Even your toddler's physical growth can catch you unawares this year. Many a two-year-old has quietly grown past the maximum weight requirement for his car seat (and perhaps also loosened the straps dangerously after months of squirming and tampering) without his par-

Since two-year-olds are more mobile and daring, parents need to be ever alert to potential dangers.

ents' knowledge. It's amazing how quickly your child can gain access to an out-of-reach cabinet or an upper-story windowsill. The danger potential is only increased by the fact that, at age two, children don't always pay attention to speeding cars, bicycles, dogs, and other hazards that you routinely avoid. Shouting "Look where you're going!" won't immediately improve this situation. Research has shown that children under age four are generally *unable* to screen out distracting stimuli or to direct their attention in an efficient way. Your child can sharpen his awareness only with time and experience.

Your child's safety is also threatened by the fact that new abilities are not always as obvious as they were the previous year. It's much easier to note that your toddler can crawl up a flight of stairs than that he has figured out how to twist the top off a bottle of cleanser. That is why it's important this year, more than ever, to *overestimate* your child's physical abilities and *underestimate* his level of experience and cognitive growth when safeguarding his environment. Even though your child hasn't yet shown much interest in jumping huge distances, for instance, and seems to acknowledge your commands to "stay with Mommy," it's still important to make sure you have a firm grip on his hand as you step onto an escalator. Even though he can't yet reach the knife drawer and has heard you warn him never to touch the knives, place them even farther out of his reach this year. He knows how to stand on tiptoe now, and he'll soon figure out how to move the stepstool. Even if he has never choked on his food, you will want to cut grapes in fourths and avoid giving him raw carrots, popcorn, hot dogs, lollipops, hard candies, and nuts. Though he has never tried to climb out of his car seat and now insists on buckling himself in, make sure you check to see that the buckle is properly closed. You never know when he will decide to start trying to climb into the front seat, and his ability to close a buckle isn't foolproof.

All in all, it is better for everyone if safety is considered ahead of time and becomes simply a part of family policy, rather than something you have to make a pronouncement about as each new situation arises. If a two-year-old is consistently told that he can't touch the iron because "that's the rule," he's less likely to try to grab it every time you start to iron your clothes (especially if you assign him an important job, such as separating the shirts to be ironed from the rest of the laundry). If your "no-candy-with-nuts" policy has been long in place owing to the danger of choking, he's used to candy without nuts and will be more likely to avoid it at friends' houses and elsewhere. Assessing your child's energy level should also become part of your family's safety routine. Note when he is becoming too exhausted to control his impulses, and point this out to him in understandable ways ("Okay, Geoffrey, you look beat. That's enough playing tag for now"). Suggest ways for him to change his pace before an accident happens ("Let's take a break. What book should we read?"). As time passes, your child will gradually learn to monitor his own activity level, becoming more vigilant and less "accident-prone."

A CHILD'S-EYE VIEW

Kickball

Ball! Two-year-old Mick spots his favorite red kickball in the corner of his room. He picks it up, enjoying the feel of it filling the space between his arms. *Roll.* He remembers how Daddy rolled it to him when they were "playing soccer" last week. He drops the ball now and throws his body on top of it. It rolls back and forth a little under his tummy. He giggles.

"Daaaaaddy!" Mick picks up the ball and wanders out of his bedroom, looking for someone to play with. There's the sound of a television downstairs, but otherwise the house is silent. Mick goes to the top of the stairs and peers down. He looks at the ball in his hands. He looks at the stairs. *Roll down the stairs?* he wonders. Laboriously, he climbs down the first couple of steps, then places the ball on a step and gets ready to jump over it.

"Mick!" Daddy has appeared at the bottom of the stairs. "I told you not to play with the ball on the stairs!" He leaps up the stairs and grabs the ball, catching Mick just before he topples backward toward the floor. "We never, *ever* do that," his dad tells him firmly. "We play with balls only outside or on the flat floor."

Mick stares at his dad, stunned. *He took my ball away!* he thinks. A feeling of outrage overwhelms him. He starts to cry.

"It's okay," his dad tells him patiently. "I know you don't like it, but that's the rule. Come on outside. I'll show you how to kick the ball to me, and I'll kick it back."

Kick the ball. Mick looks outside. He looks at the ball. Making the connection, he remembers what fun he had last time playing ball with Dad. Still whimpering, he follows his dad outside. "Gimme the ball!" he yells. "I kick it!"

"THIS IS ME": GETTING TO KNOW THE BODY

It's a fact that every two-year-old loves his body—not just the many new ways it can help him get where he wants to go, but its textures, shapes, smells, and amazing, apparently infinite variety of sensations. This is an age when it's a burden to put up with layers of clothing that chafe sensitive skin, weigh down limbs that long to move freely, and muffle contact with the outside world. You are quite likely to find yourself devising all kinds of ways to convince your two-year-old to keep his diaper on, let you help him with his coat, put him in his bath, and take him out again. The upside of this extreme body consciousness is the joy of watching your child glory in his physicality—admiring his reflection in the mirror, shrieking with pleasure as he runs naked around the house, and gently caressing the different surfaces of his face, his hair, his tummy, and his feet.

Of course, the two-year-old's passionate exploration of what he has only recently come to understand is his separate, inviolable self also includes his genitals. If he hasn't already done so, he will no doubt soon discover that this area is not only intriguing to look at but fun to touch. This is a year when most children indulge at least occasionally in self-stimulation. They talk and even brag about their penis or vagina and become curious about what others' "private parts" look like. Though curiosity about the body is perfectly normal, it's also true that frequent self-exploration makes others uncomfortable and may eventually get in the way of your child's relationships. For these reasons, it's a good idea to de-emphasize such behavior, gently diverting your child's attention without making him feel overly inhibited or ashamed. (Remember that a dramatic response will only encourage him to test your reactions again.) Talk with him about the concept of privacy and the value of engaging in certain acts only when alone. If he seems unable to stop his self-stimulation, or if it continues at a very high level for many months, discuss the issue with your child's pediatrician. But if his interest is in the normal range, remember that his fascination with his body can lead to productive—or at least preparatory—discussions about how our bodies work, the differences between boys and girls, and the advantages of using the potty.

Q & A

"Stop That!"

Q: My two-year-old, Emma, has gotten into the habit of sticking her hand down her pants whenever she's just standing around. I've asked her to stop it, but she tells me, "It's warm down there," and, "It feels good." She seems to do it as unconsciously as other kids suck their thumb. Obviously, it's especially embarrassing for me when we're out in public. Is there any way I can get her to break this habit without making her feel ashamed of her body?

A: Unfortunately, when a habit is as frequent and unconscious as this one is, it can be difficult to break. However, your child does not seem emotionally obsessed by her private parts and in fact doesn't even seem to think about what she's doing very often. The more upset you act about this issue, the worse it will get. If she realizes that she can get your undivided attention by performing this act, she will do it more often and more aggressively. By talking to her casually—both when she's performing the act and when she isn't—about the need to keep "private parts" private ("Do you want to be by yourself?"), and quickly but calmly removing her hand when she does begin to touch herself ("Emma, where should your hand be?"), you will keep the focus on the habit and not its emotional dimension. Eventually, as she realizes that she wins your positive attention more easily when she's not engaged in this awkward habit, she will start to do it less often. Even without your help, she will probably outgrow it soon enough. Meanwhile, remind yourself that it is the rare two-year-old who does not experiment with this behavior, and that the time is approaching when she will become more interested in adapting to society's rules.

"I CAN DO IT, TOO!": LEARNING TO MOVE WITH OTHERS

Two-year-olds not only take great satisfaction in learning to control their bodies but also delight in an expanded array of experiences as their movement carries them out into the larger world. Their new ability to leap, climb, and dance and their increasing familiarity with creative pursuits such as cutting and drawing open the way to pleasurable social interaction with other children their age. This is a good year to begin encouraging friendships on the playground or in the neighborhood and teaching your child simple indoor and outdoor activities that are fun to do with other kids. (These include turn-taking games such as "Go Fish," matching games like "Concentration," ball-tossing games, bowling sets, and so on.) You might even consider enrolling your child in an early-childhood gymnastics, music, or other movement-related class. Much of the time, younger two-year-olds still resemble bumper cars as they move about a room, engaging in parallel play but not really interacting much. Still, as the year unfolds, your child will benefit from the opportunity to imitate and experiment with motor skills he sees other children engaged in.

Another advantage of moving with others is that it helps to make those movements conscious—to link the *idea* of a physical act in your child's mind with the way it *feels* as he makes it. This link can be strengthened by asking your child to watch other children or adults accomplish a movement and then mimic them, or by describing a movement as your child does it. Many movement-oriented songs and games aimed at toddlers and preschoolers ("Head and Shoulders, Knees and Toes," "The Hokey-Pokey") accomplish this task, as do adults when they comment on a child's performance ("Look at you twirling around!") and early-childhood movement instructors as they work with preschoolers ("Jump high on the trampoline! Jump high, David!"). Two-year-olds frequently initiate this process themselves, in fact, narrating their own actions throughout the day ("I jump this big"). This process of linking a movement with the mental picture of it and the verbal expression—of connecting mind and body—leads to better coordination and physical confidence and is a vital part of growing up.

Q & A

What a Bully!

Q: My two-and-a-half-year-old is big for his age. When he's put with a group of kids, he usually ends up playing with children older than himself, since he appears to be their age. Lots of times this leaves him trying to take part in activities that he's too young to tackle, like T-ball or tag. When I put him back with the littler kids, however, he tends to bump into them a lot and accidentally get in their way. The other day I heard a little girl call him a bully when he pushed past her in the sandbox. What should I do?

A: Your child doesn't sound like a bully, from your description. He just sounds big. It's important to realize that his larger size can make coordination tougher. He needs plenty of opportunities to imitate others, to play in active, even boisterous ways, and to run freely without the danger of hurting others. To ease his frustration when trying to imitate children who are older than he but the same size, look for activities that are similar to "big-kid" pursuits but easier to manage, such as a plastic Big Wheel instead of a tricycle, or a soccer ball instead of a baseball. (Keep in mind, however, that there will be times when he'll want to do only the big-kid activity.) To help him in his relations with physically smaller peers, try to arrange some play experiences for your son with children who have younger siblings. By pointing out ways in which the older child helps or avoids hurting his sibling, you can introduce your son to the idea of watching out for others. Finally, when he is playing with smaller children, stay nearby to help him play without hurting them. Remind him that "these kids are smaller than you." The reality is that, being only two, he won't always be able to keep others' needs in mind. (If you're worried about other parents labeling him, you might remind them that he's just a two-year-old.) Because of his age, some of the responsibility for watching out for others is still yours.

"WATCH ME, DAD!": LEARNING TO MANEUVER IN A BIG KIDS' WORLD

It's hard to believe a year has passed, but Jesse is now three, and Peter, his dad, can certainly see the difference in the way he looks and moves. Though he hasn't grown much taller over the past twelve months, Jesse has developed much more confidence in his movement. His posture is better, he begins an action with less hesitation, and he can easily alter his direction or movement midcourse. He moves better with other kids, too, Peter notices. Exchanges with his peers are less awkward now and more like the interactions of later childhood. In fact, Peter realizes with a start (and a certain amount of wistfulness), Jesse is a "big kid" now—like the children who so outpaced him last year with their shouting and constant movement on the playground.

Peter never takes Jesse to the babies' area now. Instead, he follows Jesse as he pedals his tricycle to the larger area and carefully parks the trike next to a park bench. Usually, Peter sits on the bench and watches his son plunge into the chaos of activity, enjoying the sight of Jesse making contact with others and joining in their games. Today Jesse is mostly interested in swinging from the climbing bars, and he has managed to convince an older girl to lift him up so he can reach them. Suddenly, however, the glint of sunlight on a swing catches his eye, and in an instant he has dropped from the bars and raced toward the big kids' swings area.

"Jesse!" Peter is on his feet in an instant—much more experienced now about which equipment poses a danger for his child. As he moves toward Jesse, he sees his son hesitate at the entrance to the swings. Jesse's face takes on a serious look—and Peter almost has to laugh, it's so obvious that Jesse is mentally reviewing the rule about the swings: Never go in the swings area alone.

Almost in spite of himself, Jesse slows his pace, looks around for his father, and waits for him to take his hand. Peter joins him, relieved to know that his child has learned to some degree to be more cautious. "Want me to push you, kid?" Peter asks as Jesse leads him in a wide arc around the row of flying swings toward an empty one at the end. This time Peter won't be the parent racing to rescue his child from danger. Jesse has become an active, if still junior, partner in the effort to take care of himself.

ADVANCES

Fine- and Gross-Motor Achievements in the Third Year

Here are a scattering of behaviors that parents often see at these ages. If your child doesn't demonstrate them at the time indicated, don't be alarmed. Think of these as new territory he will probably visit soon.

24 MONTHS	May climb and descend stairs alone
	Much sturdier on feet
	Likes to dance
	Can stack three or more blocks
	May show preference for one hand

27 MONTHS	Loves to run and to play chase
	May pedal a tricycle
	Likes to walk up and down stairs
	Likes to jump off steps, walls, and other surfaces
	May unscrew lids, turn knobs, and unwrap packages
30 MONTHS	Experiments with varied movements such as galloping and hopping
	May be able to kick a ball in an intended direction
	Likes to use chalk and crayons
	May use kids' scissors
33 MONTHS	Capable of throwing a ball, eating an ice cream cone, or otherwise moving while walking
	Begins to walk more like an adult, with heel-to-toe gait
	May alternate feet when climbing stairs
	May be able to hit a baseball off a tee
36 MONTHS	Can easily ride a tricycle on his own
	Can complete a simple puzzle
	Imitates vertical and horizontal strokes on paper

FIRST-PERSON SINGULAR

Now while the issues of your child's third year of motor development are fresh in your mind, take some notes about his latest advances in learning to manage his body, ensure his own safety, and interact physically with his peers. What new skills is he developing? How is he refining the skills he already has? What is his physical style—adventurous and risk-taking, quiet and hesitant, methodical and determined? How are his physical experiences different from those described in this chapter? How are they the same?

If you have a photograph or videotape of your child at age eighteen months or so, look at it and write down some of the ways in which his physicality differs now. If possible, videotape him now—on the playground, in the backyard, with other children—so you can monitor his changes next year. These observations of your unique, actively growing child are one of your most valuable tools in getting to know him as an individual—and in helping you more effectively discern his needs, uncover any difficulties as early as possible, and lead him toward greater growth.

READER'S NOTES

_____

_____

_____

_____

_____

_____

_____

_____

_____

_____

_____

_____

_____

_____

_____

_____

_____

_____

_____

_____

_____

_____

_____

CHAPTER 3

Creating a World—My Cognitive Development

I t is often difficult for parents of two-year-olds to know when their children are "winging it" and when they truly understand what is going on around them.

Christmas has always been Deborah's favorite holiday, and she can hardly wait to experience it this year with Kaisha, her two-year-old daughter. Born in early December, Kaisha slept through most of her first Christmas Day. The next year, at age one, she still wasn't really aware of what was happening. Kaisha's speaking ability and general comprehension have now advanced so astoundingly, however, that Deborah is sure her daughter will understand the idea of Santa coming down the chimney and leaving wonderful gifts for her. In fact, Kaisha does pick up quickly on Deborah's excitement about the coming event. On weekends, when Deborah takes her daughter shopping for gifts, she explains the concept of gift-giving and informs Kaisha that she, too, will receive gifts from her family and from Santa. Later, in the evenings, as they wrap the gifts together, Deborah asks her daughter, "Who's coming on Christmas?" and Kaisha answers with an excited "Santa!" The closer they get to the holiday, the more Deborah talks about the "big day" to her daughter, and the more Kaisha mentions it in turn. At bedtime, when Deborah tells her how Santa will arrive in a sled with all his reindeer, bringing gifts for good little boys and girls, Kaisha squirms with glee.

Finally, Christmas morning arrives. Despite a late night spent putting together the tricycle and other treats that Santa has brought for Kaisha, Deborah is up early with video camera at hand, ready to capture Kaisha's expression on tape as she discovers the gifts under the tree. When Kaisha awakens, her grandmother lifts her out of her crib and lets her walk ahead to the living room for her grand entrance. Right on cue, Kaisha stumbles into the room, rubbing the sleep from her eyes, cute as a bug in her flannel pajamas. Deborah watches through the camera lens as her daughter surveys the shiny new toys surrounding the Christmas tree. She looks up at her mother with a puzzled expression. "Where Santa?" she asks.

It is often very difficult for the parents of two-year-olds to know when their children are "winging it"—trying to maneuver their way through their days through imitation, repetition, and sheer improvisation—and when they truly understand what is going on around them. At twenty-four months, Kaisha is able to mimic her mother's words ("Santa's coming!"). She can hold in her memory the sight of Santa sitting in the mall surrounded by gifts, and she can even connect that memory with the sight of gifts under the tree at home in a rudimentary way. But because her brain is still in the process of developing and growing, she has yet to make the cognitive leap beyond observation and imitation to true understanding. She isn't quite able to hold the Santa "storyline" in her mind in its entire sequence—to connect the separate facts into a logical whole.

Your child takes that leap, to a large degree, in this exciting third year of life as she moves from a one-year-old's first grappling with the concepts of language and symbolic thought to a more sophisticated ability to imagine, consider, and express herself in words and in play. The renowned child development theorist Jean Piaget described this change as exiting the *sensorimotor* stage, in which learning occurs through direct interaction with objects (banging two cups together makes a noise), and entering the *preoperational* phase, in which more complicated mental connections are made (the small cup fits inside the big one, but not vice versa). As your child learns to think in words and to connect one idea to another, she will begin to notice and think more about what's going on in her environment—from the conversations others are having about her to the fluctuating emotional climate in her family. She will become more fully aware that others don't necessarily know what she knows or see what she sees, and she will begin to adjust her behavior accordingly. A longer attention span and stronger memory will enable her to mull over the facts, feelings, verbal interchanges, and other experiences she has each day and to try to fit them together in a way that makes sense. If the conclusions she reaches are often incorrect (monsters lurk in her bedroom closet, and every adult female is a mommy), the fact that she has created them indicates an exciting growth in imagination and the beginnings of logical thought.

A PARENT'S STORY

Just the Facts

"You always read in parenting books about how important it is to talk to your child at a level they can understand," Beth, a parent and one of my adult college students, pointed out in class the other day. "I thought I was really on top of things when my two-and-a-half-year-old, Annie, started asking me 'who bringed her' to Mommy. I avoided all the technical birds-and-bees-type stuff, since it was over her head, and just told her something like, 'You were in Mommy's tummy, and you grew bigger and bigger till it was time for you to pop out.' She seemed fine with that explanation and even talked about it later when I showed her pictures of myself pregnant with her. But then the other day, when we were having lunch at a restaurant, she saw a pregnant woman walk by and started chattering away about the time when 'you swallowed me and put me in your tummy.'

"I had had no idea she'd misunderstood me that way. But the more I thought about it, the more I realized that it made perfect sense to assume that if she was in my tummy, I must have swallowed her. It just goes to show that you can't assume anything about what little kids understand. Next time she asks a 'big question,' I'll explain it to her in a few different ways."

A WORLD OF NEW IDEAS: NEUROLOGICAL ACHIEVEMENTS IN THE THIRD YEAR

If you are like most parents, one of the first things you did once your child was born was count all her fingers and toes and breathe a sigh of relief once you'd convinced yourself she was born "complete." In fact, however, scientists have been confirming over the years that infants enter this world far from fully formed, at least in the area of cognition. The neurons that make up the brain are loosely wired at birth. Some basic connections have been made through genetic inheritance and environmental stimulation in the womb, but the lion's share of brain development takes place in the three years after the child is born. As has been demonstrated more and more over the past decade, the quality and content of the child's early environment play a huge role in how her intelligence quotient (IQ) and emotional state develop over the long run.

Since birth, your child has been busily processing information in her environment, creating neuronal connections in her brain. At first, that information came to her more or less randomly—her hand happened to pass before her face, and she managed to put it in her mouth. A caregiver appeared and smiled at her, and different neuronal connections were made. Once she was able to sit unsupported at age six to nine months, however, she began to investigate more deliberately—manipulating objects, throwing them, and otherwise actively investigating their properties. Her physical development opened up a dramatic number of learning opportunities. As she learned to stand, walk, and reach higher and farther in her second year, she was able to explore more widely than ever.

By her second birthday, your child was adept at seeking out new stimulation for her still-growing brain. Veteran of countless forays into mysterious cabinets, over challenging furniture, around beckoning street corners, and through intriguing open doorways, she had long since become familiar with such physical concepts as up and down, empty and full, open and closed. Her understanding of sequence, or the passage of time, had also deepened through increased interaction with the world—she had learned to anticipate brief sequences of familiar events (such as bedtime following stories) and even to comprehend your promise that one event (a visit with Grandma) would follow another (a drive in the car).

Now, as she not only stands on her own two feet but runs, climbs, and leaps, and as she begins to use words to demand the experiences she wants and needs, she is ready to take an even more active part in her own education. She can ask questions ("Daddy come?"), test hypotheses ("Nana here?" when the doorbell rings), repeat experiments ("Do it again!"), and seek out new adventures ("Pet doggie, pweeeeze!") without having to be led. This ability to feed her intellect independently of others is quite intoxicating; as this year progresses, she will grow increasingly eager to explore the larger environment outside her home. She will enjoy walks with you, she will love to be set loose in a park or playground, and given enough reassurance that you are there to support her, she will be curious about the new people she meets. As her physical environment and everyday routines grow increasingly familiar, she will gradually become less anxious and fearful when minor changes occur. You will find that she is willing to stray a little farther from your side, and that she's beginning to understand and occasionally accept such concepts as "later" and "soon." Her increased mastery is likely to make child-care leave-takings and other routine separations easier. She will understand more fully that when you drop her off you will return for her, though she is likely to regress when routines are disrupted or her energy is at low ebb. Though she still learns most effectively in a warm, trusting atmosphere from someone she knows and loves, her more relaxed, independent attitude may allow her to begin learning from others outside her family.

By her third birthday, your little one will have traveled a very long distance from her first amazing encounters with the outside world. Her brain is now nearly fully formed physically (though its connections will certainly be reinforced by each new experience). As her learning continues, she will move through her world with ever-greater confidence and skill—and her confidence will in turn enable her to continue reaching out for more knowledge. This year, however, is when the core of her cognitive growth becomes fully formed. As far as we know now, the third year completes the most important successive period of brain development for a young child.

The Learning Game

Veterans of years of schooling, we parents sometimes tend to believe that learning is hard work—even for a two-year-old. In fact, however, young children learn best in natural, joyful interactions with those to whom they feel emotionally close. One of the easiest ways for your child to begin to familiarize herself with such concepts as counting, recognizing letters, and cause and effect—and to learn some of the many elements of social interaction, such as taking turns, sharing, following rules, and learning to win and lose—is by playing games.

Even before age two, your child probably loved such simple games as peekaboo and "This Little Piggy Went to Market." As her ability to imagine expands this year, she may create games with you that help her explore different sequences. Say, for example, that she pretends to whisper a secret to Mom, and Dad happens to respond by laughing loudly. His laughing causes mother and child to crack up, and the pleasure your child takes in this may motivate her to play the "game" again. By whispering to Mom again, she sets in motion the spontaneous "rule" that Dad will laugh. Such improvisational interaction is not only fun but helps your child explore the concepts of taking turns, cause and effect, modulation of voice, and sequence, and no one ever has to mention the word "rules."

More formal games can stimulate the minds of older two-year-olds, too, so keep an eye out for opportunities to try some. Even the simplest board or card games require players to take turns, share the spotlight, and learn how to win and lose gracefully (though, of course, she won't like losing and will have to struggle with her feelings about it). Such games also work well as a bridge between concrete and mental reasoning. (It is easier to understand the idea of "three," for instance, if she moves her marker three spaces on a board.) Your child will need your help in dealing picture cards, spinning the spinner, or matching the dominoes, but these minor challenges won't dim her enthusiasm for learning to negotiate new forms of stimulating play. Meanwhile, you can use her performance as a way of observing her mental progress. It is gratifying to see what great leaps in comprehension your child makes between one session of tic-tac-toe and the next.

"TELL ME A STORY!": THE DEVELOPMENT OF SYMBOLIC INTELLIGENCE

"I love books, and I've been reading to my daughter since before she was born," a neighbor said to me the other day. "When she was a baby, I read board books to her while she chewed the pages. When she got bigger, I let her tear up the pages and draw all over them as long as she'd let me read her another story. Frankly, I didn't care much if she was paying attention. I just liked the closeness of her sitting on my lap.

"But something's changed this past year, since she turned two. Now she actually brings books to me, and she gets mad if I have to stop before the end. It's like she actually wants to know what *happens* in the story. And she cares about the characters. She looks really sad when the kittens' mittens get lost, and scared when Hansel gets locked up by the witch. I wish I knew what happened in that little brain of hers to change her attitude toward stories. It's like she just started to get it all of a sudden. Is it because I read to her so much to begin with, or is it just part of growing up?"

My neighbor was right to be intrigued, and correct in her observation that her child's quality of attention was changing in important ways as she grew older. Nearly every infant loves to sit on her parent's lap and look at a picture book as Mom or Dad reads aloud, but not because she understands what her parent is saying. The ability to hold a sequence of mental images in the mind—to comprehend a story or even think about an object that isn't physically present—is extremely complex and will deepen tremendously this year. As this ability begins to supplement your child's sensory experiences, it will account for much of her mental progress in the future.

The roots of symbolic thinking reach deep into infancy. One of the earliest steps in learning to visualize an object is understanding the concept of *object permanence*—the idea that an object exists even when it is out of sight. As with many other aspects of babies' cognitive development, the age at which children are believed to comprehend object permanence has been repeatedly pushed back (mainly owing to more sophisticated tests devised by child development researchers) and is now believed to be around six months. Before this time, your baby was probably content to be left with a caregiver while you left the room. Once you were gone, her mind was fully occupied with the person who had taken your place. She couldn't really "miss" you because she couldn't picture you—she didn't understand that you continued to exist. Sometime between six months and one year, however, she began to realize that, though you went out the door, you were just on the other side of it, and her howls of frustration communicated her desire to join you.

Another major development in your child's thinking occurred around her first birthday, when she first began to sense that your thoughts were separate from her own, and that the two of you didn't always know what went on in each other's minds. As this awareness took root, she became increasingly curious about your responses to her actions and, in particular, your emotional state. Her experiments in this area—throwing her breakfast on the floor, for instance, to see how you'd react—evidenced her first real attempts to "think" about you as a separate entity; to predict, or picture in her mind what you might do next; and to figure out how she might influence you.

Next, at around eighteen months, great leaps in cognitive, verbal, and emotional development came together to allow her to begin to think in terms of symbols such as words, pictures, and ideas. By furnishing her mental world with spatial and time-related "landmarks,"

Everyday activities such as painting help a two-year-old's developing brain to thrive while she has fun.

she developed the ability to picture the physical layout of a familiar room and to recall and predict a brief sequence of events. These first experiences of connecting ideas in a logical sequence, combined with a steadily lengthening memory, enabled her to plan ahead to some degree, to carry out her plans, to solve simple problems, and to engage in imaginary play. Still, most of her thoughts remained disconnected as she approached her second birthday—they more often resembled a series of still photographs than a continuously flowing movie. Missing the connections between one moment and the next, she could not yet follow a very complex chain of reasoning or hold a continuous storyline in her mind. If you lose your keys, you retrace your steps until you find them, but your eighteen-month-old was not yet able to think in this systematic way. She would look everywhere for the keys (even in places she hadn't been) or look past them when they were right in front of her.

The gradual development of symbolic thinking will continue throughout your child's third year, contributing more depth and shading to her thought processes. As the months pass, she will understand more fully that ideas and words can take the place of concrete experience, both within her own mind and when communicating with others. Child development researcher John Flavell of the University of California at Los Angeles came up with a way to illustrate this change in perspective by showing a toy to young children and then asking them to tell their mothers (who were in an adjoining room) about the toy. Children closer to twenty-four months of age insisted that their mothers come and look at the toy while they described it. Apparently, they believed that their mothers had to see and touch the object to know it was there. Those approaching age three, on the other hand, were comfortable simply telling their mothers about the toy. They knew that she could picture and understand it through their words alone.

Your child's ability to rely less on direct experience and more on symbolic thinking depends on a number of underlying skills, including a decreasing level of *centration*. Centration (as in "concentration") is the tendency to focus on only one aspect of an object or situation—such as the color of a block (but not the shape), or the speed of a car (but not the color). If you and your twenty-four-month-old are playing with blocks on the floor and you ask her for the "yellow circle," she'll hand you the first yellow block she sees. As she moves closer to her third birthday, however, she becomes able to attend to an object long enough to notice more of its qualities. She may start to hand you just any yellow block but will then self-correct—putting down that block and finding the yellow round one. Another sign that she is noticing more aspects of objects is her intense need to correct imperfections in objects. You may *think* she won't notice a ripped page, a missing puzzle piece, or a broken toy—but be prepared to fix them!

Soon your child's awareness will expand to other aspects of her environment. She will notice details—sounds, images, qualities of objects, and small events—that you hardly notice or think about yourself anymore ("Mommy, listen! Airplane!"). Two-year-olds, with their brand-new ability to attend to the world around them, constantly surprise us with such comments as, "I go out through the squeaky door" (at the child-care center), or, "There's Billy! He has a green hat" (if he had one when she saw him last week). Her awareness of such details is a necessary aspect of symbolic thinking.

Another skill that supports symbolic thinking is *spatial representa-*

tion, or the ability to see things in the mind's eye. As experience with objects and people in her environment continues to create and fortify neuronal connections in your child's brain, she will be able to hold and manipulate an image or idea in her mind without relying on physical contact. Clearly, your child can think or talk about an absent object (the block tower she built) or a series of events (yesterday's trip to the ice cream shop) only if she can picture them in her mind. A lengthening attention span supports this ability, and all three skills come together to strengthen your child's memory—resulting in a new ability to reason and maintain longer trains of thought.

As with any skill, the more your child practices thinking symbolically, the better at it she will become. You can help her develop her ability to make mental pictures by using as many visually descriptive words as possible when pointing out an object ("Look at the bright red truck!") or commenting on the pictures in books ("See the big cow? What noise does a big cow make? MOOOO!"). Once your child begins to give you verbal reports of her own, be sure to ask for visual details ("What color was the ball?" "Was the boy big or little?"). By referring frequently to objects that aren't present, and to events after they have been completed, you can stimulate her memory. Review your child's daily routines with her, asking, "I forget—what happens after bathtime?" and help her visualize her local geography with such questions as, "Where are those steps?" Of course, you know that she knows the answer to the question, but asking it lets her practice symbolic thinking and gives her the experience of solving a problem successfully. Such exercises increase the kind of self-confidence that has been shown to lead to long-term success, both in and out of school. Even in preschool, teachers can see a very clear difference between children who have been encouraged to figure things out, solving problems on their own, and children who have not been encouraged in this way. A history of finding things or fixing things for Mommy and Daddy offers not only cognitive benefits, in other words, but emotional ones as well.

As your child approaches her third birthday, she will be able to solve increasingly complex problems, make more elaborate plans, and express herself more fully with words. Her ability to comprehend storylines and to create very short "stories" of her own ("We went to the zoo and saw a big deer! I feeded him") will increase as well. A few well-placed words from you whenever the opportunity arises will help her imagination take fire—enhancing her experience as she begins chatting contentedly with her dolls, building roads for her trucks out of blocks, and solemnly "purchasing" items at her cardboard-box grocery store. The development of her ability to reason and communicate will be a thrill to witness—just one reward for a year of active, involved conversation and play.

THE TOY BOX

At Twenty-six Months

It's snowing today, and David's mom, Frieda, has announced that the wind is too cold to venture outside. She lets him watch a children's TV show while she catches up on the bills, but after fifteen minutes he wanders back to her desk in search of some other distraction. "I know," Frieda says. "Let's look in your toy basket. I'll bet there's stuff in there that we've forgotten all about."

As snow falls outside, Frieda and David go through the toys in the basket that she keeps near her desk. David pulls out a fuzzy puppet. "Look!" he says, as delighted as if the toy were brand-new. "Fwoggy puppet!"

"Right!" Frieda says with a big smile. "That's the puppet Grandma gave you for your birthday, remember?" She puts it on her hand. "Remember how Grandma said, 'Ribbit,' in that creaky voice? She sounded so funny, didn't she?"

David laughs. "Wibbet!" he says, sounding just like Grandma.

His mother smiles and swoops the puppet down toward his face, but David is already digging again in the toy basket. He pulls out a busy book and hurries to undo the buttons on the cloth cover before his mother can help him. "My book," he says with satisfaction.

"Right," Frieda agrees. "Those are pretty buttons, huh? Red and yellow and blue." She turns back to the bills, giving him time to himself, but glances over a few moments later and adds, "Look, one button is round, like Mommy's eyes, one's square, and one is a triangle. All different shapes. What else is in that book?"

As David turns the cloth page and chatters on his own, Frieda returns to her work with satisfaction. Though David's use of words and other symbolic tools is still quite limited, she knows that he understands much more than he can say. In the meantime, she has helped him practice creating images in his mind by stimulating memories, describing objects' visual qualities, and comparing similar objects to one another. Now he's off on his own, elaborating on what he sees in his own developing imagination. *Not bad for a snow day,* she tells herself.

"I TRY NOW!": FROM IMITATION TO SELF-EXPRESSION

From the very first time she smiled, your little one has been a master of the art of imitation. Responding to instinctive urges, she has learned to clap her hands, say her name, feed herself, and walk and talk in much the way that you do. Clearly, she does not imitate just because it's fun. It's also a way to attract positive responses from the people she loves, to enjoy the feeling of "being just like you," to experiment with new, intriguing behaviors (as when she smashes a tower of blocks just after watching another child do so), and to learn and perfect a new skill.

From the beginning, imitation has formed the basis of learning for your child. The process of actually performing an action seems to forge deeper connections in the brain, making it easier for a very young person to recall that connection later. A study of sixteen- to twenty-nine-month-olds by Canadian researcher Leon Kuczynski and his colleagues at the National Institute of Mental Health demonstrated that a major change takes place in this type of imitation during the third year. Younger two-year-olds tend immediately to imitate an action they observe. Children nearer age three do so less often and instead re-create the action on their own a few days later. Clearly, a better memory and an improved ability to visualize actions in their minds support this change.

As your child's capabilities improve, she begins to move away from simple imitation toward *elaborating* on others' actions and her own ideas. You are likely to encounter many examples of this process every day of your two-year-old's life. If the two of you spend the morning making cookies, for example—indulging in little tastes of the cookie dough as you drop it onto the baking sheets—she's likely to elaborate on that experience by rolling out and "tasting" a piece of modeling clay that afternoon. By the middle of the year, she may begin to elaborate on ideas as well. She may respond to a friend's refusal to play by trying one ploy after another to convince him to participate, and if he won't, she may come up with more than one explanation ("Jon-Jon's tired") for his refusal.

Elaboration is a vital step in the two-year-old's process of moving beyond immediate, concrete experience toward more complex thought, and it should be encouraged whenever possible. You can reinforce your child's ability to elaborate by noting when she is beginning to run out of ideas in her play and supplying a new variation or two ("Look! Froggy's sorry he hit your doll. He's giving her a kiss"). The idea is not to *direct* your child's improvisation but to follow and support it, lending a helping hand over the difficult spots. "Post Office" is a good game for encouraging this process. Early this year, you might suggest that your child scribble a pretend letter, then help her fold it, put it in an envelope, and pretend to mail it in a mailbox. As she grows older, your child might prefer to dictate a letter while you write it. (If you always add, "I love you," at the end, she will learn to read the phrase eventually.) By the end of the year, you could start the game with, "Let's write a letter about your new kitty," or, "Let's send Nana a letter so she'll be surprised." Such elaborations help her build on a solid base of earlier knowledge and lead to increasingly higher-level thought.

By the middle of her third year, your child will probably be quite adept at elaborating on previous ideas and playing with new solutions. As a result, she will start to enjoy such problem-solving exercises as taking apart toys and trying to put them together, working simple jigsaw puzzles, and participating in creating daily routines and resolving conflicts between the two of you. Her developing symbolic thinking will also help her move from simple logic toward the beginnings of creativity.

One of the cognitive skills required for this new creativity is the

ability to compare a model of an object to the real thing. Only whe
is possible can a child draw a picture of her dog, for example, or guess
what you are drawing before you finish it. Researcher Judy S. DeLoache
of the University of Illinois has found that this ability to construct models forms quite abruptly, generally between thirty and thirty-six months.
She demonstrated this through a study in which children were asked to
find an object hidden in a room. Once they had done so, they were asked
to find a miniature version of the object in a miniature scale model of the
first room. Very few of the children aged two and a half or younger could
make the connection between the room and the model, but nearly all the
three-year-olds could. Clearly, this new understanding that one thing
can stand for another not only enhances your child's drawing ability but
enables her to think more flexibly, make more complex comparisons, and
solve problems more creatively.

You can observe how your child's symbolic intelligence is expanding by comparing her drawings over a period of several months. As her
ability to work with mental concepts increases, her drawings will
become more symbolic. Between ages one and two, she may like to
scribble but will probably not try to draw a recognizable object (though
she'll label a picture a "cat" or "dog" if you ask her to). By the time she
is approaching her third birthday, however, she may create pictures that
look something like animals or people. Harvard University psychologist Jerome Kagan constructed a study to demonstrate this development. Children were asked to copy the examiner's drawing of a face. At
sixteen months they produced just a scribble, at twenty months a rough
circle, and at age two a better circle. By thirty months, however, most
children attempted to place a few dots or lines inside the circle to represent parts of the face. The ability to "model" reality had asserted itself.

Following your child's progress in learning to solve problems and
create story sequences can teach you a great deal about how far she has
come in her ability to understand and analyze her environment. Not only
is playing with a two-year-old lots of fun, but it offers new ways to share
and compare views about each other and the rest of your world. Drawing
a picture for your child and asking her to identify what it is, mixing colors and commenting on the results, putting together a puzzle, and
exchanging little stories and memories, all encourage her brand-new

feelings of self-awareness, confirm the importance of her opinions, and provide you with insights you might not otherwise have had.

Too Much Video?

Q: My two-and-a-half-year-old has always been strongly attracted to television. She tries to turn it on practically every chance she gets. My brother gave her some computer software for toddlers recently, and now I can hardly get her to stop playing computer games. She's learned quite a few vocabulary words from both TV and the computer, and she can manipulate the computer mouse like a pro. But I wonder if she really benefits from these experiences, or if they might actually impair her development. I worry that sitting around watching TV will keep her from being a creative person later on.

A: If anyone ever doubted that children are born imitators, he has only to watch a two-year-old speak in the exact intonations of the characters in her favorite cartoon show. As two-year-olds' attention spans lengthen, they are able to spend more time actually drinking in every detail of the shows they watch and picking up every nuance of the interactions on the screen. Clearly, the content of these shows is of paramount importance, as is your presence to help interpret what your child sees. Some programs especially designed for children this age may actually stimulate her brain, especially if they reinforce what she's already doing at home (singing the ABCs, talking about sharing). Still, the essential passivity of television viewing renders it clearly inferior to direct, person-to-person interaction.

Educational computer software designed for toddlers is, in my opinion, a more valuable tool than TV or videotapes in helping two-year-olds learn to think symbolically, model reality, and practice their emerging mental skills. The best games allow children to manipulate "objects" or control events in ways that they can't yet manage in real life (completing a puzzle onscreen with a simple click, for example, months before they're able to fit pieces into a three-dimensional frame). Such experiences give children a sense of power and control—a very satisfying experience for any two-year-old. The interactive quality of computers keeps children's brains active. Well-made software adjusts itself to your child's ability, giving her plenty of chances to try again. Many games combine music, words, and visual images that tap into different abilities in the brain. Again, though, it is important to remember that nothing replaces real life in developing creativity, and computer time should be reasonably limited this year.

If you have a computer, think of the time you and your child spend with it as similar to storytime—that is, as a chance to sit close together and focus on the same activity. Make a point of playing the games with your child, talking with her about what she's learning, and drawing parallels from the ideas in the software to experiences in everyday life. Remember, the goal is for your child to have fun while learning, and the best games for this age are ones that don't have right or wrong answers but introduce concepts such as colors, shapes, and numbers, feature familiar objects, and adjust to your child's level of comprehension.

"I'M A DOGGY!": EXPLORING THE IMAGINATION

"I wonder sometimes what I did to make Miya want so badly to be something—anything—other than a little kid," Alisa, one of the members of my mothers-of-twins club, admitted to the rest of us the other day. "It seems like every morning when she wakes up, she's become a different animal or character in her mind, and if I can't guess from her behavior who she is, she won't have anything to do with me! This week, she was a puppy for two days, then Supergirl for most of the third day, and she spent the rest of the time being the horse she rode at the carnival last month. When we go out and people say hello to her, she answers them with barks or neighs or orders to 'Stand back!' Sometimes she's so into her game that she refuses to play with other children unless they play her way. I know preschoolers really get into their imaginations, but frankly I'm starting to wonder if she's going overboard."

As evidenced by the storm of anecdotes that Alisa's comment provoked at our meeting that night, parents often wonder exactly what goes on in the brain of a child who is deeply involved in imaginative play. They may worry, as Alisa did, that a child's desire to pretend means she isn't happy with the real world around her. They may see their two-year-old's interest in creating imaginary conversations as a retreat from the real human beings in her environment. Or they may suspect that their child insists on "being a horsie" as a means of wielding control. In fact, however, while any or all of these possibilities may play a minor role in your child's imaginary play, learning to pretend is a normal and vital step in a two-year-old's development—one that enables her to practice new skills, explore new concepts, and work out her anxieties and other emotions in a safe, productive way.

Even as an infant, your child used play to learn more about her world, moving more or less steadily forward in her explorations. Late in her first year, she considered a rubber ball something to squeeze and throw, and a bottle something to hold and put to her mouth. At age one, she began experimenting with more elaborate ideas—putting objects in contact with one another (a pot and a lid) and, by the end of the year, using toys as though they were real (pushing a toy car along the floor). By her second birthday, she was probably able to invent new and original uses for the objects she came across. She may have pretended to eat a ball as though it were an apple, to wear a cup like a hat, or to treat a plate like a table. *Animism*—her conviction that inanimate objects are alive—manifests itself at about this time. This is the year when you can make her food whimper, "Please eat me," and, wide-eyed, she'll do it. Soon her increasing ability to think symbolically will allow her to create simple metaphors—treating two balls of different sizes as if they were a parent and child—and to follow sequences of pretend actions with some imaginary elements, such as pretending to pour tea into a cup and drinking it. As she gets better at experimenting with a wide variety of "what-ifs," she may well become fascinated with exploring how it feels to "be" a puppy, her baby brother, her doctor, or even you for hours or days at a time. As her third birthday approaches, your child's increasingly complex thinking will allow her to direct scenes in her play rather than just physically interact with her toys. She may put a bottle to a doll's mouth, for example, rather than to her own. By her third birthday, she'll be such an experienced hand at pretend play that she'll be able to switch easily back and forth between imaginary scenarios and real ones. Now that she's a pro at pretending, she can use her imaginary play as a way to engage you in her activity ("You be the doctor, Mommy"), connect to other children, or consciously work out the answers to questions she's been pondering.

A 1994 study by Paul Harris and his colleagues at Oxford University illustrates how far two-year-olds progress in their ability to pretend. In the study, twenty-four-month-old children watched an adult pour pretend tea into a teapot and feed it to a stuffed animal. When the researcher asked what had happened, the children would talk about the animal getting "wet"—demonstrating that they accepted the pretend play as real. If the researchers tried to switch back and forth between the pretend reality and the real one, however (saying, for example, "How can he be wet? There's not really any tea"), the children would become annoyed and walk away. Clearly, holding the fiction and the reality in their heads at the same time was too overwhelming at this age. By thirty-six months, though, the children easily switched back and forth between the two, referring to the animal as real or stuffed, and the teapot as full or empty, depending on the context of the conversation. Unlike the two-year-olds, they were also able to elaborate on their play (saying the animal was sad because it had gotten wet) and to backtrack in the storyline (guessing that the animal had gotten tea poured on it when the researcher said it was wet).

In short, the quality of your child's play will be very different at the end of this year from what it was at the beginning. Yet its purpose remains the same. Whether she is banging a pot with a spoon to see what noise it makes, talking to her stuffed rabbit, or putting on Mommy's shoes to see what it's like to be a mom, your child is using play to expand on her experience—to learn more about her environment, herself, and others than she ever could in the real world. Clearly, this is a healthy and necessary process, best directed by your child herself. Just as you followed her lead when she crept around the house on hands and knees, it's best to follow her lead now in deciding what to use in her imaginary play, offering occasional suggestions to enhance the play she is already engaged in. To this end, make a point of providing an array of toys from which your child can choose. Variety is more important than quantity—she needs something to bang on or thrash about, something to share, and something to challenge the mind, but she doesn't necessarily need to have a dozen of each of these available to her every day. Once she has settled on a particular toy or activity (beads and string, for example), watch her experiment on her own, and when you see her attention start to flag or frustration building up, offer a couple of ideas to keep her imagination flowing ("What a beautiful necklace! Do you think your teddy bear might want to wear it? Look, I think he likes it").

Imaginary play cannot and should not be relegated solely to playtime. Imaginative thought and discussion can be introduced into nearly all the activities that fill your child's day—including chores, drives in the car, visits with relatives, and so on. The more effort you put into stimulating your two-year-old's thinking ("Look at that cloud. It looks like a sailboat"), the more actively and imaginatively she will stimulate her own mind as she grows older—and the more enjoyable she will be to have around.

A CHILD'S-EYE VIEW

"Want Cereal?"

Buttah, cereal, popcorn . . . thirty-month-old Reed solemnly loads a selection of pretend groceries from his cardboard grocery store into his miniature shopping cart. He loves to "go shopping" at the little store he and Mom made together. It's fun to pick out the boxes and cans he recognizes from real life, and loading them into the cart makes him feel important and grown-up.

Today, however, there's a glitch in his usual play scenario. His teenage brother, Steve, sits slumped on the couch watching

TV, oblivious to Reed's vital activity. *Soup . . .* Reed glances over at Steve again. *Why doesn't he watch me?* he wonders. Finally, having finished his shopping, Reed wheels his cart over to his brother and holds up an empty box of cornflakes. "Want cereal?" he asks.

"Huh?" Steve glances quickly at Reed, then back at the television. "Uh, sure," he says without looking at his brother. "Hand it over."

Reed ceremoniously places the box in Steve's hand. But Steve, not paying attention, drops the box. "Uh-oh!" Reed cries. "Cereal spilled!"

Steve glances at his brother and laughs. "That's okay," he says, picking up the box. "It isn't real anyway, right?"

As Steve starts watching TV again, Reed stands rooted in one place, frowning. *Looks like my cereal box,* he thinks. *When my box spills, we say uh-oh. Why won't Steve play with me?* He can't make any sense of his brother's comment. Frustrated, he grabs the cereal box out of Steve's hand, puts it back in the grocery cart, and marches out of the room. *Maybe Mommy will play store,* he tells himself.

IS IT TIME FOR SCHOOL?: LEARNING FROM OTHER CHILDREN

As your child learns to sing the alphabet song, grows curious about simple number concepts, and improves her ability to connect one thought to the next, it becomes easier to think of her as capable of learning much more about the world in which she lives. Though learning to recognize and name letters, write her name, or count beyond ten is not something every child is interested in (or ready for) at this age, there is much she *can* comprehend in the areas of social interaction, emotional self-mastery, rules and routines, the physical properties of objects, and her own physical abilities and limitations. Since imitation plays such a large role in learning under age three, and since children this age particularly enjoy copying their peers, a group education or

Note the incredible focus on this two-year-old's face as he experiments with concepts such as balance and weight.

care situation becomes a more intriguing prospect this year. In fact, an increasing number of parents (33 percent, according to a recent *Newsweek* poll) are deciding to enroll their child in preschool by age three—partly for reasons relating to child care or their jobs, no doubt, but also owing to a wider understanding of the benefits of a stimulating environment early on.

Certainly, a high-quality facility whose staff is well trained in early childhood development can provide a variety of new experiences for your child. She will have the chance to experiment with materials and specially designed equipment too expensive or messy for you to provide at home. Many children welcome the chance to interact regularly with others their age. Others enjoy a closeness with new adults that widens their view of the world. Any group care situation will allow your child to compare children's behavior patterns and adults' caregiving styles to what she has observed at home—giving you the chance to discuss such behaviors with her. She will also gain experience in learning to share, to take turns, and to cooperate—all very difficult skills that can be accomplished only with practice.

Nevertheless, group education is not the best choice for every two-year-old. As in most other aspects of your child's life, it's important to take into account her temperament, her level of security at home, and her readiness to interact socially. Before deciding to introduce her to the larger world outside her front door, observe how well she deals with separation from you and how attentive she is to the other children her age whom she meets now and then. If she still clings to you constantly and prefers to sit on your lap, she probably isn't ready to separate from you yet. Assuming that you are ready to let go of her, take gradual steps to encourage this separation if you can, such as having a teenager baby-sit for a couple of hours in the afternoons. If you have already enrolled her in group care and she is not adjusting at all, there is certainly no harm in removing her. (Just be sure everyone agrees that she's not just having a temporary problem with transition.) Enormous changes take place in two-year-olds' school readiness over the course of a few months. Your child may hate attending her group care center at twenty-four months, but love it by age two and a half. Taking her out of the group care situation until she's ready may circumvent a negative beginning that would stick with her for years to come.

Of course, every two-year-old will cry now and then when Mom or Dad drops her off with another adult, and all two-year-olds are highly self-absorbed. Still, there will come a time when your child's curiosity about others will override her attachment to you, making a group experience appear less threatening and more intriguing. Two is quite young for this transformation to occur, but it *does* occur this year for some children, especially those who have already experienced multiple caregivers. If you feel your child is ready for preschool—or if you truly must leave your child in group care whether or not she's ready—make sure that the class you pick suits her needs as closely as possible. A child who tends toward shyness, has trouble with novelty, or is very sensitive to noise or crowds would be happiest in a class that's small and relatively serene. An active and assertive child would thrive in a setting where there's plenty of time for outdoor play. No matter what type of group care you find for your child, help her begin to adjust to the idea of it before her first day. Start talking about "school" or "play group," read stories set in classrooms, take her to visit her toddler room before her first day, arrange play dates with future classmates if possible, and make plans to linger for the first few mornings until your child feels comfortable.

Once the group program has begun, don't expect your child's good-byes to be consistent at first. Not only do preschoolers respond in very different ways to separating from their parents (just watch as one of your child's fellow students forgets to kiss her mom good-bye and dives right in, while others cling and cry), but each child behaves in a variety of ways over time. Your child may cry each morning for a week and then suddenly have no problem with your leaving. Or she may respond calmly at first, but then fall apart after four weeks. Unless your child's teacher is concerned enough to discuss the issue with you, simply monitor your child's adjustment and take a wait-and-see attitude.

The important thing to keep in mind is that there is no single correct answer to the question of when to keep a child at home and when to enroll her in preschool or group care. The fear of appearing overprotective haunts parents of at-home children, just as anxiety about pushing too hard sometimes overwhelms parents of preschoolers. In the end, the choice is a personal one based on family style, finances, parents' job requirements, and the personality, interests, and needs of the child. As long as your child has plenty to do, to discuss, and to think about, it really doesn't matter whether she's interacting with half a dozen other preschoolers or mostly with you.

IF YOU'RE CONCERNED

Developmental Delays

This year can be a tense one for parents of a child who may be experiencing a delay in cognitive development. It is less reassuring now, if your child has still hardly spoken a word, to assert that "toddlers have their own timetables, and she's concentrating on other skills right now." Additional pressure springs from the fact that the cutoff age for early intervention programs is usually three years. Finally, with fewer pediatric checkups in this third year, your child's doctor is less likely to notice a serious slowing down of cognitive growth.

For these reasons, it is best to err on the side of caution. Though children this age vary widely in the pace at which they acquire language and other cognitive skills (such as an ability to classify types of objects or to follow a simple storyline), consult your pediatrician if your concerns of the previous year continue. Parents are still usually the best judges of whether there is truly a problem. Certainly, if your child demonstrates a marked inability to understand your own speech, to comprehend such simple concepts as up and down and full and empty, a general obliviousness or inattention to her surroundings, or even a lack of joy in her play and learning activities, a checkup now might prevent a great deal more trouble later on.

A SNACK FOR SANTA: MAKING MENTAL CONNECTIONS

Kaisha's third birthday has just passed, and her mother, Deborah, is deep into preparations for Christmas. Once again, she has explained the meaning of the holiday to her daughter, made and wrapped presents with her, and baked dozens of cookies. Kaisha appears as delighted with the tree and the festive atmosphere this year as she was the year before, but Deborah no longer assumes that Kaisha understands what's going on just because she seems to. She finds several different ways to explain that Christmas is all about showing other people how much you love them, and that Santa gives presents to children who share, follow the rules, and are "good" boys and girls.

On Christmas Eve, Deborah, her mother, and Kaisha prepare cookies and milk for Santa to find when he comes down the chimney, and Kaisha dictates a note for Deborah to leave for him as well. The next morning, Deborah is once again ready with the video camera as her daughter is ushered into the living room to survey her gifts. This time Kaisha is as happy and excited as Deborah had hoped. She runs to inspect her new paints and easel but pauses as she passes the plate of cookies they'd left for Santa. "Look, Mama," she says, pointing to the plate. "Santa ate our cookies!" She nods to herself. "We shared."

Deborah is delighted to have the moment on videotape—but even more satisfied to see that her daughter has begun to understand ideas more completely than even a few months ago. Her words, imagination, memory, and ability to make connections between thoughts have all come together to create a whole much greater than its many parts. To a large degree, her basic brain development is now complete, and she stands on the threshold of true childhood.

ADVANCES

Common Cognitive Achievements
in the Second Year

24 MONTHS	May understand general time-related words such as "later" and "soon," but not more specific concepts such as "in ten minutes" or "next Monday"
27 MONTHS	Able to classify objects (a cow is an animal)
	More aware of conversations around her
	May understand concept of counting (one apple, two apples)
	Able to make simple mental associations
30 MONTHS	May sort objects by colors or shapes
	Can follow a storyline
33 MONTHS	Remembers much of what you tell her
	Has trouble distinguishing real from pretend

36 MONTHS   Likes to describe events that have happened or that could happen

Engages in more elaborate imaginary play

May be able to draw a simple face

FIRST-PERSON SINGULAR

Now record your observations of your own child's cognitive development. How does she demonstrate improvements in her memory as the months pass? When does she begin to tell you about events that happened to her recently, or to look forward to what will happen later in the day? What kinds of schemes does she come up with, and how successfully is she able to carry them out? What negotiating tools does she develop as she grows older? Does she prefer to express herself through language, drawing, physical activity, or in some other way? What kinds of stories does she like best? Does she have an imaginary friend or a favorite stuffed animal with which she likes to talk? If so, write down its name and a description. She'll enjoy reading about it when she's older.

CHAPTER 4

"I See'd a Plane!"— My Verbal Abilities

N o matter what your child's level of verbal ability, the number of words he can understand dramatically exceeds the number of words he can say.

"Come on, Dylan, we've got to go pick up Daddy at his office," Linda says as she half-drags her son from the living room where our neighborhood play group has assembled. The weekly get-together has gone well, with both kids and parents eager to spend time together, but the half-dozen two-year-olds are worn out, and a number of minor crises are taking place all around the room. Dylan seems to be having an especially hard time. He's had so much fun building a block fortress with Zack that he can't imagine ever leaving this place. Nevertheless, his mother keeps pleading. "Please, Dylan," she begs as he digs his heels into the carpet. Then, lowering her voice to keep the other parents from hearing, she adds desperately, "If you come on right now, I'll stop off at McDonald's and buy you a Happy Meal."

"No way!" Dylan roars as Linda pulls on his arm. He doesn't know quite what the phrase means, but he's learned that it's quite effective in situations like this. "Gimme blocks!" Trying to make a break for it, he turns and races back toward the block fortress, but his mother catches him midstride. "Noooooooo!" Dylan roars, teetering on the edge of a tantrum. Kicking and writhing, he fights to get free of his mother. When she won't let him go, he finally sits down on the carpet, hugging his knees and clenching his fists to make himself as immovable as possible. "No go!" he announces flatly. His mother sighs and lets him go. "What am I going to do with you?" she mutters under her breath. Dylan senses her frustration, but right now he doesn't care how much he's disappointed his mom. He's effectively communicated his desire with his words and his body, and for the moment at least, he is exactly where he wants to be.

Age two is a prime time for learning new words, but for many parents a toddler's ability to "use his words" in place of kicks and crying can't come soon enough. Though your child already understands between one thousand and two thousand words and may even be able to use more than two hundred of them, sometimes in two- or three-word sentences, he still expresses himself physically much more often than through language. Limited by imperfect comprehension, intense and sometimes overwhelming emotions, and a vocabulary new enough to be easily forgotten in times of stress, your twenty-four-month-old may still hold up his arms rather than ask to be picked up. He may speak in confusingly pared-down sentences ("Mommy car!") and, like Dylan, turn himself into an immovable lump rather than discuss why he doesn't want to leave. He is as likely to repeat a word or phrase for its emotional impact as for its meaning ("Stupidhead!") as he savors all aspects of his developing verbal skills.

Fortunately, your child's communication skills will advance at a rocket pace this year—not only in the realms of vocabulary and grammar but in his ability to sustain a conversation, address adults and other children in appropriate ways, and express his desires and emotions in a socially acceptable manner. As we will see in this chapter, you and his other caregivers will act as a major force behind this growth. Your daily interactions with him will enhance his ability to converse. Your willingness to read plenty of storybooks will instill a love of language and provide structure for further learning. Your patience as he journeys from physical toward verbal expressiveness will convince him that the effort is worth the trouble. By the end of this year, your child's urgent gestures will have evolved into complex sentences, and his stubborn "No!" will have developed into somewhat more sophisticated arguments, explanations, and rationalizations. His questions will start (and won't stop), beginning with, "What dat?" and continuing with, "But why?" As he celebrates his third birthday, he will not be a perfect speaker, but he will certainly have mastered basic sentence construction and an extraordinary number of new vocabulary words—excellent tools to use in expressing himself more fully to you.

A CHILD'S-EYE VIEW

"Spoil Brat!"

Thirty-three-month-old Pete likes to go to the grocery store. The grocery cart seat seems designed just for him, and Mom often lets him pick out the treats he likes best. He is in a feisty mood today as he and Mom roll up to the checkout line, and he quickly becomes bored by the wait. He jiggles his foot restlessly, gazing around for something to entertain him.

Just then another mommy with a baby pulls her cart up behind Pete in line. *Baby!* Pete peers over his mom's shoulder at the back of the one-year-old. *Looka me!* he wills, staring at the baby, but she won't turn around and make eye contact. "Hi!" he says in a loud voice. Still no response.

Pete sighs, kicking harder against the grocery cart. Suddenly he remembers a phrase he's heard many times, most recently at the playground this morning. The words got everyone's attention. In an instant, the words are out of his mouth. "Spoil brat!" he yells at the top of his lungs, pointing at the baby.

Both his mom and the other one give Pete a shocked look—just like the mommies on the playground! Pete is thrilled, but then the other mom turns her cart so that her child's back is more fully turned to Pete. "Pete, that's not nice," his mom says loudly, very embarrassed. But Pete hardly hears her. He is determined to make contact with the baby. "Spoil brat! Poopy head!" he shrieks.

"Peter John!" The cart jerks forward, and Mom begins unloading groceries onto the conveyor belt. *Mom's mad.* Pete watches solemnly as Mom, red-faced, apologizes to the other mommy and waits for the cashier to total up her bill. Finally, Mom loads the bagged groceries into the cart, thanks the cashier, and starts pushing the cart away.

Pete perks up. He knows what to say to cashiers. "Thankoo," he coos.

"You're welcome!" The cashier waves good-bye.

Mom smiles. "That was very polite, Pete," she says, putting her head close to his as they head for the door. "I'm glad you were nice to the lady." She adds, more calmly than before, "And you should talk nicer to babies, too!"

Wow, Pete thinks as they exit the store, *some words make Mom mad. Some words make Mom smile.* He ponders this concept while she buckles him into his car seat. Then he decides, *I like it when Mom smiles.*

"GIMME MORE, PWEEZE!": VERBAL ACHIEVEMENTS IN THE FIRST THREE YEARS

"Up, Daddy." "Thankoo." "Doggie, comeer!" What can be more satisfying than hearing these early attempts at real communication from our two-year-olds? Our excitement over the prospect of getting to know our children better through their words is matched in intensity only by our children's urge to use language to relate better to their world. Both desires—ours and theirs—fuel the extraordinary leap in vocabulary and conversation throughout this year. Still, as in other areas of your child's growth, his language development began long before you heard his first words. From birth and even before, his brain began building the connections necessary to understand and use speech by taking in enormous amounts of verbal information and finding the patterns of tone, rhythm, and melody within it. This pattern-detecting process worked so efficiently, research shows, that your baby could distinguish between your language and a foreign tongue only a few days after birth. As an infant, he could tell the difference between rhymed verse and unrhymed prose. By age four months, he was sufficiently aware of the sounds of his native language to begin experimenting with sounds himself, playing with variations in pitch and loudness. Soon he could manage strings of consonant-vowel syllables ("ba-ba-ba-ba-ba"). As more patterns were perceived and more neuronal connections made in his brain, he improved his ability to mimic the sounds you made, until he was babbling with such adult-like rhythms and tones that it was easy to forget he wasn't actually talking. (It's interesting to note that deaf babies, who aren't able to benefit from this listening and analyzing process, start out making sounds like hearing children, but then begin to falter when they reach the "ba-ba-ba" stage at six months.)

Your child's brain continued to mark how often he heard particular sounds as he attempted his first words. These words were among those he most frequently heard—or at least noticed the most because they were uttered by those he loved. By around eighteen months (though the "normal" age ranges from thirteen to twenty-five months), his listening, processing, and practicing of speech reached a critical mass, and your child began comprehending (though not necessarily speaking) as many as five or six new words a day. Most were nouns, along with some pronouns ("me," "mine"), common phrases ("That's enough!"), and a verb now and then.

Now, at the beginning of his third year, your child may well have begun using two-word sentences, such as "No nap" or "Bottle juice," and attempting longer strings of words that have caught his fancy even if he doesn't know what they mean ("You are my sunshine, my only sunshine . . ."). The rate of verbal development among two-year-olds continues to vary widely, but no matter what their level of ability, their *receptive vocabulary*—the words they can understand even if they don't use them—will continue to dramatically exceed their *productive vocabulary*—the number of words they can say.

Once your child can paste two words together, it won't be long before he starts creating true sentences. Meanwhile, his vocabulary will expand exponentially as he casually picks up a word you say over breakfast and makes it his before the end of the day. The more words he commands, the more important it becomes to organize them in some way—and grammar comes to his rescue in the nick of time. By age two and a half, he will probably have begun adding "-s" to create plural forms for his nouns; soon he'll add an "-ing" to a verb or two (even when it's incorrect), and then "-ed" for the past tense. As we will see later in this chapter, researchers are still unsure how much of this sudden burst of grammatical ability is innate and how much comes from his brain's attention to the patterns of the language he hears. In any case, the result is that your child's sentences will be much more complex in structure, and clearer in content, by the end of this year. As a three-year-old, he will use words to express his ideas and feelings almost as naturally as an adult.

A PARENT'S STORY

"I'm Not Resty"

"When Nina was one, everybody used to tell me she was an incredibly verbal child," another mother told me as she watched her three-year-old play with the toys in our pediatrician's waiting room. "She only had to hear something said once, and before the hour was up she'd have repeated it two or three times. Not just single words, but whole strings of them, like 'Twinkle, Twinkle, Little Star,' or her street address.

"Then, all of a sudden, when she was about two and a half, it was like her whole ability to speak kind of disintegrated. She started saying 'eated' instead of 'ate,' 'runned' instead of 'ran.' Sometimes she talked so fast that her pronunciation went downhill, too. Lots of times we just couldn't figure out what she was saying. I started to wonder if she was having developmental problems. But then a friend of mine told me she'd read that toddlers' grammar falls apart because they're no longer imitating our speech but actually creating it on their own. Of course, kids would make mistakes in that case, with all our irregular verbs and complicated sentences!

"It was a relief to know that Nina's speech was normal for

her age, but I didn't start to really appreciate the process until right around her third birthday. We'd had a long day, and I was slumped on the living room sofa watching her wander around. She started crying over nothing, and I said, 'I guess it's about rest time, huh?'

"'I'm not resty,' she answered, snuggling against me.

"'Well, I think you are a little tired,' I said, putting an arm around her.

"'No, I amn't!' she said.

"I had to laugh. Talking with her was so hit-or-miss sometimes. But it was nothing like the 'Twinkle Twinkles' from a year ago. Back then, she probably didn't understand half of what she was saying—she just liked the sounds of the words or the reactions she got. This, on the other hand, was a real conversation. She communicated her feelings and understood my answers. She knows that words mean something now, and she can use them to get what she wants and build relationships with the people in her life.

"I still correct her grammar all the time, of course. But she's gotten better at expressing herself, and I've figured out that with talking it's the content, not the package, that really counts."

"THANKOO!": GUESSING AT MEANINGS AND LEARNING THE RULES

"Okay, Sarah," the dad said wearily to his wailing two-year-old, glancing at the impatient line behind them at the ice cream store. "I *see* that you don't want vanilla this time. How about chocolate? Just tell me what you want instead of yelling—please?"

His daughter's continued fussing must have made this dad regret having offered her an ice cream in the first place. But they had probably been having such fun shopping together—and his little girl had seemed so grown-up and well behaved—that he forgot how limited her resources still were. He was surprised when Sarah reacted to the ice cream crisis with a tantrum, yet her collapse under the pressure of her still-limited cognition and difficulty with language and the overwhelming frustration that resulted were perfectly normal for her age. She had only truly figured out the concept that words can be used to name objects about six to eight months before—and now she was faced with using them to express her feelings and get the flavor she wanted. Hard as it is for parents to keep in mind, making the journey from physical toward verbal communication is just as hard for the two-year-old as it is for those who love him—particularly when he's tired, hungry, or otherwise stressed.

If you have ever tried to learn a foreign language, you know that learning to speak is not just about memorizing words, obeying grammatical rules, and refining one's pronunciation. It also involves such social skills as taking turns in conversation, recognizing and repairing misunderstandings, and using language in polite, culturally appropriate ways. Two-year-olds must learn all these rules of communication, too—but without the experience or resources we have. To get her ice cream, Sarah must know not only how to say the words, "I don't want vanilla. I want chocolate," but how to get her father's attention, express her desire (preferably with a "please"), listen to his response, and clarify any confusion—all while controlling her strong fear that she will not end up with what she wants. This social dimension of language—its ability to enhance communication between two people—is not an instinctive process. It must be learned.

You have been helping your child learn the social skills of language practically from the day he was born. By responding to his facial expressions, gestures, and early vocalizations—and by playing such games as peekaboo—you introduced your baby to the idea of taking turns. By his first birthday, he was no doubt entranced by the rhythmic give-and-take of human conversation and had begun working hard to respond to your words with appropriate sounds, expressions, and movement. Another skill you taught your child by example was that of *joint attention*—the tendency to share a focus of conversation. When chatting with your preverbal baby, you often tried to direct his attention to particular objects or talked about things that already had his attention. As a result, he learned to use the direction of your gaze to determine which object you were labeling. This not only familiarized him with the name of the object but introduced him to the concept that the two of you were *communicating* about the object, not just making random noises. Soon he began trying to communicate back, using sounds and gestures to try to "tell" you something. If you failed to understand what he was trying to express, he probably got frustrated, but he also tried to fix the problem by repeating or changing his sounds, gestures, and behavior.

As much as the process of communicating with you thrilled your baby, he still did not really understand the fact that the words you were saying were *names* for things. When you cried, "Doggie," when a dog came up and licked your face, he didn't know whether "doggie" referred to the dog, to what it was doing, or to your feelings about it. As a result, he usually spoke his own first word ("Mama," "doggie," "cookie") because he found himself in the same situation in which he'd heard it, not because he clearly understood its meaning. Only after many more months of exposure to these words was he able to remember them, link the situations in which he'd heard them to create a category of objects that they represented, and then actually produce them. By around eighteen months, however, he began to understand that "doggie" *meant* "dog"—not only his own dog but all the other dogs in picture books, on the street, and in conversation. Once this amazing realization dawned on him, he probably dropped many of his first, improperly understood vocabulary words and threw himself into a frenzied acquisition of nouns, names, and familiar phrases, incessantly asking, "What that?"

The more words he learned, the more eagerly your toddler tried to use them to communicate his desires, feelings, and intentions to you. He crammed as much meaning as he could into his limited vocabulary. "Doggie!" could mean, "I'm scared of the dog," "Where is the dog?" "Look at that dog," and so on. As a result, you were often confused by his utterances. You frequently had to guess what he was trying to tell you in a game of fill-in-the-blank. Though he usually tried to clarify his message, he wasn't always successful. Many a one-year-old's tantrum has sprung from just such a breakdown in communication.

Now, at around his second birthday, the situation has begun to ease somewhat. A growing understanding of verbs and adjectives allows your child to create clearer, if still very short, sentences. Accustomed to figuring out the meanings of words by pointing to the object you're talking about or saying the same word each time an object appears, he can now quickly guess the meaning of a word from its context. This guessing process, called *fast mapping,* was illustrated in a 1987 study by Tracy Heibeck and Ellen Markman of the University of Pittsburgh. Experimenters exposed two- to four-year-olds to unfamiliar terms for colors, shapes, and textures. In each case, the experimenter placed the unfamiliar word in the context of familiar ones, as in, "Bring me the chartreuse one. Not the blue one, the chartreuse one." When the children were tested a few minutes later, even the two-year-olds showed that they had correctly learned the new words.

Your child's fast mapping skills will take off this year, greatly enhancing his ability to expand his vocabulary. Research using magnetic resonance imaging (MRI) has shown that a typical fifteen-month-old needs more than a second to recognize even a familiar word, like "bottle," while an eighteen-month-old guesses the word slightly before the speaker has finished saying it. By age twenty-four months, however, the child guesses the word in only six hundred milliseconds—the moment the first syllable ("bot-") is spoken. This increased speed enables him to process much more information as he listens.

Your two-year-old's desire to communicate his thoughts to you will remain passionate and intense throughout this period. Like Sarah, he will continue to feel overwhelmed emotionally at times when he realizes he's misunderstood, and he will keep experimenting with new words, tones of voice, and behaviors in his efforts to make you understand. You can help him learn new ways to communicate effectively by frequently demonstrating useful verbal formulas or routines ("Hi," "How are you?" "Bye-bye," "Please," "Thank you," "Excuse me") and tactfully raising his consciousness of the volume of his speech ("It's time to use your indoor voice") and his tone ("I can't understand you when you whine").

As he approaches his third birthday, he will appreciate your efforts to supply him with longer verbal *scripts* to supplement his still-limited ability to carry on a conversation on his own. A script, or conversational blueprint for certain situations, can provide your child with a general idea of appropriate behavior, along with a few key phrases that should see him through. By talking to him about what people say during certain encounters, rehearsing a new situation before it happens, and even prompting him gently during his first attempt or two, you can help your child ultimately hold his own while talking to grown-ups, ordering lunch at a restaurant, and so on. This is especially helpful as your child starts to interact more with children his age, who aren't yet willing or able to help him through the conversation the way most adults do.

As the months pass, your child's increasing mastery of the verbal routines and scripts you have taught him, as well as his improving ability to stifle his frustration and try again, will lead to more interesting and rewarding conversations over breakfast, on the way to the sitter's, at rest time, and during all the other little moments the two of you share each day. He will still be motivated to communicate more from a desire to get what he wants than a willingness to listen to what you have to say. (He will become much more upset if he can't make you understand that he wants the train in the toy store window than if he doesn't understand what you're telling him about his missing boot.) As the year progresses, however, he'll become more interested in your viewpoint and those of others. How quickly this happens will depend on his particular temperament, the pace of his emotional and social development, and his vocabulary skills, but by the end of this year all the tools for effective communication should be in place. The day will soon come when you realize with a start that the two of you have really started to "talk."

EASING THE WAY

Playing with Words

A great number of studies have demonstrated that the more parents talk with their children when they are toddlers, the larger the children's vocabularies will be by the time they start school. "Just chatting"—pointing out, naming, and discussing objects in the environment—is certainly an effective way to teach your child new words, but specific techniques can enhance your child's verbal growth even more.

Stay close and narrate events as your two-year-old navigates his way through an exciting new world of words and symbols.

Rhyming is a form of wordplay that all toddlers love—as you know from your experiences with nursery rhymes, children's songs, and every book by Dr. Seuss. Rhyming also stimulates your child's ear for language because it encourages him to pay attention to the specific sounds in every word. While you are helping your child dress in the morning or waiting in line at the gas station, invent funny rhymes about what the two of you are doing and encourage him to finish them. You can stimulate his thinking about the meanings of words and the rhythms of language by making up stories with him (even very short ones), making puns and word jokes ("Gooseberry? It doesn't look like a goose to me"), and talking about the different meanings of a single word. Try to include plenty of generalizations ("All taxis are yellow"), categories ("A parrot is a kind of bird"), and comparisons ("That horse hopped like a rabbit!") in your conversations. As he grows increasingly able to follow a storyline, show him how stories relate to experience by telling him tales about children his age, reading him picture books that relate to his current interests, and recalling brief stories about your childhood ("When I was two . . .").

Just be sure you're not talking *at* your child, but talking *with* him. Pause long enough for him to process your words. Wait for his responses. By really listening to what *he* has to say, you can create a pattern of rich communication that will last for years to come.

"HE RUNNED AND RUNNED!": EXPERIMENTING WITH GRAMMAR

As hard as parents work at increasing their children's understanding of how the world operates, how people interact, and how to deal with a variety of emotions, it's a relief to know that we don't have to sit our two-year-olds down and give them lessons in grammar, too. Children in the middle of their third year experience a breathtaking growth spurt in grammatical development all on their own as they move from the typical twenty-four-month-old's "Me Tarzan" type of speech toward more complex sentences that include verbs, articles, pronouns, prepositions, prefixes, and suffixes ("My name's Tarzan. What's yours?"). By his third birthday, your child will have acquired not only a vocabulary of several thousand words but, as the MIT scientist Steven Pinker writes in his book *The Language Instinct,* "a tacit knowledge of grammar more sophisticated than the thickest style manual." Best of all, he will have taken this leap with little conscious effort on your own part. Research shows that parents pay much more attention to the content of their young children's statements than to their grammar—yet most children learn correct grammar anyway.

Not only will your child develop his grammar skills this year, but he will develop them in the same order (if not necessarily the same rate) as other children his age. First, he will begin adding "-s" to his nouns and "-ing" to his verbs when appropriate. Somewhat later, you will hear a past-tense suffix ("-ed") and the "-s" suffix to form the third-person singular ("He laughs and laughs"). Once these conventions have been mastered, he will begin using contractions ("It's my turn," or, "They're funny"), and somewhere along the way he will have picked up such useful "function" words as "some," "would," "how," and "after." Of course, your child's grammar will not always be correct (there are plenty of irregular words, such as "ran" and "mice," to trip him up), but it will always be logical. Over time, his errors will diminish as he compares his own grammar with what he hears from others.

For decades, this sequence of grammatical skills was considered as instinctive for children as song for a bird. MIT linguist Noam Chomsky pointed out more than thirty years ago that virtually every language in the world is created from noun phrases ("Joey's mommy") and verb phrases ("drove the car"). Noting that two-year-olds seem to instinctively understand this structure and to use it themselves as they begin to create their own sentences, Chomsky suggested that there must be a universal grammar hardwired into the brain and shared by all human beings. Research over the past decade, however, has challenged this idea. MRI studies show that young children's brains respond to patterns in their parents' grammar in much the same way as they notice frequencies in sound and vocabulary words. Computer programs designed to simulate the working brain, called "neural nets," automatically sort words into categories—just as a child learns that certain kinds of words refer to actions while others refer to objects—and figure out some rules of word order. Neural nets even make many of the same mistakes that children do ("He jumped me the ball"). Clearly, though operating on a much more primitive level than that of a human brain, such neural nets have taken in enormous amounts of verbal information and found the regular patterns within it. Perhaps that is what your child is doing, too.

The debate between the relative contributions of nature (your child's instinctive grammatical ability) and nurture (how much he has learned by example) continues. No doubt, as with other aspects of his development, both are constantly at work as he grows. He may naturally tend to look for the grammatical elements of your speech, in other words, but you must provide plenty of that speech (and a wide variety of it) if he is to put his tendencies to practical use. At this age, you needn't strictly monitor his sentence construction, of course. (The day will come when you miss his charming mistakes.) Just provide him with examples in your everyday conversation, in storybooks, and through the media, correct him on his own efforts gently now and then, and praise him for the progress he makes.

As natural as his progression from "Up, Mommy!" to "Pick me up, Mommy!" may seem this year, it's hard not to appreciate the dramatic accomplishments of your two-year-old. Not only has he internalized and learned to reproduce the rhythms, tones, and sound combinations of his native language, but he has grown to understand their meanings in a wide variety of contexts and has learned many of the social situations in which they can be used. Not only has he picked up on what order the words must be in to make sense, but he's figured out which supporting words are necessary to flesh out his sentence and even, in most cases, which words do not follow the general grammatical rules. (If he lives in a bilingual home, he has probably learned to do this in two languages!) By the time he is three, 90 percent of his sentences will be grammatically correct. Not a bad record after only three years.

IF YOU'RE CONCERNED
Verbal Delays

Waiting for a child to move from single words to sentences can be a painful process for the parents of two-year-olds—especially since adults so frequently (and often erroneously) equate verbal ability with general intelligence. The questions and comments of friends and relatives ("What's he saying? I can't understand him.") certainly don't ease the pressure. In fact, children this age continue to vary widely in their verbal abilities, and your child's reluctance to speak may just be a manifestation of his particular temperament or unique circumstances. When considering whether his development is within the "normal" range, keep in mind that few two-year-olds (or even three-year-olds) are fully comprehensible. Most lisp, slur their words, mispronounce such letters as "l," "v," and "r," and stutter as they try to make their mouths keep up with their thoughts. Also remember that twins tend to speak later than single children— as do premature children—and their speech development may continue to lag behind a bit for much of this year. Major events at home, such as the birth of a sibling or a change in child-care arrangements, may also create a temporary pause or regression in his speech. Even under normal circumstances, two-year-olds may briefly lose their speech skills rather easily, especially near the beginning of this year. Your child's speech will probably diminish when he's deeply engaged in play, and he may well fall silent when a new person enters the room and greets him. In both cases, he simply doesn't yet have the cognitive energy to deal with the experience and create speech at the same time.

Yet there are, of course, instances when a child's relative silence may indicate a problem with speech. The first indicator is your own gut feeling about how he is progressing. Does he seem seriously out of place or uncomfortable when playing with his more verbal peers? Does he communicate with others easily through gestures and simple words, and understand what they are saying to him? What do the parents of his friends think about his speech? How long have you been worried about his progress? Often your own sense that something is wrong is the best "first warning" that will lead to help for your child. Other red flags regarding verbal development include an inability to understand differences in meaning (up versus down), to follow two requests ("Please pick up the bottle and give it to me"), to maintain eye contact during conversation, to string together two or three words, or to name common objects.

If you suspect that your child is having too much trouble with any of these aspects of verbal development, it is important to discuss your concerns with his pediatrician or a speech pathologist *as soon as possible.* If the cause is hearing loss or a neurological disorder, the earlier your child's delay is diagnosed and treated, the better the chance that his brain can reorganize, and the more easily he may be able to catch up. Even profoundly deaf children should be exposed to sign language as early as possible to take advantage of the two-year-old's critical period of language development. In the realm of speech, a parent's philosophy should be "Let's look into it now," not, "Let's wait and see."

"HE DOESN'T TALK MUCH":
THE LINK BETWEEN VERBAL ABILITY
AND INTELLIGENCE

"I love my little boy, but he worries me sometimes," a friend told me over lunch. "Mack started preschool this year, and every day when I pick him up he's off in the corner by himself, playing with a truck or a pile of blocks. Some of the other kids are talking up a storm, and even though I know he can talk when he really wants to, I almost never see him do it. My daughter was talking in whole paragraphs by this time. Frankly, I'm starting to wonder if he just isn't as smart as she is."

Such concerns are common but, as I pointed out earlier, very frequently unfounded. We have seen in this chapter that a large part of language development involves listening. The brain of a quiet child is likely to be quite busily processing not only vocabulary and grammatical rules but any of the many other concepts he must master this year. As several experts have pointed out, proof that the areas of language and cognition are quite different is found in a rare genetic disorder called Williams syndrome. Children with this disability can speak in full, complex sentences, tell a beautiful story, and employ such communication skills as looking a person in the eye as they speak, asking questions, and so on. Nevertheless, their IQ scores generally hover in the seventies—substantially below average.

Still, cognition and language are clearly linked in some ways, and one activity supports and enhances the other in your child's brain. A certain level of cognition, or comprehension, is necessary for your child to begin expressing himself through words. The development of memory and symbolic thinking (such as the ability to picture an object or action) is also necessary before a child can move forward with language. Your child's surge in vocabulary that began at about eighteen months was strongly connected to his ability to sort objects into categories. Scientists have long linked two-year-olds' block-building, memory, and symbolic play to their efforts to combine two or more words. In turn, learning new words stimulates aspects of a child's intelligence, such as curiosity. Over the past few decades, through magnetic resonance imaging, researchers have been able to watch as a new word literally forms new connections in a child's brain.

Your child's cognitive potential and rate of language development are no doubt partly inherited. Still, when so much improvement is possible in each area by making use of the other, it makes sense during this year to keep the links between them in mind. Allow your child plenty of time to play with blocks, dolls, and other kids, and don't forget to talk with him about his play. These moments spent placing one wooden cube atop another, whispering secrets to his puppet, interacting with children his age, and describing his exploits to you are the solid pedestal on which much of his future comprehension and expression will be built.

THE TOY BOX

At Twenty-eight Months

Nat is playing with his action figures on the floor of the living room while his older brother, Andrew, plays checkers nearby with a friend. "Jumped you," Andrew says, moving his piece over one of his friend's. Nat looks up, intrigued. *Jumped?* he thinks. He didn't see Andrew jump!

Nat gets up, goes over to the table where the boys are playing, and watches as Andrew's friend makes a move. "Jumped you!" Nat crows triumphantly.

The boys laugh. "No, Nat, he didn't jump me," Andrew tells him. "This is jumping. If my piece is here, see, and his piece is there . . ." Andrew demonstrates "jumping" in checkers for Nat. "Get it?" he asks.

Nat nods importantly. He likes it when Andrew pays attention to him. As the boys continue playing, he goes back to his action figures. "Take that!" he murmurs, smashing the two figures against each other. Then he gets an idea. Pressing one figure to the floor, he makes the other leap over it, much as Andrew's checkers piece sailed over that of his friend. "Jumped you!" he says excitedly. As the older boys continue their own game, Nat "jumps" his action figures again and again.

"READ ME A STORY":
DEVELOPING A LOVE OF LANGUAGE

"Wead me a story, pweeeze?" What parent hasn't heard this plea from his two-year-old—often when he was just about to settle down to the TV or the newspaper or start a conversation with his spouse. Beginning at age two or even earlier, nearly all young children become entranced by the power of a simple story accompanied by bright, comprehensible pictures. If your child has his way, you will find yourself reading much more than the occasional bedtime story this year.

If so, it will be a wonderful boon to your child as he develops his language skills, since even at this young age storytime can enhance later performance in school. Research indicates that children who are read to frequently at home learn to read relatively easily once they start school. The kind of dialogue parents typically engage in while reading ("What's that? A kitty! Right! And what's that? Yes, a hen!") resembles the kind used in school and thus paves the way for school success.

Be ready to support your two-year-old as storybooks and a budding imagination fill her head with all sorts of emotions.

Fortunately, story time—one of the few times when many active two-year-olds are willing to settle into a parent's lap and have a conversation—can be at least as pleasant for parents as it is for kids. As a result, it's one parental duty with which it's pretty easy to comply—once we set aside our beliefs about how a child should behave while we read to him. At age two, in fact, listening to a story should be an active pursuit. Ask your child to name objects in the illustrations, to fill in the blanks (especially with rhymed verse, which offers your child a clue), and to comment on the plot, the characters, and anything he's reminded of by the story. As his language skills improve, ask more complex questions about the text ("How does Red Riding Hood know that that's the wolf in her granny's nightgown?"), and introduce new books with more complex texts and pictures. Be sure to talk about the stories you've read at other times during the day ("Wow, this must be how Babar felt when the elephants made him king"). In this way, you'll teach him that books are related to life in intimate ways. Keep in mind, though, that at this age it's more important to have fun reading together than for your child to answer your questions correctly or for you to finish the story. Choosing books with characters who are already familiar to him, and series of books that you can think about together adds to his pleasure, giving him a sense of familiarity and continuity.

Q & A

"Fee, Fi, Fo, Fum!"

Q: When my daughter was born, her uncle gave her a beautiful, leather-bound book of fairy tales. The illustrations are gorgeous, and I love the book myself, so I've been reading the stories to my daughter since she was a baby. But now that she's starting to understand more of the words, and her imagination is taking off, I wonder whether they're really appropriate for her. After all, Jack climbs up a beanstalk, steals a hideous giant's personal belongings, and then kills him rather than give them back! And what about Hansel and Gretel, left to die in the woods by their parents and nearly eaten by a witch? Are fairy tales okay for children this age?

A: It can be startling, as you first begin to read to your child, to realize just how violent and frightening many traditional stories are. One reason for this is that most of them were first told or written long before children were considered children —that is, before they were understood to be different in important ways from adults. Deciding whether they are too frightening for your child is largely a personal matter, but it's unlikely that the stories will actually harm your child in any lasting way. In fact, the renowned psychoanalyst Bruno Bettelheim passionately insisted that children need fairy tales. He believed that the stories' brutality touches children's own unexpressed fears and helps them work out ways of mastering them. He was also convinced that the unreality of fairy tales offers children a safety zone in which to explore their feelings of vulnerability.

Still, be aware of the combined effect of words and pictures. (Pictures sometimes frighten two-year-olds more than words.) Since your child can't read yet, you're free to skip over some of the scarier parts. Keep in mind that more recently written books usually take children's developmental level into account and can also stimulate and entertain them when combined with more traditional tales.

"USE YOUR WORDS": MOVING FROM PHYSICAL TO VERBAL EXPRESSION

A year has passed, but the parents-and-toddlers group in our neighborhood still meets once a week. A few younger kids have joined up over the past months, and several older children have dropped out as they entered preschool, but Dylan and his mom, Linda, are still active members. Dylan continues to hate leaving at the end of a session, and his mother has decided he's a kid who doesn't like transitions. Fortunately, she's learned to plan ahead by preparing afternoon activities and other inducements to lure him home. Dylan has gradually improved in his ability to negotiate with her, too.

Today, Linda tells me, she's just grateful Dylan no longer yells "Jerk!" at her when she says it's time to leave, as he did for most of his thirty-third month. (While unsettling, this type of inappropriate language usage is very typical of the progression toward productive conversation.) In fact, Dylan's progress from sit-down strikes at twenty-four months to more reasonable requests at age three to "stay longer" has been full of detours and regressions. During a long month when his father was out of town on business, for example, Dylan reverted to shrieks and name-calling before he found his nice words again. And there are bad days even now, particularly when Dylan is tired or over-stimulated.

Fortunately, Linda has felt supported by the other moms' understanding this year, and our assurances that all our kids are facing similar challenges. She's worked hard at talking with Dylan about his experience when leaving a place, and she has read stories to him that seemed to relate to his fears about change. By now it is clear that Dylan knows his own heart better than he did a year ago and is more able to express exactly why he doesn't want to go away. "Stay five more minutes, Mom?" I overhear him asking his mom.

"No, Dylan. You know we talked about that," she responds.

"I want to play with Nathan," he announces, trying another ploy.

"Nathan's leaving now, too. Let's go home and play that new game we bought yesterday, okay? I get the green marker this time!"

Dylan considers. "I like the green one," he points out.

"Well, that's true. Green's your favorite color, isn't it? Okay, you can have the green marker if you come with me right now."

Dylan glances over his shoulder. He sees that the play group is breaking up. "Okay," he says. "But I want an ice cream cone, too."

"We'll talk about it over lunch." Linda shoots an exasperated look over her shoulder at us. We can sympathize. As all parents know, verbal interaction with a thirty-six-month-old can sometimes be almost as difficult as the nonverbal kind. Older two-year-olds love to discuss, negotiate, and demand endless explanations and concessions. In the long run, however, these first attempts at communication are well worth the effort. With your encouragement, your young child will learn to express his ideas clearly, find new ways to understand and manage his emotions, and experience the wonderful sense that others care very much about what he has to say.

Common Verbal Achievements in the Third Year

24 MONTHS	Can probably make two-, three-, or four-word sentences
	Mimics adult inflections and phrases
	Starts using pronouns (usually "I" and "me")
27 MONTHS	Speaks clearly most of the time
	Vocabulary grows rapidly
30 MONTHS	Can name some body parts
	May name some colors
33 MONTHS	Uses prepositions ("on," "in," "over")
	Carries on two- to three-sentence conversations
	Can name some objects in a book
36 MONTHS	Can follow a two- or three-part command
	Speaks in four- to five-word sentences
	Diction may still be imperfect

FIRST-PERSON SINGULAR

Your child's early conversation is sure to be a study in twisted logic, and in the years to come you will no doubt enjoy reviewing this record of his first attempts to convince you of something or tell you a story. Nevertheless, two-year-olds also come up with amazingly perceptive comments now and then, and these are certainly worth recording as well. If possible, make an audio- or videotape of your child speaking this year so that you can compare it to how he expresses himself in the years to come. You will be amazed at how completely his tone, gestures, pronunciation, and vocabulary are transformed over the next months. Capture his first expressions now before they're gone forever.

READER'S NOTES

_____

_____

_____

_____

_____

_____

_____

_____

_____

_____

_____

_____

_____

_____

CHAPTER 5

Pride and Anxiety—
My Emotional Growth

A t some point around the middle of this year, your child will make her first connections between how she feels at one moment and how she feels the next.

Marjorie isn't just having a bad day—she's having a terrible one. First thing this morning, she got a call from her soon-to-be ex-husband, Nick, demanding more visitation with their daughter, Megan. The argument that ensued made Marjorie late to work, where rumors were flying that the company was planning another round of layoffs. Marjorie has been working there for only a few months, since just after Megan's second birthday. She's pretty certain she'll be one of the first to go.

Today Marjorie has a late meeting, which makes her half an hour late picking up Megan at the sitter's. She drives as fast as she can across town, trying to fight off the guilt she always feels when she thinks about how much time Megan spends away from her now. If Marjorie and her husband had stayed together, Marjorie probably would have stayed home full-time until Megan was three or four. She still hasn't adjusted to the idea of putting her daughter in someone else's care.

Marjorie arrives to find Megan and her sitter, Catherine, baking chocolate chip cookies. The kitchen smells scrumptious, and Marjorie feels her entire body relax. "Hello, sweetie," she says, giving her daughter a hug. "Ready to go?"

Instead of returning the hug, Megan turns to her mother with a terrible scowl. "Go way!" she shouts. She turns back to the cookies as her mother, hurt but hardly surprised, wonders how to respond. Megan refuses to go home almost every evening when her mother arrives to pick her up. It's as though she's transferred her loyalty to Catherine—and it feels at times as though she almost *hates* her mom.

"Hey, now, it's okay," Catherine coos, putting down her spatula and giving Megan a little pat. "She's tired," she explains to Marjorie with an apologetic smile. To Megan she adds, "Don't you want to take some cookies home for Mommy?"

"No!" Megan shrieks, slamming a handful of cookie dough on the counter. "I stay here! Don't want you!"

Marjorie can feel her anxiety return full force. First, she tries to negotiate with her daughter—offering to play a board game or string some necklaces with her when they get home. In the end, however, she has to carry Megan out to the car kicking and screaming, while Catherine smiles uncomfortably and murmurs, "I'm sure it's just a phase."

Even in the best of circumstances, life with a two-year-old can be stormy and unpredictable. Thrilled (but also sometimes overwhelmed) by the previous year's realization that she is a separate individual with thoughts, feelings, and different goals from yours, your two-year-old is committed to fortifying her new, fragile sense of self. Her need to feel powerful and autonomous, to assert some control over her environment and herself, clashes with her equally intense need for your love, approval, and support. These opposing needs rule her life for most of the year, creating emotions so heightened and constantly changing that the adults in her life can hardly keep up. When events so often take place without her approval (whether the major changes of divorce that Megan faced or the everyday surprises of altered plans and challenging new situations), it's no wonder your child swings from baby-like clinginess to loud defiance over a span of mere moments or even for weeks at a time.

Other factors help make this period emotionally challenging for the entire family. A two-year-old's preoccupation with speech development, toilet training, or other learning processes may keep her awake nights, making her more emotional during the day. Her increasing awareness of the feelings of those around her may lead her toward frightening conclusions *(Mom's mad. Maybe she doesn't love me)*. Her limited ability to express her feelings in words is likely to frustrate her immensely— just as her developmental need to experiment with such negative emotions as anger and defiance will probably frustrate you. As a result, as Alicia Lieberman, author of *The Emotional Life of the Toddler,* points out, mild to moderate conflicts tend to take place between parent and child about every *three minutes* in homes with young children, and major conflicts happen about three times every hour. No wonder parenting a child this age feels like riding a roller coaster.

Fortunately, the same need for independence that drives your two-year-old's rebellious impulses creates some very rewarding results as well. Her growing sense of self lays the groundwork for her increasingly unique style of emotional expression, openness to novelty, and interaction with others—in short, her personality. As the months pass and she begins to explore her own imaginative, moral, and social potential, she will start to emerge from the more generic and universal behavior patterns of early toddlerhood like a butterfly from its cocoon. By the end of the year, having explored an array of new feelings (including pride, guilt, rage, tenderness, and perhaps even true empathy), she will begin to settle into a more characteristic range that reflects her *experience* as well as her temperament. The turmoil of the early months will subside as the two of you learn how to work together on expressing feelings through words rather than actions and how to find acceptable outlets for her emotions. With this goal partly achieved by the end of the year, she will have more emotional energy to interact socially with others her age and figure out how to achieve her goals in acceptable ways.

It isn't easy to give a two-year-old enough room to express her emotions while maintaining acceptable limits. Nevertheless, the rewards—in terms of her increased self-confidence, self-control, and desire to live up to your standards—are absolutely worth the effort. As you experiment with talking through conflicts, negotiating with each other, backing off at times when she's unable to talk with you, holding her when she's out of control, and using compromise, distraction, humor, and careful preparation to avoid as many rocky moments as possible, you will learn a great deal more about what works for your child and what doesn't. At the same time, you will be teaching her through example how to manage *her own* constantly fluctuating surges of desire, resentment, anger, and love. By the end of this year's journey, the two of you will have gotten to know each other—and yourselves—much better than before. You'll have a better understanding of when she needs you to guide, support, or limit her behavior and when it's okay to "give her the reins." This deeper understanding will help you both weather the many storms (and savor the triumphs) to come.

A CHILD'S-EYE VIEW

"I Won't!"

It's early morning, and Eliot's mom, Helen, is hastily getting him ready to go to Grandma's for the day. "Come on," she murmurs, shoving his legs into his sweatpants, "hurry it up, pumpkin. We're late."

Too rough, Eliot thinks grumpily, bending his legs to make the process as difficult as possible. *Want cereal!* Eliot's entire morning routine—breakfast in his pajamas at the kitchen table, time with his toys while Mommy gets dressed, and a hug from Dad before they leave—is ruined because of the early hour. *My body!* he thinks as Mommy shoves a sweater over his head. *My sweater! Mine, mine, mine!*

"Time to brush your teeth," Helen says, hauling him to his feet. Her voice sounds mad, but he's too out of sorts to care. *I can walk!* he protests silently as she lugs him to the bathroom and sets him on his stool. "Open your mouth," she commands, grabbing the toothpaste and toothbrush. "Hurry up. We're late."

"No!" Eliot clamps his jaw shut. He hates the way the toothbrush bumps against his gums. He examines his reflection in the mirror. He is intrigued by the defiant, willful face that looks back at him. His mother's obvious exasperation is satisfying, too.

"Eliot! I'm sick of this," his mother snaps. "I'm counting to three. One! Two!"

"Aaaaaaaaaaargh!" Eliot wails.

Just then, Dad's face appears in the mirror. "What? You won't brush your teeth?" he says, making a silly face at his son. Helen scowls impatiently at her husband, but steps back to give him room.

"You wanna brush your nose, then?" Dad squats down to Eliot's level.

"No," Eliot says, struggling to hold on to his anger.

"Or maybe your eyelashes," Dad says. "We have to brush Eliot's eyelashes!"

Eliot feels a giggle escape in spite of himself. "Silly!" he says with delight.

"Oh, that's not how you do it?" Dad says, giving Eliot a quick hug. "Then give me the toothbrush, Mommy. Eliot's going to show us how you *really* brush your teeth!"

With a shrug of surrender, Helen hands the toothbrush over. Proudly Eliot sticks it in his mouth and moves it around. Dad helps out a little. "So that's how it works!" Dad says. "That was great! Rinse out now, kid. We can go play while Mommy gets dressed."

Yay! Eliot hurries to rinse out his mouth. He glances at his reflection and sees a different, happier face than the one from a moment ago. He pauses. *Why was I mad?* He can't remember. But it doesn't matter. Now Eliot's the one in a hurry.

"WHERE'S MOMMY?": EMOTIONAL GROWTH IN THE FIRST TWO YEARS

"Mommy, I need a Band-Aid." The two-year-old sidles up to her mother at the playground, tears running down her face.

"Oh, honey." Her mother fumbles in her backpack for a Band-Aid and squats down to look at her daughter's knee. "Did you fall down?"

"Allie pushed me." The girl's face is a study in contrasts, the sadness over her scraped knee fighting with the satisfaction of having an interesting story to tell. "I . . . I was . . . I was on the big ladder," she explains. "I fell down."

"Well, here's a Band-Aid." Mom wipes off the scrape and ceremoniously presses the colored strip to her daughter's knee. "I'm sorry you got hurt. But you're okay now, aren't you?"

"I'm okay." The girl leans in close for a hug, her chin quivering in abject self-pity even as her mouth turns up with the pleasure of getting Mom's undivided attention. Is she sad or happy, a victim or a mother's treasured child? She hovers between opposing emotional states and self-images, not sure which to choose.

What a mixed-up, puzzling, yet fascinating experience it must be, getting through each day as a two-year-old. Veteran of an entire year's worth of independent exploration, fully aware of her status as a separate person, your child is now bombarded with a host of subtle new feelings and sensations that often do battle visibly on her face. Out on her own and looking to you less to dictate her feelings, she doesn't always know how to manage and identify the emotions that wash over her. How is she to behave when she feels both relieved and angered by the limits you impose? What words or actions can express her combined sense of excitement and fear as she enters a room full of children she doesn't know?

As an infant, your child's emotional world was a simple one—her contentment or unhappiness depended mainly on her physical state. When her stomach was empty, she wailed with despair. When she was fed, warm, and comforted, she experienced total bliss. As she began to associate these emotions with the adults who helped create them, her emotional life became somewhat more complex. She began actively looking to *you* to respond to her needs, and when you responded, her confidence and emotional ease grew.

Increasingly, the mere fact of your presence or absence influenced your child's emotional state. She felt drawn to experiment with the effects of your disappearances—playing peekaboo as long as you would let her, giggling when you covered her with a blanket and then pretended to "find" her. By age seven to nine months, she was no longer just a cute bundle to be passed easily from person to person. She was quite capable of protesting loudly whenever you left the room. Though she still studied your face for clues to how you—and she—should respond emotionally to events, she had developed her own opinions about how available you should be. As she learned to crawl, her ability to find you in the next room made her feel more confident that she could make physical contact when she needed to. This sense that you were accessible allowed her to explore both her physical and emotional worlds more freely.

The more physically independent your child grew during her second year—crawling, walking, running, and climbing ever farther out of your reach—the more emotionally independent she became as well. For the first time, she let you know that she felt differently from you about some things. "No!" became a powerful new word, and probably her favorite. Though her confidence in using it still depended on how sure she was of your support, she was well on her way to thinking of herself as her own person with her own wishes and goals.

As your toddler approached her second birthday, she may have felt relaxed enough about her physical separation from you to be satisfied with a word or smile, even across an unfamiliar room. When you prepared her ahead of time for the moments when you would leave her with others, she probably became less anxious about such situations. By age two her sense of mastery and numerous drop-offs and pickups have added to her emotional confidence. Having formed a strong attachment to you, she is able to explore the larger world of emotions, relying a bit more on herself for reassurance.

A PARENT'S STORY

"Waaaaaah!"

"My two-year-old, Josh, was watching a videotape of his second birthday party the other day," a teacher at my sons' school told me. "My sister was over, and we were talking, so I wasn't paying much attention to Josh at first. But then I noticed that he got really fascinated at one point in the tape. It was right after the birthday cake part, when Josh grabbed this red balloon off the picnic table and it popped, and Josh started wailing. 'That was sad, wasn't it, Josh?' I said to him. Josh kept staring at the TV screen with an incredibly sad expression on his face.

"'Josh is sad,' he said to us.

"'Yes, the balloon popped,' I reminded him while my sister tried not to laugh at his crushed expression. 'But then Daddy gave you a new balloon, remember? Look!' I pointed to the screen, where we could see Josh getting a new balloon. 'Now Josh is happy!'

"I thought that would be the end of it. But instead, Josh turned to us with the same solemn look. 'Wanna see Josh cry,' he demanded. 'Do the tape, Mommy.'

"He seemed really serious about it, so I rewound the tape for him. He watched it again, utterly fascinated—as though he was trying to analyze his 'sadness.' It's just amazing, I think, how many little steps it takes before kids start to understand what's really going on inside."

"HOW DO I FEEL?": EMOTIONAL DEVELOPMENT AT AGE TWO

As an independent two-year-old, your child works hard at providing some of her own emotional needs. She comforts herself when she's anxious and praises herself when she behaves well ("Yay, Casey!"). She even makes an effort to empathize to some extent with those she loves. As she increasingly experiences such new emotions as shame and pride, she grows more interested in the concepts of "good" and "bad" behavior.

Her new autonomy has its downside, too. A two-year-old's most frequently used words at this stage are likely to be "me" and "mine." She may have trouble giving up the spotlight and begin to compete blatantly with siblings for attention. Her realization that she can make things happen makes her *determined* to do so. This willfulness leads to the types of battles for which two-year-olds are well known.

There's no use fighting this period of self-centeredness, since it's just another stage in every child's emotional development. Your two-year-old's will is directly related to her developing sense of self. When this fragile sense is threatened—when she is picked up and set in the bathtub when she's trying to climb into it, or when you give her an apple when she asked for a pear—she dissolves into shrieks of fury not because she's "spoiled" or tired, but because she has lost her hold on her version of the way things are supposed to happen. Later this year, she will more fully understand that others' desires may be as valid as her own. Meanwhile, it's important to mediate between your child and others (pointing out another child's position when yours shouts, "My trike!"), but don't expect your messages to be heard at first. The desire to share, take turns, and otherwise "be nice" comes only after a great deal of cognitive development on her part and patient explanation on yours.

As her cognitive growth continues, increasingly complex emotions and attitudes begin to form within your two-year-old. She will begin to think more about who she is and how she differs from you and others in her world. This self-awareness, along with a greater ability to hold her needs in check, will allow her to experience pride, jealousy, guilt, embarrassment, and misery. Such shadings of emotion, based not on sensory input or on her parents' opinions but on *her own assessment* of her status or behavior, signify a huge step forward in her emotional journey. They add a new layer of depth, making her more interesting in some respects to herself and to others. They also motivate her to continue strengthening her emotional muscles. By the time she celebrates her third birthday, she will have learned how to redirect her negative emotions occasionally into more productive pursuits, such as active physical games or imaginary play. Psychologist Wendy Grolnick and her colleagues showed how this process works by setting children loose in an unfamiliar room filled with toys while their mothers sat nearby, reading or otherwise engaged. At age two, the children weren't very good at adjusting to their mothers' lack of involvement. They called out for their mothers, whined, and clung. By age three, though, they were able to turn away quickly from their mothers and redirect their emotional energy to their play—pretending to be Mommy cooking at the stove and in other ways working out their discomfort through their own activities.

It is impressive how quickly a typical two-year-old learns to recognize, cope with, and even make use of the constant push-pull of her emotional life. Much of the credit for the progress your child has made in managing her emotions this year should go to you. By praising her accomplishments, and by showing satisfaction with your own successes, you have helped her experience the pride born of positive self-evaluation. By working to solve an emotional conflict with your two-year-old instead of just insisting on having your way, you introduced her to the powerful satisfaction of discovering solutions by herself. By empathizing with and helping both your child and others, you reminded her that her own needs aren't the only important ones. And by putting her feelings into words when she couldn't express them herself ("You're mad at Mommy, aren't you? But I know you still love her"), you gave her a giant head start in her efforts to understand what makes herself and others tick.

With this strong beginning, your two-year-old will turn three with a more mature awareness of others' emotions and a greater sensitivity to their feelings. Though she won't always be able to control her emotions, understand what she feels, or be willing to compromise, she will certainly be much further along than she was twelve months ago. As she grows, your continued praise and support will help her learn to judge herself as gently but fairly as you have—and to extend her kindness to others.

Q & A

"I Didn't Do It!"

Q: My thirty-month-old, Angie, went trick-or-treating for the first time this Halloween and was thrilled to bring home a bag full of candy. Most of the candy was still there the next morning, and Angie wanted to eat some first thing when she got up. We told her she had to wait until after breakfast and sat her down at the table. Instead of obeying us, she waited until both adults were out of the room, then took the candy under the breakfast table and started gobbling it down. When we came back in the room, she quickly stood up straighter so she was better hidden behind the tablecloth. (I guess she didn't realize we could see her anyway.) "Angie, are you eating the candy?" my husband asked. With her mouth full of chocolate, she answered, "No." I was very upset by this obvious lying, but my husband says it's just a stage. Is it something to worry about?

A: Clearly, Angie has reached the point at which she knows she has violated a rule of behavior and feels anxiety over the fact that she's done something wrong. Since she doesn't yet know how to cope with that uncomfortable feeling, she tries to get rid of it. In this case, the first way that occurred to her was to hide. When that failed, the next stage was to try to deny her wrong doing. Your husband is right when he points out that this isn't adult-type fibbing. Angie doesn't yet understand that she's "lying" in the sense that we understand it. She knows only that she feels uncomfortable, and that she can feel less anxious through her untruthful words. No doubt, she also wants to escape the consequences of having disobeyed you.

The way to ensure that her lying remains "only a stage" is to treat it as a lesson in problem-solving. Luckily, at this age kids are terrible liars, so it is usually easy to catch them in mid-lie and deal with the behavior immediately. The best way to do this is to first "name" the situation for your child ("Daddy sees that candy in your mouth. He's sad that you disobeyed"). Repeatedly and patiently, show her how to deal with the discomfort of having disobeyed by telling the truth ("Daddy knows it's hard to behave every time. But when I ask you a question, I want you to tell me what really happened. I won't be too mad if you tell me the truth"). Keep in mind that experiments with lying are bound to happen as any young child grows and learns. What's important now is to help your child learn better ways to cope with a guilty conscience.

"THIS IS ME":
BUILDING A PERSONALITY

"I do it!" "I go upstairs!" "I want grapes, please." "Look, I catched it!" Sometimes it seems as though all we hear from our younger two-year-olds is "I, I, I," and "me, me, me." Marching through the house, narrating their actions under their breath, they are completely enthralled by the exciting drama of being themselves. And no wonder—if it's fascinating to us to watch their personalities emerge from the amorphous behavior of babyhood, it must be even more enthralling to them. Suddenly your child realizes that she doesn't like pizza even though her brother does. She nods self-importantly when you point out that Sarah hasn't yet learned to share as well as she. She attempts a new activity and, depending on how much freedom she's given to pursue it, learns a little or a lot about herself in the process.

Of course, your child has been receiving information about herself since infancy. Your care and constant presence told her how valuable a person she was. Your willingness to let her toddle away while you kept watch let her know that she was a capable, active individual. If she was uncertain about your emotional availability during those years, she may have at least temporarily become more anxious and less adventurous. Now, however, as she begins to define herself somewhat less by your responses to her and more by her own criteria, her ability to explore independently is bringing her to a fuller knowledge of her strengths and weaknesses.

The person who emerges will not necessarily be the person you expect. To some degree, your child possesses a basic, inherited temperament that makes her simply "who she is." She may have been born with a high or low activity level, a sociable or shy nature, a sensitive or generally easygoing response to change, and marked difficulty or relative ease in handling emotional stress. Another important element in your toddler's development is how well her temperament matches your own. If you're a reclusive person who likes to stay at home reading a book on a Saturday night, you probably don't enjoy your sociable child's constant efforts to chat with strangers when the two of you are out and about. When she refuses to stay by your side and instead runs off after another child to strike up a conversation, you may decide she's "rebellious" by nature when in fact she's simply different from you. Your negative feelings about her may set up a negative cycle in which each of you insists on behaving in your own way, instead of recognizing that neither way is the only "right way." One key to successful parenting lies in

Age two opens up a wide range of emotions as your child's unique personality blossoms.

choosing techniques that suit your particular type of child. Studies have shown that very active toddlers play more competently when their mothers don't intervene much, while less active toddlers benefit when their mothers are actively involved in their play. Likewise, a shy two-year-old might prefer to develop her strengths in the quiet of her own home, while a sociable child learns best from her peers. Clearly, you cannot encourage your child's optimal development simply by following generic instructions laid out by parenting experts. Instead, you need to observe your child's particular responses to a variety of techniques and then settle on the approaches that bring out the best in her.

As your child moves through the first months of her third year, she will grow increasingly aware of the many "I's" she can be: the angry "I," the affectionate "I," the good "I," the naughty "I." What she doesn't yet understand is that all of these "I's" are contemporaneously part of one person—just as *you* can be the loving parent, the impatient parent, and the tired parent all at once. Though she has a sense that she is a person who carries out actions from one moment to another ("I climb the stairs," "I give the apple to Daddy"), she does not really comprehend the fact that she can hold many different emotions inside of her and still be the same person. She can be both an angry girl and a loving girl.

Several months of cognitive and verbal development must pass before your child can come to terms with her emotional fluctuations. At some point around the middle of the year, she will make her first connections between how she feels at one moment and how she feels the next. Gradually, she will begin to compare her past behaviors and ponder the advantages of one over the other in a particular situation. She will experiment with a variety of expressions in her pretend play and compare her own emotional expressions to those of her peers, her parents, and even characters on TV. She will enjoy imitating a variety of attitudes ("I'm strong! I'm Supergirl!") in the process of figuring out which ones suit her best. As she approaches age three, her urge to explore her emotional range may even lead her to fake her emotions—by pretending to cry when someone takes away a toy, or by pouting, teasing, or showing affection to get what she wants. This primitive form of emotional manipulation is a normal part of her development. She will soon learn from your consistent responses which emotional ploys are acceptable and which are not.

Responding supportively and consistently to your two-year-old provides her with an important emotional anchor. As your child swings from one mood to another, terrified one moment, furious the next, and full of affection a moment later, she may easily wonder just where in this emotional chaos she is. At twenty-four months, the experience of feeling more than one emotion at once ("I want to be a good girl. I want to be mean. Grrr!") can be frightening and confusing. Your ability to verbalize what she feels ("It's hard to share ice cream when we want it all ourselves.") grounds her and restores her to a sense of constancy. As this feeling of constancy grows stronger—as she learns that even when she loses emotional control and acts out, you will remain there for her—her sense of self-constancy will grow. Eventually, at around age three, she will begin to understand that her self endures despite temporary glitches in relationships—that while her emotions are fleeting, the essential *her* stays the same. As her self-perception stabilizes, her behavior will grow more consistent. You, too, will begin to notice certain behavioral patterns and personality traits that may remain beyond this year. Saying good-bye to the simplicity of your child's babyhood is certainly sad in some respects, but you will be rewarded with new, almost daily discoveries about her developing self. Though there is still a great deal of room for change, by the time she turns three the essence of her personality is visible for all to see.

THE TOY BOX

At Thirty Months

Hunter has been having a grand time with the toys in his toy box while Mom is on the phone. He's spread them all over the family room and down the hall, and he's currently lugging a bag of blocks to set up in the kitchen. Just then a voice cries out from behind him, "Hunter Jackson! What on earth!" Hunter freezes in his tracks. *It's Mom!*

"Hunter, you know better than to make a mess like this. Come here right now. We're going to clean it up."

"I wanna play blocks," Hunter informs her, holding up his bag of blocks.

"I don't care what you want to do. This is a disaster!" Mommy says in her no-nonsense tone as she starts to clean. "We have company coming tonight."

"But, Mom." Hunter's shoulders droop. The bag of blocks dangles listlessly from one hand. "I wanna play blocks," he says in a tiny voice. When his mother looks up at him, he makes his chin quiver. "Waaaaaaaaaaaah!" he wails.

His mother shakes her head, stifling a laugh. She's very annoyed, but Hunter's crying act is so fake it's funny. "That's not going to work on me, kid," she says briskly, taking the bag of blocks from him and adding it to her pile of toys. "Come on now. First, help me clean up, and then I'll make you an ice cream cone."

Hunter hesitates. *Ice cream is nice,* he thinks. The crying act didn't work this time. But cleaning up usually makes Mom happy. With a sigh, he squats down and picks up a toy.

"DON'T LET HIM GET ME!": ANXIETY AND FEAR

"On the day we decided to adopt Letty, Barbara and I agreed there would be no secrets in our family," Letty's father, Dan, told me during an interview. "We planned to let her know she was adopted as soon as she could understand what that meant, and to tell her all we knew about her biological parents. Around the time she turned two, though, we started to have second thoughts. All kinds of fears seemed to surface then—not just a fear of the dark and stuff like that, but getting scared about whether we *loved* her whenever we got mad! I started to wonder whether she had these anxieties because she sensed somehow that we weren't her "first" parents—I guess most adoptive parents worry about that. Anyway, our concerns about her nightmares and fears scared us enough that we avoided even mentioning anything to do with adoption. We even stopped reading children's books with characters who didn't have parents. Looking back, I wonder if it was our own anxiety that was making Letty uneasy. I think now that it probably made things worse. If I had it to do over again, I'd definitely go back to the original plan—treating the subject in an honest, relaxed way, and dealing with our own discomfort before we looked for hers."

Of course, adopted children aren't the only ones who experience anxiety and even fear this year. Having largely mastered their movement skills and made excellent progress in language, two-year-olds are primed to look around with a more sophisticated eye at their social and emotional environment—and as any parent of a child this age will tell you, they pick up on nearly everything. For the first time, they not only notice but *think about* the fact that Mommy or Daddy looks sad today. They link the image of water draining out of the bathtub with the possibility of swirling down the drain themselves. They peer at the shadows in their room at night and see strange shapes in the darkness. And it's possible that a parent's discomfort about a particular topic (whether adoption, as in Letty's case, or household finances, or anything else) might spark some fear or anxiety.

On the one hand, these new thoughts and feelings are an encouraging sign that your child's imagination is developing right on schedule. On the other hand, certain fears and anxieties can disrupt her sleep routines, social interactions, and general attitude. As you try to deal with these negative feelings keep in mind that, though her fears may seem irrational to you, they are very real to her. She has used her very limited reasoning abilities to arrive at what seem to be logical conclusions—and your brusque assurances ("There's no way the ogre in the book can get you," or, "You know Mommy doesn't leave you at the sitter's overnight") don't convince her that she's wrong. For this reason, it's important to listen carefully to your child's descriptions of her fears so as to pinpoint the source of her anxiety. Once you understand that she's terrified of masks because she thinks they're alive, you can touch one for her, drop it on the ground, encourage her to touch it herself, and otherwise demonstrate that it's inanimate. Once you learn that she's afraid of the dark because a shadow in her room looks like a monster, you can switch the light on and off, showing her what makes the shadow, close the closet door, or install a night-light. When you realize that she's experiencing a meltdown because you punished her for a misdeed and she thinks you've stopped loving her altogether, you can explain that you were angry for only a minute. Listening to your child and carefully clarifying matters for her will reassure her much more than a command to "stop being such a baby," ignoring her fears, or encouraging her to overcome them on her own. Keep in mind that negative feelings are natural counterparts to positive ones. They're part of life—and this year she needs your help in learning to manage them.

Not all fears are based on a child's misunderstandings. Your child may experience anxiety over the death or departure of a loved one or conflict within her family. As Dan suspected regarding his adopted two-year-old, avoiding these issues does nothing to ease your child's discomfort. They can be dealt with only through repeated conversations—held at the child's level of comprehension—in which you try to clear up your child's misunderstandings, identify and discuss real dangers, and help her express how they make her feel. Children's stories that address such fears can be helpful, as can your willingness to work out these issues through play. Gradually, through such efforts, your child will come to understand that, while fears come and go, you are always there to support and protect her. You will have not only put her mind at ease but added another layer of support to her emotional base.

Coping with Anxiety

Hobbled by limited reasoning powers and a frequent inability to express their fears, two-year-olds often find themselves in a position of knowing just enough to feel anxious, but not enough to be able to reassure themselves. Such triggers as a parent's frequent absence (particularly when it's not explained), discord within the family, the arrival of a new sibling, or even a parent's overprotectiveness can cause a young child to withdraw physically or emotionally from her parents or her environment, to behave aggressively, or to dissolve into overexcited shrieks and giggles. These defense mechanisms take the place of words for the child, allowing her to express her feelings and signal her need for help.

As with simpler fears, the best way to respond to such anxious behavior is to show your child that you are there to support her and to search gently—through conversation and play—for the cause of her discomfort. Once you understand why she has withdrawn or otherwise behaved defensively, you can correct any errors she's made in interpreting events. If your child fights you off when you arrive to pick her up at the sitter's, as Megan did at the beginning of this chapter, first clarify whether she's simply having a lot of fun. If she behaves the same way consistently from day to day, consider why she's so angry and defensive. Sometimes such feelings are not caused by any real events but are brought on when a child senses a parent's ambivalence. If you feel guilty about leaving your child in someone else's care, she will probably pick up on your worry that you've "abandoned" her. If you or your partner resent the balance of child-care responsibility in your marriage, your child may internalize your resentment and express it through her behavior.

In other words, your child's anxiety may be an expression of erroneous assumptions that you can clear up with sensitivity and patience—or it may result from very real emotions and situations that threaten her sense of safety. If you cannot change the negative factors in your child's world, or the emotional atmosphere that causes her discomfort, it may be necessary to consult a professional. A sense of safety is the most essential element in a young child's development. If your child's behavior reflects a belief that she has no one to depend on, it's better to get help for her sooner rather than later.

"GIMME THAT!":
ACTS OF AGGRESSION

Overwhelmed by conflicting emotions, unable to fully understand what's going on around them and still limited in their ability to share, take turns, and postpone gratification, two-year-olds sometimes, understandably, express their frustration in physical ways. As they begin to interact with others their age, their aggressive behavior can become more of an issue. No parent likes to see his child hit or bite a playmate, and certainly no child wants to play with someone who frequently hits or bites. Factors that tend to increase aggressive behavior—family stress (a new baby), physical stress (not enough sleep the night before), or even the relative sizes of the children (the aggressor simply being bigger and stronger than her playmate)—seem beside the point when you are apologizing to your child's friend or the friend's parent.

The bad news is that there is likely to be a great deal of aggression in your child's life this year—whether it's instigated by her or the children with whom she plays. The good news is that physical aggression typically decreases over time as your child learns to curb her impulsiveness and finds other ways to handle conflicts, such as negotiation. In the meantime, it may comfort you to know that her impulsive smack on the arm of a friend isn't a deliberate attempt to hurt him—it's just that she *must* have the toy he's holding and can't make herself wait for him to let it go. According to a 1992 study by Deborah Vandell of the University of Texas and and her colleague Mark Bailey, "property disputes" occur every five minutes among two-and-a-half-year-olds. Practically all of the aggression that two-year-olds practice against one another centers on objects. Though they are old enough to know that hurting other people is bad and will bring disapproval their way, they aren't far enough along cognitively to hurt another child deliberately.

Learning to control aggression is all about learning to think before acting. Your child's ability to control frustration, delay gratification, and work out tension in more positive ways will increase naturally to some extent as her cognitive growth continues. Certainly, she will need your support a great deal as she weathers the two-year-old's typical storms of intense, if fleeting, anger. You will need to explain to her—calmly and repeatedly—why grabbing, hitting, or biting is never a good idea. You will need to show her how to employ her developing language skills, to "use her words" instead of her body. (Older siblings provide a wonderful, natural context in which to teach these lessons.) When no one is getting hurt, it's fine to let disputes between two-year-olds work themselves out. By solving conflicts on their own, children learn valuable skills for the next time and gain experience in delaying gratification as well. But keep a vigilant eye on fights in the making. It is in no way a positive, instructive experience for a two-year-old to hit a child and then be punished for it. In fact, allowing her to act aggressively and then "pay the consequences" only sets up a pattern of behavior that can be difficult for her to break. The best way to deal with her aggression is to anticipate situations that might create frustration and do your best to help her avoid them.

One way to prevent aggressive behavior before it happens is to limit the amount of aggression to which your child is exposed every day. The media are saturated with images, talk, and reportage of violent acts. According to a 1996 study commissioned by Mediascope, 57 percent of all television programs aired between 6:00 A.M. and 11:00 P.M. contain violent scenes—but 66 *percent* of children's programs do. Keep in mind that most children aged two to three watch about two hours of television a day. As your two-year-old's awareness of her environment expands, she will mimic and experiment with the aggressive behavior she sees at the movies or on TV. You don't have to unplug the radio and throw away the VCR, but you do need to be vigilant. Your child is learning from what she hears and sees.

It's also important to take note of your child's "triggers"—the kinds of situations that frequently lead her to behave aggressively. Many two-year-olds dissolve into kicks and screams much more easily when they're tired. Yours may also become easily overstimulated by crowds and respond to being dropped into the middle of a birthday party by hitting the other guests. Two-year-olds who aren't ready to share valued possessions (and most of them aren't) will probably hurt another child to get an object they want. Active children who resent being confined may strike out at those who try to pick them up and hold them. Once you have familiarized yourself with these causes of aggression, you can easily avoid a great many of them. It isn't necessary to force your two-year-old to deal with a crowd of kids if she isn't ready, for example. Your child will fare better (and so will you) if you stay by her side and help her initiate some play with another child. If she tends to grow more aggressive when she's overstimulated or tired, make a point of letting her nap before a stressful activity (including those she enjoys), and give her a brief break from the action when you see her begin to lose control. Spread events out over a day or week to prevent burnout and loss of control. Resist the temptation to leave your two-year-old unsupervised for long just because she's old enough not to need your constant help. (She's not quite ready to play peacefully on her own.) Watch her even more closely when younger or smaller children are present. And be sure to set a good example yourself of positive ways to deal with anger and frustration.

As the months pass and your two-year-old gains more experience in what constitutes good behavior—and as her sense of herself as a consistently "good" girl takes root in the latter half of the year—she will be better able to tolerate frustration and rechannel her aggressive impulses. Gradually her defiant kicks and shouts will recede as she learns, with your support and patience, to manage the frustration of being asked to do something she doesn't want to do and to wait a bit for what she wants. Your good example will go a long way in demonstrating the rewards of good behavior. The next time a telephone salesperson interrupts the family dinner, don't slam down the phone. Smile for your observant two-year-old's benefit, politely end the conversation, and get back to your meal.

EASING THE WAY

When Your Child Strikes Out

We all have our bad days, and your two-year-old is no exception. When she responds to a buildup of frustration by hitting you or biting another child, remind yourself that this is just a sign of how limited her emotional resources still are, and certainly not a sign that she is "bad." To help your child recover and teach her that such behavior will not serve her well, avoid giving her an audience during her tirade. Instead, control your (perfectly natural) impulse to scream back and, if necessary, step away until you've regained control, allowing another adult to deal with her. When you feel better able to control your own aggression, state briefly what you think she's feeling ("I understand that you're mad because I want you to brush your teeth"). Then tell her why she can't respond aggressively ("But you can't hit people just because they make you mad. It hurts them. In this family, we

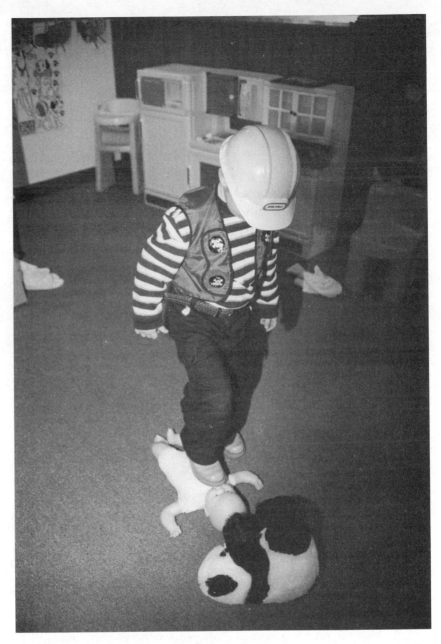

There will be times when your two-year-old's behavior will shock or embarrass you. Take heart—you're not alone!

don't hurt people"). Be sure your tone of voice conveys your conviction that this is important. She will pick up on any wavering or lack of confidence and instinctively exploit it.

Once you've acknowledged the reason for her behavior and reminded her that it's still unacceptable, give her a likable alternative if possible ("How about if we try the slides for a change? I haven't seen you slide in a long time"). You might distract her ("As soon as we leave, we can watch your new video"). If all else fails, humor usually works ("Is that an elephant on the playground? Let's go see!"). Sometimes simply giving her an extra moment to collect herself will get her back on track. Sometimes you may benefit from taking a brief time-out yourself.

There are times, however, when your child will simply be unable to stop her aggression. You may have to pick her up and put her in a place where she can work out her anger. Two-year-olds greatly resent giving up control of their bodies, and she will no doubt scream and kick as you carry her away, but don't be dissuaded. She needs the chance to calm down. Keep in mind that threats or comments aimed at inducing fear or guilt ("How could you be so bad?") are not only cruel but counterproductive. Likewise, general statements such as, "You have to share," and, "Hey now, be good!" only overwhelm and confuse her. Instead, tell her specifically what you want her to do, as in, "Let go of David's arm. It's his turn to throw the ball."

Once your child is calmer, it's a good idea to review briefly what happened with her. (The car ride home is a good time to talk, because she's confined and separated from distractions.) If you can put her feelings into words, she will feel supported and relieved. Your understanding can put the experience in perspective and help her use it to teach herself where she went wrong and how she might behave in more positive ways next time.

Finally, give your child a hug before sending her back into the fray. Her aggressive behavior is at least as upsetting to her as it is to you, and it's important for her to know that, though you don't approve of her aggressive behavior, you do approve of her. A quick signal of affection won't erase what you have said—it will only emphasize the fact that she is supported and loved even when she makes mistakes.

"I MISSED YOU TODAY!": LEARNING TO SHARE EMOTIONS

Nearly a year has passed, and Marjorie's life has settled down a bit. She and Nick have formally divorced and agreed on a custody arrangement that satisfies them both. Marjorie has weathered the layoffs at work and managed to hold on to her job. As the stresses in her life have diminished somewhat, she has been able to step back and see Megan's behavior not as just another overwhelming problem to deal with, and not as something directed purposefully at her, but as a young child's expression of her own anxiety and fear.

Today, as Marjorie climbs the steps to the baby-sitter's front door, she knows that Megan may not be eager to leave at first. Not only does Megan enjoy her time at the sitter's, but, as Marjorie has learned over the past months, she is simply by temperament not a person who makes transitions easily. At home Marjorie has learned that giving Megan a "countdown" before a new activity makes an enormous difference in her behavior. When Megan knows that "in ten minutes we'll be leaving," then "in five minutes," then "in one minute," she is reasonably ready to put her coat on by the time Marjorie is ready to go out the door.

Marjorie has also come to understand that Megan's screams ("Go away! I don't want you!") were the only way she could express her anxiety over all the changes in her life. Not only was her vocabulary still very limited, but Megan wasn't yet old enough at twenty-four or thirty months to understand her feelings. Marjorie's own ambivalence about hiring a sitter was another major factor in Megan's discomfort, Marjorie realizes now. Even when children can't identify a parent's emotion, they often pick up on it. Only after months of patient conversation, story-telling, and even compromise, when possible, has Megan begun to adjust to things as they are now.

"Come on in," Catherine says to Marjorie when she answers the door. "Megan's just finishing a picture she drew for you. It's really nice!"

"Hi, sweetie," Marjorie calls to her daughter as she steps inside. "How are you? I missed you today."

"Don't want to go," Megan responds, keeping her eyes on her work. Six months ago, these words would have devastated Marjorie and led her to question yet again her decision to work outside the home. Now, Marjorie takes them in stride. Why should Megan want to leave this instant, after all, when she's right in the middle of a project?

"Okay, you finish your picture," Marjorie says, sitting at the table near her daughter. "I'll talk to Catherine about your day, and when you're finished, we'll go home. Five minutes, okay?"

Megan doesn't answer, but Marjorie sees her relax a bit as she continues her drawing. She smiles, relieved to have avoided a crisis. "So," she says, turning to Catherine, "what kind of fun did you guys have?"

With luck and a great deal of effort, you, too, will see improvement this year in the way your moods and emotions mesh with your child's. As the two of you experiment with ways to express your emotions in positive ways, to meet each other's expectations much of the time, and to find productive means of dealing with the times you don't, you will find your daily life together proceeding much more smoothly. You will show your two-year-old consistently that there are limits beyond which you will not allow her to go, and that you are there to support her as she works to conform to those limits. In time, she will gain in self-confidence and courage to explore, and her emotional states will stabilize. With your help, she will come to appreciate the value of compromise and creative problem-solving, and she will learn that problems can be solved and despair is temporary. Best of all, as she approaches her preschool years, she will begin to internalize these lessons, and they will continue to support her emotional development as she establishes a life outside her home.

ADVANCES

Emotional Achievements in the Third Year

24 MONTHS	Self-confidence has increased
	Thrives on a reliable routine

	Can be bossy at times
	Takes pride in doing things herself
27 MONTHS	May experience frequent mood swings
	May begin to feel guilt when caught misbehaving
	Can sometimes express sadness or anxiety
30 MONTHS	May resent surrendering spotlight to siblings or peers
	Behavior is generally less impulsive
	May enjoy trying out different emotional expressions
33 MONTHS	Becomes curious about other people's moods
36 MONTHS	May show sympathy to those she loves
	Expresses affection spontaneously

FIRST-PERSON SINGULAR

Your child may be particularly interested in reading the notes you make here once she's grown old enough to wonder about her early development. She will probably want to know what her earliest fears and passions were, and how she first learned to deal with the frustrations of everyday life. Be sure to record any incidents in which she went out of her way to make another person feel better. She will need to know later that, while she was oftentimes moody, she was generally a very kind and generous child.

READER'S NOTES

_____

_____

_____

_____

_____

_____

_____

_____

_____

_____

_____

_____

_____

_____

_____

_____

_____

_____

_____

CHAPTER 6

"Play with Me!"—My Social Development

Y our child's developing awareness of the world around him will increase his ability to consider others' feelings and to want them to be happy.

"Come in!" Eileen says to twenty-four-month-old Jeff and his mother, Mary, as she steps back to let them pass into the living room. Eileen's twenty-six-month-old, Noel, sits on the living room floor beside his toy basket, playing with a wooden train set. "Look, Jeff," Eileen says to their visitor. "Noel's playing trains. Want to join him?"

Eileen has looked forward to this first play date between her son and Jeff, who met at a mutual friend's second birthday party. Eileen and Mary hit it off immediately, and the boys shared a great deal of enthusiasm for the helium balloons. Eileen hopes Jeff will turn into a regular playmate for her son, who has two older sisters but doesn't get many chances to play with kids his age.

"Jeff, say hi to Noel's mom," Mary prompts her son, but Jeff just marches past her toward the toy basket. Mary and Eileen glance at each other and laugh. *Who cares about parents,* the boys must be thinking, *when there's another guy to hang out with?*

"Would you like some coffee?" Eileen asks Mary as Jeff settles down on the floor near Noel. "I've just made a pot." Mary follows her into the kitchen, leaving the two-year-olds to play side by side. As she pours the coffee, Eileen begins asking Mary some of the questions she's saved up for this play date: how their visit to a local preschool went, how long they've been in the neighborhood, what other stay-at-home moms she's met so far, and how she likes living in this city. They are deep in conversation when a scream issues from the living room: "*My* car! Give that back!" Noel shouts.

Both mothers rush to the living room, where they find Noel up on his feet, in a rage. Jeff stands near him, clutching a toy car close to his chest and closing his eyes to withstand Noel's assault. To Eileen's horror, Noel raises his fist, which still holds a wooden train engine, and brings the engine crashing down on Jeff's head. "Give me that car!" he shouts, and then gives a shriek of utter frustration that Eileen recognizes from his constant bouts with his sisters.

Eileen rushes to pull her son off his guest. Jeff collapses, wailing, into his mother's arms. *Well, there we go,* Eileen thinks glumly as each mother tries to bring her son back into a reasonable frame of mind. *They'll never come over here again. Noel's so used to defending himself against his older sisters. He really needs to learn how to behave with kids his age—but if he hits and yells at them when they come to visit, how will he ever get the chance to learn?*

As exciting a time as this third year is for your child's social growth, it is also a year of very bumpy progress. These uneven periods, or "touchpoints," as my colleague Dr. T. Berry Brazelton describes them, involve great leaps in social ability followed by bewildering periods of regression. Parents of a verbally adept two-year-old may feel especially confident that their child understands how to interact successfully with others—only to find that he uses his many words to do battle with a potential playmate. Nothing is more discouraging than watching your young two-year-old, who says "please" and "thank you" to adults so sweetly when reminded, turn into a shouting, aggressive, and completely graceless child when you try to introduce him to a new playmate. Social skills are not innate, however, nor do they develop automatically alongside language and cognitive abilities. Your two-year-old must be taught how to behave with adults and with other children, and he must practice carrying out your instructions over and over. Finally, he must want to make deeper connections with people other than his caretakers—a desire that manifests itself only after other growth occurs.

In this chapter, we will see how a two-year-old's focus moves gradually from objects to other people, how he becomes increasingly aware that another person's point of view may differ from his own, and how he uses his interactions with others to experiment with social behavior and decide which types work best for him. A twenty-four-month-old may demonstrate his sociable tendencies by showing a caregiver an object he has found. By showing his discovery to her, he not only informs her about the object but shares his excitement about it. As he grows older, he may move from sharing or tussling over objects with a child his age to playing side by side at the same activity, and finally perhaps to "playing pretend" with him. His experience of the other child's habits, behavior, and expressions of emotion will teach him a great deal about the variety of social tools available to everyone and bring him that much further along in his social development.

As your child's ability to observe and analyze such actions improves this year, along with his skill at maintaining a sequence of social behavior ("thank you" follows "please"), he will no longer become so easily overwhelmed by glitches in his interaction with others. Rather than erupt in a rage when another child frustrates his desires, he will begin to use one of a number of social tools with which you and others have equipped him ("I'll take green. You have this one"). He will draw on an increasing ability to delay gratification, and he may even realize that the other child holds a valid point of view. Of course, his social life won't always be rosy, but if you give him patience, support, and a few well-placed instructions, he'll soon learn to maneuver through the conflicting desires that constitute a social existence. His eagerness to master this new skill will show in his eyes when, after playing for half an hour with a child he's just met, he announces, "I made a *friend!*"—though he probably hasn't even learned her name.

First Friends

"I started back to work part-time just a couple of months after Allison turned one," a mother told me while we were waiting for our kids to be released from their gymnastics class. "My neighbor had a two-year-old child, Ruby, who was cared for by a full-time nanny, and she and the nanny offered to have Allison stay with Ruby while I was at work. My neighbor had this whole fantasy about Ruby and Allison becoming best friends. I didn't see it, frankly, since the girls were six months apart in age, but I needed the child care so I went along with it.

"At first, it worked out just about as I had expected. It seemed like every time I went to pick Allison up, she and Ruby were screaming because one had hit the other or taken the other's toy or some such thing. Even when they were playing quietly, they didn't really play *together*. It was more like they'd play with different toys in the same room, mostly ignoring each other.

"Now that Allison's nearly three, though, I'm starting to think that my neighbor was right after all. The girls really do seem to be becoming friends of a sort. When they have a fight, they seem to be able to work it out faster than Allison can with other kids. And they cooperate a lot more. They have their little games that they play over and over, and they both know all the rules. The best part is, Allison seems to have picked up a lot of behavior tips from Ruby over the past year. Once Ruby figures out how to say, 'I'm sorry,' she makes sure Allison learns, too. Of course, she still doesn't want to let Allison be the doctor instead of the patient when they play hospital, but at least Allison has learned how to insist that they take turns."

"I WANT A FRIEND": SOCIAL GROWTH IN THE FIRST THREE YEARS

Of all the abilities that young children develop during their early years, social skills are perhaps the ones we parents most take for granted—and most misunderstand. Moms and dads who would naturally dismiss the idea of, say, trying to teach a three-month-old to talk, frequently meet in "play groups" where they expect their infants to acknowledge and enjoy one another. These types of get-togethers are wonderful for parents and may even benefit the babies indirectly as their parents exchange valuable information and necessary empathy. Infants, however, are necessarily focused on their own inner sensations and experiences and aren't yet cognitively advanced enough to enjoy playing with others their age. A baby must first learn that he has hands, feet, and a powerful voice before he can use them to meet, greet, and explore the world.

Since babies can't tell us what they know and don't know, it's difficult to judge exactly when they first become aware that they are separate beings in a social setting, rather than a part of their mothers and the rest of their environment. Certainly, your child's new ability to crawl between six and nine months of age led to more encounters with people and objects and thus gave him more experience of his separateness. At age one, his use of words to label objects helped him distinguish himself even more—demonstrating his understanding that a "doggie" was different from "me." As his social thinking grew more complex, he gradually began to comprehend the fact that others were not only physically separate from him but emotionally and mentally separate as well. He realized the two of you might respond completely differently to an event and would know how the other felt only if you communicated your feelings in some way. Few revelations are as mind-boggling as this one to a toddler. Your child no doubt revealed his interest through a process called *social referencing*—checking your responses to actions you both witnessed (another child crying for a bottle) and to his own actions (throwing his cereal bowl on the floor). By eighteen months, your child understood that the images of babies he saw on television were not images of himself—and that the person in the mirror *was* his own reflection. He had become sufficiently aware of his social surroundings to point out objects only if someone was there to see and hear him—instead of pointing and gesturing even when he was alone, as younger infants do.

It's easy to mistake the eighteen-month-old's awareness of others as a readiness to play with kids his age. But even the apparently natural desire to socialize requires several more developmental steps before it can be realized. The skills needed for play—taking turns, listening, empathizing, co-creating—are beyond the range of a toddler with limited language abilities and intense self-focus. Though your child was probably content to be placed in a room with another toddler, and enjoyed watching and even mimicking him, it's unlikely that the two children fully interacted. At age one, you and his other caregivers still instigated most of your toddler's social growth—teaching him verbal formulas ("Hi," "Bye-bye," "I'm sorry"), helping him find acceptable ways to communicate his feelings ("Don't whine, Troy, use your words"), and demonstrating the rhythms and body language of everyday conversation.

By now, however, your two-year-old has probably mastered the basics well enough to interact in more satisfying ways with other children as well as adults. His interest in others' emotions motivates him to reach out, while his great leaps in language ability make social interaction much easier. Now he truly enjoys the play dates you arrange for him, particularly if he's known the other child for a while. As the year unfolds, he will express a desire to share his experience with this child, saying, "Did you see that?" when he does something amazing, such as drop a ball through a net. His increased memory will allow him to think and talk about his playmates when they aren't present ("Clara likes frogs"), and his growing cognitive abilities will allow him to learn even more from them through imitation ("I hop like Mikey!"). He and his playmates may well continue to play side by side rather than together—and his emotional needs may make it hard for him to give up the spotlight to someone else—but with your encouragement and specific prompting ("Why don't we build a sandcastle together?"), he will begin to learn how to play *with,* rather than *beside,* a sibling or another child. Participation in group day care or nursery school will give him even more experience in this area. In fact, these encounters with nonfamily members can have a great impact on his social development. Studies have shown that a young child's general adjustment, competence with peers, and complexity of play are related to the quality of child care he is given and to his relationships with caregivers.

By his third birthday, your child's social world will have expanded immensely. He will have become conscious of and interested in a wide variety of adults and children he hardly noticed before. Now when you get together with a group of parents and their three-year-olds, you may enjoy the sight of two or more children playing together in the way we usually imagine. Of course, three-year-olds still often have a hard time sharing, listening, and acknowledging another child's desires, but with your patient tutelage, your child will have learned to enjoy playing hide-and-seek, chase, and "pretend" with others. He'll have begun to understand that the child he's playing with is not an obstacle but a *friend.* And he may even have learned to share the spotlight—though this will be harder at some times than at others.

THE TOY BOX

At Thirty-two Months

The entire family is watching a movie on television, and two-year-old Cam is bored. He wanders over to his toy box in the living room and rummages around, looking for something to do. Suddenly he spots his sword—the beautiful gray plastic sword his uncle gave him for his birthday. That sword has been the center of a great deal of dramatic play among Cam and his three siblings—all boys. Gazing at it, Cam remembers wonderful battles in the backyard, in the basement, and racing from bedroom to bedroom upstairs.

"Look out!" Cam shouts, grabbing the sword and raising it high over his head, just as his older brother James does. Instantly his three older brothers turn to look at him. Basking in the attention, Cam jumps forward, waving the sword. "Look out!" he crows.

As his parents laugh, two of Cam's brothers leap up and grab the sword from him. "En garde!" the older one shouts, jumping onto the back of an easy chair. "Henry, stop that right now!" his dad shouts as Henry races across the living room, two brothers in tow.

Cam stands, arms at his side, staring after his brothers. Everyone was looking at him—and now they're not! Now they're looking at *Henry,* and Henry has the sword! Cam feels a wave of despair wash over him. He tried to make something interesting happen. Something is happening, all right, but it doesn't have anything to do with him. Frustrated and helpless to change the course of events, he begins to wail. Even when his dad comes to comfort him—even when he orders Henry to give back the sword—Cam has a hard time recovering his equilibrium. Even after his brothers have turned back to the movie, he continues sniffling, wiping his face with his sleeve. *He* wants to control what happens with his toys! *He* wants to direct the play! He clutches his sword close. Next time he won't let them take it away.

"SAY HELLO": TEACHING YOUR CHILD THE RULES OF SOCIAL INTERACTION

"I have to admit, sometimes I long for the good old days," a friend remarked as we picked our kids up from preschool. "I remember when all I had to do to keep Anthony happy was to be there, smiling at him. Now that he can talk, it's, 'Let's go outside,' and, 'Gimme!' and, 'I don't *want* to hug Grandma!' all day long. All of a sudden, I have to negotiate every minute of the day. When is this going to end?"

There's no denying that, over the past two or more years, your healthy, inquisitive child has moved steadily away from the more observant state of infancy into the active role of full-fledged member of the family. Whereas initially you, as his parent, did more of the giving and he did more of the taking, your relationship increasingly became a two-way street. The remarkable cognitive, emotional, and verbal growth he achieved by age two enabled him to question your decisions, defy your orders, probe your emotions, and return your expressions of affection. Fortunately, these same advances enabled him to begin to learn the rules of social engagement—from everyone in his environment, but especially from you.

Your child has long been primed to learn from you the best ways of interacting with other people. From his first day of life, when he grasped something, kicked a foot, or performed some other random action, you responded with an eager smile, pleasant sounds, and perhaps a gentle hug. As he grew, he listened to the rhythms of your speech and watched how you approached others in your world. Peekaboo games provided him with early lessons in the turn-taking aspects of social interaction. His constant testing of your responses to his actions led to a steady stream of information on how to respond to similar situations himself.

During his third year, your child begins to express much more freely all that he has learned before. Having tested your responses and compared them to his own for over a year, he is well aware that you (or any other person) may have opinions completely different from his own. So when you offer him an apple, he may remind you that he likes cookies. When you tell him it's bathtime, he may announce (loudly) that he doesn't want to take a bath. This sudden urge to take a stand in his relations with you and others is quite trying for many parents, but at least it's a sign that he is eager to take his place as a member of his society. In fact, an inability to stand up for himself would be cause for concern in a two-year-old. As he enters the wider world, he needs to establish his place.

Your two-year-old is eager not only to achieve full partnership in his interactions with others but to learn the social rules that will best help him reach his goals. This is the year when he will learn whether a scream or a polite request is more likely to get him the TV time he longs for. Now is the time when he will begin to say "Excuse me" as a matter of course— or will deliberately not say it. Though he is still too young to understand *why* he must wait in line, refrain from interrupting, and so on, he is old enough to begin practicing these skills and to understand that it pleases you (and other important adults). As he experiments with your suggestions (saying "Thank you" when an adult offers him a toy, for example, or saying to a child, "Do you want some pizza?") and gets positive results (beaming adults, a happy playmate), he will use them more often. Of course, this progression will not be steady—he will also experiment with less positive ploys and frequently forget the good behaviors he's learned. But your approval and support are very powerful forces in his life this year. The more you reward his efforts at demonstrating correct social behavior, the harder he will try to live up to your expectations.

Another way in which you can encourage your child's social development this year is by acting as an interpreter of other people's emotions and motivations. Your two-year-old is fascinated by others' points of view, yet he often lacks the experience to understand how they feel. He will need many, many reminders this year that "hitting Bobby *hurts* him, just like Bobby's hitting hurts you," and, "People like it when you smile and talk nicely to them. Screaming hurts their ears." Only in this way can he begin to comprehend not only that other people have their own feelings, but that his actions affect those feelings in important ways.

By the second half of this year, your child will have come to rely on you to introduce him to the rules of social interaction and to explain why we behave toward one another as we do. Not all of these lessons will have been directly stated. You will have familiarized him with the practice of turn-taking by playing simple games with him, taught him the importance of reciprocity by completing chores together, and instilled a rudimentary respect for others' opinions through your casual, daily conversations.

It's important to keep in mind this year, especially when your two-year-old is misbehaving in public, that children don't instinctively understand even the basic rules of social interaction. Acceptable behavior springs almost entirely from the instructions and example that you and others give him, this year and in the years to come. As your child learns to shape his natural impulses in ways that better suit his interactions with others, he will gain a better sense of where he stands in his environment. He will possess, if not always act on, a greater understanding of what makes relationships proceed more smoothly. He will have learned to respect his own opinions, and sometimes even to respect yours.

A CHILD'S-EYE VIEW

"Say Thank You"

No more doctors! Chloe squirms on her mommy's lap, wishing she could pry open the arms clamped around her and escape this tiny room. "Doctor Dan" has already poked Chloe's tummy with a stethoscope and stuck a flashlight in her ears. His strange behavior—kneading the area around her neck, peering into her eyes—has excited her curiosity and made her feel uncomfortable at the same time. But the worst is yet to come. A lady in a white lab coat enters, saying something about "hurting just a little." Chloe recognizes that white coat. *Not good!* She struggles, but before she knows what's happening, the lady jabs a needle into her arm. "Aaaaaaaaagh!" Chloe screams, but the needle is already gone and the woman is out the door.

"It's okay, Chloe," her mother says as she carries her out to the waiting room. But Chloe cries even harder. It most definitely is *not* okay! *Who was that lady? Why did Mommy let me get hurt?*

Next thing Chloe knows, she's sitting on the counter at the receptionist's desk. "Look!" her mother tells her. "Ms. Daley has a present for you!"

Sniffling, Chloe wipes her eyes and turns to look at the receptionist. She's smiling at Chloe—but she has a lab coat on, too! *Who's she?* Chloe wonders, panic rising again. *Is she going to hurt me, too?*

"Take the cookie, Chloe," Mommy says, squatting down beside her daughter and pointing to the cookie in Ms. Daley's hand. "Don't forget to say 'Thank you.'"

Is that lady good or bad? Chloe can't figure it out. But the cookie hovers tantalizingly near. Chloe looks back and forth between Mommy and the stranger with the cookie. "Sank you," she says uncertainly.

The strange woman's face lights up in a big smile. So does Mommy's. Mommy gives Chloe a kiss. "Good, Chloe," she says. "You're so polite."

As she leaves the office, Chloe chews the cookie meditatively. *One white coat hurt me,* she thinks. *One gave me a cookie. When you get a cookie, you say "Thank you." When you get hurt, you . . .* She shakes her head. The ways of adults just bewilder her sometimes. All she knows is, she was a "good girl." She said "Thank you." And the cookie tastes sweet.

"YOU BE THE BABY": GROWING
SOCIALLY THROUGH PLAY

It would be easier, perhaps, if our children looked to us alone for information on how to express themselves socially, but one of the hallmarks of this third year is their increasing interest in other children. Your two-year-old may be quietly paging through a picture book in the library when a group of shrieking kids races into the room. Impressed, your child stops what he's doing and shrieks, too. Even if the newcomers race off and are never seen again, you may have to put up with your own child's shrieks in the library for weeks afterward, until you can persuade him that that particular form of social expression is a bad idea.

Of course, other children's influence can be a very positive force as well—a girl in the park may offer her trike to your child, modeling good behavior—and playing together allows children to practice the social rules that they've just begun to learn. Your two-year-old may not be able to sustain a friendly interaction with a child his age for more than a few minutes at a time, but during these brief episodes of mutual imitation (making a noise, responding to it, making it again), cooperation (building blocks together side by side), and pretend (talking to each other on toy phones), he will learn much about the rewards and requirements of social give-and-take. His experiences with slightly older children can prove even more stimulating as these "mentors" introduce him to more sophisticated activities such as games with rules (hide-and-seek), role-playing (teacher and student, doctor and patient), and scene enactment (conducting a tea party, escaping a monster). Since children are much more likely than adults to repeat such activities over and over, your child will be able to explore many more aspects of the game than he might if you were playing it with him.

In fact, one of the greatest forces for social growth may be living right in your home. Studies have shown that, while interacting with any child expands a two-year-old's social and cognitive awareness, playing with and observing *familiar* children has an even stronger influence on them. Not only is your child familiar with his siblings and already embroiled in a complex social relationship with them, but his brothers and sisters are frequently available for social interaction and can be observed communicating in a variety of ways with the parents. Rest assured, then, that your youngest is watching carefully—and even listening from the next room—as you talk with your other children. Whatever tactics they use to achieve their goals are bound to be imitated. You can make the best of this situation by pointing out to your two-year-old his older sibling's appropriate behavior ("Look—David helped clean up his room this morning,") and refusing to reward rudeness or selfishness, particularly when your two-year-old is watching.

Part of learning about social interaction includes learning about gender roles and gender-related behavior. Your child's general interest in classifying objects (a cow is an animal, blue is a color) will naturally spur him to classify himself as a boy or girl. At first, though, he won't have more than a vague idea of what this classification means. He may think of a girl as someone with long hair—and so will assume that a male teenager with a ponytail is a girl. His idea of a boy as, say, a short-haired person wearing pants will be so strong that you could remove the dress from a female doll, put the doll in pants, and cut its hair right in front of him, and he would call it a boy. His concept of "boyness" and "girlness" will remain vague through the end of the year, and he'll probably make many mistakes in categorizing people.

In the same way, his gender-related *behavior* will waver quite a bit. His "boy-like" or "girl-like" preferences (play fights versus tea parties), if any, will remain vague and change constantly. If he is enrolled in preschool or some other group care program, he may feel the urge to imitate others who are "like" himself and thus indulge in more gender-typical play. Consciously or not, you and your child's other caregivers will also affect how gender-typed his play is at this age, as evidenced by a 1991 study by Beverly Fagot. She showed that parents most strongly direct their children's play according to gender at eighteen months, and other studies show that parents' gender-related attitudes and behavior continue to hold sway for years to come.

As this year progresses, your child's awareness of adult interactions increases, feeding his curiosity about what it means to be a boy or a man, a woman or a girl. He will note that Daddy behaves in one way and performs certain social tasks, while Mommy behaves in different ways—and these observations will spur him to think about which way

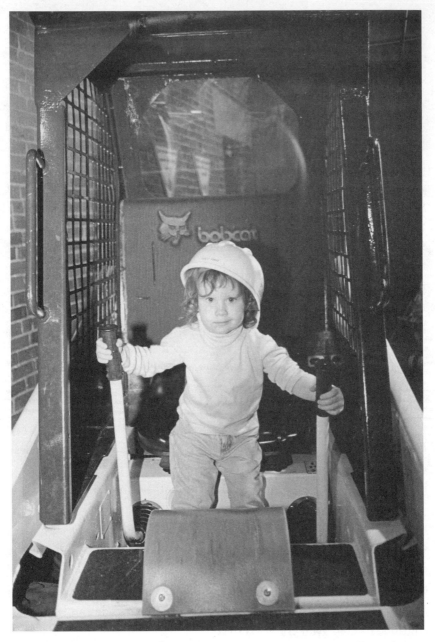

Surrounding your two-year-old with varied play experiences allows her to explore without preset limits.

he will act. At this point, he may begin to imitate his same-sex parent's social behavior—playing office like Dad and imitating his speech mannerisms or movements. Most parents unconsciously reinforce this kind of gender learning and even shut their young children down when they cross the gender line ("Donny is *not* dressing as Wonder Woman for Halloween!"). It's important to understand, however, that your child is only *observing* and *imitating* differences in behavior—he is not expressing any deeper urges. He certainly has no understanding that behaving like a member of the opposite sex means something to adults ("Is he gay?"), and his cross-gender experimentation is not necessarily an indication of his future tendencies.

If gender issues are important to you, or a source of contention between you and your partner, this is a good time for both of you to think about what your feelings and behavior are teaching your child. Any anxiety you feel about your child's gender-related behavior, or about the subject of gender in general, is far more likely to affect your child's attitudes than his actions themselves. (He will suffer from dressing up as Wonder Woman only if you or others he cares about react negatively.) It's better to keep things very simple this year—helping your child experiment with gender roles through imaginative play, keeping some nonstereotypical toys around to allow him to explore less familiar territory, and giving brief, nonjudgmental answers to his questions as a way of laying the groundwork for future discussions. Keep in mind that these issues will grow much stronger and more valid at age three and older.

Exploring and experimenting with gender roles, even at the level of a two-year-old, does give your child an exciting preview of what it's like to be an individual in the larger world. Though the persona he adopts today is no more likely to express his mature social "self" than the one he adopts tomorrow, it is a sign that he is thinking about social interaction in much more sophisticated and interesting ways. The more he is able to play with these concepts—to understand how he is like or unlike Mommy, how he resembles or does not resemble Dad, how both Mom and Dad are good at some things—the more self-confident he'll feel as he strides into the challenging world of preschool and other group activities. This confidence is very important as he interacts with and is judged by teachers, parents, and other adults who don't already know him.

Social development is not all about learning rules and studying gender roles, of course. Playing with others is fun, and we all hope our children will enjoy the pleasures of friendship. By his third year, your child interacts in much more complex and positive ways with others his age than he ever did before. He can distinguish between his playmates and even develop comfortable routines as he interacts with the partners he knows best. Though months or even years must pass before he begins to truly understand the difference between an acquaintance and a friend, the foundations for close peer relationships are being laid down this year. Slowly, day by day, he is learning to cooperate, to show affection, and to settle disagreements. He is beginning to consider the concept of fairness and to understand that his playmates have rights that may be as valid as his. As he celebrates his third birthday—surrounded, perhaps, by some of the children who've helped him explore these issues—he can surely look forward to years of rich, fulfilling, and ever-developing friendships.

Q & A

My Quiet Child

Q: My daughter, Hillary, has never seemed very interested in other kids. When I take her to any social event, she clings to my skirt and cries if I try to pry her off me. I didn't used to let it bother me much, but now that she's nearly three, her behavior is beginning to seem unusual. I'd like to enroll her in preschool next year, but I'm worried that she won't be able to handle the social aspects of it. She doesn't have any brothers or sisters, and the play dates I've arranged have all been washouts, since she refuses to interact with her guests. Is her behavior normal? If not, what should I do?

A: Your child is apparently shy by nature (many, many young children are), but whether or not this is the case, she could probably benefit from learning some specific ways to relate to other children and practicing them in simple, nonthreatening contexts. Set the bar low at first—expose her to informal encounters with other children in places she already knows, such as the children's museum, the library, or the pond where you go to feed ducks. Model good social initiatives for your child (saying to another child, "Would you like to feed the ducks, too?"). Comment on the positive results ("Look—she smiled!"). Don't put pressure on your child to talk to the newcomer, but allow them to continue their activity together, side by side. With time, your child will begin to feel more comfortable and may even respond when the child makes a move toward her.

Once your daughter seems more comfortable just being with another child, arrange for a play date, preferably with a child she already knows reasonably well. Before the play date, act out parts of it with your daughter, suggesting play ideas ("Maybe Trish will want to play ball"). Discuss which toys she'd like to share with her visitor, and help her put the others away. Structure the play date so that your child doesn't feel she must shoulder the entire social burden herself. Plan to help the two of them bake muffins, play dress-up together, or volunteer to be "it" in a game of hide-and-seek. And talk about what she should do if the other child hits, refuses to share, or behaves in any other way that she fears. When the time for the play date arrives, read a magazine nearby or otherwise stay unobtrusively within sight, so you can be there to support her if she becomes uneasy. If you can help her enjoy one play date, she is more likely to look forward to another. In this way, little by little, you can help her curb her innate resistance and find ways to begin making friends.

"GO AWAY!": SOCIAL LABELING AND REJECTION

"I'll never forget the first time I met Hector," a client told me during a visit. "I guess every neighborhood just has to have a bully, and even at two and a half, Hector was ours. Even though he was the youngest kid on the block, he was big for his age and looked about three or four. The first time I saw him was at an outdoor barbecue, and he was pushing a child to the ground for the third time since he and his mother had arrived. You should have seen the looks on the other parents' faces as his mother dragged him away from that screaming four-year-old. It didn't matter that Hector was only two and didn't know how to act as old as he looked. It didn't matter that his mom was eight months pregnant and he was probably mad about the baby. Everyone at that barbecue had already labeled Hector a bully. He's five now, and he still has that reputation. I think he's given up trying to fight it."

Few social issues are more painful for many parents than the notion that their child may be negatively labeled by his peers. Memories of children's taunts ("Tattletale!" "Wimp!" "Crybaby!") still haunt many of us, and we may worry a great deal about our own kids suffering from them. Though two-year-olds are rarely in a position to be labeled or rejected, it is not too early to teach them how to avoid the social behavior that often leads to such treatment, as my client's story illustrates. If Hector's mother had monitored him more closely, considered his angry state, and *prevented* him from pushing other children rather than pulling him away afterward, she might have been able to shape his behavior in ways that would have improved his relations with the adults in his life as well as with other children.

Refraining from aggression is not the only social skill your child will need to gain acceptance among his peers. He will need to know how to express positive feelings and how to respond to his friends' positive gestures. He will have to know how to express his thoughts and interests in ways that will engage others' attention. He must be able to lead as well as follow. He should know how to have fun and how to share his enthusiasm with others. He must also learn how to control his negative feelings rather than letting them erupt too often in angry words or tears.

Many of these prosocial abilities develop naturally from your child's interaction with you and others in his immediate circle. Some may run contrary to his natural temperament, and he may need help and encouragement from you to develop them. If you feel, for example, that your very active two-year-old routinely overwhelms other children—either physically by knocking against them frequently or invading their personal space, or verbally by interrupting frequently and refusing to listen—now is the time to begin teaching him specific ways to leave room for others. If he is a sensitive child who cries easily, it makes sense to keep his interactions short, remain nearby to redirect him in difficult situations, and talk with him frequently about how you and others manage your own anxious feelings. In general, it is important to keep in mind that younger two-year-olds are not able to interact in positive ways in many kinds of situations. As I pointed out in the previous chapter, your best bet in starting your child on the road toward social acceptance is, whenever possible, to circumvent situations that you know he can't yet handle, to teach him the basic rules and tools of social interaction, and to support him in his efforts to control his own destructive impulses.

As your child nears age three and engages in more group activity, he is more likely to encounter gender-based exclusion, particularly from older children. At this age, it is quite startling and confusing to hear two or three girls shout, "Go away! No boys here!" or vice versa. Unpleasant as this kind of rejection is, it happens all the time among preschoolers (and older children as well). Some professionals believe that exclusion serves a valuable function, helping children preserve social groups that they've only just learned to form and enabling them to hang on to a stable identity. It may also protect their play from disruption by outsiders—particularly those who are likely to play differently.

Rather than condemn exclusionary behavior when your child reports it, consider using it as an opportunity to discuss (at a simple level) the entire issue of labeling and exclusion ("It's sad when you want to make new friends but the kids won't let you play"). Such a conversation may reveal fears or anxieties you didn't know he had. Teaching him specific, concrete ways to deal with such behavior will go much further in helping him manage his world than criticizing the other children or complaining to the adult in charge. You might also read one or more of the many children's books that deal with this issue on a level he can understand. Finally, casually acknowledging the existence of certain social dynamics ("Lots of times people in a group don't want new kids to join in") lets your child know that he has not been rebuffed for personal reasons and that it is quite likely that on another day the group will accept him gladly.

Crisis Management

It's easy enough for most of us to talk to our kids about playing fairly and being gentle with those who are smaller than us— but successfully managing an actual fight can be a greater challenge. On a typical day, every playground in every neighborhood resounds with cries of "Get off me!" and "Ow!" It's hard to know what to do—or how to restrain your own emotions— when you see your child hit or pushed by another child, or even ignored or insulted by an adult. The best approach may be to look on these inevitable skirmishes as a learning experience. Since such demoralizing encounters are unfortunately part of everyone's life, you can best help your child by teaching him how to deal with them and move on.

When your child turns to you in tears after a child has hurt him, resist the impulse to, on the one hand, rationalize that child's behavior or, on the other, to label him as "bad" or a "bully." (Remember, next time the aggressor could be your child.) Acknowledge that the child "made a mistake" or "doesn't know the rules," and that "pushing was wrong." Model an effective response by putting a hand on the other child's hand and saying, "Don't do that. It isn't nice. Let's do this instead." Then, as the child demonstrates better behavior, focus on the positive by saying, "Look, he's sharing now." Ideally, the parent of the other child will cooperate in this effort (and you should certainly enlist the aid of the other parent if you can). Whether or not other adults cooperate, however, your job this year is to demonstrate a positive response for your child so that he'll be able to deal with others' hurtful behavior in the future.

"WANT SOME?": PRACTICING CONSIDERATION

Part of joining the larger world is learning to empathize and show kindness to other people. Your child's developing awareness of the

Sharing and taking responsibility are two social skills that you can begin to instill in your two-year-old.

world around him this year will increase his ability to consider others' feelings and to want them to be happy. This is a different experience from his tendency as a toddler to look concerned when you were upset, or the vague but gentle pat he may have offered last year when he found you crying. Last year he could compare your sadness to similar feelings he had felt and be moved to comfort you. Now, his mind has developed to the point where he is actually able to see things from another person's point of view (particularly those who are closest to him), to think about what might make that person happy, and to act on his empathic impulses.

This doesn't mean that your two-year-old will regularly offer his toys to restless playmates or play quietly by himself when he realizes you need a rest. Though he may *understand* the state you're in to some extent, he still finds it very difficult to put aside his own needs to tend to yours or anyone else's. When encountering another person's distress, he can easily feel threatened, his fragile sense of self dissolving in the face of the other's tears. If he sees that Brandon is scared, he may wonder whether he should be, too. This uncertainty makes him more likely to cry, act aggressively, or leave the scene than to console Brandon or try to cheer him up. In other instances, he may simply not yet know what to do to ease another person's unhappiness (such as offering his company to a child playing alone). It is also true that two-year-olds are so accustomed to seeing adults help an unhappy child that they may hang back and wait for a grown-up to make things better.

Fortunately, your child will make another discovery this year that will help him act on his empathic impulses. He will begin to understand more clearly the concept of personal agency—things don't just happen but are *made* to happen. His baby sister stops crying, for example, when he gives her a pacifier. His growing familiarity with this idea may lead to a fascination with the concept of personal *responsibility*. Once this happens, many older two-year-olds quite suddenly transform into solemn commentators on each family member's misbehavior ("Mommy, Mikey didn't share."). Annoying as this habit can be to his siblings, you can at least assure them that he's not turning into a tattletale (he's not old enough for that). He's just suddenly interested in how right and wrong behavior occur. Reward his interest by affirming his intuition that Mikey did something wrong (out of Mikey's hearing, of course) and talking about the positive behavior that Mikey might have chosen instead.

Understanding that he and others can make things happen will soon lead your child to the idea that people can affect each other's emotional states as well. Now is the time for him to begin acting on his positive urges in this area. He will need plenty of instruction on precise ways to do so. Especially near the beginning of this year, simple, concrete instructions and explanations ("Don't take that cookie away from Henry. It will make him sad") work much better than confusing general comments ("Frank, remember to share!"), which he isn't yet equipped to comprehend. As he begins to understand what behavior is expected and act correctly, you can simply acknowledge the fact that he has done so ("Look how you shared your cookie with Henry. Good for you!"). As he reaches the end of this third year, it's a good idea to talk about such behaviors even when they're not actually happening and to discuss situations that are likely to arise ("Remember, when Henry gets here, you'll need to share your toys"). It's also important to articulate the reasons behind such behavior—to talk about how a child feels when a playmate shares with him, comforts him, and so on. As your child increasingly shows interest in his own and others' feelings, comment on them frequently yourself. When reading storybooks, discuss with him how the hero feels at a certain point in the story and why, and what the hero might do to make himself or another feel better. Help your child try to remember when he felt the same way. And don't forget to talk about your own feelings, too. It is an amazing, reassuring discovery for young children to realize that their parents experience sadness, excitement, hope, envy, discomfort, and doubt, just as they are beginning to feel these complex emotions themselves.

Age two is a time to begin these lessons, but it is not a time to expect perfection in carrying them out. As in all areas of growth, your child will need to experiment with many variations in behavior before settling down to those that work best for him. For this reason, you can expect him to expend a great deal of energy violating the very types of behavior you're trying to teach him. At some point, he'll probably enjoy challenging you in ways that run contrary to your expectations about relationships ("I don't love you, Mommy!"), honesty ("I didn't do it!"), or good behavior ("I won't share!"). Difficult as it is to put up with these experiments, it's important for you to provide the correct responses. By calmly reminding your child that you love *him,* that you know he didn't tell the truth, or that if he doesn't share his friend won't want to keep playing with him, you reassure him that the world is as it should be and that the standards he is learning really are important.

By his third birthday, your child's ability to tolerate delays and to restrain his immediate impulses will have improved a great deal. These two developments will go a long way toward helping him become a kinder, more thoughtful person. As he grows, he will get better at understanding others' points of view, cooperating, and thinking of ways to express his empathy. As a result, family life should improve markedly over the next few years, if not always at a smooth pace.

IF YOU'RE CONCERNED

Social Challenges

The third year is not an extremely social one for all children, and it is not fair to expect your child to enjoy playing with other children most, or even part, of the time. He has much work to do in understanding his own thoughts and emotions before he can focus fully on others his age. Children's social skills do not really develop until between ages two and a half and five. There's no point in expecting these abilities to manifest themselves before then. However, if your older two-year-old shows *no* interest in other children, or if his behavior causes others to avoid, taunt, or complain about him, now is certainly the time to observe his interactions carefully and consider the reasons behind them.

The amount of time your child spends playing with other children is not the only gauge of how well he's growing socially. If he plays often with others but almost always takes on the same role (the follower rather than the leader, for example) or plays in nonproductive ways (constantly teasing or otherwise provoking the other child), he may need more focused attention from you before he can begin to manage relationships more successfully. A child who frequently hovers at the edge of a group of children, hoping in vain to be invited to join in, or one who smiles eagerly at a peer but doesn't know how to engage him in play, could clearly use some instruction in how to get to know someone new. If your child seems to prefer swinging all afternoon, on the other hand, or is content to go up and down the slide by himself, he is probably just not focused on social issues right now and will pick up his "people skills" easily enough when his time comes. However, if he maintains a low level of play activity beyond his third birthday, try to pull him out of himself. Too much time spent alone may lessen the amount of stimulation he receives, limit his cognitive growth, and leave him stuck in behavioral patterns that don't work well for him. Make a point of engaging him in a social activity, and show him through modeling, talk, and encouragement the joys of playing with others.

"ME, AND YOU, TOO": THE BEGINNINGS OF FRIENDSHIP

It's Thursday, and nearly time for the biweekly play date that Eileen and Mary have arranged for their two sons for nearly a year. Noel, two weeks from his third birthday, can hardly wait for Jeff to appear at his front door. "Jeff is coming today!" he keeps cheerily reminding his mom. "Jeff is my friend!" Eileen is also looking forward to the play date, which is so easy to prepare for at this point. She has a good idea of what kinds of activities each boy will want to do. She knows which toys are likely to keep them playing happily, and which ones to hide upstairs before Jeff's arrival to prevent a fight or overly aggressive play. Once she and Mary realized that it was wiser to chat in the same room with their boys than off in the kitchen on their own, they quickly picked up on the directions in which each child's personality was evolving. Fortunately, the two boys' temperaments seem to complement each other—

Jeff's generosity sometimes inspires Noel to share more readily, and Noel's enthusiasm for imaginary play leads Jeff into more complex thinking. The boys appear to sense that it's a good match, too, Eileen muses. There's a rhythm between them that allows for more fun and less conflict than earlier in the year.

Just as Eileen is pulling Noel's construction kit from the toy box, the doorbell rings. "Jeff's here!" Noel cries, running to the door. Eileen opens it and greets Mary as Jeff races past them to embrace her son. "*Finally* you got here!" Noel says with satisfaction, pulling Jeff by the hand into the living room. "I couldn't *wait* to play!" Mary and Eileen glance at each other, amused. It's really true, then, Eileen says to herself. Noel has made a friend.

ADVANCES

Social Achievements in the Third Year

24 MONTHS	Imitates other children's behavior
	Enjoys playing with older children
	May begin to share
	Sometimes empathizes with another's emotions
27 MONTHS	Siblings become more significant members of his social world
	May enjoy play groups
30 MONTHS	Begins to comprehend the concept of a friend
	Wants to be the center of attention
33 MONTHS	May benefit from group care or preschool
	Starts taking control of play with peers

36 MONTHS   Is able to learn and remember social rules and customs

Becomes more interested in the concept of gender and gender-related behavior

FIRST-PERSON SINGULAR

It's a sad fact of life that many of us forget the names of those friends who meant so much to us when we were very young. Take a moment to record here the names of your child's first playmates. Describe the activities they enjoyed most together, and those that most often led to arguments. Don't forget to record the instances when your child acted kindly to someone else, decided to tell the truth in a difficult situation, or mastered his own impulses in favor of someone else's needs. Include your thoughts on the social preferences your child seems to be demonstrating—is he sociable or solitary, active or passive, a leader most of the time or a follower? It will be interesting to find out how many of these social traits last into adolescence and adulthood—and fascinating to realize how many don't!

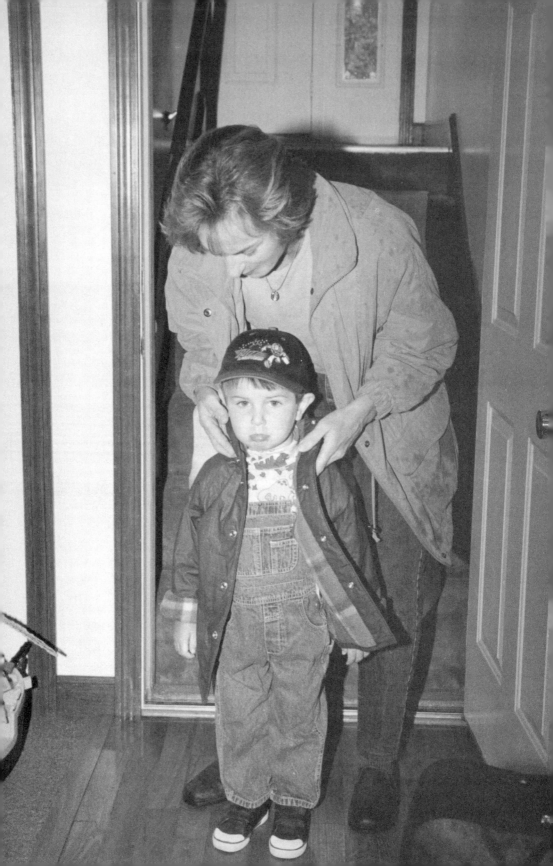

A Stable Platform—My Need for Routine

Your two-year-old is a stickler for order and correctness—at least in others.

Thirty-three-month-old Annie's caregiver, Martha, has decided to move back to her distant hometown, and Annie's entire family is sad to think that Martha will no longer be a regular part of their lives. In the two years since Martha began caring for Annie full-time, she has become a dependable partner to parents Jane and Luke, and a trusted source of love and support for Annie herself. As much as Jane will miss Martha, she's comforted by the fact that she'll be between jobs when Martha leaves, and that she and Luke can care for her daughter full-time for a while. It should be relatively simple to take up the reins in Martha's absence, Jane reasons. As the time for the transition approaches, she looks forward with increasing excitement to spending more time with Annie.

At first, the transition seems to go reasonably well. Martha and Jane both carefully explain to Annie that Martha will soon move away to be closer to her mom. Martha gives Annie a picture of herself as a memento and promises to write as soon as she arrives at her new home.

Annie clearly doesn't understand most of what Martha is saying, but she responds to this talk of change much more calmly than Jane had expected. Jane's job ends a few days before Martha leaves. After a tearful good-bye to Martha, mother and daughter begin their full-time life together.

For the first few days, the novelty of her new home situation seems to keep Annie in a daze. She gives her mom puzzled glances and asks, "Where'd Martha go?" Her behavior makes Jane nervous—is Annie going to fall apart when she realizes Martha isn't coming back? To reassure her, Jane takes her on a special field trip each day for the first week. They visit the local aquarium. They visit the children's museum. They join another two-year-old and her mom at the beach for the day. The harder Jane works to distract Annie, however, the more the little girl seems to crumple. By the end of the week, she has practically stopped talking—shrieking instead when she doesn't get her way, and crying for no reason at all. Her recent progress in toilet training has disintegrated, too. She wets her pants three times over the weekend. And every time an adult asks her to do something, she refuses with a pout and a resounding "No!"

"I just wish I knew what she's thinking," an exhausted Jane confesses to her husband Sunday night. "I mean, I know she misses Martha. But this seems like it's about even more than missing someone. She just can't seem to get her bearings."

In fact, Annie is having trouble adjusting to the changes in her life—not only the change in caregivers but the sudden disruptions in the routines embedded in her day-to-day life. Two-year-olds rely heavily on patterns they can predict—repeated sequences that allow them to believe they can comprehend their environment, thus bolstering their self-confidence. When Annie's lifelong caregiver abruptly disappears *and* her recently mastered routines of breakfast-while-Mommy-gets-dressed-for-work, bye-to-Mom-and-Dad-hi-to-Martha, coloring-with-Martha-after-breakfast, are disrupted, she feels as though all her supports have been removed at once. Her mother's well-meaning attempts to distract her from Martha's absence have in fact increased Annie's discomfort as she struggles to find something in her world that *hasn't* changed.

Even if your family has experienced no major disruptions this year (a new baby in the family, a new home, a divorce or remarriage), you will find that your two-year-old is a stickler for order and correctness—at least in other people. Determined to live in a world she can master and control, she can be counted on to make sure you stick to your routines ("Bedtime story!") and to experiment with challenging them ("No bath!"). Much of the time, her determined preoccupation with protocol may amuse you ("Kiss on the nose first, *then* on the chin!"). Sometimes it will seem more maddening than cute ("No pink pants! Blue!"). In nearly every case, however, your child behaves as she does because she has little choice—routines are her lifeboat, her major source of security in a world that's still often confusing. They're the platform from which she can launch herself toward further exploration.

Because routines are so important to your child, it makes sense to pay attention to the ones you and your child develop together this year. Ideally, they will be healthy practices that you're willing to live with for one, two, or more years to come. They should suit your child's energy level and temperament, leave some room for variety so that your child is regularly stimulated, but also come with a clear bottom line that is never violated. And they should be carried out with reasonable predictability by the other caregivers in your child's life. A regular half-hour of children's television after lunch might provide a pleasant rest, for example, for a two-year-old who is transitioning out of naptime—as long as the child is not so active that she has a hard time sitting still. Each day's changing theme provides a subject for discussion between the two of you, and your refusal to give in to her repeated demands for more TV shows her that this is a routine she can rely on. On days when someone else gives her lunch, the expected half-hour of television or videotape reassures her that life is predictable even in your absence. She begins to think of this as "her" TV time, as pleasing and satisfying as a favorite possession—and her parents enjoy the mental health break, too.

As her language and cognitive skills improve this year, establishing routines becomes easier in some respects. Your child will begin to comprehend, at least partially and at least for the moment, the *reasons* you give her for completing certain actions (a bath will clean off germs and relax her before bedtime) and the *results* of violating them (toys left on the floor can get stepped on and broken). She can also begin to contribute her own ideas about how to alter or create some routines, adding to their richness and utility. By asking her opinion on whether a night-light or an open bedroom door might best help her go to sleep at night, you demonstrate a respect for your child's needs and encourage her to start thinking of ways to structure her own daily life. It is also important to remember, however, that giving your child *too much* choice in routine matters (letting her decide what she wants to wear each day, asking whether she wants the crust cut off the sandwich bread) may lead to endless negotiating and resistance that you will regret in later years. In looking for a happy medium, focus on making it clear that you're the parent, and though your child is invited to contribute her input, you still have the final word.

Of course, predictable routines will not make all parenting problems go away this year, even if your child does help create them. Mealtimes will continue to challenge both of you if she continually refuses food and you worry about time wasted, messes made, and calories left unconsumed. Toilet training, a major routine-related issue for many families this year, is nearly always accompanied by regressions, misunderstandings, and lapses in patience on both your parts. Important routines that have no clear, immediate benefit for your child—such as cleaning up after playtime, brushing her teeth twice a day, or putting on her snowsuit before she plays outside and then taking it off when she comes back in—will be hard to implement at this age when she is still unable to think in long-term or general terms. Nevertheless, your child will look to you this year to decide which routines are important and to explain (again and again) exactly why. By meeting her need for a certain level of predictability, you will help her begin to comprehend a great deal more about why we humans live as we do, what is (or should be) important to us, and how we can move through our days productively.

Q & A

Predictability Rules

Q: Our thirty-month-old son, Kenny, is a creature of extreme habit. He hates to do anything differently than he's done it before—to the extent that we can hardly ever get him to try anything new. He refuses to try swinging on the big kids' swings on the playground because he's always swung on the infant swings. He screams his head off if he can't find his stuffed bunny at bedtime. And he absolutely will not eat anything besides the few foods he liked when he was one. It gets really tiresome trying to introduce him to new experiences when he resists them so much. How can we open him up to a little variety and change?

A: How much or how little a two-year-old is willing to leap into new experiences depends in large part on the child's temperament, as well as on his phase of development. Parents may have an effect as well, by throwing too many new experiences at a child who can't handle them or overly limiting a more active child's environment. Your two-year-old apparently leans toward the less adventurous end of the temperamental range for this age, but rest assured that nearly all parents of two-year-olds meet much more resistance to novelty than they expect. Saying no to new input—and even more challenging, suggesting their own alternative—is a relatively new skill for a thirty-month-old. Refusing or countering your offers can be a heady experience. Sticking to what he knows also gives him a necessary feeling of control and gradually increases his self-confidence.

To get a more objective feel for whether your child's resistance is abnormal, look around at other kids his age to see whether they're equally stubborn. Consider whether you're troubled about this issue because it clashes with your own temperament or because it's truly a cause for concern. Ask other parents who know your child, or have had experience with a similar child, for their opinions and suggestions. Then, if you still feel your child has a problem, talk about this issue with his pediatrician at his next checkup. Keep in mind that most two-year-olds begin to grow a little less rigid during the second half of this year. By age three, if he hasn't been pushed too hard to experiment beyond his comfort level, he should begin to feel somewhat more secure about things as they are and become more open to experiencing something different. He'll probably still rely on routines as he grows older, but the influence of friends and other acquaintances should increase his flexibility.

"LEAVE THE LIGHT ON": SLEEP PATTERNS IN THE THIRD YEAR

"I always felt so lucky when other parents complained about their kids' sleep habits," Andrea, a mom I met on the playground, confessed to me recently. "I don't know why, but my son, Eugene, settled into a great sleep routine at about nine months of age and never really fell out of it until he was two. Then, when I decided he was ready to start skipping his afternoon nap, everything fell apart. I couldn't get him up in the mornings, so then he wouldn't go to sleep till late that night, he'd sleep late again the next day, and the whole time he acted tired and cranky. I tried having him take a nap again, but he couldn't settle down. It took me half the year to work things out with him."

Andrea didn't know it at the time, but her experience with Eugene was actually quite common. By the time your child is two, you have no doubt created some kind of bedtime routine with her—whether it consists of a bath, a story, and her security blanket at eight-thirty or falling into your bed together, exhausted, at ten or eleven. Whatever the routine, she's grown accustomed to it, and even as she resists the nightly ritual, she has begun to understand that there's no avoiding it. At around this time, however, a number of elements come into play that can affect her reliance on (or resignation toward) her usual routine. Her verbal growth may leave her so mentally stimulated at the end of the day that she finds it hard to stop talking and settle down. Once alone, she is now able, owing to recent cognitive developments, to imagine spooky creatures in the darkness and even to experience a nightmare or two. Her improved physical skills enable her to climb out of her crib, if she's still sleeping in one, or to come to your room at night if she sleeps in a bed. Finally, the tendency of all young children to test and retest their parents' resolve will come into play again at bedtime this year.

As always when developing or changing routines with your child, it's best to tailor her bedtime ritual to her particular temperamental style, developmental stage, and home situation. If your child is a night owl and you want to start moving her toward an earlier bedtime, you may need to initiate some kind of physical activity in the evenings, such as a walk around the block or a mock-wrestling session, to help her adjust to the new schedule. If she is in a particularly resistant phase of development, encourage her to create some of her own rules for bedtime (one story plus an "extra," or three kisses from Mom plus a story on tape) so that she feels she's in control even as she falls asleep. If she shares a room with one or more siblings, it might be a good idea to put her to bed an hour before the others so that she'll be fast asleep by the time they enter the room. It is much more effective to observe the results of these experiments and change the routine in positive ways to suit your child than to adhere to the cookie-cutter bedtime rules laid out in many parenting articles and books.

Nap time is a particularly effective tool to use this year when adjusting your child's sleep schedule to better fit her own and the entire family's needs. Your child probably doesn't need to sleep as much during the day anymore, but a nap might help regulate a schedule that's gone awry. A non-napping child who's just started coming home from group child care at noon, for example, may be so tired that she frequently falls asleep around 5:00 P.M., wakes up an hour later, and finds it impossible to go to bed again until nearly midnight. If this child is encouraged to take an early nap right after coming home, she may adjust to her new schedule more easily. Even when you feel that any daytime sleep keeps your child up too late at night, it's still useful to build a regular rest period into her daily schedule. A brief rest can help your child learn how to create quiet time for herself, and it can regulate disrupted sleep schedules much as naps do. Andrea, for instance, might have reinstated a rest period for Eugene at least until he adjusted to a schedule without naps, to avoid having him swing unpredictably between a high-energy state and exhaustion.

For a number of reasons, sleep routines tend to grow easier as the third year progresses. Your child becomes able to work through her uneasiness about bedtime through conversations with you, imaginary play, an ability to narrate a book to herself or talk herself back to sleep, and greater understanding that you'll come back to her room in the morning. Outside routines may also make bedtime easier. Waking early to attend group care or preschool will make your child quite tired by the time dinner is over, and she will be more likely to fall asleep easily. (It's not a bad idea to wake her up at the same time on days when she does not have school, to keep her system on schedule.) Your own schedule may have become more predictable now that your toddler's life is more regulated, making it easier for both of you to stick to predictable routines. By your child's third birthday, you will at least have learned a great deal more about what helps your child get to bed on time, even if she still strenuously resists bedtime or has a hard time falling asleep. As you continue to build on those reliable aids—keeping the stuffed bunny on her pillow, for instance, while changing her waking-up and going-to-bed hours—the two of you should eventually be able to create a routine that works well enough for everyone.

A PARENT'S STORY

Jack's Room

"My son, Jack, slept in our room with us until he was two and a half," a neighbor told me recently. "He loved to snuggle with us and didn't really like sleeping in the crib next to our bed even when he was a baby, so I was worried about how I was ever going to get him out of there. Finally, my husband and I had had enough of sharing our space. We moved our two older boys into the same bedroom and gave the empty one to Jack.

"As it turned out, two and a half was the perfect time to make the change. Jack was at the height of his 'do-it-myself!' phase, and he really got into helping decorate his very own 'big-boy' room. He couldn't get over how cool it was to have his own real bed, like his big brothers', instead of a crib. He got to decide which stuffed animals got to stay on the bed and which had to go up on the top bookshelf. I let him pick out his own bedside lamp at the hardware store, and we made sure it had different settings so he could leave the light on low without admitting to his brothers that he was scared of the dark.

"Of course, the transition didn't happen all at once. For about six months or more after that, I spent plenty of nights keeping him company in his room till he fell asleep, and he would wake up in the middle of the night and come to our room at least two or three times a week. But we kept emphasizing how great it was that he had his own room now, and we let him control his own activities in there—letting him move around and look at books, as long as he stayed in bed. Over the long run, it really worked. Bedtime became a positive process instead of something painful that he had to force himself to go through."

"I *HATE* IT!": NEW EATING ROUTINES

Feeding issues are often a major concern throughout the first three years of a child's life as parents move from breast-feeding or bottled-formula issues to introducing solids to trying to ensure a balanced diet in their child's daily life. The good news is that this is the year when many feeding challenges can finally be resolved. You will learn more about your two-year-old's responses to various eating routines, and she will become more interested in eating as a social activity. The bad news is that children who were picky eaters as one-year-olds will probably continue to be so, especially during the first half of the year, when their resistant behavior may even make matters worse.

It helps to keep in mind, when trying to ensure that your child's eating routines lay the groundwork for proper nutrition, that two-year-olds don't need to consume as much food as parents sometimes assume. The American Academy of Pediatrics recommends that children between ages one and three consume about forty calories per inch of height a day. If your child is thirty-four inches tall, she should eat enough food to provide 1,350 to 1,400 calories per day. These amounts vary somewhat according to your child's metabolism, build, and level of activity, and she may eat a great deal one day and practically nothing

One way to reduce the inevitable feeding battles this year is to encourage your two-year-old to take control of some eating-related routines.

the next. Fortunately, studies have shown that young children display a natural tendency to consume the correct number of calories over the course of a week if a range of foods is provided for them. Your job as parent is to make sure that the foods containing those calories are healthy ones—fruits and juice, vegetables, dairy products, whole grains, and meats or other proteins rather than (or at least much more than) soda, chips, sweets, and other non-nourishing treats. Of course, you don't have to offer a fresh-cooked meal three times a day, but do try to resist giving in to the ever-tempting convenience factor. Bad eating habits can be very hard to break.

As your two-year-old moves out of her high chair and takes a place at the family table, feeding issues may become more prominent and divisive than before. In particular, you and your partner may find yourselves embroiled in the "eat-everything-on-your-plate" versus "whatever-you-want-is-fine" debate. It is certainly true that frequent pressure on your child to eat what she doesn't want will most likely lead to stubborn refusal and even tears—and can even have a negative impact on her eating habits in years to come. On the other hand, preparing special meals just for her or allowing her to leave and return to the dinner table throughout the meal doesn't provide the structure she needs to learn to feed herself well. The most effective eating routines at this age seem to occupy the middle ground: cooking one meal for the entire family (but not making your two-year-old taste every dish); insisting that she stay at the table until she's finished eating (but not forcing her to stay until everyone else is done); encouraging her to try a new food by reminding her that she doesn't have to eat more than a bite if she doesn't like it; letting her help prepare the food she eats; letting her control what she puts on her food (parmesan cheese, butter, and so on); and refraining from criticizing or commenting on how much she has or hasn't eaten. This is a very difficult process for parents (and especially grandparents) who worry that the tiny amounts of food their children take in can't possibly sustain them. But the fact is that children never starve themselves as long as food is made available to them. When your child is hungry enough, she will stop demanding cold cereal and try a bowlful of spaghetti with tomato sauce instead.

Your child continues to be physically active this year, and there's nothing wrong with dropping a small snack into that little hand as she races by. Healthy finger foods such as bread, bagels, banana chunks, cooked carrot, cooked chicken, and cereal can go a long way toward providing the calories your child needs without forcing her to sit down and put her exciting life on hold. A wide and frequently changing variety of foods may also encourage her to eat more and try new foods. As you expand her diet, however, take care not to give her too much of a new food before you assess its effect. Two to 5 percent of children under age three suffer from food allergies, resulting in a range of reactions from skin rashes, diarrhea, watery eyes, sneezing, or a swollen throat to spasms or difficulty breathing. Pediatricians agree that most children outgrow the majority of these allergies by around age three, but it's important for her health as well as her enthusiasm for eating that you monitor her food intake until then.

As your child moves through the second half of this year, her increasing interest in social interaction may motivate her to spend more time at the dinner table, trying to participate in the family conversation. At this age, she will no doubt enjoy learning, practicing, and monitoring others' table manners (though she may start to resist if you put too much pressure on her to conform). Her skills won't be perfect by any means—she'll frequently use her hands instead of her spoon, wipe her face with her sleeve instead of her napkin, and knock over her "big-girl" cup of milk—but her inclusion in the group will mean a great deal to her, and she will work hard to earn her position. As she listens to her siblings describe a new video game between bites of the yucky food she refused a month ago, she may grow more curious about what everyone else is eating. Gradually, her resistance to newness may fade in the face of this new communal experience, and your child will learn to actually eat her food "like a big girl," too.

A CHILD'S-EYE VIEW

Broccoli Again

Mommy has just finished cooking dinner, and the house is filled with wonderful smells. Almost-three-year-old Rachel and her big brother, Gary, have finished setting the table (Rachel's job is to lay out the five napkins), and now everyone is taking a seat. *Meat,* Rachel says to herself eagerly as her dad lifts her into her toddler's chair. A big roast sits in the center of the table. Rachel breathes deeply, hardly able to wait till her mom slices a piece off and cuts it up on her plate.

"So how was work today?" Rachel, her eyes fixed on the meat now being cut up for her, is only vaguely aware of her parents' conversation. As soon as the knife pulls away, she grabs a piece and stuffs it into her mouth. *Mmmmm. Yummy.* She savors the juices, the texture of the beef, as Daddy's voice drifts toward her from the next chair: "Rachel, use your fork next time, okay?"

It takes a while for Rachel's hunger to abate, but after half a dozen more pieces of meat (two eaten with her hands, the rest with a fork, with Daddy's help), she feels relaxed enough to look around the table. Gary is talking about a chicken crossing a road. It's a joke—she can tell by his big, silly gestures and the way the others are smiling at him. Suddenly everyone erupts with laughter. Rachel is so preoccupied that she hardly notices her mother adding broccoli and mashed potatoes to her plate.

"I know a joke!" she shouts, bouncing in her chair and waving her arms around. To her great satisfaction, everyone now looks at her. "Okay," her brother Mike says. "What is it?"

For an instant, Rachel experiences only blankness where a joke should be. Then she remembers a phrase from a book her preschool teacher often reads. "Why'd the chicken cross the street?" she demands.

"Why?" asks Dad, smiling.

"Uh . . ." Rachel thinks for a long, painful moment. Then, spotting the first object in front of her, she says, "Because it was pepper!" To her relief, everyone laughs.

"Now I'll tell a joke," Mommy says. "But everybody take a bite first."

Jokes are fun. Rachel, beaming back at her family members, picks up a piece of food without looking and pops it into her mouth. *Yuck! Broccoli!* She starts to take it out. But then she hesitates. *Oh,* she thinks. *Butter. This is good.* Rachel chews thoughtfully, looking around the table as the conversation continues. She likes it here. She talks like the others, and she eats like them. She is a part of this family.

"I NEED GO POTTY": TOILET TRAINING

Few changes in routine are anticipated with more excitement and dread than toilet training as parents look forward to discarding expensive diapers and worry about pushing their children too hard. Certainly toilet training is one of the more difficult routines to establish, since there is no biological reason for a child to use a toilet rather than a diaper, and all her motivation must come from her environment. Nevertheless, parents of two-year-olds have a better chance of success than they would have had the year before. By age two, children are at least physically able to control elimination voluntarily—and the two-year-old's need to be a "big kid," with all the paraphernalia (including underwear and a potty or child's toilet seat), is a powerful motivating force. Near the beginning of the year, your child's preoccupation with the concept "mine" opens the way for you to present her with her very own personal potty. You might even give it to her as a birthday present and let her climb in it, turn it upside down, tote it from room to room, and otherwise claim it as her own. Her urge to imitate other children may motivate her to use the potty just to be like her older siblings or the girl across the street. Her love of order may increase her interest in learning where her body waste should go.

For these reasons, toilet training is probably *possible* this year, but it certainly isn't *necessary.* Don't be surprised if your two-year-old's periodic contrariness and sporadic attention get in the way of success. In general, it's best to keep the process positive (making the potty chair an attractive object, but not treating diapers or pull-ups as something for "babies") and not to push too hard or expect too much at this age. If you find that your child has lost interest or is actively resisting your efforts to get her out of diapers, drop the subject for now and wait for the next emotional and cognitive "window of opportunity." (Remember that toilet training is much more important to you than it is to her.) Times of major change—pregnancy, a move to a new house, a marital crisis—are certainly not the time to begin training. Even without such a major event, there's no real need to begin toilet training before age two and a half or three, unless she's required to be toilet-trained before entering a group program you have planned for her.

As with all aspects of your child's growth, you can most easily encourage her development by observing what her interests are at a given time. If she's becoming interested in the fact that you or her siblings use the potty, she'll show you in several ways: by choosing a book about potty use for her bedtime story, by hiding behind the couch when it's time to poop, or, like the little girl Denise in Chapter 1, by acting excited about the idea of wearing underwear. Once you've begun to note some of these signs, build on her interest by showing her a picture of a potty (and when you're ready, buying one for her) and talking about how all children learn to use one eventually. Let her spend time with you in the bathroom, just hanging out as you get dressed for the day. Let her watch you using the toilet—and if possible, other children using the potty—and buy some pull-ups or underwear for her to use when she's ready. Chances are good that your child will be eager to learn more about this mysterious process and will go along with your suggestion to sit on the potty with a book or toy once a day, even if she doesn't actually use it yet. Boys should be encouraged to sit on the potty, too, at first, so that they'll be in position when it's time to defecate. Later, when they begin to use the toilet more reliably, they can switch to a standing position—preferably with Dad's example and guidance.

Once your child is familiar with the general idea of a potty, it's time to prepare her to use it. First, she must make the connection between needing to eliminate and going to the potty. To help her do this, begin emptying her dirty diapers into the potty, explaining that this is where the poop goes. Once she's comfortable with this idea, start watching for moments when you see that she's about to have a bowel movement and offer to place her on the potty ("You look like you might want to go poop. Why don't we go find the potty?"). She may refuse, but at least the link between elimination and the potty will have been reinforced. (During this period, it's a good idea to let her wear underwear around the house—or nothing at all—so that you can get her to the potty quickly and easily once she does consent.) It will probably not be long before you manage to get your child into proper position at the right time. When she sees that she has actually accomplished the action you and she have been talking about, she will feel very proud.

It's important to praise this first accomplishment, but don't overdo it. You don't want your child to feel as though she's failed when she has an accident. Proudly inform the rest of the family about it, and make sure they praise her, too. This positive attention will convince your child that she is moving forward into the world of "big people" and motivate her to improve her skills even more. Don't expect her to follow up on her success right away. She needs time to process what has happened. In the meantime, praise *every effort,* follow her lead on diapers-versus-underwear and diapers-versus-potty, continue to put her on the potty just to sit once a day, offer her the potty when she's about to have a bowel movement, and talk about the issue in positive ways.

Gradually, her desire to imitate others and be a big girl will have its effect, and she will follow up more and more on her understanding that the potty is where she should eliminate. The two-year-old's love of step-by-step processes—pulling down her pants, sitting, getting toilet paper—should also motivate her. However, it's important to realize that there will be *many* exceptions, now and in the months and even years to come. Your child will probably wet her pants when she is upset, when she is too preoccupied with an activity to leave it, or when she is in an unfamiliar place. Her ability to wait to urinate is still quite minimal, and you will have to get her to a bathroom quickly once she announces that she needs to go. Be aware that some children feel uncomfortable, and therefore have difficulty, using an adult toilet, particularly away from home—so much so that they "hold it in" for an unhealthy length of time. Furthermore, young children who are already fully toilet-trained during the day may have trouble staying dry at night for quite a while. In fact, nearly half of all children in this country still wet the bed at age three. Most child development experts consider occasional bed-wetting normal until about six.

These accidents can be frustrating to a parent who believes that the toilet-training process is completed—and, of course, embarrassing when they happen in public. The adult often experiences such an incident as a failure on his or her own part, or as stubbornness or lack of cooperation on the child's part. It is vital to keep in mind, even when your child has urinated on the floor for the third time that day, that she is not doing it on purpose. Responding negatively, punishing her, or otherwise criticizing her efforts may well undo all your hard work up to this point and even make it necessary to start the training process over again. (If she gets a sufficiently emotional reaction from you by having an accident, she may just do it again soon to see whether you react the same way.) Instead, respond as you wish another adult would respond to you when you break a glass or accidentally cause some other kind of damage: sympathize with her, downplay the situation, and suggest a positive solution ("Oh, well, you'll get to the potty next time. Let's get some fresh underwear from your room"). Take a change of clothes along with you whenever you go out, to ease your own tension as well as her discomfort when something goes wrong. If her accidents continue occurring frequently, you might suggest pull-ups or even diapers again. Keep in mind that as long as you and her other caregivers are patient and maintain the routine for using the potty, she will conform to it when she's truly ready. By her third birthday, her desire to be a big girl and more frequent opportunities to observe other children her age who are toilet-trained (particularly in preschool and group care) will have given her another push to complete the process. And if she continues to resist, remind yourself that it is her body, after all, and that there's still plenty of time.

IF YOU'RE CONCERNED

Regression

Toilet training is a very uneven process, with many leaps forward and nearly as many leaps back. Most children move back and forth between the potty and diapers a number of times before settling on potty use most of the time. For some reason, boys tend to take longer to reach this settling point than girls do. Even twins sometimes pick widely different times to adjust to a potty or toilet, despite equivalent treatment. Overall, the toilet-training process may take several months to complete—not the couple of weeks that parents frequently expect when starting out.

Nevertheless, some children who are truly trained suddenly seem to forget their elimination routine over the course of a day or two and remain stuck in a regressive stage for a perplexingly long period of time. Usually, this regression is caused by an event that has distracted the child and occupied a great deal of her energy. A move to a new house, a change in caregivers, extended travel, or even a struggle to adjust to other changes in her life, such as a new sleep schedule or a big-kid bed, can cause your child to revert to diapers just when you were looking forward to moving on to other issues.

Such regression can be a minor problem for you, as you resign yourself to more cleanups and diaper purchases, but it need not be a major failure for your child if you have avoided treating accidents as a negative experience and telling her that diapers are "for babies." Simply offer her the pull-ups or diapers, wait for the distracting event to pass (or for your child to grow accustomed to it), and then begin training again. Reassure her that she "did it before and can do it again," stick to forward-thinking language ("Next time" and "Pretty soon"), keep her actively involved in the process (letting her pick the stall in the public bathroom, and letting her wash her own hands), and she will soon let you know that she's interested in trying again.

"WHERE AM I?":
PLANNING AHEAD FOR TRAVEL

Many parents recall with dismay their attempts to travel with their one-year-old child. The one-year-old's desperate urge to keep moving, the ease with which she became disoriented and confused, and her short memory and attention span combined to make it a very difficult year to go for a long drive, much less get on a plane and visit someone cross-country. Fortunately, matters improve somewhat this year. Two-year-olds' longer attention span and greater ability to sit still make long periods in a car seat or airplane seat more bearable. The travel experience itself becomes more rewarding as young children's interest in other people and their surroundings increases. Still, two-year-olds' love of routine and occasional fearfulness or anger when their routines are disrupted can create new challenges.

When planning a trip, it helps to consider the prospect from your child's point of view. With only a tentative hold, if any, on new eating, sleeping, and elimination routines, she may feel her world slipping out of her control when the food she likes to eat is unavailable when she expects it, when she must fall asleep in a car seat instead of in her crib at home, or when she must try to use the bathroom on a noisy, uncomfortable airplane toilet. Many children respond to this challenge by either tightening up on routines (insisting on their usual foods, bedtime comfort objects, or potty) or abandoning them altogether and regressing. Since neither solution is ideal, it's best to try to keep your child's daily routines as close to normal as you can possibly make them. Pack her favorite foods for the trip, and try to give them to her at the usual times. Bring her favorite books or audiotapes along for the car, plane, or train ride. An activity book is an ideal way for a two-year-old to enjoy a regularly scheduled play period while remaining buckled into her seat. A simple pad and pencil, with which you can play tic-tac-toe and draw, can keep her calm for long stretches at a time. Once you're settled someplace for the night, be sure to produce her favorite stuffed animal and any other comfort object she needs to fall asleep. You might even pack a couple of familiar bath toys to help her through the trip.

One advantage your child has this year is her new verbal ability. You can use this skill to prepare her for the trip she's about to take and to interpret events for her as they happen. Talk to her about the trip and your destination, and show her pictures. Read a book about airports to her. She may not understand exactly what it means, but if you take the book along, you can point out a few bits of information when you arrive at the airport and refer to the book once you've boarded the plane.

The more you can prepare your child for any surprises or sudden changes, the more relaxed she'll feel about the travel process. Remember that even child-appropriate sights, such as a costumed character at a theme park, can frighten a young child who hasn't been told to expect it. Keep your senses attuned to unfamiliar sounds (an airplane's engine as it takes off), smells (the bathroom at a highway rest stop), textures (the stiff sheets at a hotel), sights (a camel at the zoo), and tastes (the bread in a foreign country) that are likely to set off her fear of the unknown, and comment on them in a calm, informative, even positive way.

In short, your child is capable of enjoying some vacation travel this year—but probably not much, and probably not often. The more calm and methodical you are about the process, the more likely she will be to let go of her fears and go along with your new, temporary travel routines. In the meantime, however, don't be surprised if she doesn't leap right into the exciting new experience you've planned for her this year. It doesn't mean she's unadventurous. It only means she's two.

EASING THE WAY

A Child's Itinerary

Many parents look forward to the day when they can take their children out into the world, introducing them to all its wonders. Two is an early age to begin this process, obviously, but there are ways to enhance your child's cognitive, emotional, and social growth through travel. The first rule to keep in mind is that your two-year-old retains much more information than is evident through her words or behavior. If you read her a children's book about camping in the mountains several times before leaving on your own trip, for example, she may not start spouting the names of different birds, but she *will* experience the trip much more fully than she would have otherwise. Not only will she be better prepared to enjoy the new sights, but she'll make countless interesting and stimulating connections between the characters and information in the book and what she sees in the actual place. By exposing her to this kind of experience, you're establishing a learning routine that can act as a valuable stepping-stone toward more active learning later on.

Emotional growth can be enhanced as your child learns that familiar routines are transferable to unfamiliar places. When you travel, do you like to take one or two familiar objects along with you, pack the same pajamas for each trip, or sleep on your usual side of the bed? Your child will experience the same reassurance these practices provide for you, but much more intensely. Be sure, then, not only that she brings a couple of comforting objects along, but that she participates in some of the same everyday activities—going for an evening walk, riding bikes, picnicking—that the family likes to do at home.

Social growth can be encouraged by making it easy for your child to interact with others. Traveling by train rather than plane allows her to walk with you from car to car, chatting occasionally with other passengers. If you fly, waiting to board allows your child to work out her energy in the airport, improving her chances of social success on the plane. A leisurely travel schedule leaves her with the energy and opportunity to meet people along the way.

By planning ahead, you can teach your child that traveling is a positive experience. Perhaps next year, she'll actually look forward to the family vacation.

"I HELPED!":
SHARING AND COMPLETING TASKS

Two-year-olds long to be older, more powerful, and more in control of their day-to-day lives than they are. As they move toward age three, they are increasingly eager to take their place in the world, acting and being treated as equals in their family. Simple daily chores, far from being an imposition on them, allow them to "do it themselves"—to contribute to the family's well-being and thereby win the status they crave. Such chores should be real ones that provide assistance in a concrete way that the child can understand, and simple enough to allow her

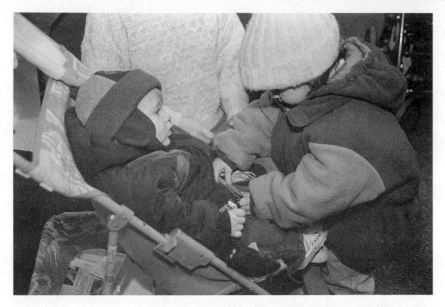

Your child's desire to help can be encouraged by welcoming her involvement in daily tasks.

to complete them successfully. Laying out the place mats and napkins for dinner or holding the dustpan for you while you sweep up the dust lets your child experience tasks on a visceral, concrete level. When you or other family members comment on how well the job was done, your child swells with pride and her self-confidence increases.

It isn't necessary at this age for your child to have many tasks. Limiting her to a single duty each day is fine, as long as she is able to accomplish it herself from start to finish. Finishing the task for her defeats the purpose and may even teach her that there's really no need to finish things in the future. When initiating tasks, start small and simple. You might begin by asking your twenty-four-month-old to help you carry the laundry basket to the laundry room when you're ready to wash the clothes, thanking her profusely as she does so and commenting on how heavy the basket is. When she's a little older, you can assign her a two-part job, such as fetching the mail and then throwing away the empty envelopes as you go through it. Finally, you can let your child help decide which task she'll take on next. Let her choose from two tasks, and then be patient as she learns to do them well. Remember, this process is not about the task. It's about learning to cooperate, follow instructions, and stick to a commitment. It's about being part of the family.

Your two-year-old will benefit even more from completing tasks if they are a part of a routine that continues through the week. When she is expected to accomplish her chores each day, even when doing so isn't very convenient for parent and child, your child enjoys the satisfaction of knowing what to expect and of participating fully in family life. To help her mark her progress, create a chart listing each of her duties and let her attach a sticker for each task completed. You need not include only typical duties such as bringing the dog's food bowl to the kitchen to be filled or wiping off the table after dinner—you can add the personal tasks she's learning to accomplish such as using the potty or brushing her teeth. Don't forget to maintain such routines during play periods as well—insisting that toys be picked up (at least a little) and the caps replaced on markers before your child moves on to another activity. It is wonderful to see how proud and happy a two-year-old is when her chart is full. "I did it!" is a common cry for happy two-year-olds who feel they've done their share. An added bonus is her new, growing respect for your own work. A child who has her own responsibilities may more readily understand that you have to get chores done yourself.

THE TOY BOX

At Thirty-two Months

Glen has spent a long, fruitful morning playing with his blocks, train set, and a number of other toys. At eleven-thirty, he sits back on his heels, surveying his room. *Hungry!* he thinks. He doesn't know what time it is, but something tells him that the next event for the day is for him to sit at the kitchen table while Mom serves a peanut butter and jelly sandwich.

"Glen? Are you hungry?" Mom enters the room and stands beside him, looking at all he's done this morning. "Ready for a peanut butter sandwich?"

Glen's tummy rumbles in response, and he jumps up and tackles Mom in a bear hug. "Hungry!" he says.

"Okay," Mom says in a somewhat sterner voice. "But first we have to pick up some of these toys. What a mess it is in here!"

Glen steps back from his mom, confused. *But she said lunch!* he thinks. He sits down among his blocks. His hunger—combined with the discomfort caused by his mother's tone of voice—is about to overwhelm him, and he begins to cry. "I'm hungry!" he says.

"I know," his mom acknowledges, squatting down beside him. "It's lunchtime, and you want a sandwich. But you know that we have to clean up a little after playtime. Here, I'll help. I'll hold the block box, and you throw the blocks in."

At first, Glen refuses to cooperate. *Sandwich!* he reminds himself stubbornly, folding his arms and looking away. But Mom continues to hold the block box for him. "Where'd that helping boy go?" she says playfully, tossing in the first few blocks.

Glen likes the sound the blocks make. *My job!* he thinks. Quickly, he grabs some blocks and throws them in the box. With Mom's help, they're finished before he knows it.

"Good job, Glen," his mom says, picking him up. "We can put up the rest of the stuff later. Right now, let's go get you something to eat."

I did good, Glen tells himself with great satisfaction, giving his slightly neater room one last look over Mom's shoulder as she carries him out of the room. *Picked up blocks. Now I can eat!*

CHANGE CAN BE GOOD: MOVING TOWARD NEW CHALLENGES

A year has passed, and Jane feels it has been an unusually trying but rewarding one. Owing to the fluke in her career trajectory that left her at home for the past twelve months, she has had the chance to spend a great deal more time with her daughter Annie than she'd ever expected. As week followed week, Jane began to get a sense of how important a predictable schedule and daily routines were to her daughter. Though she didn't want to go along with all of the routines that Annie's sitter had created, she and Annie have had a good time creating their own. Now Jane looks forward almost as much as Annie to rest time after lunch, when Jane reads her daughter several storybooks and Annie snuggles up against her mom. Annie loves "Freaky Friday," when she and her mom go off on a spontaneous adventure (a picnic in the park, a drive to the country), giving Annie a chance to be stimulated by new experiences and Jane a way to avoid cabin fever.

Now, as Annie looks forward to her third birthday, Jane considers the possibility of accepting a new job outside the home. She knows that taking the job would create yet another major change in Annie's life. But she believes that she knows better now how to prepare Annie for it—by talking about it frequently, demonstrating what will happen in concrete ways (such as showing Annie her new office and letting her draw pictures to decorate its walls), and understanding that even when Annie doesn't seem to be paying attention to what's happening she is really processing on some level what's going on. Fortunately, Annie's progress this year has somewhat reduced her need for everything to remain the same. She's even had a few new sitters since her first one left. Annie will start preschool this year, and her increasing interest in children her age will take some of the focus off Mom's activities. In fact, Jane looks forward to comparing notes with her daughter as they both venture out into a new group situation. If they can share their feelings about meeting new people, adjusting to new routines, and separating from one another, Jane hopes, they can both not only survive these major changes but actually thrive.

How the Need for Routine Evolves in the Third Year

24 MONTHS	Enjoys family routine
	Major changes (such as a new sibling or a move) may trigger regression
27 MONTHS	Need for order increases her attraction to routines
30 MONTHS	Likes accomplishing daily chores
	May show interest in using the potty
33 MONTHS	Grows more tolerant of minor disruptions in familiar routine
	Enjoys "discussing" plans for the day
36 MONTHS	Shows pride in her place as a full-fledged family member
	More willing to conform to family practices
	Shows increased interest in trying new things

In so many instances throughout this year and the next, conflicts between parent and child can be magnified or resolved with a simple change in routine. A stubborn refusal to lie still and go to sleep after the bedtime stories are finished, for example, may be remedied by playing a story on tape for your child to drift off to. As you work your way through this year, tinkering in one way or another with the routines that work best with your child, take notes on what works and what doesn't. Is your two-year-old the type who responds best to humor when she begins to feel overwhelmed, or does she need a hug and a quiet talk? Does she feel better when her routine is pretty much the same each day, or does she thrive on variety within a basic predictable framework? Does she experience "fads" during which she wants to do only one activity (play with clay) for days on end, and then switches allegiance abruptly to another activity (cutting with scissors) for the rest of the week?

Observing and taking notes on your child's attitudes toward routines can help you arrange her world so that she moves through it most effectively—the first step in teaching her to manage her environment more wisely by herself. A written record of what has worked and what hasn't in the past will save both of you time and effort in structuring her habits in the future.

_____

_____

_____

_____

_____

_____

_____

_____

_____

_____

_____

_____

_____

_____

_____

_____

_____

_____

_____

CHAPTER 8

"But I Want To!"—My Need for Limits

S tudies have shown that parents' consistency in limit-setting is much more important for toddlers than it is for infants.

It's seven in the evening when Mark hangs up the phone, and he hasn't even started dinner yet. He was late leaving work, got hung up at the child-care center when Lawrence, his two-year-old, insisted on showing him around the playhouse, and then had to stop by the grocery store. As soon as they got home, Mark dropped the groceries on the kitchen floor and collapsed on the living room sofa, while Lawrence wandered over to the television, switched it on, and sat down on the floor to watch.

Luckily, the television was tuned to the public station, because Mark was too exhausted to get up and change the channel. After an hour's rest, he managed to answer the phone when it rang. It was his wife, Mia, calling from her evening shift at the hospital. On opposite work schedules, she and Mark had hardly seen each other in three days, and it took them some time to catch up.

"Love you, too." Mark finally hangs up the phone and looks up with a dazed expression. *Wow. It's dark already,* he realizes. *Lawrence has been watching TV for . . .* he checks his watch *. . . one and a half hours!* Guilt-stricken, Mark snaps off the television midprogram. "That's it, buddy," he says to his son. "Too much TV for one day. Come on. Dad needs help making supper."

"Whaaa . . . ?" Lawrence stares up at his father, stunned by his action. "I wanna watch TV!"

"That's enough TV!" Mark repeats. He hates it when Lawrence begs to watch television. It makes him feel like a bad parent. "Come on—I'll let you put the pasta in the water."

Mark strides off toward the kitchen, expecting Lawrence to follow him. Instead, the moment Mark's back is turned, Lawrence marches over to the television and turns it on. As the brightly colored figures reappear on the TV screen, Lawrence sits down on the floor again, very pleased with himself.

Mark hears the sound of the television and turns around. He can't believe Lawrence deliberately disobeyed him. His guilt increases as he marches back to turn the television off. *He's a complete addict!* he says to himself. "Young man, you will *not* turn the television on when I say the time is up," he snaps, grabbing Lawrence's arm and pulling him to his feet. "You come with me right now. We're cooking dinner, and you're helping." Mark starts back toward the kitchen, pulling Lawrence along with him.

Mark's insistence makes Lawrence all the more determined to have his way. "Let go!" he yells, and squirms out of his father's grasp. Before Mark can stop him, Lawrence races back to the television and turns it on, standing two inches in front of the screen exactly as his parents have always told him not to.

"That's it!" Mark's exhaustion rolls over him in a wave, and he feels himself lose control. He grabs Lawrence's hand and slaps it, hard. *"Bad* boy, Lawrence! Go to your room right now!"

Lawrence's eyes widen as he stares at his hand, then looks up at his dad. Mark has never hit him before, and Lawrence can hardly believe he did it now. Slowly, his expression changes from shock to fury. "Nyaaaa!" he yells, right in his father's face. Before Mark can react, Lawrence races away.

Mark starts to chase him, but then suddenly stops himself. *What am I doing?* he wonders, leaning against the wall. *Chasing a two-year-old around the house? Spanking him because I'm mad? I'm behaving worse than he is.*

Mark may deeply regret his actions toward his son, but at least he can remind himself that he's not alone in feeling pushed to the limit by such behavior. Few parenting challenges are more difficult than effectively managing the perfectly normal, healthy surges of defiance that all two-year-olds express on the road toward independence. It has often been said that age two offers a preview of what adolescence will be like. As you struggle with your child's bouts of rebellion, extreme emotion, and stubborn refusal to cooperate, you may agree. But as difficult as it is to believe for much of this year, your two-year-old's frequent misbehavior is a necessary step toward a valuable goal. Once he has tested the boundaries of his world—learned what the rules are, what will happen if he breaks them, and whether you will be there for him even when he's naughty—he can move beyond this chaotic phase toward greater self-confidence and self-discipline.

Your job, then, is to help your child come to respect these boundaries, reminding him what the limits are, teaching him to control his emotions, and explaining why certain behaviors are unacceptable. As your child moves through different phases of cognitive, verbal, and emotional development, this will not be an easy process. When rewarding his best efforts or responding to deliberate misbehavior, it's necessary to take into account his level of understanding, his particular temperament, his physical and emotional capacities, and your own emotional state at the moment. The parent of a two-year-old must understand that this is not the year to tell him to "clean up his room" (such a vague command only confuses and overwhelms him) or that his leaping about the kitchen is "driving you bananas" (he isn't ready to think about your feelings to that extent and will only puzzle over that interesting phrase), or to take him to the circus "because he's been good all month" (he can't remember details that far back or generalize in that way). On the other hand, his progress in cognitive development will increase his understanding that actions have consequences; his language skills will help him understand your explanations and express himself more often through words; and his longer memory will help him remember what's off limits and what's okay. As the year progresses, his ability to control his emotions will improve, and new feelings of empathy will begin to curb some of his more aggressive behavior. The key to maneuvering through this difficult period lies in keeping your rules or commands simple and specific, noting which responses work best during each particular phase, changing your methods to suit new situations, and keeping in mind your long-term goal—a confident, aware, *self*-disciplined child.

A PARENT'S STORY

"No, Timmy! Hot!"

"My daughter, Zoe, is a real handful," a colleague told me at a conference recently. "She's constantly getting into one fix or another, and when she was two, she was so physically active that I was never sure she even heard me when I tried to explain how she should behave. She'd grab another kid's toy and run off with it before I could deal with the situation. I remember how upset I used to get, thinking that she was going to grow up to become a selfish brat and everyone was going to blame me.

"Then, about the time she turned three, there was this total change in her behavior. She started getting interested in how other kids acted, and she loved to tell them when they were doing something wrong. I still remember how happy she sounded saying, 'No, no, Timmy, hot!' whenever the little neighbor boy came within a foot of our stove. She loved to tell her best friend, Sheila, that sharing made everybody feel better, and she got to be a real stickler for whose turn it was when I played board games with her. Of course, we made a lot of jokes about what a dictator she was turning out to be (and we did have to teach her to tone down the bossiness a bit), but it was great to know she'd been *listening* to me all those years—or at least that she'd learned something from hanging out with other kids. Once I saw that she recognized bad behavior, I was able to talk with her more about her own manners. She got a lot better about following the rules over the next couple of years. I guess I just had to wait for her physical energy to slow down some and for her listening ability to improve.

"Two is a hard year because other people's kids always seem to 'get' the idea of following rules before yours does, and then you feel like a failure as a parent. But all you really need to do, I think, is stay consistent and keep the faith. It's hard to believe it, but two doesn't last forever."

"THAT'S THE RULE": SETTING CLEAR LIMITS TO LIVE BY

As you race from one discipline crisis ("Ray, give Sarah back her doll!") to another ("Ray, no jumping on the bed!"), you can be forgiven for believing that your two-year-old invented the concept of testing limits this year, but the fact is that he has been experimenting with his behavior and your responses to it practically from birth. Back then, as you cuddled him when he smiled and looked unhappy when he yelled, your infant came to understand which behavior created the best results. As the year progressed and you rewarded his positive social interactions, good eating habits, and more adaptable sleep patterns, he continued to learn what the limits were in each of these areas and molded his behavior to meet them to some degree. Only when he had learned to crawl and then to walk, however, did the two of you begin to encounter classic limit-setting situations. As your one-year-old began to interact with a wider range of objects and people, you responded more often with, "Don't touch that," "Good boy," and, "Say thank you." Your words and actions intrigued him, stimulating his developing interest in the ways your attitudes differed from his. He became fascinated by your concept of limits and began to experiment with ways of figuring out where they were exactly and whether you responded in the same way every time to these experiments.

Now, in his third year, your child's cognitive, physical, and emotional development have come together to enable him to concentrate more on the issue of limits. This can be extremely trying, of course, but it also presents a wonderful opportunity to *teach* him more about his world. By accepting your two-year-old's many behavioral blunders as necessary steps in acquiring a new skill—rather than as attempts to embarrass you in public or drive you out of your mind—you can take advantage of this window of opportunity. Look back on how you might have felt the first time you ate at a traditional Japanese restaurant—did you know to take your shoes off, to sit on the floor, and use chopsticks? Did you apply the right sauces to the right foods? Your two-year-old must learn to cope with an equally bewildering array of rules, expectations, and unspoken conventions. He needs your help.

The keys to success in this teaching activity are to *keep it simple* and *be consistent.* Just as you had to start with the basics when entering the Japanese restaurant ("Where do I put my shoes?"), your child needs to start with the simplest rules before he can expand his thinking to more general concepts. By speaking in simple, concrete ways that your two-year-old can understand, you make it possible for him to succeed at obeying and create a positive cycle in which he *wants* to follow the rules to win your approval.

Increasingly, part of making rules comprehensible will include explaining *why* they should be followed (always at a level he can understand). Your child's experiments with the concept of cause and effect have already taught him that his actions have consequences, and he will remain fascinated by this fact throughout this year. You can use his interest to help him focus on proper behavior by linking action and consequence as closely as possible. It's good to tell your young two-year-old, "Don't take Harold's toy," rather than, "Be nice to Harold"—but as he moves through the year it becomes even more effective to say, "Look, you took Harold's toy, and now he's crying. Give him back the toy so he'll feel better. Here's another toy for you." Your child may not want to cooperate with your instructions—he may not even appear to understand them at first—but with repetition he will gradually begin to comprehend the reasons behind your behavioral rules. Of course, some restrictions—particularly those involving your child's safety—are too important to wait for your child to achieve a thorough understanding of them. Fortunately, your child is old enough to accept the fact that he can't run into the street or wander off at the shopping mall because "that's the rule." Gradually, you will be able to shorten your more com-

To best capture your two-year-old's attention, try to set brief, consistent limits—ideally made face-to-face.

mon demands to code phrases. Simply saying, "Parking lot," as you get out of your car at the mall will remind your child to hold your hand as you walk across the lot, refrain from running, and look both ways before crossing the street.

Maintaining a close link between actions and their consequences is important in responding to your child's behavior as well. His cognitive skills and memory are not sufficiently developed for him to think about and analyze his past actions very well. To create a mental link between his behavior and its results, then, it's important to respond immediately and clearly. When your child takes a playmate's toy, explain *at that moment* that he should give it back (and why), rather than waiting until after the play date is over. As MRI studies have shown, your words routinely create new neuronal connections in your child, and strengthen old ones. In other words, they literally shape his brain.

When responding to misbehavior, try to keep your response factual and instructive, rather than emotional and judgmental. Though it's true that your negative response is always a good motivator for your child to change his immediate behavior (particularly as he approaches age three and grows more interested in pleasing you), shouting at him or calling him a "bad boy" will only distract him from the lesson you really want him to learn (not to take toys from other children). Instead, add a brief, matter-of-fact, "I don't like it when you take other children's toys away." (Make sure, however, that you just as readily say, "I like it when you share.") It also helps to look at the situation from your child's point of view. After all, taking away a playmate's toy means that he has the toy—a very powerful motivator for a two-year-old. To start to override this, point out to him that "See, you got the toy for a second, but then Mommy took it away. Grabbing toys from people is not the way to keep a toy. Next time, ask for the toy, and if he gives it to you, you can play with it."

"LISTEN TO ME!": ADJUSTING YOUR STYLE TO SUIT YOUR CHILD

As with every other aspect of parenting a young child, your knowledge of your two-year-old's unique temperament is one of your best tools in setting effective limits. A very active child may not hear you if you ask him to "stop it" and may need a touch on the arm or direct eye contact before he can pay attention. A sensitive child may crumble when you express your disapproval and respond to your instruction only when it's couched in the most positive language. A child who cries easily will need a moment to master his emotions before he can focus on what you are trying to say. A child who is shy or easily embarrassed may need privacy when you talk to him.

Even a child's "family temperament" has an effect on which techniques work best for him. A child whose family interacts in more dramatic, extroverted ways would probably expect, or at least be less fazed by, a more emotional response to his misbehavior. A child with highly verbal parents may respond better to logical explanation and negotiation and resist the statement, "That's the rule." For these reasons, it's best to listen to the general advice of child-care experts and other experienced parents, and then tailor that advice to your child's specific needs and circumstances, and your own.

Once you have decided which kinds of responses work best for your child at this particular point in his development, keep your responses as consistent as possible. As difficult as it is sometimes to refuse your child a snack at bedtime when he didn't eat much supper, and awkward as it can be to enforce a rule in the middle of a birthday party or other public event, consistency is the key to developing good habits and (eventually) reducing the number of conflicts you and your child experience. Keep in mind that on an unconscious level your child is monitoring the number of times his behavior (crying for candy) leads to a desirable response (getting the candy) and how many times it leads to an undesirable one (refusal to give in and provide a treat). Just as your frequent smiles encouraged his happy expressions as an infant, your *consistent* responses now will mold his actions in the future. Though there is always room for the occasional exception (he can have candy before lunch this time), in general each time you say, "Okay, just this once," you set him back a bit in his progress toward desirable behavior.

Studies have shown that parents' consistency in limit-setting is much more important for toddlers than it is for infants. Just as important as one parent's consistency is the level of consistency between both parents' approaches. Parents should agree this year not to undermine each other's rules and parenting style. Two-year-olds easily pick up on the differences between their parents' approaches to discipline and are able to use these disagreements to get around restrictions. We have all seen older children who have developed this skill to a fine art.

Of course, it's easy for parents to acknowledge that they need to decide on a single parenting style, but much harder to go along with a partner's methods when one passionately disagrees. Our parenting philosophies usually depend a great deal on how we were raised ourselves—whether we're inspired by those memories or are reacting against them. Our intense recollections of how we felt when certain methods were used ("When Mom sent me to my room, I thought she didn't love me") make it especially difficult to discuss these matters objectively. As you try to work out with your partner a "game plan" for limit-setting, keep in mind that your child will be capable of accommodating differences in your attitudes to some degree. (Experiencing moderately different styles that aren't in direct opposition can even be a good experience.) It is more damaging when one parent contradicts, sabotages, or ridicules the other parent's techniques in front of the child. Keep your emotions out of the discussion as much as you possibly can, and don't debate parental techniques in front of your child. When designing a parental strategy on which you can both agree, start with your general philosophies and work toward specific strategies. Try to reach a compromise on the important issues *before* you begin to enforce them frequently. Avoid getting hung up on each other's inflammatory buzzwords ("You're too permissive," "You're too strict"), and focus on identifying which approaches actually work best with your child at this point in his development. The sooner you find a way to settle such disagreements the better, since the same disputes are likely to come up again and again throughout your life with your child.

As your child approaches his third birthday and socializes more frequently with other children, he'll begin to realize that rules vary widely from family to family. Comparing and judging these different approaches to discipline is a favorite activity for some children—and a sign that he's accepting your own rules as part of "how his family is." The clearer and more consistent you can be about your rules, and the more consistently you can enforce them, the firmer your child's footing will be as he tries out his learned behavior in the larger world.

EASING THE WAY

When Parents Disagree

"I wish Scott and I had compared parenting philosophies before we got engaged," a friend once said to me. "If I knew then what kinds of fights we would have about how to raise the kids, and how hard it would be on our children, I don't think I would have married him." Certainly, few issues run so deep, and linger as long, as fundamental disagreements over how to raise a child. Still, even if you and your partner find yourselves on opposite ends of the parenting spectrum, there are ways to make it easier to design a viable strategy.

First, it is important to back away from the kinds of global statements that do little more than set you up in opposition to one another. Claiming that you believe in "setting a child free to be creative" will only alienate a parent who believes in "obedience and proper behavior." Instead, look for some small areas in which it's possible to compromise, even if the large issues remain unresolved. Agree to let your child choose her first chores, for instance, and agree to make sure she does them. Discuss specific situations until you've agreed exactly how to address them ("When Ralph wants ice cream and he hasn't eaten all his dinner, we'll insist that he take one more bite and finish his milk before he can have dessert"). Talk about ways in which each of your deepest parenting convictions can be carried out in real, day-to-day life ("I don't believe in spanking. If you feel the urge to spank Ralph, give him a time-out and let me take over"). Decide what to do when a new issue comes up and only one of you is present ("Handle it within our general guidelines, and we'll discuss it alone as soon as I get home"). Most important, use your home life as a miniature lab experiment: Observe your child's response to a particular parenting technique, review the response with your partner, and use your new knowledge to help design more techniques that will work best with your particular child.

With frequent reminders to one another that you share a common goal (a well-brought-up child) and that your love for him is what motivates you both, you are likely to get better at such compromises over time. If your conversations fail to improve the situation over the course of the year, however—or if you and your partner just can't seem to discuss the matter— this is a time to think seriously about obtaining outside guidance, whether it's a parents' support group, a professionally run workshop, or family counseling. Discipline issues will continue to arise throughout your parenting careers. Your child will benefit greatly from your determined efforts to settle on a game plan early in his life.

"I TAKE TURNS LIKE BEN!":
THE POWER OF IMITATION

Fortunately, your child's very strong urge to imitate is even more powerful when it comes to family members than it is with other children. Given a choice between imitating your behavior and a neighbor child's, your child will (eventually) settle on yours. Setting a good example for your child becomes one of the most effective means of shaping his behavior and enforcing limits.

Sometime around your child's second birthday, he probably became much more interested in observing other children and began to enjoy imitating their behavior. At first, this imitation was practically his only way of interacting with others—he signaled his interest in another child by mimicking whatever action or noise that child happened to make. Soon he began to imitate other children's more general behavior as well, both in their presence and later, when he was on his own. Often this was a good thing—many two-year-olds have learned to hold a crayon correctly, count to ten, and even use the toilet simply by imitating the children in their lives. Sometimes, of course, the results were not so good—as when your child began hitting other children after playing with a child who hit.

If your two-year-old has learned to hit by watching the child next door, you can show him how to settle differences in more positive ways, and then consistently demonstrate your methods through your own behavior. Studies have shown that setting a good example themselves is one of the most effective ways in which parents socialize a young child. Though it's only human to notice most often your child's negative imitations, work at noting and praising his positive imitations, too.

During this third year, your child will begin to respond to many other influences in his world. It's extremely important to take into account the examples offered by television, movies, and other adults. Rather than ignoring these influences, or trying to shield him from them completely (an impossible task), use them as opportunities to discuss in simple terms your reasons for requiring that he behave differently. Certainly, as he nears his third birthday, your child is old enough to understand that you don't approve of punching people like the cartoon characters on TV because "it isn't good to hurt people." Keep in mind that young children really don't understand the difference between fake and real violence. As you watch a program with him, comment on the behavior you see ("Oh-oh, that's going to get him into trouble"). Narrate what you would do if you were in the same situation ("Wow, that guy needs a time-out"). By hearing you observe and comment on different modes of behavior, he will gradually learn to judge the behavior he witnesses instead of blindly imitating it—a valuable skill to acquire for later life.

THE TOY BOX

At Thirty-six Months

Grace's twin cousins, four-year-old Will and Ryan, have come for a visit, and Grace is proudly showing them the objects in her toy basket in the family room. Will and Ryan are very active boys, and Grace increasingly finds herself pushed to the side as they pull out and toss away toy cars, rag dolls, dress-up clothes, and several varieties of blocks. "Look, a train!" Ryan says, spotting the box of train tracks and cars wedged behind the basket. He pulls it out, opens the box, and starts setting up the equipment. Meanwhile, Will has found a soft ball and begins bouncing it against the piano.

"No, no, Will," Grace says to her cousin. "No throwing!" Will continues to throw the ball. "It's fun," he tells Grace. "Here, you try it."

Will hands the ball to Grace. She's tempted to throw it at the piano. It makes a nice, solid *thud* when it hits the wood. Besides, she's thrilled that Will, a big kid, has offered to play with her. But Grace can't shake a vague idea of what her mother might do if she sees what they're doing. In the end, Grace wanders away from Will, still holding the ball and still shaking her head no. "My turn," she says to Ryan, squatting down to play with the train set. She smiles to herself. Mom, watching from the doorway, is pleasantly surprised. Grace didn't like Will's behavior, and so she broke the cycle of imitation in the only way she knew how—by leaving the scene.

"GOOD FOR YOU!": REWARDING GOOD BEHAVIOR

If you have ever worked for a boss who criticized your performance constantly without showing you how you *should* do your job, you may understand the frustration a two-year-old feels practically every day. Confused about proper behavior, often too overwhelmed emotionally to behave in positive ways, told to "stop that" several times a day or even several times an hour, it's little wonder that children this age are known for their tantrums, defiance, and other forms of emotional meltdown. You can improve your child's morale—thus making him *want* to behave well—by praising his efforts in ways he can understand. Again, the best kinds of responses to good behavior are simple and immediate. A simple "Good job," when your child completes a chore may work better than a longer analysis ("I'm so proud of you for picking up your blocks. You clean up your room better than anyone I know. I bet you'll be a very neat person when you grow up") because it doesn't distract him with tangential thoughts or emotions. Two is a good age to begin awarding stickers on a chart listing four or more positive behaviors you expect. By putting a gold star next to the heading "Clean up Toys," you teach your child to take pride in his accomplishments and inspire him to continue behaving well. Promising a treat or activity in exchange for good behavior really isn't a bribe, no matter what your friends say. It's an acceptable form of conditioning that will help your child figure out how to accomplish good behavior, and it won't "spoil" your child as long as you don't promise a treat for *every* act of compliance every time. In general, rewards do not have to be as consistent as other responses to behavior—your child doesn't have to get a gold star every time he cleans his room for gold stars to be effective. (In fact, research has shown that sporadic reinforcement is the most effective method.) But they should occur frequently enough for your child to understand that you are focusing on his behavior and that you appreciate his compliance.

Stickers and treats make for wonderful rewards at this age, because they are concrete objects that your child can look at or hold in his hand. Still, the most powerful reward he can receive at any age is your attention and approval. As you keep your focus on your child's positive behavior and ignore some of his less acceptable actions, you may well see those negative behaviors diminishing steadily as the year goes by. Children—even two-year-olds—want more than anything for their parents to approve of them. Of course, there will be times when simple positive reinforcement isn't enough to ensure that your child behaves safely and responsibly. As pointed out earlier in this chapter, firmness and consistency have their place, and there are even times when "because that's the rule" is the best way to guarantee good behavior. In the long run, however, your goal for your child should center on teaching him to control his own behavior, rather than following someone else's arbitrary rules. To this end, showing your child that you like what he's doing—and helping him understand what's in it for him—is one of the best ways to encourage him to set limits for himself.

Q & A

Naughty, Naughty

Q: Since before I ever even had any children, I've believed in the idea of positive discipline. I always thought that if I were firm and set a good example for my kid, he would learn to behave like I did. But my two-and-a-half-year-old daughter, Eileen, is such a pill nearly all the time. If I put her in her car seat, she tries to unbuckle it. If I take her to a movie, she makes so much noise that we have to leave. If I take her to the playground, she hits another kid with a sand toy. I know she's two and it's expected that she'll misbehave sometimes. But I end up practically in tears by the end of every day. Am I going to have to start spanking her?

A: You're right when you acknowledge that all two-year-olds misbehave, but you're wrong if you think spanking is the magic answer. Misbehaving is part of the process of learning limits and growing up. If your daughter's behavior is starting to overwhelm you, there are some steps you can take to improve the situation this year. First, try to make it as easy as possible for her to behave *well*. Part of this process involves praising her when she does meet your expectations, but it also includes very simple practical considerations, such as providing her with a toy to play with while she's in her car seat, or removing the knife from her setting at a restaurant before she smashes it against her plate. Avoid situations that are beyond her ability to cope with now, such as movies, large crowds, or long separations from you. Consider her physical and emotional state as you plan her day. If she didn't get enough sleep last night, skip the trip to the playground—she won't have the emotional control to deal with other children. If she's hungry, cut the visit to your mother's short and go home for lunch, where you know you'll have fewer eating problems.

Sometimes when our two-year-olds' misbehavior has us down, we wonder whether all of our parenting strategies are completely misguided. Often, however, it turns out that our mistakes are in the details. And we may find ourselves, despite our best efforts, attending only to the negative behaviors we want to correct. Acknowledging your child's progress, keeping an eye on her shifting capabilities and preparing for her needs will help you smooth the journey toward age three.

"TIME OUT!": CREATING EFFECTIVE CONSEQUENCES FOR BAD BEHAVIOR

However much you encourage good behavior in your child, there will be plenty of instances—probably several each day—when he violates the rules of conduct you've created for him. At these times, try to keep in mind that testing your limits truly is one of his most important activities this year—part of his struggle to be more independent. Much as he seems to rebel against your rules, however, it is vital for you to

Stickers or a similar reward system are valuable positive reinforcements as you "catch your child being good."

show him that you expect him to comply with them. Only in this way can his world begin to take shape, with parameters for behavior on which he can rely.

As in all aspects of setting limits, the best approach is a matter-of-fact focus on cause and effect rather than a global condemnation ("Bad boy!") or an emotional response ("How could you do such a thing?!"). Keep your responses to misbehavior simple and specific, and make sure the consequences occur immediately after the action. Negative consequences will be even more effective if they proceed naturally from your child's actions. If he throws his food on the floor in a fit of rage during dinner, for example, you might respond by calmly cleaning up the mess and then refusing to give him a treat. (As he approaches age three, it even makes sense to have him help with the cleaning.) By refusing to share his anger and making the consequences both consistent and just, you will eventually convince your child that there's little satisfaction in misbehaving.

A common mistake I see parents of two-year-olds making is expecting their child to have a greater ability to self-regulate than he's capable of at his stage of development. Though it's true that your child can understand the words "stop that" when he's breaking every crayon he has in half, he isn't necessarily able to come up with a way to stop his activity once he's started it. He may not even understand the problem—maybe he thinks that he's providing himself with twice as many crayons! By substituting an alternative activity (getting out the felt-tipped markers and suggesting he draw a picture of his cat), you can help him escape a bad situation while teaching him positive ways to change his behavior.

It's also important to limit your "No's" so that your child doesn't feel overwhelmed by the sheer number of rules he has to follow. Start with the most important issues involving safety and the protection of important property, and work your way gradually down your list toward the details of good manners and social behavior. Working on only a few issues at a time helps your child feel that good behavior is possible. By arranging his environment so that he has fewer opportunities to misbehave (limiting his choice of activities, diverting him while you dress him or brush his teeth, keeping dangerous objects out of reach), you limit his "failures" to a manageable number and help him believe that he is a "good boy" overall.

When your child does misbehave, consider his developmental level as you respond. A two-year-old's sense of time is quite different from an adult's. A two-minute time-out will feel like two hours to him. Use a timer that beeps at the end to let him know when his time out is over. After the time-out, be sure you explain—clearly, simply, and without undue emotion—why he had to be alone for a while. Point out that it's his behavior you disapproved of, not him. Tell him you're sure he'll do better next time—that everyone makes mistakes and the important thing is that we learn from them. Then give him a quick hug to let him know that you love him no matter how he behaves. If your child responds with anger or defiance, don't be too concerned. Committing a "crime" and being punished is a disorienting experience for a two-year-old. In trying to reestablish his sense of self-control, he may feel the need to tell the world, "This is how I am—like it or not!" If you've ever resisted a hug from your partner after an argument, you may understand how he feels.

A CHILD'S-EYE VIEW

The Other Side of the Door

Eva, who's nearly three, is bored. Her mom's on the phone, and her six-year-old brother, Nicholas, is in his room with a friend. Eva wanders over to her brother's room and stands in the doorway, watching the boys arm up with water pistols for an outdoor game. "I want one," she says, walking over to grab a water gun.

"No way!" Nicholas shouts, grabbing the toy and holding it out of her reach. "You can't play with us, Eva. Go away!"

Meanie, Eva thinks. *I want to play, too.* "Gimme that!" she yells, reaching for the water gun. When Nicholas refuses, she starts to scream.

"Eva, you stop that noise this instant!" Mommy is standing in the doorway, looking very mad. "Come on out of Nicholas's room. He wants to play with his friend right now."

Eva is unhappy that Mommy's not agreeing with her. She

remembers how boring it is outside this room, wandering around the house by herself. *Don't want to go,* she decides. Unable to keep her impulses in check, she has to move. "My turn!" she yells at her mother, and grabs the gun from her brother.

"All right, young lady. That's it. You're having a time-out!" Eva's mother marches her to her own room. "Stay here for two minutes," she says. "I said no. There's no screaming in this house. I want you to think about how much your screaming hurts people's ears."

The door slams, and Eva finds herself alone in her room. This is even worse than before! She smashes the door with her fist, but there's no response. She starts to cry and sits on the floor. *Hate being alone!* she thinks as tears run down her face. *Bad Mommy! Bad Nicholas!* The sounds of the boys running outside to play only make her cry louder.

When Mom opens the door, Eva's still out of sorts. She doesn't want to listen to Mom tell her about her bad behavior. She sniffs, wipes her nose on her sleeve, and stalks into the play-room. The plastic knight's helmet, sword, and shield her daddy gave her rest invitingly against the wall. Eva picks up the sword and waves it around with great satisfaction. *My sword!* She whacks a nearby sofa a few times with the sword, enjoying a new sense of power. "Give me that gun!" she demands, and whacks the bed again.

"DON'T HIT ME!": AVOIDING THE TRAPS OF PHYSICAL PUNISHMENT

"How many times have I *told* you not to hit other kids?!" *Whack.* What parent hasn't felt the temptation to respond this way when their child strikes out physically for the umpteenth time? Perhaps you've thought, if only fleetingly, "If a *grown-up* talked to me like my child just did, I'd want to punch him in the mouth!" The fact is, however, that two-year-olds are not at all like grown-ups. Not only do they have very little concept of the effects of their actions and words, but physical punishment such as a slap or spanking violates their still extremely fragile sense of self, smashing apart their sense of how the world works in ways that no adult can completely understand. Clearly, such an experience eclipses any behavioral lesson the punishment was meant to give. What it does teach children is that aggression is an acceptable way to control others— in other words, as countless studies have shown in recent decades, it teaches children to hit back. In fact, I've never met a parent who felt good about having spanked a child—justified, yes, but not good.

As difficult as it is to control our own behavior when a two-year-old lashes out for what seems to be no reason or misbehaves in the same way for the two-hundredth time, refraining from physical punishment is one of the most important goals this year. Keep in mind that your two-year-old is *testing* your responses, and do your best to pass that test. Think in advance about the positive ways you'd like to see your child respond when he is frustrated or angry, and set a good example by responding in those ways yourself. Be aware of the times when you or your child are feeling stressed or otherwise vulnerable, and try to avoid confrontations or challenges at those times. Plan your environment in ways that discourage physical aggression—maintaining clear, nonphysical consequences for misbehavior, taking time away from your child when you're beginning to feel burned out, and sharing your frustration with other adults rather than taking it out on your child.

Ironically, one of the reasons parents today may feel pushed to react *physically* to a child's behavior is the popular belief that setting strict *verbal* limits stifles young children's self-expression and leads to lowered self-esteem. It is easy to worry that saying no too often will prevent our children from learning to negotiate and from feeling free to share their feelings with us. As a result, we may grit our teeth and put up with a great deal more whining, arguing, or defiance than we would like to— until the moment when we are pushed past our tolerance level and simply blow up. If you find this to be the case, consider how much better it would be to decide ahead of time how much negative behavior you can tolerate, firmly tell your child no well before you reach the point of no return, and put up with his inevitable angry response while you are still able to control your temper.

As important as it is to encourage children to express themselves fully, setting clear and even strict limits is not a bad thing. Limits help your child build internal controls that will fortify him throughout life. Point out to him that grown-ups have to follow rules, too. Give him examples ("Mom was mad, but she didn't yell"). By demonstrating your own conscious, thoughtful ways of preventing and controlling your own outbursts of anger, you will show him that physical aggression is not the answer. By keeping limits in your lives together, you will not only enjoy a more tolerable day-to-day life with your two-year-old but teach him the value and methods of *self*-discipline—which, of course, is every parent's ultimate goal.

Controlling Your Own Anger

When your child loses control of herself and refuses to listen to reason, the urge to strike out physically can be overwhelming. What begins as a firm hand on her shoulder ends with a sharp twist or an angry shake; what starts out as a lesson in logical consequences ("This is what hitting feels like! Do you like that?") ends with shock and tears on your child's part and horrible feelings of guilt and regret for you. Ironically, the best way to avoid losing control of yourself with your child is the same way you help her control her own behavior—by heading off difficult situations whenever possible and by monitoring your emotional state and implementing simple, concrete solutions for the times when you're past your tolerance level. A great deal of conflict occurs, for example, when parents try to cram more activities into the day than their young children can keep up with. By *underestimating* how much you can get done and leaving more than enough preparation time, you can avoid those moments of desperation when you realize you're late to an appointment and your child insists on playing with her tea set instead of putting on her shoes. Other problems occur when we expect too much from a child at a certain point in her development—restrained behavior from a curious toddler at a relative's house, for example, or adult-type patience while shopping, eating in a restaurant, or waiting in line. Relaxing your expectations and remembering that your child has not had even three full years to learn all the rules may help you maintain equilibrium as your child stomps on Grandma's foot, spreads her toys all over the living room, or punches the ATM buttons *again* when you just told her not to. It is also important to remember that you, your partner, and the rest of the family need scheduled time away from your child. A life dedicated wholly to satisfying a two-year-old's demands would send nearly any parent over the brink.

No matter how careful you are to build relaxation into your lifestyle, however, your child is bound to inspire your anger now and then. Your goal at these times is to know when you've passed your own tolerance level and to choose from one of several ways to back off. A client of mine once told me she makes a point of not touching her child at all when she's angry. "I read once that a good way to discipline a child is to take them by the arm and lead them physically through what you want them to do, since it's easier for them to learn by doing stuff than by hearing about it," she said. "But I noticed that when I did that—marching Carol into the bathroom and actually guiding her hand to brush her teeth—it was really easy for me to lose control of my anger and *jerk* her really meanly through the process instead. She would say, "Mom, you're hurting me." I just couldn't trust myself to be gentle when I was mad at her, so instead I learned to put my hands behind my back or in my pockets, breathe deeply, and talk her through it instead."

In general, it's a good idea to avoid trying to discipline your child when you yourself feel out of control. At these times, you're not likely to discipline well or wisely, and you may well find yourself unable to avoid physical action. Instead, give yourself a time-out. If necessary, avoid touching your child, as my client did. Shut yourself up in the bathroom for a minute if you have to. Call a sympathetic friend to substitute for you, and go for a short drive. You'll find that your sense of reason returns very quickly given the chance—and you will have avoided actions that you would later regret.

"LET'S START OVER": MOVING BEYOND DISCIPLINE

Is family life always going to be this exhausting? Mark arrives home with Lawrence, now nearly three, so tired he can barely fit his key into the lock of the front door. Once inside, he drops onto the living room sofa while Lawrence putters around the room as usual. "So—how was your day?" he asks his son, putting his feet up on the coffee table. "Did you play with the big boys today?"

"Uh . . . no," Lawrence says distractedly. "Daddy, can I watch TV?"

Mark appreciates the fact that Lawrence at least stuck to their agreement that he would ask to watch television instead of just switching the TV on. They've talked a lot about this issue over the past year, and Lawrence seems to understand now that he needs permission to watch a show or two a day. For a while near the beginning of the year, Mark tried to cut out television altogether, but he had to accept the fact that he is just too tired at the end of the workday to start interacting directly with a young child right away. A half-hour show gives him the time he needs to unwind and lets Lawrence feel that he has some say in what he does at home. Lately, Mark has noticed that watching the show with Lawrence, and talking with him about the characters and what they're doing, is a good way to phase into the evening's activities. As Lawrence has gotten better at expressing himself through language, their conversations have become more interesting. Mark actually feels closer to his son as they talk about the issues raised on the show.

"Okay, pal, that's it," Mark says 30 minutes later as the show's credits roll. He gets up quickly and turns off the television—having learned not to let Lawrence focus on the ad for the next show. "I brought some paper clips home from the office," he says. "Do you know how to make a paper-clip chain? Come on, I'll show you how." Mark knows now that distracting Lawrence helps him make the transition from TV to another activity. Stringing paper clips will keep him busy at the kitchen table while Mark makes dinner.

"But, Daddy . . . ," Lawrence says, reaching longingly for the TV.

"Look, here are the paper clips," Mark repeats, pulling them out of his pocket. "Come on. I'll race you to the table!"

To his surprise, Lawrence takes him up on his challenge. All in all, he has to admit that parenting Lawrence has gotten easier over the past few months. Lawrence seems less rebellious and more committed to trying to please his dad. He's learned some basic behavior that takes the pressure off their relationship. Best of all, he's accepting some of the house rules that Mark feels are most important. A couple of times, Mark has even watched Lawrence stop himself from misbehaving instead of waiting for his dad to distract him, correct him, or otherwise help him change direction. Of course, not every day is as easy as this one when they get home, but the easier days seem to happen more and more often.

ADVANCES

Moving Toward Self-Discipline in the Third Year

24 MONTHS	Begins to understand simple time-related concepts ("soon," "after breakfast," etc.)
	Learns a great deal of behavior through imitation
27 MONTHS	Starts to rely more on words to communicate feelings
	More attentive to parents' commands
30 MONTHS	Behavior becomes more logical, less randomly defiant
	Remembers behavioral rules more easily

33 MONTHS	Increasingly eager to please parents and be a "good boy"
	Somewhat better able to wait for what he wants
36 MONTHS	Observes others' behavior and compares it to his own
	Can follow a two- or three-part command
	Starts to experiment with negotiation

FIRST-PERSON SINGULAR

Every child responds to various limit-setting techniques in his own unique way. By observing your child's responses and trying to understand the feelings that inspire them, you can better tailor your discipline techniques to suit him. Write down which techniques you have tried and what the results were. At what times of day, or on what days of the week, is it most difficult for your child to behave well? Which of his behaviors threaten to send you over the edge, and what have you done to remedy this situation? When your child reveals in his own words how he feels when you respond to his behavior, record his words here. He will be interested to know what went through his mind as a two-year-old, and you'll be able to refer to his refreshingly honest comments in the years to come.

READER'S NOTES

_____

_____

_____

_____

_____

_____

_____

_____

_____

_____

_____

_____

_____

_____

_____

_____

_____

_____

_____

_____

_____

CHAPTER 9

Looking Ahead—I'm Three

One of the greatest leaps your child will take next year will be in the realm of her imagination.

What an eventful year this has been for the children we've observed in these chapters and for you and your family. Over the past twelve months, Amy and Kaisha, Dylan and Jeff—and your two-year-old as well—have learned to skip, turn a somersault, and hold a pencil; to enjoy an interesting conversation; to share (sometimes) with friends; and to use predictable daily routines as a base for further exploration. We have watched their unique personalities assert themselves as they learned to express their feelings more clearly, use imaginary play to work out conflicts, and creatively resist the rules and restrictions they did not like. Your own development as a parent has been no less impressive as your time spent playing with your child and observing her actions showed you new ways to shape and encourage her growth. This expanded knowledge will support you through the next year as you witness the continued blossoming of your three-year-old's fascinating personality. Next year an array of skills she has worked so hard to develop will come together at last, creating a whole that is truly far greater than the sum of its parts. The more you understand your two-year-old today, the more you will be able to enhance and enjoy this next step in her growth.

"WHO ARE YOU? WHO AM I?":
WHAT YOUR CHILD HAS LEARNED

Verbal and emotional growth dominated your child's development this year, though giant steps were certainly also taken in other areas. This has been the year when your child really began to talk to you—picking up new phrases, words, and inflections at a breathtaking rate and gradually substituting language for tears and physical expression. As the months passed, she grew more confident that, with language, she could control at least a limited part of her world (negotiating for a later bathtime, explaining why your actions made her sad). Her moments of defiance probably decreased over the course of this year, and she began to interact in more reasonable ways. By her third birthday, the two of you have probably worked out a number of verbal formulas—a special rhyme while brushing her teeth, an exchange of thoughts at bedtime—to get her through her daily routines and inevitable emotional roadblocks. In the future, as your voice takes its place in her own inner dialogue, she will learn to use similar techniques to encourage herself and manage her emotional ups and downs.

Your two-year-old's emotional dramas were strongly linked this year to her need to establish herself as a presence in her world. As her language skills enabled her to express newly hatched opinions and desires, she experienced a strong urge to see that her opinions were recognized and her desires realized. No doubt her insistence on "doing it herself" or having her own way sometimes had you tearing out your hair in frustration. But such interactions ideally also sparked new, creative methods for the two of you to compromise and get along. Now, as the year ends, your child has a clearer idea of where you stand on behavioral issues, what her limits are, and how she can please you while still, whenever possible, achieving her goals. She has found ways to establish her presence beyond simply stomping her foot and shouting, "No!" She has learned that sharing, taking turns, listening to others, and other prosocial behaviors win her the attention she craves. Gradually, over the year to come, she will experiment with these new ideas to carve out a place for herself in the wider world of social interaction.

Of course, none of this verbal, emotional, and social growth would have been possible without a great deal of cognitive development over the past year. By piecing together bits of knowledge gained from careful observation, your two-year-old began working to create a coherent understanding of how her world works and the meaning behind certain events. Her theories often led to amusing misconceptions (candles at dinner don't necessarily mean it's your birthday), but day by day her accuracy improved. As she became more aware of the currents of emotion, adult conversations, and other fluctuating elements surrounding her, she experienced new fears and anxieties. Fortunately, an expanding imaginative ability allowed her to begin working her fears out through her play. Now, on the brink of turning three, your child is much more familiar with the world of ideas. She is able to remember and think about events that occurred quite a long time ago. She can use logic to some extent to negotiate for what she wants. She can puzzle over problems and come up with solutions, all in her mind. In the next year, this ability to "hold her world in her head" will come to fruition. She will be able to recognize symbols, such as numbers and letters, written with a crayon. She will draw an actual shape or a face instead of simply scribbling with a crayon. Her "magical thinking" will increase dramatically, and she will come up with fascinating answers to such questions as, "What makes the clouds move in the sky?" and, "What happens to a flower when it dies?"

Perhaps most satisfying of all this year, your two-year-old's experiences with other children have prepared her for a sea change in her relationships with peers. As she played side by side, and increasingly face to face, with children her age and older, she observed other children's behavior patterns and began to imitate them. By the end of the year, her interest in other children has probably fully asserted itself. She enjoys getting together with others her age and may even have become interested in the concept of having a "friend." As she enters her fourth year, she will particularly treasure her connections to one or two specific children and will learn a great deal from her time with them. Depending on her temperament, she may even benefit from a preschool, group-care situation, or a "threes and fours" gymnastics or music class.

LISTENING AND RESPONDING: WHAT YOU HAVE LEARNED

This third year of your life as a parent has also been full of great discoveries. Over the past twelve months, you have learned which of your own and your partner's traits your child has picked up, and you've spotted some personality quirks that are her very own. You've seen where her temperament and yours rub up against each other now and then, and where they meld perfectly. You've used your lifelong experience dealing with your personal traits—shyness, an abundance of energy, a tendency to be a night owl—to help your child adjust to her own. Meanwhile, your close observation of her physical, mental, and emotional growth has helped you adjust your parenting style to her changing needs and capabilities. As she has established herself as a presence in your home, you have moved to make room for her. Now much more than before, your relationship consists of two individuals communicating, reaching compromises, and using one another as springboards for further growth.

This trend will continue as your child enters her fourth year. Her leaps in verbal ability will greatly enhance your interaction, putting her on a more equal footing as the two of you continue to work toward her further development. The more she is able to tell you about how she feels, what she needs, and how she views the world, the better you'll be able to understand and support her, and the richer your own experience will be. Certainly, in the next year, the truism that "the child raises the parent" will become even clearer as so much of the care, energy, and thought you've put into raising your child comes back to reward you (as well as challenge you) many times over.

COMING ATTRACTIONS: DEVELOPMENTS IN THE FOURTH YEAR

One of the key concepts in the life of a three-year-old is independence. Your child's insistence on "doing it herself" this past year will result in her new ability to put on her shoes and even get a snack from the refrigerator without your help—though her shoes may end up on the wrong feet and you may not approve of the snack. Her physical coordination will improve enormously next year. She will be able to ride a tricycle, jump, and even hop on one foot, though it may still take quite a bit of concentration. Her fine-motor development will also improve—she will more frequently draw recognizable outlines of things instead of simply scribbling. All of these advances in physical and cognitive mastery please your child enormously, making her easier to get along with (much of the time) and more eager and able to please.

One of the greatest leaps your child will take next year will be in the realm of her imagination. Her ability to model real and fictional worlds in her mind will improve tremendously in the months to come. As a result, she will be able to work out a number of her emotional, social, and cognitive conflicts through pretend play, storytelling, and other mental activities. New fears will most likely surface as her imagination increases, but she will begin to settle on ways to handle these fears. She may even invent a fantasy friend next year to use as a scapegoat for bad behavior, help work out emotional dilemmas, and provide herself with a playmate who's always available on demand.

As her verbal skills continue to improve (a typical three-year-old's speaking vocabulary is between three hundred and nine hundred words), she will ask questions constantly about how the world works, where important people in her life are right now, and what she will do today. Her questions will be a sign of her continued cognitive development, which will allow her to explore her world on a much deeper level than before. Her curiosity will make her quite an interesting conversationalist and enhance her social life. Certainly by the middle of the year, she will be able to play more agreeably, to share, and to enjoy such social delights as secrets and surprises. She will be fully aware of her gender and will probably gravitate toward friends of her own sex. Her increasing ability to focus on one activity for a longer period of time will allow her to start playing more structured games, such as tag or "Go Fish." For all these reasons, more group activity, such as a preschool program or a gymnastics class, can open new vistas for her, helping her get to know herself better as well as learning more about others. By the end of the year, your more experienced three-year-old is likely to comment frequently and affectionately on herself as an individual, as in, "I *hate* potatoes," and, "I *love* dogs."

Of course, it won't all be smooth sailing in the fourth year. Parents often tell me they are surprised by the extent to which three-year-olds continue the defiant, resistant behavior they are better known for at age two. Unfortunately, their determination to have their way is a necessary part of moving toward creating their own routines, rules, and limits. Like many of us, they tend toward inflexibility while in the early stages of learning this new skill. (Think of how *you* react when your partner "helps" you as you struggle with a difficult new recipe or try to program the VCR.) Other behavior issues may come to the fore as your child enters preschool or another group situation. Other adults' negative responses to your child's actions may call your attention to issues you hadn't noticed before. Such incidents are unpleasant for any parent, of course, but they also provide a chance to help your child fine-tune her social skills and to address problems that had become so familiar you no longer noticed them.

Assisting your child on the road toward successful interaction with others, and supporting her in her continuing eagerness to learn about her world, will probably remain your prime goals for most of the coming year. Your three-year-old's better language skills, improved impulse control, relaxing focus on herself, and increasing ability to understand rational explanations will eventually help her win the struggle between babyish outbursts and more socialized behavior. As the year draws to a close, she will develop stronger resources with which to cope with such new demands as extended group activity and the need to obey rules—even when you're not around to remind her. She will be equipped with a hard-won sense of right and wrong and may well enjoy pointing out others' good and bad behavior. Best of all, she will understand that even when she does have problems with others or with herself, you and other loving adults will be there to help her see the way toward greater mastery.

FIRST-PERSON SINGULAR

Now would be the ideal time to look back at the predictions you wrote for your child when she was twenty-four months old. Chances are your predictions were more accurate this year than the year before. As the months passed and your child's temperament and personality became increasingly clear, you were able to observe and understand her with a much more educated eye. Still, there were probably a number of ways in which your child surprised you, whether through a new behavior quirk or remarkable progress in an area of development where she had lagged before. Now that you have a better sense of who she is, get out your videotapes and photographs of your two-year-old, marvel at her progress, and think about where you want her to go. What are your goals for her, for yourself as a parent, and for your family as a whole next year? How would you most like to see your child grow? Have you noticed any particularly strong skills in your child that you might help her start to develop in the coming months? As we've seen, the better you know your unique child, the better equipped you will be to encourage her growth in the future. Thinking about her with pen in hand provides you with tools for a better future as well as precious souvenirs for the years ahead.

_____

_____

_____

_____

_____

_____

_____

_____

_____

_____

_____

_____

_____

_____

_____

_____

_____

_____

_____

_____

I'm Three

Every Parent's Guide to the
Charming and Demanding
36- to 48-Month-Old

The couple sat down in front of me at the movie theater, attacking their sodas with the relief most parents feel when they finally have an evening to themselves. Still, like many moms and dads, they couldn't resist talking about their child on their night out. I listened in as the woman reviewed their daughter's day in her preschool's "threes'" class.

"Melissa's teacher told me something interesting today," the woman said, taking a sip of her soda. "You know Malcolm, the little boy with the red hair? He dropped the caterpillar he'd made at the art table and it broke in half. He cried and cried over it, just inconsolable, and no one could get him to stop. Then Melissa walked over, picked up the pieces and handed them to him, and said, 'That's okay, Malcolm. Now you have two!' Malcolm took the pieces and smiled, and after that he was fine."

"Wow. She did that on her own?" Melissa's dad sounded impressed. "She has been acting a lot nicer to people lately."

"Yeah. I really feel like everything's starting to come together for her now." The woman leaned back in her seat as the theater lights dimmed. Then she added wryly, "And not a moment too soon."

It *is* amazing to witness the transformation that takes place in your child between her third birthday and her fourth. So many improved physical, cognitive, verbal, emotional, and social skills combine to create a full, unique individual whose personality unfolds almost magically from day to day. Your three-year-old not only wants to please you but increasingly knows how to. She not only enjoys drawing pictures and creating stories, but she takes pride in her work and expects others to appreciate it. As she nears her fourth birthday, she may go beyond just sympathizing when others are unhappy to actually trying to help them solve their problems and feel better.

Such delightful developments are a great reward for the hard work and patience you provided during your child's early years. But don't expect them to happen right away. The integration of a three-year-old's personality is a *gradual* process that takes place bit by bit over the course of this entire year (and it doesn't stop there). In the meantime, certain behavioral glitches may become more pronounced and difficult to deal with as your child gets better at imposing her will and circumventing rules. For parents who have eagerly anticipated the end of toddler-type conflicts, these new or stepped-up negative behaviors—refusing to eat the pancakes she asked for, insisting on a Band-Aid for every tiny scratch, scribbling on the furniture right after she was told not to, and so on—are especially upsetting. Confused by their children's behavior ("She talks like she's ten, but acts like she's two!"), parents look to friends, books, and other resources for help. Sometimes the advice they receive is useful, but often it is too general to work in a particular situation. Quite often, it fails because it doesn't suit the temperament or developmental stage of the child in question.

As a developmental psychologist and as the mother of twin eight-year-old boys, I am intimately aware that children are very different from one another, even when they are the same age or in the same family. They are *growing* beings whose comprehension, skills, needs, and desires evolve over time, and parenting itself is a process that constantly gets refined as a parent learns more about his or her child. I know from experience that applying a general parenting technique (such as time-outs) to an individual child may lead to success if the technique happens to suit both child and parent but can actually cause harm—a child's sense of emotional abandonment or a parent's failure to discuss or correct the behavior—if it doesn't. How much more effective it is to observe the child's personal style (verbal or physical, affectionate or independent, timid or adventurous), acknowledge one's own strengths and weaknesses, and combine these with knowledge of normal three-year-old development. This is the ideal way to create a parenting strategy that truly works for all.

Recent scientific research on the workings of the developing brain tells us that young children are active partners who interact with their environment with a purpose, not passive recipients of knowledge spoon-fed to them by adults. Now that your child can run, jump, speak, pretend, and make plans on her own, she is less dependent on you as the main source of her knowledge than she was the year before. Learning to overcome obstacles on her own and solve problems in her unique way is one of her primary challenges and achievements this year. Over the months, the two of you will need to make many adjustments as you begin to step back while she steps forward in her learning activities, physical experimentation, imaginary play, social interaction, and even in the setting of limits. You will have to decide when it's best to assert yourself in your role of parent and when your child will benefit more from experimenting (and perhaps initially failing) on her own. You will need to know when her behavior is a result of her natural limitations (an inability to wait very long for what she wants; confusion over the meaning of your words), when it is a form of testing limits, and when it signals an opportunity for real progress. The only way to make these decisions, moment by moment and day by day, is to observe your child accurately *with an educated eye*, and then implement your knowledge to support her climb toward greater maturity.

My goal in presenting this series of books is to help you see the world from your child's own point of view—and to show you how her thinking differs from yours in profound ways—so that you can use this knowledge to better understand, support, educate, communicate, and deepen your bond with her as she grows. In these pages, I will suggest many ways to do this in practical situations that most parents encounter with their children in the course of everyday life. I will offer glimpses into the lives and experiences of other parents like yourselves. I will give you a general idea of what to expect from someone your child's age, so you can more easily apply that general information to your child's situation and personality. It is my hope that this book will help you understand the development of your three-year-old so that the entire family will grow together with an ever-increasing sense of wonder, discovery, and joy. Welcome to the world of threes.

CHAPTER 1

What I'm Like

A three-year-old needs to know that he can learn to master his environment.

Nobody said it was going to be easy. Parenting a young child takes an enormous amount of energy and skill, but by the time our children turn three we can begin to really enjoy the results of all our efforts. Dave Parker thinks about this as he tends the hamburger grill at his neighborhood's block party and watches his son Pete play with his friends. At three and a half, Pete trades jokes and silly noises with his best friend, Russell, plays a decent game of tag, and even stops to comfort a toddler who's fallen and bumped her knee. Dave realizes that the preschool bunch have in fact been playing for ten whole minutes without the intervention of adults. "It's a whole different ball game now, huh?" he says to Henry, Russell's dad, nodding his head in the boys' direction. Henry grins. He doesn't even have to ask Dave what he's talking about.

Dave glances back at the kids and sees that his son has wandered over to the picnic table where the refreshments are laid out. He's reaching for one of the giant open soda bottles (again), an entranced expression on his face. "Pete, get away from there!" Dave yells, waving his spatula. Pete looks at his dad, startled, and walks away. A minute later, though, he sneaks back to the table when he sees that Dad is distracted.

Moving fast, he grabs the soda. As he tries to take a drink, the bottle slips out of his hands and soda spills on the ground.

"Pete!" Dave strides toward him, embarrassed and angry. "I told you no!"

"I didn't do it!" Pete cries, looking up at his dad. "It was a naccident!"

Dave is startled by Pete's deliberate misbehavior—and the obvious lie. Who taught his son that it was okay to act this way? "It's worse than when he was two," he points out to his wife, Rita, later that night when the party is over. "Back then, he got in trouble because he couldn't really control himself. Now it's like he does bad things *on purpose*. I could practically hear the neighbors thinking, 'Boy, Pete doesn't listen to his parents.'"

Rita sighs. "The other moms say their three-year-olds do it, too," she tells him. "But I don't see it. Sometimes I wonder if Pete misbehaves just to find out what we'll do."

What a strange and challenging year this is, when the same developments that so delight parents also lead to such mystifying behavior. Nearly all parents would agree that watching their child learn to manipulate his environment is an exciting experience in many respects. Yet it can also be confusing as children's improved skills convince us they're more capable of understanding and coping than they really are. True, your child will take much more initiative this year, seeking out and even creating situations that stimulate his growth. This same initiative will sometimes spur him to go after what he wants whether or not you want him to have it. His improved physical skills will make it easier for him to get into trouble and harder for you simply to pick him up and remove him from a situation. You will find it more difficult, due to his developing verbal abilities, to end a dispute with a simple "No." His need to reanalyze situations on a higher, more complex level will cause him to rehash old behavior issues you thought had been laid to rest. And the same emerging sense of self that allows him to sweetly promise "I won't" enables him to shout, red-faced, "I will!"

For all of these reasons, three can frequently be the best of times and the worst of times for parents—as well as, possibly, for children themselves. The good news is, as your child's skills continue to improve he will resort less to negative behaviors to get his way, and a refreshingly mature emotional and social persona will begin to emerge. The bad news is, this journey toward greater maturity is littered with misunderstandings, defiance, and frustrating regressions just when you thought the hard months were over. Your three-year-old will certainly struggle with such concepts as telling the truth, keeping a promise, and finding ways to dovetail his needs with yours. Fortunately, his expanding comprehension makes this a year when your firmness, patience, and repeated explanations may have their most beneficial and lasting effects.

A PARENT'S STORY

"Say Hello"

"I used to dread taking my Rose to preschool when she was three," a colleague told me as we were comparing parenting notes. "We live just a few blocks away, so I walked her there on my way to work. Naturally, we'd run into other parents and their kids on the way. Every one of them would say, 'Hello, Rose, how are you, how have you been?' And Rose would never say a word to anyone. She'd march down the sidewalk with her eyes on the ground, never even looking up. Every morning, the maintenance man at the front door would greet her by name, and she never once acknowledged his existence. I knew she knew *how* to be sociable, because the second she walked into the classroom she'd start smiling and saying hi to everyone in sight. But that walk was embarrassing. I thought she was the only three-year-old with absolutely no manners.

"Finally, I talked to the head of the preschool about it. I still remember how relieved I was when she told me that lots of three-year-olds are that way. She said they're so preoccupied with all the information coming at them when they're outside or just entering the school that they don't have any mental room for remembering their manners. She said that Rose probably literally didn't hear people greeting her. She wasn't deliberately being rude. Once in her classroom, though, she felt secure and relaxed enough to start using the verbal meeting-and-greeting routines she'd just started to learn.

"Later I started to notice other kids in Rose's class behaving the same way. It's just part of the age, and all you can do is keep prompting them, acting as a role model and explaining over and over why they should acknowledge other people, until they have a good enough hold on their environment to follow your lead."

"I WANNA DO IT!": YOUR CHILD'S PROGRESS AT AGE THREE

The pediatrician's waiting room was packed with parents and children this afternoon, but two-year-old Molly and Hanna, aged three, had managed to secure two seats at the child-sized drawing table. It was amusing to observe the differences in how the two girls pursued their tasks. Molly, a typical two-year-old, narrated her drawing activity in a soft contented voice—literally telling herself what she was doing. Hanna was old enough to conduct her narration in her head and made much more of an effort than Molly to draw people and animals instead of just scribbling. The girls' developmental differences were highlighted even more when a younger toddler suddenly snatched their drawings away. Molly looked surprised, but then simply picked out another marker and started a new drawing. Hanna turned on the little boy, clearly upset—though she pulled back a little when she saw how young he was. "Hey, that's my picture!" she said loudly, looking to the toddler's caregiver for backup. Hanna's mother offered her a fresh sheet of paper, but this failed to make Hanna happy. Only when the toddler's caregiver returned the original picture was she able to take her seat and start working, silently and very industriously, on her original creation.

If your three-year-old has ever collapsed in tears when his sister erased his Etch-a-Sketch drawing, or gotten mad when you took his painting off the refrigerator, you know how committed he has become to the product as well as the process of his creative efforts. This pride in his accomplishments is a sign of his emerging awareness of himself as a consistent, unique person with developing talents and skills. Last year your child lived from moment to moment, happy one instant and crying the next but not able to comprehend the bigger picture. Now, his improving memory, deepening experience, and expanding emotional and thinking skills allow him to hold on to a somewhat fuller sense of self. Rather than trying out each new skill sequentially, he is beginning to use them in concert, and this takes him to an entirely new level of thought, action, and feeling. He is becoming a more integrated individual, justifiably proud of what he can do yet still eager for your praise and recognition.

This new integration will begin to manifest itself not only in his pride in his work, but in nearly every other aspect of your child's development this year. As we will see in Chapter 2, his ability to hold an entire process in his mind from beginning to end will help him learn more complex movements such as hopping and skipping, to move with greater smoothness and coordination, and to participate in organized games. His expanding spatial awareness will allow him to complete more crafts activities (with your support), write his first name (though it may take him ten minutes to do so), and solve some gravity-defying Lego problems. It will also increase his perception of danger in his environment. A new fear of playing in the water, climbing trees, or working with knives or scissors is not a sign of weakness but a healthy indication that your child is beginning to understand and internalize your own safety concerns.

A charming aspect of your three-year-old's higher level of thinking is bound to be revealed in his increasingly sophisticated sense of humor. At age two, he probably laughed at slapstick scenarios, funny faces, and silly noises. This year, as we will see in Chapter 3, he will become more interested in what is reasonable and what isn't—and silly situations will send him into fits of giggles. Your child may pretend to catch butterflies with his new butterfly net—and then crack himself up by "catching" Daddy's head! As the year progresses, your child will start to sense why a comment may be funny and acceptable in one context but not in another (such as saying, "You silly-head!" to his brother but not to the counterperson at the fast-food restaurant). With your help, he may even learn to use humorous wordplay or funny role-playing to jolly himself (or you) out of a bad mood.

One of the greatest leaps your child will take this year will be in the realm of his imagination. His ability to model real and fictional worlds in his mind will improve tremendously. He'll be able to work out a number of emotional, social, and cognitive issues through pretend play, storytelling, and similar activities. His imagination will inspire intense curiosity about the world around him, and he'll begin to ask such questions as, "What makes it rain?" and "Where does the wind go?" Much of the time, he'll invent his own answers to these questions, and his theories will both amuse and amaze you. Clearly, this deeper level of thinking will lead to more satisfying conversations, particularly near the end of the year.

In fact, your child's continued astonishing verbal growth can present an interesting new problem for both of you. It becomes quite easy at times to assume that he understands what adults are saying even when the discussion is far over his head. As we will see in Chapter 4, children this age frequently use words and verbal "scripts" that they don't fully comprehend or can't yet consistently follow. (He may promise not to splash in any more mud puddles, but that doesn't mean he knows to stay out of clear *rainwater* puddles as well.) Though his understanding of context (a place and a time for every comment) will improve this year, you can expect a large number of embarrassing questions ("Mommy, where'd that man's hair go?") as your child's intellectual curiosity takes over his tongue. By age four, your child will gradually learn to use his enthusiastic "outside voice" and softer "inside voice" appropriately, to (occasionally) refrain from interrupting when you're talking with someone else, and to speak more simply and gently to a baby than he would to an older child. He may even be able to wait half a minute or so before whispering (all too loudly), "Mom, why is that man's belly so big?"

Justifiably excited about his growing ability to understand and interact with his world, your three-year-old will probably become almost obsessive about regulating certain aspects of it at some point during the year. He may refuse to put on his shoes before going out—particularly if he senses you're in a hurry—or have a meltdown if you order him ice cream in a cup instead of a cone. His need to dictate how his life will proceed is one of the most challenging aspects of his developing personality—particularly as he *appears* increasingly capable of listening to reason—but such temporary willfulness is an inevitable part of growing up. In Chapter 5, we will explore ways for both you and your child to survive this difficult period, which usually peaks around the middle of the year or even a little later. Meanwhile, it's encouraging to realize that such willfulness is part of an exciting process of self-definition. As your little

While three-year-olds seem "grown-up" in so many ways, they will still need your comfort and affection during rough times.

one puts his hands on his hips and declares his preferences ("I *love* soccer!" "I *hate* brushing my teeth!"), he understands more about who he is and who he isn't. With your help, he can use this knowledge to become a more independent four-year-old who's confident enough to live with compromise.

In Chapter 6, we will explore the many ways in which social interaction can help your child hone his personality, by allowing him to practice managing his emotions and stretch and test his imagination. His developing sense of self will allow him to better understand others' feelings and points of view. As a result, he will grow more responsive to other children and even to unfamiliar adults.

Predictable routines will also continue to provide the reassurance and sense of security that lends itself to a more relaxed, generous attitude by age four. As your child learns to recite the days of the week, he will enjoy rattling off each day's events ("Library on Monday, play date on Tuesday, gymnastics on Wednesday . . ."), and may even begin informing you of *his* "plans for the day" by the end of the year. In Chapter 7 we will see how the simple act of posting a monthly calendar on your child's bedroom wall, filled in not only with "things to do today" but also "things I learned today," can enhance his sense of mastery and confidence. Such positive convictions will affect all areas of his future development.

In Chapter 8, we will trace the wonderful transition a young child makes from following your rules in order to please you toward following your rules to feel good about himself. The success of this important internalization process depends a great deal on parents' consistency in enforcing limits, individually and as a team. As your three-year-old continues to experience cognitive growth, he will be able to "listen to reason" for the first time—that is, to comprehend and accommodate your logical explanations regarding why your limits should be obeyed. As the year progresses, his increased verbal comprehension will enable him to understand more of your rules, and his lengthening memory will help him stick to them. Of course, verbal dexterity also leads to negotiation, and more complex thinking means a greater ability to circumvent limits. Fortunately, it is usually not hard to stay half a step ahead of a three-year-old. It's important to do so this year, so that respect for your commands becomes a natural part of your child's ongoing behavior.

Q & A

"Mommy Said I Could!"

Q: Our daughter, Kenya, is a very verbal little girl. Lately, it seems as though her imagination has caught up with her vocabulary. When she wants to do something—say, have some more pudding for dessert—and Mommy has told her no, she goes to Daddy in another room and asks him for the pudding. (She knows he's less strict about sweets.) My husband knows better now than to just give it to her, but if he asks Kenya if Mommy said it was okay, Kenya says yes! On the one hand, we have to admire her ingenuity at such a young age. On the other, we know that consistency between parents is important. Besides, she's not telling the truth. What should we do about this?

A: Kenya's behavior is very typical for a three-year-old. Imagine how exciting it must be for a very young child to realize that just by saying a certain thing (even if it happens to be untrue) she may be able to get what she wants or avoid punishment. Playing one parent against another becomes more common now because dads typically become more actively involved parents as their children leave toddlerhood. Endless negotiation (just one spoonful of pudding? just half a spoonful? just a little taste?) is another common tool this year. Still, I cannot emphasize enough how important it is to remain consistent when it comes to rules—and to make sure you're sufficiently in sync as parents to keep your child from finding and exploiting many loopholes. Three-year-olds are now able to consciously search for and identify the acceptable limits to their behavior, and because they are beginning to internalize these limits they will probably act accordingly for many years to come. Cute as it may be, your daughter's manipulation is not something you still want to be dealing with when she's six, eight, and thirteen. It's not necessary to chastise her at length for her efforts to get what she wants (you can't blame her for trying!), but take care to be as clear as possible about your rules, and—just as important—be sure both of you enforce them as consistently as possible. Your daughter does sound precocious, but you and your husband are still more savvy than she is. In short, next time she tells Dad that Mommy said it was okay, Dad should say, "I hope you're telling the truth," and then he should double-check.

PROBLEM-SOLVING: LEARNING TO MASTER HIS WORLD

From birth or even before, the world has seemed a complex, utterly fascinating place to your child, and he has devoted an enormous amount of energy to solving the puzzle of how it works. During his first year, he struggled with such basic concepts as up versus down and here versus not-here. As he learned to crawl and then walk, his expanded access to physical objects enabled him to explore the fascinating intricacies of in and out, you and me, and yes and no. Last year, as he grew better able to think in symbolic terms, his problem-solving activities moved more toward the verbal, emotional, and social realms. He began to experiment with trying to get his way, playing successfully alongside other children, and communicating in a rewarding manner. As a three-year-old, he will attempt to master more complex situations within all of these areas and elsewhere, and to a large degree his successes and failures will determine his behavior and mood. Think about the times last year when you and your child played with his blocks. He may have tried to build a tower atop a triangular block, been surprised when the tower fell down, and then responded by scattering the blocks in a fit of fury or bursting into tears of frustration. Still, he would have moved on easily enough if you helped him build a new tower or diverted him with another toy. This year, he's more likely to try to solve the problem of the falling tower by, say, replacing the triangular block with a rectangular one. The huge satisfaction he experiences from having resolved this situation is a hallmark of this year—as are his angry outbursts when you try to solve the dilemma for him. A three-year-old *needs* to know that he can learn to master his environment. This is the age when children start to form basic assumptions about their own ability to succeed. Recent research by Dr. Carol Dweck and colleagues at Columbia University shows that by age four children can already be divided into "non-persisters," who doubt their ability to achieve, dwell on their failures, and give low evaluations of their work, and "persisters," who respond optimistically to new tasks and bounce back easily when they fail. Since these attitudes have such an obvious effect on a child's social and academic success, this is certainly a year in which to encourage your child to tackle reasonable challenges on his own.

Thinking about your child's behavior in terms of problem-solving can help you understand his motives, even in the most trying situations. Of course, it is a joy to watch a three-year-old struggle to master the task of learning to write his ABC's or move his marker the correct number of spaces on a board game. Keep in mind, though, that his urge toward mastery will also be expressed in less positive yet equally natural ways. Your child may continue climbing that dangerous fence behind the house even after you've told him not to, just to see whether he really will fall and hurt himself. He may continue to squeeze the pet cat too tightly, despite your warnings, because he feels compelled to figure out how to make the animal stay still.

Social problem-solving of all kinds plays a major role this year as well. By spending time with others his age, your child can practice remedying conflicts, repairing misunderstandings, and learning a variety of ways to get along with others through words, gestures, and other actions. It is a delightful experience to watch a group of older three-year-olds interact in a preschool or other structured environment. The numerous ways in which these young children spontaneously express affection, comfort one another, and share in lively, interesting conversation may make you wish that all grown-ups' social skills were as well developed. Of course, not all of your child's attempts at social problem-solving will succeed (his idea of offering his half-eaten Popsicle to a crying child may not go over as well as expected). Still, he should be applauded for his efforts to "fix" so many of the emotional, social, physical, and cognitive challenges that present themselves this year. It's a fact of life that problem-solving involves both rewarding and trying behavior, and that all of this is a necessary part of the package.

THE TOY BOX

At Thirty-six Months

Tara loves her tricycle. In fact, she's ridden it so often and so hard that the seat has come loose, and it now rocks crazily from side to side as she pedals. Mom started to fix the trike last night, but only got as far as removing the seat completely. This morning, Tara is ready to ride. But the tricycle is broken! "You'll have to wait till Mom comes home from work," Stacy, her caregiver, tells her.

Last year, Tara would have burst into tears when told she couldn't have her tricycle, but today she responds by thinking for a moment, then moving to Plan B. Picking up the seat, she tries to put it in place herself. When this doesn't work, she brainstorms some more. Stacy, amused, keeps an eye on her but lets her experiment with sitting on the spot where the seat used to be—too

uncomfortable!—and standing in back and pushing—too tiring!
Finally, Tara realizes she can sit on the low bar in front of the seat,
push the trike with her feet on the ground, and steer by reaching
way up to the handlebars. She can't go as fast this way, but at least
she solved the problem. Tara has such fun riding her trike this
new way—and is so proud of her own ingenuity in the face of distressing obstacles—that it's almost a disappointment when Mom
bolts the seat in place that evening.

SECRETS AND SURPRISES: EXPERIMENTING WITH POINT OF VIEW

A major theme you will observe running through your child's development this year has to do with point of view—the idea that different
people can possess different information about and different views of an
object or event. Your child's expanding realization that he may know
something you don't or feel differently about something than you do—
what developmental psychologists call a *theory of mind*—is a major step
in development that affects every aspect of his growth and behavior.
Research has shown that at around thirty-six months few children
understand that another person may not necessarily know what they
know. If your three-year-old spots his older brother in the yard through
the living room window, for example, he may wave and start chattering
away to him—not realizing that his brother can't hear him because of
the glass. He'll refer to events that happened in your absence as though
you were there ("Let's play that game I played yesterday at Jodi's!").
He'll assume that Grandma knows he's nodding "yes" when he talks to
her on the telephone, and that if he runs around to look in the
viewfinder of the video camera, he'll see himself where he was standing
a moment before ("I wanna see me!").

As the months pass, though, these errors in perception begin to
fade away. Your child will begin to understand, if still on a very basic
level, that each person's perspective depends on who he is and what has
happened to him. Once your child realizes that his mind is like no
other, he will become intent on discovering just what his mind is like.

You'll know he's entered this stage when he begins announcing his likes and dislikes, chatters about himself and his characteristics ("I'm strong like Superman!" "Margie doesn't share, but I do."), and frequently "borrows" others' viewpoints by pretending to be an animal, storybook character, or cartoon hero in his imaginary play.

As he gradually forms an idea of who he is as opposed to all of these other creatures, he will become more interested in what others do and do not know, and what they feel. This stage of development is characterized by a fascination with secrets and surprises, riddles (especially when he knows the answer and you don't), hide-and-seek games, and perhaps even an older relative's magic tricks. This is an age at which "knock-knock" jokes are told over and over again—with your three-year-old crowing in delight each time he reveals the pun that you apparently didn't anticipate. He may even reinvent the game of hiding-under-the-blanket that he so loved when he was one—though this time he's not exploring here-then-not-here, but I-know-I'm-here-but-you-don't!

Again, your child's interest in establishing what you know and what you don't know plays itself out in both enjoyable and difficult ways this year. It's common for a child at this stage of development to tell his parent to "not look" when he wants to do something forbidden (his belief that he's going to get away with something is so sincere that most parents can't help but laugh). He may experiment a great deal with lying, constantly testing whether you really don't know what he isn't telling you and figuring out what that fact means in practical terms. Fortunately, his efforts to manipulate the truth are still primitive (When you ask him what he's eating, he may simply hide his hands behind his back and say, "Nothing."). It's a fairly simple matter for most parents to firmly confirm their child's suspicion that lying is not only an ill-advised act that's "against the rules," but that it will not get them what they want for long. At this age, a child is still too young to be lectured to about lying. In fact, just as with physical misbehavior, too much focus on the lying only draws attention to a perfectly normal stage. You and your child are better off with a brief reprimand focused on the positive ("Joey, I like it better when you tell the truth. Now give me the cookie behind your back."). And then move on.

As your child becomes more sophisticated in comprehending differences in viewpoint, he will begin to interact on a deeper level with his playmates. Whereas at age two he usually just snatched a toy he wanted from the hands of another child, this year he becomes increasingly aware of and interested in influencing the other child's point of view ("It's my turn, then your turn—okay, Chloe?"). He is able to use reason to help another person see things his way; to relate a story about something he experienced in a relatively entertaining way; and to offer a satisfactory solution to a child who seems distressed ("Wanna play dolls with me?"). He will probably also show a new interest in other families' rules and customs. The fact that another mom believes in spanking or a dad lets his son cross the street without holding hands will deeply fascinate him and will open the door for more discussion later in the year about the reasons why you've instituted the rules you have.

A great deal of experimentation with point of view, styles of behavior, and the truth as each person sees it is necessary for your three-year-old to begin developing an idea of who he is and where he stands in relation to the rest of society. By thinking about his behavior in terms of this need to experiment, it is easier to understand why he does what he does, and to respond appropriately. Your explanations and support as he tries out new roles and techniques will help him strengthen his social skills, paving the way for rewarding relationships in the future.

A CHILD'S-EYE VIEW

Ready or Not, Here I Come!

"What do you wanna play?" Thirty-six-month-old Gloria squirms happily, grinning at her friend, Tracy, from child care. It's their first play date, and both girls are thrilled with the idea of visiting at Gloria's house.

"I know!" says Tracy. "Let's play hide and seek!"

"Okay!" says Gloria. "You hide first! I count!"

As Gloria covers her eyes and starts counting (missing a number now and then), Tracy looks around. There happens to be an empty plastic laundry basket by the wall a few steps away. *Inside!* Tracy thinks, picturing how she'd fit in there. Without a moment's hesitation, she jumps into the laundry basket and hunches over, closing her eyes so that *she* doesn't see.

"Ten!" Gloria announces, finishing counting. She opens her eyes and sees Tracy right in front of her, huddled in the basket. "Found you!" she crows, running to touch the other girl. Both girls giggle, and Tracy leaps out.

"Now your turn to hide," Tracy says. Covering her eyes, she starts counting.

Gloria looks around. *Where can I hide?* She thinks. *What's a good hiding place?* Then she remembers. *Laundry basket!* Instantly, she leaps into the basket, hunches over, and covers her eyes.

Tracy opens her eyes, spots Gloria right away, runs to touch her on the back, and cries, "Found you!"

The girls erupts into giggles again, and continue taking turns hiding in the laundry basket for several more rounds. By the end of the year, they will have learned that closing their eyes doesn't mean they can't be seen. They will have figured out that it's better to hide somewhere other than right in front of the seeker. They may even have realized that the last place a person hid is not the best place to hide the next time. But for now, they're happy with what they do understand about the rules and the ultimate goal of the game, and they're having an enormous amount of fun.

"ME FIRST!": THE GROWTH OF INDEPENDENCE AND THE DEVELOPMENT OF WILL

"I remember how relieved I was when the 'no's' finally started to go away," the mother of a three-year-old confessed recently at a parenting meeting I attended. "I thought my Asa and I were finally going to get along. But fat chance. Along came the 'I won'ts!' and the 'I *hate* baths!' and the 'Gimmes!' I'm really trying to be understanding with him, but I have to tell you, a lot of the time he just seems to me like a downright selfish kid. Am I going crazy or is this normal for a three-year-old?"

As I assured this parent, and as I pointed out earlier in this chapter, negative behavior does not end on the third birthday, but simply changes form. Defiance and willfulness will probably increase, in fact, as your three-year-old learns new ways to resist your wishes and enforce his own. (This tendency usually peaks at around the middle of the year or even later.) It may help to understand that, just as your two-year-old's "No!" signified not just simple stubbornness but an attempt to establish his individuality, your three-year-old's "I won't!" is a normal and important part of the process of developing a sense of independence and personal autonomy. This development of will is the third major theme that continues throughout this year, and it, too, will manifest itself in both positive and negative ways in every aspect of your child's daily experience.

A desire for independence and to have one's own way springs in large part from an expanding sense of self that manifests itself so impressively in the early months of this year. The new pride your three-year-old takes in his creative work and his personal qualities tells you that he will soon feel a need to extend his influence further into his environment. This is why he becomes so angry when well-meaning adults try to help him with everyday accomplishments. He *must* demonstrate that he is able to put on his own jacket, thank you very much. He needs to know that others respect his amazing array of strengths and talents, that they will listen to his words, and that they will take his opinions seriously.

At around the middle of the year, this need to establish a more "public" persona may reach its emotional peak. As your child tests his position in his world, making sure he will receive his fair due, he may become quite a stubborn conversationalist—absolutely sure he's right and not open to persuasion. Experiencing the heady thrill of becoming one of the players in each day's human interaction, he may take objects just because he wants them ("Gimme! That's *mine*!") and assert himself in inappropriate ways ("*My* turn! Me first!"). As he moves beyond simply establishing his presence toward all-too-normal attempts to dominate his surroundings ("Go away, Mommy! I don't like you!") shaping and limiting his behavior becomes a priority. Explaining why his behavior is unacceptable, responding consistently to it, and modeling a more easy-

Consider presenting your child with new challenges this year, as his determination and physical abilities soar.

going attitude won't stop your child's expanding will in its tracks (nor would you want it to). But this is an age at which your child can gradually come to understand that there are limits to any person's freedom. The key is to help him learn to change his unacceptable expression without overly stifling his desire to affect his world. By the end of the year, your child should be sufficiently confident to solemnly inform another child, "Andrew, you shouldn't hit people," and look to you for approval.

EASING THE WAY

Supporting Your Child's Independence

We all need to feel we have some influence on our world, and your child is no exception. As a parent, you can foster his sense of independence and self-confidence by allowing him to make choices whenever possible—in the foods he eats, the clothes he wears, the games you play together—while keeping his options simple in age-appropriate ways. At restaurants, for example, take advantage of the fact that your child can't yet read and narrow the menu to two or three items. When he greets you at breakfast with a list of activities he intends to accomplish that day, play along for a while. Chances are his memory is still too weak to allow him to remember all of his goals, so you won't have to worry about satisfying every one. Meanwhile, he will have gained a sense of importance by supposedly making decisions and plans on his own.

Despite all the bluster, three-year-olds really do appreciate their parents' supervision. Your child will probably feel relieved if he senses that you don't expect him to make the big decisions, as long as you give him some freedom to make the little ones. It's certainly comforting to have a parent who will say "no" when he or she senses that the child is afraid. By offering your three-year-old this kind of support, and gradually easing up as he conquers his early anxieties and becomes more responsible in making his own decisions, you allow him to test his strength while knowing he's safe and secure.

A MAGICAL YEAR:
YOUR 48-MONTH-OLD

A year has passed, and the neighborhood block party is in full swing again. Pete, a good three inches taller, is participating in an energetic round of soccer with his friends. As Dave once again tends the hamburgers, he enjoys watching his son kick the ball toward the goal. Pete's movements are so much better coordinated this year, and he actually gets the idea that the ball is supposed to go into the net. He still isn't very successful at the game, but Dave sees a big improvement over twelve months ago, when Pete had no idea what "soccer" meant.

Dave notes that Pete has managed, miraculously, to kick the soccer ball within a yard from the proper goal. Unfortunately, a slightly older goalie stands in the way, waiting to give the ball a kick in the opposite direction. Dave watches his son look at the goalie, look at the ball, and then look at the goalie again. To Dave's embarrassment, Pete runs closer to the goalie, sideswipes him out of the way, and kicks his ball to the goal.

"Hey! He pushed me!" the goalie yells, getting to his feet.

Pete looks over his shoulder guiltily. "No I didn't," he protests instinctively. Then he sees his father watching him, and a shadow of guilt crosses his cherubic face. "It was an accident," he stammers, trying to shed the discomfort he feels. But clearly that doesn't work either. Wanting to make things right, Pete tries a new tack. "I'll get it," he offers, and picks up the ball. Handing it to the still-disgruntled goalie, Pete offers, "I'll be goalie now."

Dave is relieved to see how effectively his son realizes his error and finds a way to make up for his mistake. Pete's willingness to switch places is a more mature gesture than he might have expected—and the reward is a wary nod and a "That's okay" from the goalie. Dave relaxes and turns back to the barbecue grille. All those promptings, explanations, and refusals to back down on behavioral issues really have paid off. Three seemed like a confusing wilderness to Dave and his wife (and probably Pete) a lot of the time, but for now he guesses they've found the right path.

Parenting Concepts for the Third Year

In the rush, chaos, and onslaught of unexpected challenges that fill the lives of families with three-year-olds, it's easy to lose sight of the parenting goals you've created or the new approaches you've been meaning to try. Here you'll find a few general pointers to keep in mind as you guide your child through the months ahead. By considering these general guidelines with your partner and your child's other caregivers, and discussing how they might improve specific situations in your family, you can create a working parenting plan and improve your family's daily experience as a result.

BE POSITIVE. Focus on your child's accomplishments rather than his lapses. Look for and point out positive examples for him to follow in his environment. Praise good behavior sincerely, to ensure that it happens again.

THINK ABOUT "WHY." When your child is driving you crazy, think about why he's doing it. Imagine yourself in the same situation. Chances are he's not trying to get to you, but is responding to frustration. Instead of criticizing, help him find a way out of his behavioral impasse.

DON'T EXPECT TOO MUCH TOO SOON. Your child's new verbal skills may convince you that he's further along in his development than he really is. Remember, he's only three. He will still frequently behave impulsively and respond in illogical ways.

USE HUMOR AS YOUR ALLY. A good-spirited joke, a funny face, or a silly play on words can diffuse anger, stop tears, and offer you both a fresh perspective in the face of conflict.

MAKE FRIENDS. Whether informal (other families) or formal (child care or preschool), this is really the year to expose your child to social interaction. Group activities will stimulate his cognitive development, improve his behavioral and emotional skills, and take some of the pressure to entertain him off you.

BE CONSISTENT. Three-year-olds love to find the exceptions to any rule, and will capitalize on any inconsistencies you allow. Because they're internalizing rules this year, it's especially important to keep limits simple, clear, and predictable. Consistency doesn't mean a perfect batting average, but if exceptions are made, be clear in explaining why.

SET A GOOD EXAMPLE. Your three-year-old responds less to what you say than what you do. If you want him to choose books over television, avoid bad language, and eat well, be sure to do so yourself.

PROVIDE A SUPPORTIVE SCAFFOLDING. Let your child manage as much of his behavior as he can this year, but be ready to intervene when he ventures out of his depth. Think of him as a junior partner who needs your encouragement and support to learn to do his job.

FIRST-PERSON SINGULAR

Now as always, the most effective tool in successfully parenting your three-year-old is your own observation of his behavior, needs, personality, and style of expression. Take a moment now to think about what you have already learned about your child. How is his personality expressed in his daily actions? Is he generally friendly and talkative, or quiet and observant? Is he happiest out on the playground, wandering around a museum, working on group projects at preschool, or playing imaginary games with his stuffed animals in his room? Which of his behaviors worry you most this year, and which would you like to encourage? At what times or in what circumstances do the two of you lock horns ("You will!" "I won't!") in ways that you would prefer to avoid? By writing down your thoughts, ideas, and observations now, you can compare them to your feelings about your child twelve months hence—and ponder the ways that his temperament, his environment, and your actions and ideas have brought the entire family through another year of growth.

READER'S NOTES

_____

_____

_____

_____

_____

_____

_____

_____

_____

Hop, Pedal, and Skip— My Physical Abilities

Your child naturally desires to take greater control of her body, behavior, and self-expression.

It's four o'clock, time for three-year-old Josie's gymnastics class. This is the first formal class experience that Josie has ever had, and her mother, Rebecca, enjoys watching her through a large window at one end of the room. It's a relief to see that Josie appears able to follow directions and clearly enjoys the child-sized trampoline, balance beam, and other equipment designed to stimulate preschool-aged children's motor development. Having already figured out that Josie has a careful, methodical temperament (like her dad), Rebecca isn't surprised to see her practice these skills step by step rather than throwing herself head-long into a new movement. Her cautious approach is particularly obvious when seen in contrast to that of others in the class—active and sometimes distracting Omar, adventurous and even reckless Miya, and shy, fretful Benjamin. It's fascinating to watch each child approach a piece of equipment and tackle it in his or her "typical" way.

As Rebecca watches, the children are guided one by one in a flip over a low horizontal bar, after which they must climb to the top of a triangular-shaped padded structure and somersault to the bottom. As Josie finishes her flip over the bar, Rebecca leans forward expectantly. Josie is the only one in the class who hasn't mastered a somersault. *Come on! Give it a try for once,* Rebecca silently urges as Josie climbs to the top of the triangle, then glances back uncertainly at the instructor. *How are you going to learn if you don't practice?* But the instructor has already turned toward the next child on the horizontal bar. Left undirected, Josie quickly tiptoes down the slope, instead of somersaulting, and jumps onto the trampoline. When the instructor turns back to her, he sees her dutifully bouncing up and down. "Great job, Josie!" he calls. Josie smiles brightly, while her mother covers her face with her hand. She looks around furtively, embarrassed by her daughter's sneaky behavior.

As in many areas of your child's growth, physical skills will expand at an impressive pace this year, though perhaps not always as quickly or easily as you might anticipate. As a three-year-old begins to choose her activities more deliberately, she is able to control the focus of her own development more than before. Her temperament plays an increasingly important part in determining whether she learns the skill you want her to now or a little later. She may suddenly balk at learning to swim, though she's the one who begged to go to the pool. She may insist on finishing every maze in her workbook, even if it takes twenty minutes and you desperately need to get to work. Part of the reason for this behavior is her normal desire to control her environment. Another reason might have to do with her increased focus on the product rather than the process of accomplishing a new skill: she may fear that the results won't pass her own judgment, or may need to know she's finished a task perfectly before she can stop. Whether your own child currently shies away from challenges or attacks new skills with a fervor that scares you, you can best support her motor development by allowing (not pushing) her to experiment physically as much as possible while keeping an eye out for potential hazards. Rest assured that, while her basic style of learning may remain the same, your understanding and encouragement will bolster her confidence, stimulate her interest, and increase her awareness of her physical world.

Maybe Tomorrow . . .

Sparkly! Clint loves the way sunlight reflects off the surface of the lake near his family's summer cottage. Every summer of his life has been spent here, and he has vague but happy memories of watching his two older brothers cut through and noisily splash each other. This year, Clint is determined to join them. Fortunately, his frequent marches toward the shore have convinced his parents that they'd better teach him how to swim.

Come on! Clint waits impatiently for Dad to grab a couple of towels and walk him down to the water's edge. Clint's brothers are gone for the day. *When they get back, I'll swim with them!* Clint tells himself.

"Okay, kid," his father says, taking his son's hand and leading him toward the shore at last. "Let's see what we can teach you."

Clint walks down the hill toward the shimmering water. It's nearly evening already, and a cool breeze chills his belly, which until now was always reassuringly covered by his life jacket. He pulls back a little, but just then his dad swoops him up and carries him into the water. *Cold!* Clint flinches. "Hey, what's the matter?" he hears his dad say. "I thought you wanted to swim!" Dad playfully splashes his son, getting a little water on his face.

For an instant, Clint can't see because of the water in his eyes. *Aaaugh!* He kicks his father in a sudden panic. "Let go a' me!" he yells, squirming to get back on shore. As soon as his father sets him back on dry land, Clint runs to the beach towel his mom is holding up for him. "Mommy," he whimpers, "I *hate* that lake!"

"Oh, don't be silly," his mother says, drying him off. "Don't you want to get in the water and learn to swim like Jack and Luke?"

Clint frowns and cuddles up against her. "I *never* do that again."

Mom rubs his back thoughtfully. "How about if I get you some goggles like the ones Jack has? Then the water won't splash in your eyes."

Goggles? Clint pictures them in his mind. Jack's goggles look funny. He nods, starting to smile. "Yeah," he says enthusiastically, "then I can swim like Jack!"

The lake still sparkles enticingly in the sunlight. Tomorrow, if he has the goggles, he'll go in the water, he decides. But nobody better splash him, or he'll get right out again.

"LOOK WHAT I DID!": PHYSICAL PROGRESS AT AGE THREE

"When I remember my years of parenting preschoolers, I always think of what I call 'the lesson of the winter coat,'" a colleague told me the other day. "I had three kids under four back then, and we were always in a hurry. One day I completely lost it while trying to get my oldest, Harry, who was three, to dress himself for school. He took forever with his coat—he just couldn't get it on. I stood there yelling at him to hurry up while he kept insisting I was giving it to him wrong, and of course the twins started wailing. It was awful. Then, that afternoon when I picked Harry up from school, I was getting his things together when his teacher came over to help me. She grabbed his coat, dropped it upside down on the floor in front of Harry, said, 'Here you go,' and walked away. To my amazement, Harry squatted down, stuck his arms into the sleeves, flipped the coat over his head, and it was on. I couldn't believe it! You should have seen the look he gave me—like, 'See, Mom, I *can* do it myself.' It made me think about how much easier life with a three-year-old is—and how much better for the child—if you keep his 'challenges' within the realm of his abilities."

It is true that by their third birthday, most children are so agile that their parents forget that some skills are still beyond their ability. Your three-year-old no longer needs to concentrate on the mechanics of walking, running, or climbing stairs. She can probably ride a tricycle, move nimbly, run fast, dress herself, pour herself a bowl of cereal, and even catch a ball with her arms stiffly outstretched. But watch her try to do jumping jacks (she can probably do each part separately, but not together); stand quickly from a squatting position; balance on one foot; or hop from one square to the next in a game of hopscotch, and you will see how extensive her physical limitations are. Certainly, nearly every three-year-old is eager to practice such new movements. Given an environment in which she is challenged to experiment but not pushed too hard, she will quite likely learn all of them by the time she turns four.

If watching your child learn to skip, turn a somersault, and walk a balance beam is a satisfying experience this year, witnessing the development of her fine motor skills can be even more exciting. As the months pass, your child will develop both the focus and the muscle control she needs to draw more precisely and even, if coached, attempt to write her name. At the beginning of the year, she can probably already move each finger independently, hold a pencil or crayon like an adult, and scribble on a piece of paper. When drawing a person, she may create a circle with two dots for eyes and perhaps two lines sticking out of it for arms. Soon, though, her improving dexterity—fueled by cognitive growth—will allow her to move toward a classic stick figure with circles for hands on the ends of the stick arms, a smiling mouth, a nose, and perhaps even ears or hair on the head. Her nimbler hand movements will delight her as they increase her mastery over her world. As her abilities improve, she will probably grow more interested in working with clay, paint, crayons, puzzles, and scissors designed for children. Though she'll probably play with these tools randomly at first, figuring out what she's created only after she's finished ("It's a . . . um . . . it's a cat"), by the time she turns four she'll frequently decide what she wants to make ahead of time and then make it quite effectively.

Not only will your child's physical movements become refined and enhanced through her natural development this year, but her improved spatial awareness will allow her to direct those movements in more effective ways. Spatial awareness makes your three-year-old more conscious of the relationships among objects and prompts an appreciation for orderliness, symmetry, aesthetics, and so on. It is also responsible for what some parents see as the "pickiness" with which their child insists that no food touch any other food on her plate; that pieces be arranged

Note the intense focus as this three-year-old carefully creates her masterpiece.

just so on a game board; and that no one help her set the table, no matter how long it takes. If your child is exhibiting this type of behavior, consider it a small price to pay for her improving ability to carry objects without spilling them, build a tall block tower that won't fall over, and even to write the letters of her name in the proper order.

By the end of the year, the quality of your child's movements will have improved in visible ways that the entire family can appreciate. A child who tore at the wrapping of her gifts on her third birthday will probably open gifts more methodically on her fourth. She will not only put on her coat, but also zip it up. Whereas at age two she may have just stood and stared when a friend tossed her a ball at the child-care center, she'll now pick up the ball and toss it back rather accurately. As she approaches age four, your child will probably also learn to skip, walk along a low wall, stop and turn quickly, and hop for a few steps at a time. Such mastery will help her broaden her experience even more as she extends her physical range and joins in a variety of childhood games.

Q & A

Are You Done Yet?

Q: My son, Mac, was fully toilet trained by the time he turned three. I was relieved that the process went so smoothly, and even happier when he stopped insisting that I accompany him on his every visit to the bathroom. The problem is, now that he goes to the bathroom alone, he takes forever to come out again. He has to sit on the toilet for about fifteen minutes, talking and singing to himself. Then he has to tear off exactly three squares of toilet paper, and if he doesn't manage to tear it off perfectly along the perforation he has to start over. Then he has to pull his step stool to a certain exact spot in front of the sink, and turn the water just so to wash his hands. We only have one bathroom, so this behavior is driving the rest of the family nuts. What can we do?

A: Picky behavior is typical for a three-year-old, especially when he's just beginning to master a new skill. While Mac's bathroom marathons are obviously annoying to his family, to some degree he just has to get through this phase before he can speed up his sessions. You might find it worthwhile to start accompanying him to the bathroom again so that you can show him more efficient ways to finish and get out—or remind him of something fun he'll get to do as soon as he's finished. The good news is that this period probably won't last for more than a few months. In the meantime, instead of focusing on what he hasn't perfected yet, think of all the advances he's made. He recognizes the feeling that he needs to use the bathroom, pulls down his own pants, knows to wipe, and can climb onto his step stool and turn on the faucets, all in the correct order. From his standpoint, this is quite an accomplishment. No wonder he's singing.

"GO PLAY!":
ALLOWING YOUR CHILD
TO EXPERIMENT

One of the great discoveries parents of three-year-olds tend to make is that for the first time their children enjoy spending significant periods of time on their own. You may realize one day that your child has been shut up in her room for the past half hour—and see when you peek in that she's happily involved with her stuffed animals or rocking in her child-sized chair while looking at a pop-up book. Physically, three-year-olds need to practice new skills that keep them busy outdoors or in safe-play areas much longer than last year.

Obviously, this is a wonderful advance for parents and other caregivers who have grown tired of trying to keep their kids occupied from morning till night. It's a relief to see your child start to come up with her own ideas for play and recreation; encourage herself with the same words you've used since she was born; stick to an activity without your urging; and even to start internalizing and expressing your own rules about safety ("Hang on tight, Dolly."). Three-year-olds are old enough to play alone, unsupervised, in childproofed areas for short periods of time. Yet it's important to remember that they still lack the awareness, self-control, judgment, and coordination necessary to protect themselves in riskier or more distracting situations (when they're around dangerous equipment, near traffic, or with other children). Their greater access to their environment, increased curiosity, and increased size and speed can get them into greater trouble than when they were two. Statistics show that more accidents occur among preschool-aged children at home than in child-care situations. As your child ventures out into the neighborhood more frequently, oversee her safety by making sure that she:

- wears a helmet when she rides her bike.

- knows to stop and wait for you before crossing a street.

- never goes near swimming pools, ponds, or streams without an adult and uses water wings in the water (or learns how to swim).

- turns on the correct faucet before washing her own hands or brushing her teeth.

- is still unable to reach knives in kitchen drawers and on restaurant tables, and can't get to medicines, matches, and poisonous substances at home.

- walks alongside you in the grocery store if she won't sit in the baby seat (if she sits in the main body of the cart, it can easily tip over).

- continues to stay buckled into a car seat until she weighs more than forty pounds—and is then moved to a booster seat in the backseat. (Adult-sized seat belts restrain your child but aren't designed for her body; if an accident occurs, she could be harmed by the seat belt as well as the impact itself.)

As the months pass, you and your child's other caregivers will be able to teach her to actively watch out for her own safety as well. This is the year for her to learn not to run holding sharp or breakable objects; to stay clear of matches and fires in fireplaces; to obey rules regarding traffic (particularly in parking lots, where three-year-olds don't think of cars backing out); and to keep her head above water if she falls into a pool or lake. The better your child gets at looking out for herself, the more confident you will feel in allowing her to explore further. As a result, she'll gain more freedom to practice her physical skills and experiment with new ones.

Ideally, by the end of the year, your child will have begun to internalize your safety messages, adopting your rules as her own. Along the way, she may have seesawed a bit from behaving in ways you consider too reckless or too cautious. Many three-year-olds express a new fear of water, climbing trees, or trying new play equipment at some point during the year. This apprehension is actually a good sign in most cases. It demonstrates your child's move toward self-monitoring and her increasing awareness of the elements in her environment. Try not to criticize for this extra-cautious behavior or dismiss her fears. At this age, it's really better for a child to be wary rather than impulsive—and as your child completes the process of internalizing your safety values, she will loosen up and become ready to try new skills again.

EASING THE WAY

Encouraging Physical Mastery

Three-year-olds delight in using their bodies to master their environments, and their expanding skills make physical activities more fun for the entire family. There are many ways you and your child's other caregivers can stimulate your child's physical development this year that promote closeness as well as a sense of fun. Fine motor skills can be stimulated through the use of sewing cards especially designed for preschoolers; simple jigsaw puzzles, crayons, clay, wooden blocks, and drawing or painting pictures. The fine muscles of the hand get a good workout with pegboards, too, as well as stringing large beads, building sand castles, pouring water into various-sized containers, and dressing and undressing dolls. It's a good idea to ask your child to help you do simple chores around the house, thus giving her a chance to manipulate a screwdriver, spade, butter knife, eggbeater, and other tools. Gross-motor skills can be stimulated through opportunities to climb, run, jump, pedal, and swim. Reward her efforts as much as her successes. As she tackles each new task, don't forget to tell her what a big girl she's becoming!

"READY, SET, GO!": LEARNING SELF-CONTROL

"Not yet," Wanda cautions, holding a hand up to still the group of three-year-olds in her preschool dance class who are about to race across the room together, leaping over a rope along the way. The preschoolers surge forward, then turn and march back to their places as their teacher reminds them to be still. One or two children break loose from the pack and are halfway across the room before Wanda's assistant stops them and returns them to their places. As Wanda's hand remains raised, the tension proves almost too much for the three-year-olds. They *must* move forward, now that the idea is in their heads. They simply can't stop themselves!

Finally, Wanda drops her hand and says, "Now go!" With a cry of relief, all eight children race across the room, leap over the rope, and laugh out loud as they throw themselves against the opposite wall and collapse in a heap. How good it feels to carry out the action they'd imagined. Holding back any movement is still very difficult for them, and learning to wait until an adult says "now" takes practice, focus, and determination.

As many experts, including Dr. Ross Thompson of the University of Nebraska, have demonstrated, the ability to keep from starting a physical action until given a signal is indeed a skill that develops only gradually during the preschool years. If your child is already starting to reach for the sugar bowl, she is probably *physically* unable to stop her movement the instant she hears you say, "Stop that!" If she has already spotted a toy she wants on a shelf at the toy store, it will be difficult for her to stop herself from reaching for it even if you've told her not to touch anything. This body-brain limitation is the cause of many, many misunderstandings between parent and child this year, as parents mistakenly assume their child is deliberately defying their orders rather than just completing an action that is impossible for them to stop. Since the ability to physically start and stop is related to a larger range of abilities to monitor and direct, regulate, and control one's own behavior (such as delaying gratification, tolerating frustration, and adjusting one's behavior in accordance with one's surroundings), it is easy to see how preschoolers labeled "defiant" or "spoiled" may simply have yet to adequately develop this skill.

Of course, the fact that your child isn't always *good* at stopping or starting an action on command, controlling her tears when she's told she can't have something, or lowering her voice when she's in church or in the library, doesn't mean she shouldn't try. You can help her improve her self-control by creating a *supportive scaffolding* for this skill—by treating her as your inexperienced junior partner, as described in Chapter 1. ("I know you're trying to help, but you can't snap all the peas," you might say to your angry child. "Here, you take half and I'll take half.") By understanding where your three-year-old is now (still largely impulse-driven, easily overwhelmed by physical and emotional urges) and where you want her to be by the end of the year (able to monitor her movements, regulate her behavior, and control her emotions to a greater degree), it is easy to visualize the steps she needs to take to reach this goal. First, your child needs to know that you understand how hard it can be to "behave" on command. ("Hey, sweetie, I know you want to go fast on your trike, but this is a hill.") Next, she needs your specific guidance on how to practice inhibiting an action. ("Go slow until the bottom. Then you can pedal as fast as you want on the sidewalk.") It doesn't hurt to gently guide your child's movement (pacing the speed of the trike by holding on to it), physically demonstrating how her body should respond. Finally, summarize what she has accomplished in words to help her fix the experience in her memory ("See, you didn't tip over. That's because you pedaled just right."), and be sure to praise her on this and any other occasions when she manages to successfully master her actions.

Your child naturally desires to take greater control of her body, behavior, and self-expression. Supporting her in this area of her growth may be a little difficult in the short run, but the rewards are certainly worth it as she learns the self-regulation and mastery that are necessary for physical, social, and academic success later on.

Three-year-olds love to announce their physical strength. Here, a group of boys practice their superhero stances as they ward off "bad guys."

"Can't Catch Me!"

"When Ryan was two, my husband and I made the big mistake of playing 'chase' with him down the sidewalk—encouraging him to race ahead of us while we lumbered behind him making silly monster noises," a friend told me. "Of course, Ryan loved it, and it helped us get wherever we were going faster. The problem was, he still loved it when he was three, and at that point he could race off to the end of the block and nearly into traffic while we ran up behind him, scared to death. It took us forever to get over that problem, but we finally figured out a way.

"Instead of playing 'chase,' we started playing 'freeze.' When we started on our walk we'd say, 'Okay, Ryan, you walk five steps ahead of me.' He'd count out the steps, and of course soon enough he'd start to increase the distance. When he did, we'd say, 'Freeze!' or 'Baby steps!' He'd have to either stay still or take tiny steps until we caught up. Then we'd let him go five steps ahead again. That way, he still got the thrill of being ahead of us, and we still got places pretty fast, but he didn't get so far away he was in danger. Later on, we came up with other ploys, like telling him he had to consider us old, tired grown-ups and slow down for our sake, and reminding him that if he couldn't see us he'd gone too far. What didn't work at that age was trying to explain logically why it wasn't safe to run ahead. Running is just too much fun—it's not possible for a three-year-old to stop and listen to reason."

THIS IS ME:
LEARNING ABOUT THE BODY

As your child continues to master new skills and explore her physicality, her curiosity about all her body's parts and functions will naturally continue to expand. The interest she showed in her genitals last year is likely to continue, though she may begin to show some awareness of the fact that certain parts of the body are "private." Her increasing self-control may discourage the two-year-old's tendency to idly fondle or explore her genitals while watching television or otherwise sitting or standing unengaged. As before, your role as parent is to ignore the self-stimulation that occurs in private, tactfully redirect her actions when she is behaving inappropriately, and remind her about what's appropriate to do in public and in private.

Meanwhile, as this year progresses, your child will pass through new developmental stages that may present fresh challenges in this area. For example, as your child becomes increasingly aware of the fact that it's possible to know something that others don't know, she will become more interested in and fascinated by the idea of secrets and revelations. Obviously, the concept of "private parts" proves irresistible to some children in this stage. Though they're now able to understand that certain parts of their body are private, they may temporarily experiment with "revealing" these parts, hiding them, and (usually giggling mischievously) revealing them again. This is but another example of children wanting to control their bodies and their actions. As your child's verbal dexterity improves, she may also pick up sexual language or terminology from her environment and try it out on you (usually in public, and usually very loudly) for effect. Her expanded awareness of her surroundings will cause her to notice (or more awkwardly, stare at) your body and to make such comments as "What's that?" and "Look at that big bottom!" while you're getting dressed. Finally, your three-year-old's expanded ability to engage in pretend play with others her age may lead to games of "doctor" and other scenarios in which children shed their clothes and take a look at each other's bodies.

All of these actions are understandable from a developmental point of view, and will soon pass if they don't get a strong reaction from you or her other caregivers. If you are consistent in pointing out that our private parts are private and that it's "the rule" to explore them only alone and in private—and if you casually suggest more acceptable games to play with friends—your child will learn to monitor such impulses. Meanwhile, keep in mind that this period when your child is taking another, clearer look at the workings of her body is an excellent time to tackle toilet training, review the reasons why it's important to take baths, read books about mother animals and their babies, and help your child develop a positive and healthy view of her physical self.

What Sound Does *That* Make?

Fred likes it when Lilly comes over to play, because her mom always stays for a long time and Lilly doesn't go home till it's nearly time for supper. Today, as usual, the moms are in the kitchen drinking coffee and talking, and the two three-and-a-half-year-olds are alone in Fred's room. "What's that?" Lilly asks, pulling a long, black contraption out of Fred's toy box.

"A stessoscope," Fred tells her proudly. "You listen to your heart. Aunt Rosie gave it to me."

Frowning, Lilly examines the stethoscope. "Where do you put it?" she asks.

"Look." Fred takes the stethoscope and puts in on his ears. He places the other end over Lilly's stomach. "See? It goes bum-bum, bum-bum."

"Lemme try." Lilly grabs the stethoscope and places it crookedly over her head. "It doesn't work." Fred repositions it over her ears. She plants the other end on Fred's stomach. "It's broken," she says.

"Here." Fred lifts up his shirt and places the end of the stethoscope against his skin. The two children frown as they wait for Lilly to hear something.

"Can I hear your foot?" she asks.

Fred giggles. "Okay." He takes off his shoe and sits down so Lilly can listen. Laughing, they switch the stethoscope back and forth, listening to different body parts.

A few minutes later, Fred's bedroom door opens and both moms' faces appear in the doorway. "Frederick Wilson!" his mother cries out loudly. Startled, Fred removes the stethoscope from Lilly's chest. The children have removed all their clothes in their effort to listen to the sounds their bodies make.

"Lilly!" Lilly's mother says. "Get your dress on right now!"

Startled, Lilly and Fred look at each other. *What are the moms so upset about?* Startled out of their play, they realize that they're standing there, naked and exposed. Lilly starts to giggle. "You look funny!" she says, pointing at Fred. "You don't have no clothes on!"

"You don't have no clothes, too!" Fred says, laughing. As their embarrassed mothers hastily get them dressed, the two young friends excitedly tell them all about their stethoscope adventure. "Lilly's tummy makes a loud noise," Fred concludes proudly. "But my penis doesn't say nothing at all."

The two moms roll their eyes, but don't say more than, "That's true. Only hearts and tummies make noises." Fred suspects he and Lilly shouldn't have stripped, but at least he's learned something new today. He hears the two moms talking about the You and Your Body books they've been reading to their kids. "Where is that book?" he demands of his mother. "Can you read it to me now?"

ONE POTATO, TWO POTATO: ENJOYING ORGANIZED GAMES

One of the great advantages of turning three is the new ability to comprehend the point of some of the games that adults and older siblings always want to play. Instead of digging randomly in the sandbox, your child may now enjoy helping her brother build a sand castle or create a system of rivers and dams. Instead of just running, falling, and running some more in the backyard, the park, or the playground at preschool, she may prefer riding a trike, playing tag, or even trying to throw a ball back and forth. Though she won't always comprehend all the aspects of a game (you put the ball *where?*), she will delight in simple games with easily understood rules ("Statues," "Duck, duck, duck, goose," "Rock, paper, scissors"), and the feeling of mastery they give her.

As your child explores through games not only her physical potential but concepts that include timing, sequence, sharing, and fair play, don't forget to consider the possibility of more formal training as well.

Swimming, gymnastics, and dance classes, widely available for three-year-olds, give your child a chance to practice accommodating to the rules of adults other than parents and caregivers; socialize in a new way with children her age; experience the process of practicing regularly to achieve a particular goal; and become part of a larger culture in which such skills are usually rewarded. Allowing your child to partake in such an activity signals to her that you consider her a "big girl" now—and that's a wonderful message for any three-year-old to receive.

Signs of Difficulty

As was true in earlier years, three-year-olds vary in the pacing of their development of physical skills, but the sequence of skill development is largely the same from one child to the next. If the three-year-old next door can take tentative steps on ice skates while your child can barely stand up, think about this difference in terms of temperament as well as ability. Is your child focused on another area of development at this particular stage of life? Does she not work hard at new physical skills because she's easily frustrated or doesn't like to fail, or because she really can't manipulate her body that way? Does she hold back from climbing the big slide because she's a cautious kid, because she has a fear of heights, or because she doesn't have a good sense of balance? Resist the temptation to compare her to the star of the gym class or the playground. Some children are truly physically gifted; those who have older siblings are often more advanced or daring; some have parents who happen to have emphasized physical risk-taking.

If your child's skills lie somewhere between those of the top performers and those of younger or less coordinated children, she's probably doing fine. However, there are certain skills that should be achieved by the end of this year—including throwing a ball overhand, jumping in place, grasping a crayon between her thumb and fingers, scribbling on paper, and making a tower of at least four blocks. If your child is still unable to accomplish these tasks by her fourth birthday—and if you believe this is part of a larger pattern of tardy development—talk with your pediatrician as soon as possible. The earlier such delayed abilities are diagnosed, the easier they often are to deal with. As always in such cases, it's better to follow up on your concerns early so that you can allay your fears as soon as possible or get your child the help she needs.

"WHAT A BIG GIRL!": GAINING PHYSICAL CONFIDENCE

"That'll be fifty dollars, please." Rebecca shakes her head, writing out the check for yet another session of gymnastics classes. Money's tight this month and it's hard to budget for this extra treat, but Josie loves the classes so much and has made so much progress that Rebecca feels it's worth the cost. Last week, for the first time, Josie managed a somersault all on her own, and the proud smile she flashed her mom, who was watching through the observation window, was truly a sight to see. Rebecca is pleased to see how often Josie tries out her new skills when playing outside of class, too. She often spies Josie practicing standing on one foot and stretching her arms out in an "airplane," trying to stand on her head, and swinging from a low tree branch in the backyard. Of course, Rebecca knows that she could teach Josie to stand on one foot herself—and she frequently does demonstrate new skills. Still, it's a pleasure to see Josie experiencing this growth with others her age—learning to take turns, to praise others' efforts, to help those who need it, to follow an instructor's directions, and feeling like such a "big girl" as her abilities improve. In addition, gymnastics class has given Rebecca new ideas for games and activities to introduce to Josie and her friends at home. Until she watched Josie play hopscotch with the other kids in gymnastics class, for example, she'd forgotten how much fun it could be!

Physical Achievements at Age Three

Parents often see a scattering of behaviors at these ages. If your child doesn't demonstrate them around the time indicated, don't be alarmed. Think of these behaviors as new territory she will probably visit soon.

36 MONTHS
Throws a ball overhand

Rides a tricycle on her own

Completes a simple puzzle

Copies vertical and horizontal strokes on paper

Uses children's scissors

42 MONTHS
Hops or stands briefly on one foot

Walks up and down stairs without support

Draws circles and squares

Begins to copy some capital letters

48 MONTHS
Moves forward and backward with agility

Catches a bounced ball most of the time

Throws with increased accuracy

Draws a person with three parts

Now, while your questions, hopes, and concerns relating to your three-year-old's physical development are fresh in your mind, take some notes about her latest developments in learning to manage her impulses, ensure her own safety, and interact physically with her peers. What new skills is she developing? How is she expanding on the skills she already has? What is her physical style—adventurous and risk-taking, quiet and hesitant, methodical and determined? How are her physical experiences different from those described in this chapter? How are they the same?

It's fun and often informative to look back at photographs or video-tapes of your child at age one and two and write down some of the ways in which her physicality differs now. If possible, videotape her frequently this year as well, so you can monitor her progress as she grows. (You might also ask your parents or in-laws if your child resembles you or your partner at that age in terms of physical style.) These observations of your unique child's development are one of your most valuable tools in getting to know her as an individual—in helping you more effectively discern her needs at a given time, uncover any difficulties as early as possible, and help lead her toward greater mastery.

_____

_____

_____

_____

_____

_____

_____

_____

_____

_____

_____

_____

_____

_____

_____

_____

_____

_____

_____

_____

_____

_____

CHAPTER 3

A Richer Understanding—
My Cognitive Development

T he point this year is not to achieve a certain outcome but to enjoy the process of learning.

"So this is Sam!" The three-year-old's great-aunt Lilly bends lower to get a good look at the newest member of the clan while Sam's mother, Evelyn, looks on. The family reunion is huge this year, and relatives who have never met are enjoying the chance to finally get to know each other. "What a big boy you are," Lilly remarks to Sam.

"I'm almost four," Sam announces proudly, holding up four fingers close to Lilly's face.

Lilly smiles. "Soon you'll be a grown-up," she tells him. "You'll have your own children."

"And I'll be their grandma!" adds Evelyn, smiling at her son.

Sam turns to his mother, his confident expression starting to dissolve. "I don't want you to be their grandma," he says, his voice quavering. "I want you to be my mommy!"

Surprised, Evelyn and her aunt burst out laughing. At this, all of Sam's composure vanishes and he starts to cry. "Don't laugh!" he blurts out when his mother tries to console him. "It's not funny!"

Poor Sam, Evelyn says to herself as she gives her crying son a hug. He hates to be laughed at. And, after all, why should he understand that he'll always have her as a mother, even when he's grown and has children of his own? Family relations are the kind of thing one can only learn through years of experience. It must be frustrating trying to figure out how such systems work at age three. "I'm not laughing at you, sweetie," Evelyn says to her son. "I was just surprised, that's all. You know I'll always be your mommy, no matter how big you grow."

One of the most fascinating aspects of parenting a three-year-old is trying to pin down the perfectly logical but frequently erroneous assumptions they make about their world. Ask your child what creates the waves in the ocean, and he may tell you that the fish are rolling over in their sleep. Ask him what makes the clouds move across the sky, and he's likely to answer, "The grass wiggles and makes them move, silly!" Such fanciful assumptions are a delightful sign that his mind is working very hard at arranging the bits of information into a coherent, comprehensible whole. Though he is usually pretty good at understanding how familiar aspects of his environment operate, more novel situations still cause him to misinterpret the evidence in fundamental ways (when Daddy and his friends yell at the TV during a football telecast, it doesn't mean they're angry). Basic concepts of subjectivity (who knows about something and who doesn't) and appearance versus reality (the world you see through sunglasses isn't really green) still trip him up. Correcting such mistakes is usually easy; the challenge for most parents is keeping in mind that they will probably occur, being patient when your child is adamant that he is right, and making allowances for such gaps in understanding.

THE TOY BOX

I'm Winning

Chutes and Ladders is three-year-old Jessica's favorite board game, and she's thrilled that she's managed to persuade her older brother Geoff to play it with her after dinner. "Four!" Geoff announces, and moves his marker along the board. Land-ing on a space with a ladder, he moves his marker several rows up on the game board. "Your turn," he says to his sister.

Jessica studies the game board with a frown. Something has happened, and she's not sure it's a good thing. After a moment, she spins the spinner. When the pointer comes to a stop, her face lights up. "Six!" she says, pointing to the spinner. "I'm winning!"

Geoff glances at his mother, who's washing dishes nearby. Then, with a theatrical sigh, he says to his sister, "Want me to help you move?"

"I wanna do it!" Jessica says proudly, getting up on her knees to be able to reach her marker. Mimicking Geoff's manner of moving his marker from space to space while counting, Jessica occasionally counts twice on one square and skips another, but with her brother's tactful guidance she finally lands on the correct spot.

"Look," Geoff says, pointing to the square he'd spotted as soon as Jessica had announced the number. "It's a chute. You have to slide down."

"Okay!" Jessica says with a smile. Proudly, she slides her marker down, practically to the bottom of the board. "I got a big number," she announces to her mother. She doesn't notice her big brother rolling his eyes in exasperation. *Look at her!* his expression says. *All she knows is that her number was bigger. She doesn't even know she's losing!*

His mother smiles to herself as she continues straightening up the kitchen. Better not to interfere, she decides. Geoff is being patient, and Jessica will learn the dynamics of the game with experience. Meanwhile, they're having a fine time doing something together.

"I SPELT MY NAME!": COGNITIVE GROWTH AT AGE THREE

Three-year-olds' cognitive errors are so often amusing to us adults that it's easy to overlook how amazing their mental growth is this year. The improvement in your child's thinking is not just quantitative, but qualitative—a true coming-together of many different skills as a number of neurological developments gel. As an infant, your child explored and understood the world solely through his senses. Now he can use "symbolic thinking," or mental representation, to think about objects or events that aren't present. He can predict the consequences of many of his actions, combine symbols to express more complex ideas (putting words together into sentences, for example), figure out how a toy works, and tap memories of earlier experiences to try to explain why and how events take place. The result is an increasing coherence in his thinking— a new, deeper ability to reason, analyze, and wonder why.

Such new skills spur three-year-olds to become ever more active and competent partners in their own education. Your child's natural desire to seek out general patterns and rules will inspire him not only to observe and narrate events but to make a real effort to explain them. A tremendous increase in his attention span will allow him to process his thinking long enough to come up with some plausible, if sometimes erroneous rules. Without any specific prompting on your part, he will begin implementing these rules in his grammar ("The glass breaked, Mommy"), in his behavior (refraining from yelling because it gets him into trouble or frequently whining because it gets him what he wants), in his emotional expression ("I hurt my knee, but I'm okay"), and in his social awareness ("He hits me a lot. He doesn't know the rules yet."). These advances, along with greatly improved communication skills and memory, enable your child to interact more successfully with others, thus garnering even more feedback about the world and his efforts in dealing with it. As he begins to learn whether his concepts or "rules" are shared by others, he refines his expression further. In fact, children improve so much in this area that the biggest risk for parents is in overestimating their capabilities. We may be so impressed by a three-year-old's interest in taking responsibility for his actions (his pride in brushing his teeth each night, his ability to resist grabbing toys from his brother) that we fail to realize that telling a lie is the flip side of exploring such concepts as intention and point of view. His ability to spell his name aloud may make us so proud that we're disappointed when he spells his name in cookie-cutter letters upside down. We thrill to his growing ability to count a group of objects, but are disappointed when he skips or repeats a number, or has to start over again each time he's distracted.

All of these errors are part of the learning process, of course. Rather than worrying about the long-term significance of our children's mistakes (errors that are only natural), we should keep in mind how startling their growth in awareness continues to be. Yes, your three-year-old may continue to "read" books upside down for a while—but the fact that he has made the association between those marks on the page and a story is truly earth-shattering. With your encouragement and gentle, positive support, your child's errors in perception will fade and true competence will assert itself—especially if you try to follow his lead by helping him expand on his interests rather than trying to direct his attention in ways you'd prefer it to go. If all goes well, you will soon hear your child begin to announce proudly, "I couldn't do that when I was two." This sense of being a big kid is your child's well-deserved reward for a great deal of mental work. By celebrating his discoveries with him, you can help set the stage for better comprehension in the years to come.

EASING THE WAY

Helping Your Child Learn

A child's mind is like a sponge, soaking in information and analyzing patterns inherent in whatever the world sends his way. Yet now more than ever, the higher quality the information you offer him, the faster and more efficient his cognitive growth will be. Sometimes this can be accomplished in small details. Place mats that contain letters and numbers, for example, are preferable for him to look at while eating than a decorative tablecloth. Educational videotapes are better for his learning brain than cartoons interrupted by overstimulating commercials. As always, the best way to help your child learn is to follow his lead—noting his interests and asking open-ended questions that spur him to progress further in his thinking and comprehension. If he has developed a passion for dinosaurs, for example, feed his love of learning by teaching him the names of several of his favorites.

Discuss which of these dinosaurs were carnivores and which ate only plants, which ones lived during the same period, which have spikes and which ones don't. If his preschool class has been talking about jungle animals, check out a book about jungles from your local library and help him find out more about them. If your child is not yet enrolled in preschool (a place full of cognitive and social opportunities, as Chapter 6 shows), you can utilize the same tools a teacher would at home. When accomplishing chores around the house, take the time to show him how to perform them himself. He may make a mess the first dozen times he prepares his own bowl of cereal, but his confidence will soar as he discovers he can improve his performance with practice. Meanwhile, you can stimulate his thinking about his physical actions by pointing out, say, that the farther he tips the cup of milk into his cereal bowl the more milk he'll get. Of course, your three-year-old won't remember in detail all that you tell him. Still, the positive reactions from adults when he repeats what he does remember will teach him that learning brings a great deal of satisfaction.

Games continue to serve as a pleasurable means of learning about the world. Simplified forms of charades (say, imitating an animal instead of acting out a song title), stimulate your child's imagination and allow him to experiment with the concept of subjective points of view (he knows the answer; you have to guess!). Knock-knock jokes introduce him to the joys of language. Board games that involve counting and taking turns encourage his mathematical thinking and reinforce social growth. Such games as I Spy and Which Hand Is the Nickel In prod him to use his developing logic skills. Even computer games can lead him further in his experimentation than he would otherwise go due to physical limitations (he may be able to complete a puzzle more easily on a computer screen than in the real world), though such games obviously lack the hands-on benefits of real blocks, books, and toys.

Open as your child is to your input and proud as he is of his accomplishments, the point this year is not to achieve a certain outcome but to enjoy the *process* of learning. Many parents fall

Thanks to magical thinking, this three-year-old believes since he can "hear" the ocean in the shell, there must be water inside!

into the trap of trying to help their children finish an activity and get it right (making sure they complete a jigsaw puzzle, for example, even if they have to guide their child's hand themselves). Instead, try to applaud the effort, not the outcome. Three-year-olds should know that all one should have to do is to try one's best, and that it's okay for an accomplishment not to be perfect at first.

WHERE DID THE MOON GO?: USING REASON TO COMPREHEND THE WORLD

The party had been organized to celebrate our neighbor Nat's fourth birthday, but half a dozen of the guests had brought their younger siblings along as well. At such gatherings, it is fascinating to observe the differences in cognitive development that manifest themselves in different-aged children. On this occasion, I enjoyed the sight of very young guests grappling with the challenge of playing pin the tail on the donkey. The first guest to play, two-year-old Andrew, categorically refused to put on a mask. Handed a donkey tail, he marched off with it toward the refreshment table, flapping the tail up and down, enjoying the movement and forgetting all about the game. Next, three-year-old Sharon took her turn—agreeing to put on a mask, but peeking out from under it as she pinned the tail on the paper, but nowhere near the donkey's rear. When a parent reminded the next child that the object was to pin the tail *on* the donkey, Little Sarah shouted, "Don't hurt him!" and burst into tears. Next came Nat, the birthday boy. Like the others, he was playing the game for the very first time, yet he clearly understood the concept—putting on the mask, moving toward the donkey, and pinning the tail pretty close to the correct position *without* peeking.

I could not have asked for a clearer demonstration of the great progress in the ability to reason that takes place between ages two and four. Nat's ability to infer relationships between ideas (playing a game) and objects (a mask, a picture of a donkey, and a paper tail), to arrange a series of concepts in logical sequence (put on the mask, take the tail, and pin it to the donkey), and to relate a specific situation to a general rule (when playing a game that involves hiding your eyes, don't peek), allowed him to play this new game with ease. Of course, his comprehension isn't perfect (he didn't care that he missed the donkey, for one thing). Still, even this much progress is impressive considering three-year-olds' difficulty with such issues as centration (an inability to pay attention to more than one aspect of a situation at a time), appearance-reality problems (difficulty distinguishing what one sees from what's actually happening), and memory limitations (difficulty following multiple steps in a series of directions).

Ask a two-year-old to hand you a square yellow block, and he's likely to give you either a yellow block or a square one but not necessarily a block with both characteristics. Give him a toy airplane as a gift, and he may say, "Wait, it can't fly. It has wheels." Such errors are examples of problems with centration—the tendency that kept Andrew focused on the dreaded mask at the birthday party and unable to see the "bigger picture" of the Pin-the-Tail game. Centration kept Sharon so tightly focused on reaching the donkey that she didn't think about cheating when she peeked. Centration is also the reason why Jessica, described playing Chutes and Ladders earlier in this chapter, was only able to focus on the high number she spun on the spinner, missing the fact that it caused her to land on a bad spot on the board. It is easy to imagine the many ways in which centration can trip up a young child in his efforts to use reason to decipher his often confusing world. (A nickel may be bigger than a dime, but it isn't worth more.) This tendency usually fades over the course of this year, and by age four most children are able to hold more than one characteristic of an object, event, or process in their minds at once, allowing for much greater sophistication in their thinking, conversation, and behavior.

The challenge of distinguishing between appearance and reality most often confuses three-year-olds when they find themselves in unfamiliar situations. Studies by Dr. John Flavell and colleagues at the University of California at Berkeley have demonstrated that when children this age look at a white object, then look at it again through a colored filter, and look at it once more without a filter, they believe that the object has actually changed color—and they assume that objects that look like other objects (a sponge that looks like a rock, for example) really are what they resemble (the sponge must therefore be a rock). Appearance-reality confusion accounts for a child's belief that pregnant women have babies in their tummies because they swallowed them, or that the ant he just stepped on is simply sleeping. The same confusion (along with a tendency toward *animism,* which I'll discuss later in this chapter) led Sarah to believe she'd hurt the donkey if she pinned a tail on it. Studies have shown that even younger three-year-olds already have some concept of the difference between appearance and reality (they often use the word "real" to distinguish between toys and real objects, and "really" to distinguish between play and real life), but this skill will expand greatly over the course of this year. By age four, your child will be more open to your explanations about how things really work, somewhat better able to understand that a sad event in a book or on TV is "just part of a story," and much nimbler in leaps between imaginary play and interaction in the real world.

One reason behind your child's progress in these areas is the remarkable increase that takes place in attention skills and memory. A challenge for all preschool-aged children is the ability to tune out background noise and distractions and focus on whatever conversation or activity is taking place in the foreground. This is why your child sometimes doesn't respond to your questions or demands even after you've repeated them several times, and why it's so easy for him not to notice a speeding car or careening bicycle when he's outside. As he approaches age four, his ability to prioritize his attention improves, making it easier for him to isolate and think about different aspects of a new experience, follow a train of logic, play organized games, and participate in other group activities. His memory will also progress from what is already an impressive ability to recall long lists of dinosaur, vehicle, or superhero names to remembering and implementing "rules" of logic or behavior (don't hide in the same place every time in a game of hide-and-seek). He will be better able to draw on his experience to piece together a coherent picture of his world. Even by age four, however, he probably won't have mastered the ability to deliberately remember something as older children and adults naturally do. He doesn't yet understand that repeating a phrase over and over ("Take your goggles to swim class," or reciting his address) will help him recall it later. As shattered as he's likely to feel when he forgets to take a treasured object along on an outing, he isn't capable of reminding himself ahead of time to take it with him (and he will self-righteously blame you for forgetting). Throughout this year and well into the next, he will depend on you to plan ahead and help him remember what needs to be done.

All of these cognitive limitations are typical and normal for your three-year-old, and there is not really much you can do to erase them. (In any case, who would want to when so many of his misunderstandings prove so delightful?) Still, as with other aspects of your child's development, growth occurs more easily when you remain a half step ahead of your child, leading him toward more sophisticated thinking. While you can't really expect him to remember to take his jacket home from child care, for example, you *can* show him how to create memory strategies that will one day allow him to do so. ("Let's check your cubby before we go. That way we can see if there's anything we forgot today.") While you must still watch out for threats to his safety that he might not notice in the confusion of the outdoors, you *can* teach him to "stop, look, and listen" at every street corner. Appearance-reality confusion can gradually clear up as you talk with your child about stories that are "just pretend," provide masks, puppets, and costumes for playtime, and provide clear, simple explanations for events that leave him mystified. Even centration issues can be addressed by pointing out that, say, the airplane has wheels so it can land on the runway, or explaining that spinning a one rather than a nine on the board game's spinner may be necessary to win. Your child may not retain much of what you tell him at first, and he may continue to make the same mistakes for quite some time ("But nine is *bigger*, Mommy!"), but at least you've given him something to think about—clarifying the facts and feeding his natural desire to reason.

A PARENT'S STORY

When We Move Away . . .

"When we moved to Chicago when Lisa was three, I was sure I had the whole scene under control," a colleague told me at a recent seminar. "A fellow psychologist told me about the wild ideas preschoolers get if you aren't incredibly specific and concrete with them, so I told Lisa every single detail about the move—or so I thought—to make sure she was prepared. I talked about how we were looking for a house, and then how we found one, and how I'd arranged to have the furniture moved, and how we were going to have to help the cat get used to the new backyard. I still hadn't packed Lisa's stuff, thinking I'd leave that for last. Finally, just about a week before the movers came, I mentioned something about transferring all the pots and pans to the new kitchen, and Lisa, looking kind of uncomfortable, said to me, 'Are you going to leave my toys here?'

"'Of course not,' I said. 'Why would I do that?'

"She looked a little sad, and said, 'So I'll have something to play with after you move away.'

"I was dumbstruck. I couldn't believe she'd been thinking all this time that we were going to move without her. But when

I thought back, I realized I'd always said 'we,' which could have just meant Daddy and me, and never actually told Lisa that she was coming, too. For months, I guess, she just assumed she was going to end up all alone in our house. Looking back, I see that I should have talked a little less and listened to *her* talk about the move a little more, to be sure she understood what was happening. As it was, she took the facts she had and put them together in a way that made sense to her. The poor thing looked so relieved when she found out she was coming, too."

ONE, TWO, THREE, FIVE . . . THE BEGINNINGS OF MATHEMATICAL AWARENESS

One of the areas in which your child's search for patterns and rules is most evident this year is in the realm of mathematics. This is a year in which many children become fascinated by such mathematical concepts as more versus less ("I have more toys than you"), bigger versus smaller ("Mikey is bigger than me, but I'm bigger than Sam"), and division ("Can I have half?"). It's interesting to observe how naturally three-year-olds seem to comprehend these concepts—easily dividing a plateful of cookies by handing one to you, one to himself, until each of you has an equal share. Your teaching may also have introduced your child to the concept of numbers and counting. If so, he probably enjoys reciting numbers (though he often skips or repeats a number, and will easily lose his place if distracted and have to start from the beginning again), and counting all kinds of objects (though he easily miscounts, skipping an object or counting it twice, or has to physically move each object as he counts it).

An awareness of mathematical relationships helps a great deal in the reasoning process, and three-year-olds are quick to use whatever awareness they have regarding size, quantity, volume, and time in creating hypotheses about their world. The fact that your child lacks full abilities in all these areas doesn't slow him down a bit. He simply reasons according to what researchers call the *primitive rules* that he's managed to create so far—rules that lead to personally satisfying (if wildly incorrect) conclusions.

In a 1990 study, Dr. Karen Wynn of the University of Arizona at Tucson pointed out that if you ask a younger three-year-old to count a set of objects and then ask how many objects there are, he will have to count them again instead of just telling you, "four." By age three and a half, he may be able to tell you without counting if there are only two or three objects, but will probably have to count them again if there are more than that. It's clear from this evidence that three-year-olds' mastery of the idea of quantity is still quite tenuous—partly due to their trouble with memory, their still-new understanding of symbols, and their tendency toward centration. Still, their understanding expands greatly this year. Your child may still mistakenly feel cheated if you divide his brother's sandwich into four pieces and his into only two—but he'll demonstrate his understanding of addition, at least, by transferring some of his brother's dessert to his own plate.

Appearance-reality problems create difficulty this year with the related concept of conservation—the idea that the amount of something

Three-year-olds are very interested in the correct order and sequence of objects, as this girl demonstrates with her puppets.

remains the same even if its form, shape, or appearance changes. Three-year-olds are unable to comprehend that a pint of water in a measuring cup is still a pint, even when it's poured in front of them into a wide, low bowl. They assume that a widely spaced row of six pennies is greater in number than a closely spaced row of ten. Two ropes that stretch for the same length must be equally long, a three-year-old assumes, even though one rope is stretched straight and the other is wavy and loose. Other measurement issues prove problematic as well: your child may guess that a very small wrapped gift he receives for his third birthday contains a "great big dog," though he's not likely to make that mistake on his fourth birthday. For parents, these miscalculations often go unnoticed unless they result in a conflict ("Hey, his half is bigger!"), but they are constantly under way this year.

On another front, three-year-olds' comprehension of sequence and time has improved enormously since infancy. Having observed and experimented with such cause-and-effect events as smiling at you and seeing you smile back, and dropping an object and watching you pick it up, your child has long understood that some things happen in a certain order. This understanding expanded to include a growing sense of sequence of events (wake up, eat breakfast, get dressed, play) and an ability to predict what will happen next ("I don't want my stories yet. I'm not sleepy!"). By age three, your child may have become sufficiently familiar with his regular routine to trace the rhythms of his days (library day, gymnastics day, lunch-with-Grandma day) and even develop an interest in others' daily rounds (the garbageman, the mail carrier). He may enjoy reciting or singing the names of the days of the week and is aware that certain holidays occur now and then, but the idea of a year or even a month as a whole is still beyond him.

In general, you will find that your three-year-old is better at *relative* mathematical judgments (this group is bigger than that one) than *quantitative* ones (how much bigger something is). Still, the obvious pleasure he takes in counting, measuring, dividing, and comparing reflects the satisfaction he takes in discovering all kinds of patterns and rules in his daily life. By praising his efforts and building on his enthusiasm as it occurs (helping him count the squares in the sidewalk outside, arrange his building blocks by size, and count down the days until his birthday on the calendar), you can set the stage for further development in mathematical understanding.

Q & A

A Little for You and a Lot for Me . . .

Q: I had always heard that sharing gets a lot easier at age three, but my daughter Eleni doesn't seem to follow that pattern. If she's eating a chocolate bar and her brother asks for a piece of it, she gives him the tiniest possible flake. If he asks for more, she gives him a tiny pinch more, and then stuffs the rest of the chocolate bar into her mouth. Is she selfish, or is this normal for her age?

A: Your daughter's behavior may appear selfish, but she is in fact displaying a perfectly normal, and even admirable, mathematical awareness that she probably didn't have when she was two. Last year, she may have handed over the entire bar—not because she was more generous, but because she didn't realize she wouldn't get any chocolate back. She understands now that the more chocolate her brother has, the less is left for her. It's hard to blame her for trying to use this new discovery for her own benefit. Certainly, it's not a sign of a fundamentally selfish personality. By understanding why your child responds in this way, reminding her, "In this family, we share," and praising her when she does so, you can help her overcome this tendency before much more time has passed. Besides, while she's busy counting each tiny square ("One for you, one for me . . ."), she will be so caught up in her math ability that she won't realize how much she's given away.

"THE CURTAINS WAVED AT ME": MAGICAL THINKING

It was a brisk winter's day, and Dorrie was not surprised to see as she hurried along the sidewalk that her three-year-old, Connor, had hidden his bare hands inside his jacket sleeves. "Wanna hold my hand?" she asked her son. Instantly, Connor stuck his left hand out of his sleeve and snuggled into Dorrie's palm. "Where's your other hand?" Dorrie asked playfully as they continued walking. Connor frowned. "It's not coming out," he told his mother. "It's sleeping."

Animism—a child's tendency to attribute life or humanlike qualities to nonliving things—crops up frequently in the lives of preschool-aged children, with all kinds of surprising results. Your three-year-old may develop a sudden friendship with a rock in your back yard, converse at length with his favorite blanket, or become convinced that the jacket hanging from a hook in his bedroom at night is a menacing monster. Such conclusions are based on his still imperfect reasoning skills coupled with an exploding imagination. This combination is also responsible for what is often referred to as *magical thinking*—the conviction that burning logs in the fireplace feel pain, that a swing feels dizzy, or that a kite gets scared when it flies high in the sky. As you have surely observed, this kind of thinking takes up a large portion of your child's inner life this year, as he moves back and forth freely between fantasy and reality throughout the day. Many children this age actually become so involved in imaginary scenarios that they can't tell where they end and reality begins. Their fantasy lives may spill over into real-world interaction to the point where your three-year-old insists that you refer to him as "Superman" for several hours or even a day or two.

Some parents become quite concerned over this tendency, particularly when their children refuse to reclaim their real identities when it's time to eat supper, go to bed, or otherwise call an end to playtime. You may feel some concern over whether your child is able to tell the difference between pretend and reality, and start to wonder whether he's at all in touch with the actual world around him. Although such renowned child-development experts as Jean Piaget once believed that children this age really don't understand what's real and what's not real, more recent research has shown that in situations that are familiar to them their sense of what's real is in fact quite grounded. Your child may believe that the clouds pull the sun up into the sky each morning (after all, he's never been up there to see how it works), but he probably knows that his favorite toy superhero isn't really alive and that the bathroom drain isn't thirsty. Still, he continues to indulge in pretend play and magical thinking for the sheer enjoyment it offers him as well as the chance to work out problems and explore concepts in an unrestrained way. It makes sense, then, for you and your child's other caregivers to respect his desire to experiment with his imagination. By refraining from teasing or belittling his fantasies, you will be better able to observe them and thus learn more about how he feels about things and where he is in his development.

A CHILD'S-EYE VIEW

"I Could Just Gobble You Up!"

Christine is nearly four, and a very big girl. She's also very brave, so when the doorbell rings and Uncle Charlie walks into the house, she doesn't run to her room even though she'd like to. The sight of big Uncle Charlie brings memories rushing back to Christine—memories of him holding her up in the air, saying, "I could just eat you alive!" and then hugging her and adding, "You're the tastiest little girl I ever saw."

"Well, hello there, Chrissie!" Uncle Charlie booms through his bushy brown beard when he sees her hovering in the corner of the living room.

Christine recoils visibly but holds her ground.

"Aren't you going to say hi to me?" Charlie says, moving toward her.

Not scared, Christine tells herself, holding on to the couch. Uncle Charlie is a very big man, though, and somehow he keeps getting confused in Christine's mind with a storybook picture of a big brown bear.

"Hmm." Uncle Charlie looks at Christine's mommy, who hovers protectively nearby. "Should I hang her upside down? You think she'd say hi then?"

"No!" Christine blurts out as her mom says in a warning tone, "Charlie."

"I know," Charlie continues obliviously. "I'll give you a tickle. *Then* you'll say hi, won't ya?"

Uncle Charlie reaches toward Christine. Her mind starts to plan her escape. "Stop it!" she yells, clenching her fists. "I don't want to!" She scrambles behind the couch, thinking, *He can't reach me from here.* Then she heads down the hallway toward her room.

I'm okay, Christine says to herself a moment later, hovering behind her closed door with her heart beating fast. *He can't get me here.* She hears her mom talking to Uncle Charlie in the distance. She looks around at her stuffed animals, her dolls, and her familiar toys. This is her place. No bear-man can grab her and hang her upside down while her friends are protecting her. She puts the stuffed bear behind a chair where he can't see her. She sits down on her bed, thinks for a moment, then picks up her bear and hugs it.

"I DRAWED A FIRE TRUCK LIKE JIMMY": THE COGNITIVE BENEFITS OF GROUP PLAY

In the late 1970s, psychologist Lev S. Vygotsky introduced a new concept to the science of developmental psychology called the *zone of proximal development.* According to this theory, any child can improve his understanding and performance through contact with a person with higher skills. The most obvious person would be a parent, teacher, or other concerned and competent caregiver. But, as studies have subsequently shown, even more competent children aged three or older can have a profound impact on your child's level of performance.

You may have observed this theory in action if your child has already taken part in a structured group program or preschool. Though you may not have spent much time yet teaching him to recognize letters, he may have come home from preschool one day pointing out the *A* in the word "Monday" on the calendar. Another child who happens to have a non-English-speaking parent or caregiver may have taught your child a word or two in another language. Certainly, exposure to different family customs (taking shoes off when inside), behavior and emotional responses ("David doesn't know that you don't push people"), and social roles ("Daniel's mommy is a painter. She makes pictures of people.") is a fascinating exercise for any three-year-old and feeds his desire for as much information as possible with which to create his hypotheses about his world. By coming together in this way, parents and children can pool their resources for the benefit of each child. Of course, it's true that negative ideas and behaviors can be transferred just as easily (or perhaps even more easily) than positive ones, either by other children or adults. It's easy enough to discourage new negative actions and encourage positive ones by observing your child's daily behavior, pointing out why you don't tolerate some things and redirecting your child to actions that you do approve of.

As we discuss in Chapter 6, not all three-year-olds are ready to take the plunge into group life. Emotional, behavioral, cognitive, and financial issues all come into play when deciding whether to introduce your child to preschool or some other regular group activity. The potential benefits are great for children this age, however, as they direct their attention increasingly outward and develop a greater curiosity about what others know and how they feel.

IF YOU'RE CONCERNED

How Smart Is He?

Early childhood classes or other group activities not only offer three-year-olds a chance to learn from others, but they provide parents with what is sometimes a first chance to observe their child in a regular group setting and compare him to others his age. This experience can come as quite a shock at times, as parents note their children's relative difficulty separating at the beginning of the day or their tendency to act out their frustration instead of using their words, as other three-year-olds may be able to do. One of the more potent sources of anxiety for parents in this situation lies in the cognitive realm. When watching another three-year-old write his name, then your own child's name, it's hard not to worry about your own child who has not even learned to copy the letter *A*. Listening to your child's classmate chatter on and on to her teacher about what kinds of foods various animals prefer to eat, you may wonder why your child is content to play alone in the corner with a set of blocks.

In most cases, however, such anxiety is ill-founded and will soon pass as you observe more aspects of your own and other children's skills and abilities. As we have seen, three-year-olds display a remarkable talent for recalling "lists" of names or attributes relating to objects that interest them, such as dinosaurs, cartoon heroes, or butterflies. Such skills as rudimentary writing and reading are also displayed startlingly early in some children. In most cases, the appearance of these skills doesn't signify greater intelligence as much as the natural unevenness of skill development during this period of life (or the fact that others have consciously or unconsciously worked with the child earlier). It's easy to over- or underestimate your child's (or any other child's) reasoning or thinking ability this year. Your child's preschool teachers or child-care providers can serve as sounding boards if you're convinced your child is truly behind the others. Don't hesitate to raise your concerns, but don't be surprised if their advice is to avoid making judgments that aren't based on formal testing. Adopt a "wait-and-see" attitude toward all the three-year-olds you get to know this year.

FOREVER MOM: MOVING TOWARD GREATER AWARENESS

"Mommy?"

"Yes, Sam?" Evelyn snuggles deeper into her favorite easy chair, cuddling Sam, who's nearly four now, in her lap. It's bedtime and Sam should be under the covers by now, but Evelyn can't resist hanging on to this moment of sleepy affection just a little longer.

"I love you," Sam murmurs, leaning against his mom and closing his eyes.

"I love you, too, Sam." Evelyn smiles and rests her chin atop his head.

"When I grow up, I'm going to have lots of little kids," Sam continues, reciting a prediction that's become quite familiar over recent months.

"And I'll be their grandma," Evelyn adds on cue.

Sam sighs and snuggles in deeper. "Yeah," he says, his voice already drifting toward sleep. "But you'll still be my mommy. You'll always be my mom . . ."

Glancing at her husband with a wry smile, Evelyn picks up her son and carries him to bed. It took months of conversation and careful reassurance before Evelyn managed to convince her son that yes, she *would* always be his mother, no matter what happened. Ideas and concepts that Evelyn hadn't even considered had to fall into place ("Don't grandmas have gray hair?") before Sam could fully understand that what she said was true. Once he mastered the facts, though, Evelyn could see that this new comprehension provided Sam with a real feeling of relief. It isn't easy understanding this big, confusing world, Evelyn reminds herself, pulling the covers over her son's sleeping form. But one by one, thanks to the hard work put in by children and their caregivers, ideas start to clarify themselves. In the end, the results of all that questioning, reasoning, and hypothesizing are so satisfying, it's no wonder children work so hard to achieve them.

ADVANCES

Cognitive Achievements in the Third Year

36 MONTHS	Knows two animal actions: which roars, which flies, etc.
	Engages in simple fantasy play
	Spontaneously classifies an object by color or shape, but usually not by both without prompting
42 MONTHS	Understands the concept of counting and may know a few numbers
	Begins to have a clearer sense of sequence in directions (first, next . . .)

	Recalls parts of a story
	Understands the concepts of "more" or "less" in quantity
48 MONTHS	Can classify an object by two or more properties: for example, color and shape
	Initiates deceptive strategies
	Engages in extensive fantasy play

FIRST-PERSON SINGULAR

Every three-year-old's cognitive development follows a unique path—and even a single child's abilities appear markedly different from day to day. It's not only fun but instructive to observe how and when your child picks up new concepts and demonstrates new skills. Take some time to record the ways in which you see his reasoning skills at work. How does he demonstrate improvements in his memory as the months pass? What has he learned from his friends or teachers recently? What amusing forms of magical thinking or animism has he come up with? If he doesn't often divulge his hypotheses to you, try asking him direct questions about how he believes a merry-go-round works or what cotton candy is made of. You are likely to get some surprising answers that he'll enjoy reading about in the years to come.

READER'S NOTES

_____

_____

_____

_____

_____

_____

_____

_____

_____

_____

_____

_____

_____

_____

_____

_____

_____

_____

_____

_____

_____

_____

CHAPTER 4

"Guess What?"—
My Verbal Abilities

Many studies estimate that a dozen or more words a day are added at this age.

"Forgive us our trespasses . . ." Steven intones, helping his three-year-old daughter, Bethany, recite her bedtime prayers.

"Forgive us our trusspesses," Bethany echoes solemnly, her hands pressed together and her eyes shut tight.

Steven has to suppress a smile. Bethany looks so cute, cuddled under the covers in her pajamas, trying to pronounce such difficult words whose meaning she doesn't really understand. Understand or not, instilling this habit is important to Steven, so he continues right up to the end—when Bethany "repeats" his final phrase, "Lead us not into temptation, but deliver us some e-mail. Amen."

Amusing slipups such as this one frequently delight parents of three-year-olds—partly due to the startling realization that our children's verbal dexterity doesn't mean they understand everything they hear. Still, by her third birthday, the typical child in this country has a spoken vocabulary of about 300 to 900 words. She can speak in relatively complex sentences of five words or more and make many of the word sounds that stumped her just a few months before. Language comes alive for her as her ability to attach meaning to symbols improves, and she savors, experiments with, and even sings all the interesting new nouns, verbs, and (unfortunately) expletives that she encounters every day. If she lives in a bilingual home, she will expand her skills in this way in both languages, though the double load may slow her progress in one or the other language temporarily.

Your child's progress is not only a matter of learning new words and refining her pronunciation. Her cognitive development prompts her to use language as a tool, both to get more information about the world and to involve you in conversation and keep your attention focused on her. This is the year when she will begin to ask "Why?" a dozen or so times a day and, as the title of this chapter suggests, start many conversations by grabbing your arm and demanding, "Guess what?" Her persistent questions about the people she encounters and the events she observes are likely to be quite embarrassing in public due to her still limited awareness of others' feelings and points of view, as well as the "rules of society." Awkward as these situations can be, it's essential for your child to feel free to ask you about people and events. With patience, you can help her learn to heed the context in which she asks her questions. Meanwhile, her efforts to practice new words (efforts that may lead to constant chatter at some times) will improve her ability to think, create, and tell you what's going on in her very active mind.

THE TOY BOX

"I Wonned!"

Wow! I matched 'em all! Three-year-old Victor stares at the computer screen, thrilled that he won a "certificate" by matching all the pairs of animals in a game of Concentration. *Gotta tell Dad!* He climbs down from the desk in his father's home office. He can hear Dad on the phone in the kitchen. He races toward him. "Dad, guess what?"

"Just a second, Victor," Dad says, putting a hand over the receiver. "I'm talking to Aunt Jo."

Dad turns back to the telephone. Victor stares in disbelief. *I have to tell him!* he thinks with an almost physical urgency. Grabbing his father's arm, he says, "Guess what, Dad? I wonned the game!"

"That's great, pal. Hold on." Dad turns back to the phone.

I matched the dog with the other dog. And then I found the mouse, and the other mouse on the other side of the 'puter . . . Victor can picture exactly what he wants to say, but there are so many words that he can't get them all out. *I have to show him,* he decides. He grabs his dad again—this time by the leg. Trying to pull him toward the computer, he shouts, "Daddy, I wonned! Come look, okay?"

"OKAY!" Annoyed, Dad gets off the phone and follows his son to the computer. "Why do you have to show me? I get it— you won."

Victor doesn't answer. He's too excited, and it's so complicated to explain. "Look!" he says triumphantly once he finally arrives in front of the screen with Dad in tow. "I did it by myself!"

Dad relaxes when he sees the certificate with Victor's name on the computer screen. He grins at his son, who's bursting with pride. "That's great, Vic," he says, patting him on the shoulder. "You matched all the pictures, and you won the game. See, you got a certificate that says you completed that level. Now you can go to the next one. Let's do it together, okay?"

Victor feels the intense relief of hearing his thoughts put into words. *Yeah!* he thinks. *I wonned that level!* Having learned to frame what he wanted to say, he climbs into his father's lap for another round. Maybe someday he'll be able to wait until Dad's off the phone before sharing his news. For now, though, he needs Dad's patience and translation skills when there's just too much for a three-year-old to say.

"I ATE *ALL* MY LUNCH!": VERBAL PROGRESS AT AGE THREE

It probably feels like eons ago when your child blurted out her first recognizable words. Her early efforts consisted much more of sound imitation than real communication: she knew that the sound "Mama" elicited an amazing response from Mom but didn't really understand that the word *meant* "Mom." Such a concept—that sounds or marks on a page could stand for ideas—was still many months away, and only fully developed near the end of last year. By her third birthday, however, your child not only "gets" but is thrilled by the process of expressing ideas in words. Her interest in expression, along with a new desire to make sure everything is correct and in place, leads to an increasing interest in refining her speech. By age three and a half she will recognize a mispronunciation when she hears one. She may even begin to self-correct at times and correct her friends' mispronunciations when she notices them. As a result, her speech will become much more easily understood by people outside her family. Compared to last year, conversations will become much more two-sided, to everyone's relief.

Although three-year-olds clearly understand that the purpose of language is to communicate, they still encounter roadblocks in achieving this goal. When describing a process to you (for example telling you how a toy works, or how they climbed to the top of the biggest slide and slid down by themselves), they still find it easier to take you to the place where the event happened and *show* you (like Victor), rather than try to narrate the entire process in words. At age two, they didn't really comprehend the fact that you could understand what happened without having been there. This year, they know *you* don't have to see what they're talking about, but *they* may still have to see it to effectively describe what happened—just as we adults process information better by physically attempting, rather than just talking about, a new skill.

A general difficulty with abruptly starting or stopping any action can also get in the way of your child's conversation this year. Difficulty stopping (along with a tendency to be easily distracted) is often the reason she asks you a question five times in three seconds. Once you've given her an answer, she may have to repeat it several times (or ask you the question again to get you to repeat the answer) in order to secure it in her memory. Annoying as this process can be—particularly when you're in a hurry and she insists on hearing *again* why she has to put on her raincoat when it's not raining outside right now—it is a perfectly normal aspect of a three-year-old's conversation and will fade as the year progresses and her memory improves. Meanwhile, try to resist the temptation to groan, "I already told you that." It may help to keep in mind that the first time you answered her your child might have been listening to your grammar, the second time she may have been absorbing a new vocabulary word, and the third time she was probably busy associating what you said with an idea or memory of her own. These are all productive activities and part of the learning curve, and thus they deserve your patience.

Another source of errors results from children's natural ability to categorize new words by associating them with what they already know. While this is a useful skill, it's often incorrectly applied by preschoolers, resulting in wonderful creations like "tiger horse" for zebra and "bubble water" for seltzer. If your child uses and actually seems to prefer some of these terms, don't worry. They may not match your expectations, but they're the correct result of logical associations, and thus are a sign that your child is doing well.

You can help your child improve her verbal confidence this year by expanding on her experiences with language. At this age, new words spur new ideas, and new ideas call for more words. The better your child's mastery of language, the more effectively she will be able to think—to follow a train of inquiry, to maintain a sequence of ideas in her head, to analyze situations, and to plan ahead. She will hardly need your encouragement to seek out new words. Preschoolers are amazing learners and will soak up new vocabulary on their own—from songs on the radio, the teacher's lessons at preschool, and your own conversations no matter how private you think they are. You can spur your child's verbal development even more by deliberately building on the words she already knows and adding new ones. (Victor's father did this in the example above by adding the new phrase, "You completed that level," to his "I wonned!") As you help your child add nuance and shading to her verbal expression (responding to her "I like swimming," with "Me, too. I like the way big waves *crashhhhh* on the sand! What do you like about the beach?"), you will demonstrate the pleasures of exchanging information. As you engage in rhyming games, funny songs, and improvised stories, you'll introduce her to the pleasure of wordplay and experimentation. As she learns that verbal expression is not only necessary but fun in its own right, you will be amazed at how creative she becomes at developing the verbal ideas you've planted.

Verbal Progress

Nearly every three-year-old shows an increased love of language and a strong urge to communicate. Frequently, parents of children this age become so accustomed to verbal progress in most areas that any lingering problems start to concern them. Your child's increasing awareness of the sounds in her environment helps her begin to correct some of her pronunciation errors, for example, but some sounds, such as "r," "th," and "l," are still very difficult and will take time to perfect. At the beginning of this year she may still mispronounce as many as half the speech sounds she uses, with more correct speech only beginning to emerge midway through the year and remaining imperfect many months later. Pronouns may also continue to pose difficulties this year. Your child may occasionally use her name instead of saying "I" or "me" ("Cindy do it!") or "Mommy" instead of "you." Grammatical errors will occur quite frequently as your child naturally imposes general rules on exceptional cases ("I eated it all up!"). Because children this age can clearly understand so much more now, parents tend to clamp down hard on their verbal errors. In fact, correcting your child's pronunciation or grammar at this age will probably only confuse or frustrate her more, and may even make her so self-conscious about her expression that she won't experiment as much. Since most of these mistakes will disappear on their own within a year or so, it's usually best either to correct them very gently (responding to "I eated it all!" with "Yes, honey, you ate it all up!") or to ignore the error but continue setting a good example through your own speech.

Of course, there are some cases in which a parent is right to be concerned. If, as the year progresses, your child doesn't use "me" and "you" appropriately or doesn't use sentences of more than three words, point this out to her pediatrician at your next visit. Mention any consistent articulation disorders, such as dropping all end consonants or saying "woo" instead of "you." A tendency to rely on visual cues or gestures instead of words or to respond to your remarks only if she's looking directly at you may signal a need for a hearing test. If your child's errors make it hard for people to understand her, so that people tend to look to you to translate, she may have a speech delay. According to medical experts such as Dr. James Coplan of the State University of New York, speech delay is the most common disorder in early childhood, with 5 to 10 percent of all preschoolers so diagnosed. In most cases, such delays are not related to intelligence level or cognitive development but are specifically a speech issue. Most can be efficiently remedied through speech therapy or other clinical procedures.

If your child still stumbles frequently in his verbal expression but shows *progress* in his abilities, he's probably just moving along at his own pace (perhaps focusing more on other skills for the time being). Keep in mind that those *r*'s pronounced as *w*'s at the beginnings of words are usually the last to go (*r*'s at the ends of words are easier). Children in bilingual homes, who must work twice as hard to master both languages, may make a few more mistakes or seem to struggle a bit more than others their age, but as long as your child continues to make a fair amount of progress in both languages research shows that she will catch up by next year or certainly by age five.

". . . AND THEN YOU KNOW WHAT?": LEARNING TO COMMUNICATE EFFECTIVELY

As anyone knows who has ever tried to get a word in edgewise while chatting with a tireless motor-mouth, good communication involves more than a large vocabulary and a mastery of pronunciation and grammar. Other skills are needed, such as determining how much information another person needs in order to understand what one is saying—which ideas must be spelled out in detail, which will be understood without explanation, and which ones just need a little clarifying. As we will see in Chapter 5, part of being three is experiencing a decline in egocentrism—that is, developing a new ability to understand and appreciate another person's perspective, needs, and point of view. This new skill will naturally lead to your child adjusting her conversation depending on whom she's talking to—speaking in a high baby voice to a toddler, giving more information to a stranger who doesn't know much about her background, knowing she needs to wait her turn, and so on. You can support her increasing awareness of this necessity by discussing it with her beforehand ("Now, remember, Uncle Leo doesn't hear very well, so you'll have to speak up"), praising her when she figures it out on her own ("You were so nice and patient with Sandy's baby brother"), and remaining calm when she occasionally slips up. Just interacting within the family may also encourage these skills. Several studies have shown that in families with more than one child, each child takes more turns in family conversations, and conversations are three times longer, than in conversations between mother and child alone. The more your child interacts with her siblings in this way, the better she will get at adjusting her conversation to different listeners' needs.

Other kinds of communication skills begin to develop this year as well. Your three-year-old's growing awareness of her environment makes it easier for her to remember to monitor the volume of her speech (whispering in the library, speaking up at preschool, shouting on the playground). Her deeper understanding of others' emotional experience allows her to understand why she shouldn't tease, label ("Joey's bad. He tooked my toy."), or frequently tattle on other children. Her experience with interesting words and phrasing helps her spice up her own conversation with attention-getting tricks that will make her a more entertaining conversationalist. She'll soon begin to say things like "What?" or "Huh?" to extend a conversation and to clarify when she needs more information. She'll also learn quite a lot about maintaining eye contact and a steady conversation rhythm—and respecting others' personal space—just from interacting with you.

It's important to keep in mind that though these abilities begin to develop this year, your child won't always use them unless you encourage her to do so. A three-year-old who's never reminded to lower her voice while in the library will probably not do so spontaneously. A child who's never talked with an adult about how unpleasant it feels to be tattled on will probably have no qualms about informing her teacher every time a child misbehaves. As with all aspects of your child's development, it pays to deliberately focus on these new abilities as they begin to appear. By supporting, encouraging, and helping expand your child's awareness of the subtler side of human interaction, you can help her successfully socialize with her caregiver, teacher, relatives, and playmates, and to tell you more accurately what went on at the child-care center, during a play date, or in other situations where you weren't around.

A PARENT'S STORY

Speak Up!

"Daniel's always been shy," a new neighbor said about her three-year-old son during a party held to introduce her family to our block. "I kind of hoped he'd grow out of it, but he got even more quiet around the time when we moved. I got pretty worried about it since he was already registered for preschool here, and I really wanted him to go and make some friends. I mean, I know it's just his way to play by himself a lot, but I wanted him to be able to get along with other kids when he felt like it. Finally, a couple of months ago, my husband and I discussed some of the basic skills we thought would help him. Basically, we wanted him to feel comfortable talking more—you know, showing his enthusiasm so maybe other kids would want to play with him.

"Once we figured out what we wanted him to do, we started trying to deliberately steer him that way. I don't mean we criticized him or told him to talk louder all the time or anything. But when we ran into other kids and their parents, we made a point of chatting with them and then leading Daniel into the conversation—like asking a kid at the natural history museum which dinosaur was his favorite and then saying, 'Daniel's favorite is the Apatasaurus, right, Daniel?' We started *listening* to him more, too—waiting till he got past his stammering and actually expressed himself, singing songs together but letting him do the chorus by himself, leaving the last word off every line in a familiar

Pretend play becomes more verbal this year, with three-year-olds "talking like" Mommy and Daddy as they act out familiar scenes.

story so he could fill it in—anything to encourage him to enjoy speaking. We made sure to talk about emotional stuff, like how he was feeling about the move and starting preschool and so on. He started to talk about it more, once we gave him the chance.

"I can't say that what we did made all the difference when he started school. But he didn't have any major problems starting, and he seems to be blending in with the class okay. Some of the other more aggressive boys are actually having more problems than he is. Daniel still prefers his own company a lot of the time, but when I pick him up at the end of the day he usually has at least one or two other kids chatting away with him at the art table."

"WHAT DO YOU SAY, DEAR?": LEARNING AND UNDERSTANDING VERBAL SCRIPTS

"Robby, what do you say to the nice lady? Say, 'Thank you for the candy.' Mommy likes manners." Such parental direction is commonplace for most three-year-olds, with good reason. At an age when input from the environment can still so easily overwhelm (*Mmm, candy! That lady's looking at me. But I don't know that lady. She has big teeth. Uh-oh, is Mom talking to me?*), it is often difficult to negotiate a conversation or come up with the right thing to say. By prompting your child with phrases you've taught him, you provide him with "scripts"—verbal blueprints for the appropriate response for a particular type of interaction.

Your three-year-old adopts a wide variety of scripts even without your deliberately teaching them. If you and your partner regularly say "Excuse me," before breaking into a conversation, she will most likely pick up this habit, too. She probably uses phrases similar to yours when interacting with her teacher, with adults at a birthday party, with her friends, and with other people the two of you encounter every day. (She may amuse you by how precisely she mimics your posture, tone, and language in these cases—just another reminder that very little goes unobserved by children this age.) She even demonstrates her awareness of verbal "roles" in her pretend play, changing her voice and language to suit the mean witch, the sweet fairy, the superhero, the scared little fawn, and so on. Still, despite this apparent dexterity regarding verbal attitudes, there will be many instances this year when your child finds herself tongue-tied, frustrated, or even excluded from conversation because she doesn't know the proper thing to say. You can increase her verbal and social confidence tremendously over these months by helping her learn useful verbal formulas for, say, ordering food at a restaurant, joining someone else's conversation, asking for clarification when she doesn't understand something, and stating her feelings when she feels she's been slighted or treated with disrespect. Sometimes she will ask you directly for help ("Mommy, he hitted me. I want him to stop it."). Sometimes you will need to step in and provide her with a little help ("Sheila, ask Laura if you can use her bike."). She may not accept your prompting in every situation, but her natural interest in collecting such scripts ensures that she will listen and consider the usefulness of what you have to say.

Interestingly, verbal scripts are even more helpful when your child is interacting with other children than when talking with adults. This is because adults are better able and willing to overlook a little unintentional rudeness, such as interrupting a conversation, without saying,

"Excuse me," while young children don't yet have the skills to fill in for a person who doesn't provide the proper verbal cues. If a child takes his toy back from your three-year-old, for example, he may not understand why your child has started to cry (after all, it's his toy). The other preschoolers might merely look on in concern, but an adult would ask, "What's wrong?," offer a substitute, or explain why he took the toy. For this reason, it's especially important to focus on assembling some scripts if your child is about to enter preschool. You will ease his transition to group experience considerably if you teach him verbal scripts to:

- enter a group activity ("Can I play, too?" instead of "Lemme have it!")

- divide up a task ("How about if you get the train and I'll make the tracks?")

- engage others ("Hey, what are you doing?")

- express emotions ("That makes me mad," instead of "Quit it!")

Preschoolers don't automatically know how to substitute words for behavior. The more scripts you teach your child, the better your child's chances of success.

Q & A

"Excuse Me . . ."

Q: My son's preschool allows parents to drop in and observe the class on any Wednesday, and I've done this several times since the school year began. I've noticed that during story hour and major projects, my son tends to interrupt the teacher a lot to comment on the story or tell one of his own. Obviously, he talks so much because he's having a great time and I love the fact that he's so enthusiastic—but I get the impression that his interruptions really get on his teacher's nerves. Should I try to get my son to tone down his responses in school, or should I just let this go?

A: Enthusiasm for school and any other such activity is a wonderful thing, and it's easy to understand why parents hesitate to do anything to dampen their children's excitement. On the other hand, your child's frequent interruptions make it hard for the teacher to communicate with the group as a whole, and may even prevent her from finishing the story or project before the group's time is up. In a one-on-one situation this might not be such an issue, but at school it is easy for a child who behaves this way to be labeled as, say, having problems with impulse control. Studies have shown that once a child is labeled in this way, his caregivers tend to respond to him differently, and these responses tend to reinforce the original behavior. The fact is that some kids are physically squirmy, while others, like your son, happen to express their energy verbally. It is sad to see a child whose intentions are good be punished for not knowing the precise formula that will win him the approval he deserves.

For this reason, it's a very good idea to engage the preschool teacher as soon as possible on this issue. No doubt she's a veteran of many such situations. She may welcome your concern or even reassure you that your son is not as difficult as you think. Once you have a clear idea of where your son stands, start to work on his listening skills one at a time. If he's jumping up and shouting as well as interrupting with his own stories, pick the habit that bothers you most and address it first. Try having him count to three before he says something, and teach him to say, "Excuse me," when he feels he absolutely must interrupt. (He'll soon learn that good manners go a long way.) Be sure to notice and comment when he handles his impulses well. There is certainly no reason to get angry or exasperated with a child who hasn't yet reached a stage of cognitive development that allows him to listen to an entire story without talking back. (Have you ever been to a movie with a group of three-year-olds?) Just remind yourself that by offering him appropriate verbal formulas in positive ways, you are providing him with tools for success with his teachers and peers. As his new verbal techniques start to reap more positive responses from the adults in his life, his enthusiasm for school is likely to increase rather than diminish.

"I'M JUST SO ESSASPERATED!": FOSTERING A LOVE OF WORDS

All three-year-olds love language. Most are just waiting for the adults in their lives to share their delight in all things verbal and to stimulate what is already a phenomenal increase in vocabulary. (Many studies estimate that a dozen or more words a day are added at this age.) Keeping in mind that an increased vocabulary stimulates thinking of all kinds, you will certainly want to devote some time and energy this year to encouraging your child's natural interest in verbal comprehension and expression. The best way to instill a love of language in your child is to demonstrate that sort of appreciation yourself. Knock-knock jokes, simple puns, and other word games keep your child occupied during errands and in the car, and keep you both laughing and engaged with each other. Songs with silly lyrics will capture your three-year-old's attention, and sad or moving songs will stimulate his imagination. Certainly, this is a year to read to your child as much as possible. Stories will convey to her the power that words can have, add to her experience of the many ways words can be put together, and add enormously to her vocabulary without her even realizing what's happening.

An improved vocabulary enhances your child's social interaction, too, of course. We see how much better our children do with their peers when they can explain why they are angry (rather than just hitting their friend) or persuade a playmate that the game they want to play is worth playing. Perhaps this is why it's so distressing to hear our children erupt with inappropriate words and phrases that diminish social success (although milder words such as "poopyhead" and "pee-pee brain" may actually win them laughter, thus confusing matters). If you find that your child's ability to soak up new vocabulary words is extending into the realm of the unacceptable, try ignoring her eruptions and see what happens. She may simply be imitating something she's heard on the playground and will forget the word if you don't call attention to it. If she continues to use the word (which will certainly happen if she manages to get an emotional response from anyone within hearing range), you will have to put your foot down. Explain clearly and matter-of-factly that, "We don't use words that make people feel bad," or "That word is rude. Don't say it again." She will probably try saying it again—perhaps under her breath—just to see what happens. When she does, respond with a time-out or other mild, but firm, deterrent. (If you happen to hear her practicing the word by herself, however, it's fine just to ignore her. She's probably acting it out with her toys or otherwise trying to get it out of her system.) Remember, "bad words" only work if they get a rise out of someone. If your response is boring or you provide a substitute word, your child will move on to more positive behavior.

One aspect of vocabulary that few parents consider at this age is its ability to shape a person's general attitude. When talking with your child, you have the power to direct your language and hers in either constructive or destructive ways. Simply put, it's best to stress the positive whenever possible. If she's trying to tie her shoes and erupts with a frustrated, "I can't do this!" respond by saying empathetically, "You mean you're having trouble?" If she persists with "I can't," say, "I'm sure you'll be able to soon." Show her what progress she's already made and add, "Last year you couldn't do this at all, remember?" Reminding her of her "big-girl" self can help a child with perfectionist tendencies to focus more on what she *can* do. Sooner than you may imagine, she will begin to internalize these more positive messages ("Dad, I need help. I'm having trouble with my coat buttons."). As a result, she will face future challenges with more confidence and optimism.

EASING THE WAY

Giving Your Child Words

A large vocabulary is not the same as intelligence, but strong communication skills do make your child appear smarter—certainly not a bad thing as she approaches school age. To help your child increase her vocabulary as much as possible, keep providing her with new words even when she doesn't ask. If she points to a car and says, "That's a big car," you could answer, "Yes, it has no top.

It's called a convertible." If you're walking along together and spot a dog coming toward you, say, "Look at that Doberman," instead of, "Look at that dog." Don't ignore her frequent "What's this?" questions—answer them as fully as she'll allow. If she asks a question to which you don't know the answer, take her to the library and find it together.

As the year progresses, your child will grow increasingly able to frame in words her ideas about objects and events that she isn't witnessing at that particular time. You can help her in this transition by prompting her to describe her ideas, stories, and dreams in her conversations with you. If she tells you that Grandma read her a story about swimming in the ocean, ask her if the water was calm or full of big waves; if the island in the story was a desert island or full of big trees and thick green vines; if any people lived on the island or only animals. During the early months of this year, it's best to stick to concrete questions that lead her to give you specific details ("Where did we see that Doberman? I've forgotten.") Later, you can add open-ended questions ("I wonder where that dog is now?") that require her to answer with more words and stimulate her imagination or memory.

It is mind-boggling what great leaps in self-expression children can make when stimulated in this way. As your child moves on to more complex sentences and lively speech, other adults are likely to ask you if she's unusually smart—but you'll know she has simply learned to think in words.

"WHY IS THAT LADY SO FAT?": COPING WITH EMBARRASSING QUESTIONS

"Mommy, what happened to that man's hair?" "Wow, Aunt Trudy, your hands are so wrinkly. You must be very old."

What parent hasn't heard their child utter such tactless sentences and wanted to sink through the floor from sheer embarrassment? Unfortunately, asking questions without a sense of who might overhear them or how they might make others feel is a perfectly normal part of being three.

If you're lucky, the person your child is talking about knows perfectly well that, say, his hair looks funny and will understand that your child is just being a child. (I remember one instance when a woman in our gym's dressing room generously forgave my son for asking "what those scratches on her back were." She explained that she'd recently had an operation and then added to me, "Don't worry about it, honey. I have kids of my own. You have to let 'em ask those questions or they'll never learn.")

Though it is indeed true that there's nothing wrong with asking such questions, it is possible for your child to begin learning *when* and *where* to ask them before the year is over. By around the middle of the year, your three-year-old's cognitive development will help her start to understand you when you point out that other people can hear her and that it's best for her to talk about them in a whisper or wait until they're gone. (She still won't always remember to do so, but at least she will begin to understand the concept and be able to wait.) The idea that her questions might hurt another person's feelings is a bit harder to comprehend, and she will probably only truly heed your warnings in this regard as she approaches her fourth birthday. You can help speed up this understanding somewhat by asking her how she might feel if someone asked a similar question about her. In general, tactfulness is a gift that requires much patient prompting on your part and a certain amount of neurological growth on hers. By age five, you will laugh at your child's earnest efforts to hold on to a question until its subject can no longer hear it ("Dad, you made me forget my question!"). Until then, try to maintain a sense of humor about your child's curiosity and hope that other adults can do the same.

A CHILD'S-EYE VIEW

Did You See That?

Yum! Three-year-old Arthur opens his box of chicken nuggets and sticks a straw in his carton of milk. Mom has had a long day and so has given in to his request for a fast-food dinner, and he's savoring every moment. "Did you get nuggets, too, Mom? Hey, Mom, did you get nuggets, too?"

"Yes, yes," Mom says wearily, sitting across from him in the booth and unwrapping her own meal. Arthur eyes her with curiosity. *Mom's not talking much. Maybe she needs a nap*, he thinks.

Just then, his attention is distracted by the family in the booth behind his mother. Another mom is sitting there with her daughter, a girl about Arthur's age. As Arthur watches, the mom snaps at her daughter, and then suddenly jerks her out of her seat and spanks her on the bottom. The little girl starts to howl.

Arthur stares, stunned. "Mommy!" he says in astonishment. "Did you see that?!"

"Sssh," his mother responds uneasily. "Be quiet and eat your chicken."

"But Mommy!" Arthur can't believe his mother doesn't share his amazement. "That lady hit her little girl! She HIT her! Did you see that?"

"Arthur Louis, lower your voice this second! I'll talk to you about it later." Arthur notices that the other mom is glaring at them, ignoring her own little girl, who's still sniffling.

"But, Mommy," Arthur continues, lowering his voice a little and squirming with anxiety, "why did she hit her? Was that girl bad?"

"Okay, mister, that's it. One more question and we'll leave right now."

While Arthur sits in glum, confused silence (*What did I do?*) the other mother and child pack up and leave. "Okay, Arthur," his mom says with relief as soon as they're out the door, "it wasn't right to talk about that family right in front of them. But we can talk about it now."

As she explains the situation as best she can, Arthur starts to relax. *That's better,* he tells himself, satisfied with what she's told him. *I'm glad Mom's not mad at me.*

A WORLD OF EXPRESSION: LEARNING TO LIVE WITH LANGUAGE

It's way past Bethany's bedtime, and Steven has been trying to get her through the Lord's Prayer for fifteen minutes already. The good news is that with her fourth birthday still two weeks away Bethany has memorized the entire prayer—and Steven has patiently reexplained all the phrases she misunderstood when she was younger. The bad news is that practically every time she recites a line of the prayer, she interrupts herself to ask a question, relate an anecdote, or express a new thought to her father. "Not again," Steven groans inwardly as the phrase "forgive us our trespasses" inspires Bethany to ask, "Daddy, does God forgive *all* the bad guys?"

"That's enough, Bethany," he says, preparing to leave. "Come on, now. Finish your prayer. It's time to go to sleep."

"But, Daddy . . ."

"Bethany. Finish now."

"But, Dad . . ."

"Bethany!"

"But I was just thinking that . . ."

"One . . . two . . ."

"O-KAY! If you say so, Dad." Bethany closes her eyes and starts reciting again. Steven watches her, a smile of bemusement on his face. She's just used one of his favorite phrases, he realizes. It isn't always easy having such a little conversationalist around the house, but at least it's never boring. He has to admit, some of her questions have really challenged him. He's sure that brain of hers will come up with something to completely stump him pretty soon. In fact, he can't wait to hear what she'll come up with tomorrow.

ADVANCES

Verbal Achievements at Age Three

36 MONTHS	Vocabulary is about 300 to 900 words
	Holds a two- to three-sentence conversation
	Names at least four animal pictures
	Uses "and" and "but" to combine sentences

42 MONTHS	Counts to five
	May repeat words or questions
	Asks questions constantly, especially, "Why?"
	Speech is understood by people outside the family
48 MONTHS	Knows her first and last names
	Enjoys talking and singing to herself when alone
	Starts using elaborate pretend conversation in play

FIRST-PERSON SINGULAR

Your child's verbal errors will no doubt amuse you a great deal this year, but they can sometimes offer insights into the ways in which your child's thinking is developing. If you experience such incidents, be sure to record them here. It will be interesting to find out later whether your child remembers some of these misapprehensions. In any case, as your child grows she will probably enjoy reading about how cute she was as a talkative three-year-old.

Don't neglect to record your child's verbal advances as well. In what ways has she learned to cope with everyday situations and social challenges through language? How has she used words to reveal her thoughts, dreams, and fantasies to you? Has she created a collection of favorite jokes or stories? What are her favorite books, and how have they affected her perception of the world around her?

If you can, make an audio- or videotape of your child speaking this year, so you can compare it to how she expresses herself in the years to come. You may be surprised at how similar her later style of expression is to the way she comes across this year. By capturing her verbal expressions now, while they're still forming, both of you will better understand what went into creating the adult she will eventually become.

READER'S NOTES

CHAPTER 5

"I'm a Big Boy . . . Right?"— My Emotional Growth

P ositive exchanges between you and your child help him think of himself as competent, effective, good, and likable.

It's Wednesday evening, and as usual in the middle of the week, everyone in the Worlitzer family is in a rush. Andrea, just back from a long day at the office, is setting out the ingredients for a quick dinner. Her husband, Max, has already called to say he'll be at the office late tonight. Twelve-year-old Jodi practices the clarinet while ten-year-old Jena plays in her room with her best friend from next door. As often happens at times like this, three-year-old Noah is left to pretty much fend for himself. He wanders into the kitchen, eager for attention from his mom after a long day at preschool. "Can I help cook?" he asks his mom.

Andrea glances over her shoulder at him. "Okay," she says, "pull up the stepstool. You can stir the spaghetti." A delighted smile crosses Noah's face.

Just then the phone rings. Andrea answers it. Noah's smile fades now that Mom's no longer focusing on him. His gaze falls from her to the kitchen counter. There's the forbidden cookie jar, right next to the coffeemaker. They look so good . . .

As Andrea continues talking with her back turned to Noah, the hungry three-year-old pulls the step stool up to the kitchen counter. Nimbly, he climbs the steps, opens the cookie jar, and sticks his hand in. He is just savoring the first sweet bite when his mother's voice freezes him in mid-taste: "Noah! What do you think you're doing?"

Noah turns to look at his mother. "Nothing," he says in a small, guilt-ridden voice.

"You're eating cookies! I *told* you not to do that without asking me if it's okay. We're eating dinner soon!"

Noah stares at her, his eyes wide. *She's mad at me!* Shattered, he searches his memory for some way to fix this situation, but nothing comes to mind. He starts to panic. How can he make this "angry" mom—and this "naughty" boy—go away?

Andrea grabs the cookie jar and pushes it to the back of the counter. Then she grabs Noah's hand. "Come on," she says. "We need to wash you up."

Her rough handling only intensifies Noah's panic. The hopelessness of the situation overwhelms him, and he starts to cry.

"Oh, come on. I didn't even yell at you," his mother says more gently. "Just say you're sorry, and don't do it again."

Noah, a sensitive little guy, struggles mightily to swallow his tears. *Mom doesn't sound mad, and I like the new faucet in the bathroom. After I wash my hands, Mom will be happy.* He feels better just thinking about it.

Many parents of children just past their third birthdays will recognize Andrea's frustration at dealing with her child's deliberate misbehavior. On the one hand, children this age often seem to deliberately provoke parents with expressly forbidden behavior. On the other, they dissolve in tears and misery when their parents respond in ways the children should have expected. No wonder so many parents wonder whether their three-year-olds have regressed emotionally, are suffering from some hidden source of distress, or are responding to less-than-perfect parenting techniques. The reality is this sort of testing behavior is a normal and even vital part of your child's emotional growth this year. Doing something forbidden—and then watching one's world dissolve into accusations and anger—is a highly distressing experience for a very young child. This year, your three-year-old will begin the highly complex process of figuring out that the "angry" mommy and the "happy" mommy are the same, continuous person; that the "good" child and the "bad" child are just different aspects of himself; and that he can survive and even partly control the transition from one state to another.

Such comprehension, important as it is to your child's sense of stability, does not come easily, and it requires quite a lot of testing. Early in the year, your child will probably misbehave as Noah did, getting himself into that chaotic emotional situation he so fears, denying his transgression, and then crying when he fails to find a way out. As the year progresses and he continues to experiment with the emotionally powerful sequence of misbehaving, observing your reaction, and responding in different ways, he will learn that saying "I'm sorry" is one effective way to make the angry parent fade away and ease his discomfort. Hugging you is another. Promising not to misbehave in that way is a third. Explaining *why* he misbehaved is yet another, more challenging way to manage the transition from anger and guilt to forgiveness. As your child gains more experience with repairing emotional breaks and feels increasingly sure that he can resolve them, he will be less driven to deliberately misbehave in order to practice these skills that reassure him you still love him. I often tell parents that this emotional roller coaster is good practice for the same challenges they'll face in the teenage years. As he tests your responses, try to push your own natural frustration aside and focus on maintaining the firm limits he's looking for; showing him effective ways to repair the emotional break he's created (helping him clean up the mess or pick up the pieces) and demonstrating through your forgiveness (once he apologizes) that relationships continue despite the occasional disruption.

Certainly in the latter half of the year, your child will increasingly want to please you, his preschool teacher, and other adults important to him. He will probably delight in shared secrets, surprises, and exchanges of affection, and will more often understand that others' feelings are important, too. But three is also an age of turbulent emotions and a great deal of defiance as your child fights for the right to "do it himself," whines when he doesn't get his way, faces new fears brought on by his active imagination, and explores both negative and positive moods. Many parents of three-year-olds thus find themselves thrown for a loop when it comes to their children's behavior. By educating yourself about the steps of your child's emotional growth, you can prepare for and better understand the conflicts, tests, and even happy surprises that are bound to come your way.

"Honey, Mom Has to Go . . ."

"I just knew Beatrice would be one of the kids who had a hard time handling separation at preschool, and I was right," I overheard a woman tell a friend at my local coffee shop. "Every morning we'd talk about how it was a school day and I was going to leave her there for a little while, but I'd come back and get her in the afternoon. It didn't do any good. She screamed her head off the minute I even glanced toward the door of the classroom and grabbed my leg tight so I couldn't leave. I mean, this went on for two whole weeks—with the other kids just somberly watching us the whole time. It was total agony. I thought about giving up on preschool altogether, but my sister made me talk to the teacher about it first.

"That turned out to be a good idea, because the teacher was obviously experienced in this area. She said it was best to say good-bye quickly, so Beatrice could get the painful part over with and move on to figuring out how to feel better. She showed me how I could help Beatrice do that by focusing on the feelings of coming back—saying, 'I'll be so psyched to see you for lunch'—instead of dwelling on 'I'll miss you.' She said it was okay to do the separation in steps—so for a few days I hung around for a minute outside the window where Beatrice could see me, and then I'd just wave good-bye and leave. The teacher also got all the parents to put pictures of themselves in the kids' cubbies, so they could look at them when they wanted to.

"At first, it didn't really seem like all this stuff was getting through to Beatrice. She still had a really hard time saying good-bye, and I didn't know what to do. I mean, it was hard on me, too. But then one day after a couple of weeks, we walked into the classroom and she said out of the blue, 'I'm gonna draw a picture, Mommy.' She went over to the crafts table and sat down with

558 | WATCH ME GROW: I'M THREE

some markers. 'This is gonna be great,' she said. 'And when you come back and get me, Mommy, I'll give it to you!'

"I said 'bye and left, but she was so busy she hardly even looked up. What a little trooper. I don't know if her teacher gave her that idea for getting through the 'good-bye moment' or if she thought it up herself, but it sure worked for her. She still has some bad days, but if I can get her focused on making something to give me that afternoon, she manages so much better than she did."

"LOOK—THAT'S ME!": EMOTIONAL GROWTH AT AGE THREE

There's no denying that growing up has been a very exciting nonstop process for your active three-year-old. Utterly captivated as an infant by the sights and sounds surrounding him, your child eagerly grabbed the chance to learn more about his world as he learned to roll over, sit up, and grasp a wide variety of fascinating objects. Last year, he thrilled to his new power to walk, climb, and use words to get what he wanted. It came as quite a shock, then, when as a toddler he realized that there were limits to his independence, and many of these limits came from you. Every parent of a preschooler is long familiar with the cries of outrage, bitter defiance, and possibly even angry tantrums with which their children have greeted the word "no." Issues of safety, propriety, or fairness mean nothing to a child whose urge to explore and experience more has been stymied—yet in the end there is no getting around the fact that the grown-ups are in charge.

This year, to everyone's relief, your child's development will allow him to find a solution to this conflict. By *identifying* with you, or adopting your attitudes, rules, and characteristics as his own, he can share in your power instead of constantly opposing it. Like a boxcar hitching itself to a powerful engine, he can use your greater capabilities and experience to add to his own store of feelings and behaviors ("Me and Dad are brave guys. We aren't scared of the dark."), define his values ("Our family is nice to little kids."), solve problems ("When I get mad at Dad, we don't yell."), and more fully define himself ("Mom and me played on the computer today. We like the dinosaur game."). In most cases, this identification process leads to a new level of harmony in the family and is largely responsible for the widespread conviction that life with a three-year-old is often easier than it was the year before.

Your influence on his emotional sensibility has been building since birth. For the last year in particular, he's been watching how you handle yourself and is now basing his behavior on yours. A child who has regularly seen a parent who gets upset, talks about her feelings, and tries to resolve the situation calmly will learn those skills. A child faced with constant turmoil, aggression, or emotional tirades will imitate those tactics. If you do your utmost to provide a healthy emotional climate, odds are good that the constant conflicts will fade away. The two of you will feel better attuned, and the confidence your child gains from this parent-child team allows him to be more cooperative, generous, and patient in his dealings with you. He is able to relax and feel more secure and open to the many other emotional and cognitive changes that dominate the second half of this year. As a result, all of his emerging capabilities begin to coalesce into a new *coherence* of personality that seems to unfold magically before your eyes. His progress in understanding his own and others' emotions combines with his ability to express himself verbally—making for a much more insightful conversationalist and fewer outbursts. His increased confidence in regulating his own feelings (calming himself down, for example) joins with his greater emotional awareness to improve his general mood and interactive style. By age four, you may be surprised at how much more complex, capable, and perceptive your child is now than he was even six months ago. He will have moved from a somewhat fragmented, emotionally volatile late-toddler state to the full, rich, and fascinating condition of early childhood.

A CHILD'S-EYE VIEW

"We Don't Do That"

Empty! Greta peers through the open doorway into Daddy's study. The door to this "forbidden" room is rarely open, and Greta stares in awe at the mysterious computer equipment, heavy furniture, and book-lined shelves. Looking behind her, she sees that no one knows she's here. With a tingly feeling of guilt, she tiptoes into the room.

Big desk. Greta climbs up on Daddy's enormous leather desk chair and examines the items on the desktop. Paper. Pens. More books. Computer keyboard. With a thrill of delight, she notices her own framed photograph there. *Daddy's pen!* Greta stares at the shiny fountain pen lying unguarded on the desk. Daddy never lets her touch it. He says it's too messy. Greta picks it up.

"Hey, what's going on here?"

Excitement turns to anxiety at the sound of Daddy's voice. Greta drops the pen on the desktop. Daddy joins her beside the desk and picks up the pen. "Greta, were you playing with this?"

Greta looks up at her father's face. *Is Daddy really mad? He doesn't look mad.* She thinks about what to say. "It's so pretty," she says coyly.

Dad nods, then returns the pen to the table and picks Greta up. "In this family, we don't touch grown-ups' things without asking. Isn't that right?"

Greta looks very serious. Then she nods. "Sorry, Dad."

To her relief, her apology seems to have fixed things. Daddy carries her out of the room and lets her go. Greta runs to her room and closes the door—only to find her little brother, Benjamin, mouthing Binnie, her stuffed duck.

"Hey!" Greta yells, outraged. Benjamin looks at her, wide-eyed. *Benjy looks scared. This feels like when Dad saw me with his pen,* Greta realizes. Softening her expression and her tone, Greta approaches her baby brother and carefully removes the duck from his hands. "You have to ask to touch my stuff," she tells him firmly. Then she opens her door. Sounding as grown-up as she can, the nearly-four-year-old says, "Get outta here."

"NOT TILL AFTER DINNER": LEARNING TO MANAGE THE EMOTIONS

"I don't know what to do about Joey," I overheard a woman telling a friend as they stood in line at the dry cleaners one afternoon. "It seems like he has meltdowns over every little thing—more than he did when he was littler, I think. I keep telling him he's three years old now and big boys don't cry, but that doesn't seem to have any effect. I was at the playground with him the other day, and another kid pushed ahead of him in line for the swings, and he just stood there and cried instead of doing anything. I have to tell you, the first thing I thought was, 'What's the matter with him?' I don't want him to grow up to be a wimp."

It is very hard, sometimes, to be a three-year-old—wanting so much to please his parents and himself, yet still having such a tenuous hold on the skills he needs to succeed. Children this age are usually expected to maintain a reasonable level of self-control in spite of their strong emotions, to express their feelings in acceptable ways, and to adjust the intensity of their expression to suit a particular situation. These are complex and difficult tasks, made even harder by the fact that three-year-olds usually interact with so many more people now and may face sharply different situations outside their homes. (An only child, for example, may be humored at home when he loses his temper, but find that his preschool classmates won't play with him when he behaves that way.) Though your child's expanding experience will eventually help him learn to adjust his behavior according to where he is, it's important to keep in mind that learning to manage one's emotions takes practice, experience, parental support, and time.

Before your child can control his emotions, he has to begin to understand them. This year, your child will continue to learn a great deal about emotions through experience, conversation, and imaginary play. (Play especially allows him to experiment with "risky" emotions—by reprimanding his toy soldiers when he's angry at you, for example, or demanding that his action figure hurry up when he's impatient with his baby sister.) As a result, his comprehension and use of emotional words will expand rapidly. He will begin to understand more complex emotions such as jealousy, pride, embarrassment, and misery. By the end of the year, he'll have grown much better at identifying others' positive expressions, though he probably still won't be very good at interpreting negative ones. (He may not respond immediately to a critical adult, for example, but instead stare or smile at her in confusion.) Due to his trouble with appearance-reality distinctions (discussed in Chapter 3), he may also have a hard time distinguishing what people really feel from what they appear to feel (tears of joy don't make sense at this age).

Your child's better understanding of emotions, along with certain other cognitive developments, will improve his ability to tolerate frustration. In general, three-year-olds are less angry and tantrum-prone than younger children, especially later in the year (though those with certain temperaments still struggle to manage their emotions). Older three-year-olds are also better able to stick with a problem despite their frustration and respond in more productive ways, such as seeking direct help or moving from "Plan A" to "Plan B." (If your child has not already come up with these techniques on his own, teach them to him so he doesn't blow up so readily when things go wrong.) An expanded awareness of their environment allows three-year-olds to learn to adapt the level of their emotional expression to suit a particular situation. With your support and guidance, your child can now learn to use an "inside voice" and an "outside voice," line up quietly for recess at preschool but then run, shout, and play during recess, and so on. As he experiences more success in these areas, he will begin to drop less effective behaviors such as whining, crying, and outright defiance. Obviously, this will improve his relationship with you and other adults a great deal.

In gauging your own child's emotional maturity it's important to keep in mind that while three-year-olds do make remarkable progress in this area month by month, they still need your help and guidance to work on such skills as weighing future consequences when deciding how to act; stopping and thinking of possible ways around an obstacle; controlling their emotions when they're prevented from achieving a goal; blocking out irrelevant thoughts and distractions when working to reach a desired objective; and doing more than one thing at a time. These abilities aren't fully developed even by kindergarten, yet many parents of three-year-olds tend to get discouraged early in the process as they compare their child to the "perfect" kid next door who never seems to cry and wonder what they've done wrong. Keep in mind that different children develop these skills according to different timetables, dictated in large part by their natural temperaments (and anyway, how do you *know* that that other kid never cries?). They also tend to make progress in sudden spurts, often after long periods of relative stability or even regression. Changes in your child's life, such as a move to a new house, the arrival of a new baby, a new caregiver, or entry into preschool, will make it more difficult for him to manage his feelings for a while (not unlike adults). At these times, just tell yourself to hang in there a little longer. As long as you are supporting your child in his efforts to find ways around his frustration, demonstrating concrete strategies as these situations arise in everyday life, and letting him know that you understand and applaud how hard he's trying, he will learn to cope with his feelings more successfully in the months ahead.

EASING THE WAY

Mastering the Emotions Through Play

This year, your child probably spends much more time playing successfully by himself than he did when he was two. If you listen in on some of his solitary play sessions, you will probably hear him talking to himself or to his toys—perhaps acting out scenarios in different voices. If he has recently had a bad scare or other disturbing experience, or watched a violent show on TV, he may well act out the situation in his play. He may also cuddle his toys like a parent, lecture them like a teacher, or examine them as his doctor examines him. Clearly, your child is not just having a good time during these activities—nor is he only exploring social roles. He's also exploring the emotional content of these scenarios, working out any feelings of anxiety, and, by reversing roles with adult characters, resolving feelings of powerlessness. These activities not only improve your child's current emotional state, they also help him develop ways to maintain a healthy emotional balance throughout life. Now is the time when he begins to learn how to recognize an emotional problem, confront it, and do something about it, rather than simply avoid it or "act out."

For this reason, it's a good idea to let your child continue with such play uninterrupted whenever possible. This is his chance to learn techniques for emotional mastery that work best for him. Unless he is upsetting others or risks hurting himself (punching the pillow is okay, but punching the headboard is not), don't be disturbed if much of his play centers around negative topics—violence, arguments, being mean. Because fear and anger are such powerful emotions, preschoolers often focus much more on these issues in their play than on more benign feelings. If you notice that your child seems stuck in one scenario, try joining him in exploring it—taking one of the principal's roles and providing open-ended questions that will help him move toward a resolution. ("That leopard sure is mad at the bear. I wonder what the bear did," or "Ouch, that dinosaur really bit the other puppet hard. I wonder why?" If there's no answer, help him find a solution by adding, "Do you think he's hungry . . . or sad?") Reading a children's book on the topic might also help. Most important, remember that play is play—it's not real life. If your child feels the need to throw his stuffed bear onto his bed in the privacy of his room, allow him the freedom to work through this emotion. He will benefit from having a safety zone in which to experiment.

"I'M STRONG AND BRAVE": DEVELOPING A POSITIVE SELF-IMAGE

If you own a video camera, you may have noticed an interesting evolution in the way your child responds to the sight of himself on a video screen. As an infant, he cooed and kicked with delight at the sight of any baby's face on TV—but he clearly didn't recognize himself as the baby. At age two, your child no doubt recognized himself onscreen, but didn't really understand that he was still the same person as the one who had been videotaped earlier. In other words, he had no sense of the *continuity* of self—that the child being photographed was the same child watching television later, or that the "him" who was angry one moment was the same "him" who was happy the next. He might go so far as to stop in his tracks and say to the tape, "Why is that boy sad, Mom?" Only at around age three and a half, as your child's neurological development allows him to start to comprehend the flow of time and the concept of self-constancy (I am the same person this morning that I was when I went to bed last night), can he begin to combine these impressions into a unified sense of who he is. In short, his improved cognitive skills help create a richer emotional experience this year.

You will be able to observe your child's immersion in the process in many different ways—for instance, during his increasingly frequent "pretend" sessions in front of the mirror. As a three-year-old, your child not only enjoys playing the role of Superman or of a hairdresser at a beauty shop, but enjoys watching himself do so. As Dr. Dennie Wolf of Harvard University demonstrated in one 1990 study, most preschoolers can uncouple various aspects of experiences—they can pretend and at the same time observe themselves pretending. In fact, this magical experience of being me-but-not-me, and me-observing-me, fascinates young children, and is a sign of profound deepening of their concept of self-image.

It is a short step from observing oneself in action to "telling the story" of oneself. As a two-year-old, your child had already begun to narrate his concrete actions to himself. Now he moves beyond physical examples of himself to include emotional narratives ("I'm scared. I don't like that dog."). When interesting emotional scenarios don't happen to present themselves naturally, he may create them in his pretend play. Using his action figures to reenact conflicts he's observed or experienced not only offers your child a wonderful opportunity to explore complicated feelings but helps him define where he stands and how he wants to respond. Any child or adult who happens to be available will probably get pulled into the drama. Your child may even try a game of role reversal with you—pretending to be a stern parent, carefully observing your portrayal of him, and getting quite upset if your performance doesn't meet his expectations.

As he experiments with different stories about himself, he begins to generalize these experiences, creating a firmer concept of what sort of person he is and even a sense of personal history. You'll know he is far along in this process when you hear him boast on the playground, "When I was little I was scared of the big-kids' swings," or see him confiding to a friend, "I used to hate peanut butter. But now I know better."

The more your child comprehends the idea that he is who he is, no matter how he feels or acts at a particular moment, the more irresistibly drawn he will be to test whether this is true of other people, too. This is when he may misbehave in ways that mystify you (as we saw with Noah and the cookie jar at the beginning of this chapter) because you thought he'd gotten over those particular misbehaviors long ago. Once you understand the motivation behind his actions, however—to cause a rift between you so he can see whether and how it's patched up and the two of you become "you" again—it makes perfect sense for him to choose an act that he *knows* you will not like. As your child studies this process of righting wrongs and repairing relationships ("I'm sorry, Mommy"), you can help him understand that a bad situation can be reversed and it's not the end of the world. By not getting unduly upset over a mistake or an accident, letting him know that all people make mistakes and the important thing is to try to make it better, you support him in his efforts to become a better partner in regulating his emotions and correcting his behavior. By this age, your child is usually aware when he's crossed the line. If your "practice sessions" have been sufficiently positive and low-key, you will soon be able to just give him a warning look and he will automatically try to get his emotions in check and his behavior in line. Eventually, he will even self-correct—getting that "uh-oh" look when he tosses a wad of paper at the trash can and misses, looking at you, and then putting the paper in the can on his own without a word said. As he learns to begin taking responsibility for his actions, his sense of satisfaction will soar. He will bask in your praise or gratitude. Such positive exchanges between you and your child help him think of himself as competent, effective, good, and likable. As his idea of who he is begins to gel this year, this attitude will be extended to others in his world. Naturally, the better he feels about his own disposition, the more positively others are likely to respond to him.

All of these elements will contribute to your child's coalescing opinion about himself—his basic *self-evaluation*. This opinion will differ from how he felt before because it's based not on what you do or say about him but what he knows about himself. He can now feel genuine guilt about a specific act when he does something wrong (rather than the more global, all-encompassing shame he felt when you chastised him last year), and he understands the possibility of making up. He also feels pride when he does well (as opposed to the flush of pleasure he experienced when you praised him at age two), and this pride is also increasingly linked to specific actions. Toddlers often show just as much pleasure when an adult solves a problem as when they solve it, but preschoolers are usually happier when they find the solutions themselves. Your child's feelings of pride are also much stronger and more frequent when the problem he's solved or the task he's accomplished is slightly difficult. To satisfy his own higher standards of performance, help him up the ante a bit. This is an age when children start to get very bored with some of their old toys. By providing him with new, somewhat more difficult challenges (keeping the solution within reach, of course), you help him practice his problem-solving skills and give him something to brag about when his other parent comes home at night.

Fierce concentration takes the place of frustration this year, as three-year-olds improve their self-help skills.

"Faster!"

Three-year-old Amanda spins around and around in the bathtub, water splashing in all directions. Her dad, Lou, sticks his head in the bathroom and gives her a stern look. "Exactly what are you doing?" he asks his daughter. Amanda beams at him, ignoring the mild censure in his expression.

"Look, Dad, I'm spinning!" she says excitedly. "See, there are three settings. This is the easy setting." Drawing her knees up to her chin, Amanda spins around slowly in the bathwater, hardly splashing at all. "This is the medium setting." She spins around again, a little faster this time, splashing just a cup or two of water on the floor. "And this is the hard setting!" she cries, spinning around as fast as she can, with plenty of effort and a lot of splashing. "Isn't that great?" she demands when she's finished, grinning proudly at her father. "I can spin so fast! I bet I'm the bestest spinner in the family!"

Lou grins wryly. "You're a good spinner, all right." He grabs a towel and starts mopping the floor. It's good to see Amanda taking pride in her abilities and acting so satisfied with herself, even when she's playing alone. He just wishes it weren't such a messy process.

"I CAN DO IT MYSELF": MOVING TOWARD GREATER SELF-RELIANCE

"Mommy, I'm cold."

"Your sweater's hanging on the peg in your room, Sam. Just go get it and put it on, okay?"

"Moooommmy, you do it!"

"Sam, I'm busy right now. The sweater is right there on the peg. Go get it and bring it to me."

"Mooommmy, I'm cold."

Sometimes it seems as though our three-year-olds, who appear so competent and sophisticated in so many ways, can regress nearly back to infancy at a moment's notice.

Our expectations about what they can do soar this year, and as a result we adults tend to lose patience when they actually act their age. Your child will confront and master an enormous number of emotional, cognitive, physical, and verbal challenges this year. Sometimes, as for all of us, the pressure gets to be too much and he'd like nothing better than to be a baby again. Many three-year-olds actually demonstrate this to their parents—cuddling against their mothers' stomachs and pretending to drink from a bottle, for example.

Such moments are understandable, and it is a good idea to keep in mind that your child is, after all, only three. Still, by this age many parents long for an end to the clinginess of babyhood and look forward to the day when their child begins to look to himself a bit more in the face of difficulty. When this starts to happen depends on a number of issues, including your child's natural temperament, the events in his life, and your and his other caregivers' ability to help him learn to help himself.

Much of your child's sense of self-reliance comes from his experiences in the real world. By learning to tie his shoes, he not only keeps his feet covered but starts to think of himself as a person who can take care of himself in this (and, eventually, other) ways. As his abilities in all areas improve over time, and as he repeatedly experiences the satisfaction of managing his world in a host of tiny ways, his confidence increases and he takes pleasure in caring for himself. Clearly, if these minor tasks are usually done for him (if you always tie his shoes because it's too difficult for him to do, pour his cereal for him every morning because you're in such a rush, and hurry to comfort him after a scraped knee or hurt feelings instead of helping him figure out how to recover on his own), his progress toward self-reliance will be slowed considerably. Helping a child in this way certainly takes effort, but the long-term benefits are more than worth the energy spent. Resisting that first impulse to snap, "Boys don't cry," or "It's not that hard," and instead *showing* your child how to do things for himself is a start. Weaning him from emotional dependence on you by commenting, "You must be proud of yourself," instead of "I'm proud of you," bolsters your three-year-old's self-esteem even further and thus increases his desire to accomplish more.

Certainly, there are aspects of your child's life that affect his level of self-reliance yet are impossible to control. Some children are clingier than others by nature. A major life change (a parent's serious illness is one clear-cut example) will cause your child to look to you more often for emotional support than would otherwise be the case. Still, there are strong forces at work in your three-year-old's development that eventually come together to support greater self-reliance in an almost irresistible way. Each of these new skills reinforces the others, creating a newly *coherent* or *integrated* state of emotional independence. Your child's increasing ability to control his emotional expression (for example, not whining when he needs to wait his turn), his improvement in communication skills, and his greater physical abilities will encourage adults to trust him more to manage himself—and so he will. As he succeeds time after time, he will develop high self-esteem. Research shows, in fact, that by age four such successes in self-management will have led a child to assume routinely that others will respond positively to him and, as a result, they usually do. For this reason, no matter what obstacles stand in the way of your child's journey toward self-reliance, now is the time to help him experience the satisfactions (and reap the rewards) of "doing it myself."

IF YOU'RE CONCERNED

Emotional Dependency

It is usually easy to spot a preschool child who is struggling with dependency issues. He is the one who constantly hovers near his teacher, sits in her lap during story time, needs her help to perform such simple tasks as fetching his jacket from his cubby or playing with Play-Doh, demands constant feedback during free play, and maintains physical contact not just when upset or feeling affectionate, but nearly all the time. Such overreliance on adults is sometimes harder to see at home, where long habit tends to blur our vision. In general, you are right to be somewhat concerned if by the end of this year your child still clings to you frequently in everyday situations, acts out without any self-control when he's upset or angry (depending on you to calm him down), routinely resists dressing, sleeping, or using the toilet on his own, or doesn't engage in fantasy play without you.

If you have worked to encourage your child to experience the tiny successes that are necessary before he can attempt bigger ones (allowing him to succeed at putting on his jacket before you expect him to button all the buttons), and he continues to show no interest in performing such acts for himself, now is the time to address it. Talk with your child's pediatrician, caregiver, preschool teacher, or other adults who know your child well. Dependent behavior can prod adults to treat your child as needy—tolerating his behavior and doing things for him—thus encouraging the tendencies you are trying to correct. Look for ways in which all of you can allow your child to feel the satisfaction of small successes, thus starting a new positive cycle of behavior and expectations. Maybe it means encouraging your child to try something twice before he asks for help, or perhaps guaranteeing success by giving him tasks you know he can complete (folding a facecloth rather than a pair of pants when doing laundry together), or letting him choose what's for lunch and thanking him for bringing you the ingredients. Be sure to keep an eye on your own responses to his needy behavior and make sure they're not meeting your own needs. (This can be particularly true with first- or last-born children, whose parents tend to consider them the babies of the family.)

By starting small, and making sure that all adults concerned are working with your child rather than reacting to him, you should be able to deal with any immaturity that would otherwise stand in the way of his emotional and social success. Meanwhile, your child will have learned that he is capable of meeting emotional challenges and conquering them, and does not have to wait to be rescued.

"I'M OKAY NOW": COPING WITH STRESS

"I have a question about something I saw at a birthday party last week," a mother announced at a parenting meeting in my neighborhood.

"There were a dozen or so three- and four-year-olds at this party, and each one of them got a helium-filled balloon. Needless to say, at least half of the balloons got away and floated off into the sky before the party was over. When this happened, some kids would completely freak out, sobbing like it was the end of the world, and others would just watch it go in utter fascination and then run off and play. My question is, what's the difference between these kids? What makes one three-year-old break down when things go wrong while another one picks himself up, brushes himself off, and goes on his way?"

It's true that very young children respond in widely varying ways to all kinds of negative or stressful situations. Some of this variability has to do with their stage of emotional development. A child may be too young to realize that a balloon that gets away is gone forever, or young enough to be easily distracted until he forgets the balloon. Studies have shown that younger three-year-olds, while capable of recognizing an emotionally stressful atmosphere, will ignore it and move on if given a reassuring hug. As the months pass, though, a child's cognitive growth spurs him to wonder why the people around him are sad and what he can do about it. During my years at Children's Hospital in Boston, I frequently saw toddlers crying in frustration when their mothers ignored them—whereas older three-year-olds worked hard to figure out what was wrong ("Mommy, can you hear me? It's noisy in here!"). Clearly, a child who feels able to identify a problem, deduce its cause, and resolve it successfully ("I'll hold on to my balloon really tight next time") is likely to be more resilient in times of more serious stress. You can help your child stock up on emotional resilience for the times when he may need it by talking with him about a wide variety of negative as well as positive emotions, exploring options for solving dilemmas ("Sometimes people who are crying feel better if you give them a hug."), and helping him find solutions to everyday problems ("Would tying the balloon to your wrist next time help?").

Another predictor of how resilient your child is has to do with his relationship to you when he was younger. Drs. Alan Sroufe and Byron Egeland of the University of Minnesota found that, among children they studied who had encountered problems in preschool, those who were close to at least one parent from an early age recovered more quickly and fully than those who were less securely attached. This does not mean that your child is necessarily compromised if the two of you were prevented from maintaining emotional closeness in earlier years, nor does it guarantee problems if your child was, for example, adopted at a later age. (The researchers also found that the quality of a preschooler's current care also affects how well he functions, and that *improvement* in that care has positive effects even if his relationships were imperfect earlier.) What it does mean is that closeness to an adult at any age promotes a vital sense of security in a child, and that feeling of security is a primary requirement in the process of becoming resilient.

If you sense a certain fragility, insecurity, or lack of control underlying your child's approach to stressful situations this year, try addressing these issues of closeness and support in your relationship with him. Strike a balance between overseeing his behavior under stress and encouraging his efforts to become more independent. Remember, resilience is a quality that is built up over time. Keep in mind, too, that temperament—your child's inherited personality and style—also plays a role in how he responds to stress. If your child needs more cuddling than the three-year-old next door, it doesn't necessarily mean you haven't raised him well. Children are born with different personalities, and some children are naturally more volatile or sensitive than others. If you suspect that this is the case for your child, you may need to change your parenting accordingly. Make a point of introducing your child to new experiences gradually. If he doesn't do well in physical competitions and is miserable when he loses, avoid exposing him to losing in public when possible until he has learned to deal with these feelings. If he is an active child who responds to his emotions in physical ways, enroll him in a karate class or gymnastics program for preschoolers. Try to avoid such parenting extremes as overprotectiveness and insisting on a "stiff upper lip." In general, it's important to give your child room and space in which to *learn* to deal with stressful situations. By maintaining awareness of what makes your child feel insecure and avoiding focusing on immature emotional behavior, you demonstrate your support while he wades through challenges in his effort to grow.

Getting Through the Hard Parts

Q: I am in the middle of a messy divorce that includes a custody fight over our three-year-old daughter. What should I look for, specifically, in figuring out how my daughter is responding to the situation?

A: Divorce is never easy for a child, but the preschool period is a time of such rapid cognitive and emotional development that major stresses can make children feel particularly vulnerable. One of the first responses you may notice in your child is a tendency to regress. Recent advances may fade away as she gets upset or angry during even routine separations (being dropped off at child care) and minor transitions (stopping a game to accompany you to the grocery store). She may grow more clingy or may act just the opposite way, pushing you away when you try to help or comfort her. She will probably revert to acting out physically rather than using her words. In short, at least some toddlerlike behavior may return as she redirects her energy toward grappling with this new, unsettling problem.

All of this behavior is to be expected, and since it is sparked by an actual troubling situation is not in itself a cause for alarm. The fact is, though, that preschool children can be quite vulnerable to conflict between their parents. Three-year-olds are cognitively mature enough to notice and worry about the emotional disruption in their family, but not yet old enough to understand that the breakup isn't their fault. In the 1980s, Drs. Judith Wallerstein and Joan Kelly interviewed a large number of three-and-a-half to six-year-olds following their parents' divorce, and found that self-blame was the predominant response. They also found that preschoolers fantasized more than any other age group that their parents would get back together. If this notion comes up in conversation with your child, point out firmly that though there's no way that's going to happen, you both love her and you'll both be there for her. Expect that both parents will need to repeat this statement several times during the next few months before it starts to sink in. Meanwhile, monitor your emotional expression to be sure you're remaining available to her. A preschooler's anxiety over divorce is greatly amplified if the primary parent is depressed or emotionally withdrawn. Do your best to keep your anger, anxiety, or depression out of your dealings with your child. Make sure you get time out for yourself during this time so that you're really present and involved with her when you're together.

It also helps a preschooler if you maintain your routine together, even if it's not always convenient. (If you've always gone to dance class with her, keep it up now.) You will probably feel some relief at spending time together doing normal, everyday things, and your daughter needs to know that divorce changes relationships but is not the end of the world. As the weeks pass, keep a vigilant eye on her behavior. Most studies show that young children's adjustment improves markedly by two years after the divorce, provided parents can agree to handle disagreements cooperatively.

"I DON'T DO THAT . . .": MOVING TOWARD GREATER MATURITY

It's another Wednesday, and Noah is in the kitchen again—this time gleefully helping Mom bake a cake for his fourth birthday. With Andrea's help, Noah has chosen the type of cake, flavor of icing, and color of sprinkles to put on top. He has even made use of his new flour-sifting skills and is now placing the butter in the mixing bowl for creaming. Andrea observes the pride with which he follows all the rules of cake making—rules that he learned bit by bit through many harried Wednesday cooking sessions when Andrea would have given anything to be slumped in front of the television instead. The effort was obviously worth it, Andrea acknowledges as Noah solemnly announces, "And now for the creaming," and holds tightly to the mixer. What a difference she's seen of late. Noah doesn't get impatient when she stops to answer the phone. He sings happily to himself while she gathers ingredients. And even when he's grumpy he can usually be jolted out of it with a silly question like, "Should we make a cake as big as a house?"

As he waits for the butter to be thoroughly creamed, Noah's gaze moves toward the cookie jar at the back of the kitchen counter. *Oh, no,* Andrea thinks with a sinking feeling, *I should have put that thing away before we started.* Before she can move, Noah's hand has already reached out for the jar. But then, amazingly, he hesitates and frowns slightly. He glances at his mom, pulls his hand back, and looks Andrea full in the face. "We don't need cookies if we're having cake, right, Mom?" he says. And then he can't help but add, "But maybe I could have a little one?" He cocks his head and puts on his most angelic, hopeful face.

Andrea laughs, and reaches for the jar herself. "Sure, Noah," she says. "One cookie is okay. And good for you for asking first instead of trying to sneak one."

Noah looks very serious as he accepts a cookie. "I don't do that, Mom," he says somberly. "I follow the rules."

ADVANCES

Emotional Progress at Age Three

36 MONTHS	Increasingly inventive in fantasy play
	Argues with forcefulness
	Fears are common
42 MONTHS	Pretends to be "Mom" or "Dad"
	Negotiates solutions to conflicts
	Delights in secrets and surprises
48 MONTHS	Cooperates with other children
	Takes great pride in accomplishments
	Can wait for something he really wants

FIRST-PERSON SINGULAR

This year is such an eventful one emotionally that you will probably have plenty to record in this space reserved for your own observations. You will be able to write down your increasingly confident predictions about your child's personality as it becomes more fully formed. Record the solutions he comes up with to solve emotional dilemmas or conflicts or to deal with stressful situations. These solutions may come in handy again when he's older. You can both illustrate his high self-esteem and support it by taking notes on which activities he's proudest of. You might even paste one of his favorite drawings into this book, so he can discover on some future date what an active, creative, ambitious preschooler he was.

READER'S NOTES

CHAPTER 6

"Can I Play, Too?"— My Social Development

child's ability to get along with peers is one of the strongest predictors of later success.

"I played chase with Rhonda today. She's my new friend," three-year-old Maddy chatters excitedly to her dad, John, as he picks her up from preschool one afternoon. "She's in the fours' class. She's bigger than me. She can run fast. She says when I'm four I can maybe run fast like her. Fast as the big boys!"

"Wow," John says, exchanging an amused glance with another parent. Then he remembers. "Those are the boys you were talking about before, right? The ones who wouldn't let you play with them?"

"Yeah. The *bullies*." Maddy's expression darkens for a moment, but then her smile returns. "But Rhonda plays with them. They knock her down and she doesn't even cry."

Loaded down with lunch box, artwork, and a printout from the school, John ushers his daughter out of the classroom. He enjoys seeing Maddy so stimulated by contact with the other kids in her school and interested in learning how to get along with them. At the beginning of the year, she complained frequently about the older boys who wouldn't let her play with them and called her names. Now, through her new friendship with her four-year-old mentor, Maddy seems to be finding ways to deal with this social problem. John is also pleased to learn that this new social contact has Maddy looking forward to the day when she can climb trees "just like Rhonda." Just six months ago, he worried that she was too cautious on the playground. Now he makes a mental note to keep an eye out for risky experiments.

Social interaction expands and deepens quite a lot this year as three-year-olds start to note one another's behavior, wonder about the reasons behind it, and try out new approaches themselves. Not all children this age will express themselves so well or reach out to their peers with Maddy's eagerness and physicality. (Many three-year-olds prefer to hang back and quietly observe others, or to putter about on their own unless someone joins *them*.) Still, your child will probably be more friendly and outgoing than she was last year and will almost certainly have more opportunities to interact. Aided by such improving skills as sharing, taking turns, and participating in the rhythm of social give-and-take, your child will make connections that reap both emotional and cognitive benefits. As she compares her behavior to that of other children, discusses their personalities in still-limited ways, visits their homes and investigates their rooms, their toys, and their ways of interacting with their parents, she will begin to place herself in a social context—learning more about who she is, what she's like, and where she stands in the society of three-year-olds. As a result, her world and her view of it will expand immensely.

"SHE'S MY FRIEND": SOCIAL DEVELOPMENT AT AGE THREE

"Play nice, Claire." "Stop pushing, Andy." "Look, Cindy, there's Eileen. Remember, she's your friend from the park!" For months now, you have probably been nudging your child toward successful social relationships in all kinds of ways—only to feel perhaps a bit frustrated by your child's perceived lack of cooperation. We've all seen one-year-olds completely ignore the other child in the sandbox, two-year-olds playing back-to-back, and younger three-year-olds walk right past a smiling child to plunge their hands into a pile of clay. But when it's our child who acts this way, we feel it's a personality flaw. Mildly disappointing as these first forays may have been for you, they at least clearly demonstrated that making (and even desiring) friends takes a great amount of cognitive and emotional development and skill. Like it or not, the fact is true friendship isn't a social development that can be rushed, and the path to deeper relationships is paved with a certain amount of pushing, weeping, and self-interest.

It may come as something of a surprise, then, when your child does show a marked increase in social curiosity and activity at around the middle of this year. Though she has been preparing for this moment in many ways—learning to recognize and respond to others' emotional states, developing physical skills that enable her to participate in games, and working on her verbal skills—the same coming-together or coherence that so enhances her personality this year also adds new depth, complexity, and potential to her social interactions. When you stop and think about it, it is clear that your child's improved memory and other cognitive growth allow her to understand many subtleties in the social interactions going on around her. She has not only begun to notice other people's emotional responses but has begun to wonder what makes them feel or behave in certain ways and to try to predict what they will do next. Her new appreciation for the fact that others don't necessarily know what she knows or feel what she feels allows her to communicate more effectively. She makes more of an effort to explain or demonstrate her thoughts to others, to make sure they've understood her, and even to clarify her message if they seem confused. She enjoys telling jokes and studying her friends' reactions; suggesting activities to pursue together and watching others (sometimes) go along with her suggestions; comforting a child who's sad; and otherwise altering others' emotional states through her own actions and words. As her fellow three-year-olds also intensify their efforts to maintain contact with her, her relationships with her peers become much richer and more meaningful than before.

Many parents are especially pleased to find that group activities such as preschool or group child care become easier as their child starts to appreciate the company of others her age. Separation anxiety often begins to taper off more after the middle of this year (though it may return on days when your child is tired, you are rushed, or your morning is otherwise stressful). There will probably be less talk of how much your child missed you (or how she "hates school" or "won't go back") and more chatter about the children she played with, the activities she engaged in with the teacher, and (always a fascinating topic) what the other kids had in their lunch boxes. Through group interaction, whether on play dates, in the classroom, or even with older siblings, she will have a chance to experience longer, more complex fantasy play than you were probably willing to engage in. She will also learn a great deal very quickly about such issues as fairness and reciprocity, and may pick up useful techniques for repairing relationships ("I'm sorry. You can have the next turn."), recovering from a misadventure ("I hurt my knee, but I'm okay"), and even explaining others' behavior ("Joey's tired today"). Of course, not all social interaction involves positive behavior in children or adults. Therefore negative techniques such as hitting and manipulating can also be learned through social interaction, and it will become increasingly necessary to modify such learning through conversations with and conscious role modeling for your child.

As your child picks up new skills and techniques in one arena (at preschool) she transfers them easily to another (her relationship with her sister). This process of generalizing what she learns enhances her social competence enormously. For perhaps the first time, you may see her come up with a solution to a social challenge in a way that is effective but that you never consciously taught her (faced with only one bike and an envious friend, she gets off and says, "Here, you sit down and I'll push"). By praising these efforts and discussing which approaches work best, you can help her begin to actively choose how she will interact with others in her world. This process of creating and being comfortable with her own social style represents another giant step in becoming who she is.

IF YOU'RE CONCERNED

Social Competence

Some kids seem "born" to be social. From the get-go they are expressive, engaging, and fun to be around. They are fortunate, too. Research has shown that the preschool traits that most strongly predict social success include an ability to show enthusiasm, to positively engage with and respond to peers, to take the lead as well as follow, and to sustain a reasonable level of social give-and-take. Children who display one or two of these traits usually display most of the others as well, since they tend to develop in conjunction with one another.

On the other hand, your child may have a more independent, solitary temperament that is finding expression naturally as she matures. This is not a bad thing. Studies have shown that such children, who play alone happily and act according to their own agenda, tend to have a good sense of who they are and easily resist peer pressure when they're older. It's wise to keep in mind, too, that even very social children enjoy playing by themselves in group settings sometimes, and should be allowed to do so.

More important than your child's *willingness* to interact with others is the *tone* of the encounters she does have. If your child's contacts are mostly aggressive or consistently one-sided (with your child always following or bossing others), or if she tends to hover near a group of children but seems unable to join in, she may simply need to learn a few verbal scripts or other tools to grease the wheels of social interaction (such as following up "That one's mine," with "Here's one for you.").

When helping her learn such techniques, it's best to start small. Keep the social pressure minimal by inviting just one other child over for a play date—ideally, a child whose social skills are a bit more advanced. Three-year-olds can learn an enormous number of effective social skills from competent, tolerant friends their age. After the visitor leaves, praise your child for the ways she and her friend managed to agree on what game to play, share the toys, or cooperate on a project. Talk with your child about which actions or words made the play date more fun, and which ones caused arguments or tears. Later on, deliberately practice these same techniques when interacting with your child ("I'll start with yellow and you can have green 'cause it's your favorite.") and encourage her to do the same. As she gains experience with a variety of new social skills, her confidence will increase and you can gradually expand her circle of friends.

If you have focused on social skills a great deal this year but still see little progress, ask other parents what they think of your child's social competency and ask how they've handled similar social problems. Other adults who know your child may be able to offer a more objective view, and their tips are often right-on. Keep in mind, too, that successful interaction is still quite a challenge for any preschooler. Like their parents, three-year-olds have their good days and their bad days when it comes to dealing with others.

"I WANT THE PINK ONE!": LEARNING ABOUT GENDER

As your three-year-old participates in group activities more often and grows more aware of what's going on in her environment, she will start to notice and talk about the differences between the ways that boys and girls—and adult males and females—talk, dress, play, and perform distinct social roles. As we've seen in earlier chapters, the process of identifying with one of her parents will spur her toward thinking more about gender and what it means. By her third birthday, she may already tend to choose toys designed for her gender and play more frequently with others of her sex (though both of these behaviors are often strongly influenced by parents' actions and comments). As the year progresses, she will pick up increasingly on your opinions about "proper" behavior for a boy or girl, on the attitudes put forth by the media, and on others' responses to her own actions. She will probably begin to attribute positive attributes to her own gender and (in many cases) negative qualities to the opposite one. Near the end of this year, she may even become involved in more overt types of gender segregation in part as a result of the reinforcement she gets from her peers ("No boys allowed!" "Go away—you're not a girl!"), though this phenomenon is much more widespread at age four.

Some parents find their three-year-olds' single-mindedness regarding gender distressing, as it brings up issues of sexism and sexuality that are quite meaningful to us adults. It helps to keep in mind that your child is usually not dealing with those issues but is instead focusing on simple questions such as "What does Mommy do?" and "What does Daddy do?" Of course, the answers to these questions do contain larger implications. If stereotypes are important for you to deflect, you can expand your child's awareness of the *variety* of possible social roles by pointing out that dads cook dinner sometimes, moms run businesses, girls can win races, and boys can go to dance class. You might also want to monitor the gender assumptions made by other adults who spend time with your child. The pioneering work of Dr. Eleanor Maccoby at Stanford University, most recently documented by Dr. Beverly Fagot at the University of Oregon, has shown that ideas about gender come from many directions, including your child's caregivers, teachers, adult relatives, and parents of friends. Think of the obvious gender stereotypes found in the media, or of the pink and blue aisles of your local toy store. Other influences are more subtle but just as powerful. As just one example, the typical preschool class is often set up in remarkably gender-stereotyped ways, with play kitchens or dress-up areas in one space where it is assumed girls will usually play, and block corners and trucks in another to which boys are expected (and subtly encouraged) to gravitate. Caregivers or teachers may reveal a bias they didn't even know they had with such comments (often cheerfully offered) as, "Joey spent an awful lot of time in the kitchen area with the girls today!" You can counter such remarks, and tactfully convey your desire to allow your child room to experiment, by saying something like, "Oh, I'm not surprised. He helps me around the house all the time, and that's our special time together."

Certainly, some differences among children that you will see this year are biologically determined. In general, three-year-old boys around the world tend to be more aggressive than girls, while girls are generally more verbal; preschool girls are more interested in nurturing babies (or dolls) than boys their age; young girls usually prefer to play with one other child at a time, while boys prefer group activities. Beyond these generalities, your child will experiment with a wide range of attitudes and behaviors as part of the process of exploring social roles. Some preschoolers certainly go to extremes in acting out their own gender's stereotypes (a girl insisting on wearing frilly dresses to school or a boy who carries pretend guns everywhere). Others, or the same children at a different time, experiment with behavior typical of the opposite gender (a girl fighting on the playground, a boy adorning himself with necklaces), often as a result of having spent time with children of the opposite sex or from a different culture or background. Such mimicry is perfectly normal, and can be an excellent social tool, since a boy who's willing to join in a tea party may be more readily accepted by a female friend, and a girl who will help reenact the exploits of a male group's favorite superheroes is more likely to be accepted by them. Often the attention she gets from her peers for acting "different" actually reinforces the behavior.

Your responses to these actions are particularly important this year, since your child's gender identity will have become well established by the time she reaches kindergarten. As in other areas of development, a strong negative reaction from you will create anxiety around that issue and may result in an even stronger need to experiment or a feeling of shame when she engages in it. I've seen parents get particularly worked up, for example, in the case of boys who want to copy Mommy and wear nail polish and, to a lesser extent, toward girls who like to roughhouse with the boys. If your child's behavior is so stereotyped for the opposite gender that you fear it may lead to her being taunted or unfairly labeled, let her try out the behavior at home in private, so that she gets to experience a new action or style of dress. Often this is enough to allow her to move on. It's best to remain low-key in your responses, balancing your discomfort with her natural curiosity. If you (or your partner) are truly distressed by such behavior, you can find ways to dissuade it—offering alternatives ("Usually girls wear shirts, but I guess you can wear just an undershirt this time"), but be prepared to deal with your three-year-old's ability to note exceptions ("But that girl baby's not wearing a shirt. How come?").

A PARENT'S STORY

Where's My Leotard?

"Since Ralph was my first child, I tended to sign him up for lots of activities. So I didn't think twice about signing him up for ballet class," a colleague at Boston Children's Hospital said to me. "His friend Tracy had signed up the semester before, and Ralph fell completely in love with her little leotard and begged me to get him one, too. So I did, and since he was such a physical little boy I signed him up for ballet while I was at it.

"Needless to say, he was the only boy in the class of three-year-olds. He didn't care, the other kids didn't seem concerned, and his teacher was very politically correct, treating him just as she treated the girls. And Ralph just loved it. He wore his leotard every day that spring, and practiced his steps all the time.

"The problem, though, was the four-year-olds who waited outside the classroom for their class that immediately followed the threes'. There weren't any boys in the group, and the girls spent at least ten minutes before each class comparing their outfits, twirling like little dolls for one another, and otherwise just hilariously overdoing the ballerina thing. Most of their mothers played right into it, too—brushing their hair, telling the girls how cute they looked, and so on. When the threes' class was over and my Ralph walked into the waiting room in *his* dance outfit, you could hear a pin drop, the room went so quiet. It was really almost comical, how unnerved those little girls—and their mothers—were to see a *boy* in ballet clothes. Ralph didn't even notice it for the first half-dozen classes— though it really burned me up, I have to admit. But after a while I started to see him kind of falter a little when he entered the waiting room, and act a little self-conscious. There was just a lot of social pressure there from both parents and kids, and the older he got the more aware he became that he was not acting the way they expected a boy to act.

"So after a while he stopped wearing the leotard, and when I asked him if he wanted to sign up for another semester of ballet, he said no. But he still loves to be on the stage, so we joined a drama class where he can still dress up and be as dramatic as he pleases. I'm not sorry he had the ballet experience. I just wonder how many times we adults stifle good, creative urges in kids because we don't know how to handle someone who challenges the world as we see it."

"GIVE IT BACK!":
DEALING WITH AGGRESSION

Most parents of three-year-olds feel like old hands at dealing with aggression, from a one-year-old's smacking their nose with her head as she struggles to get down, to a two-year-old's pushing, to a three-year-old's grabbing a toy out of a playmate's hand. Although all of these kinds of behavior are aggressive, they represent different levels and types of aggression. As your child moves from the generally impulsive aggression of a toddler toward more overt aggression in which she *intends* to hurt someone, you may experience new concerns about how much of your child's behavior is acceptable and what to do to curb it.

Intending to hurt someone or to cause distress involves a level of cognitive development that takes full effect this year. As a toddler and younger three-year-old, your child may lash out more frequently than later in the year, but her behavior is usually just the result of immature verbal and emotional skills. As she begins to understand the concept of social agency (the idea that she can *make* something happen to someone), and explores ideas relating to fairness and justice ("She hit me first!"), she becomes capable of acting deliberately to cause distress. Just as a toddler learns that it's okay to turn the knobs on her toys but not on the radio, a three-year-old must try to figure out why it's okay to play-wrestle but not to push. These differences are hard to distinguish, since they're based on degree and consequences (someone getting hurt), not the action itself.

As parents and caregivers, we contribute to the confusion when we're not consistent—laughing at or overlooking a deliberate act of aggression one minute and getting angry about it the next. This year, while your child is experimenting with and learning to control her new ability to deliberately hurt someone, focus on teaching her the boundaries. Demonstrate how to ask first if someone wants to play instead of diving right in on the person and to stop as soon as the other person says to. Observe the context in which she becomes aggressive: Is she trying to achieve a goal (snatching a toy from another child), or is she just being hostile (pushing or taunting a child who wasn't harming her)? The former type of aggression, often called *instrumental aggression,* is a normal part of development for three-year-olds. Children this age who are very social are often the most aggressive in this way, partly because they play more often with other children. This type of aggression will gradually decrease as you firmly and consistently show your child other ways to get what she wants (trading toys, for instance). The latter type, called *hostile aggression,* in which a child bullies others with no visible goal, is more serious and should not be tolerated. If you see your child push a playmate to the ground, bite him, taunt him, or otherwise make him cry for no reason other than to create distress, remove your child from the scene immediately and don't let her return until she's calmed down. Eventually, she will associate such aggression with the experience of having no fun and will rely on it less and less.

No matter what type of aggression your child indulges in this year, your job as a parent is to show her how to resist the aggressive impulse and move on to other, more positive responses. Don't just punish your child for snatching a toy from a friend; show her how to ask nicely for the toy, offer something in exchange, or suggest taking turns. Don't just sit silently with your child once you've removed her from an aggressive situation. Talk with her about better ways to get and maintain a playmate's attention—by using her words, or participating in what the other child wants to do. In the latter half of this year, you can help your child begin to understand how her playmate feels when she's been victimized by reminding her of a time when she felt that way. Once she understands what she's done wrong (and only then), have her apologize to her friend or otherwise make amends (hand over the toy). Keep in mind that you may have to go through this process many, many times before the message sinks in. She may miss much of the content of your explanations until she's nearly four. In the meantime, consistency, repetition, and nonjudgmental firmness are key in teaching your child alternatives to deliberate aggression. Your own consistent avoidance of aggressive behavior is also a vital way to communicate its unacceptability to your child. Yelling at your child to stop hitting other kids or you're going to spank her will not teach her to stop hitting.

It's important to note that preschoolers have lots of role models besides their parents when it comes to aggression. Most three-year-olds watch more television now than they did when they were younger (an astounding three hours a day on average, according to one recent survey), and parents tend to lighten up on restrictions for what their kids watch, especially regarding animated shows. And kids, left to their own devices, rarely monitor their own viewing choices. Yet studies have shown that watching violent television shows translates quite often to aggressive behavior in young children. Your child doesn't have to watch police thrillers to start thinking more aggressively. Cartoons, with their slapstick humor and animated violence, give three-year-olds compelling ideas for new kinds of aggression that they wouldn't have otherwise. (As proof, just watch a preschooler play in the five minutes after a cartoon or computer game.) The combination of a child primed to explore deliberate aggression and a television program that provides fascinating new forms of it is a potent cocktail. It's easy to see why limiting the amount and content of your child's television viewing is so important this year. I always advise parents to try to keep TV time down to an hour or so a day, to make room for less passive activities and more time for reading, drawing, and game playing. If you find that you must occasionally use TV as a baby-sitter for brief periods, at least provide familiar videos (often available free at your local library) whose content doesn't make you uncomfortable. Parent-oriented magazines provide updates on age-appropriate videotapes as well, or you can borrow from or trade with a trusted friend. Luckily, three-year-olds will watch these same tapes over and over.

As your three-year-old spends more time with friends her age, she is also more likely to become the victim of other children's aggression, both random and deliberate. Painful as these experiences can be, if handled well they can serve as opportunities to further emphasize and expand on your feelings about this issue. If the other child's aggressive behavior is relatively minor (a slight push, a mean comment), it's best to let your child try to find a solution to the problem on her own (eventually she will have to deal with these situations by herself anyway). If your child starts to appear over-whelmed or is seriously hurt, you will have to step in. This is best done by going directly to the other child rather than his parent, making eye contact, and saying calmly and firmly, though in a sharp enough tone of voice to get his attention, "Hey, we don't do that." Then take the toy away or get between the children if that's what it takes. If you know the parent, you may toss her a look ahead of time to warn her that you're going to interfere, but don't be shy about making your move even if you don't know who or where the child's parent is. The child will probably listen more carefully to you, a less-familiar adult, than to his parent who's probably told him to "play nice" a thousand times—and it's important for your own child to know that serious aggression will not be tolerated. In any case, most parents will back you up, and a brief discussion after the fact will reinforce the lesson for your child that hurting others is wrong.

A CHILD'S-EYE VIEW

"Stupid!"

There. Good castle. Now I need a moat. Louis concentrates hard on his sandbox creation. Playing in the sand is his all-time favorite activity, and he's become an expert builder of castles. He sticks his fingers deep into the sand, digging a moat where the sea monsters will go. He glances over at his mom, who's sitting on a bench chatting with friends. She grins and gives him a thumbs-up sign. Turning back to his work, Louis mutters to himself the words from a book about castles that Mom read him last night. "Lower the dawbridge," he says in a low, commanding voice. And then, in a different voice, "I will not! No way!"

"Hey, what're ya doin'?" A kid's sneaker appears on the sand half an inch from Louis' moat. The three-year-old looks up to see a bigger boy scowling at him.

"Digging," Louis answers solemnly. "This is a moat."

"What's that supposed to be?" the boy says, indicating the castle. "A mountain?" He sits down on the sand next to Louis, stepping on the moat in the process.

"It's my castle!" Louis backs up a little, feeling wary. *I don't like him*, he thinks.

"That's a *castle*? Looks like a stupid one to me." The older boy reaches over and casually smashes Louis's castle with his fist.

"Hey!" Louis yells. "Stop that!"

"You baby. There!" With one swipe of his sneaker, the older boy finishes obliterating Louis's castle. "I can make better castles than that," he boasts as Louis starts to cry.

Mean! Louis is so overwhelmed with fury and frustration that he doesn't know what to do. He wails loudly, and tries to kick the older boy, but misses—which only makes him feel worse. Almost immediately, he feels two hands under his arms pulling him up and out of the sandbox, away from this bully. He sees his mom lean down and talk directly into the other boy's face. "We don't talk like that," she says sternly. "And we don't smash each other's stuff, either. Go find your mom."

Louis's mother carries him over to the park bench, where she cuddles him on her lap. "You're okay," she tells him. "That boy didn't know how to behave. But look—his mom will tell him he was wrong. He'll leave you alone next time."

Louis wipes his eyes and looks over at the sandbox. The boy's mom is standing over him now, yelling really loud and pointing toward them for emphasis. The yelling makes Louis uncomfortable, so he puts his hands over his ears and stares. He's relieved when he hears his own mom call over his head, "It's okay. We fixed it, it's over." The other mother looks toward them and then yanks her son away.

"No wonder that boy's so mean," Louis's mother mutters. Louis doesn't understand what she's talking about, but he realizes he's no longer angry (even if he is still a little sad). "Tell you what," Mom says. "Why don't I help you build a new castle, and then we'll do the big slide?"

"I wanna slide now," Louis says, hopping to the ground and running off. He feels better now that the big kid is gone, and he's ready to play again.

"PLAY NICE": ENCOURAGING PROSOCIAL BEHAVIOR

Fortunately, the same "I can make it happen" ability that enables your child to deliberately hurt someone also allows her to direct her behavior in more positive ways. Three-year-olds are generally much better than

Three-year-olds thoroughly enjoy imitating one another, and in general play together more cooperatively.

toddlers at sharing, taking turns, and asking politely for things, though they won't always choose to use these improved skills. Their better memory and their emerging understanding of others' feelings helps them understand why such social gestures make sense, though. The more practice they have with social interaction, the more adept they will become at getting along with others, especially if you continue to prompt, praise, and otherwise support them in their efforts. Fortunately, as their sense of their own identity strengthens near the end of the year, they will not need your prompting as often. This new social dexterity is another pleasant aspect of parenting an older three- or four-year-old.

Of course, the understanding that she can direct social interaction has its downside, too. (There's a difference between making your wishes known and getting your own way all the time.) As your child adds an increasing number of polite scripts to her repertoire, she is bound to experiment with using them to get her own way (sweetly telling a younger child, for example, "I know you like chocolate, so I'll let you have this piece tomorrow"). As she begins using words in place of aggressive actions, she will also start to negotiate for what she wants and will continue negotiating as long as you let her. Amusing as these "nice" ways to manipulate others can be, it's not a good idea to let her see you laughing at her efforts or indirectly reinforce her for having found this new method to get her way ("Nice try"). She will bask in your (perceived) positive reaction and immediately step up her efforts to use language to accomplish her wishes, in contrast to yours. Soon, every time you ask her to sit still at a restaurant or on the bus, she will want to negotiate how long she should sit still and in exactly what position; when you tell her she must finish dinner before playing a computer game, she will negotiate you down to ten bites, then eight, then seven, then two. By age four, she will have become such an expert negotiator that you may regret every sign of approval you gave her—so calmly nip these attempts in the bud before your child forgets who's the parent.

Part of developing good social skills involves progressing out of the toddler's typical self-centered nature or egocentrism. Though your child has long shown a certain awareness of your feelings and has now begun to note others' emotional states, she will only grasp the significance of those feelings and start to understand her effect on them at a very simple level this year. Even when she does finally understand that a sad expression on her friend's face means she might have made her feel bad, she won't necessarily act on her perception. (For one thing, out of sheer habit, toddlers and younger three-year-olds generally wait for any adult in the room to solve such social problems.) During the first half of this year, consider it a victory if you can get her just to think about others' emotional responses ("Well, maybe next time you'll share your crayons with Judy, and then you can both be happier"). As she shows signs of paying more attention to others' actions and expressions and using them to infer their point of view, show her ways she can affect those feelings through her own actions—by sharing, comforting, cooperating, and otherwise finding ways around a potential conflict. In the meantime, don't get too worried if your younger three-year-old still sees no reason to share or take turns. Research shows that even at this age spending 40 percent of playtime in nonshared activities is the norm. As long as she is making some progress beyond her toddler state—and you and her other caregivers are supporting and keeping a watchful eye on her—she should eventually realize that treating others well not only feels good but encourages others to return the favor.

Setting a Good Example

Positive social behavior is an area in which your influence as a parent can make a particularly strong difference, and this is an effective year in which to teach such skills. Studies show that one of the greatest influences on a young child's social behavior is the parents' style of caregiving. If you empathize with your child's and others' feelings and make an effort to be helpful, your child will behave more empathetically than if you just tell her to be nice to her friends. If you listen to your child with respect, use "please" and "thank you" when interacting with her and others, and control your aggressive behavior, she will behave the same way while picking up some valuable self-regulation techniques.

Understanding the stages of your child's social development and responding to your child's behavior accordingly is another way you can act as an effective social guide. As pointed out earlier, your thirty-six-month-old is probably not yet able to understand that the friend who wasn't allowed to share her crayons is as bereft as she would be in the same situation—much less the fact that her refusal to share *caused* her friend's sadness. *She can go find other crayons,* she might be thinking. Or, since her memory is still so short-lived, she may actually forget about her friend as she gets absorbed in her drawing. It's important not to expect too much while your child is still developing these abilities early in the year. Still, even before your child can fully understand you, start talking about these issues so that when she is ready (probably somewhat before you notice a change), you will be there supporting and encouraging her growth. Even at thirty-six months, take the time to clearly (if briefly) explain to your child what's making the other person sad ("Judy's crying because you wouldn't give her a crayon"), tell her what the rules are for social behavior in this case ("We always share with our guests"), and speak with enough emotional intensity (but not anger) to let your child know that this issue is important. Later, when you have quiet time together—while riding in the car or reading a book—walk her through what she might have done. What could she do to fix this problem, and how would that make her feel? Fantasy play can also help your child explore social rules and concepts ("Look, Bear wants to play with the other animals. What can he do about it?"), and find the techniques that are most effective for her.

One step that many parents neglect in teaching their children good social skills this year is to step back gradually as their child begins to deal competently with others on her own. All young children, including three-year-olds, need plenty of practice in putting new skills to good use. As you see your child's capacity grow in handling conflicts and other social situations, make it a goal not to dive in to fix every potential problem. Wait and see whether your child can figure out how to make two kids happy with one cookie, to give a friend some crayons to make her stop crying, or to distract a child from aggressive behavior by suggesting a new game. Research has shown that holding back in this way greatly improves preschoolers' social problem-solving skills. Older-three and four is not a bad age for your child to join the other kids in the neighborhood on her own two feet and start finding out where she stands, provided watchful grown-ups are nearby to intercede if necessary.

"COME TO MY HOUSE": DEVELOPING EARLY FRIENDSHIPS

As your child's language and social skills continue to grow, her relationships with children her age become more meaningful and coordinated. Three-year-olds form budding friendships that can last for a year or even longer. At this point their friendships are based on pretty superficial characteristics, such as liking the same toys, having the same level of physical activity, living next door, and so on. Parents' support is one reason for these friendships; another is that children this age tend to see one another more frequently in such venues as preschool, at the child-care center, or in the neighborhood. By age four your child will have developed the ability to make friends on her own and to remain invested in those friendships over time. Next year, these relationships will become even more important to her.

You may have noticed that your child now behaves somewhat differently with children she considers her friends than she does with non-friends. Friends this age tend to cooperate more often and interact more positively in other ways. They also disagree more often than non-friends do, but such conflicts are often less heated, end in fairer solutions, and don't as frequently cause the children to separate. Like adults, kids this age seem to understand that some relationships are more important for them to maintain. Their desire to get along motivates them to practice, experiment with, and use the social skills they're beginning to learn. If your child's friend happens to be somewhat more advanced in her social skills, interaction with her may speed up your three-year-old's progress.

As we've seen, this is a year brimming with magical thinking and animism in many forms, so it's not surprising that your child may count nonliving objects (a doll, blanket, or stuffed animal) or imaginary play-mates among her closest friends. Statistics vary regarding the frequency with which preschoolers invent imaginary friends (estimates range from about 30 to 50 percent of all children this age), and it is certainly a difficult number to estimate when such friends may last for a day, for six months, or for several years. In any case, it's comforting to know that though imaginary playmates do "appear" more often to children without siblings than to those in larger families, they are apparently more a product of a developing imagination than a sign of loneliness or emotional stress. In most cases, such relationships provide an excellent forum for your child to experiment with different social behaviors, emotional expressions, and other activities. It is not surprising, then, that imaginary friendships generally have a positive, stabilizing effect on children and, research shows, are often found in children who are more creative, cooperative, independent, and happy.

If your child is in the thrall of a stuffed elephant or an invisible play-mate, you will certainly want to respect her pretend play and accept her friend, but there's no need to go overboard. Three-year-olds are old enough to know the difference between "pretend" and reality, and your child will know you're fooling if you act as though her friend is real. Allow her to use her friend to talk with you about her feelings or other subjects that may be difficult for her—but be aware of three-year-olds' tendency to try to manipulate. On those inevitable occasions when she blames her friend for a mess she made, assure her that the friend can help *her* clean it up.

THE TOY BOX

"Bimmy's Bad"

For the past fifteen minutes, Paul has been playing alone in his room. His dad, Frank, who's making lunch nearby, has overheard enough to know he's talking to Bimmy again. Bimmy is Paul's imaginary friend who appeared shortly after Paul's third birthday and has been hanging around pretty regularly in the six months since. The conversation in Paul's room sounds pretty intense, so Frank is prepared when Paul emerges with a somber look on his face.

"Daddy, Bimmy's sad," Paul says, his chin quivering.

"What's the matter, son? Did he lose his blankie?" (The blankie is Bimmy's favorite accessory.)

"No. He's sad 'cause he misses Snowy. He can't find her."

"Oh, I see." Frank puts down his spatula and turns down the burner on the stove. Snowy is the family's pet cat who died several months ago. Frank knows that Paul has had a hard time under-standing what happened to her. When he was two, he refused to acknowledge his parents' explanations about Snowy's death, insist-ing, "No, she just went out for a long walk." In the months that followed, he revisited the issue occasionally, sometimes crying for five minutes or so, sometimes asking questions before he dropped the subject again and went off to play. Frank is relieved in a way that Bimmy has finally gotten involved in this problem, because he has always come in handy in helping Paul figure things out.

"Paul, you remember that Snowy died, don't you?" Frank says, squatting down to Paul's level and talking in his gentlest tone of voice. "Did you tell Bimmy about that?"

"Yes," Paul says tearfully. "But he doesn't believe me."

"Well, tell him that it's true. Snowy died, and that means we won't see her again. I miss her, too. But new kittens are born every day."

Paul, still looking a bit confused, says, "Are we going to get a new kitten?"

Dad says, "Not right now, but maybe when you're four. We can go to the pet store and look at some if you want to."

Paul frowns thoughtfully. "Just a minute," he tells his dad. He turns partly away from Frank and engages in a long, pantomimed conversation with his invisible playmate. Frank waits patiently until Paul turns back to face him. "Bimmy says he's better now," Paul says. "He says we can go look at kitties after lunch."

"Okay," Frank says, giving his son a quick hug. "I'm glad you and Bimmy could talk about it."

"IS IT A SCHOOL DAY?": CONSIDERING PRESCHOOL

This year, it's a sure bet that your child will experience more frequent and meaningful encounters with other children and with adults outside her family. These opportunities to soak up the customs and values of her culture, experiment with tools for interacting successfully, and begin to get an idea of where she stands in the world, will help her understand how she compares to others, and how she feels most comfortable dealing with people. In these years before kindergarten, preschool or any other group situation offers valuable social experience. If your child seems reasonably comfortable and competent during one-on-one play dates and separates from you without too much anxiety, she may benefit from the gradual introduction to group life that small, high-quality preschool classes provide.

It is important to consider, however, that both positive and negative experiences shape your child's self-concept and style of interaction. In other words, group interaction has the potential to increase her social confidence and skills enormously—and has the same potential to decrease or delay them. This is why the quality of the preschool or group care facility is such an important factor in choosing whether or not to enroll your child. Smaller groups are preferable for children with no previous group experience. They allow your child to move from single-person relationships to a group experience at a rate and in ways she can handle. Children with extensive child care or group experience may do fine in much larger groups, but you should make sure that the preschool does meet the standards of the National Association for the Education of Young Children (NAEYC). Placing your child in a chaotic situation in which her social interactions are largely unsupervised can be worse than forgoing group situations this year, especially if she doesn't have a highly sociable temperament.

Ironically, parents and preschools often put more emphasis on physical readiness—that is, toilet training—than on emotional readiness. But your child's stage of development is something to consider carefully. If your child has not yet achieved the ability to empathize with other children—to understand that they have feelings and a valid point of view—she may encounter social or disciplinary problems that will make her group experience largely negative. If she has not learned some basic social skills such as (usually) listening to children who are talking to her, stopping an action when asked to, or sharing and taking turns reasonably often, she may end up feeling disliked or rejected by her teacher or peers. A number of recent studies have shown that a child's ability to get along with peers is one of the strongest predictors of later success in social adjustment, psychological health, and even school achievement. It's therefore a good idea, when possible, to wait to introduce a group experience until your child stands a good chance of succeeding.

If work or personal considerations leave you with no choice about timing, take extra care to locate the best-quality environment you can and plan to support your child more than usual as she struggles to adapt to this new situation. Keep in mind that many parents notice a great improvement in their children's group experience after age three and a half, once their empathic and other social skills begin to assert themselves. If your child experiences a rough transition into group care or other trouble at any point in the year, resist the impulse to blame it on the program or to pull her out prematurely. (It may make her anxiety even higher when reentering next year, when the group will have coalesced without her and she will have missed the chance to make friends.) Instead, support her with some remedial experiences: one-on-one play dates in which she can practice her skills, conversations with you about how to handle certain situations, and, if possible, more focused help and attention from her caregivers. If you can, volunteer to occasionally come and help at the preschool. Even your sporadic presence can provide her with enough reassurance. Little things like being early at pickup but not early for drop-off can also make a big difference to a child who is still unsettled or anxious about separation. Consider car-pooling with a classmate. The car time together is a good transition period for most kids. Keep the separation brief and focused on the reunion, or on an activity she can do while you're gone ("Look, Susan and Laurie are stringing beads. Why don't you go make me a necklace? You can give it to me when I come back.") With your guidance and understanding—and good communication with the adults in charge of her care—your child can overcome a difficult beginning to interact more effectively in the group, thus paving the way for greater social success.

Q & A

Suspended!

Q: My three-year-old was sent home from school the other day for sassing her teacher one time too many. Specifically, she refused to clean up her art materials before recess and when her teacher insisted, she put her hands on her hips and snapped, "You can't tell me what to do!" The head of the school decided to send her home for a day or two until she was ready to behave more appropriately. I didn't even know preschoolers could be suspended! Naturally, I'm appalled by her behavior, but I'm also worried that she feels like she's failed at school. What should I do?

A: Three-year-olds can be masters of defiance, and it sounds like your daughter hasn't yet understood who's in charge in the classroom when you're not around. The first thing you need to do is talk with your child's teacher and make sure you have the story straight before you address your child. Once you have a pretty good idea what happened, sit down with your daughter and explain the preschool situation—that the teacher takes your place when you're not there, and that she does indeed tell the children what to do. Next, ask her why she didn't want to do what her teacher suggested. She will probably try to duck the question (she may not remember why she acted in that way), but however she responds, explain calmly and nonjudgmentally that certain routines must be followed, that we all have to clean up after ourselves, and that if she has a problem with that she should talk with you about it instead of yelling at her teacher.

All of these are lessons that your daughter will easily learn over time, as long as you are consistent and firm in reiterating them for her. Your more important concern, as you stated, is that she not feel she has failed utterly as a member of her preschool group. To prevent this, help her figure out a way to repair the situation. Perhaps have her draw a picture for her teacher showing how sorry she is, make a card and write her name on it, or otherwise do something concrete that will give her an avenue back into her teacher's good graces. The day before your daughter returns to school, call her teacher and discuss ways to make her reentry a positive experience. Then bring your child to school with her picture, card, or other creation, and, if at all possible, allow her to approach her teacher herself. I'm sure the teacher will meet your daughter more than halfway—and your child will have learned a very important lesson not only about good manners in the classroom but about forgiveness.

"I'M WITH THE BIG KIDS": BECOMING PART OF A GROUP

"I'm not a three anymore, Dad. From now on, I'm a *four*." Maddy throws her backpack over her shoulder with all the bravado of a "threes"-class graduate and leads the way out of the classroom on her last day of school. Her dad, John, dutifully follows her, marveling at the confidence with which she waves good-bye to her schoolmates and pauses to give the head of the preschool a farewell hug.

"I guess next year you'll be able to teach the three-year-olds how to play with the boys," John suggests as they load her end-of-school projects into the car.

"Those boys are going to kindergarten, Dad. They won't bother us anymore."

Well, there will always be more boys, John thinks, buckling her into her booster seat, but he doesn't want to bring up a touchy subject now. The fact is, with the help of her friend Rhonda, her teachers, and her parents, Maddy has learned how to negotiate many of the social challenges that were so difficult for her a year ago. Not only has she really enjoyed going to school most mornings for the past few months (a big change from the wailing John suffered through back in September), but her verbal and cognitive skills have soared due to so much interaction. Looking back on the year, John wonders briefly whether they had started Maddy in preschool a little earlier than was best for her, but her supportive environment and her natural resiliency had carried the day.

Not a perfect experience, but a good enough one, John decides as he starts the car and waves good-bye to the other parents outside the school.

"Hey, Dad," Maddy says from the back seat. "There's my friend Rhonda! Can she play at my house tomorrow?"

ADVANCES

Social Milestones at Age Three

36 MONTHS	Aware of what being a girl or boy means
	Imitates others in more complex ways
42 MONTHS	Starts to play more agreeably
	Able to share, even with unfamiliar children

Enjoys secrets and surprises

Likely to prefer same-sex playmates

48 MONTHS   Wants to please, especially adult caregivers

Friends are important

Adjusts better to new situations

Expected gender roles are firmly laid out

FIRST-PERSON SINGULAR

Your three-year-old's social life will become increasingly important to her this year, so make a point of recording the names of her friends and their favorite activities. Observe which social skills she picks up easily and which ones she has trouble with. (It will be interesting to compare this list with a similar one ten or fifteen years from now.) How does she respond to inappropriate behavior from other children or adults, and how might you help her respond more effectively?

Be sure to write down those instances when your child accomplished an utterly unselfish or kind act, and record those instances when her amazing insight into people's relationships blew you away. If your child has invented an imaginary friend this year, describe it here and write down the ways it was included in the family. Finally, if your child has entered group care or preschool by now, describe the ways she found to adjust to her situation, and predict how she might use similar techniques when confronting future unfamiliar situations (such as a change to elementary school, taking music lessons, or a first sleepover). It will be interesting to show her what you wrote later on—and she may even pick up a few helpful tips from her younger, innovative self.

READER'S NOTES

CHAPTER 7

A Guide for Life—
My Need for Routine

T here's no such thing as too small a job at this age.

For the second time this week, Janet is running late to her early-morning class at the university. She races around the apartment grabbing books, glasses, car keys, and three-year-old Shane's coat, muffler, and mittens, calling to Shane to hurry up and finish getting dressed. Grabbing her own coat out of the hall closet, she notices a big strawberry jelly stain on the sleeve—a souvenir of yesterday's lunch with her son. Frantic now, Janet races into the bathroom to scrub the stain off, yelling, "Shane, are you ready to go?"

"Yeah, Mom. I put on my favorite clothes!" Shane shouts back from his bedroom. Janet relaxes a little. Thank goodness he's started insisting on dressing himself for the past few weeks. He seems to like being an active player in their morning routine, and Janet, a busy single mother, is all for supporting him in this new development.

"See, Mom? Look at me!"

Janet looks up from scrubbing to see her son standing in the doorway, the picture of self-satisfaction. He's wearing, on this February morning, bright red bathing trunks (his favorite color), a pair of sandals from their trip to the beach last summer, and a faded red T-shirt with the name of his soccer team emblazoned on the front. *Where did he find that stuff?* Janet wonders. Struggling for a tactful response to his getup, she says lamely, "Uh, that's great, Shane. You might need some long pants today, though." She checks her watch, gives up scrubbing her coat, and then tosses it on top of the laundry basket in the corner. What's the use? She's never going to get to class today. "Come on, kid," she says, taking Shane's hand. "Let's see what else you've got in your closet."

Old enough to participate in the routines of daily life, but too young to be always effective at them, three-year-olds once again find themselves caught in the bind of appearing more competent than they really are. As your child becomes increasingly interested in controlling at least some aspects of his day-to-day care, he will begin to insist not only on dressing himself but on brushing his own teeth, pouring his own bowl of cereal, and perhaps even making his own bed. Chances are he will not accomplish any of these tasks even close to perfectly. Still, it's important for him to take his place as an active (if still decidedly a junior) partner in his care. Routines continue to provide your three-year-old with an important sense of stability, predictability, and self-confidence. By making it easier for him to participate in the activities of daily life (keeping only clothes you like him to wear in his dresser drawers; buying easy-to-handle pint-sized cartons of milk for him to pour on his cereal; using just a fitted sheet and a comforter for his bed so he can make it quickly) and overlooking those unbrushed molars or clashing colors now and then, you can help him begin to provide that sense of stability for himself, and start him on the road to self-management.

A PARENT'S STORY

Unexpected Benefits

"I think I did a lot of good things for my kids as a first-time parent, but lots of times for the wrong reasons," a friend told me as we watched her kids, now teenagers, playing with my boys at the local swimming pool. "I remember when Robby was three, I enrolled him in a half-day of preschool mainly because I was desperate to have some time to myself. Luckily, Robby was ready to spend time out of the house. In fact, after a few months, I started to notice that a lot of stuff we did together at home had started to get easier. It used to be impossible for me to get Robby to put anything away after he'd finished playing with it, but now he loved to announce, 'Time to clean up!' and sing the cleanup song they'd taught him at school while we put things away. His teacher assigned different duties to each of the kids, too, so Robby started insisting on passing out the napkins at dinner or carrying the glasses to the table. By the end of the year, he'd even gotten better at falling asleep at night listening to a story on tape the way he did at school at rest time. I didn't even know back then that all of this stuff was so important to kids that age. He got plenty of mental stimulation at home, and had enough friends on the block to play with, but I'm glad I sent him off for a few hours anyway so he could learn the routines he didn't get from me."

"ONE MORE STORY. . .": SLEEP ROUTINES AT AGE THREE

It is quite a relief to parents of three-year-olds to say good-bye to the up-three-times-a-night routines associated with babies and toddlers. This year, your child needs and may often get ten to twelve hours of sleep per night. Still, these months are not without their bedtime challenges. A number of new events such as the elimination of nap time, serious attention to toilet training, and schedule changes caused by starting preschool or other new activities may disrupt his sleep and, therefore, the rest of your family's as well. Fortunately, these disturbances are usually short-lived or easily handled. Even new night fears inspired by his expanding awareness and imagination become easier to conquer with a three-year-old's greater experience and your continued help. As a result, you are likely to notice a marked overall improvement in your child's sleep habits—especially after the middle of the year—and by the time he turns four you should all be able to sleep through the night much more soundly.

The key to helping your child maintain healthy sleep habits lies in observing his natural activity levels, assessing your needs, creating a sleep routine that suits these requirements as closely as possible, and then sticking to the routine as strictly as circumstances allow. If your child is a night owl who's much more energetic in the evenings than the mornings, and he still spends his days at home—or you are only able to spend much time with him if he's awake for several hours after your arrival home from work—there's no harm in adjusting his schedule so that he wakes up and goes to bed a little later than the child next door. If you and your partner desperately need a solid chunk of quiet time alone in the evenings in order to recharge for the next day, it's important to wake your child early enough each morning so that he's sleepy by, say, seven-thirty or eight o'clock. If he is used to waking up late but has just started preschool, you will need to institute an earlier bedtime as well as a wake-up hour, and probably lengthen his total sleep time to help him recover from his highly stimulating days.

Such changes are themselves disruptive in the short run, and you can expect your child to experience some grumpiness or sleeplessness as he struggles to adjust to his new routine. But it's easier this year than last year. Now he can understand patterns, delay gratification to some extent, understand multiple directions, and better regulate his behavior. Understandable as it is that he doesn't want to go to bed at eight o'clock just because he now has to get up earlier, be firm in insisting that he follow the guidelines you have set. Within a week or so, his body will adjust to his new schedule, and he will fall and stay asleep more easily unless his routine is disrupted again. If external needs have had to take precedence over his own temperament (if your work schedule or his siblings' requirements call for an early bedtime even though he's a night owl), it's even more vital to avoid bending the rules. Just one late bedtime or unplanned nap can spoil his body's sleep rhythms all over again, and it will probably take days to get him back on schedule. A slightly early bedtime or late wake-up call is acceptable if toilet training or other issues have disrupted a good night's sleep—and a fifteen-minute nap is fine when he's completely worn out—but this is not a year when major schedule disruptions can be easily accommodated. So resist his age-appropriate efforts to test your resolve through endless negotiation, escapes from bed, and constant calls of, "Daddy, I'm thirsty/hungry/scared!" Provide him with a predictable sequence of bed-time story, quiet talk, tucking under the covers, and nightlight on, and then firmly leave the room and close the door.

EASING THE WAY

Saying Good-bye to Naps

It's often said that nap time is designed more for tired parents than it is for young children. Your three-year-old will soon be, or is already physically able to forgo regular daytime naps. You will know this is the case when falling asleep at an acceptable hour becomes difficult on days when he's napped well. Parents respond in different ways to this period when their children *can,* but perhaps *shouldn't,* sleep during the day. Some, reluctant to give up their quiet afternoons, insist on a full nap and must then struggle with a child who cannot sleep through the night. Others give up nap time altogether, only to find that their three-year-olds fall asleep, utterly exhausted, at five o'clock, wake up two hours later, and are then unable to start their night's sleep until eleven o'clock.

To avoid such traps, it's best to phase out the naps yourself rather than letting your child take the lead. Accepting the fact that your child no longer needs to sleep during the day (except perhaps after an extra-stimulating morning), allow him to lie in bed at nap time without actually sleeping but instead looking at a book or chatting to himself. If he falls asleep, wake him up after fifteen minutes or half an hour. Such breaks are excellent for both of you, providing a welcome pause in otherwise hectic schedules and teaching your child how to manage and maintain his own energy level. This is an especially useful skill if your child attends a group program in the mornings and comes home either wound up or completely worn out. If he attends a full-day program, he no doubt rests in this way with the group.

As the year progresses, your child will probably stay awake more and more often during nap time. Eventually, you can do away with this time in bed altogether, substituting the solitary play at which he's becoming more adept. By the end of the year, you may actually be able to put your feet up yourself while your child plays happily and relatively quietly nearby. His sleep habits will have become much more like an adult's (one long nighttime sleep), with nap time reserved for those days when he really needs it.

"I'M NOT HUNGRY": EATING ROUTINES

By age three, your child's temperament and personality have grown remarkably clear, and these "typical" behaviors include his attitudes toward food. A picky eater at age one is quite often a picky eater at age three, while a toddler who eats everything in sight often grows into a chubby and very hungry preschooler. As your child explores new aspects of himself this year and develops a clearer idea of who he is, his eating tendencies become part of his identity, and his relationship with food changes from a natural tendency to a more deeply ingrained habit that can be difficult to change as time goes by. Certainly, this is the year to start seriously addressing eating habits in overweight or underweight kids. Now—when your child is able to sit still at the table and follow rules (no dessert until after dinner; no playtime until all the broccoli has been eaten), ready to expand his food experience (helping choose vegetables at the grocery store, helping cook, adding favorite elements to familiar recipes), and isn't yet able to argue too much (as he will next year)—is the time when he can best change unhealthy practices. The habits he ends up with by the end of the year are likely to stick with him throughout childhood. Again, when working on this issue it's important to focus on process versus outcome. Don't expect too much at first. You might count sniffing as a step toward trying a new food— then progress to licking the spoon, and then to tiny mouse bites. Reward him for foods he does try—adding each new food to a list on the refrigerator and letting him place a happy-face sticker to the foods he likes and a sad-face sticker to those he doesn't. (Chances are he'll want the list to "look happy.") Occasional treats are fine as a reward for finishing the meal. You may also find that going to restaurants, where your child gets to pick what he wants from a menu, helps him become more adventurous in his choices.

As with sleep routines, the most successful eating regimen is likely to be one that reasonably accommodates your child's natural temperament and physiology, your own requirements, and the situation in which you find yourselves. If your child loves to eat and is somewhat heavy, you can offer him frequent snacks but control the number of empty calories or pure sugar these contain (substituting graham crackers for cookies, or fruit for candy). If your child rarely cleans his plate and is underweight, you might try leaving nutritious snacks around the house (grapes, cheese sticks, raisins) as a supplement to meals, extend mealtimes by conversing with your child while he slowly eats, and allow such partly nourishing after-dinner treats as ice cream, muffins, and oatmeal cookies. Many parents of preschoolers find that work schedules preclude making a full home-cooked breakfast, lunch, and dinner. This is not a problem when most three-year-olds are just as happy with—and as nourished by—cereal with milk instead of pancakes for breakfast, a peanut butter and jelly sandwich instead of homemade soup for lunch, and a dinner of a boiled egg, cooked baby carrots, and ice cream instead of roast chicken and asparagus. In general, healthy eating routines that are built around the way your child and your family actually live are much more likely to last and are certainly better than berating your child for eating too much or too little, or criticizing yourself for time restraints you can't help. Look at what you eat as well, and model good food habits for your child. If you eat healthfully, your child has a much better chance of avoiding serious food problems.

When designing an eating routine, keep in mind that a little food goes a long way this year. Compared to age one or two, age three is not a time of rapid physical growth, so your child will probably not have a huge appetite. As long as you consistently offer small servings of meat or other protein, milk products, and fruit, vegetables, and bread or other grains each day—and your child samples several foods from each group over the course of a week—you have probably done as well as can be expected. Don't ask, "Do you want some?" because you'll get a "No." Just leave plenty of healthy food lying around, and your child will eat it as he dashes through the kitchen to his next activity. Rest assured that a three-year-old who is offered nutritious food will not starve. His desire to control his environment may lead him to reject his dinner on Monday and even Tuesday, but by Wednesday he will no doubt be ready to bolt down his serving and his sister's, too. His idea of who he is and what he likes may inspire him to eat four bananas a day for a week, but he will move on to pears or peaches after that time. In the meantime, look forward to the hungrier, more adventuresome fours and supplement his food intake with a good-tasting chewable multivitamin.

A CHILD'S-EYE VIEW

"Bet You Can't!"

A napkin for Daddy, a napkin for Mommy, a napkin for Jimmy, a napkin for me . . . everybody got a napkin! Three-year-old Jenny surveys her work with supreme satisfaction from her place at the dinner table. *Good job. Daddy will give me a sticker.*

Jenny is so absorbed in savoring her accomplishment that she hardly notices that Mommy has piled a steaming heap of spaghetti and meatballs on her plate. "Go ahead and start eating, Jenny," Mommy tells her. "Doesn't the spaghetti smell good?"

Jenny looks down at her food. The tomato sauce looks so bright against the white pasta. The meatball has rolled over to one side, and looks crumbly, brown, and dry. *Yuck.* "I don't want that," she announces, pushing her plate away.

"Oh, Jenny, not again!" Her mother's exasperation sounds clearly in her voice. "You *love* spaghetti and meatballs, remember? You ate a whole plate last week."

"I *hate* it!" Jenny turns her face away. She loves making definite statements about herself. They give her such a feeling of satisfaction. "Can I go watch Bugs Bunny now?"

"You will sit right there until you've eaten every bite," her father commands.

Jenny glares at him. She *hates* being told to sit still. She *hates* being told what to do about anything. "I wanna watch Bugs Bunny!" she yells.

Daddy starts to get out of his chair. But just then eleven-year-old Jimmy's voice sounds from the end of the table. "Hey, Jenny," he says, "did you know that when you were a baby, spaghetti with meatballs was your favorite food?"

"I want Bugs Bunny," Jenny says sulkily.

Jimmy smiles at her. "You know how you used to eat it? You'd get one end of the spaghetti in your mouth, and you'd suck it up like this." Jimmy demonstrates, getting tomato sauce all over his face. "Bet you can't do it."

Jenny thinks about this challenge. *When I was a baby, I loved spaghetti.* This is another definite statement about herself. She likes the idea. Suddenly, she's as determined to "play baby" by eating the spaghetti as she was determined not to eat it a minute ago. She puts a forkful in her mouth and sucks up the spaghetti, sauce flying everywhere.

"Great!" Jimmy says. "But that was a baby bite," he teases.

"Jimmy!" his mother warns.

"Shhh," says Jenny's father. "As long as she's eating . . ."

Jenny hardly hears them, she's so intent on acting out her new role. *Baby Jenny loves spaghetti!* she says to herself, and gobbles down some more. *Pretty good,* she realizes, surprised. Indeed, the spaghetti tastes so delicious that she forgets she's supposed to be a baby and wolfs down the rest of her dinner without a word.

"Congratulations," Mom says in jest to Jimmy. "You can take over for a while." But Jenny is more focused on the nice, warm fullness in her belly than the family conversation. Her face covered with sauce, she holds her plate out to her father. "Daddy, can I have dessert?"

"I HAVE TO GO": TOILET TRAINING AT AGE THREE

"Charlie, do you have to go to the bathroom?"

"No, Mom."

"You're dancing all over the place. Are you sure you don't have to go?"

"No, Mom."

"Look at how you're holding yourself. You must have to go."

"I don't, Mom. . . . Whoops."

The "bathroom dance" can be a frustrating one for both parents and children in many senses this year. As your child grows older and your friends, relatives, and even preschool staff start pointedly asking when you plan to toilet train him, you may feel a great deal more pressure than you did last year to successfully complete the process. At the same time, your three-year-old's increased curiosity, still-short attention span, and expanded awareness often distract him from the task at hand. He may have an accident while engrossed in a project, refuse to go to the toilet as a way of imposing his will, or use his developing language skills to inform you that he simply doesn't want to use the potty like a big boy yet. As new events and experiences in other arenas demand greater reserves of mental and emotional energy, he may even regress in his training, reverting to pull-ups for a while, or wetting the bed at night. Certainly, toilet training progress is often uneven among three-year-olds, and some children remain in pull-ups at night well into the next year. Unless you plan to enroll your child in a group program that requires your child to be toilet trained (though there are many high-quality facilities that don't require this), there is no real need to worry unduly if your child prefers to put off the potty until the end of the year or even a bit later. However, if your anxiety over the issue has begun to affect your relationship with him or if his repeated accidents seem to be hurting his feelings of self-esteem, there are ways to hasten the process along.

Certainly, your three-year-old is physically able to use the toilet if he wants to. By age two, most children can control elimination voluntarily, and this skill becomes even easier once your child turns three. As the year progresses, his investment in demonstrating his competence as a "big boy," and his growing tendency to compare himself with his peers, will motivate him to give the potty a try—especially if you encourage this. Casual conversation about potty use is a real possibility this year and can also help move him toward considering this major change in routine.

Impatient as you may be to get the toilet training process over with, the first rule in successful training is to keep things positive. Your child will sense any anxiety or frustration you feel, and his typical willfulness may well spur him to dig in his heels. In a sense, the more eager you are for your three-year-old to move from diapers to his potty, the more important it is to be casual regarding the issue when you bring it up with him. Deal with his resistance by quietly watching for the moment when his attention turns toward toilet training. He might demonstrate this interest by describing the potty at preschool, talking about how his friend uses the potty, hanging around the bathroom while you use the toilet, hiding behind the couch when he feels the need to poop, sitting on or playing with the potty you've provided, or asking to wear the big-kid underwear you bought for him the other day.

Once he appears open to the topic, take advantage of the situation by providing the potty, underwear, and attention he needs. Watch carefully as he wanders about the house without a diaper, and gently but firmly put him on the potty the moment you see he needs to go. (Boys should be encouraged to sit down at first so they'll be in position to defecate. Later, when they have begun to use the toilet more reliably, they can switch to a standing position—preferably with Dad's example and guidance.) Stay with him while he's on the potty, chatting and keeping him company as he tries to eliminate. If he's successful, praise him sincerely and let him hear you bragging to other members of the family about what he's accomplished. (There is no feeling as wonderful for a three-year-old than the sense of pride over a job well done.) If he doesn't manage to eliminate, cheerfully tell him, "Good try," and remind him that he can try again whenever he feels the need. Children this age often love to talk about their efforts to accomplish new skills. Listening to his musings in this area may give you new clues about how to encourage the practice.

Often, to their parents' disappointment, children who have begun the process of toilet training drop it after a few tries, whether or not they were successful. If your child acts in this way, try not to overreact. He has no doubt learned a lot on this first go-round and may simply need time to mull over this new experience before he starts trying again. (Unlike adults, he doesn't "know" that he's made progress, and so he needs to be told he succeeded.) Keep in mind, too, that major life changes such as a new baby, a move to a new house, a marital crisis, and so on, will almost certainly interfere with toilet training progress. Also, he may get different cues, rules, or pressures from different adults that confuse him. Regression for whatever reason should be tolerated whenever possible. Your child's desire to be like his parents, older siblings, and other kids will cause him to renew his efforts soon enough. In the meantime, keep suggesting (without insisting) that he sit on the potty at least once a day, offer him the potty when he's about to have a bowel movement, read kids' books on the topic to him, talk about having to go use the toilet yourself, and praise him *every time* he remembers to sit on the potty in time to use it.

Over time, your obvious interest in the subject of elimination will catch on with your child, and he will try harder to use the potty in part to win your approval. His progress, once he truly commits himself to toilet training, will probably be much faster than it would have been at age two. Still, it's important to know that accidents will occur frequently both during the initial adjustment process and long after the training process is complete. Your child will "forget" to go to the bathroom when the events around him are too exciting to miss; when he's overwhelmed with anxious or fearful thoughts; and when he's very tired or asleep. Certainly, nighttime training generally takes longer to accomplish than daytime potty use. Even an unfamiliar bathroom (a public bathroom, perhaps) may discourage your child from making use of the skills he's only recently learned. Throughout these errors and regressions, continue to maintain a positive attitude. (Watch out: he's old enough now to feel shame.) Keep in mind that toilet training is much more important to you than it is to your child. He is doing his best to conform to the customs regarding elimination that his culture imposes. Soon enough he will conform perfectly. In the meantime, he needs your support.

IF YOU'RE CONCERNED

Bed-Wetting

"Lizzy was toilet trained during the day by the time she was two, but she was nearly four before I got her trained at night," a friend told me while we sat chatting on a bench at the playground. "I swear, I tried everything. I even added 'Potty at night' to her list of chores and pasted a big sticker on it that said 'Great job!' every morning that Lizzy's bed was dry. I thought that was going to work, too, till one morning when she woke up, peeked around the corner of my bedroom door, and said, 'Mommy, is there a sticker that says, Oops, you wet the bed again?'"

It is a great satisfaction to parents when their three-year-olds no longer need diapers during the day—but this euphoria may increase the frustration they feel at how long it takes to leave behind nighttime diapers or pull-ups. If you are in this situation, you can at least comfort yourself with the knowledge that occasional bed-wetting is common for children up to five years (especially in families when either parent had similar difficulties as a child). Obviously, circumstances such as extreme sleepiness, emotional stress, fear of the dark, or a recent major life change, will increase the chances that your child will not wake up and call you to take him to the bathroom or even go there on his own. A three-year-old's love of determining his own course—deciding that it's easier to defy your wishes and wet the bed than to get up to use the bathroom—may also have its effect. Whatever the cause, practical measures may work best for everyone in most cases. First, make sure that your child sits on the potty immediately before going to bed. He may protest occasionally (or frequently) but will usually urinate when placed in the proper position. (You might consider a "wake up and pee" routine before your own bedtime as long as your child is able to fall back asleep easily.) Second, be sure that you can hear his call for assistance at night by keeping your bedroom door open if necessary. Third, praise every successful effort to use the bathroom instead of wetting the bed. A chart such as the one my friend used is not a bad idea, despite the minor setback she described. Such evidence of your child's increasing success at nighttime training will encourage him to try even harder in the future. Some parents have also learned that a mild reminder ("Yikes, the bed's wet. It feels better to wake up dry, doesn't it? Next time, call me when you need to pee, and I'll take you to the bathroom.") spurs children who have not really

Be patient this year as your three-year-old tries hard to act like a "big kid" and do more for himself.

thought much about the issue to contemplate the advantages of using the toilet.

Finally, try to remember that this period really won't last forever. With your encouragement, your child will probably remain dry virtually around the clock by the time he turns four. In the meantime, place a plastic-lined pad under your child's bedding and insist that your partner do a little sheet-changing, too.

"YOU GET THE NAPKINS": THE IMPORTANCE OF CHORES

Among the most delightful traits of three-year-olds is their eagerness to take their place as a contributing member of the family. Show your child how to crack open an egg, and he will gladly help you make pancakes every Sunday morning. Assign him the job of filling the dog's water bowl, and he will proudly fill it when reminded, even if he's unable to remember on his own. Performing regular assigned tasks expands three-year-olds' sense of who they are and how they fit into their world, thus giving them a great sense of satisfaction and fulfillment.

As with so many aspects of life with a three-year-old, the greatest challenge for parents lies in keeping expectations reasonable in the face of what looks like amazing competence. Your three-year-old may behave as though he's able to set the table with plates, silverware, napkins, and glasses. And he may be able to do each of these jobs separately. He may even insist that he can and wants to perform this task every evening. Yet, if you agree that he can be the table-setter for the family, the other members are likely to stand around impatiently (and increasingly hungrily) each night while he tries to remember where the forks go, carefully places each glass in its place one at a time, and yells at anyone who tries to grab the dinnerware from him or otherwise hurry him along. Such a negative scenario, repeated each evening, is not the way to instill good work habits in your child. Far better to assign him the job of distributing napkins, allowing him to experience success and learn that doing his part can be fun. As he easily manages to place a napkin beside each plate, he savors the experience of family life and avoids the discouragement of an impatient parent taking his job out of his hands.

Whenever you start to create a list of duties for your young child to fulfill, be sure to start small. There's no such thing as too small a job at this age. If you're doing laundry, let him put away the socks. When you make his bed, have him line up the stuffed animals on top of the blankets. Keep in mind that three-year-olds are easily distracted by whatever is going on around them, and their attention span remains quite short. Even if your child wants to be a "big boy" and help you around the house, he's quite likely to abandon his task halfway through. This is not the year to insist that he finish every chore, since such perseverance is still beyond him. Try to help him strengthen his abilities a bit by insisting that he pick up or put away "three more things," and then let him go play.

Satisfying as tasks are at the moment your child is accomplishing them, they are even more significant in terms of his long-term growth. The ability to accept a job, assess its difficulty, know when to ask for help, and bring the job to completion profoundly affects a child's later ability to achieve academically, in the workplace, and even in terms of personal relationships and other commitments. By considering your three-year-old's task performance in terms of such long-term goals, you can see more clearly how important it is to introduce the concept of commitments and responsibilities at an early age—and to make meeting them a pleasurable and fulfilling experience. The goal this year, in other words, is not to get your child to single-handedly clean his room, set the table, or wash the dog. The goal is to get him to *enjoy* helping with cleanup chores, to view such activities as a natural part of everyday life, and to take pride in his developing ability to complete them.

Q & A

Cleanup Time

Q: As my three-year-old has started to spend more time with other kids her age, I've noticed that most of her friends are better at cleaning up after themselves than she is. Other kids cheerfully pick up their blocks at the end of a play date, but when I tell my daughter to pick up she just looks at me, says she doesn't want to, and leaves the room. What can I do about this?

A: Much of a three-year-old's behavior regarding cleanup tasks depends on the preparation they received at age one and two. Toddlers who are taught to associate picking up toys with a cleanup song will clean up more or less habitually (though not perfectly) when they are three. By now, though, your child is aware that her point of view can differ from yours—that she can *not* want to clean up even though you want her to. As a result, persuading her to help with the task will now be more difficult. Still, it's easier this year than next, when she will be better able to argue, negotiate, and use subterfuge to avoid cleanup—so the earlier you start to institute new rules, the better it will be for both of you.

The key to interesting your three-year-old in such chores is to make them a quick, fun, and relatively painless activity at first. Make up a cleanup song to sing with her, and pitch in and help her with the chore. Insist that she stay in the room and help you, but suggest a treat or fun activity as a reward for a clean room. When other children are around, lavish positive attention on those who are doing their share. She'll want some of that praise, too. Let her peers apply pressure ("Jody's not helping"), and encourage her to join them. Don't expect her to pick up more than two or three toys at first, and thank her sincerely for her effort when she does so. As she becomes more accustomed to this new responsibility, she will be able to help out more—and will even point out to you a bit self-righteously that "Mary never cleans up her messes," or "Tim forgot to put up his plate." Reinforce her pride in her own contributions by creating a chart of daily duties and giving her a gold star for each task accomplished. And don't forget to set a good example by cleaning up the messes you yourself create—or you may find your three-year-old lecturing *you* about chores.

"LET'S GO SEE GRANDMA!":
TRAVEL ROUTINES

"Finally!" a neighbor said recently when I congratulated her on her child's having turned three. "Now we can travel again! I hated carrying all that baby stuff around so much, we haven't taken a vacation since she was born." Many parents look forward to the day when they can travel unburdened by diaper bags, security blankets, stuffed animals, and a child so dependent on his routine that he cries at the sight of a suitcase. Much of this is possible as your child turns three, but once again it's important not to expect too much from him at first if you want him to learn to love travel as you do. When packing for a trip this year, focus first on taking along such safety-related items as a car seat or even a bed rail. Next come stress-relieving items, such as a mattress pad in case of bed-wetting and a sippy cup for spill-proof drinks in the car. The greatest space saver for your suitcase this year is in the number of comfort objects and toys you need to take from home. Your three-year-old, so interested in and curious about the world around him, will probably feel sufficiently secure with just one favorite doll, stuffed animal, or action figure. Much more verbal, imaginative, and able to sit still than last year, he may now need only a pad and markers to get him through the plane ride to Grandma's. (Still it's a good idea, if you have room, to bring along an Etch-a-Sketch, travel-sized games, or some audiotapes just in case.) As the months pass, you will find that travel with your three-year-old involves less careful re-creation of home routines and gradually more sightseeing, chatting, relaxing, and actual enjoyment of the ride.

One travel-related concept that three-year-olds still find difficult is the passage of time. Your child does not yet understand how long a week is, much less two weeks, and may become anxious about when he will be returning home. The best way to deal with this is to be as concrete as possible when talking about the length of a trip (or your own absence from home). "I explain it to my son in terms of how many sleeps we'll be away," one mother, Kathie, told me. "When I tell him we'll be going to Nana's for three sleeps, or that Dad'll be back after two sleeps, he feels less anxious because he knows what that means." Other ways to help your child make the leap from the *idea* of traveling to the actual experience is to draw your route on a map, and then describe the route to him in terms of scenery (if it's a car or train trip) or sequence of events (if you're traveling by plane). Reading stories that involve the mode of travel you'll be using or that are set in areas you will visit also enhance his understanding of what's in store for him, or where you are going on your own. His memory has improved to the point where you might even be able to remind him of how much fun he had on previous trips—but he may not remember well enough for reminiscences to invariably help.

Sophisticated as three-year-olds can be when traveling, they are still three—with all the cognitive, emotional, and physical limitations we have discussed throughout this book. By planning ahead for your child's special needs—frequent bathroom breaks, leg-stretching opportunities, snack times, and quiet moments without a need to get somewhere in a hurry—you will find your trip proceeding with greater ease than you might expect. Slowing down to a three-year-old's pace is not a bad way to ensure that you, too, enjoy your time away from home.

THE TOY BOX

"I Feel Sick . . ."

Scared! Sarah sits, fists clenched, next to her mother on the airplane. The flight attendants are preparing for takeoff, and Sarah is so anxious about flying that she can't relax. *Too many people! It's noisy here. And that stranger's sitting too close to me.* "Mommy . . ." she whimpers as her mother double-checks her seat belt. Remembering how she felt last week on the plane, Sarah says, "I feel sick."

"Don't worry, honey. Everything's fine," her mother says, sounding a bit helpless in the face of her daughter's vague anxiety. "We were okay on the flight over, right? And now we're just flying back home!"

"But the plane can crash," Sarah says, clutching a toy.

Sarah's mother blinks. "It won't, though, sweets. I promise."

But Sarah has picked up on the uncertainty in her mother's voice. "My tummy hurts," she moans.

Just then, the airplane's engines rev up and the plane begins to move down the runway. The pilots speaks over the intercom, and the passengers sit up straighter, ready for takeoff. "Oooooh. . ." Sarah moans as the plane speeds up. "Oooooh. . . !" The plane starts to lift from the runway. Sarah screams, "Mommy!"

Just then, a face appears from around the back of the aisle seat in front of Sarah and her mom. It's the face of a lady who's sitting with her own little boy. "Hi, there!" the lady says to Sarah. "I bet you've never seen this." She holds up a Rubik's cube. As Sarah watches, the lady moves the pieces of the cube around. "Wanna look at it?"

Sarah's body relaxes a little. She glances at her mom, who is giving the lady a smile of relief. "Okay," she says tentatively. She takes the puzzle, and the nice lady tells her how to move the pieces around. "It's pretty," she admits when the lady asks if she likes it.

"You can play with it as long as you want," the lady tells her. "My son is tired of it."

Sarah smiles. She likes moving the colored parts of the cube, though she's too young to understand that there's a goal to be achieved. The unfamiliar toy is attractive and complex enough to hold her attention, however, and before she knows it half the flight is over with. "Sarah, you want some milk?" she hears her mother ask. She looks up from the puzzle to see a flight attendant smiling at her from behind a rolling drinks cart. *The next lady will bring me pretzels,* she remembers. "Uh, okay," she says. Still clutching the puzzle, she relaxes into her seat. *I'm flying high,* she thinks, looking out the window. Her mother unhooks her little tray table. *Airplanes are fun.* She looks at the phone in front of her. "Can we call Dad?"

"I DID IT MYSELF": HELPING YOUR CHILD MANAGE ROUTINES

Miraculously, considering the pressures of parenting and supporting her family, Janet managed to complete her bachelor's degree. This year she's a graduate student with a part-time job as a teaching assistant, which means she still has to be on campus early most mornings. It's a relief as well as a delight, therefore, that Shane has grown increasingly competent at managing the routines of his daily care. Having experienced small successes and much encouragement as he strove to "make" his own breakfast of cereal and milk, dress himself, brush his teeth, wash his face, and even comb his hair after a fashion, he feels very much a part of the family as he and Mom rush around getting ready for their day. Janet knows that Shane's ability to complete such tasks has added to his level of self-confidence and self-esteem. She understands now why children of single mothers are often shown to be more independent than their two-parented peers.

Today, however, is a school holiday, and Janet is enjoying a rare day off with breakfast and the newspaper in bed. She's so engrossed in the paper that she doesn't hear Shane rummaging around his room, already awake. As she reaches for her coffee cup, though, she hears a noise from that direction. "Shane?" she calls.

"Yeah, Mom! I'm getting dressed!"

"Oh . . . great!" Janet answers. She hesitates, then adds tactfully, "Remember, it's chilly outside today. You'll need to wear warm clothes."

"I know, Mom! I remember! I got my flannel pants!"

A moment later, Shane appears, beaming with pride, in Janet's bedroom doorway. "Here I am!" he announces. Janet looks up from the paper and nearly drops her coffee cup.

"Uh, you're wearing that?" she stammers. Shane is dressed in red plaid flannel pants and a red-and-white striped shirt.

When Shane sees her expression, his face falls. "What's the matter?" he asks innocently. "The colors match. See—red, red. White, white!"

Well, it wasn't his fault, and not mine either, Janet tells herself wryly. (If they weren't going to the mall she'd just let it go, but as it is she helps her son change his shirt.) Having learned from experience over the past year, Janet had pruned the choice of clothes in her son's dresser drawers, leaving only those clothes appropriate for the season. Having chatted with him about which colors go together and weathered countless tussles over shoes, socks, and other fashion choices, she thought she had nothing to fear. *But he is still only three, for two more weeks at least,* she tells herself. She has to laugh at how creative Shane is when he tries to be a big boy. "Good job," she tells him sincerely when they've buttoned up his solid-red flannel shirt. "You'll be nice and warm today, and you figured out how to get ready all on your own. You should be proud of yourself." She gives her son a hug. She can tell by his answering hug that he's indeed very proud.

ADVANCES

How the Need for Routine Evolves at Age Three

36 MONTHS	Shows pride in his place as a full-fledged family member
	More willing to conform to family customs
	Shows increased interest in trying new things
42 MONTHS	Sleeps through the night without a daytime nap
	Frequently makes his own plans for the day
48 MONTHS	Reasonably well toilet trained at night
	Ability to complete self-care routines has greatly improved

FIRST-PERSON SINGULAR

The key to helping your child learn to manage the routines of daily life is to allow him to experience small successes before he attempts larger challenges. By noting here his early achievements in self-care, you will be better able to appreciate the progress he makes over the course of the year. Older three-year-olds love to talk about all the things they couldn't do when they were little that they can do so easily now. As your child approaches age four, show him what you've written here so that he, too, can celebrate how much better he is now at eating all his supper, going to the potty, visiting Grandma, and brushing his teeth. You might even note here, and discuss with your child, which methods worked best in helping him take responsibility for himself. Is he a deliberate person who prefers to accomplish tasks at his own slow pace, or does he prefer to move from one activity to another quickly, returning to finish them later if necessary? Does he respond better to your reminding him repeatedly about what needs to be done, or to your helping him make a joke or a story out of his activity? By talking these issues out with your child (on a simple level, of course), you continue to support his self-management abilities—a vital skill for later academic and personal success.

READER'S NOTES

_____

_____

_____

_____

_____

_____

_____

_____

_____

_____

_____

CHAPTER 8

"Just One More?"— My Need for Limits

L et your child know that telling the truth is the most important thing and that you'll love her even if she breaks a rule.

"Lori, sit down in your chair!" Walt glares at his daughter from behind the menu of the neighborhood diner, where he's taken her for dinner as a special treat. A divorced parent, Walt has his daughter for the weekends only and doesn't want to spend their time together cooking. Unfortunately, the lively music on the diner's speaker system makes it hard for Lori to sit still, and she's gotten down from her chair to jump and dance to the rhythms. The other adults in the restaurant smile indulgently, but Walt is not amused by her behavior.

"Lori! Sit down right now, or we're leaving!"

"No! I won't!" The three-year-old gives him a defiant look and continues waving her arms and kicking her legs.

"I'm counting to three! One . . . two . . ."

Lori dances even more enthusiastically, a stubborn smile on her face.

"All right, that's it." Walt gets out of his chair, grabs his three-year-old by the arm, and sets her a little roughly back in her seat. "And stay there!" he mutters as he returns to his own chair.

He starts to pick up his menu again, but just then catches a glimpse of Lori's expression. Her little face has crumpled. She looks completely crushed. "You meanie!" she shouts at him and bursts into very loud tears. "I don't want to eat here. I wanna go home!"

Hunching his shoulders in embarrassment, Walt glances at the other diners. Their kind smiles have turned to disapproving frowns, and they're frowning at *him*. *What did I do?* he wonders as he tries more quietly to shush his daughter. *She was naughty! I had to discipline her! Does that make me a bad dad?*

Walt is correct in believing that three-year-olds not only need reasonable limits, but that they are ready and at least sometimes able to respect parents' rules. This is a time of notable developments in the realms of self-control, self-reliance, and self-regulation, as well as a year when it becomes much easier to talk to your child and believe that she understands what you have to say. As you observe these impressive changes in your child's comprehension and behavior, you will naturally begin to expect much more of her in terms of obedience and compliance. While last year you didn't count on her to control her own impulses or to be able to direct her own activities without you, you may now assume that she is much more capable of controlling her emotional outbursts or physical aggression and managing her own time. In some cases this is true, but she will still quickly revert to toddlerlike behaviors throughout this year when she is tired, in an unfamiliar environment, confused, or otherwise stressed. She will also understand much less of what you say than she appears to, as her verbal growth outstrips real comprehension. Meanwhile, your assumptions about her capabilities have a profound impact on her developing ideas about who she is and what she's like. If you consistently expect more than she can give in terms of self-regulation, she may come to think of herself as incompetent, naughty, or bad. She may even increase the behavior you dislike, convinced that that's just "the way she is." On the other hand, if you expect too little, she may decide that you're right in assuming she can't control her behavior and continue to look to you to direct her every move. This dilemma is why discipline in general presents a parent like Walt with such difficulty. Within reasonable limits, punishment choices (time-outs versus yelling versus spanking) are each family's responsibility. But when parents ask my opinion, I try to present them with the facts—

that discipline is more than about punishment, and that some methods, as we'll see later in this chapter, work better than others.

It isn't easy to walk the thin line between being too strict and overindulging this year. You will probably find that, as in other aspects of her growth, the best approach is to try to remain just *half a step ahead* of what you know she can do (expecting her to stay in her seat at the restaurant, but looking the other way as she plays with the sugar packets); to pick your battles (insist that she take her dishes to the kitchen after a meal, if that's important to you, but not making her eat everything on her plate if that bothers you less); and to specifically criticize the action, not your child, when enforcing limits (saying, "We don't hit," or "Hitting is wrong. It hurts people," instead of "What are you doing? Bad boy!").

A PARENT'S STORY

"How Many Times?"

"My son, Victor, was a real gabber by the time he turned three," a woman at my sons' day camp told me the other day. "He was so good at arguing, negotiating, carrying on conversations, and picking up and using phrases he'd just heard once, that it was easy to forget that he didn't always understand what we were talking about. I remember one time I completely lost my temper when he let our outdoor cat into the house for about the fifteenth time, after I'd told him not to. 'How many times did I tell you not to let the cat into the living room?' I yelled at him. He looked up at me with that perfectly innocent little face and said, 'Three.' 'And how many times should I *have* to tell you?' I yelled. He just blinked like he was confused, and answered, 'Four?'

"That was when I realized that the two of us looked at things in completely different ways sometimes, and it wasn't fair to expect his agenda to always be the same as mine. Eventually, I figured out that I had to explain things more clearly to him, even when I thought he'd understood. I made sure he was looking at me when I asked him to do something, to make sure he wasn't distracted or only half-listening. I told him to nod or say, 'Okay, Mom,' so that I knew he'd heard me. I also learned to ask him, 'What are you going to do?' and to correct anything he'd gotten wrong. And if he got in trouble, I worked harder on making sure he knew what had gone wrong. I'd ask him, 'What's the rule? What'd you learn from this?' That was the only way I could find out if he really got the message."

"I DIDN'T MEAN IT!": HOW YOUR CHILD LEARNS TO OBEY LIMITS

If you have ever had to break in a new employee at work, you probably expected him to make a few mistakes at first and were prepared to tolerate them. If a seasoned employee had made the same mistakes, on the other hand, you most likely would have been much more irritated. An experienced worker should know what he's doing, and is more likely to have erred out of carelessness, thoughtlessness, or apathy. When teaching your child how to behave according to your rules, the same mechanism often comes into play. Last year it was obvious that your two-year-old understood little about why or how she should control her impulses, so you didn't usually hold her responsible for bad behavior. At age three, however, she is clearly much more interested in and able to comprehend the reasons behind your limit-setting. She knows that hitting hurts other people, that taking turns allows everyone to participate, that it's necessary to be quiet indoors so that other people can hear, and even that brushing teeth and taking baths is necessary to stay clean and keep from getting sick. For this reason, her disobedience now seems more deliberate and thoughtful. Believing she should know better, you are likely to become more aggravated with her more easily, just as she's on the verge of being able to improve her behavior.

The fact is, however, that unlike the experienced coworker who slacks off on the job even though he knows better, your three-year-old is still moving *very gradually* from the impulse-driven, emotionally unstable condition of a two-year-old toward the more considered, mature awareness of age four. While it's true that she understands more about the reasons why good behavior is necessary, she easily forgets these reasons in emotional or stressful situations. Though she has grown better at tolerating frustration, she still has a hard time systematically figuring out what to do when an obstacle blocks her goal (for example, when a child repeatedly refuses to let her have a turn on the slide) and will probably lose control of the situation and her emotions unless you step in and help. Three-year-olds are not much better than toddlers at filtering out irrelevant sounds, sights, and thoughts when it's time to focus on an event or activity, so your child may not hear you or respond if you address her while she's watching TV or involved in imaginary play. She also continues to find it difficult to focus on more than one issue at a time (her need to stop kicking the chair leg at the dinner table *and* her need to eat), is largely unable to weigh future consequences when deciding how to act (not understanding that sneaking a snack now leads to an inability to eat dinner), and still thinks of you as so all-powerful that she can't comprehend the idea that you can't or won't fulfill her wishes (why *won't* you give her that beautiful parrot at the zoo?).

For all of these reasons, it's important to pause and consider the causes behind your three-year-old's misbehavior before you respond. Ask yourself whether your child actually heard your command. If so, are you sure she really comprehended what you were saying? Did you demand too many things of her at once, overloading her ability to respond correctly? Did she misbehave because she was unable to find a productive way out of the situation she was in? By making the effort to understand what caused the misbehavior, you can provide the small bridge your child probably still needs to get from a frustrating situation to a positive solution.

Responding to her normal limitations in a positive way—looking for the problem, coming up with a solution, and showing her how to implement that solution—not only gets the two of you through difficult moments more easily but has a profound effect on your child's general behavior as she matures. Recent studies by Dr. Grazyna Kochanska of the University of Iowa and others have demonstrated that three-and-a-half and four-year-olds are much more likely to comply with a parent's wishes, *even in the parent's absence,* if they typically experience frequent positive limit-setting exchanges with that parent. This kind of compliance is called *committed compliance,* and it is best encouraged by making your child *want* and *feel able* to please you. Just as you probably do your best work for a supportive, responsive employer, so your child will best learn to behave if you actively help her with problem-solving skills rather than lecturing, criticizing, or nagging.

As the months pass, your three-year-old will get better at impulse control, emotional problem-solving, and other basic behavioral skills. Your assurance that she can overcome everyday challenges to her tolerance and patience, and your consistent help in devising ways to do so, will have enhanced her concept of herself as a competent, controlled, and well-behaved person. As her skills develop, her experience deepens, and her confidence expands, she will need your direct support less often and will benefit more from explanations about *why* she should behave in a certain way. She'll even remind others to follow established rules, particularly about safety-based limits ("Be careful," to a friend holding scissors). These are positive signs of her *internalizing* your rules by making them her own.

Her increasing awareness of the difference between right and wrong may, however, lead to a host of distressing new behaviors. Your child may try asking you "not to look" while she indulges in forbidden behavior; deny that she did something wrong when you confront her with the evidence; or tell you each time she's caught transgressing that "It was an accident," or "I didn't mean it." As adults, our first instinct is to think, "Oh no, now she's lying." In reality, such acts are early signs of the development of a conscience. Clearly, your child now feels uncomfortable inside when she commits (or even thinks about committing) a forbidden act and is trying to get rid of that discomfort in the only ways she knows how. By gently (but firmly and consistently) pointing out that you know what she did and that it was wrong—and then providing her with a positive alternative behavior ("You know you can't have more than two cookies at a time. How about some grapes instead?")— you can once again teach her how to move from unacceptable impulse to acceptable act. Let her know that telling the truth is the most important thing, and you'll love her even if she breaks a rule. Without a doubt, this is a valuable lesson at any age.

By around age four, you should see a huge difference in both the quality and quantity of your child's misbehavior. At that point, she will probably be more obedient than she was when she'd just turned three, while her rarer "naughty" incidents will result much more from an urge to test her limits than from simple loss of control. If you find that she has not eliminated much of her impulsive behavior, now is the time to insist a bit more. At this age, she is mature enough to be able to obey rules with reasonable consistency and should know how to ask for help or support when she can't. She needs to know that the limits you have set are important and that you mean to stick to them. Certainly, you do not want to promise discipline ("One more time, young lady, and you're getting a time-out!" or, as in Walt's case, "We're leaving!") and then fail to carry through when the misbehavior continues. Just as we adults are more likely to obey parking regulations when we know they're strictly enforced, your child will learn to stick to your limits only if there are consequences for disobeying.

EASING THE WAY
Letting Your Child Be the Judge

Good behavior, particularly as it relates to aggression and morality, is a hot topic for many parents and an aspect of your child's development that's likely to cause at least some social embarrassment, discomfort, and self-doubt. For this reason, many parents keep an eagle eye on their children's behavior from a very early age, moving in to correct and instruct at the first sign of trouble. But the fact is your child can only learn to manage her own behavior (and to deal with others' misbehavior) through experience. While she needs your support and problem-solving suggestions, she will also increasingly need to practice her developing skills on her own.

To help her do this, try to intervene only when truly necessary in situations where you see real trouble brewing. Instead of constantly jumping into disagreements between your child and a playmate, telling her exactly what to say and how to act, experiment with such responses as, "You two are going to have to work this out so that neither one of you gets her feelings hurt. I know you can do it," and see what happens. Three-year-olds are old enough to know

Three-year-olds inevitably end up in conflicts with one another, but they are often best left to figure out solutions on their own.

they've done something wrong or that they have a conflict and to know that Mom's watching. This motivates them to find a way to solve the problem on their own, instead of running to you with a complaint every five seconds. (Of course, if it turns out that they are unable to reach a compromise, you will be there to show them how.) I've always been impressed at how well children, left to their own devices, can assess situations, determine what's fair, and come up with an agreeable solution. Teaching your child to look to herself for solutions to conflicts at this age will pay off enormously later, when you will not be around as much to help her out of difficulties. It also enhances her concept of herself as a self-sufficient, self-regulating person—moving from "I'm telling Mom" to "Wanna try this?"

"IS IT ME OR MY KID?": PARENTING STYLES AND CHILDREN'S TEMPERAMENT

As adults, we are sometimes unaware of the different parenting styles out there (in our family of origin, our community, and even our parenting partners) until after we have our children. Your partner's or another adult's approach to raising and disciplining children may be quite close to or completely different from your own. In an effort to determine what general styles of parenting are most common in the United States and which styles are most effective in the long run, developmental psychologist Diana Baumrind and colleagues at the University of California at Berkeley conducted a number of longitudinal studies over recent decades. Their research identified three major approaches to child raising: *permissive parenting,* in which parents fail to set firm limits and are slow to require correct behavior; *authoritarian parenting,* in which adults control behavior in relatively harsh, inflexible ways and are unresponsive to their children's wishes; and *authoritative parenting,* a nurturant, supportive, and responsive approach that includes a willingness to set firm limits. As might be expected, Baumrind's studies showed that preschoolers with permissive parents tended to be impulsive and unable to regulate their own behavior. Those with authoritarian parents were more easily frustrated, hostile, and anxious. Young children with authoritative parents were for the most part better adjusted and more emotionally responsive, nurturant, energetic, curious, and self-reliant than others their age. It is important to note that one of the most important positive parenting traits Baumrind identified was the clear expression of care and concern for the children. She pointed out that when this caring attitude is evident in other parenting styles in certain environments (such as through a sterner, more authoritarian approach in dangerous neighborhoods), those styles may prove just as effective. This year, as your child is learning to comprehend and respond to your messages regarding discipline, it is important to think about which parenting style works best in your world, with your particular child, and with your partner.

"My son is such a talker," I once overheard a neighbor say. "No matter what I tell him to do, he has to talk about it for ten minutes before he can even think about starting to do it. I've figured out that with him I have to just give the order and leave the room, or we'd spend the whole day discussing the issue." You yourself probably know by now whether your child is a natural negotiator, a rebel, or a sweetly compliant soul. Such expressions of each child's temperament are another important consideration when choosing a parenting style. A quiet, shy child would probably be badly frightened by authoritarian commands or even loud, jocular comments, while a more high-energy three-year-old (particularly one who's accustomed to highly assertive caregivers) may not pay attention to anything less. If you find that your child rarely responds well to your directions as the year progresses, ask yourself if her frequent defiance or avoidance might be a response to your approach. Try speaking to her more quietly rather than shouting orders; letting her come up with her own solutions to problems instead of showing her what to do right away; or making a point of getting her attention (even if you have to speak up more) before you ask her to perform a task.

Children's requirements regarding parenting style depend not only on temperament but on their stage of development as well. As an infant and toddler, your child required a great deal of warmth, emotional responsiveness, and positive expression from you to begin learning such skills as empathy, cooperation, and social competence. While she continues to rely a great deal on your emotional responsiveness to continue this development (and will fashion much of her own behavioral style on what she has learned from you), she increasingly needs to experience *consistency* in your approach to discipline. As three-year-olds' awareness expands, they are able to note and become confused by varying responses to the same behaviors or responses that are stricter in public than in private. Confronted with such contradictions, your child will feel compelled to reenact the behavior again and again, or in some other way challenge your patience, in an effort to figure out whether it's acceptable or not.

Even if you yourself are careful to respond to a behavior problem in roughly the same way each time no matter where you are (shouting at a grown-up is never allowed), it's also important to keep your responses consistent with your partner's, your child's teacher's, and her other caregivers' as much as possible. Anyone who's ever watched a savvy three-year-old try to get her way knows how persistent she can be in her responses. ("Grammy lets me." "Daddy gave me a lollipop before dinner." "That was my last piece.") If you can enlist other adults in addressing any inconsistencies you see early on, it will be better for everyone. However, such efforts can get tricky at times, so keep your emphasis on the child as you explain why you prefer a certain discipline style. Rather than stating things in a way that could be taken defensively ("I don't want you to let Riley watch too much TV"), try a more child-oriented approach ("If you let her, Riley would sit in front of the TV forever. Can you back me up and keep it off when she's around?") and offer alternatives ("Riley really loves to look at books"). Point out that your child is smart enough now to figure out that sometimes it pays off to remind you when exceptions were made to the rule. The more alike everyone's responses are in style and content, the more quickly she will learn to behave appropriately—which means fewer prolonged negotiations with all of her caregivers.

As your child strives to master her emotions, control her own behavior, and regulate her world, try to give her enough room to experiment without harshly criticizing or punishing her for her failures. She is bound to try flatly refusing to eat her vegetables at least a few times to see what will happen (is "no veggies, no dessert" *always* the rule?). It's your job to firmly show her that this is not a productive ploy without calling her "rude" or "naughty" (or indirectly making her feel that way). Such anxiety often leads preschoolers to repeat inappropriate behavior rather than correcting it. ("Maybe if I hide the peas under the plate, Dad won't see them.") By keeping your lessons positive—especially by demonstrating positive behaviors and tone of voice yourself—you can help her achieve the flexible self-control you hope for.

THE TOY BOX

"No Ball Bouncing on the Deck!"

It's early evening, and Dana and Bob are enjoying their ritual half hour of relaxed conversation on the backyard deck before it's time to start dinner and give Colin his bath. Bob is deep into a description of today's run-in with a coworker when Colin appears on the deck beside him, bouncing his new basketball against the floor, watching it roll away, chasing it, and bouncing it again. "So I told him . . ." Bob continues, but then breaks off, looking exasperated, as the noise of the bouncing ball continues.

"Colin, stop that!" Dana commands. "Dad's trying to tell me a story!"

Colin, focused on the feel and the sound of the bouncing ball, doesn't seem to hear her. He bounces the ball again, and this time it careens under the wrought-iron table and knocks against Bob's legs. Bob moves his feet, not bothered, but Dana stands up, frowning, and points angrily at Colin.

"I told you to stop that bouncing!" she says. "Why don't you listen to me?"

Bob can hear the fatigue in Dana's voice. She's been alone with Colin all day. "The ball doesn't work. It's running away from me," Colin protests. Bob looks at his son, who is now clutching the basketball, frozen in place with his eyes fixed anxiously on his mother. Colin is a quiet boy, Bob knows, and seems to get really frightened when people yell at him. Clearly, he's focused much more on his mother's negative emotions than on what she's telling him.

"I know what," Bob says, reaching over to put a reassuring hand on his son's shoulder. "How about if I show you how to dribble, just like they do on the basketball court? I'm in the middle of telling Mommy something now, though. Go see if the ball bounces over there on the driveway, and in three minutes when I've finished my story I'll come play with you."

Colin relaxes visibly. "Okay, Daddy," he says gratefully, and runs to the driveway a short distance away.

"So anyway, as I was saying . . ." Bob says, turning back to Dana, who has had enough time to relax into her chair again and is actually smiling at him. Bob smiles back, glad to have found a way to resolve the situation without directly contradicting his partner (he and Dana work really hard on that). Even better, he's shown Colin a way out of a difficult situation by redirecting his attention (for three minutes anyway), and he'll soon be giving Dana a much-deserved parenting break.

"I'M COUNTING TO THREE!": FINDING ALTERNATIVES TO PHYSICAL PUNISHMENT

Eager as we are to teach our children to regulate their emotions and behavior, it is sometimes hard for us to do the same as we face frequent outbursts of defiance, inexplicable, toddlerlike regressions, and refusals to admit wrongdoing. Normal and typical as all of this behavior is, it's still maddening—and is even more difficult to put up with as a child's verbal abilities fool us into believing that she understands more than she really does. Parents of three-year-olds sometimes find it harder to control their responses toward their children just because they *appear* so mature now, relative to their two-year-old state. "I didn't spank Lisa when she was littler, but I do now," a woman once told me as I interviewed her for a research project. "Now she can understand the connection between what she did and the spanking, and she can understand my words when I explain it to her." Perhaps this is why, according to the 1990 National Longitudinal Survey of Youth, 60 percent of parents of three- to five-year-olds had spanked their children at least three times in the previous week for an average 150 times per year. (A year 2000 study by the well-known Zero to Three Organization revealed the same 60 percent reliance on physical punishment, despite the fact that the parents surveyed understood that spanking may lead to greater aggression in children.) The assumption that three-year-olds are "old enough to know better" may be understandable, but the facts simply aren't that black-and-white. While a younger three-year-old can understand the meaning of each word in the sentence, "You broke the dish after I asked you to put it down, so now I'm going to have to spank you," she can't really comprehend its logic. What she does understand is that you believe it's okay to hurt her (and therefore others) when you are angry; that hitting is okay if one can't immediately come up with a better solution; and that working verbally through a conflict is not worth the trouble. Your actions have taught her these lessons. For children this age, actions speak much louder than words.

Since how you deal with her misbehavior is so carefully observed and mimicked by your three-year-old, this is an especially important time to find nonaggressive ways to deal with your preschooler. Many parents find that they are better able to maintain control of their own actions if they keep in mind that they're acting as role models for their child. If you can find a nonaggressive way of responding to repeated shouts of "No, I won't!" you may help your child figure out nonviolent ways to defend herself against, say, a playground bully in the future. "I try to picture my son in a similar situation, and act like I hope he would act," one father told me. "When he's done something not too serious, like splashing in the tub, I try to joke or tease him out of it sometimes by saying, 'I hope the fish don't run out of water.' If it's a big deal, I flat-out explain why he needs to stop what he's doing. If he doesn't stop, I usually give him a choice of two consequences—'You're out of the tub now or you clean up the mess'—and ask him which one he thinks is fairer. That starts him thinking about why the behavior was bad, how bad it was, and how the situation can be fixed. If he can fix the situation, then he's one of the good guys, right? If I hauled off and hit him, he'd just feel 'bad.'"

Clearly, this parent has learned the difference between punishment—which may end misbehavior for the moment but does nothing to promote self-control in the long run—and the kind of calm, confident setting of limits and enforcement of consequences that leads to adoption of your values and increased self-discipline. Studies have shown that the fearful, anxious emotional state caused by physical punishment actually gets in the way of the adoption of parents' values necessary for learning self-discipline. The more you spank your child for misbehaving, the more she will feel unable to resolve the conflict positively, and the less responsibility she will take for her own actions. No parent wants their child to turn out like that.

Sparing the Rod

Most parents who spank their children tell me they would prefer not to. They say that they resort to physical punishment only when other approaches seem futile. If you find that you are spanking your child with increasing frequency as she moves through the typical three-year-old stages of defiance, greater experimentation, and testing behavior, try taking a step back and thinking about how such extreme measures might be avoided ahead of time. Certainly, we are more likely to spank or hit our children when we ourselves feel too stressed to control our behavior. Sometimes, this stress level is created by the circumstances in which we live. At other times, we may have tried to cram too many activities into a day. Or we may ignore or endure a child's repeated misbehavior until we suddenly reach our breaking point and lash out physically instead of positively resolving the situation.

Whatever the cause of our stress, it's important to take note of our own inner warning signs and heed them immediately. If you feel pressured by work or financial concerns or haven't had enough sleep, make a point of getting some help with child care if possible *before* you reach the end of your rope. If you find that you're beginning to routinely lose your temper as you try to stick to a hectic schedule, drop a few items from your list of things to do. If you realize you've reached your limit, tell your child you need to be by yourself for a minute or two. It's better to plant her in front of the TV for a short while so you can call a friend or otherwise emotionally refuel than to lash out at her. As you implement these tools to regulate your own emotional state, explain what you're doing occasionally to your child. ("Mommy's really mad about the mess you made. I need to be alone to calm down right now.") Preschoolers are fascinated by all possible solutions to emotional dilemmas, and at some level will appreciate the "Mommy time-out." By talking to your child about how you handle your own frustration, you will help her learn to handle hers.

"WE DON'T DO THAT": INTERNALIZING FAMILY VALUES

Relating to your preschooler in a supportive, responsive, yet firm manner not only feels right as a parent, but it also helps speed the process of *internalization,* or adoption of the parents' values, that leads to consistent good behavior. The better the quality of your relationship with your child, the more effortlessly she will take on your rules and values as her own as soon as she is cognitively able. Internalization is also a necessary step in developing such moral qualities as real concern for other people, an understanding that some behaviors are right and others wrong, and a desire to repair damage done to others. At age two your child may have stopped a harmful act if you told her to, but she wouldn't have thought about it much. At age three, she is increasingly able to consider why the action is wrong. As she ponders such issues and adopts your values when defining both good and bad behavior, she begins to regulate her own actions more easily and feel guilty when she doesn't meet her own standards. Drs. Robert Emde and Helen Buchsbaum of the University of Colorado demonstrated in a 1990 study that children at this stage of development will typically show signs of distress when persuaded to do something against their parents' rules in the parents' absence, and often confess when the parent returns.

Clearly, internalization is an extremely valuable aspect of your family's development—not just because it's flattering to watch your child trying to imitate you, but because it provides such an energy boost to her social and emotional growth. While you may have noticed it starting to happen in your own family, in some respects, it's a phenomenon that can't be rushed. Your child must be able to discern and comprehend your feelings and values before she can internalize them—a development that usually isn't in place before the middle of this year. There are ways, however, to lay the groundwork for your child to easily and smoothly commit herself to your and your partner's point of view. Research has shown that the strength of the attachment you and your child formed during infancy and toddlerhood plays a major role in determining the ease with which she adopts her family's values, even before she's capable of fully understanding what those values imply. Attachment leads to a sense of security and oneness with the family, so that when your child learns that certain behaviors are the "family's rules," she adopts them without a second thought. As she grows older, the way in which you enforce rules affects her willingness to internalize them. When you clearly convey to your child what the rules are and take the time to explain why they are there ("Mary, you know we don't eat ice cream before we've finished our peas. It keeps us from getting the vitamins we need."), your child may test them now and then but will probably accept them easily enough. If, on the other hand, you depend on your power as a parent to enforce rules ("Mary, put that ice cream back and eat those peas RIGHT NOW!"), you increase your child's anxiety about them and cause her to avoid thinking about, rather than internalizing, those rules.

Of course, it's important to keep your explanations short and simple enough for your child to understand ("Hold my hand when we cross the street. I don't want you to get hurt," versus "This is a busy street. Cars can go by very fast and you never know if the driver's paying attention. I need you to hold my hand so I know the driver will see you and you won't get in the way of the cars.") and to tailor your responses to her behavior to suit her stage of development as she matures. Whereas you had to respond in strong, simple, very direct ways when your child was two ("No no! Don't push!"), you can now help her take a more active self-regulating role by making more general, indirect comments ("What a good girl to let Andrew help make cookies, too"). As your child gets better at initiating her own good behavior, you can recognize and reward this new ability by setting her up to succeed ("I know you'll share your crayons with Leah. You're always so generous.").

The key to acting as a role model for your child, in other words, is to behave toward her (as closely as possible) in the same calm, clear, and open way that you hope she will behave toward you. By the end of the year she will probably have internalized your values so fully that you may have to give her no more than a stern look, or hold up a finger for her to wait a moment, for her to correct her behavior and even (sometimes) apologize. She will have spontaneously begun to obey such rules as saying "please" and "thank you" without your having to prompt her. Her manners may have improved so much by the end of the year, in fact, that she may take pains to remind *you* now and then, "Don't point, Mommy, it's not nice."

Q & A

"Rachel Hit Me!"

Q: My three-year-old, Daphne, often reports other children's bad behavior to me. Lately, though, I've noticed that what she says sometimes isn't really true. If a friend jostles her as she goes by Daphne says, "Rachel hit me." She told me once that a girl sitting next to her at snack time in preschool kept telling her she was "a bad, bad girl," but the teacher says that never happened. It's upsetting to hear these false reports, and it's getting to the point where I don't know whether to believe anything Daphne tells me. What should I do about this?

A: No parent likes to think their child is a tattletale or, worse yet, a liar, so it's natural that you're upset. But children, like adults, sometimes exaggerate. Sometimes it's on purpose, to get a reaction. Other times they're acting on partial or incorrect information, or they witnessed something rather than experienced it themselves. It's important to discern which is the case with your daughter, who may just be responding to the preschooler's urge to rank or quantify—to figure out exactly how bad you think such negative incidents are, whether or not they actually happened. When in doubt, remind Daphne that it's important for everyone to tell the truth, whether the misbehavior is her own or someone else's. She pays close attention to your responses, since they confirm the values she's already begun to internalize. When she reports something that's clearly impossible ("Mommy, James made the doggy eat all the sugar cookies"), gently correct her ("Now, the dog wasn't inside

At age three, children find joy in their own—and others'—successes as they internalize the rules their parents have set.

the house, so I know that didn't happen. Who really did eat those cookies?"). If she tells you, point out that what happened wasn't nice, and remind her of what she can do to resolve the situation. Try not to intervene directly in the children's interaction, especially if you didn't witness the event. I always tell parents that as long as no one is hurt they shouldn't reward the tattler by getting involved. When preschoolers argue, simply say, "Figure it out. I know you can do it." Otherwise you set up a dynamic of getting pulled into every little disagreement. (An exception to this is power struggles between siblings who are mismatched—one is significantly larger, older, or otherwise more powerful than the other. In such cases it's best to intervene early, demonstrating positive ways to play, to keep such battles from escalating.) If you continue to respond to your daughter's reports in a calm, consistent way, she will soon tire of these experiments, and you will be able to rely on her to tell the truth most of the time.

"GOOD JOB!": USING LIMITS TO BUILD SELF-ESTEEM

Many parents these days worry that saying "no" to their preschool-aged children, or forbidding them to indulge in certain behaviors, will negatively affect their developing creativity or cause them to lose self-esteem. On the contrary, as we have seen, setting reasonable, consistent limits to behavior helps your child begin to master her actions—a necessary step in gaining confidence and a positive self-image. As your child learns a reasonable number of do's and don'ts from you and adopts them as her own, she becomes increasingly able to take over the reins in her environment, and the satisfaction she gains from this is enormous. You can help her experience the pleasure of knowing how to behave—and of reaping positive responses from others—by keeping her list of choices short enough to allow her to succeed early and often.

How often have you heard a parent yell at an out-of-control preschooler to "Stop that right now!"? In most cases, a younger three-year-old may not be able to physically stop behavior fast enough, or may wonder what she's supposed to stop—or she's so distracted by Dad's tone of voice that she loses the content of the message. If a parent instead tells her to "sit down or we leave," or "share those cookies with Shawn or put them away till after he goes home," the child has enough information to make a successful choice. Telling your defiant child, "Either brush your teeth or go back to bed"—and then calmly *enforcing* her choice every time—allows her to feel that she's choosing her behavior and is in charge of what will happen next. This method works best when the consequences spring naturally from the behavior—a display of temper leading to a time-out in her room, or eating all of her dinner leading to a favorite dessert. Just as with adults, the more a three-year-old experiences the logical results of a wrong action, the more motivated she is to change it. The better she gets at determining her fate in this way, the better she will feel about herself.

You can speed this process even more by offering positive choices rather than "don'ts" whenever possible. Tell your child that if she's patient while you're on the phone, you'll take her to visit her cousin later. (If she doesn't comply, you may have to move on to punishment-based choices such as forfeiting computer games, but at least you've given her a chance to make something good happen for herself.) It isn't necessary to keep coming up with exciting activities to persuade her to improve her behavior. She's young enough for you to use routine activities as inducements. Let her "earn" the detour to the ice-cream store (which you were going to take anyway) by patiently accompanying you while you shop for clothes, and she will have had an extra experience in good behavior leading to a positive outcome. Stickers, which hold a natural fascination for preschoolers, are another easy way to help your child to see the rewards that good behavior can bring. You can give her stickers for good deeds and matter-of-factly take them away if she misbehaves. If five stickers will get her an ice cream, she will soon learn how much better it is to be good.

By showing your child that the behavior *she chooses* leads to predictable consequences, you put her much more in control of her own behavior and experience. By keeping your approach to her behavior matter-of-fact, you will help her focus on controlling the behavior rather than the nonproductive emotions caused by guilt, resentment, or blame. Berating your child for being naughty throws her into a confusing well of bad feelings and also feels bad for you as a parent; telling her that what she did was "against the rules" and offering her ways to resolve the situation is not spoiling her. It gives her the feeling of control that is necessary for high self-esteem. Explaining that another preschooler who has misbehaved "hasn't learned the rules yet" relieves your child's anxiety about the incident and demonstrates that good behavior isn't inherent, but has to be learned.

A CHILD'S-EYE VIEW

"Sharing Is Good"

Adam has been asking all week for Luke to come over for a play date after their morning session at preschool. Finally, the day has arrived, and the two three-year-olds are busily exploring Adam's room. "I have a sword!" Adam says, proudly brandishing his plastic weapon.

"I have a sword at home, too, *and* a helmet," Luke tells him, continuing to rummage through Adam's toys.

"I have a helmet, too," Adam says hesitantly. At least he thinks he does. He wonders where it is.

"Oh, look!" Luke says suddenly, pulling a race car set out of the corner. "I have this at home! Daddy gave it to me 'cause I was good for three stickers!"

Adam frowns and looks around with dismay at his old toys. Luke has everything. *Adam* wants something! With a defiant, "Hey!" he grabs the plastic track out of Adam's hands. "That one's mine!" he says. Luke stares at him, then starts to howl.

"What's going on in here?" Adam's mom sticks her head into the room. "I was just fixing you guys a snack. Are you fighting already?"

"He tooked my toy away!" Luke yells, pointing at Adam.

"It's *my* race cars!" Adam shouts, his face red with fury.

"Hey, hey now." Adam's mom enters the room, gently disengages the track from Adam's hands, and sets it out of sight. "We're here to play, not fight," she reminds the two of them. Getting down between them, she looks from one to the other. "Now, you have a choice," she says, though she knows the answer in advance. "You can have cheese and grapes for your snack, or you can help me make chocolate chip cookies."

"Cookies!" Adam says, already over his tiff with his friend. But Luke looks hesitant. He's in a new place and he's not having fun yet. Adam watches him, growing anxious, as his mom adds, "The rule at our house is whoever helps bake the cookies gets to eat some dough."

Luke's face brightens. "Okay. Cookies," he says. Adam beams, and jumps up and down with excitement as they head to the kitchen. "Luke can sit here." Adam graciously points to his chair. *I'm sharing my chair,* he's thinking. *This is better than fighting with my friend.*

"WHAT'S THE RULE?": SETTING LIMITS WITHOUT JUDGING

It's the weekend before Lori's fourth birthday, and Walt has taken his daughter out to dinner again as a special treat. Lori has grown three inches taller over the past year, and Walt is amused by how composed and grown-up she looks as she takes her seat, picks up a menu, and gazes at it upside down. Since this is her birthday celebration, Walt had considered taking her to a fancier place, but he knows she likes the music at the diner so he's brought her there again.

"I'll have a grilled cheese sandwich and french fries, please," Lori says confidently, putting her menu down. "And a glass of milk." Looking at her dad mischievously, she adds, "Chocolate milk."

"Sounds good," Walt says, nodding judiciously as he continues reading his own menu. He's learned not to laugh at Lori's efforts to act grown-up. She hates it when he teases her.

The waitress arrives, and Walt starts to place their order when he notices that the music on the loudspeakers is getting pretty lively. He glances over at Lori, and sure enough, she is wiggling to the beat and getting ready to squirm out of her chair. "Uh-uh!" he says mildly, giving her a stern look. "What's the rule in restaurants?" Lori hesitates, then quickly settles back down, though she still taps her fingers on the table and kicks her feet to the beat.

What a difference from last year, Walt thinks as he turns back to finish talking to the waitress. But Lori's better behavior certainly didn't happen all at once. It took months of hard work on both their parts, he reflects—first his establishing limits and methodically sticking to them, and then her figuring out how to comply. It got easier, too, as the stress of the divorce faded somewhat and as Walt learned to express his opinions in calmer, more matter-of-fact ways. Certainly, Lori's ability to control her physical movements helped, as did her increased understanding of when certain behaviors were inappropriate. What Walt appreciates most, though, is her obvious desire to please adults through her behavior. At last, it's possible to have a conversation with his daughter rather than having to discipline her all the time. And Walt can see, as he asks her about her day and she begins to tell him, that the ability to communicate and behave in acceptable ways makes her a much happier, more confident little girl.

ADVANCES

Moving Toward Self-Discipline at Age Three

36 MONTHS	Observes and comments frequently on others' behavior
	Can follow a two- or three-part command
	Starts to experiment with negotiation
42 MONTHS	Begins to comply with your wishes even when you aren't there
	Feels uncomfortable when others engage in forbidden activities in her presence
48 MONTHS	Adopts your methods to solve conflicts and ease social situations
	Needs minimal reminders to correct most behavior

FIRST-PERSON SINGULAR

As your child's personality continues to emerge, you can better observe how she responds to various parenting techniques aimed at improving her behavior. Some children behave better when reminded of their actions' effects on others' feelings; others respond more quickly to discussions of fairness. Your child may behave better with frequent direct support from you, or with less assistance, preferring to figure things out on her own. By observing her responses to your interventions and trying to understand the feelings that inspired them, you can better tailor your disciplinary techniques to suit her personal style. Write down which methods you have tried and what the results were. What times of day or days of the week seem most difficult for your child, behavior-wise? Which of her behaviors tend to make you lose your own sense of control, and what have you done to remedy this situation? As your child begins to come up with her own ways to resolve conflicts or deal with frustration, record her solutions here. She will be interested to know what went through her mind as a three-year-old as she tried to manage her emotions and her behavior.

_____

_____

_____

_____

_____

_____

_____

_____

_____

_____

_____

_____

_____

_____

_____

_____

_____

_____

_____

_____

CHAPTER 9

Looking Ahead—I'm Four

Your firmness when he was three will go a long way in stemming unpleasant scenes when he is four.

It seems as though just yesterday the children in this book, as well as your own child, were celebrating their third birthdays, and now it's nearly time for their fourth. It's been a year of very satisfying progress—so much progress, in fact, that it's hard to imagine how they managed to fit it all into twelve short months. Over the past year, Pete and Bethany, Maddy and Shane—and your three-year-old as well—have learned to ride a bike (with training wheels), to draw a picture of a person, to use their words to make friends or resolve a dispute, to work out their anxieties through elaborate pretend play, and to sleep through the night almost as easily as an adult. We have watched their behavior steadily evolve as they encountered and tested your rules and values, adopted many of them, and even began to impose them occasionally on their stuffed animals and younger siblings. Your own evolution as a parent has been equally impressive as you observed your child's development, adopted new parenting strategies based on his stage of development and personal style, and found ways to turn negative situations into opportunities for growth. Your increasing experience and mastery as a parent will help make next year all the more rewarding as you witness the further blossoming of your four-year-old's capable self. Next year, your child's new cognitive, emotional, and social capabilities will take him much further toward independent thought and action, verbal sophistication, and true friendships with his peers. The deeper your understanding of the processes at work in your child today, the better able you'll be to support, encourage, and thoroughly enjoy these new advances.

DO YOU KNOW WHAT I KNOW?: WHAT YOUR CHILD HAS LEARNED

The past year has been one of integration of a wide array of important skills, leading to much deeper comprehension, expression, and self-mastery for your child. This is the year when your three-year-old learned effective ways to impose his will and personality on his surrounding environment—to dress himself (often in very creative ways), communicate his feelings more clearly to you (and perhaps an imaginary friend), persuade a friend to join him in a game or activity, and negotiate with others to get his way. As the months passed and he experimented with the ways in which his behavior affected his relationships with others for better or worse, he developed new interactive techniques based on his experiences. He learned that you did not always know what he was thinking or feeling unless he revealed his thoughts to you; that his misbehavior made you angry, but that he could repair the damage done by apologizing, cleaning up the mess, and behaving better next time. He discovered that play dates and preschool weren't much fun if he or his playmates frequently gave in to aggression, and so he developed new ways to resolve conflicts, express positive emotions, and substitute words for blows. Your example played a large role in helping him learn to manage himself and others in this way and will continue to lead him into the larger world as the next year begins.

Of course, none of this progress would have been possible without the amazing cognitive growth your child has experienced over the past year. His increasing ability to associate ideas, follow a line of reasoning, make comparisons, and ask "Why?" has played a huge role in supporting and directing his behavioral development. An improving ability to focus his attention, follow multiple directions, and remember has also helped him manage his world more effectively. Continued encounters with appearance-reality issues and other confusing situations have stimulated him to try to find answers to his questions that fit the evidence as he sees it. As a result, he has no doubt accumulated a fascinating variety of logical but inaccurate convictions about the natural world and the objects in it. He may believe that tree branches blowing in the breeze are waving at him; that his dog can understand his speech; and that his toys have grand adventures at night while he's asleep. His ability to discern the truth about his world will improve next year. In the meantime, his tendency toward animism and magical thinking stimulates a great deal of creative thought and pretend play.

One of the most enjoyable aspects of your child's development this year has probably been in the realm of his imagination. As the months have passed, he has spent longer periods alone with his dolls or action figures, creating exciting dialogue and changing his voice and manner to suit each character he plays. His emerging creativity is also evident in his drawings, which have grown much more sophisticated this year—moving beyond circles and squiggles to stick figures with eyes, nose, mouth, fingers, and hair. As his urge to please you increased near the end of the year, he probably began showering you with such handmade gifts as clay sculptures, beads on a string, and other forms of artwork. You may have overheard him inventing stories for himself when alone in his room, or seen him thoughtfully turning the pages of a picture book. His growing imagination and creativity even enhanced his social life as he engaged other children in his pretend play and joined in theirs. As he turns four, these interactions will support steadily deeper and more complex friendships. Chances are that as he expands his experience in the world outside his door, your four-year-old will find one or two other kids his age who are especially fun playmates to have around.

MAINTAINING LIMITS AND EXPANDING BOUNDARIES: WHAT YOU HAVE LEARNED

It must be said that three-year-olds make great parenting instructors as they continuously test our rules and respond instantly to any exceptions, inconsistencies, or mistakes we make. If you have learned one thing about caring for your child this year, it may be that setting reasonable limits and sticking to them (with perhaps a few exceptions) is the best way to help him learn to manage his behavior and to generally avoid conflict. This parenting skill will become even handier next year as your child gets better at negotiating, arguing, and spotting and remembering inconsistencies. Your firmness when he was three will go a long way in stemming unpleasant scenes when he is four.

As your child began to internalize your rules and values, his ability to regulate his own behavior improved considerably. As a result, you found that you could begin to take down some of the supportive scaffolding you'd erected over the years. When he got into an argument with a playmate, you learned to hold back and let him try to resolve it positively himself. When he fell and skinned his knee, you discovered that he'd get up, brush himself off, and tell *himself,* "I'm okay," if you let him. As you showed your child new ways to actively engage with his world—to help set the table, try to fix a broken toy, choose his bedtime story, and draw a picture for Grandma on her birthday—you observed the pleasure he derived from accomplishing these tasks on his own. This new independence saddens some parents, who see it as a loss. In actuality, it's strong evidence that you've been there for your child enough for him to feel comfortable taking new risks, knowing you'll always be available for backup. As he turns four, he will continue to rely on you to stand in the wings as he hones old skills and learns new ones.

COMING ATTRACTIONS: DEVELOPMENTS AT AGE FOUR

By the time he turns four, your child will have become a much more independent individual, with a clearer concept of who he is and where he stands in the world. He will take pride in his ability to master his environment and take care of himself to some degree. He will enjoy talking about himself to adults and other children—discussing his likes and dislikes, expressing his opinions, and comparing himself favorably to others his age or younger. Family life will become more pleasant as

As your child turns four, her unique personality will shine through as she tackles her world with confidence.

his self-confidence increases, as he learns ways to win positive responses from others, and as he both desires and improves his ability to please you and be good to others.

The development of his gross- and fine-motor abilities will tend more toward quality than quantity of new skills, and this refinement will continue next year. If he hasn't already, he will soon move from a tricycle to a bicycle with training wheels; from somersaults to hopscotch; and from simple games of hide-and-seek to more complex organized games. As he continues to take great pride in his accomplishments, his desk work will evolve from drawings of a face with two eyes and a mouth to pictures of his house and family, and perhaps even the letters of the alphabet. Your child's cognitive development will support this leap into more sophisticated drawing and writing. It will also pave the way for such budding skills as considering and planning for the future; comprehending the passage of the seasons, a week, and even a year; and wondering about such "big issues" as God and the cycles of life and death.

Your child's imagination and creativity will continue to expand considerably next year. He will grow even more eager for stories from books, anecdotes from your childhood, and stories about the places he visits and the people he knows. His wondering "why" will lead him into more magical thinking, though greater experience helps feed his rational side. As new associations, ideas, and influences enter his awareness he may develop some new fears, but here, too, his improved ability to comprehend your explanations, remember them, and invent strategies with which to manage his own emotions will help him maintain balance.

Your child's urge to know more will spur his verbal development this year, and he will grow more perceptive about the meaning of words and their impact. You are likely to hear him use a number of your habitual phrases ("Be careful . . ."; "Would you do me a favor?") as he experiments with new ways to make a verbal impact. He'll also grow even more entranced by the wonderful effect that jokes can have on others. Expect to play many a "knock-knock" game and listen to a lot of puns this year—and try not to flinch when he triumphantly cries, "Get it?" for the fourth time in a row. As you continue to play with language through funny songs, poems, word games, and other activities, his vocabulary will grow and his enthusiasm increase. By the end of the year both his pronunciation and grammar will have improved sufficiently to enable him to communicate with just about anyone with ease.

Four is a year of relatively placid emotional development, as your child's sense of self (including his sense of gender) solidifies and his self-management skills continue to improve. Largely reconciled to your brief absences (due to experience and a better concept of time), he will probably react less negatively and for shorter periods to your dropping him off at preschool or child care. Of course, temperament still plays a major role in your child's emotional expression and experience, but difficulties relating to shyness, fears, aggression, and manipulativeness can be more easily addressed as he becomes better able to respond to your rational explanations, support, consistency, and good example.

Because four-year-olds are often at a relatively stable stage emotionally, many parents find this to be an excellent year to introduce their child to preschool. Not only do most four-year-olds love to hang out with children of their age and gender, but their cognitive development has a reached a stage at which sit-down activities such as creating artwork, doing jigsaw puzzles, and trying to write the letters of the alphabet become more manageable. Your child will no doubt also benefit from increased opportunities to engage in pretend play with others, to practice his social skills, and to observe the rules, customs, and varying styles of others outside his home.

In fact, four-year-olds typically love routines and the feelings of group acceptance and well-being that accompany them. Your child may start to enjoy putting his toys in order if you encourage and support this, even if he showed little interest a year ago. He's likely to spend a contented morning sharpening each one of his colored pencils and replacing them in their box and will want to complete every maze in the coloring book he asked you to buy. Stickers and gold stars continue to spur him toward good behavior. He will eagerly wash his hands, feed the fish, help with the laundry, and straighten his room if it means every space on the sticker chart gets properly filled in.

Obviously, these orderly tendencies will diminish the frequency of conflicts in your home. You will find it easier to maintain discipline as your child continues to internalize your values, and you will find it easier to talk to him (and thus control your temper) when he strays. It's no surprise that physical punishment diminishes markedly in most American families as children turn four. Parents find that behavior that required a sharp command or active intervention last year now needs only a disapproving look—and they have been parenting long enough to learn that physical punishment creates negative results in the long run. On the other hand, your child's better verbal skills mean a sharp increase in negotiating, arguing, and pointing out your own inconsistencies. This is the first year when you might find yourself actually losing an argument with him.

All in all, you will find your four-year-old moving clearly from discipline to self-discipline. As a result, it's an excellent year for parent-child relationships. Look at it as your reward for several years' work well done.

FIRST-PERSON SINGULAR

Your child is nearly four, but before you put this book away, look back at the predictions you wrote for your child twelve months ago when he turned three. Chances are your sense of his personality and temperament and years of accumulated experiences allowed you to make some pretty accurate guesses about where he'd be right now. Certainly, by educating yourself about the typical stages of every young child's development, you've been able to observe and understand him much more fully than might otherwise be possible. Still, it's a good bet that your child surprised you in many ways this year—whether through a new quirk of behavior, an astounding insight, an unexpected expression of kindness or empathy, or remarkable progress in an area of development where he had lagged before. Now that you have a better sense of your child, get out your videotapes and photographs of your three-year-old, marvel at his progress, and think about where you want him to go. What are your goals for him, for yourself as a parent, and for your family as a whole next year? How would you most like to see your child grow? Have you noticed any particularly strong skills that you might help him develop further in the coming months? As we've seen, the better you know your unique child, the better equipped you will be to support his growth in the future. Thinking about him with pen in hand provides you with tools for a better future as well as precious souvenirs for the years ahead.

READER'S NOTES

Bibliography

Begley, Sharon. "Your Child's Brain." *Newsweek,* 19 February 1996.

Brazelton, T. Berry. *Touchpoints: Your Child's Emotional and Behavioral Development.* Reading, Mass.: Perseus Books, 1992.

Brownlee, Shannon. "Baby Talk," *U.S. News & World Report,* 15 June 1998.

Cole, Michael, and Sheila R. Cole. *The Development of Children,* 3rd ed. New York: W. H. Freeman and Co., 1996.

Dunn, Judy. *The Beginning of Social Understanding.* Cambridge, Mass.: Harvard University Press, 1988.

Epstein, Randi Hutter. "Fix Speech Problems Early, Experts Now Urge." *New York Times,* 30 November 1999.

"Fertile Minds." *Time,* 3 February 1997.

Gopnik, Alison M., Andrew N. Meltzoff, Patricia K. Kuhl. *The Scientist in the Crib: Minds, Brains, and How Children Learn.* New York: William Morrow & Co., 1999.

Hancock, LynNell, and Pat Wingert. "The New Preschool." *Newsweek,* 19 February 1996.

Jabs, Carolyn. "Computers and Kids." *Sesame Street Parents,* November 1999.

Kopp, Claire B. *Baby Steps: The "Whys" of Your Child's Behavior in the First Two Years.* New York: W. H. Freeman and Co., 1994.

Lieberman, Alicia. *The Emotional Life of the Toddler.* New York: Free Press, 1993.

Markman, Ellen M. *Categorization and Naming in Children: Problems of Induction.* MIT Series in Learning, Development, and Conceptual Change. Cambridge, Mass.: Bradford Books, 1991.

Newcombe, Nora. *Child Development: Change Over Time.* New York: HarperCollins, 1996.

Perry, Bruce D., Lea Hogan, and Sarah J. Marlin. "Curiosity, Pleasure, and Play: a Neurodevelopmental Pespective." *NAEYC Advocate,* 15 June 2000.

Perry, Bruce D. "Gray Matter." *Forbes,* 30 November 1998.

Pinker, Steven. *Words and Rules: The Ingredients of Language.* New York: Basic Books, 1999.

"Read*Write*Now*" http://www.ed.gov.

Rhodes, Sonya, with Lee Lusardi Connor. "Discipline ABCs." *Sesame Street Parents,* November 1999.

Shore, Rima. *Rethinking the Brain: New Insights into Early Development.* New York: Families and Work Institute, 1997.

Sroufe, Alan, Robert G. Cooper, and Ganie B. Dehart. *Child Development: Its Nature and Course,* 4th ed. New York: McGraw Hill, 2000.

Stern, Daniel N. *Diary of a Baby: What Your Child Sees, Feels, and Experiences.* New York: Basic Books, 1998.

Windell, James. *Discipline: A Sourcebook of 50 Failsafe Techniques for Parents.* New York: Macmillan, 1991.

"Your Child: From Birth to Three." *Newsweek Special Issue,* Fall-Winter 2000.

Recommended Reading

1. What I'm Like

Brazelton, T. Berry. *Touchpoints: Your Child's Emotional and Behavioral Development.* Reading, Mass.: Perseus Books, 1992.

Kopp, Claire B. *Baby Steps: The "Whys" of Your Child's Behavior in the First Two Years.* New York: W. H. Freeman and Company, 1994.

Shelov, Steven, and Robert E. Hanneman, eds. American Academy of Pediatrics. *Caring for Your Baby and Young Child: Birth to Age 5.* New York: Bantam Doubleday Dell, 1998.

2. My Physical Abilities

Spock, Benjamin and Stephen J. Parker. *Dr. Spock's Baby and Child Care,* 7th ed. New York: Pocket Books, 1998.

3. My Cognitive Development

Gardner, Howard. *Frames of Mind: The Theory of Multiple Intelligences,* 10th anniversary ed. New York: Basic Books, 1993.

Greenspan, Stanley, and Serena Weider, with Robin Simon. *The Child with Special Needs: Encouraging Intellectual and Emotional Growth.* Reading, Mass.: Perseus Books, 1998.

Stern, Daniel N. *Diary of a Baby: What Your Child Sees, Feels, and Experiences.* New York: Basic Books, 1998.

4. My Verbal Abilities

Gopnik, Alison M., Andrew N. Meltzoff, Patricia K. Kuhl. *The Scientist in the Crib: Minds, Brains, and How Children Learn.* William Morrow & Co., 1999.

Pinker, Steven. *The Language Instinct: How the Mind Creates Language.* New York: HarperPerennial, 1995.

———. *Words and Rules: The Ingredients of Language.* New York: Basic Books, 1999.

5. My Emotional Growth

Chess, Stella, and Alexander Thomas. *Know Your Child.* New York: Basic Books, 1987.

Greenspan, Stanley, and Nancy Thorndike Greenspan. *First Feelings: Milestones in the Emotional Development of Your Baby and Child.* New York: Viking, 1985.

Kagan, Jerome. *The Nature of the Child.* New York: Basic Books, 1984.

Lieberman, Alicia. *The Emotional Life of the Toddler.* New York: Free Press, 1993.

Pruett, Kyle. *Fatherneed: Why Father Care Is as Essential as Mother Care for Your Child.* New York: Free Press, 2000.

6. My Social Development

Dunn, Judy. *The Beginnings of Social Understanding.* Cambridge, Mass.: Harvard University Press, 1988.

Greenspan, Stanley, with Jacqueline Salmon. *The Challenging Child: Understanding, Raising, and Enjoying the Five "Difficult" Types of Children.* Reading, Mass.: Addison-Wesley, 1997.

Hopson, Darlene Powell, and Derek S. Hopson. *Different and Wonderful: Raising Black Children in a Race-Conscious Society.* New York: Fireside, 1992.

Kagan, Jerome, and Sharon Lamb, eds. *The Emergence of Morality in Young Children.* Chicago: University of Chicago Press, 1988.

7. My Need for Routine

Roberts, Susan B., and Melvin B. Heyman, with Lisa Tracy. *Feeding Your Child for Lifelong Health.* New York: Bantam, 1999.

Wilkoff, William G. *Coping with a Picky Eater: A Guide for the Perplexed Parent.* New York: Fireside Books, 1998.

8. My Need for Limits

Brazelton, T. Berry. *Touchpoints: Your Child's Emotional and Behavioral Development.* Reading, Mass.: Perseus Books, 1992.

Windell, James. *Discipline: A Sourcebook of 50 Failsafe Techniques for Parents.* New York: Macmillan, 1991.

Organizations and Support Groups

ADVICE AND RESOURCES FOR PARENTS

Family Resource Coalition

(312) 338-0900

Chicago, IL

This service puts callers in touch with state and local branches for accessible community support.

National Parent Information Network

(800) 583-4135

Largest parenting database in the United States. Parents can call for free professional referrals, advice, and printed articles. Weekdays, 8:00 A.M.–5:00 P.M., CST.

Zero to Three

734 15th Street NW, Suite 1000

Washington, D.C. 20005

(202) 638-1144

http://www.zerotothree.org

Call this child advocacy group for a general information kit, or access the website for excellent information on all aspects of infant and toddler development.

American Academy of Pediatrics

http://www.aap.org

The academy provides a wealth of information on the most recent scientific findings on teething, nightmares, toilet training, and countless other issues affecting children and their families.

Babycenter.com

http://www.babycenter.com

This website provides frequent updates on your child's development, as well as answers to parents' questions and a large database of information for parents.

Connect for Kids

http://www.connectforkids.org

An action and information center for citizens, businesses, and parents who want to make their communities work for kids.

Family.com

http://www.family.com

Sponsored by Disney, this website provides forums for parents to meet and talk online.

ParenthoodWeb

http://www.parenthoodweb.com

Answers to frequently asked questions. Pediatricians and psychiatrists also respond to parents' e-mail questions.

Parenting Q&A

http://www.parenting-qa.com

Offers answers to parents' questions, reading lists and activity suggestions for kids, and other family services.

ParentSoup

http://www.parentsoup.com

A good source of online advice for parents in nearly every challenging situation.

ParenTalk Newsletter

http://www.tnpc.com/parentalk/index.html

An online collection of articles by psychologists and physicians for parents.

U.S. Department of Education

http://www.ed.gov

Provides ideas and resources for parents relating to early childhood education, including the excellent Read*Write*Now* Early Childhood Kit.

CHILD CARE

Child Care Aware

National Association for Child Care Resources and Referral Agencies (NACCRRA)

1319 F Street NW, Suite 810

Washington, D.C. 20004

(800) 424-2246

http://www.naccrra.net

Provides referrals to local licensed and accredited child-care centers anywhere in the United States. They also offer a free information packet on how to choose quality child care. Weekdays, 9 A.M.–4:30 P.M., EST.

Families and Work Institute

267 Fifth Avenue, Floor 2

New York, NY 10016

(212) 465-2044

http://www.familiesandwork.org

Publishers of the excellent book for parents and professionals, *Rethinking the Brain: New Insights into Early Development* by Rima Shore, this organization provides information relating to the changing nature of work and family life.

SPECIAL NEEDS

Mothers United for Mutual Support

150 Custer Court

Green Bay, WI 54301

(414) 336-5333

Support and networking for families of children with any disorder, delay, or disability.

National Organization of Mothers of Twins Club

P.O. Box 23188

Albuquerque, NM 87192–1188

(505) 275-0955

Offers advice and information to parents of twins and refers callers to local chapters.

CRISIS INTERVENTION

ChildHelp National Hotline

(800) 4-A-CHILD

Twenty-four-hour advice and referrals from counselors with graduate degrees for children and adults with questions or in crisis.

National Clearinghouse for Family Support/Children's Mental Health

(800) 628-1696

Twenty-four-hour information and referrals to local family clinics, support groups, and therapists.

SUPPORT GROUPS

Home-Based Working Moms

P. O. Box 500164

Austin, TX 78750

(512) 918-0670

http://www.workHomMom@aol.com

Provides networking opportunities and newsletter for mothers working from their homes.

National Association of Mothers' Centers

336 Fulton Avenue

Hempstead, NY 11550

(800) 645-3828

Provides referrals to mothers' support groups and centers in your area, as well as information on how to start a group.

Parents Anonymous

Claremont, CA

(909) 621-6184; (800) 932-HOPE

Provides referrals to state and local affiliates, which offer support groups, counseling, referrals. Weekdays, 8:00 A.M.–4:30 P.M., PST.

Parents Without Partners

401 North Michigan Avenue

Chicago, IL 60611

(312) 644-6610

National organization with local chapters providing support for single parents.

Acknowledgments

Both formal and informal "teachers" have helped me understand children and parenting and, therefore, have made writing this three-volume set possible. The diverse families I have met through my work at Children's Hospital in Boston, Temple University, and the Institute of Child Development at the University of Minnesota taught me so much about the essence of parenting. My mentors at these institutions deserve special thanks, as they showed me how to turn my innate fascination with children into observational skills that apply to real-life family situations. In particular, T. Berry Brazelton and my colleagues at the Brazelton Touchpoints Center have deepened my appreciation for the expertise of parents. My own family of origin helped shape me immeasurably, of course. So, thanks Mom and Dad, Jim, Tom, and Trish, as well as the extended O'Brien-Garcia clan for all your support and for your example.

The Watch Me Grow series has been a collaborative effort, with several team players. Foremost, Sherill Tippins is a wondrous writing partner—insightful, humorous, and real. Elise Donoghue's photographs bring the stories vividly to life. Lynn Sonberg and Meg Schneider of Skylight Press and the team at HarperCollins/William Morrow, especially Rome Quezada, round out the "behind-the-scenes" supporters. Thanks also to the folks who graciously opened their doors for photos: the Boston Children's Museum, Bright Horizons, Children First, Lori Mitcheroney, and numerous parents.

I am indebted most of all to my husband, George, for his steady encouragement, and to my kids, Alex and Matthew. They are the heart and soul of my existence and continually delight me with the joy of discovery and endless surprises that are the rewards of family life.

—*Maureen O'Brien*

Index

NOTE: Italicized page numbers refer to picture captions.

Bailey, Mark, 346
ballet classes, 588–89
"bathroom dance," 617–18
baths, 165, 260, 365, 500, 638
battles, choosing, 238
Baumrind, Diana, 643–44
bed-wetting, 402–3, 618, 620–23,
    626
bedtime, 103–4. *See also* sleep
The Beginnings of Social Understanding
    (Dunn), 105
behavior
    child choosing, 655–57
    control of, 191, 496
    future consequences of, 563
    and gender issues, 586
    general principles of, 197
    as learned, 656
    positive alternative, 640
    rules of, 209
    See also bad behavior; good
        behavior; inappropriate
        behavior; models
behavior modification, 191
Bettelheim, Bruno, 321
bigger-smaller concept, 520
bilingual homes, 77–78, 90, 305, 308,
    315, 533, 539
biting and hitting
    and alternatives to physical
        punishment, 648, 649
    and coping with embarrassing
        questions, 550
    and emotional growth, 111, 114,
        346, 347, 348
    and imitation, 428–29
    and limits, 193, 194, 196, 234,
        428–29, 436, 637, 638, 648,
        649, 652–54
    and social development, 138–39,
        148, 234, 358, 360, 366, 373,
        376, 584, 590, 591
    See also aggression

body
    connecting mind and, 262–63
    control of, 350, 496, 499
    fascination with, 260–61
    getting to know, 260–61
    learning about, 498–501
    and physical abilities, 498–500
body language, 134, 362
books, 67, 68, 69, 211, 513. *See also*
    reading; stories
bossiness, 420, 585
Boston Children's Hospital, 1, 172,
    573, 588
boys. *See* gender issues
brain
    and cognitive development, 48–50,
        221, 274–76, 279, 296, 372
    development of, 2, 9, 14, 19, 28, 47,
        48–50, 66, 84, 90, 221, 274–76,
        279, 296, 304, 372, 423, 459
    as fully formed, 275–76, 296
    and interaction with computers, 287
    and motor development, 28
    and neural nets, 314
    new knowledge about, 48–50
    size of, 5, 14, 233
    and verbal abilities, 77, 84, 90,
        304, 305, 306, 314, 317
    See also magnetic resonance imaging;
        neurological development
Brazelton, T. Berry, 2, 9, 93, 176, 221,
    358
bribes, 191
Bruner, Jerome, 221
Buchsbaum, Helen, 650
bullying, 263–64, 373–74, 376, 591,
    594
"busy books," 244–45
"bye-bye" waves, 36, 134

Campos, Joseph, 108
car seats, 29–30, 254, 256, 258, 494,
    626

caregivers

and achievements of two-year-olds, 209

changing, 125–27

and cognitive development, 53, 56–57, 528

and emotional growth, 106, 125–27, 327, 351

later effects of attachments formed with, 106

leaving of, 389–90

and limits, 197, 645

multiple, 293

and parent coping with own physical limits, 255

and parenting style, 645

as part of extended family, 125–26

and personality, 220

quality of, 57, 125

and readiness, 225

and routines, 179–80

selection of, 57

and social development, 134–36, 141, 146, 359, 362, 369, 587, 603

and verbal abilities, 545

See also child care; child-care centers

caring, importance of, 323, 644

"catch me" games, 250

categorization. See classification/categorization of objects

Categorization and Naming in Children (Markman), 84

cause-and-effect concept, 17, 18, 195, 199, 208, 276, 422, 425, 522

centration, 280, 516, 519, 521

The Challenging Child (Greenspan and Salmon), 117

Chapieski, M., 6–7

charades, 514

Chess, Stella, 115

child care, 292–94, 316, 345, 362,

393, 394, 574. *See also* caregivers; child-care centers; group care

child-care centers, 118–19, 140, 197. *See also* caregivers

child development

Piaget's theory of, 272–73

as process, 2

unevenness in, 229, 237, 250–52

See also brain: development of; cognitive development; emotional growth; motor development; social development; verbal abilities

child-proofing, 39–40, 199, *200,* 201

children, other. *See* friendships; imitation; others; peers; social development

"A Child's-Eye View," 3, 225–26, 474–75

on cognitive development, 60–61, 290–91, 625–26

on emotional growth, 330–31, 560–61

on limits, 195–96, 435–36, 656–57

on motor development, *37*

on physical abilities, 259–60, 487–88

on routines, 166–67, 398–400, 616–17

on social development, 144–45, 366–67, 593–94

on verbal abilities, 85–86, 303–4, 549–50

choices, making, 189–90, 238, 390, 478, 486–88

Chomsky, Noam, 314

chores

and cognitive development, 290, 514

completing, 624

of four-year-olds, 669

and motor development, 253–54

comprehension, 224, 235
    and cognitive development, 52,
        271–72, 273–74, 275, 277, 278,
        281, 283, 287, 295, 513,
        515–19, 528, 668
    and development delays, 295
    and emotional growth, 344, 557,
        562–63, 567
    and experimenting with point of
        view, 473
    of four-year-olds, 668
    growth in, 10, 14–15, 18, 231–33
    and internalizing values, 650–51
    and limits, 422, 636, 638, 639,
        650–51
    and routines, 388, 389, 390
    and rules, 199
    and social development, 361, 366,
        379
    of three-year-olds, 463, 467, 468
    and verbal abilities, 80, 82, 302, 305,
        307, 317, 318, 536, 546, 549
    and "winging it," 271, 272
compromise, 336, 352, 446, 643
computer software, educational, 67,
    286–87
Concentration (game), 534–35
confinement, frustration caused by, 10,
    29–30, 118
conflicts
    adults' involvement in settling,
        328, 335, 654, 666
    avoiding, 185–86, 190–91, 666
    and choosing battles, 238
    and cognitive development, 284
    diminishing, 669
    distractions in, 185–86, 190–91,
        236–37
    and emotional growth, 329, 336,
        344, 346, 560
    of four-year-olds, 664, 666, 669
    and limits, 425
    managing, 376

between parents, 425–27, 575–76
    remedying, 471
    resolving, 229, 284
    and routines, 413
    and social development, 376, 599
    talking through, 329
    of three-year-olds, 641, *642, 643*
    and verbal abilities, 329
connections, making, 225–26,
        231–33, 537, 664
    and cognitive development, 273,
        279, 283, 285, 291, 295–96
    and emotional growth, 327, 340
    and physical abilities, 259–60
    and routines, 406–7
    and social development, 359, 372
conscience, development of, 640
conservation, concept of, 521–22
consideration of others, 357, 376–80
control
    parent's loss of, 418
    See also type of control
conversation, 6, 210, 445
    and cognitive development, 282, 517
    and emotional growth, 345, 560, 562
    family, 398, 540
    imaginary, 288
    interruptions in, 544–46
    about limits, 636, 639–40, 669
    "pretending" to hold, 80
    rhythms of, 88–89, 540
    about routines, 393, 618
    sharing focus of, 308–9
    and social development, 366, 584,
        603
    spontaneous, 86–87
    of three-year-olds, 467, 533, 536
    and verbal abilities, 80, 86–87,
        88–89, 94–95, 304, 307, 308,
        322
    and willfulness and independence,
        475
    See also scripts

achievements in, 106, 128–29, 209, 331–33, 352–53, 446, 577

and appropriateness of emotions, 329, 562, 563

as challenging, 327–29

and cognitive development, 49, 110, 273, 274, 278, 281, 288, 291, 335, 340, 346, 512, 560, 563, 565–66, 575

and consistency, 340, 341, 352, 669

and control/management of emotions, 245, 329, 330, 336, 419, 420, 561–64

and coping with stress, 572–74

and deliberate misbehavior, 555–57, 576–77

development delays in, 114–15, 145, 571–72

and development stages, 329, 334–35, 337, 344–45, 563, 573

expanding boundaries in, 127–28

and explanations of misbehavior, 557

and expressing feelings, 148, 151, 225, 307, 308, 309, 328, 329, 336, 341, 344, 350, 351, 352, 362, 544, 562

and faking emotions, 340, 342

in first year, 104–6, 331–33

of four-year-olds, 668, 669

and future consequences of behavior, 563

if you're concerned about, 145, 344–45, 571–72

and internalizing values, 650

and limits, 188, 198, 201, 329, 332, 419, 424, 430, 432, 557, 559, 636, 639, 640, 650, 655

and motor development, 42, 109, 333, 343

and "nurture," 113

of one-year-olds, 101–31, 331–33

and parent-child relationship, 559–61, 572–74

and parenting style, 108–10, 121–24, 210

and physical abilities, 332, 333, 346, 571

regression in, 556, 564, 570, 575

and "risky" emotions, 562

and routines, 160, 165, 180, 343, 406, 407, 564, 576

and self-comforting, 334

and sharing emotions, 351–52

and social development, 106, 111, 137, 139–40, 143, 148, 329, 343, 362, 364, 467, 582, 583, 590, 602

and swings in emotion, 212–13

and thinking before acting, 346

of three-year-olds, 335, 465, 466–67, 470, 555–79

and transitions, 120–21, 125–27

and "triggers" of children, 347–48

of two-year-olds, 212–13, 327–56, 339

and understanding emotions, 562–63

and verbal abilities, 102, 302, 307, 308, 310, 311, *319,* 322, 327, 328, 329, 336, 340, 341, 343, 344, 346, 350, 351, 352, 362, 540, 542, 544, 547, 560, 562, 571

The Emotional Life of the Toddler (Lieberman), 329

emotional readiness, 602

emotional separateness, 108–10, 209, 278, 328, 361

empathy, 207, 209, 211, 228, 229, 235

and cognitive development, 52

and emotional growth, 106, 110–11, 114, 329, 334, 336

and limits, 420

modeling of, 597

and parenting style, 644

and social development, 143, 144–45, 362, 376, 378, 380, 597, 602

375, 583–84, 587, 604–5
and verbal abilities, 544
See also group care; preschool
guilt
    and emotional growth, 329, 335,
        337, 350, 556, 557, 560,
        567–68
    of four-year-olds, 479
    and limits, 186, 655
    of parents, 345, 418
Gunnar, Megan, 108
"gut feelings," 34, 69, 314, 316

hand-eye coordination, 36–37, 38
Harris, Paul, 289
hearing, 70, 76, 91–92, 316, 539
Heibeck, Tracy, 310
"Hello," saying, 234, 463–64
here and not here. *See* object
    permanence
heredity, 49, 113, 115, 274, 318, 329,
    338, 656
hide-and-seek, 363, 368, 473, 474–75,
    668
high chairs, 169, 397
hitting. *See* biting and hitting
hostility, and parenting style, 644
household dangers. *See* child-proofing;
    safety
humor, 207, 211, 228, 329, 350, 465,
    549
Huttenlocher, Janellen, 49–50
hypotheses testing, 275

"If You're Concerned"
    and cognitive development, 69–70,
        294–95, 527–28
    and differences among children,
        250–52
    and emotional growth, 145,
        344–45, 571–72
    and limits, 201–2, 438–40, 649–50
    and motor development, 33–34

and physical abilities, 250–52,
    502–3
and routines, 172, 403–4, 620–23
and social development, 145, 146,
    380–81, 584–86
and toilet training, 620–23
and verbal abilities, 145, 315–16,
    538–39
imagination, 211, 227, 232, 445, 447,
    465–67, 468–69
    and cognitive development, 273,
        276, 279, 281–82, 283, 284,
        287–90, 296, 372, 514, 524,
        525
    and emotional growth, 340, 343,
        557
    of four-year-olds, 449, 665, 668
    in play, 52, 95, 162, 209
    and routines, 611, 626
    and social development, *234,* 467,
        599–601
    and verbal abilities, *319,* 320, 546
    See also friendships: fantasy
imaginative play
    and cognitive development, 279,
        287–89, 290, 525, 669
    and emotional growth, 335, 340,
        562, 571
    of four-year-olds, 665, 669
    and physical abilities, 499
    and point of view, 473
    and routines, 393
    and sexual issues, 499
    and social development, 359, 371,
        382, 584, 598, 599, 669
    of three-year-olds, 449, 459,
        466–67
    of two-year-olds, *234*
    and verbal abilities, *542,* 543
    See also friendships: fantasy
imitation, 17, 211, 447
    and cognitive development, 55–57,
        64, 283–86, 291–92, 372, 511

imitation *(continued)*
  and emotional growth, 340, 559–61
  and internalizing family values, 650
  and limits, 428–30, 650
  and motor development, 245, 252
  and physical abilities, 250, 262–63
  and routines, 173, 175, 400, 402
  and social development, 137, 141,
    143, 211, 229, 234, *234,* 362,
    368, 369, 371, 588, *595*
  and verbal abilities, 76, 79, 86–87,
    94, 305, 306, 543, 546
impulse control, 544–46, 636, 638,
  640
impulsive behavior, 544–46, 636, 638,
  640, 641
inappropriate behavior, 606, 645–46,
  658
independence
  and cognitive development, 71
  and emotional growth, 105, 106,
    122, 127–28, 329, 333, 559,
    571, 574
  of four-year-olds, 448–49, 666
  growth of, 475–78
  and limits, 189, 419, 559, 666
  and motor development, 40–41, 42
  of one-year-olds, 7, 8–12
  and routines, 159, 169, 629
  and social development, 599
  support for, 478
  of three-year-olds, 467, 476
  of two-year-olds, 208, 227
individual differences
  and cognitive development, 66,
    515–16
  in development stages, 2, 3, 8, 20,
    33, 42, 69–70
  and emotional growth, 106,
    114–15, 573
  and motor development, 33
  and physical abilities, 250–52
  and social development, 587

inductive reasoning, 199, 211
infants, 28–29, 278. *See also specific topic*
instincts. *See* "gut feelings"
intelligence
  and cognitive development, 66–67,
    277–82, 283, 284, 285, 286,
    288, 527–28
  concerns about, 527–28
  symbolic, 277–82, 283, 284, 285,
    286, 288, 317
  types of, 66
  and verbal abilities, 76, 91–93,
    315, 317–18, 539, 547–48
  See also thinking
intelligence quotient (IQ), 49, 106,
  122, 274, 317

jargoning, 78, 140
jealousy, 335, 562
joint attention, 308–9

Kagan, Jerome, 113, 145, 285
Kelly, Joan, 575
knock-knock jokes, 473, 514, 546,
  668
Kochanska, Grazyna, 639
Kuczynski, Leon, 283
Kuhl, Patricia, 77–78

labeling, 373–75, 376, 540, 545, 588
Lamb, Michael, 121–22
language
  body, 134, 302
  learning to live with, 550–51
  love of, 319–20, 538, 546–47
  sexual, 499
  sign, 316
  as tool, 533
  See also conversations; verbal
    abilities
*The Language Instinct: How the Mind
  Creates Language* (Pinker), 85,
  313

limits *(continued)*
 setting of, without judging, 657–58
 and social development, 146–49,
  187, 426
 of three-year-olds, 199, 459,
  461–62, 468, 635–61, 665–66
 of two-year-olds, 211, 417–43
 and verbal abilities, 188, 198, 199,
  419, 437, 438, 468, 636, 647,
  648, 670
 and willfulness and independence,
  475, 477
 and window of opportunity, 422
 See also "No!"; praise; rewards; rules;
  testing
lisps, 315
listening, 313, 317, 343, 362, 363,
 446, 448, 520, 541, 545, 602
loving relationship/environment, 53,
 56, 66, 115, 330
lying, 336–37, 462, 463, 468–69,
 473, 512, 635, 640, 652

Maccoby, Eleanor, 587
magical thinking, *515,* 523–25, 599,
 665, 668
magnetic resonance imaging (MRI),
 310, 314, 317, 423
making sense, 273, 291
making up, 568. *See also* apologies
manipulation
 emotional, 340
 and experimenting with point of
  view, 473
 by four-year-olds, 669
 of ideas and images, 281
 and limits, 201
 of objects, 274, 286, 496
 of parents, 468–69
 and social development, 584, 596,
  600
 by three-year-olds, 462, 468–69

manners
 and emotional growth, 335
 and limits, 652
 parent modeling of, 597
 and routines, 398
 and social development, 365,
  366–67, 594–96, 597, 604
 of two-year-olds, 211, 237, 304,
  308, 335, 365, 366–67, 398
 and verbal abilities, 304, 308,
  542–46
Markman, Ellen, 84, 310
mathematics, 514, 520–23
mealtimes, 223–24. *See also* eating
Mediascope, 347
memory, 9, 208–9, 220, 231, 235,
 447, 465
 and cognitive development, 55,
  273, 279, 281, 282, 283,
  285–86, 296, 372, 512, 516,
  518, 525
 and independence, 478
 and limits, 419, 423, 468, 639
 and routines, 627
 and social development, 362, 583,
  595, 597
 strategies for, 518
 and verbal abilities, 90, 209, 317,
  536–37
mental representations, 512
metaphors, 288
mimicking. *See* imitation
mind-body, connecting of, 262–63
Minnesota Parent-Child Project, 106
models
 and emotional growth, 330, 348,
  560, 561, 564
 of good behavior, 191–92, 193
 and internalizing values, 651
 and limits, 191–92, 193, 428, 438,
  475, 477, 646, 651
 reality, 285, 286

and routines, 615, 620, 625
and self-management, 664
and social development, 139, 144,
148, 373, 376, 381, 464, 584,
591–92, 597–98
and verbal abilities, 538
and willfulness and independence,
475, 477
morality, 142–44, 145, 229, 235, 450,
640, 641
more and less concept, 520, 523
motor development
achievements in, 25, 28–29, 42, 43,
207, 208, 246–48, 265–66
and brain development, 28
and cognitive development, 42, 66,
247
and development delays, 33–34
and development stages, 188
and emotional growth, 42, 109,
333, 343
and experimentation/exploration,
35, 37, 40–41, 42, 252–53, 262
and first steps, 25–26, 28, 33
of four-year-olds, 449, 668
and hand-eye coordination, 36–37,
38
if you're concerned about, 33–34
and imitation, 245, 252
and individual differences, 33
and inductive reasoning, 199
and limits, 198, 200
of one-year-olds, 9, 10, 18, 25–46
and play, 61, 66, 254
and refining movement skills,
252–55
and repetition, 252, 254
and rhythm, 31, 33
and routines, 161, 165, 169
and safety, 29–30, 31, 32, 35,
38–40, 257
and social development, 361

of three-year-olds, 445, 465
of two-year-olds, 211, 224, 227,
229, 246–48, 249–50, 253–54,
265–66
and verbal abilities, 81
See also fine-motor development
moving of household, 519–20

name
saying, 283
spelling, 512
writing, 291, 465, 489, 491
naps, 160, 161, 164, 389, 392, 393,
611, 613–14
narratives, self, 566, 665
National Association for the Education
of Young Children (NAEYC),
602
National Institute for Child Health
and Development, 125
National Institute of Mental Health,
283
National Longitudinal Survey of
Youth, 647
nature vs. nurture. See heredity;
"nurture"
needs and motivations of child, 293,
294, 334, 335, 336
negotiation
and emotional growth, 329, 346
of four-year-olds, 664, 666, 670
and limits, 468, 645
and routines, 390, 612, 625
and social development, 595–96
of three-year-olds, 322, 329, 346,
390, 469
and verbal abilities, 322
neural nets, 314
neurological development, 14–15,
274–76
and cognitive development, 49,
51–52, 53, 55, 56, 281, 512

neurological development *(continued)*
   "critical windows" of, 15
   and emotional growth, 565–66
   and limits, 423
   and verbal abilities, 305
night terrors, 160–61
nightmares, 160, 342, 392
"No!"
   child telling parents, 10, 19,
      80–81, 116, 175, 219, 220, 224,
      228, 302, 303, 330–31, 333,
      336–37, 388, 446, 475, 648
   and consistency, 195–97
   and disruptions in routines, 388
   and emotional growth, 116,
      117–20, 330–31, 333, 559
   and limits, 187, 188, 195–97, 434,
      648, 654
   parents telling child, 6–7, 187,
      188, 434, 478, 559, 654
   and toilet training, 175
   and verbal abilities, 80–81, 302,
      303
novelty, 180–81, 254, 329
nudity, 260
numbers, 276, 287, 291, 520. *See also*
   counting; mathematics
"nurture," 57, 113

object permanence, 48, 54–55, 208,
   278, 281, 362
objects
   animism of, 288
   child's focusing on, 346
   classification/categorization of, 231,
      295, 317, 369
   comparison of, 283, 285
   labeling of, 361
   manipulation of, 274, 286, 496
   naming, 308, 309, 316, 320
   visualization of, 278, 280–81, 283,
      317
"One potato, two potato," 501–2

one-year-olds
   achievements in, 20–21, 25, 42, 43,
      71–72, 80–81, 128–29, 152–53,
      182, 203, 208–9, 274–75,
      296–97
   overview about, 1–4, 5–23
   progress in, 8–12
   See also specific topic
open and closed concept, 275
opinions
   developing own, 333
   importance of child's, 286
orderliness, sense of, 173, 669
organizations and support groups, 1.
     See also specific group
others
   awareness of, 336, 361–62
   consideration of, 357, 378–80
   and coping with embarrassing
      questions, 548–50
   and emotional growth, 106, 122,
      328, 336
   emotional responses of, 583, 596
   explaining thoughts to, 583
   feelings of, 467, 540, 557, 560, 595
   influence of, 368, 581–82
   interacting with, 10
   interest in, 6, 311, 368
   learning from, 233–35, 275,
      291–94, 526–27, 585, 599
   learning to move with, 262–63
   point of view of, 472–74, 540
   positive and negative expressions of,
      562
   respect for, 366
   and self, 134, 209, 596
   and social development, 134,
      138–41, 362, 372, 581–82
   toleration of, 179, 226–27, 228
   watching out for, 264
   See also empathy; play
overindulging children, 637
overprotectiveness, 294, 344, 574

parenting
   adjusting style of, 424–26
   and cognitive development, 67, 68,
      69
   consistency in, 645
   as constant challenge, 221
   creativity of, 207
   and development stages, 644–45,
      663
   differences between partners in,
      643, 645, 646–47
   different styles of, 425–27
   and differing points of view, 625,
      637
   and emotional growth, 108–10,
      121–24, 210
   and limits, 424–26, 643–47
   one-size-fits-all, 2
   and social development, 597–98
   and temperament, 643–46
   for three-year-olds, 448, 480–81
   for two-year-olds, 237–40, 448,
      480–81
   undermining other parent's, 425–27
parents
   achievements of, 210, 445, 448,
      663
   anger of, 418–19, 437, 438–40,
      556–57, 576
   anxiety of, 619
   child's identification with, 559–61,
      586
   closeness of child and, 228
   consistency between, 468–69
   coping with physical limits of,
      255–56
   disagreements between, 425–27,
      575–76
   emotional connection between
      child, 15
   feelings of failure of, 421
   frustration of, 437, 619
   guilt of, 418

"gut feelings" of, 34, 69, 314, 316
hands-on experience in child
   development of, 2
identification of child with,
   559–61, 586
isolation of new, 1–2
loss of control by, 418
manipulation of, 468–69
meshing of moods and emotions of
   child and, 352
mismatch between expectations and
   abilities of child and, 224–25
as preschool volunteers, 603
self-control of, 438–40
self-regulation of, 649–50
talking about feelings of, 379
time-outs for, 439
and trusting yourselves, 210
See also parenting; "A Parent's Story"
"A Parent's Story," 15–16, 230–31,
   463–64
   and cognitive development, 50–51,
      66, 273–74, 519–20
   and emotional growth, 103–4,
      333–34, 558–59
   and limits, 189–90, 420–21,
      637–38
   and motor development, 29–30
   and physical abilities, 248–49, 498
   and routines, 160–62, 394–95,
      610–11
   and social development, 149–51,
      360, 588–89
   and verbal abilities, 89, 306–7,
      541–42
Parke, Ross, 121–22
patterns, 304–5, 306, 512, 520, 522,
   612
peek-a-boo, 62, 63, 276, 308, 332,
   365
peer pressure, 625
peers. See friendships; others
perfectionism, 547

permissive parenting, 643
"persisters," 470
personal agency, 378–79
personal space, 540
personality, 207, 220, 228, 236, *339,*
    445, 457, 467
  and cognitive development, 294
  coherence and integration of, 458,
    560
  and development stages, 251
  emergence of, 103, 209, 448
  and emotional growth, 103, 114,
    329, 337–41, *339,* 560
  of four-year-olds, 664, *667,* 670
  and limits, 659
  and negative feelings about child,
    338, 340
  and routines, 467, 614
  and social development, 381, 467,
    583
  and temperament, 113
physical abilities
  achievements in, 264–66, 488–91,
    495, 502–3, 504
  and appearance, 227, 228
  and being a "big kid," 263–65,
    502, 503
  and choosing activities, 486–88
  and cognitive development, 244,
    247, 248, 258, 274, 291, 489,
    514
  and development stages, 499,
    502–3
  and developmental delays, 502–3
  and emotional growth, 332, 333,
    571
  of four-year-olds, 449
  and idea of physical act, 262–63
  if you're concerned about, 33–34,
    250–52, 502–3
  and learning about body, 498–501
  and limits, 244, 255, 420, 421,
    432, 658

  of one-year-olds, 6, 10, 11, 17–18,
    19, 25–46
  over- and under-estimating child's,
    258
  and parents trusting themselves,
    210
  and routines, 392, 397–98, 400,
    613, 618
  signs of difficulty concerning, 502–3
  and size, 263–64
  and social development, 260–61,
    262–64, 502, 583, 602
  and starting and stopping actions,
    495–97
  and strength, *497*
  of three-year-olds, 459, 462,
    485–507
  of two-year-olds, 208, 209, 212,
    220, 224, 243–69
  and verbal abilities, 263, 321–23
  and willfulness and independence,
    476
  See also motor development; walking
physical punishment, 193, 197–98,
    418, 436–38, 647–50, 670.
  See also spankings
physical readiness, 602
Piaget, Jean, 272–73, 524
pickiness, 489, 491–92, 614
Pin-the-Tail game, 516–17
Pinker, Steven, 85, 313
planning, 9, 209, 224, 227, 668
  and cognitive development, 52, 55,
    279, 281, 518, 668
  and emotional growth, 118–19, 329
  and frustration, 13
  and independence, 478
  and limits, 432, 437
  and motor development, 254
  and physical abilities, 249–50, 254
  and routines, 160, 164, 404–6
  and social development, 373
  and verbal abilities, 321, 537

play, 6, 8, 10–11, 20, 449, 461
  age-appropriate, 254
  and cognitive development, 17–18,
    19, 52, 57, 61, *62*, 63–67, *68*,
    69, 276–77, 279, 282, 285–86,
    288, 289, 290–91, 525, 526–27
  complexity of, 362
  and control, *62*
  and development delays, 295
  and development stages, 380–81
  and emotional growth, 335, 340,
    341–42, 344, 345, 347–48,
    564–65, 569
  and experimentation, 61, 63, 65,
    492–94
  and frustration, 13
  and gender issues, 586
  importance of, 16–18, 61, 63–64
  lack of joy at, 295
  and motor development, 61, 66,
    254
  pacing, 65–67
  parallel, 140, 262
  parent-child, 64, 67, *68*, 69, 287,
    335, 340
  and physical abilities, 250, 254,
    262, 263–64, 492–94
  and playing with rather than beside,
    362
  purpose of, 289–90
  and routines, 393, 409, 614
  and siblings, 64
  and social development, 134–36,
    137–42, *140*, 141, 149, 229,
    359, 360, 362, 363, 368–72,
    370, 371, 372, 375, 380–82,
    585, 586, 587, 591, 593–96, *595*
  solo, 64, 140, 492–93, 541,
    564–65, 569, 585, 614
  symbolic, 63
  and verbal abilities, 69, 78–79, 95,
    301–2, 316, 317, 318, 541, *542*,
    543

  See also groups; imaginative play;
    play dates; play groups,
    neighborhood; The Toy Box; toys
"play baby," 617
play dates, 225, 664
  and cognitive development, 294
  and experimenting with point of
    view, 474–75
  and limits, 189, 194
  and physical abilities, 255
  and social development, 137–38,
    141–42, 149, 151, 357–58, 362,
    372, 373, 381–82, 584, 585,
    601, 603
play groups, neighborhood, 301–2,
  321–23
"Please," saying, 597, 652
point of view, 424, 472–75
politeness. *See* manners
Power, T., 6–7
practice
  and cognitive development, 281,
    283, 286, 293, 372
  and emotional growth, 557, 567, 568
  and limits, 641
  and physical abilities, 489, 492,
    495, 496, 502, 503
  and social development, 149, 365,
    368, 373, 376–80, 467, 471,
    585, 595, 598, 599, 603
  and verbal abilities, 305, 533
  See also repetition
praise, 26, 465
  and cognitive development, 56, 522
  and emotional growth, 334, 336
  and limits, 191, 202, 428, 430,
    432, 654–56
  and physical abilities, 496
  and routines, 169, 175–76, 402, 408,
    410, 619, 620, 621, 625, 630
  and social development, 149, 584,
    595
  and verbal abilities, 315, 540

predictability
  and cognitive development, 60–61,
    66
  of limits, 196–97, 390–92
  of routines, 158, 159, 166, 171–72,
    239, 389, 390, 394, 410–11,
    610, 613
  of rules, 390–92
preoperational stage, 272–73
preschool
  benefits of, 669
  and cognitive development, 281,
    292–94, 514, 527, 528, 669
  considering, 601–3
  and emotional growth, 562, 563
  in fourth year, 450
  parent as volunteer at, 603
  and physical abilities, 496
  quality of, 602
  and routines, 394, 403, 411, 611,
    612, 618
  and social development, 293, 369,
    371, 372, 583–84, 587, 601–3,
    606, 664
  suspension from, 603–4
  timing of placement in, 602
  and verbal abilities, 537, 544–46
pretending, 17, 227, 232, 449
  and cognitive development, 519,
    524, 525
  and emotional growth, 566
  and physical abilities, 499
  and social development, 363, 368
  and verbal abilities, 80
  See also fantasy friends; imagination;
    imaginative play
pride, 228, 465, 666
  and emotional growth, 329, 334,
    335, 336, 562, 568, 569
  and motor development, 668
  and routines, 619, 624, 625, 630
  and verbal abilities, 535
privacy, 261–62, 424

problem solving, 221, 227, *232,* 447,
    479
  and cognitive development, 55, 71,
    279, 281, 284, 285
  and emotional growth, 336, 352,
    559, 568, 573
  and limits, 639, 640, 641, 642, 643
  and safety, 470–71
  and social development, 471, 584,
    598
  of three-year-olds, 459, 465, 469–72
professional help, seeking, 252, 261,
    295, 316, 345, 424, 503,
    538–59, 571
promises, 463, 557
property disputes, 346
prosocial behavior, 143, 199, 211, 374,
    446, 594–96
Pruett, Kyle, 122
punishment
  alternatives to physical, 647–50
  choices of, 636–37
  and emotional growth, 347
  of four-year-olds, 670
  and limits, 186, 193, 194, 197–98,
    418, 436–38, 636–37, 670
  negative results of, 670
  physical, 193, 197–98, 418,
    436–38, 647–50, 670
  and social development, 591
  and verbal abilities, 545
  See also spankings

"Q&A," 3
  and cognitive development, 53,
    56–57, 523
  and emotional growth, 124–25,
    126–27, 336–37, 575–76
  and limits, 197–98, 431–32,
    652–54
  and motor development, 39–40
  and physical abilities, 261–62,
    263–64, 491–92

and routines, 162–63, 390–92,
624–25
and social development, 134–36,
372–73, 603–4
and verbal abilities, 87, 93–94,
320–21, 468–69, 544–46
questions, 449, 467, 668
and cognitive development, 275
embarrassing, 467, 548–50
open-ended, 548
persistent, 533
and verbal abilities, 303, 533, 536,
551
"Why?," 533, 664, 668

Ramey, Craig, 14
"Read*Write*Now*," 78
"Reader's Notes," 22–23, 240–41,
453–54, 482–83, 671
and cognitive development, 72,
298–99, 531
and emotional growth, 130–31,
354–55, 578–79
and limits, 204–5, 443, 660–61
and motor development, 44–45
and physical abilities, 268–69,
506–7
and routines, 183, 414–15, 631–33
and social development, 154–55,
384–85, 607
and verbal abilities, 97–99,
324–25, 553
readiness, 11, 173, 175, 225, 293,
362, 474–75, 602
reading, 208, 319, 668
and cognitive development, 67, 68,
69, 277–78, 294, 528
and developing love of language,
319–20
and emotional growth, 342, 344,
565
fairy tales, 320–21
and following storyline, 320

as fun, 320
and learning to read, 284
and limits, 199
parent-child, 67, 68, 69, 75–76, 94,
165
and routines, 165, 620, 627
and school performance, 319
about sexual issues, 500, 502
and social development, 375, 379
upside down, 513
and verbal abilities, 75–76, 79, 94,
302, 312–13, 319–21, 546
See also books; stories
reasoning
and animism, 524
and cognitive development, 279,
282, 468, 515–19, 520, 528
concrete and mental, 277, 279–80
and emotional growth, 343, 344
and experimenting with point of
view, 474
inductive, 199, 211
logical, 343
symbolic, 277–82
See also thinking
receptive speech, 80
referencing, social, 136, 361
reinforcement
and gender issues, 586
and limits, 191, 431, 433
and routines, 625
and social development, 371, 586,
588, 593, 596
rejection, social, 373–75
relationships
quality of, 106
repairing, 557, 561, 567, 584, 591,
604, 652, 664
See also friendships; social
development
repetition. See practice
responsibility, 377, 378–79, 512, 567,
624, 625, 638

of three-year-olds, 467–68, 609–34
of two-year-olds, 225, 229,
    387–415, 445, 446, 618
and verbal abilities, 162, 388, 389,
    392, 405, 618, 626
violation of, 389–90
See also chores; cleaning up; eating;
    rules; sleep; testing; toilet
    training; travel
rules, 7, 209
    and cognitive development, 276,
        291, 512, 520, 522
    of communication, 308
    and emotional growth, 337, 576–77
    internalizing, 640
    and limits, 655–56, 657–58
    predictability of, 390–92
    primitive, 520
    and routines, 390–92, 614, 625
    of social interaction, 364–67
    and verbal abilities, 307–11
    See also limits

safety
    and cognitive development, 518–19
    and emotional growth, 345, 559
    and limits, 194, 196, 199, 200,
        201, 265, 422–23, 434, 640
    and motor development, 26–27,
        29–30, 31, 32, 35, 38–40
    and physical abilities, 238, 243–44,
        245, 248, 255, 256–59, 257,
        265, 492, 493–94, 498
    and problem solving, 470–71
    and routines, 162–63, 626
    of three-year-olds, 465, 470–71
safety zone, for experimentation, 565
scaffolding
    secure, 221
    supportive, 496, 666
school
    achievements in, 106, 602
    performance in, 319

starting, 542
scissors, 248–49, 250
scripts, 310–11, 467, 542–44, 585,
    595
second year. See one-year-olds; specific
    topic
secrets and revelations, 473, 499, 557
security
    and emotional growth, 102, 104–6,
        107, 116, 123, 125, 560, 574
    and independence, 478
    and internalizing values, 651
    and preschool, 293
    and routines, 158, 159, 161, 172,
        389, 391–92, 467, 626
self, 450, 465, 467, 669
    and cognitive development, 275
    continuity of, 565–66
    effect on others of, 596
    and emotional growth, 328, 329,
        335, 341, 556–57, 565–66, 669
    and limits, 437, 640
    and others, 134, 209, 596
    and point of view, 473
    and social development, 362, 371,
        467, 595, 601
    talking to, 86, 140
    and willfulness and independence,
        475
    See also play: solo
self-assessment, 335
self-awareness, 286, 335, 464
self-centeredness, 334–35, 337–41,
    363–64, 378
self-comforting, 334
self-confidence, 467, 667, 668
    and cognitive development,
        275–76, 281
    and emotional growth, 104, 105,
        106, 329, 352, 560, 570
    and independence, 478
    and limits, 419, 654
    and motor development, 41–42

shame, 228, 261–62, 334, 568, 588, 620

shapes, 27, 36, 283, 287, 522

sharing, 10, 18, 211, *212,* 225, 226, 229, 235, 445, 446, 449
  and cognitive development, 276–77, 286, 290, 292, 523
  and emotional growth, 111, 335, 345, 351–52, 557
  and limits, 190–92, 199, 420, 424, 656–57
  and physical abilities, 501
  and routines, 407–9
  and social development, 138, 144, 146, 149, 151, 359, 362, 363, 373, *377,* 379, 382, 582, 585, 595, 596, 602

shopping, going, 290–91

shyness, 372–73, 424, 541–42, 669

siblings
  and cognitive development, 290–91
  and emotional growth, 334, 344, 346
  and physical abilities, 245, 264, 501, 502
  and play, 64
  and routines, 398, 400
  and social development, 358, 368–69, 378–79, 584
  and toilet training, 173
  and verbal abilities, 90, 540

sick, feeling, 627–28

sign language, 316

situational compliance, 189

size, physical, 148, 346

sleep
  and emotional growth, 343, 571
  and how child goes to bed, 165–66
  and limits, 187
  of one-year-olds, 159–60
  and physical abilities, 254
  resistance to, 254
  rhythms of, 254

and routines, 158, 159–67, 177, 229, 343, 392–95, 413, 611–14
  of three-year-olds, 571, 611–14
  of two-year-olds, 212, 228, 392–94

social agency, 590

social development, 224, 229, 233–35, 237, 446
  achievements in, 136–37, 152–53, 207, 382–83, 605–6
  and being a "big kid," 604–5
  and cognitive development, 136, 276, 291, 361, 364, 382, 512, 514, 582, 583, 605
  and consistency, 590, 591, 604
  and crisis management, 376
  and debriefing, 148–49
  development delays in, 380–81, 584–86
  and development stages, 138, 380–81, 597, 602
  and emotional growth, 106, 111, 137, 139–40, 143, 148, 329, 343, 362, 364, 467, 582, 583, 590
  and expressing feelings, 362, 374
  in first three years, 360–63
  of four-year-olds, 479, 664, 665, 669
  and gender issues, 369, 371, 375
  and "good" versus "bad" behavior, 139
  and identifying with parent, 586
  if you're concerned about, 145, 146, 380–81, 584–86
  and inductive reasoning, 199
  and internalizing values, 650
  and labeling, 373–75
  as learned, 358–59
  and limits, 146–49, 187, 426, 650
  and morality, 142–44, 145
  and motor development, 361
  of one-year-olds, 10, 11, 18, 133–55
  and parenting style, 597–98, 644

verbal abilities (*continued*)

and symbols, *312,* 533

and talking to self, 86

and talking to versus talking with, 313

of three-year-olds, 301–26, 445, 448, 449, 450, 467, 468–69, 470, 533–54

of two-year-olds, 211–12, 220, 224, 225, 226, 227, 229, 231, 238–39, 309–10, 315, 323

See also bilingual homes; communication; conversation; grammar; language; speech; vocabulary

videotapes, 96–97, 267, 296, 324, 333–34, 513, 552, 565–66, 592, 670

violence, 592. *See also* aggression

vision, and developmental delays, 70

"visual cliff" experiment, 108

visualization, of objects, 278, 280–81, 283, 317

vocabulary, 10, 209, 228

and cognitive development, 65, 286

of four-year-olds, 668

and intelligence, 547–48

and love of words, 546, 547

productive, 305

receptive, 305

of three-year-olds, 449, 468–69, 533

and verbal abilities, 79, 81, 84, 92, 302, 303, 304, 305–6, 309, 310, 311, 313, 314, 317, 351, 537

voices, "inside" and "outside," 563

Vygotsky, Lev, 526

walkers, use of, 33

walking, 10, 207, 226, 227, 247

critical periods for, 50

delays in, 33–34

experimentation with, 250

and first steps, 25–26, 28, 33

and learning to walk, 28–29, 30–33, 274, 283

and limits, 187

and routines, 160, 169

See also motor development

Wallerstein, Judith, 575

willfulness, 462, 467–68, 475–78, 476

Williams syndrome, 317

windows of opportunity. See critical periods (critical windows)

winning and losing, 276–77

Wolf, Dennie, 566

Wolff, Richard and Maggie, 223–24

words

meaning of, 307–11, 312, 315, 316, 533, 668

playing with words, 78–79, 311–13

plural words, 306

work space, toddler's own, 41–42

writing, 284, 291, 465, 528, 668, 669

Wynn, Karen, 521

Zero to Three Organization, 647–48

zone of proximal development, 526